Duxbury Press
North Scituate, Massachusetts

POWER
AND
POLITICS
IN
AMERICA

Third Edition

LEONARD FREEDMAN

University of California, Los Angeles

Library of Congress Cataloging in Publication Data

Freedman, Leonard.
  Power and Politics in America.

  Bibliography: p.
  Includes index.
  1. United States—Politics and government—1945—   I. Title.
JK274.F923   1978   320.9'73'092   77-27900
ISBN 0-87872-159-2

Duxbury Press
A Division of Wadsworth Publishing Company, Inc.

Power and Politics in America, 3d ed. was edited and prepared for composition by Randy Foy. Interior design was provided by Dorothy Thompson and the cover was designed by Nancy Gardner.

ISBN 0-87872-159-2
Printed in the United States of America

1 2 3 4 5 6 7 8 9 – 82 81 80 79 78

Contents

To Vivian

_____

What This
Book Is About

Power and Politics in America is a book cast in terms of controversy. It provides the reader with basic information about our system of government and politics, and interprets this information from five sharply differing points of view.

Chapter 1 sets up a political spectrum, along which five "perspectives" are identified: a centrist position, which sees the American system as a remarkably effective model of self-government; liberal and conservative flanks, which argue that there are serious shortcomings in the way our system operates; and radical left and radical right poles, which express still harsher dissatisfaction with our political system. The debate thus established among these five doctrines is then pursued throughout the book.

In Part One we look at the processes of American politics through which individuals, groups, and the mass of the people seek to influence the course of public policy. As we examine the electorate, parties, elections, and interest groups we are brought face to face, time and again, with the problem of power in a democracy. Do the people at large rule? Can they? Should they?

In Part Two we analyze the institutions of government—the presidency, Congress, the federal bureaucracy, the Supreme Court, and state and local governments. And we ask: Is the system of checks and balances a good idea? Is it working today?

Part Three applies everything we have dealt with up to this point to some of the major issues of our time—poverty, race, the environment and energy, and foreign policy. We look not only at the issues themselves but also at the way in which the principal political and governmental institutions have approached these issues. Then we ask from various perspectives: Has the system been responsive to these issues? Has it been effective?

In the final chapter we sum up, reviewing the strengths and weaknesses of government and politics in America as weighed by each of the five perspectives in turn.

This way of looking at government and politics through rival interpretations has grown out of my own teaching in introductory courses. Why do I use this method? For one thing it reflects the real world of politics; for democratic politics, especially the American brand, is made up in large part of conflicting ideas and interests. Then, too, this approach helps students shape their own interpretations out of the various alternatives presented. While I hold strong beliefs of my own, I am much more interested in seeing students develop *their* capacities for independent critical reasoning than in having them adopt my positions.

However, like all organizing principles this one presents certain difficulties.

First, categorization is as dangerous as it is indispensable, and, at the close of Chapter 1, I provide some warnings on the distortions that can result if my categories are used without great care and flexibility.

Then, it did not prove possible to give equal attention to all five perspectives in each chapter. This, after all, is a book about the decision-making process, and the principal actors, the decision makers, have been mostly centrists. Again, I have drawn heavily on political science scholarship; and most of the scholarly writing in this field is by people who operate within a framework of centrism or liberal dissent. There is a growing amount of conservative writing, though conservatives have generally been less prolific than liberals. The body of radical left writing has been expanding, and in recent years there has been a significant increase in the number of social scientists of the left. However, proponents of the left tend to see economic institutions as more fundamental than governmental and political institutions; thus few of them have written in much detail about the latter. As for the radical right, the only scholarly sources are *about* the right and not *by* the right, so we cannot make more than a few basic points about them in this book. Nonetheless, in each chapter there will be at least some discussion of all five perspectives.

Another difficulty in our emphasis on conflicting interpretations is that it may imply that nothing matters but opinion. But this book is aimed at the development of *informed* opinion. That is why we have described, in as much detail as we felt was useful, the basic elements of the system. Accordingly, in each chapter, the essential context of information is provided first. Second, this information is interpreted in the context of varying perspectives. Third, a concluding section attempts to sum up commonalities and divergencies among the perspectives, and suggests some prospects for the future.

A final difficulty is to provide all this information and all these interpretations on so many topics within the span of one book. So I must remind the reader that this text is intended only as an introductory work aimed at opening up the workings of the American system in light of contemporary controversies. More exhaustive study will have to be undertaken of each of the subjects dealt with here if the reader is to arrive at more definitive answers to the very large questions I have raised. Accordingly, a Selected Bibliography is offered at the close of the book to help provide further dimensions and more precise formulations and distinctions.

Changes from the Second Edition

Although the general structure of the second edition of this book has been retained, the new edition constitutes a substantial revision.

First, there has been a major expansion of the first part of each chapter—the basic presentation of facts and analysis. The most important deficiency of the earlier editions was that the reader was plunged into the arguments before he was provided with an adequate background of data to enable him to understand the arguments fully. I have therefore added a considerable amount of information which instructors and students felt was lacking in the second edition. The result (since I did not want to cut seriously into the unique feature of this text—the rival perspectives) is a longer book. I believe, nonetheless, that the increased clarity of organization in each chapter will make the material easier to grasp and thus will not take more time to master. The publisher's editorial and production staff have also helped considerably in this respect by creating a more handsome and readable layout, and by encouraging me to use more charts, tables, and other illustrations. Also in this edition, the U.S. Constitution is reprinted as an appendix for easy reference when discussing such questions as the balance and separation of power among the three branches of the federal government or the division of power between the federal and state governments. In addition, a list of presidents of the United States has been appended.

Second, a new edition is an opportunity for updating. So I have taken account of a good deal of new research. And I have responded to the unceasing march of events, problems, and crises. The second edition went to press early in 1974 in the midst of the Watergate crisis. Now we have been able to take the reader through the final stages of that crisis, notably the resignation of Richard Nixon; then on through the Ford administration, the 1976 elections, and some interim assessments of the presidency of Jimmy Carter. And, of course, there has been a flood of developments in each of the public policy areas. We have again focused on poverty, race, energy and environment, and foreign policy—with one change in the treatment of the poverty issue: in this edition, our discussion of poverty is set in the context of economic policy in general.

Needless to say, even this cannot make a new edition totally current. Events persist in attacking us in bewildering profusion. Our purpose, however, is to establish a framework of concepts within which contemporary developments can be analyzed. So the reader must take it from here, and revise the material in the light of subsequent developments.

It is impossible to give credit to all of the very large number of teachers, colleagues, and friends who have been formative influences in the development of this book. The revision has been much affected by the comments of students who were assigned the first edition. I was greatly helped, too, by the suggestions of several faculty people who used the first edition in their courses, and provided invaluable assessments of its strengths and weaknesses as well as specific comments on the manuscript of the new edition which led to a number of major improvements. Among these were Paul Brennan, Saddleback Community College; Donald J. Devine, University of Maryland; F. Chris Garcia, University of New Mexico; Allen F. Repko, Oral Roberts University; John Schultz, Fullerton Junior College; Jack Soule, San Diego State University; and Ann Wynia, North Hennepin Community College.

Then there were the enormously important contributions of Mr. Robert Gormley, the publisher of this book, and several members of his staff. Among these two call for special mention. Ms. Victoria Pasternack undertook the role of "developmental editor." This is a role which does not begin when the draft of the manuscript is completed, but rather while the manuscript is being written, and it calls for detailed analysis of concepts organization and style with a view to increasing the accessibility of the book's ideas to the reader. To the extent that this has been achieved much of the credit must go to Ms. Pasternack's insight, exacting standards, tact, and ability to grasp and help clarify complex ideas. Then, the final detailed editing of the manuscript was in the capable hands of Ms. Randy Foy.

Invaluable research assistance was provided by Mr. Peter Proehl and by Ms. Magdalen Suzuki. Ms. Suzuki also shared the arduous task of manuscript typing with Ms. Patricia Nicholas, and supervised the various stages of preparing the manuscript for the editors with her invariable skill, dedication, and patience. To all of them, my grateful thanks.

Five Perspectives

on the American Political System

In America today many people are dissatisfied with the way our system of government and politics is working. Evidence points to a general erosion of trust in institutions and leaders over the last 20 years. But we cannot hope to change anyone's mind merely by asking for a reaffirmation of faith. The times call for a thorough reassessment of the American political system. This book undertakes that task. However, its purpose is not to provide a single, definitive resolution of the problem. Rather, the intent is to help each student work toward his or her own conclusions. The method adopted for this purpose is to present and debate a number of rival positions.

Political Power:
The Theme of the Debate

Basically the debate is about *power*—who should have it and for what purposes it should be used. We shall be talking about *the power to make public policy through government and politics*. Since this statement is made up of key terms that will be used over and over again in this book, we had better begin by defining them.

Power, which has been defined in a great many different ways, will mean in this book *the capacity to play a significant part in the making of decisions*. In many instances it will be very difficult to distinguish power from *influence*, which is *the capacity to have an impact on the making of decisions*. On the other hand, power is not necessarily the same as *authority*, which is *legitimized right to make decisions* and to wield power. In other words, some people who have legal authority have very little power to make decisions, whereas others exercise vast decision-making power even though no one has granted them the authority.

Public policy is *an official guide to action on issues,* (health, education, the environment, national security, and so on) *that affect the entire community.*

Government consists of *the institutions that provide the official decision points for public policy.* These institutions establish the laws through legislation, executive action, and judicial interpretation. Then they put the laws into effect through persuasion, financial rewards and penalties, and, ultimately, through the threat of organized coercion. Force may be commonplace today; but only government has the legal authority to use or approve its use.

Politics is defined as *the process through which a multitude of individuals and groups try to impress their ideas and interests upon government.* Politics enters into the processes of electing government officials and of influencing them once they are elected.

At this stage these definitions may seem very general and abstract. But we shall discover that the questions they imply are of far more than theoretical interest. Enormous amounts of money are involved, for governmental decisions can create prosperity or depression and can make or break very large fortunes. Today competition for power is involved on a scale never before dreamed of. Divergent but passionately held beliefs about justice are at issue. And survival itself could hang on the outcome of the debate, for the wrong kind of political decisions could intensify the forces that threaten to wreck havoc on the human race. So the subject matter of this book is a series of conflicts in which the stakes are very high.

A Political Spectrum

The contemporary debate on power in America cannot be reduced to a simple pro and con formulation. Conflicting and strongly held views multiply in all directions. For the purposes of our debate we can set forth a spectrum of opinion from left to right. Then we can divide the spectrum into five broad *perspectives*—ways of looking at and interpreting the political system and the policies produced by the system (see Figure 1–1).

The first of these five perspectives is that of the *centrists*, those who belong to the great American middle-of-the-road consensus. Flanking the centrists on either

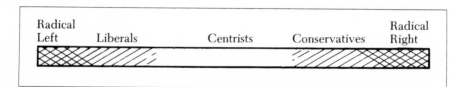

| Radical Left | Liberals | Centrists | Conservatives | Radical Right |

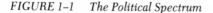

FIGURE 1–1   *The Political Spectrum*

side are two smaller bands of opinion made up of people who dissent from that consensus—on the one hand, the *liberals*, on the other, the *conservatives*. Toward the two poles of the spectrum are two still smaller groups—the *radical left* and the *radical right*—defined as radicals because their rejection of the middle-of-the-road position is much more deep-rooted or fundamental than that of the liberals and conservatives.

Please take special note of four features of Figure 1–1. First, it does not pretend to reflect a precise quantitative distribution of support among the five perspectives but only a very rough indication. Thus the centrists make up the broadest band of opinion. Next in the number of adherents come the liberals and the conservatives. The smallest numbers are in the left and right radical groups. Second, each perspective is not a single point on the spectrum but a band of opinion within which there are wide divergencies. They are distinctive categories because, despite the differences within each grouping, all within that category share certain beliefs that distinguish them in significant ways from the people in any other category. Third, the perspectives are not separated by high, unscalable walls. They shade into each other, so that some of the people we shall be discussing bridge the categories. And, fourth, many people are difficult to categorize, sometimes taking a centrist stance, other times a liberal, conservative, or even radical position, depending on the issue.

Despite these qualifications—which I shall expand on at the end of this chapter—the spectrum describes in an approximate way the main divisions of opinion over government and politics in America today. Thus it gives us a useful point of departure for discussing the issues treated in this book.

The Perspectives Introduced

To introduce our perspectives we take a brief look at the spokespersons, groups, and principal ideas associated with each.

The Centrists

The centrist category comprises the largest body of opinion in the country. In this part of the political spectrum we find many political scientists, sociologists, economists, and historians. Most high school and many college texts on American history and government express a centrist perspective. The larger number of viewpoints expressed in the mass media are centrist, and most elected public officials are centrists.

This is not to say that they speak with a single voice. Large differences are found among them, ranging from the more conservative centrists, such as Gerald Ford, to more liberal centrists, such as Jimmy Carter.

Just the same, all centrists tend to agree that the American political system is fundamentally sound. All of them will concede that it has its faults, and some frequently draw attention to shortcomings and failures and the need for change. Thus centrism is not a simple, stand-pat doctrine, defending the status quo in all circumstances. Still, centrists of all shades of opinion claim that, whatever its defects, the American political system serves the people at least as well as, and probably better than, any other system in the world today.

The Liberals

To the left of the centrists on the spectrum we find a body of opinion that expresses a much deeper dissatisfaction with the American political system than is felt by even the most liberal of the centrists. The liberals do not agree that the system is working well. They see it riddled with inequities between rich and poor, powerful and powerless. They believe that it repeatedly fails to handle the problems facing the vast majority of people. They argue that major reforms are urgently needed.

Among these liberal critics are several political scientists, including James MacGregor Burns, some economists, notably John Kenneth Galbraith, political activists such as Ralph Nader, and such political leaders as Senator George McGovern, and Representatives Ronald Dellums and Robert Drinan.

The New Republic and *The Nation* are magazines of liberal opinion. The Americans for Democratic Action, a political pressure group that rates candidates and members of Congress on its own political spectrum is one of the leading liberal organizations. Also included in this camp are the various groups founded by Ralph Nader.

The Conservatives

On the other side of the centrist band is a group of conservatives who argue that the American governmental system, as designed by the framers, was brilliantly conceived and had served the country well for almost a century and a half until it was undermined by the liberals' faith in an all-powerful federal government which has dominated official thinking since the New Deal of the 1930s.

This group includes a considerable number of economists, among whom Milton Friedman will be quoted frequently in this book. Then there are the political analysts and commentators who write for the magazine *The National Review*, including William Buckley and William Rusher. Conservative elected officials include Senators Barry Goldwater and Strom Thurmond, as well as ex-Governor Ronald Reagan.

Conservative organizations include the Americans for Constitutional Action, the American Conservative Union, the Young Americans for Freedom, the Society for Individual Liberty, and the American Enterprise Institute for Public Policy Research. Conservative periodicals, apart from *The National Review*, include *Modern Age* and *Human Events*.

The Radical Left

On the far left of the spectrum, beyond the liberals, we find a variety of *radical* groups. Some are commonly described as the *old left*, whose principal intellectual sources are Karl Marx and Nikolai Lenin (real name: Vladimir Ilich Ulyanov). Included here is the Communist party–U.S.A. and rival groups such as the Socialist Labor party, the Progressive Labor party, the Socialist Workers party, and the Young Socialist Alliance. Marxist writers and scholars include Paul Sweezy and the late Paul Baran; *The Monthly Review* is the leading Marxist journal.

Then there is the *new left*, a term that covers a great many very small groups drawing upon diverse strands of doctrine and strategy. Marxism is a strong influence among all these groups, along with the variation of Marxism associated with Mao Tse-tung, Maoism. But so is anarchism, the doctrine of total opposition to both governmental power and private property. Thus one of the most important expressions of the new left is the youth "counterculture," which grew out of the campus revolts of the 1960s against all kinds of established authority. Sociologist C. Wright Mills and philosopher Herbert Marcuse are among the scholars most frequently quoted by the new left.

In the 1960s the main new left organization was the Students for a Democratic Society, founded by Tom Hayden; but by the 1970s it had been succeeded by a variety of organizations, such as the Weather Underground, the New World Liberation Front, the Red Guerrilla Family, the Revolutionary Union, and the October League.

Most of the new left groups have only a few hundred members. They consist predominately of young white people from upper-middle-class backgrounds, which limits their ability to form alliances with the more militant members of black, Chicano, and American Indian groups. They differ widely on tactics, some advocating and practicing terrorism, others preferring education and organization among workers and students.

Still, a significant number of younger university faculty members in such fields as sociology, history, and economics are included in their ranks. And the new left believes that, although its active supporters are currently a small minority, there are very large numbers who were radicalized during the campus turmoil of the 1960s and whose basic attitudes have not changed since then.

Despite the ideological and tactical disagreements that divide the new left and set the new left off from the old left, all on the radical left agree that the American political system is controlled by monopoly capitalism, or big business, which is inherently unjust and antihuman; that the liberals are merely a minor variation of the centrists and the conservatives; and that only root-and-branch, radical, and perhaps revolutionary changes can cure the sickness of the system.

The Radical Right

At the opposite pole of the spectrum we find a cluster of groups, including extreme, militant organizations such as the American Nazi party, the Minutemen, and the predominately southern Ku Klux Klan; organizations that draw upon religious as well as political doctrine, such as Billy James Hargis's Christian Crusade; and, the most publicized of contemporary right-wing groups, the John Birch Society.

Although there are sharp differences among these groups, all agree that American government and politics are run by a small group of insiders who are leading us toward communism or a similar kind of dictatorship.

All these groups together constitute only a tiny fraction of the electorate. The largest among them are the Birch Society, which says that it has about 80,000 members, and the Ku Klux Klan, whose claim of membership running into the hundreds of thousands contrasts with much lower FBI estimates. There are deep divisions about beliefs and tactics not only between but within each of these organizations. The secrecy with which most of these groups enclose their meetings and their membership lists, and the intensity of their rhetoric, cause most people to reject them as "extremists."

Still, like the far left, the radical right cannot be ignored as a factor in American politics. The Birch Society, under its leader Robert Welch, publishes weekly and monthly magazines, including *American Opinion*, and a number of books sold through its own network of bookstores. It also operates a speakers' bureau. At least two members of the society serve in Congress.

John Schmitz, a southern California Birch Society member, gained over a million votes when he ran for president in 1972 on the ticket of the right-wing American Independent party. Schmitz's predecessor on that ticket in 1964 and 1968 was George Wallace; and Wallace, who received a good deal of his backing from radical right groups and espoused a number of right-wing attitudes, succeeded in attracting support from wide segments of the public.

The Basic Differences

Having defined each of the five perspectives briefly, we must explore further the differences between them. To do this we shall look at their views on three types of questions.

We begin with questions about *values*, for these include our assumptions with regard to how people should behave toward each other. We shall ask: What should be the guiding principles of human behavior?

Then we turn to the problem of *power*, and ask: Who has power in America today?

Having done this, we shall find that a gap exists between the answers to the first group of questions about values (how things ought to be) and the second group about power (how things actually are). To bridge the gap between the actual and the ideal, *change* is necessary, and we ask each of our perspectives: How much change is needed, in what directions, and by what means should it be achieved?

Values

At the heart of the disagreements between the perspectives is a conflict of values. Our values are our beliefs about what is good or bad conduct, what is right and wrong. They are statements of ideals to which we at least pay lip service, even though we fall far short of them in practice. For example, statements such as "human life is sacred," "government officials should be honest," "there should be no limits on free speech," and "private property is the essential condition of liberty" are all expressions of values. We cannot, given the present state of knowledge, prove or disprove any of them. Whole societies have existed for long periods on assumptions quite different from these. And within our own culture there is a great diversity of beliefs, intensely held, and sometimes brilliantly argued, on these and other issues.

We can organize all the value questions considered in this book around two concepts that have appeared persistently from the earliest political philosophers: *equality* and *liberty*.

Attitudes toward *equality*—equality of income, possessions, status, power—constitute the most reliable litmus test of whether people stand right or left of center on the political spectrum. In general, as we move toward the left we find increasing support for the idea that justice cannot be achieved in the face of large inequalities; and as we move toward the right we find more emphasis on recognizing and rewarding differences of ability and effort.

When we turn our attention to *liberty*, however, we find that the task of differentiating among the various perspectives becomes much more complicated. At the most superficial level, in fact, it seems useless to look at liberty as a means of distinguishing among the perspectives, for all of them proclaim deep and undying devotion to the principle that the individual should be free from governmental tyranny.

However, beneath this bland consensus there are sharp differences on what constitutes governmental tyranny. As we move right of center, we encounter opposition particularly to interference by government with our right to do whatever we want with our property. Thus the emphasis is on *economic liberty*. On the left side of the spectrum, the primary concern is with freedom of expression and personal behavior, that is to say, with *civil liberty*. On the other hand, right of center there is strong support for government action to protect the social order against subversive, disruptive, or debased ideas and conduct, while left of center there is enthusiastic endorsement of measures to regulate private business and property.

So, with a few exceptions to be noted later, everyone favors governmental action in some areas, and whether or not this action constitutes a denial of our liberty depends on which perspective we are talking about. With these generalizations in mind we can proceed to examine in more detail the views of each of the five perspectives on the basic values of equality and liberty. Since the centrists' values tend to be middle-ground positions between the conflicting ideas on either side of them, we shall begin this part of our discussion by examining the left-of-center perspectives, then those right of center, and then the centrist beliefs.

The liberals.   Equality is a prime value of the liberals. They do not believe that a just society should tolerate the enormous disparities that exist in America between those at the top of the income scale and those at the bottom. They accept some differences of income, wealth, and status as inevitable and legitimate. But the large inequities that exist today mean that the needs of the poor are simply not attended to in the same way as the interests of the rich, for in politics money talks with a loud and clear voice. So liberals call for a major redistribution of the privileges now enjoyed by the well-to-do groups to the poor, blacks, Chicanos, Puerto Ricans, American Indians, and others who have been left behind in the struggle for success.

If this is to be accomplished, government must play a leading role. The key economic decisions cannot be left in the hands of great business corporations and wealthy individuals, for they will see to it that these decisions will protect their privileges. Government must intervene in ways that we shall detail in later chapters, all to the end of setting limits to the accumulation of private property and changing our policy goals from protecting powerful special interests to benefiting the community at large.

Achieving the goal of *equality* seems to present a paradox, in that the liberals' push for a large role for government imposes serious infringements on the *liberty* of individuals. The liberals' explanation is that, indeed, they are proposing to limit the liberties of some individuals. But unless these limits are imposed, liberty will be the exclusive prerogative of those who own most of the property, for they will dominate the economic life of the society. And where this is allowed to happen, the freedom of the rest is lost. So the liberties of the few must be restricted to expand the freedom of the many.

In any case, say the liberals, liberty should not be defined primarily in economic terms. We are free to the extent that we can say and write whatever we please, consort with anyone we want to, and control our personal lives and individual relationships as we see fit. Government should not interfere with these basic freedoms—those civil liberties clearly defined in the Bill of Rights, most particularly the First Amendment to the Constitution—except where the pursuit of our own liberties directly interferes with the personal liberties of others or immediately endangers the safety of the community as a whole.

The radical left.   Equality is the core value of the radical left, and they criticize the liberals for being willing to leave wide variations in income and property, and for failing to face up to the root cause of our present inequities. That root cause, say the radicals of the left, is the system of capitalism, which is based on private ownership of industry and agriculture. Capitalism thrives on inequality. It promotes competition, which sets people against each other in a struggle to gain more than the next person. It brings out the worst in people by encouraging greed, instilling the lust to own more and more goods. Moreover, it is a system of exploitation, in which members of the capitalist class make their profits and expand their property holdings from the efforts of the laboring masses. Capitalism must be abolished and replaced with socialism, a system in which, as

Karl Marx put it, "the means of production, distribution, and exchange" are owned by the whole community. Under socialism, cooperation would eventually take the place of competition, and inequality would give way to a sharing of resources, so everyone would have enough and no one too much.

Socialism, in the doctrines of the left, will not only bring social justice based on equality. It will bring true liberty to the masses of the people—unlike capitalism, which reserves freedom for the capitalists. But if liberty is a professed value of the left, achieving it confronts them with some awkward contradictions. To examine these contradictions we must distinguish between the old and new left.

The old left, particularly the Communist party, sees a strong central government as the mechanism for taking over power from the capitalists, and they urge that private businesses, especially the big ones, be nationalized, that is, taken over by the national government. Now the enormous power that this action would vest in the government is seen as a temporary phenomenon. Karl Marx predicted that, when social justice at last prevailed and everyone had a fair share of the abundance that socialism would produce, there would no longer be any need to ride herd on people and control them with laws. Government, including the entire machinery of bureaucracies, courts, and police forces, would "wither away," and the individual would, for the first time in human history, enjoy complete freedom.

However, this is the eventual goal, the final stage of "communism," which succeeds the interim system of socialism; and there is a problem of getting there from here. Even when capitalism is abolished, the selfish attitudes it generates will not be immediately eradicated. So there needs to be an interim "dictatorship of the proletariat," during which government, acting on behalf of the masses, will take steps to get rid of the vestiges of capitalist thought and behavior.

Now it happens that in the Soviet Union, which the Communist party of the United States has generally held up as its model, the "dictatorship of the proletariat" has lasted since 1917 and there are as yet no signs of Marx's "withering away of the state." On the contrary, government is immensely powerful, and dissenting opinions are still treated with great harshness. The communists' response to this dilemma is that dissenting voices persist because capitalist countries stir them up and give them encouragement; and the maintenance of a large governmental and military establishment results from the need to defend the Soviet experiment from the aggressive hostility of America and other capitalist powers.

The new left is not satisfied with this response. They have been highly critical of the Soviet Union because of its centralized bureaucratic structures of power and its continued suppression of artists and other critics. The new left grew out of the rebellion of students and others against the oppressiveness of all large institutions. Individuals must be free to determine their own lives. In the language of the sixties, they must be able to "do their own thing" without interference. So new left theorists could see little advantage in replacing the tyranny of great industrial corporations with the tyranny of big government agencies. Although they are advocates of socialism, which means moving economic decisions out of private into public hands, the institutions they want to create are small scale, with control in the hands of communities or of workers, not huge, remote governmental or-

"I drifted from socialism to Marxism, but now I'm into anachronism!"

Richard Rice

ganizations. Unlike the old left, they do not equate public control with nationalization, and they have little use for the supreme example of total nationalization, the Soviet Union.

And yet the new left, like the old, sees total freedom as part of the long-term goal, not the short-term tactic. When the just society arrives, there will be no need to suppress vicious, destructive ideas because no one will harbor such ideas. But, under capitalism, racism, militarism, and other such affronts to human dignity are very much alive. Liberty does not extend to the advocacy of race hatred and imperialist war, and we should not tolerate such antihuman beliefs.

The conservatives.   Conservatives do not share the attachment of liberals and the left to the concept of equality. On the contrary, as conservatives see it, people are intrinsically unequal. They are endowed from birth with differing qualities, personalities, and preferences. These differences should be cherished, and diversity should be encouraged.

Conservatives also place heavy emphasis on motivation, effort, and thrift. People should strive to develop these virtues to the full, and the best means of stimulating them to do so is to provide them with competition. The social system should be so constructed that, if they compete successfully, they should be rewarded to the full extent justified by their performance.

The social system that embodies all these ideas is capitalism. The capitalist system is based on individual effort, enterprise, thrift, competition, and rewards for effective performance. It is the most successful economic system the world has ever seen. It has produced an abundance that socialist countries have dismally failed to achieve. Nor is this abundance limited to the few. Under capitalism the exceptionally able and talented can acquire very large fortunes. But, when the system is working properly anyone who is responsible, hardworking, and ambitious is able to acquire a comfortable share in the fruits of the economy. Thus, along with a wealthy upper class, a large middle class emerges, as has been the case in America.

What about those who lack the essential qualities of diligence and motivation, and, as a result, remain poor? The conservatives do not suggest that we do nothing about them. A sense of obligation is a key element in conservative doctrine. So conservatives are willing to support a certain amount of action by government to ensure that the poor will not go without the minimum requirements of food, clothing, shelter, and education. However, conservatives prefer private charity to government programs. In any case, they argue that the best way of providing enough to go around for everybody, including the poor, is to allow capitalism scope to generate ever more economic abundance.

And yet, say the conservatives, wherever capitalism exists, there are attempts to interfere with its functioning in the name of equality. This interference is misguided on two grounds. First, it is self-defeating. Equality can never be achieved. Differences in wealth and status—not to mention differences in abilities from birth—are so natural that they cannot be extinguished without the ruthless use of massive power; and those who exercise this power, as in communist countries, become a self-perpetuating elite whose existence contradicts the very notion of equality.

Second, interfering with capitalism undermines liberty. In the conservatives' perspective, liberty is associated primarily with the right of the individual to acquire and use property and conduct his business without hindrance from government. Thus capitalism, which is based on private property and the private ownership and operation of business, is inseparable from liberty. "Capitalism," says the conservative economist Milton Friedman, "is a necessary condition for political freedom."[1] This is because capitalism, or private enterprise, or free enterprise, disperses decision making among a large number of individuals and groups, instead of concentrating it all in government, and thus protects us from governmental tyranny.

Now Friedman and other conservatives do not completely rule out any role for government in the economy. We need government to set up and referee the rules of the game; to help define and protect property rights; to resolve conflicts among the freedoms of different individuals; and to control the supply of money without which the economy cannot function. But beyond these minimal functions of government, the cardinal principles underlying a free society are economic individualism, or free competition among private businesspeople, and property rights, or the ability to own and use without restraint a home, a business, and whatever else we can legally acquire with our money.

In the area of civil liberties, on the other hand, most conservatives are inclined to support more governmental intervention than are liberals. Conservatives agree that the freedoms contained in the Bill of Rights are of great importance. But they argue that those freedoms are possible only within a framework of order and stability. The latter are preserved by respect for tradition, patriotism, religion, and the family. They are undermined by communist subversion, the disruption stirred up by the new left, the youth culture's total rejection of traditional ideas and beliefs, pornography and the abandonment of all sexual taboos, and the surging wave of violent crime. Thus conservatives see a major role for government in formulating stronger laws and vigorously enforcing them to control these destructive elements. Moreover, the conservatives tend to believe in a strong, nationalist foreign policy as a defense against international communism, which they see as the great threat to liberty in the world. This leads them to support high levels of military spending, which paradoxically entails a large government bureaucracy and the tax outlays to support it—both of which they dislike as infringements on our liberties.

There are some exceptions to this assessment. There is a group of conservative *Libertarians*, who are consistent in their opposition to government intervention not only in economic affairs but also in questions of sexual behavior, the right to smoke marijuana, and so on. These Libertarians have some strength on college campuses and their influence within the conservative movement may be growing. However, the larger number of conservatives still tend to emphasize the individual's right to unfettered economic liberty while supporting governmental action to preserve the social order in the area of civil liberties.

The radical right.   There are a number of contrasting strands within the radical right on the question of equality. Some, like John Birch Society members, incline toward an extreme version of conservative thought, deeply antiegalitarian, and strongly supportive of unlimited competition and rewards for superior performance. The other is "populist" in character; that is, it claims to speak for the people at large against established wealth and power. This right-wing populism has been particularly characteristic of the lower-middle-income people who have supported the Ku Klux Klan, the right-wing fundamentalist religious groups, and George Wallace during the 1960s. However, this populism is not truly egalitarian. Although it expresses resentment of the rich and well-born, it is also directed downward against the demands of groups traditionally at the bottom of the status scale—the very poor, the blacks, and the ethnic minorities.

In fact, the older, more extreme radical right organizations, such as the Ku Klux Klan and the Nazis, hold virulently antiblack and anti-Semitic prejudices. The John Birch Society, on the other hand, strongly denies any taint of racial or ethnic bigotry. Still, the Birch Society, like all right-wing groups, bitterly opposes the quest for equality associated with the civil rights movement.

Whatever differences may exist among right-wing groups on the issue of equality, they do not differ very much on the question of liberty. Freedom is the right to develop our capacities, to own, buy, and sell property, to practice religion, and to live according to traditional standards of patriotism and morality. The enemy of all these values, and thus of freedom, is socialism, which to the radical right is indistinguishable from communism. According to the radical right, communists believe "that a collectivist society should swallow up all individuals, make their lives and their energies completely subservient to the needs and the purposes of the collectivist state. . . ." In contrast, the "true American" believes that "the individual should retain the freedom to make his own bargain with life, and the responsibility for the results of that bargain. . . ." We should get back to the beginnings of our republic, when there was very little government. "The greatest enemy of man is, and always has been, government. And the larger, the more extensive that government, the greater the enemy."[2]

However, since atheism–socialism–communism is destructive of freedom, government may have to be used to prevent its spread. Whatever pernicious things may have been done to this country through the infiltration of communism, our nation and flag are still symbols of true patriotism and Americanism. So it is a contradiction in terms to provide people with the "liberty" to advocate unpatriotic or "un-American" ideas.

The centrists.   In relation to both equality and liberty, centrist views reflect their location on the spectrum: the middle ground between left and right doctrines.

Thus equality is one of the constant themes in the accounts of the American creed found in centrist high school texts, and much is made in these texts of the doctrine of the Declaration of Independence that "all men are created equal." Yet what centrists have in mind is a degree of equality that goes further than the conservatives prefer but stops well short of the proposals of the radical left or even of the liberals. The key to the centrist approach is *equality of opportunity*. This requires that no one can be denied the chance to develop his full potential because of prejudice or discrimination or lack of access to education. As the concept of equality of opportunity has expanded over the years, it has come to include equality before the law, equality of voting rights, and the equal right of all to a standard of living needed for survival and human dignity. Once these basic rights are provided, however, people should be able to use their opportunities to move ahead of others, so that equality of opportunity does not produce equality of condition.

The centrists' inclination to find the middle ground is also shown in their attitudes on economic liberty. They are for free enterprise, private ownership, capitalism. Yet they believe that government should regulate business to prevent monopoly and other practices that hurt the consumer and the public at large. They favor laws that set minimum wages for workers and protect their right to organize into labor unions. They also feel that government has a crucial responsibility to intervene in the economy with budgetary, fiscal, and tax policies to keep the economy on an even keel, preventing massive unemployment on the one hand and runaway inflation on the other.

Finally, in the area of civil liberties, centrists seek a judicious, moderate position between the demands of freedom on the one side and the need for order on the other. They regard the guarantees of the Bill of Rights as an indispensable part of our democracy. Yet, they say, there is no such thing as complete freedom, for the liberties of each of us are constantly coming into conflict with the liberties of others. Thus we need a framework of law and government to settle individual and group conflicts. Moreover, people have a need for some degree of stability in their lives. So government has a right to protect society and itself against disruption and the threat of violent overthrow. Thus centrists allow extensive scope for civil liberties, but they are more prepared to accept limits on those liberties than are the liberals.

Power: Who Rules America?

So far, in discussing the values of equality and liberty, we have distinguished among the five perspectives on the basis of their underlying beliefs on how the world *ought* to be. Now we turn to their perceptions of reality, of how the world actually *is*. In particular we ask them: Who has the power in America? Who rules? And from each perspective we receive a different answer.

In brief, the closer we get to the center of the spectrum the more likely we are to be told that power in America is widely distributed among a considerable number of people and locations; whereas the farther we move away from the center the greater is the prospect of our hearing that we are ruled by a small elite group.

The centrists.   Although on this and all other topics in this book there are many differing positions within the centrist band, the most typical centrist view of the realities of the American system is that power is limited and diffused. To begin with, there is the framework of the Constitution. At the heart of the document devised by the Founding Fathers was the insistence on limited government. They came together in Philadelphia to create a central government. But the framers of the Constitution were fearful of the power that they were now concentrating in a national government. So they proceeded to establish an ingenious and intricate series of limits on that power.

First, they deferred to the fears of the separate states, which were seeing their roles reduced. The principle of *federalism* was built into the Constitution, which divided power between the national and state governments, and reserved to the states all the powers that were not specifically assigned to the federal government.

Having *divided* the power between the different levels of government, the framers of the Constitution also *separated* it between the different branches of the federal government. Congress was to make the laws, the president to execute them. The two houses of Congress and the president were elected for different terms of office and, even more important, from different constituencies—the president from the entire national electorate and the members of the Congress from particular states or districts.

The principles of preserving different electoral constituencies for the two houses of Congress and the president, while making government more directly responsible to the people at large, has resulted in each institution's responding to different power bases and has also created a permanent tension between the three institutions. Each has developed its own history, its own identity, and its own purposes. Sometimes these purposes will coincide; but at other times they are bound to collide.

Power conflicts among the institutions can occur at several points in the governing process. The president, says the Constitution, may veto an act of Congress; but Congress can override the veto by a two-thirds vote of both houses. The president can send policy messages to Congress, but Congress can ignore them. The president can nominate officials and ambassadors, but the Senate can refuse to confirm them. The president has the power to make international treaties, but the treaties go into effect only if upheld by two-thirds of the Senate.

Even where harmony prevails between the president and both chambers of the national legislature, there is still another point of power in the system at which decisions might be overturned. If the third branch of government, the Supreme Court of the United States, finds a duly enacted law incompatible with the principles of the Constitution, that law may be rendered null and void. Although it is not clear from the language of the Constitution that the framers meant to give this power to the Court, it was pretty well established in 1803 by the case of *Marbury v. Madison* (as we shall see in Chapter 9).

Beyond the Supreme Court there is still a further recourse against the dangers of excessive power in one branch of government. The Constitution provided for its own amendment. The process is not easy. A potential amendment must first receive a two-thirds vote of both houses of Congress (or a constitutional convention called on petition of the legislatures of two-thirds of the states), and then requires approval by the legislatures or conventions in three-fourths of the states. Even so, the first 10 amendments, the Bill of Rights, soon followed the ratification of the Constitution, and 16 additional amendments have subsequently been adopted.

Thus we have an elaborate structure of checks and balances, severely limiting the power concentrated in Washington. The centrists concede that the balance has not always been perfect. The power of the presidency, in recent years especially, has grown far beyond what the Founding Fathers originally conceived. However, the way the system has responded to abuses of power (such as the Watergate scandal in 1972–74) is proof to the centrists that the constitutional structure has a way of generating self-correcting forces which lead to a restoration of a reasonable balance.

Nor do we have to rely entirely on the Constitution for constraints on power. Many statutes have been passed that protect the rights of individuals and minorities. Federal and state courts maintain the rule of law, that system by which everyone, including government officials, is subject to carefully devised and impartially applied rules of conduct. A free press, television, and radio provide a constant stream of information and criticism to prevent government from conducting its affairs secretly and irresponsibly. Competition between two major political parties and a variety of small ones is a constant reminder to any administration that it must not wield power without concern for the wishes of the people.

Finally, the centrists are reassured of a balance of power by the fact that we have an incredible array of groups, representing small business and big business, labor, farmers, the professions, ethnic and racial minorities, and religious, civic, fraternal, and other causes. Many of these vie for influence over the shaping of public policy. Some are more potent than others. Yet none of them, and no combination of them, is powerful enough to control the government, for they compete with each other, they are watched over by the media, and they are regulated by government. To complement the constitutional balance, then, we have a group balance.

So, through the separation and division of powers in the Constitution, the courts, the media, the parties, and the interplay of groups, centrists maintain that we have a system of *pluralism,* or many sources of power. The majority does not run things directly. Leaders (elites) in government and private organizations carry out most of the decision making. Still, the elected leaders may be replaced if they have failed to carry out the majority's will. And this, together with the dispersal of power to many locations, clearly establishes our claim to be a representative, constitutional democracy, a society in which the wishes of the majority are carried out by elected representatives according to orderly, generally accepted procedures.

The liberals.   Unlike the centrists, the liberals perceive an *imbalance* of power in America. Certain groups, particularly businessmen and those who possess large amounts of money and property are overrepresented in the policy-making process and have a much greater impact on government decisions than other groups. The liberals also perceive and are critical of a gravitation of power in recent years toward the military, power that results in absurdly inflated outlays on weapons, and which is used in pursuit of a foreign policy that is too responsive to the interests of American business.

The liberals concede that this disproportionate power is not completely unchecked and that some of the limits which the centrists point to are significant. Still, they are not sufficient, in the liberals' view, to prevent some people from obtaining a degree of power that is inconsistent with the idea of democracy, or rule by the people.

One cause of this disproportionate power is the very large inequities in the distribution of wealth in America. Another is the nature of our governmental system, which is vulnerable to those who possess large amounts of wealth. The very checks and balances that the Founding Fathers invented in order to set limits to power have instead provided people with money and property the opportunity to exercise undue power. Our decision-making machinery is so fragmented that well-organized and well-financed interest groups are able to maneuver among and infiltrate the decision points. The political importance of wealth is also demonstrated in large contributions to election campaigns, which puts elected officeholders under an obligation to rich contributors.

Consequently, business and monied interests generally far outweigh such groups as the poor and the racial–ethnic minorities in the governmental system. Indeed, in the face of such power, the interests of the majority are poorly served.

Liberals also argue that it is not easy for the majority to see how they might correct these inequalities and bring the process back into their own hands. To understand their interests clearly, people need to have alternatives from which they can choose. But there is no clear presentation of alternatives. The two major parties do not offer sharply distinguishable programs. Candidates in elections are reluctant to deal directly and in detail with policy issues. The separation of powers makes it difficult to determine who should get the credit or the blame for a policy. Thus possible alternatives are not formulated. This makes it difficult, if not impossible, for the people to make rational judgments on policy issues. Without this ability, the power of the people at large is seriously undermined, and they are unable to assert their interests effectively.

The radical left.   Within the left there are various definitions of who has the power in America. There is general agreement, however, on the following propositions. To begin with, power in America is not widely diffused but is concentrated in the hands of a small stratum of the population, a ruling class. The top leadership of this ruling class comprises the key decision makers in America—the "power structure," or "the power elite." Next, the dominant element in the ruling class and the power elite is big business, corporate capitalism. Economic power is the crucial kind of power, and the controllers of most economic power are the boards of directors and top executives of the largest industrial and financial institutions. Working with the industrial and financial leaders are the top figures in a number of other institutions. Among these are the corporate law firms of Washington and New York, skilled in manipulating the law in the interests of business. And a climate of ideas favorable to corporate capitalism is established by the mass media, the universities, the great philanthropic foundations, such as Ford and Rockefeller, and opinion-molding associations in foreign affairs, such as the Council on Foreign Relations and the Trilateral Commission, and in economic affairs, such as the Business Council and the Committee for Economic Development.

Further, the key institutions of the federal government—the presidency, the major Cabinet departments and regulatory agencies, the FBI, and the military—are dominated by the power elite. The various elements of the ruling group—the leaders of corporations, law firms, opinion-making organizations, and the federal government—work closely together. They are not a completely integrated, single executive committee. But they are linked in a number of ways. For example, their social backgrounds are similar. Most come from upper-middle- to upper-class families, and often their power has been inherited from their power-elite fathers. They are predominately male, white, Anglo-Saxon Protestants, though an increasing number of Catholics, such as the Kennedys, and some Jews, such as Henry Kissinger, have been making it into the inner group. Moreover, they see a good deal of each other, for they belong to the same exclusive clubs (and many went to the same expensive, private preparatory schools and Ivy League universities). In addition, their institutional bases overlap, for they move easily from one location of power to another and then back again.

Another assumption of the radical left is that the power elite works through great, technological bureaucracies which treat the mass of the people as cogs in the organizational machinery. (This factor has become so important in the minds of some new left analysts that they suggest that the men at the top are themselves mere agents of the technological system.)

Last, the ruling group subscribes to a common set of beliefs in capitalism and private property, and in the domestic and foreign policies that correspond with those beliefs. This is not to say that there are no differences among the rulers. There are liberal and conservative wings within the elite. But even the liberal wing accepts the values of private property and capitalism, subject to a certain amount of governmental guidance, and they agree that our foreign policy should protect those values from their opponents, specifically the communist powers.

Thus our political parties, the media, educational institutions, and so on offer the people only a very narrow range of alternatives—a range contained within the consensus established by the power elite. Outside that consensus the mask of tolerance is dropped, and police power and the courts are used ruthlessly to suppress opinions and actions that offer radical alternatives. And in all of this the masses of the people are nowhere—bewildered, unrepresented, and, to all intents and purposes, powerless.

The conservatives.   The conservatives, too, see excessive power in the hands of a small stratum of the population. They believe that power has been skewed in the direction of an elite, which they call the "liberal establishment." It differs in a number of important respects from the radical left's version of the ruling group. It is considerably broader, less unified, and not nearly as dominant. And the conservatives see its bias as left of center, whereas the left's power elite is clearly perceived as being on the right. However, their analysis of the liberal establishment actually includes some of the same elements found in the radical left's power-elite analysis.

Thus the conservatives believe that tremendous power has gravitated to the institutions that produce information and ideas, with special reference to Harvard and other Ivy League universities; the major foundations; opinion-leading associations such as the Council on Foreign Relations; public policy research organizations such as the Brookings Institution; the television and radio networks; such newspapers as *The New York Times* and *The Washington Post;* and such periodicals as *Harper's Magazine, Atlantic Monthly, The New Yorker,* and *Foreign Affairs.* These harbor, according to William Buckley, "the intellectual plutocrats of the nation, who have at their disposal vast cultural and financial resources."[3]

Then there is Wall Street. It may seem strange that conservatives, who champion the business system, should be critical of the great center of eastern finance and corporate law; and they certainly do not agree with the radical left that corporate business runs America. But their complaint is that important elements in the New York financial world have betrayed the true interests of American business. Conservatives feel betrayed because Wall Street's financiers have heavy investments aboard, and they try to protect these by having our government placate international communism instead of standing up against it.

Working with the knowledge industry and Wall Street is the White House and the vast array of bureaucracies that are controlled by the president. And until the early 1970s the Supreme Court, too, was seen as part of the establishment, though, as we shall see in Chapter 9, this view has been somewhat modified by some of the decisions of the Court under Chief Justice Warren Burger. Finally, the leaders of organized labor are believed by conservative analysts to be close allies of these other liberal establishment elements, working out agreements with them that expand the role of government and undermine the free-enterprise system.

These establishment groups, say the conservatives, claim to speak for the great consensus of American beliefs. This simply is not true. Its members live and work in cities in the Northeast, in an artificial, insulated world of ideas. They are totally different from, and cannot represent, the great numbers of people who live in the "heartland" of America, the Midwest; or in the South and West, where conservatives do not have to be apologetic about their creed. They are the "eastern establishment" and the only consensus they express is that of the liberal intellectuals and the eastern financiers and lawyers.

People drawn from the ranks of the liberal establishment have ruled America since the 1930s. Consequently, limited government has been gravely compromised. The separation of powers has fallen before the dominance of the executive branch. Thus the division of powers has been lost as states' rights were overridden by the federal juggernaut. The only limits advocated by the liberal establishment are the wrong kind—limits on the ability of the police to preserve the public order, and limits on the military budgets needed to halt the spread of international communism.

Consequently, we need alternatives to the rule of the liberal establishment. And, like their liberal counterparts, conservatives argue that clearer choices should be made available to the electorate through the party system, so that the people can perceive that their interests have not been well served by those who have ruled them for 40 years and that others should now be entrusted with the task.

The radical right.   Ever since the Russian Revolution of October 1917, the radical right in America has warned that communism was spreading throughout the world and was conspiring to take over the United States. As time went on, the right became increasingly convinced that communists and their socialist-cum-liberal allies and dupes had won several vantage points of power in America and were steadily increasing their hold on the system.

As Robert Welch of the John Birch Society put it in 1965, "The Communist conspiratorial apparatus is now steadily closing in, with every conceivable pressure and deception, on all remaining resistance to the establishment of its police state over our own country."⁴ The apparatus was gaining control of the media, the universities and public school systems, and the philanthropic foundations.

It was even reaching for the presidency itself, and in 1961 Welch wrote that "Dwight Eisenhower is a dedicated, conscious agent of the Communist conspiracy."⁵ This was too much for many, perhaps most, members of the John Birch Society. However, the belief remains widespread among the radical right that communism has taken over much of the world, runs the United Nations, and is rapidly gaining ground in America with the insidious help of its intellectual apologists.

Recently, a variation of this view has been advanced in some radical right quarters, including the John Birch Society, that the rulers of America are not communists as such, for they are not eager to allow Moscow to tell them what to do. Just the same they constitute a group of "insiders" who are out to establish a collectivist dictatorship which, from the point of view of most Americans, will not be very different from communism. These insiders, notably the Rockefellers and their allies in government, eastern finance, the universities, and the media, aim to divide up the world with the communist powers into spheres of influence in each of which the ruling groups can preserve their privileges intact.

Change

We have already discussed ideal values, or what principles should guide human behavior, and power, or the reality of who runs America, from the point of view of each of our five perspectives. In each case we have found a gap between the ideal and the perceived reality. To bring what *should be* closer to what *is*, each perspective suggests certain changes in our political system and advocates various methods to achieve them.

The centrists.   Of all the perspectives the centrists see the greatest degree of concordance between what is and what ought to be. But it would be a mistake to interpret the centrist position as being an uncritical defense of the status quo.

It is true that centrists tend to defend the accomplishments of the American political system. They argue that at home the system has produced an incredible abundance of material goods; an unparalleled provision of educational opportunities; and an impressive array of programs designed to give the less privileged members of society a share of the American heritage. Internationally, we have protected the national security against periodic aggression, yet displayed a willingness to negotiate in the quest for peace.

Still, along the way there have been blunders, failures, and even disasters, such as the Civil War and the Great Depression, which made clear the need for significant changes. Fortunately, our system, from its beginning, has included mechanisms to produce change. The Founding Fathers designed a Constitution of great flexibility, which has evolved to meet the political and economic stresses of each successive era. Change, then, has been a permanent part of the American experience.

However, the key to the centrist approach is that change must come gradually, step by step, incrementally. Rapid, sweeping changes put people under great psychic stress, raising the level of anxieties and endangering the fragile network of relationships that holds a complex society together. Moreover, changes undertaken faster than a step at a time, leaving insufficient opportunity to test the results of each move, usually make matters worse rather than better.

Within the system the means are readily available to produce incremental change. Our political system provides for open discussion of the issues. Free elections are held regularly. Then there is the interplay of organized groups, which are constantly engaged in a process of negotiating and bargaining. As the interests of the various groups come into conflict with each other, the conflicts are resolved by *compromise.*

This process of compromise is the key to the way governmental decisions are made in America. Agreements are arrived at, and then we move on to one negotiation after another as conditions change. It takes time to hammer out each accommodation; and by its nature a compromise represents a moderate advance over previous conditions. Yet the process has taken care of the grievances of one group after another throughout American history.

On the other hand, the system cannot satisfy those who refuse to accept gradualist measures and insist on drastic and immediate transformation of policies and procedures. In fact, if they resort to tactics that threaten violent disruption, government has the obligation to take firm countermeasures. Certainly a democratic government should use its authority with restraint and give the widest possible latitude to the free expression of even the most hostile views. But where the law is breached, a democratic government must enforce it. For democracy is in essence a system that provides for orderly change within a framework of law.

The liberals.   The liberals are not satisfied with the centrists' position. They concede that there have been real accomplishments under our system of government and politics. But they feel that, in large measure, these gains have been made because of the persistent criticism and pressure that the liberals have applied. Moreover, the achievements fall far short of what is needed. All too often, government in America has not been effective. The structure of government is ill-equipped to handle the pressing problems of our age. Its movement is so slow and erratic that we are unable to evolve broad policies and long-range plans. Consequently, although we have managed to struggle through most of our great crises, we have not been able to forestall them. Our system is characterized less by coherent decision making than by inertia and deadlock, interrupted by occasional spurts of activity.

We suffer, says James MacGregor Burns, from "government by fits and starts . . . a statecraft that has not been able to supply the steady leadership and power necessary for the conduct of our affairs."[6] So the cities are allowed to deteriorate, and the poor and minority groups are neglected. And our foreign policy is still based on outmoded militaristic and nationalistic conceptions instead of reaching toward a new kind of conciliatory, internationalist posture, which the liberals advocate as necessary in a thermonuclear age.

Traditionally, liberals tended to look to the federal agencies, and particularly the presidency, to make government more effective. And they have at times been fascinated by the British model of parliamentary or cabinet government. This model does not contain the principle of separation of powers and is able to produce faster results than our system. Yet the British can make as strong a claim as we to the title of democracy; for theirs, too, is limited government.

We shall note in Chapters 6 and 7 that the liberals' faith in the presidency and their tendency to want to follow the British example of government have been considerably reduced since the mid-1960s. Nonetheless, it remains their general view that we should simplify our tremendously complex system; assign responsibility clearly instead of diffusing it; and replace delay with action.

To bring about the necessary changes will, the liberals admit, take time. They accept the necessity of negotiation and compromise. They also believe that change must be accomplished within the framework of law and that revolutionary methods are both impracticable and undesirable.

Still, they are much less inclined than the centrists to accept a slow pace of change. Bargaining and compromise may be necessary, but in America they have become ends in themselves.

The liberals argue that we are now confronted by an unprecedented array of social, political, and ecological crises so intense as to pose serious questions about the prospects for further progress and even to raise doubts about the possibility of human survival. Given the dire nature of our situation we need major changes in both our institutions and our policies.

If these changes are to be supported by the majority, as they must if we are to remain a democracy, they will have to be accomplished incrementally. But if we cannot find ways of speeding up the process, of accomplishing more substantial increments at a time, the system may break down. And although liberals are usually believers in progress and optimists, they no longer rule out the possibility of the ultimate failure of the American system of government.

The radical left.   The radical left are as impatient with the liberals' proposals for change as the liberals are with the centrists'. As the left perceives it, the system is effective only in serving the interests of the ruling elite. Although the rulers' purposes may be subjected to some harassment, delay, and even an occasional veto, they are able to hold onto their power and to achieve public policies that serve their ends. From the point of view of the true interests of the people, however, American government is profoundly ineffective. Its principal outputs are not those factors making for the good and the just society, but rather racism, a mindless pursuit of economic growth with little regard to a fair distribution of the product or the damage inflicted on the environment, and a continuing buildup and application of military force.

Consequently, the system is blindly unresponsive to the new forces struggling for expression in the country, which cannot indefinitely be suppressed. And internationally the paranoiac obsession with the menace of international communism is leading us toward the thermonuclear holocaust.

Given the dreadful intensity of the crises we face, it is clear to the left that the centrist belief in the effectiveness of gradualism is absurdly wrong. Given, furthermore, the nearly inaccessible structures of power, the strategies of the liberals are irrelevant. We can no longer accept the kinds of changes that merely provide pacifiers to keep the system going. The game of compromise and expediency, which the centrists adore and the liberals are all too ready to accept, is worn out both morally and practically. We need radical change that will replace the present relationships of power with a new system based on humane values.

But how is this to be accomplished? Here there is disarray on the left. For the ruling elite has at its disposal an overwhelming machinery of official force. The left comprises only a small minority of the people. The complacency of the rulers is not likely to be shaken unless the left can win impressive support from the masses of the people.

But the people at large are difficult to reach. The combination of affluence and mass media manipulation have attached them to the system. They have internalized its values. Their servitude is "voluntary"—they are not even aware that they are not free.[7]

A variety of strategies is proposed. A few small groups have advocated terrorism and guerrilla warfare. A larger number, while rejecting this kind of calculated violence, adopt the tactics of militant confrontation as a means of forcing the masses into awareness of the realities and of radicalizing students and intellectuals—in which task government can help by responding with an excess of official force. Others go out to live among the poor to undertake community organization or work in factories to convert the workers to socialism. A common theme among all these groups is the plea to look beyond the national context and aim at an international socialist revolution organized by the "Third World," the poor, nonwhite nations whose populations greatly outnumber those of the white nations.

Others again urge withdrawal from all efforts to challenge the society directly. Some of these emphasize individual contemplation and inward exploration. Some engage in the establishment of new communities in which radically different ways of living may be tried—forms free from technological pressure, acquisitive urges, and bureaucratic regimentation. Although these experiments may lack political impact in the short run, it is the hope of many of their proponents that they will demonstrate to the people at large the viability of other ways of living and make them so attractive that they will become the models for the society and politics of the future.

Still others accept the power-elite analysis generally but believe that the system provides vantage points from which concessions may be won and experience gained for the long haul. So they organize pressure, seek out campaigns in which they can work for candidates who stand against militarism and racism, and create new political parties to achieve their goals.

This is by no means an exhaustive list of strategies. Nor are they mutually exclusive. Individuals and groups within the left may adopt combinations of these and shift from one to the other in a determined search for ways of bringing about the rapid transformation of the American system.

The conservatives.   The conservatives perceive American government as having become profoundly ineffective. Since it has fallen into the hands of the liberal establishment, our position has deteriorated both domestically and internationally. At home the expectations of the poor and the blacks have been raised to the point at which they are in a perpetual state of unrest and dissatisfaction; crime proliferates; the young are permitted to endanger lives, property, and morality; and the authority needed to preserve public order is denied by the courts. Abroad, communism has extended its sway since 1945 over Eastern Europe, Cuba, China, and parts of Southeast Asia—and our withdrawal from Vietnam has opened the way for further encroachments.

What is needed, then, is not change in the direction advocated at different speeds by the left, the liberals, and the centrists, but on the contrary, a restoration of the principles proposed by the Founding Fathers—notably, limited govern-

"*I guess I'm a conservative, if you mean do I put up a lot of jams and jellies.*"

Drawing by Weber: © 1976 The New Yorker Magazine, Inc.

ment and respect for private property. This is not to say that we can turn the clock back and revert completely to the system as it was established. It does mean that the purposes for which the Constitution was designed should be reasserted and restated in contemporary conservative terms.

To accomplish this reversion conservatives propose procedures that the system itself provides. The only force to be used is legitimized force to restore "law and order," relying on the removal of what they regard as unreasonable restraints on the authority of the police. In the political realm they rely on education and advocacy, organized pressures, and the support of candidates sympathetic to their cause.

To operate through the electoral process means the use of compromise and bargaining to some extent. This is acceptable to the conservatives up to a point. However, like the liberals, they are seeking far-reaching policy changes, and these do not usually emerge from the existing methods of negotiation and accommodation. Thus they have worked with particular enthusiasm for such candidates as Barry Goldwater and Ronald Reagan, who call for more basic changes from existing policies than do most politicians.

The radical right.   The radical right include spokespersons for a number of conflicting approaches to the problem of change. All of them see the situation as desperate, so drastic measures are called for to produce, in effect, a counter-revolution. A few extreme groups, such as the Minutemen, have armed for violent insurrection (or, as they claim, for the defense of the Republic against violent insurrection from the left or imminent invasion by communists from abroad). Others, like the John Birch Society, oppose illegal tactics but maintain secrecy of membership, adopt authoritarian leadership, and use tactics of infiltration—all as ways of countering the methods which, they say, the communists and other subversive groups are using to take over America. However, the Birch Society, and most other right-wing groups, also enter the electoral fray from time to time, giving strong support to very conservative candidates for various offices.

Summary

Table 1–1 sums up the differences between the five perspectives with respect to their views on the values of equality and liberty; the question of who has power in America; and the problem of how much change is needed and how it is to be brought about.

Some Warnings

Having set up the categories and discussed the differences between them, we must recognize some dangers about the use and possible misuse of categorization in general and these categories in particular.

TABLE 1-1   *The Five Perspectives: A Summary*

		Radical Left	Liberals	Centrists	Conservatives	Radical Right
Values	Equality	Full social and economic equality	Substantial redistribution of wealth, status, power	Equality –of opportunity –before the law –voting rights –right to basic standard of living	Differentiation Rewards for ability and effort Competition	Two strands (1) strong emphasis on differentiation (2) populism
	Liberty — Civil Liberty	Individual authenticity, freedom of personal behavior; but ban on militarism, racism, etc.	Freedom of expression and personal behavior	Balance; freedom and order	Freedom within framework of "law and order," tradition, antisubversion, antipermissiveness	Loyalty Authority Control of left
	Liberty — Economic Liberty	Socialism	Severe limits on business, property rights	Mixed economy	Economic individualism, property rights Government only as rule setter and referee	Unrestricted private ownership
	Power — Who rules America?	Power elite, corporate capitalism	Imbalance favoring business, money, military	Checks and balances Pluralism	Liberal establishment	Small elite working with or controlled by international communism
	Change	Radical/revolutionary	Faster	Gradualism; compromise	Restoration	Counterrevolution

All categories distort.   Categories are artificial constructs that our minds impose upon reality to make our experiences more comprehensible. Categories are, at best, rough, simplified approximations of reality. This must certainly be true of an attempt to compress the entire range of American political opinion into just five perspectives. Thus we should constantly remind ourselves of a number of qualifications, some of which were mentioned earlier and are elaborated here.

First, each category represents not a single distinct point on the spectrum but a broad range of opinion. This is particularly so in relation to the centrist position. It is important to note that most of the debate in Congress and in election campaigns takes place within this category. But there is also conflict, often very bitter in nature, within each of the other categories we have defined.

Second, by definition, a spectrum is not a series of separate entities but a continuum in which each position gradually shades into the next. This means that some political thinkers will bridge two of our categories. For example, left of center there have been efforts to combine the best qualities of the liberal and radical left positions; and right of center there is a group of people, such as Irving Kristol, Nathan Glazer, and Daniel Moynihan, who bring together centrist with conservative themes and have come to be called neo-conservatives.

Third, many people fit into one category on some issues, and another category on other issues. They may be liberals on questions of economic liberty (supporting massive intervention in the economy to attack unemployment), yet conservatives on matters of civil liberty (such as using government to suppress pornography). This refusal to be ideologically consistent is especially marked among political leaders. This does not imply that all politicians are completely unprincipled. Some are, but others have strong convictions about the public issues they deal with.

However, as we shall see throughout this book, even highly principled politicians must deal not only with ideas and values but also with power. To be effective they must be elected; and once elected they must deal with the realities of officeholding, including the need to represent their constituents, who hold many differing views. In so doing, politicians are likely to fall into inconsistencies. The only exceptions to this rule of political expediency will be members of minor political groups that have no immediate prospect of gaining any degree of power and thus can remain ideologically consistent.

Fourth, other inconsistencies are frequently found between people's political outlook on the one hand and their personalities and lifestyles on the other. Thus many businessmen who are devout advocates of the conservative attachment to tradition are adventurous and constantly innovative in their business lives. Conversely, many university professors who identify with liberal proposals for sweeping political and social change resist change within the structure of the university.

We should also be wary of assuming that extremist politics go with maladjusted personalities, although there may be some evidence for this association. For example, psychologist Bruno Bettelheim found most of the militant student leaders of the radical left in the 1960s to be "consumed by a self-hatred they try to escape from by fighting any establishment."[8] And Richard Hofstadter described the role of the right wing in American history under the title *The Paranoid Style in American Politics.*[9]

Yet psychiatrist Kenneth Keniston has challenged the identification of left-wing radicalism with disturbed personalities, and described the militant student leaders he talked with as being sensitive, humane, and highly intelligent people, alienated from society not because they are neurotic but because society is maladjusted.[10] Similarly, various studies by social scientists have questioned whether the John Birch Society, for example, can be understood primarily in terms of individual psychopathology. According to these studies, the larger numbers of its members are not suffering from psychological disturbances and seem to cope with their personal lives and careers about as effectively as do most other people.[11]

Have all these qualifications, contradictions, and inconsistencies rendered our five categories meaningless? Of course not. All categories, all labels, distort reality to some extent and must be used with caution. But despite the popular distaste for using labels (and especially for being labeled), we cannot think, analyze, or approach an understanding of any problem without categories. Political science itself is a rather vague category, yet it serves some useful purposes to set it off from other categories, such as sociology and economics.

The five perspectives discussed in this book are quite widely used in political discussion and analysis. The division into left, right, and center, with the additional subdivisions, of liberal, conservative, radical left, and radical right, provides a commonsense reflection of the principal controversies over politics in America. If handled with care, these categories will provide us with a useful framework for an introductory survey of American government and politics.

Opinion is not enough.   It would be easy to conclude from all this talk of values and perspectives that nothing matters but opinion and that anyone's opinion is as good as anyone else's if the opinion is seriously held. This would be a totally erroneous conclusion. An opinion is not worth much unless it is based, first, on a solid understanding of the pertinent facts, and, second, on a process of careful, cogent reasoning. And opinions of that quality are difficult to come by.

Getting at the facts is a complicated, often frustrating task. To begin with, there are certain rudimentary problems of observation. Five witnesses seeing the same accident will typically provide five different versions of what actually happened. The difficulty is compounded when the facts in question are immensely complex. Thus wide variations are found in investigations in the so-called "hard" sciences. According to one study: "At least half the data reported in scientific journals are either wrong or else supported by so little evidence that readers can't tell how reliable they are."[12]

When we relate this phenomenon to the study of politics, we find that the difficulty is still further compounded by our habit of observing facts selectively through a screen of values. We tend to see what we want to see. We have already noticed this in the five perspectives' five different pictures of who actually has power in America. We shall encounter the problem repeatedly throughout this book. For example, in Chapter 13 we shall find alternative accounts not only of how acute the energy shortage is, but of whether there is a shortage at all. In Chapter 14 we shall explain how scientists argued with great bitterness over the antiballistic missile program. They debated not only whether the ABM was desirable for national security, but also whether it would work; and in most cases those who were for it because we needed it said it would work, and those who claimed we did not need it said it would not work.

This difficulty of getting agreement on the facts is discouraging enough. But in addition to having a good grasp of the facts, we have to interpret them carefully through a process of critical reasoning. Again, our values tend to interfere with clear analysis, for they make us reluctant to follow the logic of an argument wherever it leads unless that is where we want to be led. Moreover, in political science our tools of analysis are still relatively crude. Many of the most significant political questions do not lend themselves to exact study, for we are dealing with human behavior with all its contradictions and absurdities and imponderables, on the largest and most complex scale. The data available are often fragmentary, and rarely can we draw upon controlled experiments or make accurate predictions.

When all this is said, we need not conclude that systematic study of politics is impossible. There are many facts on which everyone—or at least all scholars—agree, no matter what their position on the spectrum. Moreover, the amount of pertinent data has been increasing rapidly in recent years, especially in such fields as public opinion, voting behavior, and legislative behavior.

Nor is controlled experimentation the only technique that qualifies as scientific method. The behavioral sciences are becoming more sophisticated in the development and use of analytical tools. Political scientists today are using case studies, survey research, intensive interviews, and statistical techniques. Familiarity with these techniques is not necessary to an understanding of this book. However, some of the results gathered by these means will be considered in various chapters.

Nor does the impossibility of completely excluding personal value judgments from the topics considered here mean that any interpretation is as good as any other. Passion and commitment are highly desirable attributes to bring to the practice of politics. But in studying politics, feelings will not suffice in place of intellectual rigor. So it makes good sense before we make final judgments, first, to seek out the pertinent data; second, to set forth alternative interpretations of that data; third, to select the most convincing alternative; then, and only then, to make proposals for action.

Notes and References

1.   Milton Friedman, *Capitalism and Freedom* (Chicago: The University of Chicago Press, 1962), p. 10.

2.   Robert Welch, *The Blue Book of the John Birch Society* (Belmont, Mass.: John Birch Society, 1961), pp. 67–68.

3.   William Buckley, "The Genteel Nightmare of Richard Rovere," *Harper's Magazine*, August 1962, pp. 51–55.

4.   *Bulletin of the John Birch Society*, July 1965, p. 4.

5.   "The Conspirator," letter by Robert Welch circulated within the Birch Society.

6.   James MacGregor Burns, *The Deadlock of Democracy* (Englewood Cliffs, N.J.: Prentice-Hall, Inc. [Spectrum Books], 1963), p. 2.

7.   Herbert Marcuse, *An Essay on Liberation* (Boston: Beacon Press, 1969), p. 6.

8.   Testimony before the Senate Committee on Government Operations, Permanent Subcommittee on Investigations, *Hearings on Riots, Civil and Criminal Disorders*, 91st Congress, 1st Session, May 9, 13, and 14, 1969, Part 16, pp. 3069–79.

9.   Richard Hofstadter, *The Paranoid Style in American Politics* (New York: Alfred A. Knopf, Inc., 1952, 1954, 1964, 1965).

10.   Kenneth Keniston, *Young Radicals: Notes on Committed Youth* (New York: Harcourt, Brace & World, 1968), and *Youth and Dissent: The Rise of a New Opposition* (New York: Harcourt Brace Jovanovich, Inc., 1971).

11.   See, for example, Ira S. Rother, "Social and Psychological Determinants of Radical Rightism," in *The American Right Wing: Readings in Political Behavior*, Robert A. Schoenberger, ed. (New York: Holt, Rinehart and Winston, Inc., 1969). See also Wolfinger et al. in *Ideology and Discontent*, David Apter, ed. (New York: The Free Press, 1964), pp. 262–93.

12.   "Scientific Data: 50 Pct. Unusable?" *The Chronicle of Higher Education*, Vol. 10, No. 1 (February 24, 1975), p. 1. This is a report on a study undertaken by the National Bureau of Standards.

1 Part One 1

Politics and the People

IN THE NEXT

four chapters we explore the broad context of American politics, the basic forces that contend with each other to influence the decisions of governmental officials.

We begin in Chapter 2 with the electorate at large and discuss the relationship between public opinion and government. Then we assess the extent and quality of the electorate's participation in politics, finding that the majority of the people are still not very politically conscious, despite an increase in political awareness in recent years. So we ask: How serious a problem is it when only a minority are well informed and politically active?

In the next three chapters we look at the mechanisms through which individuals, groups, and the people at large express their political ideas and interests. Thus in Chapter 3 we study political parties and debate the implications of the general decline in support for the two major parties. Chapter 4 deals with elections and asks whether the electoral process provides significant choices of candidates and policies or whether elections are merely exercises in distortion and manipulation. Then in Chapter 5 we describe the groups that organize the multiple interests of the people and analyze the effect of these special-interest groups on the political process; and we ask whether there is a reasonable balance among these groups or whether a few of them tower over the rest in their ability to influence political decisions.

In this first section three key questions define the debate among the five perspectives: *Do the people at large rule? Can they? Should they?*

Photo: Stock, Boston; Patricia Hollander Gross.

2

Public Opinion

Who Cares about Politics?

Democracy, the dictionary tells us, is a form of government in which political power resides in all the people. But there are more than 215 million of us in America, so we cannot all exercise our power directly. A great many decisions have to be handled by relatively small numbers of leaders. Still, the democratic ideal requires that the leaders be responsive to the voice of the people, to what is commonly called "public opinion." Actually this phrase is misleading. We are not a single, undifferentiated mass of people holding a single opinion. We are made up of many "publics" holding a diversity of opinions.

In this chapter we shall begin by looking first at the factors that shape the opinions of these publics, then at the ways these opinions express themselves politically. After that we shall examine some disturbing data on the amount and distribution of political participation in America. This will set the stage for a debate among our five perspectives on the extent to which the people at large are equipped to exercise political power.

What Influences Our Opinions?

We all like to consider ourselves self-determining thinkers, independent of the categories that bind other people. In fact, even if we assume that we retain an ultimate measure of free will, our ideas and behavior are powerfully influenced by a great range of factors when we make political decisions. For one thing, part of our response to politics springs from our deepest hopes and fears, our drives and impulses, our frustrations and aggressions—from that level of our personalities that is not fully subject to rational control. Then, too, our family background is an important factor in determining our personalities and our political values. There is a strong tendency for people to reflect their parents' attitudes and political leanings, even though their living conditions and lifestyles may be totally different from their family background.

At this stage, however, we shall not dwell upon these elements of individual behavior, for our concern must be with opinions in the aggregate, that is, in groups and in the mass. Let us begin by investigating the socioeconomic influences on our opinions.

The Socioeconomic Context

Our political outlook is heavily influenced by a range of factors that can be used to distinguish among the various segments of the population of the United States. So we shall first look at some basic characteristics of the social and economic makeup of the American people, and then explain the political implications of these characteristics.

Income.   The United States is easily the wealthiest country in the world. Its median family income in 1976 was $14,350, which means that half the families in the country earned more than this, the other half less. This is a remarkable level of affluence, which has created a large middle class. However, there are also very considerable variations in income, with some earning hundreds of thousands of dollars a year, while others (officially estimated in 1976 at over 12 percent of the population) live below the designated poverty line of $5500 for a family of four.

Occupation.   The civilian work force in the United States consisted of almost 95 million people in 1976. The most significant developments affecting the labor force in recent years are, first, the fact that the proportion of jobs requiring substantial training and skills has increased greatly. Almost a quarter of all jobs today are in professional, technical, managerial, or administrative categories. Unskilled laborers make up barely 7 percent of the work force, as compared with 15 percent at the beginning of the century. Then, the number of people employed on farms has declined drastically from 38 percent of the population in 1900 to not much more than 3 percent today. Next, there has been a shift from producers of goods to providers of services—salespeople, secretaries, administrators, entertainers, and so on. Today almost half the jobs are in "white-collar" fields, as against about 37 percent in "blue-collar" occupations.

There has also been a dramatic growth in the number of women seeking jobs, some for the sake of augmenting the family income, others becoming the primary family provider after a divorce, others wanting the satisfaction and the independence derived from pursuing a career or occupation outside the home.

Finally, the number of employees in government has expanded, especially at the state and local levels. About one-sixth of the work force is now employed by government, and some projections indicate that this could rise to one-fourth within a few years.

Education.   In the United States more people go to college than in any country in the history of the world. By the 1970s the proportion of the college-aged population who actually entered college was around 45 percent, up from 32 percent in 1960. At the other end of the scale the high school dropouts had fallen to about one-quarter of their age group by the 1970s as compared with well over one-third in 1960, and one-half in 1950.

Race and ethnicity.   Except for fewer than a million American Indians everyone in this country comes of immigrant stock. The immigrants arrived here from Britain, Ireland, and northern Europe, and later from southern and eastern Europe. Several million blacks were brought here from Africa as slaves. Immigration laws from the early 1920s were designed to keep down immigration from areas outside northern Europe, especially Asia. However, in recent years considerable numbers have come here from Canada and Mexico. And new laws in 1965 have resulted in a large increase in immigration from Asia.

Today the biggest ethnic group in America consists of the descendants of immigrants from Great Britain. But large numbers derive from Germany, Africa, Ireland, Mexico, Puerto Rico, Italy, Poland and other East European countries, and Japan and other parts of Asia.

The first settlers established the dominance of the English language and the Anglo-Saxon legal system, and the schools and other agencies undertook the task of trying to Americanize the successive waves of immigrants into the great "melting pot." Still, various ethnic heritages are very much alive. Indeed, spurred by the resurgence of racial pride and identity among black Americans in the 1960s, a number of groups, especially those of Spanish, eastern and southern European, and Asian origin, have reasserted their historical roots and made their ethnicity an important factor politically.

Religion.   According to a Gallup poll in 1976 Americans are "extraordinarily religious people" when compared with citizens of other industrialized countries. In the United States 56 percent of those interviewed said that their religious beliefs were "very important" to them, compared with 36 percent in Italy, 23 percent in Britain, and 12 percent in Japan. Only in part of the Third World—India, Africa below the Sahara, and Latin America—was the percentage higher than here.

Some 60 percent of Americans are Protestants, among whom close to half declare that they have had the "born-again" experience—that dramatic conversion to the preaching of Christ which became a topic of intense political interest during the presidential campaign of Jimmy Carter. The next largest religious group, the Catholics, comprise over a quarter of the American population. Jews make up less than 3 percent of the population. And there are a large number of other faiths and denominations, including non-Western beliefs, such as Buddhism.

Geography.   Increasingly, Americans have become an urbanized people, with over two-thirds of the population now living in metropolitan areas—cities of 50,000 or more people and their surrounding suburbs. Through the first half of this century masses of people were moving into the big cities of the Northeast and Midwest. Since midcentury, however, there have been three major geographic trends. First, large numbers, especially whites, have moved out of the cities and into the suburbs. Second, there has been a shift away from metropolitan areas into smaller towns. Third, population growth has almost stopped in the Northeast and is occurring mostly in the western states and, since about 1970, in the South—reversing a period of declining population in the southern states.

Age.   The United States now has a steadily aging population—a fact that has already brought to an end the national preoccupation with the attitudes and behavior of young people that marked the 1960s. The number of teenagers was over 29 million in 1976 but will fall to less than 26 million by the mid-1980s. In the same period the over-65 population will rise from under 23 million to over 26 million, and by the year 2030 more than one person in six in the United States will be 65 or over.

A number of factors have contributed to the trend toward an older population, including a significant decline in the death rate due to improved medical care. But most important has been a dramatic decline in the birth rate. It soared after World War II, reaching its peak in 1957. Then it began to sink, until it fell below the rate necessary to keep the level of the population stable (apart from immigration).

Sex.   There are more women of voting age than men. Although slightly more boys are born than girls, women's average life expectation is almost eight years more than men's: 75.9 to 68.2. Almost half of all women, a total of about 39 million, are now part of the work force.

Linkages.   The socioeconomic factors we have listed are intertwined in a number of ways. This can be seen most readily if we start with income and trace its connections with other elements. Thus the more highly skilled jobs generally pay more money. More years of schooling tend to generate higher income. On the average, blacks earn considerably less than whites. Geography affects income: concentrations of poverty are found in the inner cities (where there are large numbers of blacks) and in rural areas in the deep South. Middle-aged people earn more on the average than the young and the elderly. And women tend to earn less than men.

The relationship becomes more complicated with respect to ethnicity and religion. The later immigrant arrivals, mostly Catholics, Jews, and Asians, began at the bottom of the income ladder. Now they are moving up. The average annual income for Jews, in fact, is now the highest of any religious–ethnic group, and Irish Catholics are in second place. Japanese-Americans have also established a high average-income ranking. Each of these groups also has a well-above-average number of years of schooling.

Implications for Political Attitudes

What do these socioeconomic factors mean in terms of our political attitudes and opinions? Answering this is an immensely complicated task. But it is possible, before we proceed to the complications, to make some very crude, approximate generalizations. Chief among these is that those segments of the population that feel least advantaged by the system, who have a sense of being "out-groups," are most likely to stress the need for more equality, and in that sense to be left of center on our political spectrum. Most often these people will be found at the lower end of the income scale and in the less skilled occupations. They are likely to have fewer years of schooling than the average. Many of them will be black or have Spanish surnames, and will live in the inner cities. Others will be descendants of the later waves of immigration, who have a sense of grievance that those who got here first are the "established" groups who are reluctant to give the newer groups their place in the sun. Conversely, the more affluent, business and professional, college-educated, strata of the population, living in the suburbs and descendants of the earlier settlers, tend to feel that they have the most to protect and thus to be less enthusiastic about egalitarian notions.

This simple scheme is useful as far as it goes. But, as we look at the strands of opinion more closely, we see that they move in all directions, producing extraordinarily complex patterns, sometimes breaking down into a bewildering maze. Thus some well-to-do, college-educated people—perhaps because of their personality structure and family background—have a strong social conscience that impels them to advocate strong measures on behalf of the poor. At the other end of the scale, poor whites in the South may be so resistant to the claims of blacks that they oppose policies that help the poor because they also help the blacks.

Then, as we look at the question of civil liberties, we are more likely to discover liberal or left-of-center attitudes among the affluent, college-educated segment of the population. Thus a survey in 1972 indicated that, among people with no more than a grade school education, only 22 percent would be willing to allow freedom of speech to an admitted communist; the figure for college graduates was 84 percent.[1]

We come across further complexities when we examine the political attitudes of certain ethnic and religious groups. Thus Catholics still tend to feel that they are not fully accepted into the system, which they believe to be dominated by Protestants. This inclines them left of center on a number of issues. Yet they are pulled in a different direction by their increasing affluence; and also by the tenets of their church on such issues as abortion and school prayers. Jews represent another political anomaly. Their average income is high; they have more years of schooling than any other group; and many of them occupy highly skilled professional positions. Yet the Jewish people's long history of suffering, discrimination, and near-extermination in Nazi Germany created in them a sense of being outsiders. Consequently, they have tended to ally themselves politically with underprivileged groups. (However, as we shall see in Chapter 12, many Jews have opposed the positions of black and other minority organizations on such issues as school busing and affirmative action.)

Finally, there is the factor of age. Young people are on the whole more liberal, more disposed toward equality than their elders. Partly this is a matter of economics, for the young earn less and have much less property than older people. But even the young who are affluent tend to be more liberal than older people in the same economic bracket. As people grow older, their tendency is to become more protective of what they have acquired, more resistant to social experimentation, and thus more conservative. But even this statement must be qualified, for people over 65, who tend to conservatism on many issues, are overwhelmingly in favor of such egalitarian policies as Social Security.

So we experience once again the problem we encountered in Chapter 1. We suggest some generalization and then we go on to describe a large number of exceptions that complicate the picture immeasurably. We shall encounter this exasperating difficulty again and again throughout this book. Even so, the generalizations represent an important aspect of reality. They are useful starting points for analysis. Thus, despite all the exceptions and crosscurrents that we have mentioned, we must not lose sight of the important relationships that exist between our socioeconomic status and our political opinions.

Political Cues from Opinion Leaders

Now let us look at the political cues we receive from people in positions of leadership or authority, since there is more to the formation of political opinions than their association with social and economic conditions. Political opinions have to be articulated, and we receive help in articulating them from other people. Probably the most important source for our opinions is those individuals who form our network of personal relationships—parents, spouses, relatives, friends, and other acquaintances. They are closest to us, they tend to share our own socioeconomic background, we trust them more than other people, and thus they help to formulate and to reinforce our ideas and values.

Public and private schools, from kindergarten onward, provide another setting in which attitudes with significant political content are conveyed. Teachers, administrators, curriculum designers, and textbook authors play key roles in the process of *socialization,* or communicating to us the prevailing climate of social and political ideas. Then, too, we receive political cues from a variety of leaders, people who have attained some level of prominence or status and have developed relatively clearly stated opinions of which they try to convince us. Among these are leaders in politics and government, in private organizations, and in the institutions that disseminate information and ideas.

Political and governmental leaders.　At all levels of government, elected and appointed officials transmit political ideas to us. The president is the nation's most potent shaper of opinions. The Cabinet, Congress, the Supreme Court, and state and local representatives bombard us with political data. Political party activists, both professionals and involved amateurs, try to reach us with their messages. We are the objects of speeches, debates, news conferences, and newsletters. And the barrage becomes deafening during election campaigns when the contending candidates strive to attract our attention and convince us of their qualifications. We shall have much more to say on the impact of political leaders on public opinion in the remaining chapters of this book.

Organizational leaders.   Leaders of business, labor, professional, civic, and many other kinds of organizations play important roles in the formation of public opinion. These leaders and their staffs represent an extraordinary diversity of interests and opinions. Their jobs require that they be better informed than anyone else in the fields in which their organizations operate, and that they educate their membership, the political leaders, and the public at large to understand and accept their views. Organizational leaders, as we shall see in Chapter 5, are not always able to carry their own memberships along with them on political issues, a problem most likely to occur in mass membership organizations such as labor unions. Still, their claim to speak for very large numbers of people is usually not without foundation; and their expertise in their own field gives their views a particular authority in such complex or obscure areas of public policy as energy, transportation, interest rates, law, and weapons systems.

Professional Opinion Makers

Although political and organizational leaders have to be very much concerned with public opinion, influencing other people's views is only one of their many functions. However, this is the primary role of the professionals who work for those institutions which specialize in the field of information and opinion—the mass media, colleges and universities, research institutions, and philanthropic foundations.

The mass media.   Addressing themselves to the broadest mass public are television, radio, and newspapers. Television has become preeminent among these as a source of political news. About two-thirds of the American people say that they get most of their news from television. This is especially true during great crises. The national trauma of the assassination of John F. Kennedy was experienced largely through television. It was television, through its coverage of the resistance to the civil disobedience movement in the South, that gave the civil rights movement its impetus. The eruptions of violence in the cities in the 1960s, from Watts to Detroit, were a series of television events, and had a great impact on the public consciousness. The bloody battlefields of Vietnam, coming into American homes at the dinner hour night after night, helped to turn opinion in the country against the war. And the televised Senate and House investigations and debates over the Watergate scandal were a principal means of establishing the climate of opinion that led to Richard Nixon's resignation from the presidency.

As for presidential elections, they are fought increasingly in the arena of television. Even the traditional personal tours of the candidates are scheduled to get the best coverage on the local television stations. Vast amounts of money are poured into television commercials. And in 1960 and 1976 the televised debates between the major party candidates probably had a critical effect on the election results.

Radio, a potent instrument of mass persuasion for political leaders in the 1930s and 1940s, has now fallen to a secondary role. However, the increasing number of all-news stations is an important source of information for people driving to and from work and for housewives, and a respectable portion of election campaign budgets is assigned to radio advertising.

Thus newspapers are no longer the public's prime source of political information and opinions, and most of the major papers have been losing circulation. They cannot bring home to us, even in photographs, a candidate's style, gestures, expressions, or the terror of riots and wars, or the drama of a debate or a cross-examination. They can, however, explore issues in depth, give the full background to a news story, deal with problems which, though of crucial importance, are difficult for television to deal with visually. Not all newspapers do this. But those that do have great influence over public opinion. Newspapers such as *The New York Times*, *The Washington Post*, *The Christian Science Monitor*, and *The Los Angeles Times* contain enormous amounts of thoughtfully written information. They also offer opinions through their editorials, and through columnists whose national syndication gives them a readership in the millions. Nor is the impact of newspapers solely on the general public. *The New York Times* and *The Washington Post* are read regularly in the White House and in Congress. And many political and organizational leaders, like the public at large, don't know what to think about a given subject until they have read David Broder or Joseph Kraft or James Reston.

It is important to note, however, that television news and newspapers are not unrelated sources of information. The most likely watchers of the television network news programs are newspaper readers; and the day after a major story has appeared on television, newspaper circulation will generally rise, for many people want to know more about the story than they can glean from the usually superficial coverage given it on television.

Is there a particular bias in the presentation of news and opinions in the mass media? We shall have more to say on this question later in the chapter. For the moment we can indicate that some process of selection is inevitable in the presentation of news, since it is impossible to cover everything that happens, and the values and preconceptions of the individuals who decide what is important and what is not cannot be completely excluded from the selection process. In general, it appears that the majority of journalists are centrist to left of center, and the majority of publishers, whose editorial views are carried by their publications, are centrist to right of center.

In addition to the mass media, we have an array of specialized journals speaking to particular publics. Magazines with a primarily political emphasis offer analyses that cover the complete spectrum of opinion. In the center, *Time* and *Newsweek* have the largest circulations in this category (*Newsweek*, which is owned by *The Washington Post*, being slightly more liberal than *Time*); then comes the more conservative *U.S. News and World Report*. Liberal weeklies such as *The New Republic* and *The Nation*, and the conservative *The National Review* have much smaller circulations; and a great many organs of opinion on the far left and the far right speak to still smaller constituencies. Then, among the vast number of weekly and monthly publications that appeal to various tastes, hobbies, professional activities, and leisure-time pursuits, some give at least occasional attention to politics. Thus such business publications as *Fortune* and *Forbes* give a good deal of coverage to the relationships between government and industry; and the rock music paper, *The Rolling Stone*, provides some well-written coverage of political events from a liberal to left vantage point. Finally, a number of scholarly journals, especially those in political science and economics, bring the findings of recent research to bear on governmental affairs.

Institutions of higher learning.   An important source of opinion in any society are the intellectuals, people whose primary interest is in philosophical, social, aesthetic, scientific, and political ideas. They work in a diversity of professions, but the bulk of them are to be found in colleges and universities, where they can undertake the most characteristic functions of intellectuals: research, writing, and teaching. They influence opinion in the first place through their impact on their students and their peers. They reach the public at large through lectures, articles in the press and popular journals, and radio and television appearances. They also act as consultants to government and, as in the case of Henry Kissinger, are even appointed to high official posts.

In general, college and university faculty members are considerably to the left of the public at large. However, there is no one pervasive ideology common to all academics. According to one study, 64 percent of the social scientists and 57 percent of the humanities professors call themselves "liberal" or "very liberal." And the more distinguished universities with the largest number of research awards tend to have more politically liberal faculties than is the case with the less prestigious schools.[2] However, in business and engineering 60 percent of the professors describe themselves as "conservative" or "very conservative." The governing boards of universities and colleges are generally considerably more conservative than their faculties, a fact that has occasionally caused acute conflicts.

Other opinion-making institutions.   There are three other kinds of agencies concerned with the development of ideas. First, there are social science research centers—the Rand Corporation, the Brookings Institution, the Hudson Institute, the Hoover Institute, the American Enterprise Institute, the Institute for Policy Studies, and others. Then there are organizations, such as the Council on Foreign Relations and the Committee for Economic Development, which help top-level business and professional people explore political and economic issues, as well as other organizations, such as the Foreign Policy Association, that are concerned with the education of the broader citizenry. Finally, several of the private philanthropic organizations, including the Ford and Rockefeller Foundations, have provided large amounts of money over the years to facilitate research into many areas of public policy. However, philanthropic foundations may jeopardize their tax-free standing if their grants are used for partisan political purposes.

The Influence of Events on Public Opinion

One other set of external forces acts upon us to affect our political opinions—great events or major changes in the circumstances of our total society. Some of these are accidents or freak occurrences: drastic changes in the climate, earthquakes, fires, floods, and assassinations. Other events—wars, oil embargoes, the collapse of foreign currencies—result from deep-rooted international problems. Technological advances such as television, atomic energy, or computers have an enormous impact on our lives and attitudes. So, too, do certain social forces, such as

"In our view, the rapid pace of events on both the domestic and the international scene and the continuing uncertainty of the economic climate preclude any expression of voter preference at this particular time. I will say this, however. Both my husband and I will continue to monitor developments across the entire political spectrum, and we look forward confidently to rendering a fair and equitable judgment in November."

Drawing by H. Martin; © 1976 The New Yorker Magazine, Inc.

the movement for equal rights for women and the transformation of sexual attitudes and behavior.

Somehow a bewildered public, staggering from crisis to crisis, must confront all these pressures for change, absorb them into their value systems, and eventually react to them politically—deciding for or against the Equal Rights Amendment, the construction of nuclear energy plants, or judging government's performance in dealing with international crises and natural calamities. To some extent, political, organizational, and other leaders of opinion can influence the reaction of the public to critical events and may even have an impact on the direction and pace of change. But of course they cannot fully control all these events and, like the public at large, leaders find themselves groping for understanding, desperately trying to avoid being overwhelmed or bypassed by the surge of unpredicted, sometimes unpredictable, developments.

How Do We
Express Our Opinions?

We have reviewed the various forces—socioeconomic factors, political leaders, professional opinion matters, and events—that go into creating political opinions. Now we reverse our approach and examine the ways in which publics try to make their opinions count. Voting is the most common way in which people express their political opinions. Suffrage, or the right to vote, now includes the entire adult population. This was not the case at the beginning of the Republic, when only male property owners could vote. These comprised a fairly high proportion of the people at the time, for a great many of them were independent farmers. However, as more people became industrial workers, city dwellers, and tenants, property restrictions became discriminatory and pressures rose to do away with property and taxpaying qualifications for voting. By the middle of the nineteenth century most of these restrictions were gone.

There were still three other major obstacles to universal suffrage in this country, but each of these was finally abolished after a long struggle. Although the right of black males to vote was guaranteed by the Fifteenth Amendment to the Constitution in 1870, not until Congress passed the Voting Rights Act of 1965 did this guarantee become effective for black people in the South. The right of women to vote was bitterly resisted until the passage of the Nineteenth Amendment to the Constitution in 1920. And the Twenty-sixth Amendment, which was ratified by the states in 1971 in the record-breaking time of two and a half months after approval by Congress, lowered the voting age to 18.

Voting is not the only means by which people express themselves in political campaigns. They also attend political meetings; they undertake a variety of tasks at campaign headquarters—stuffing envelopes, telephoning voters, writing speeches, and organizing motorcades and rallies. They put bumper stickers on their cars. They contribute money to candidates and political parties. They go from door to door in precincts to present their candidate's case and to get out the vote on election day.

Outside the election campaigns there are many other kinds of political participation. People are active in organizations that take political stands. They write letters to their representatives and to the editors of newspapers. They talk to relatives, friends, and fellow workers. Where people's feelings are particularly strong and they are frustrated by the traditional channels of political communication, they engage in protest activities—marching, demonstrating, picketing, in some cases occupying buildings, obstructing traffic, and in extreme cases resorting to violence.

In addition to these various forms of active participation there is another, essentially passive, means by which the opinions of ordinary people find expression in politics. This is through the medium of public opinion polls. The George Gallup Poll and the Louis Harris Survey are the best known of these. In addition, there are national polls conducted by the Yankelovich and Roper organizations; presidential and other major candidates retain their own pollsters; and there are several statewide polls. In addition, there are some university-based organizations, such as the Michigan Survey Research Center. All of them use a carefully devised *sampling* method for determining public views on a candidate or issue, which means that the people interviewed are taken to be representative of larger segments of the population. Gallup usually relies on a sample of about 1500 interviews, Harris about 1600.

How can such small numbers accurately represent the entire electorate? Pollsters claim that the sampling method has been shown to be valid through two tests. First, when the number of interviews is greatly increased, the results do not change very much. Second, polls taken just before an election are measured against the actual election results. Questions about the accuracy of polls persist, as we shall see in Chapter 4. Nonetheless, in recent presidential campaigns the Gallup and Harris final preelection polls have been accurate within their admitted 3 percent margin of error. And on other questions we can reasonably use poll results as indicating the general, approximate trends of opinion in the country. In any case, most political leaders pay close, even hypnotized, attention to the polls, both to see how their policies are being accepted by the public and to determine the acceptability of future course of action. So, as a means of conveying the opinions of people in this country, opinion polls are potent tools indeed.

The Big Question:
How Much Interest in Politics?

Several crucial questions arise from our discussion of what influences political opinions and how people express these opinions: How much do people care about politics in America? What proportion of the people have strong political opinions? How many take part in the political process? In general, the answer is that, although the number who care and participate has increased significantly in recent years, politics is still not a consuming passion of the majority of the American people, and a sizable minority has no interest at all.

Knowledge, Interest, and Ideology

Not many Americans are well informed about politics. Some of the top political leaders are simply not known to a high proportion of the electorate. According to a Gallup poll in 1970 only about 53 percent could name their congressman. Other studies in the same year showed that proportions ranging between a quarter and a third could not name the speaker of the House, the Senate majority leader, and the secretary of defense. In 1973 Gallup reported that over a fifth of the public could not correctly identify Henry Kissinger as President Nixon's foreign policy adviser. Or consider another Gallup poll in late 1974 which asked a sample of the electorate about possible Democratic candidates for the presidency in 1976. The question was: "Which of these people have you heard something about?" Among the responses were:

Candidate	Percentage
George Wallace	94
Hubert Humphrey	91
George McGovern	86
Ralph Nader	73
Eugene McCarthy	68
Thomas Eagleton	59
Morris Udall	38
Walter Mondale	38
Frank Church	27
Lloyd Bentsen	13

Now it is true that there was not a great deal of publicity about Udall, Mondale, and Church until the election season was further advanced. However, the poll was conducted only two years after McGovern had run for the presidency, and 14 percent of the electorate had heard nothing about him. Eagleton had been the center of a tremendous furor during the 1972 campaign, for McGovern had selected him as vice-presidential running mate, then dropped him when the news broke that Eagleton had once had electric shock treatment for a nervous condition; two years later 41 percent of the sample had no recollection of Eagleton at all. And over a quarter of those polled knew nothing about Ralph Nader. Still other surveys have revealed widespread ignorance about the structure of American government and about the provisions of the Bill of Rights.

Much the same story applies to political issues. Thus, in September 1963, at the height of a great debate over the ratification of a nuclear-test-ban treaty, the

Gallup poll found that 22 percent of the electorate had not heard of the issue. George Gallup found cause for reassurance in this. After all, 78 percent had heard of it, and 78 percent, said Gallup, was a high awareness figure as compared with what the public knew about other issues. This was borne out in August 1964, when 33 percent had never heard of the John Birch Society. Then in September 1972, three months after the arrest of seven men for the "bugging" of the Democratic National Committee Headquarters in the Watergate building in Washington, 48 percent of all voters had never heard of the incident, despite the public uproar that had followed the arrests. It is true that by June 1973 the awareness figure had reached 97 percent. Still, there had been a considerable amount of public discussion of Watergate by September 1972, but it had not entered the consciousness of almost half the electorate. This confirms other evidence which suggests that even when politicians and the mass media develop a topic to the point of obsession so that it seems impossible for anyone, anywhere, to avoid being saturated with information on the question, there will still be a quarter, even a third, of the adult population who have not the remotest idea that such a question has ever been raised. And of those who have heard of the issue a considerable proportion will have only the haziest notion of what it is about.

One reason for the widespread apathy and ignorance is that many of those who do not know much about politics do not *want* to know much about politics. This becomes apparent every time a major political event is televised and preempts a popular program. Thus, when the Watergate hearings conducted by Senator Sam Ervin's committee were televised in 1973, they received good ratings. But 44 percent in a Gallup poll complained that the media were giving too much coverage to Watergate. And many angry viewers called local television stations to complain about not seeing their favorite soap opera. As one caller said, "When I come home in the afternoon and put the kids to bed, I want to see 'As The World Turns,' not the damned Watergate." At the 1976 Democratic Convention Hubert Humphrey ruefully noted that his speech was competing against another network's coverage of the baseball All-Star game; baseball outdrew the senator two to one. And Jimmy Carter's acceptance speech at that convention, though carefully scheduled during prime television time, was twenty-seventh on CBS's weekly ratings and twenty-eighth on NBC's.

Another index of the level of public interest in politics is the style and substance of most election campaigns. Candidates and their campaign staffs, whose careers depend on an accurate reading of how to attract the public's attention and support, usually avoid placing any strain on the intellects of the voters. While praising the good sense and wisdom of the people, candidates conduct their campaigns on the assumption that a high proportion of the voters know little and care less about politics. Accordingly, as we shall see when we discuss national elections in Chapter 4, a large part of the budgets of most candidates for high office goes into short television and radio commercials, which inevitably oversimplify the issues and commonly emphasize the candidate's personality rather than public policy issues.

This type of evidence seems to support the conclusion of one of the major studies of the electorate, *The American Voter,* published in 1960. That conclusion was: "We have . . . an electorate almost wholly without detailed information about decision-making in government . . . almost completely unable to judge the rationality of government actions. . . . "[3] The authors of this study recognized that a segment of the population were well informed, followed politics very closely, and had some kind of ideological framework which helped them place candidates and issues on a liberal–conservative spectrum. But this "attentive public," as political scientist Gabriel Almond called them, constituted only a small minority. The greater part of the population was poorly informed and did not have any conceptual framework to help them assess whatever information they had. The majority, said *The American Voter,* were not able to think in ideological terms. They did not have any set of thoughtful, reasonably consistent political beliefs to which they could relate their impressions of events, candidates, and parties.

However, more recent studies have revised this assessment of the electorate upward. This reassessment was a major theme of a 1976 work, *The Changing American Voter.*[4] According to this book the American electorate has become much more politically aware and sophisticated since the fifties. The proportion able to think in ideological or near-ideological terms has risen considerably, as indicated in Figure 2–1, which traces the voters' ability to relate presidential candidates to some kind of basic framework of ideas. The "ideologues" in this figure are those who can define candidates in such terms as "liberal," "conservative,"

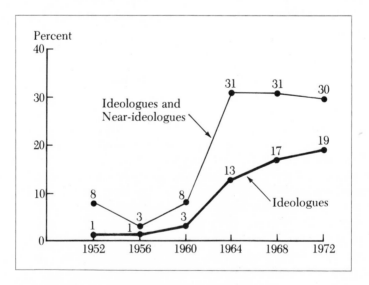

FIGURE 2–1   *Ideological Evaluation of Candidates, 1952–72*   (Redrawn from Norman H. Nie, Sidney Verba, and John R. Petrocik, *The Changing American Voter* [Cambridge, Mass.: Harvard University Press, © 1976, the Twentieth Century Fund], p. 113.)

"socialist," and so on, and also relate these to specific issues and the effect of those issues on particular groups in the population. The "near-ideologues" are people who use some ideological terminology, but do not relate it specifically to the issues or to the groups affected by the issues. Thus we see an increase from only 3 percent in the ideologue and near-ideologue categories in 1956 to 30 percent in 1972. Another sharp increase is recorded in the voters' ability to evaluate the political parties. In fact, if we combine the perception of candidates and parties, we find that practically half of the entire electorate can be classified as either ideologues or near-ideologues in 1972, as compared with only 18 percent in 1956.[5] So *The Changing American Voter* concluded that since the 1950s there had been a substantial improvement in the quality of reasoning and the capacity to think in ideological terms about parties, candidates, and issues among the general public.

What accounts for this improvement? In part, it is a matter of definitions. The authors of *The Changing American Voter* use less stringent criteria for what constitutes ideological awareness than the *American Voter* scholars, and this produces a considerably higher figure in the 1972 study than their predecessors' work would support. Still, even by the earlier criteria the trend would show a sharp increase in the public's ability to think in ideological terms. So the explanation is to be found primarily in two other factors.

The first is the increasing educational level of the electorate. Between 1956 and 1972 the proportion of the population that had been to college increased from under 20 percent to almost 30 percent. However, this is only part of the answer, for the increase in political sophistication is greater than the increase in education, and there is discernible improvement also among many of those who have not been to college.

The other explanation is the nature of the times. The fifties were a relatively quiet period in American politics. There were few deeply disruptive issues. The majority were reasonably content with their government and the political system. Politics did not intrude very much into their lives.

But from the early 1960s there has been a succession of shattering events and issues. John F. Kennedy, Martin Luther King, and Robert Kennedy were assassinated and George Wallace crippled in another assassination attempt. The cities were torn by race riots and the campuses by student upheavals. We have been through Vietnam and Watergate, inflation and recession at the same time, and an oil embargo. Crisis has crowded crisis out of the headlines. And all of this has been driven into the consciousness of the American people by an enormously potent medium that was only in its infancy in 1956—television.

However, it is important not to overstate the extent of the change in the American people's political awareness. In *The Changing American Voter* the average members of the public are not viewed as deeply informed citizens, constantly engaged in a process of cogent political analysis. Their ideological capacity is judged by whether they refer to parties, candidates, and issues in such terms as "liberal" and "conservative"; and, although the proportion that does this has risen considerably, we still have 50 percent or more of the general public that falls below even the not very stringent category of near-ideologues. Moreover, there are still very large numbers of people who hardly follow politics at all or know much about political leaders and thus lack the informational base on which to build carefully reasoned structures of political analysis. So, while the trend of the past 20 years has been toward growing political awareness and conceptual understanding, it remains true that a majority of the people are not particularly knowledgeable about political leaders, events, and issues.

Participation

Our next concern is: what proportion of the American public participates in the political process? Apparently about a sixth of the population takes part in one way or another in political campaigns. This was the case, for example, in the 1972 presidential campaign. In that campaign about a tenth of the population gave money to a candidate and attended one or more meetings, and 5 percent did other things to help a candidate or party. Close to a quarter of the electorate claim to have taken part in an election at some time. Slightly over a quarter say that they have written a public official to express an opinion. About 7 percent have written a letter to an editor.

The proportion who participate in campaigns has increased since 1952. On the other hand, with respect to voting we find a significant decline since the early 1950s. In presidential elections the percentages of the population of voting age who cast their votes are as follows:

Election Year	Percentage of Eligible Voters Casting Ballots (rounded to the nearest whole number)
1952	62
1956	59
1960	63
1964	62
1968	61
1972	56
1976	53

Thus in 1976 almost half the potential electorate did not vote; and Jimmy Carter's 51 percent share of the votes cast actually reflected the votes of not much more than a quarter of the population of voting age.

In congressional elections the voter turnout is lower still. In midterm years, when there is voting for Congress but not the presidency, the voter turnout is typically in the low- to mid-40 percentage range, and in 1974 it fell to 38 percent of the voting-age population. Even when members of Congress are being elected on the same ballot as the president, fewer people bother to vote for Congress than for president. Typically the gap is about 3 percentage points; and in 1968 and 1972 the congressional voting averaged a full 5 points below the presidential balloting of 61 percent and 56 percent, respectively.

These are considerably lower percentages than are found in most other democracies. One major reason for this is that, in order to reduce the voting frauds that were commonplace during the nineteenth century, many states introduced procedures that required the potential voter to take specific steps to register. This cut down on the fraud, but it also reduced the voting rolls, for many people forgot or did not bother to go to a voting registrar's office, especially since registration had to be completed some time before an election when interest in politics is rarely high. This contrasts with the practice in most other democratic countries, where automatic registration eliminates any requirement that residents of a district initiate steps to ensure that they are on the district's voting roll.

However, this explanation is not sufficient in itself. Changes in registration laws in many states have been making it easier to register. In 1972 the Supreme Court, in *Dunn* v. *Blumstein*, established a maximum residence requirement of 30 days to qualify for voting in any election. The 1965 Voting Rights Act greatly increased the numbers of blacks who could register and vote in the South. Yet the proportion of the potential electorate casting their votes has continued to decline.

The Distribution of Involvement

So far in this section we have examined briefly the extent of political knowledge, conceptual ability, and participation in America. We have seen that, while there has been a significant increase in awareness and conceptual ability, there are still big gaps in information and understanding. We have also observed that, though the numbers involved in campaign activities have grown since the 1950s, voting proportions have fallen. Now it is time to take a more detailed look at the figures, relate them back to our socioeconomic data, and thus determine who is most likely and who least likely to be actively interested in politics.

The most important finding is that people with higher incomes, more education, and the most highly skilled jobs are more likely than people lower down the status scales to keep up with politics, to be actively engaged in campaigns, to join and be active in organizations, and to vote. Thus a Gallup study in 1970 showed that among people who make more than $15,000 a year, over 70 percent knew who their congressman was and over 40 percent knew something about his voting record. Among those who made under $7000 a year, less than half could name their congressman, and only an eighth had any idea how he had voted.

So our "attentive public"—the people who read political periodicals and the editorial page of the newspaper, who watch the public affairs documentaries on television, who go to political meetings and write letters to the editor—are drawn disproportionately from the upper socioeconomic groups. Of course, there are many lower-income, less educated people who are deeply interested in politics, and who work very hard in campaigns. Labor unions, for example, draw considerable numbers of their members into active participation in elections. And there has been a dramatic increase in the amount of campaign activity by blacks since the early 1950s. By and large, however, poor people, those who have not graduated from high school, blacks, Chicanos, and other disadvantaged groups are less likely than other segments of the population to follow politics closely, to take part in campaigns, to vote, and, of course, to contribute money to candidates.

The second, most important dividing line between the involved and the uninvolved is age. Young people are less inclined than their elders to care about politics and to vote. The year 1972 saw the addition of 25 million young people to the voting age population. Of these, 11 million between the ages of 18 and 20 were enfranchised by the Twenty-sixth Amendment, and 14 million between 21 and 24 had not been old enough to vote in 1968. The voting turnout in this group was 15 percent below that of the population as a whole. In the 1974 elections two-thirds of the 18- to 20-year-old group did not register, and, almost 80 percent did not vote. Again in the 1976 presidential election, the proportion of young people voting was significantly below that of the total electorate.

Before the 1972 Supreme Court ruling, the problem was in part that registration requirements tended to discriminate against the young, for they are the most mobile group in the population, and so they often found difficulty in satisfying the residence qualifications for voting in their district. However, there is also the problem of attitude. Most young people have not yet established their own family, settled into a community, placed children in the schools, and put down the kind of social and economic roots that tend to make people aware of their political environment. The young are also typically preoccupied with starting their careers, building personal relationships, and, in general, finding themselves, rather than worrying about national and international problems.

Among the young, college students are more likely than those in the work force to think about politics and to vote. However, even during the campus turmoil of the 1960s there was much less commitment to political action among the young than was generally assumed. One study of students at Berkeley and Stanford published in 1968 found that a large majority of students were still "privatists" in their outlook, ranking their careers and future family life far beyond involvement in international, national, or civic affairs.[6] A similar study in the early 1970s would probably have shown an upsurge of involvement, spurred by the U.S. invasion of Cambodia, the shootings at Kent State, and so on. But most observers of campus life since then report a falling off of political interest.

At the opposite end of the age scale, the over-70 group, we again find less political activity than the average. But much of this is due to ill health and transportation problems. And if the elderly are less politically active than the population as a whole, they are still more involved than the young. There are other factors that influence the degree of involvement. Women, for example, tend to be less politically active than men; but the difference is not great and it has narrowed considerably over the years.

To sum up, the typical member of the attentive public is middle aged, college educated, doing skilled work, and earning over $20,000 a year. The typical member of the politically unconcerned, inactive citizenry is young, a high school dropout, in a low-skilled job or unemployed, and earning less than $5000 a year.

The Decline of Trust in Government

The data we have been reviewing contain a puzzle, an apparent contradiction. On the one hand, we have noted that educational levels and income have been rising; that these factors are associated with higher levels of political awareness and activity; and that, indeed, there is more awareness today than 20 years ago, together with increased sophistication and conceptual ability. On the other hand, the proportion of the population engaging in that most fundamental of all kinds of political activity—voting—has been going down.

The key to this riddle may be the change in attitude mentioned in the opening paragraph of this book: a general erosion of trust in government.[7] Surveys by the National Opinion Research Center at the University of Chicago indicate this trend in the percentage of people who agreed with the following statements about government from 1964 to 1973:

Statement	Percentage Who Agree			
	1964	1968	1972	1973
You cannot trust the government to do what is right.	22	37	45	66
Government is for the benefit of a few.	30	42	57	67
There are a lot of crooks in government.	30	27	38	57
Public officials don't care much what people like me think.	37	44	50	56

Other studies tell much the same story. A Harris survey in 1975 reported that the proportion agreeing with the statement "The people running the country don't care much what happens to you" had increased from one-third to two-thirds in 10 years. And other Harris surveys have shown a sharp decline in public confidence in all our governmental institutions—the presidency, Congress, the bureaucracy, the Supreme Court, the military—from 1966 to 1976. (In fact, in 1975 the only group, public or private, that commanded the confidence of over 50 percent of the population were the garbage collectors, who scored 51 percent.) There are some signs that since 1976 the decline of trust may have been arrested and even reversed. But we are still far below the levels of confidence of the fifties and early sixties.

Along with this erosion of confidence in government has gone a decline in the electorate's self-confidence. The University of Michigan's Survey Research Center data show a sharp increase since 1960 in the proportion of the population that believes that political effort is futile. There has been a decline, in other words, in what social scientists refer to as *efficacy*, the sense that what we do makes a difference.

Now all the previous studies have shown that, not only in the United States but in a number of other countries, the better-educated, more affluent people tend to feel efficacious.[8] They believe that political activity is worthwhile. In contrast, the poor tend to feel that no matter what they do they will continue to be ignored and discriminated against. This distinction has not yet been invalidated. As we have said, we still find more political activity, including more voting, as we go up the income and educational ladders. However, a significant number of well-educated, well-to-do people who are very interested in politics, very much aware of what is going on, and deeply concerned about the future have decided that voting is useless. Since political leaders and institutions are corrupt, remote, and unresponsive, why bother? So nonvoting is no longer merely a sign of apathy and ignorance. It is also the result of a positive decision to abstain on the part of a number of politically conscious citizens.

Five Perspectives
on Public Opinion

The Centrists:
A Favorable View, Nonetheless

Centrists can hardly take pleasure in the statistics showing a decline in voting, in trust in government, and in the sense of efficacy. These are all indications of a troubled electorate and of some undesirable trends in American politics. Still, centrists insist that there is no cause for alarm. They persist in their belief that the data we have examined do not nullify their claim that we have a basically sound and responsive democracy in America.

First, they note the evidence presented in *The Changing American Voter* and other studies of significant increases in the level of political understanding. But they also argue that even those people who do not have a detailed knowledge of a large number of specific events and issues still have a pretty good idea of how government policies affect their interests. If many people are still not able to attach ideological labels to their thinking, this does not mean that they cannot make effective judgments. In a general way they know what they want from government, and they have a sufficient understanding of what the candidates and the parties stand for. Nor are they easily fooled by the trivia and advertising techniques used in election campaigns. Centrists have more to say about this, as we shall see in Chapter 4. But for the moment we need only emphasize the centrists' belief that, despite the lack of conceptual sophistication, the majority know where their interests lie and are able to see who in politics is most likely to serve their purposes.

Moreover, the voice of the majority is expressed in important ways, and it is listened to by the policy makers. Elections are still crucial events. Even the authors of the now outdated *The American Voter* qualified their dismal conclusions by declaring:

It would be altogether wrong to suppose that the electoral process does not profoundly influence the course of government. Unquestionably it does. The decisions of the electorate play a role primarily in defining broad goals of governmental action or very generalized means of achieving such goals.[9]

Those same authors also point out that shifts in the tide of opinion *between* elections are closely followed by government. Those shifts are measured in many ways, but the public opinion poll is now firmly established as a powerful link between the mood of the public and the decisions of government leaders.

We should also note, say the centrists, that whatever deficiencies there may be in the dialogue between the mass of the people and the government are remedied by the lively presence of that active minority, the attentive public. Even if we accept the lowest estimates of what proportion of the electorate should be placed in this category—perhaps a tenth or even less of the total—we are still talking about several million people. These are people who follow politics closely and worry about the state of the nation. Sometimes they may become frustrated, feeling that events are getting away from them and that their voices are not being attended to. In some instances they may even, for a while, refuse to vote. But most of them stay with it despite their dissatisfactions.

The active minority have a good deal of influence, more than most of them realize. Since the majority do not have much detailed knowledge of political issues, they are likely to be influenced by others who are more knowledgeable. And since, as we have noted, the prime influences on our opinions are personal contacts—family, friends, acquaintances at work, fellow members of organizations—those people we know who are better informed and more articulate than the average are likely to have a disproportionate impact on our political thinking. Then, too, the active minority is especially prone to write letters to congressmen and to the newspapers; and decision makers in government tend to be very much impressed with a few hundred, even a handful, of letters if they are thoughtfully expressed.

Moreover, public officials are forced to account for their policies not only to the general, politically interested citizenry. On every issue there is an abundance of organized groups, whose leaders and staffs are specialists on that issue, and who bring information and a diversity of opinion to the attention of government and the electorate. In addition there are the media, the journals of opinion, the universities, and other institutions that contain a wealth of knowledge and insight into public affairs. Hence we should never assume that all or most of the expertise in the system is contained in a narrow world of officialdom. Between government and the mass of the people is a stratum of interested, involved people who force government to explain and defend its policies publicly and who provide the general electorate with alternative sources of opinion from those presented by government.

The final element in the centrists' argument on this subject is that it is by no means clear that the health of the system demands that a much greater number of people be more actively involved in the political process. First, becoming an informed citizen today is an exacting and time-consuming undertaking. Issues and crises crowd one upon the other, each enormously complex. Even the experts, the scholars in the field of public issues, must confess to wide areas of ignorance, and they are forced to specialize in order to preserve a degree of authoritativeness in, at most, a few fields. The lay person cannot acquire more than a superficial knowledge across the range of public affairs. Moreover, to proceed from knowledge to action demands further large commitments of time and energy, for it is admittedly difficult for the ordinary person, however active, to have a substantial effect on public policy.

Thus, if most people were to dedicate themselves to the effort to make their mark on public affairs, other pursuits of high importance to society would be neglected. The family, already much weakened as an institution, would suffer further. People would have no time to advance their careers. The arts and other leisure-time pursuits would not get the attention they deserve. A democratic society does not demand that we turn away from all these pursuits in favor of politics. Only in the totalitarian society do the leaders try to make everything political—the arts, science, work, even sex.

Second, lack of information does not result only from apathy, but also from "the need not to find out." [10] One of the reasons that people do not want to know is that the news is too oppressive. There are many neurotic reasons for people's wanting to shelter themselves from the intrusions of public life. [11] But in view of the multiplication of horrors contained in public issues in our era, the ability to screen out much of the suffering is a necessity of mental health; it may therefore not be a contribution to the good society to try to make everyone feel guilty for not paying more attention to issues that are likely to increase personal tensions. Hence it is entirely natural and reasonable that many people are irritated when their favorite television programs are ousted in favor of coverage of a political controversy. For instance, one of the people who called to complain about the preempting of a soap opera by the Watergate hearings in 1973 was an old lady who explained that she could not understand what was being said at the Senate hearings, and that, since her eyes were going bad and she couldn't read, television was all she had to pass her time. Thus NBC may well have made a good choice in March 1975, when it delayed its broadcast of President Ford's speech on a tax-cut bill to finish televising a national, semifinal basketball game between UCLA and Louisville.

Third, it is doubtful that a democratic society could stand the strain if everyone became stirred up about political issues and became intensely involved in them. Tempers would rise, antagonisms erupt, and conflicts grow unmanageable.

We are much better off, then, with a specialization of functions between the mass of the people and the attentive public. On the one hand, the masses are given periodic choices of leaders and policies, and between times careful attention is paid to shifts in their attitudes and opinions. On the other hand, the attentive public takes care of political activity, of scrutinizing the conduct of government, and of shaping and debating alternative public policies. This active minority tends to be better educated than the average, which is all to the good, since education equips people to deal cogently with issues. It is not an exclusive minority, for anyone who has motivation and the energy can join its ranks.

The results of this system, despite the obvious deficiencies of knowledge on the part of the majority of the people, are reasonably good. It is true that we are going through a period in which cynicism about politics and politicians is rife. However, some of this should be discounted as the normal attitude toward politicians found in all democratic societies. And to the extent that it has increased recently it is the consequence of a series of unusual failures, such as Vietnam and of scandals such as Watergate. If we can just manage to get through a few years without any more foreign disasters or gross abuses of power, we shall see the levels of confidence rise again to those which prevailed in the 1950s. If our system can only meet this requirement of providing reasonably competent, reasonably honest government, then the electorate will not have to spend so much time worrying about politics, tensions will be reduced, and a healthy relationship between government and the electorate will be restored.

The Dissatisfied Liberals

The liberals are not convinced by the centrists' argument. They believe that the centrists are too ready to settle for a level of participation that is insufficient for a vital democracy. In a society that has lavished so much of its resources for so many years on education, it seems sadly unimpressive to liberals to claim that the majority of the people are *not completely* uninvolved or without influence on their government. Nor do the liberals worry as much about the dangers of increased political activity. They do not believe that a stepup in involvement and interest would necessarily increase tensions. On the contrary, political involvement is usually associated with a greater sense of efficacy, which is a positive, healthy feeling. And liberals do not accept the centrist's suggestion that greater participation would result in the neglect of other important aspects of American life. After all, the minority that are now actively engaged in politics also tend to be successful people in their careers and energetic devotees of the arts and various community causes. To the liberals, broader participation is a means of producing a more sophisticated citizenry, more competent to cope with the pressures that constant change imposes on our society and better equipped to force government to adopt alternatives to the present unsatisfactory policies.

More important still to liberals is the fact that wider participation means bringing into politics those segments of the population that are currently underrepresented in the system. The existing activists, the attentive public, consist predominately of the higher-income groups. This is an obviously unsatisfactory state of affairs for liberals, for equality is one of their core values. We are not likely to move very far toward a reduction of the present inequalities of income and status as long as those who suffer most from those inequalities are the least involved politically. So liberals urge measures that will encourage fuller participation by the groups who are presently uninvolved or underinvolved—the poor, blacks, Chicanos, the young, and women.

But here the liberals have to face two difficulties. The first is that the very groups who feel the most disadvantaged, and have the most to gain by government programs, are the least likely to try to gain the government's attention. Then why don't these disadvantaged groups do more to help themselves politically? The second problem for liberals is that bringing more people into the system would not always help liberal causes. As we have noted, devotion to First Amendment freedoms is more likely to be found among well-educated, more affluent people than among the less educated poor. And liberals believe in civil liberties as strongly as they believe in equality.

The liberals' response to these dilemmas is that the system is to blame in various ways. First, there are the barriers that our election procedures place in the way of voting registration. These discriminate, as we have seen, against the young, and also against the less educated segments of the population. Even the court decisions that allow people to register until 30 days before an election have not done enough to change this, for many states still maintain archaic registration procedures, and registration offices are often not conveniently available to the electorate.

Then there is the inadequate way that politicians present the issues. Election campaigns are full of distortions and irrelevances. Issues are neglected in favor of personalities. For those who do not have the benefit of a college education an election could be an extraordinarily useful education forum. This opportunity is systematically ignored by our political leaders. The media do a little better. Some of the major newspapers are excellent sources of information and interpretation. But most papers around the country are not of the quality of *The New York Times*. And if the national television networks provide occasionally superb coverage of political events, the newscasts over the local stations are full of trivia, with staffs chosen primarily for their good looks and winsome personalities, presenting stories that emphasize action, violence, and the weather rather than the great issues facing the people.

Finally, the very inequalities with which American society is riddled discourages whole segments of the population from participating. If poor people feel politically weak, it is because they *are* politically weak. They see the great influence of organized business groups in shaping the climate of opinion and in the making of government decisions, and they are quite realistic in believing that they are not likely to overcome business power by their efforts. They know that money talks very loud in elections and in organizing pressure on public officials, and they have no money to contribute. So, if the poor do not have a strong sense of political efficacy, this results not so much from apathy and ignorance as from a shrewd realization that their political participation is much less likely to be effective than participation by more affluent people.

The liberals' proposals to improve the situation follow directly from this analysis. First, they want to make registration easier. They strongly support the legislation that has been before Congress for some time which provides for postcard registration forms to be sent to every address in the nation. Voters would simply fill these out and mail them to local registration offices. Short of this, liberals would like to see all the states adopt certain procedures—already in operation in some states—such as letting people register right up until election day; keeping registration offices open evenings and weekends and moving them into the neighborhoods; keeping people's names on the registration rolls even if they fail to vote in one or two elections. These reforms at the state level could, according to some studies, increase the number of voters in presidential elections by as much as 14 million. Liberals also call for strict enforcement of the 1965 Voting Rights Act, which has been enormously helpful in getting southern blacks to the polls. They are also pleased with the additional provisions of the act passed in 1975 which help Spanish-speaking and other minority people by requiring districts with 5 percent or more language-minority voters to print ballots and other election materials in their languages.

Then liberals favor vigorous programs by political parties and other groups to encourage the involvement of politically underrepresented groups. They are pleased with the increase in political activity by blacks that has been generated by the civil rights movement, by legislation and court decisions, and by the increase in black consciousness that has developed since the 1960s. They are impressed, too, with the surge of activity by the women's movement, and they urge passage of the Equal Rights Amendment, which provides that equality of rights under the law shall not be denied or abridged on account of sex.

Finally, liberals believe that we will not get the needed levels of interest and participation without significant changes in the system. As we shall discuss in later chapters, liberals want politicians and the media to do a more effective job in presenting the issues and in helping the people see the relationship between politics and their everyday concerns. They want political parties to provide clearer choices to the electorate. They seek ways of reducing the power of business by building coalitions of the poor, working people, minority groups, the young, intellectuals, and those members of the more affluent classes who recognize the need for major changes in politics and society. And they look for new political leadership that will appeal to the aspirations rather than the fears of the people, and thus help to rebuild a sense of confidence in our institutions. This will not only encourage new segments of the population to enter the political process. It will also bring back those who have become disenchanted by the failures of government and the inertia and corruption of so many of our leaders.

The Radical Left: Power to the People

The radical left slogan "Power to the People!" captures their belief that ordinary people should control their own destinies. To the left democracy means the most active participation by the mass of the people in the political process. It also means that the people must no longer tolerate a system in which decisions are made for them by a small group of corporate rulers. But the left's own analysis of power in America indicates that convincing the mass of the people of this is a very difficult task indeed. For, as the left sees it, the corporate elite controls the institutions that communicate and interpret information, and this gives them an enormous influence on public opinion.

Most of the top professional opinion makers are members in good standing of the power elite. The mass media are owned by the corporate rich. The metropolitan newspapers and the three major television networks are big corporate enterprises. The leading magazines of opinion are owned by wealthy publishers. Although some diversity of opinion is allowed within the media, the political views of the owners and the pressures of the advertisers prevent the expression of any radical alternatives to capitalism. And, although there are some radical left periodicals, they lack the financial backing and advertising revenue needed to reach a wide audience.

The country's entire educational system is dedicated to the perpetuation of the established values. Public schools teach the virtues of the "free enterprise system" along with a jingoistic version of patriotism. At the university level there are some young faculty members, especially in the social sciences, who subscribe to radical left views. But their situations are generally precarious, especially if they participate actively in radical politics in the community.

Although many other faculty members think of themselves as politically liberal, they do nothing significant to challenge the prevailing policies of the ruling class. This is not surprising since both liberal professors and their institutions are heavily dependent on federal research funds. An important part of this funding is for military-related purposes, the grants coming from the Pentagon and even, in some cases, from the CIA. Moreover, a number of faculty members act as consultants and advisors to government agencies. And there has been a steady flow of personnel between universities and the federal government, with Henry Kissinger working for Republican presidents, McGeorge Bundy, W. W. Rostow, and Dean Rusk for Democrats, and Patrick Moynihan for both. So the notion that the universities are dedicated to independent critical reasoning and to challenging the conventional wisdom is a myth. They are part of the established system of ideas. It could hardly be otherwise when their ruling bodies, the boards of regents or trustees, are made up mostly of successful men in the fields of business, finance, and law.

The left also sees such organizations as the Council on Foreign Relations as instruments through which the corporate rich inject their ideology into foreign and domestic affairs. They note that the council restricts its national membership to some 1400 people, most of them holding high posts in business, law, finance, communications, and education; that its board of directors always includes men who have held top positions in the federal government; and that it forms public opinion by spreading its doctrines through seminars and lectures around the country and through the influential quarterly *Foreign Affairs* (whose editor, William Bundy, was a high State Department official during the Vietnam years). Then there are the "think tanks," such as the Rand Corporation and the Hudson Institute, which are always ready to serve corporate and militarist purposes, and the even more conservative Hoover and American Enterprise Institutes. The left has its own think tank, the Institute for Policy Studies, where Marcus Raskin, Richard Barnet, Arthur Waskow, and other scholars produce books, pamphlets, and journals and organize conferences to disseminate radical views. But the left complains that this is pathetically underfinanced as compared with its centrist and conservative counterparts.

So it will not be easy to challenge the manipulative power of these men and their institutions. However, the left believes that the brainwashing of the people is beginning to lose some of its effectiveness because the failures and corruption of the men at the top have become too blatant. The task of the left is to alter the established values by persuading the people—especially blue-collar workers, the poor, minorities, and students—that the proper response to the present situation is not withdrawal and noninvolvement but militant action. The people have the capacity to take things into their own hands, to refuse to accept any longer a system under which a small elite makes the decisions for them, and to insist on the creation of a true "democracy" in which all the people can participate in all the decisions that affect their lives. This, say the radicals of the left, is incompatible with capitalism, and requires the establishment of a socialist society.

The Conservatives: Manipulation by the Liberal Establishment

As we saw in Chapter 1, conservatives believe that much too much power in America is in the hands of a liberal establishment, and that this establishment is able to exercise so much power largely through its ability to influence public opinion.

Conservatives perceive the mass media as heavily biased in favor of liberalism. The several conservative newspaper publishers in the country cannot prevail against the leftward slant of the majority of reporters and columnists. Moreover, no other newspapers can match the influence of the liberal *New York Times* and *Washington Post*, which are carefully read every morning by the top decision makers of the federal government. As for the television networks conservatives believe that, under the guise of balanced objective news reporting, broadcasters such as Walter Cronkite, Eric Severeid, John Chancellor, and David Brinkley present the news in a manner that persistently leans toward liberalism. Patrick Buchanan, a speech writer for President Nixon who later became a newspaper columnist, put the conservatives' case against the network news staffs this way:

> Simply stated it is that an incumbent elite, with an ideological slant unshared by the nation's majority, has acquired absolute control of the most powerful means of communication known to man. And that elite is using that media monopoly to discredit those with whom it disagrees, and to advance its own ideological objectives.[12]

The universities, too, are attacked by conservatives for pretending to pursue the ideal of objective scholarship while in fact teaching an overwhelmingly liberal line. As one conservative commentator put it: "Our colleges and universities have conformed themselves over the past two decades to the orthodoxy of secular liberalism."[13] Nor do the conservatives have any more use than the radical left for the Council on Foreign Relations. They note that its board of directors has been made up of such men as Averill Harriman, an old establishment hand dating back to the New Deal years, and David Rockefeller. Conservatives have also aimed their fire at the Brookings Institution, a policy research organization that has supplied Democratic administrations with many of their economic ideas and personnel. Conservatives take some encouragement from the growing stature of the American Enterprise Institute; but they insist that the preponderance of professional social science research is still on the liberals' side.

The result of this dominance of the institutions of knowledge and ideas by the liberal establishment is an artificially imposed consensus behind bigger and bigger government at home and conciliation of our enemies abroad. Fortunately, the liberal establishment has not been able to indoctrinate the people completely. In the face of rampaging crime, for example, most people cry out for law and order despite the liberals' apparent concern only for the rights of criminals. And the majority were infuriated in the 1960s by the refusal of liberal professors to stand up to the totalitarian demands of radical students.

Still, in all too many areas the values of the liberal establishment have prevailed. They must be challenged, say the conservatives, by more active participation by the citizenry. In this sense, then, conservatives, like liberals, are calling for a reversal of the recent trends toward noninvolvement. However, the conservatives differ from the liberals in a very important respect. The liberals view the present registration laws as discriminating against the poor, minorities, and the young, and they advocate postcard registration, for example, to remedy this. But conservatives see no reason to go this far. It is one thing to insist that people should not be prevented from voting by intimidation and by artificially contrived legal barriers. It is quite another to spoon-feed the electorate and remove any procedure that requires the slightest degree of initiative by the voter. Registration today is not an onerous task. If people are too uninterested or too lazy to take even the small amount of time needed to register, why should we go to additional effort and expense to get their attention? As for the liberals' proposals (backed by President Carter in 1977 but rejected by Congress) to allow people to register as late as the day of the election, this would act as an open invitation to widespread voter fraud.

The liberals complain that the larger number of those who do not register or participate are poor. But conservatives remind us that these people also happen to be the least educated, the least informed, and the least equipped to make careful, reasoned judgments on the issues. It makes no sense to dilute the quality of our public dialogue and decision making even further by dragging into the electoral process people who have no interest in politics and who know nothing about candidates and policies. What is true of the poor also applies to the young. When they are settled down, own property, and begin to worry about matters other than starting their careers and "finding" themselves, they are more likely to become involved and to vote. There is no need to force the pace; events should be allowed to run their natural course.

So conservatives are advocates of stepped-up participation; but their concern extends to those segments of the population who have a sufficient financial stake in the community and enough education to play a meaningful role in political life. This, they argue, applies to a majority of the population, for the majority are homeowners, pay substantial taxes, and have at least some interest in and knowledge of political affairs. As for the rest, they should have equal opportunity to participate, but we should not bend the system out of shape in an attempt to coerce them into involvement.

I DISAGREE, WE NEED TO BEGIN TO EDUCATE EVERYONE NOW AND

The Radical Right ENCOURAGE ENVOLVEMENT OF
and the "Left Conspiracy" EVERYONE.

There are, as we have observed, two differing strands of thought on the radical right. One, of which the John Birch Society is the most prominent, is elitist. Robert Welch and other Birch Society members argue that America is supposed to be a republic not a democracy—that is to say, the framework established by the Founding Fathers is based on rule by the best qualified rather than by the masses of the people. The framers' republic was a system of indirect election in which the voters (who qualified by owning property) elected delegates who then, after careful deliberation, chose the president and the members of the Senate—only the House being directly elected. But now senators are directly elected and the electoral college is only a ceremonial body for ratifying the wishes of the voters at large. Moreover, the franchise has been extended to include just about everybody. We have gone from republic to democracy, and in the process abandoned the precepts of the Constitution.

The other radical right strand is populist, in the sense of voicing the dissatisfactions of considerable numbers of people of fairly low socioeconomic status who feel that the system has ignored them. In the 1960s, leaders such as George Wallace articulated these frustrations and stimulated intense political interest and involvement on the part of their followers.

Both the elitist and the populist factions of the radical right, however, are united in their hostility to the left-wing elites who conspire to control the country by controlling the minds of the people. There is an intense dislike of intellectuals, of what George Wallace used to call the "pointy-headed pseudo-intellectuals." Universities are perceived by the right as spawning grounds for vicious attacks on traditional values. The Ford and Rockefeller Foundations are criticized for using their tax-exempt status to give financial support to left-wing research and political activity. And the command post of the communist or quasi-communist conspiracy is said by some right-wing commentators to be located in the headquarters of the Council on Foreign Relations, with strong support from the liberal internationalist business group, the Committee on Economic Development.

The television networks and the major newspapers are other mouthpieces of the conspiracy. Overwhelmingly, they expound the doctrines of the left. And legal technicalities are invented to keep dissenting views off the air. Thus the Federal Communications Commission (FCC) has invoked the "fairness doctrine" to harass two spokespersons for the right, Dean Clarence Mannion and the Reverend Carl McIntire. The doctrine imposes on television and radio stations the obligation to provide substantially balanced coverage of controversial issues under threat of losing their licenses. Stations carrying Mannion's and McIntire's broadcasts were informed by the FCC that they must give equal time to other points of view. Even those station owners sympathetic to the right might not be able to afford to do this and would therefore be inclined to drop the programs. Moreover, McIntire lost his license to operate a Pennsylvania radio station after complaints from such liberal groups as the American Civil Liberties Union, the National Urban League, the United Auto Workers, and the National Council of Churches that the station did not give time to opponents of McIntire's position—though the FCC did nothing about the overwhelmingly leftist slant of many other radio stations.

In their efforts to combat the thought control exercised by the left-wing "insiders," the radical right engages in several very active forms of politics. The populist right organizes rallies, which are sometimes large and enthusiastic, and buys time on television and radio, particularly in the South and Texas. The John Birch Society is deeply involved in small group meetings of its own members, in providing speakers for various groups, and in publishing and distributing its ideas through a national network of Birch Society bookstores. Like all radicals at both poles of the spectrum, people on the far right reject existing kinds of politics but are second to none in the intensity of their political activity.

Conclusion

It is difficult to find much comfort in the material we have covered in this chapter. Large numbers of people care very little and do very little about politics. A high proportion of these are the poor and the minorities—those who have most reason to be dissatisfied and most to gain from governmental action. The young are also heavily represented among the uninvolved; yet it is their future that is being decided now by the policy makers. It is true that there has been a substantial increase in political awareness and sophistication over the last 20 years. But there are several reasons not to be delighted about this. First, the level of sophistication after all this improvement is impressive only in comparison with the past. Next, it has been accomplished only partly by increased educational levels. Even more important is the fact that people have been shocked into political awareness by a series of crises, catastrophic events, and the failures of government's performance. Finally, now that people follow politics more closely than in the past, they do not like what they see, and more and more of them are refusing to vote.

It may well be that the centrists are right. While they express concern about the situation, they are convinced that the erosion of trust and the decline in voting are temporary phenomena and that better and more honest performance by government can turn things around. But what if government, beset as it always has been by a proliferation of extraordinarily complex problems, is not able to perform well enough to satisfy an increasingly alert and critical populace? What if the voting proportions continue to fall, and the surveys on trust in government reveal a persisting decline? Will we at last fall below those minimal levels of participation and confidence necessary to sustain democratic institutions?

Of course, we cannot know precisely where those minimal levels are nor if we will in fact approach them. For the moment, at least, only the radicals believe that we have already passed the point of no return. There is still a good deal of hope on the part of most political analysts that the worst will not happen. However, on the evidence of this chapter and of chapters to come, that hope must be expressed in guarded terms.

Notes and References

1. General Social Survey, National Opinion Research Center, University of Chicago.

2. Everett Carll Ladd, Jr., and Seymour Martin Lipset, *The Divided Academy* (New York: McGraw Hill Book Company, 1975).

3. Angus Campbell, Philip E. Converse, Warren E. Miller, and Donald E. Stokes, *The American Voter* (New York: John Wiley & Sons, Inc., 1960), p. 543. See also Bernard Berelson, Paul F. Lazarsfeld, and William N. McPhee, *Voting* (Chicago: The University of Chicago Press, 1954).

4. Norman H. Nie, Sidney Verba, and John R. Petrocik, *The Changing American Voter* (Cambridge, Mass.: Harvard University Press for the Twentieth Century Fund, 1976).

5. Ibid., p. 115.

6. Joseph Katz and Associates, *No Time for Youth* (San Francisco: Jossey-Bass, Inc., Publishers, 1968).

7. See Arthur H. Miller, "Political Issues and Trust in Government: 1964–1970," *The American Political Science Review*, Vol. 68, No. 3 (September 1974), pp. 951–72.

8. See Gabriel Almond and Sidney Verba, *The Civic Culture* (Princeton, N.J.: Princeton University Press, 1963).

9. Campbell et al., *The American Voter*, p. 545.

10. Robert E. Lane and David O. Sears, *Public Opinion* (Englewood Cliffs, N.J.: Prentice-Hall, Inc., 1964), p. 65.

11. See Robert E. Lane, *Political Life: Why People Get Involved in Politics* (New York: The Free Press, 1959), pp. 113–14.

12. Patrick J. Buchanan, *The New Majority* (Philadelphia: Girard Bank, February 1973), pp. 20–21.

13. Stephen J. Tonsor, "Alienation and Relevance," *The National Review*, Vol. 21, No. 35 (July 1, 1969), p. 661.

Chapter 3

Political Parties:

Do We Need Them?

In the last chapter we saw that there has been a general erosion of confidence in American governmental and political institutions. A number of surveys have indicated that, of all our institutions, none is distrusted as much as the political parties.

There is nothing new about this. George Washington warned "in the most solemn manner against the baneful effects of the spirit of party . . . ," and criticism of parties as divisive and corrupt has been a recurring motif throughout American political history. But we seem to be in a particularly antiparty period today. Since 1952, the number of people willing to identify with one or the other of our major parties has declined sharply. In 1952 almost half the electorate called themselves Democrats, over a quarter said they were Republicans, and around a fifth described themselves as Independents. By 1974 the declared Democrats had declined to about two-fifths of the total, the Republicans to only about one-fifth—whereas the Independents had almost doubled to close to two-fifths of the electorate. From this and other evidence some political observers have concluded that we might be approaching the end of the American party system. A noted political scientist fears that me might be caught up in a "trend toward the gradual disappearance of the political party in the United States."[2] And *Washington Post* columnist David Broder has suggested that "with growing public cynicism and continuing proof of the ineffectiveness of the party system, the nation may eventually witness the disintegration of the two major parties."[3]

In this chapter we shall examine the reasons for the decline of support for the parties and assess whether or not the predictions of their eventual demise are justified. Our procedure will be to look first at the functions of political parties; then at the reasons for our having essentially a two-party system; and then at the nature of the differences between the parties and the forces that narrow the range of those differences. After that we shall provide five perspectives on the performance of the parties and on what, if anything, should be done to reform them.

Why Parties?—Their Functions in the Political System

In view of Washington's warning against parties and the persistent hostility to political parties throughout our history, the question we must start with is not why they are in decline today, but how and why they got started in the first place and how they have survived so long.

Parties began in this country in pretty much the same way they begin everywhere. A group of people who agree on one or more public policy issues get together to try to persuade other people to accept their ideas. Then, in order to make their persuasion effective, they give themselves a label, a brand name, and they put forward from among their number candidates for public office under that label. These are the two essential concerns of any party: policy and power. There must be a program, and there must be an attempt to acquire the political power to put the program into effect by placing members of the party in government positions.

These were precisely the elements that came into play even while Washington was warning against the baneful effects of party. People who agreed with him that we needed a strong national government banded themselves together, called themselves the Federalists, and set about the task of ensuring that Washington's successor would agree with their view. A rival group, clustered around Jefferson, wanted a more decentralized system, came to be known as the Anti-Federalists, and organized to get people who agreed with them into the federal government. The Federalists and Anti-Federalists were very loose associations; but in a rudimentary form the key ingredients of party—programs and efforts to get people elected on those programs—were already there.

After that the parties slowly grew more structured and became an integral component of the American political system. They survived because they fulfilled a number of functions which, here as in all democratic countries, have been of great importance to the functioning of the system. What are these functions? They are of two kinds, the first pertaining to the electorate at large, the second to the institutions of government.

Parties and the Electorate

The primary service that parties render to the public is to help them make *choices*. Parties organize alternative programs and candidates. Without the parties the electorate at large would be faced with a very large number of individuals, each of them claiming to offer the best program and to be the best qualified to run the government. But in a country as large and varied as ours it would be well-nigh impossible for even the most politically aware members of the electorate to make intelligent choices; and, as we have seen, the majority are not especially attentive to politics. Parties act as intermediaries in the process of election by organizing behind the major issues and screening candidates for office. By putting their label on policy proposals and candidates they make it possible for people to choose among the labels rather than among all the individual proposals and candidates, just as a brand name is designed to give the consumer a sense of the nature and quality of a product without his having to test every single batch.

Parties and Government

In providing a systematic means for organizing alternative programs and candidates, parties fulfill functions of great importance to the operation of a democratic government. They help establish coherence and consistency within the executive branch, for presidents choose most of their Cabinet members and other top officials from their own party. Parties also encourage a degree of coherence within the legislature; if this were lacking, if there were nothing to bind all the separate legislators together, it would be very difficult to get anything done. Parties also provide an important link between the executive and legislative branches, since presidents appeal to the leaders of their party in Congress for cooperation. This establishes a bridge across the separation of powers.

Next, the party system provides one of the means by which the government is subjected to constant scrutiny and cross-examination. The parties outside the government are not merely trying to make life difficult for those in power. The opposition parties' purpose is to demonstrate that they are better qualified than the present government to exercise power, and are ready to do so as soon as the electorate gives them the chance. Thus parties offer alternative governments; and they are instruments for arranging the orderly transfer of power from one set of policies and leaders to another.

Finally, parties are means of recruiting and preparing people for public office. Almost all top officeholders have used the machinery of party to attain their position. Richard Nixon had not thought much about a political career before his local Republican party organization, looking for a young, articulate candidate with a suitable war record, approached him to run for Congress in 1946. Even Dwight Eisenhower, whose political leanings were so little known that in 1948 he was approached by both Democratic and Republican party leaders to see if he would be their presidential candidate, finally became president by accepting the label and the organizational and financial support of the Republican party. And Jimmy Carter, the great outsider, who won his nomination by battling the established forces within the Democratic party in the primaries, would have had no chance of winning the presidency if he had not carried the Democratic label in the general election.

Why Two Parties?

Ours is basically a two-party system. It is true that we have had an abundance of parties. Some have been one-issue parties, such as the Prohibition and the Vegetarian parties. But most have offered platforms concerned with the whole range of public issues. In 1976 several of these parties put up slates of candidates for offices from the presidency on down. They included the American Independent party, the American party, the Libertarian party, the Communist party–U.S.A., and the Socialist Workers party; and Eugene McCarthy ran for president as an Independent. But none received as much as 1 percent of the vote. Others have done better than this in the past. Theodore Roosevelt's Progressive party won enough votes in 1916 to take a victory away from the Republic party and make Democrat Woodrow Wilson the president. Robert LaFollette ran as a Progressive in 1924, and he, too, rolled up an impressive vote. And in 1968 George Wallace's American Independent party gained close to 10 million votes. Here and there in our history cities and even states have voted majorities for Socialist, Progressive, or Farmer–Labor candidates. Yet the rule has been for two parties to dominate, and only once has a new party ousted one of the two major parties. This happened in 1860, when the established Whig party (the party rivaling the Jacksonian Democrats) collapsed, and its place was taken by the newly created Republican party.

Now the two-party system is the exception rather than the rule in the world today. In most nondemocratic countries there is only one party. As the ruling party its job is not to present alternatives to the people but rather to marshall opinion behind the government and to see to it that the government's policies are carried out. The nations that we regard as democracies, on the other hand, all have more than one party, and most have several. France, Italy, West Germany, the Netherlands, Switzerland, the Scandinavian countries, and Israel all have at least three or four substantial parties and several others that cannot be ignored. Great Britain is among the few other democracies in the world in which two parties tower above the rest. But Britain is a much smaller, more homogeneous country than our own. How did such a huge, populous, diverse country as the United States come to coalesce around only two major parties?

One reason is habit. We started out that way, with the Federalists against the Anti-Federalists, who soon gave way to the Jeffersonian Republicans (or Democratic Republicans). After a period of complete dominance by the Jeffersonians, a new alignment formed in 1828, the Whigs against the Jacksonian Democrats (the inheritors of Jeffersonian Republicanism). With the disappearance of the Whigs we come to the rivalry that has lasted from 1860 until now: the Republicans (the "Grand Old Party," or GOP) versus the Democrats. Thus a pattern emerged at the outset; it fulfilled the functions of policy and power, which we described earlier, and so it survived; and once it had established its survival value, we grew attached to it, assumed that was the only way to do things, and were reluctant to break the habit.

The second reason for the dominance of two parties is that our electoral system makes it difficult for minor parties to gain a foothold. The principal problem they face is that we have *single-member constituencies* in federal elections. In congressional races we elect only one member for each district; and in most states whoever gets a *plurality* of the votes—that is, more votes than anyone else, even if that number is not a clear majority—is the winner. Similarly, in presidential elections, whichever candidate receives a plurality of a state's popular votes wins all that state's electoral college votes.

Now minor parties sometimes attract strong and enthusiastic followings and considerable numbers of votes. But rarely can they muster the plurality of votes needed to win in a district, for they are generally more homogeneous in their membership and more ideologically pure than the major parties—and thus less likely to appeal to a broad range of voters. So, even if a minor party could get 5 or 10 percent of the total number of votes cast in a national election, it could finish up with *no* seats in Congress (because it lacks sufficient strength in each separate district to gain a plurality) and *no* states in a presidential race.

With nothing tangible to show for their strenuous efforts in election campaigns minor party activists tend to become discouraged; and many voters who are attracted to a minor party's program fail to cast their ballot for its candidates because they feel that they are throwing their vote away.

Still other elements in the electoral process reinforce the preeminence of the two major parties. Thus in 1976 Eugene McCarthy and other minor party candidates for the presidency protested bitterly about the television networks' giving time for the Ford–Carter debates and ignoring the other candidates. The media, said McCarthy, were establishing in the public mind the idea that only two parties were to be taken seriously and that the rest were of only trivial interest. So, for a variety of reasons, our system tends to arrange the choices available to the electorate around two main clusters of ideas and interests.

Distinguishing
between the Parties

As we have seen, a primary function of parties is to present alternative sets of policies to the public. In Chapter 1 we set up a left-to-right political spectrum as a means of helping us to distinguish between alternative policies. This spectrum provides us with a convenient device for testing whether or not the two major parties in America, the Democrats and Republicans, are fulfilling the function of providing choices to the electorate. According to the breakdown along the spectrum, this would require that one of the parties represent a left-of-center, more or less liberal tendency; and the other, a right-of-center, more or less conservative tendency.

Liberal-Conservative Policy Differences

Before we check to see if the parties actually offer such alternatives, let us remind ourselves of what these liberal and conservative tendencies mean in relation to stands on the issues. For this purpose we take five main policy areas—welfare programs for the poor; civil rights programs to help minority groups; federal intervention in the economy; civil liberties; and foreign policy—and see how the various perspectives respond to each issue.

With respect to the first two of these, welfare and civil rights programs, the strongest support for government programs is found in the liberal direction and the greatest resistance is found in the conservative direction. The same is true with respect to government intervention in the economy. Left of center we find approval for federal spending and government regulation of business, whereas right of center there is more concern for individual property rights and the unrestricted freedom of business. In the civil liberties area there is a much greater predisposition on the conservative than the liberal side of the spectrum to assert the claims of law and order and traditional values against dissent and change. In foreign policy the left-of-center, liberal inclination is for reduction of armaments, support for international organizations, and economic and technical aid for the world's underdeveloped nations, whereas the right-of-center, conservative preference is for stronger military preparedness against communism, unwillingness to weaken our national sovereignty, and a reduction of aid to the poor nations.

By and large, the differences between the parties in these five policy areas are the ones most commonly used in discussions of contemporary American politics. When the Americans for Democratic Action rate the votes of members of Congress in terms of their degree of liberalism, they are looking for support of government welfare and civil rights programs, federal action to boost the economy and help the consumer, the protection of nonconformist ideas and behavior, and a lessening of the military emphasis in foreign affairs. On the other hand, when the Americans for Constitutional Action rate members of Congress by their degree of conservatism, their criteria are resistance to increased welfare spending and civil rights legislation, opposition to budget deficits, support of the rights of private property and business, protection for traditional values, and stronger military preparedness.

So we apply all this to our discussion of the two-party system, and pose the question: Do the Democratic and Republican parties differ along liberal–conservative lines? Is one left of center and the other right of center? The answer is yes, but only to a moderate extent. The Democratic party has generally been somewhat more liberal than the Republican party with respect to its programs, its elected leaders, its active members, its group support, and its ideological appeal. To explain this, we shall look first at the nature of the differences between the parties, then at the factors that hold these differences down.

"*And so I say ask not for whom the bell tolls. It tolls for moderate Republicanism.*"

Drawing by Ed Arno; © 1975 The New Yorker Magazine, Inc.

Ways in Which the Parties Differ

Party platforms. Over the years there have been significant liberal–conservative divergencies in the content of the Democratic and Republican party platforms, drawn up every four years by their national conventions. Some issues selected from the 1976 platforms are particularly good indications of these tendencies and are shown in Table 3–1.

But do these platform differences mean anything? They tell us something about the distinctions between the parties only if the programs are generally acted on. And there is widespread skepticism on this score, the general belief being that the platforms are insincere, usually unfulfilled promises. According to political scientist Gerald Pomper, this is not so. After studying the platforms of 1944 through 1964, he concluded that "pledges are indeed redeemed." Slightly over half the pledges were translated in considerable measure into congressional or executive action. Others were partially carried out. Altogether "only a tenth of the promises are completely ignored."[4]

Elected leaders. Next, there are differences in the policies of Democrats and Republicans when they are elected to office. Franklin Roosevelt, Truman, Kennedy, and Johnson were much more inclined to take vigorous governmental action on behalf of the lower-income groups and the blacks as well as to regulate

TABLE 3–1   *Party Platforms from the 1976
National Conventions*

Issue	Democratic Platform	Republican Platform
Welfare	Supports "a simplified system of income maintenance, substantially financed by the federal government."	Opposes a guaranteed annual income and opposes shifting the funding of welfare from the states to the federal government.
Health	"We need a comprehensive national health insurance system with universal and mandatory coverage."	"The Republican Party opposes compulsory national health insurance."
School busing	". . . a judicial tool of the last resort."	Though segregated schools are wrong and unconstitutional, "we oppose forced busing to achieve racial balances" and "favor consideration of an amendment to the Constitution" to ban it.
The economy	Supports a bill proposed by Senator Humphrey and Congressman Hawkins to reduce unemployment to 3 percent within four years.	Opposes the Humphrey–Hawkins bill, and calls for an end to deficit spending.
Taxes	Calls for overhaul of the tax structure to close loopholes favoring high-income and business people.	"The best tax reform is tax reduction." Favors tax incentives to encourage more capital investment by business.
Energy	Urges breaking up the big oil companies into separate producing and marketing units. Calls for a minimal dependence on nuclear energy.	"We vigorously oppose" the breaking up of the oil companies. Favors "accelerated use of nuclear energy through processes that have been proven safe."
Abortion	Opposes a constitutional amendment to ban abortion.	Supports the efforts of "those who seek enactment of a constitutional amendment" to ban abortion.
Vietnam amnesty	Supports "full and complete pardons for those who are in legal or financial jeopardy because of their peaceful opposition to the Vietnam War"; deserters to be considered case by case.	No mention.

TABLE 3-1   (continued)

Issue	Democratic Platform	Republican Platform
Defense	Urges a $5 to $7 billion defense-spending cut, and delay on the decision to build the B-1 bomber until February 1977.	Calls for a "period of sustained growth in our defense effort," and endorses the B-1.

business than were Eisenhower, Nixon, and Ford. Generally speaking, the Democratic presidents have worried more about unemployment than about inflation. The reverse has been true of the Republican presidents. As for Congress, we shall see in Chapter 7 that the Americans for Democratic Action find far more support for their liberal positions among Democratic representatives and senators than among Republicans.

Party activists.   Active Republican party leaders are much more likely to be conservative than are active Democrats. Studies of delegates to the Democratic and Republican national conventions confirm what is obvious to the most casual viewer of these events on television—that the tone, the attitudes, and the policy views of Republican delegates are very much more conservative than their Democratic counterparts.

Group support.   In Chapter 2 we saw that there is a relationship between socioeconomic background and political attitudes. To a significant extent this relationship carries over to political party affiliation. Before we explain this, we should sound two cautionary notes. First, we are making very approximate generalizations, allowing for large numbers of exceptions. Second, since twice as many people call themselves Democrats as Republicans there are few socioeconomic groupings in which the Democrats are not well represented.

However, with respect to income, occupation, and education the tendency has been to find particularly heavy concentrations of Democrats at the lower end of the scales. To the extent that the poor vote, they mostly go Democratic, whereas the Republicans' base is stronger among the more affluent income groups. With respect to occupations, a majority of blue-collar workers call themselves Democratic; the Democrats' margin is smaller among clerical and sales people; and the highest proportions of Republicans are found at the business and professional level (except among academics who, apart from business and engineering faculty, are heavily Democratic). Educationally, the greatest Republican strength has been among the college educated, whereas Democrats have been especially well represented among those with a high school education or less. Racially, blacks are overwhelmingly Democratic. In the context of religion, Republicans find their strongest support among Protestants, and Democrats among Catholics and Jews. As for age, Democrats are more heavily represented among the under-30 group than among the population as a whole.

Some recent studies suggest that Democrats have been gaining ground in recent years among younger, college-educated, higher-status whites in the North, thus giving the Democrats growing strength at the top as well as the bottom of the socioeconomic scales.[5] However, this development has not yet invalidated the very general distinctions we have made, which can be summed up as follows. Democrats are found in especially high proportions among the poor, blue-collar workers, people with a high school or grade school education, blacks, Catholics, Jews, and the young. Of these categories, the widest Democratic margins are usually found among blacks and Jews. Republicans find their greatest strength among the well-to-do, the business and professional people, the college educated, and Protestants. The most characteristic Republicans, then, are found among affluent business people who are Episcopalian or Presbyterian.

We encounter the same kind of distinction when we turn our attention from broad socioeconomic categories to organizations. Business organizations tend to support the Republican party and business executives to contribute to its campaigns. Labor unions have long been mainstays of the Democratic party, their money and manpower being vital elements in many Democratic campaigns. So, in very general terms, we can distinguish between the Democrats as the party of the working class and the "outgroups," and the Republicans as the party of business and the groups most wedded to the status quo.

These distinctions have been true of the two parties in considerable degree throughout most of their histories. For a while Abraham Lincoln's Republican party won the support of many working people and blacks, and Republican Theodore Roosevelt attacked big business; conversely, under Cleveland the Democrats gained a good deal of backing from business. But, more typically, thrice-defeated Democrat William Jennings Bryan gathered together poor farmers and laborers against eastern money and Democrat Woodrow Wilson spoke out against business power. Then Franklin Roosevelt and his New Deal programs in the 1930s solidified the lineup that we have described as differentiating between Democrats and Republicans. It was Roosevelt who won the blacks over from the Republicans to the Democrats; who confirmed the Jewish attachment to the Democrats by appointing Jews to high posts; who offered so many new social and economic programs to blue-collar workers that their gratitude to the Democrats lasted through generations. At the same time the groups antagonized by the New Deal became more firmly identified with the Republican party.

Ideological support.   In Chapter 2 we described a rising ideological consciousness among a considerable proportion of the electorate. As people become more ideological, more inclined to call themselves "liberal," "conservative," and so on, the awareness of their differences of attitude with people of other ideologies increases. Accordingly, there has been a growing polarization of the electorate. This can be seen in Table 3–2, which indicates that the proportion of voters in the center declined from about two-fifths of the total voting-age population in 1956 to not much more than a quarter in 1973. The table suggests not only a shift from the center but also from the moderate left and right positions to more extreme positions.

TABLE 3–2   Percentage Ideological
Distribution of the Electorate

Year	Leftist	Moderate Leftist	Centrist	Moderate Rightist	Rightist
1956	12	19	41	15	13
1973	21	12	27	17	23

Source: Data from Norman H. Nie, Sidney Verba, and John R. Petrocik. *The Changing American Voter* (Cambridge, Mass.: Harvard University Press for the Twentieth Century Fund, 1976), p. 143.

Moreover, the polarization indicated in this table is paralleled by a sharper distinction between the views of Democratic and Republican voters—a significant change from the 1950s, when there was not very much difference between the rank-and-file members of the two parties in their views on the issues.[6]

Finally, on a number of issues "a fairly substantial degree of difference is . . . perceived between the two parties" by substantial majorities of the people.[7] These differences are especially clearly recognized by the more ideological members of the public. People who call themselves conservatives identify themselves as Republicans by large margins, and the self-declared liberals are very much more likely to be Democrats than Republicans.

In sum, there are differences, which are perceived by a majority of the electorate, in the programs of the two parties. These distinctions reflect the differences between party activists, interest groups, and bodies of ideological opinion lined up behind each of the parties. Yet we cannot conclude from the analysis thus far that the parties are poles apart. In fact, they differ in degree, not in kind, and the degree of difference is fairly limited.

Why the Differences
between the Parties Are Narrow

Although there are significant contrasts in the platforms that the parties draw up every four years, the rival platforms do not challenge certain fundamentals of policy. If the two parties disagree on the extent of government involvement in the economy, neither rejects the prevailing system of capitalism, private enterprise, and private property, and neither calls for the abdication of government responsibility to take action against unemployment and inflation. Despite the arguments over foreign and defense policy, Democrats and Republicans alike call for strong military preparedness against the dangers of international communism, and both insist on their dedication to peace.

Next, although it is true that platform proposals cannot be dismissed out of hand as idle promises, they typically encounter considerable delays and a good deal of dilution before they are finally put into effect. And, finally, as election campaigns move on beyond the conventions, candidates usually try to broaden their electoral appeal by blurring the edges of the platform proposals, hedging their earlier promises, and moving closer to one another's stands. So, in the final stages of the shaping of issues for the electorate's consideration, the candidates of the two parties emphasize their moderation, and the policy alternatives become less distinct.

There are several factors that set limits to the degree of difference between the Democrats and Republicans, some relating to the nature of the parties themselves, others to the American electorate, and others again to our governmental structures.

The Parties Are Loose Coalitions

In reducing the number of major parties in America to only two, we have made it almost impossible for either of them to be a cohesive, well-integrated organization with a sharply defined set of policies—for this is an enormous and very diverse country. To build a national party with enough strength to win the support of a majority of the electorate requires a strenuous effort to reach across vast differences of class, race, ethnic group, religion, and region and weld together a coalition from these many sources. A party that is identified with one income group, one religion, or one region cannot hope to win a presidential election. Nor can a party that appeals only to the strongly ideological liberals or conservatives, for there are not enough of either of those to elect a candidate.

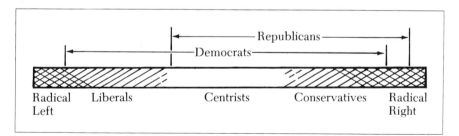

FIGURE 3–1   *Alignment of Parties on*
the Political Spectrum

As we see from Figure 3–1, the Democratic and Republican parties have both recognized the need to construct broad coalitions. Both contain a great many differing elements, sometimes to the point of seeming incompatibility. Thus Republican party officeholders include a few members of the John Birch Society, such very conservative people as Senators Strom Thurmond of South Carolina and

Jesse Helms of North Carolina, such moderates as Senator Jacob Javits of New York, and even a few rather liberal congressmen such as Paul McCloskey of California.

However, this range is still more limited than the scope of the Democratic coalition. Among the more prominent Democrats are several who are clearly in the liberals' camp, such as Congressman Ronald Dellums of California and former Congresswoman Bella Abzug of New York. But there is also a strong representation of conservatives, mostly from the South.

This antithetical element in the Democratic party, the southern conservative, has long been part of the Democratic coalition. The bond between Democrats and the South goes back to the early stages of the development of the party system, and it was reinforced by the Civil War and the era of Reconstruction which followed. The Democrats spoke for the South; southerners were grateful and voted overwhelmingly for the Democrats. In fact, they voted almost exclusively for the Democrats, making the South practically into a one-party region.

The southern one-party system served two purposes. First, it avoided the danger of a two-party system in which one of the parties sooner or later would seek to build its strength by going after black voters. Keeping political competition within one party made it easier to maintain white dominance. Second, as long as there was little or no Republican competition, the same people could be re-elected to Congress over and over again. This enabled them to build up seniority and ascend to those committee chairmanships which are the strongholds of power in Congress. So for southerners the Democratic party was built into their culture, commanding such strong loyalties that for a southerner to think of defecting to the Republicans was almost tantamount to rejecting one's birthright.

Franklin Roosevelt was careful not to challenge these loyalties. In fact, he absorbed the South into his New Deal coalition. There was a certain logic to this. The South was the poorest region of the country, and suffered under the disdain and condescension of the North; so it qualified for the "outgroup" status of the other elements in the Democratic coalition, and economically it benefited substantially from the New Deal programs. Still, the South's attitudes on race and other issues were very different from those which prevailed among northern Democrats, and Roosevelt paid a high price for his southern alliance in the frustration that he experienced at the hands of southern committee chairmen in Congress.

Eventually, the hold of the past over the mind of the South had to weaken. Industry came to the South, much of it from the North, and this brought to the region a number of people whose traditional voting habits were Republican. The Democratic party in the North was becoming increasingly the party of civil rights, and Republican Presidents Eisenhower and Nixon were noticeably more reluctant than Democratic presidents to force the pace of integration in the South. So the attachment of white southerners to the Democratic party was undermined. In 1952 about three-quarters of all southerners called themselves Democrats. By 1972 the proportion was down to less than one-half. Although only about a sixth were ready to call themselves Republicans in 1972, this was not much below the national average. Moreover, in presidential elections from 1952 onward, many of the Democrats tended to vote for Republicans, and in 1972 the once solidly Democratic South was solidly for Nixon. There were Republican gains, too, at the congressional level. By 1973 there were seven southern Republicans in the Senate, and 34 in the House of Representatives. The South was on its way to becoming a two-party region.

Still, the process is slow and subject to reversals. In 1974 the backwash of Watergate cost the Republicans a net loss of seven southern seats in the House of Representatives. And in 1976 Jimmy Carter brought most of the South back to the Democratic presidential ticket. So for some time to come the Democratic party will remain a great, incongruous coalition, and black liberals such as Ronald Dellums of California and white segregationist conservatives such as Senator James Eastland of Mississippi will all be identified as Democrats. When one party includes people who are so far apart on everything from race to foreign policy, it is no wonder that the Democratic party finds it difficult to present a clear, consistent set of programs to the nation. As a popular humorist of the 1930s put it: "I'm not a member of any organized political party. I'm a Democrat."

Party Organization Is Weak

Our national parties are loose associations of state and local parties. They build upward from precinct or ward organizations (or local clubs where, as in some parts of the West, there are no precinct organizations), through county and state central committees, and then to national committees made up primarily of representatives of the state committees. However, there is very little power at the top. The national committees raise money and provide some funds for presidential and congressional races. But they are not the major sources of income for local party organizations, and there is very little they can do to compel local or state organizations to follow the national party line. And this greatly complicates the task of offering clear policy positions to the electorate, for here again the national organization must try to hold together a large number of organizations, many of which are pulling in opposite directions.

Another source of weakness in party organization is the lack of clear definition of party membership. In most other democratic countries party members *join* their party. They belong to a local branch of the party, and through that they are members of the party nationally. They pay dues, part of which go to the national headquarters; they are involved in the selection of candidates and in debates over policy; they are bound by majority rule in their organization. This is another of the factors that makes it possible for a party, after it has conducted its debates on the issues and the candidates, to take its case to the country and contrast it with that of the opposition party. But in the United States we have no agreement on what we mean by a Democrat or Republican. Sometimes we mean an active member of a party organization or club; sometimes someone who registers Democrat or Republican in order to vote in the party primary elections; sometimes merely one who votes Democratic or Republican more or less consistently. Thus the ambiguity of party policies is a reflection of the ambiguity of party membership.

Two other developments of recent years have tended to undermine the strength of party organizations. The first is the growing importance in elections of television. Candidates usually regard an appearance on a television news or interview show as a much more fruitful use of their time than speaking to the faithful at a local party meeting.

The second new threat to the importance of party organizations is public financing of presidential campaigns, which we will discuss in Chapter 4. Party organizations have always been of great value to candidates in raising money for their election campaigns. Although parties still have a role under the new system, the federal exchequer has now taken over the larger part of their fund-raising role for presidential (though not congressional) races.

The Majority of the Rank and File Are Moderates

Parties, we have seen, are instruments for organizing and trying to win election campaigns. This means that they must study very closely the attitudes of the electorate. As they do so, they find a number of reasons that compel them to soften the policies that party activists favor. *Rank-and-file party voters are predominantly less militant than party activists.* The mass of party voters are, generally speaking, less ideologically committed than the dedicated party workers and more inclined to subscribe to middle-of-the-road views. They are also less inclined to be consistent from one issue to another.

Although some studies indicate an increase in issue consistency over the years—that is, more people who are liberal or conservative in one or two areas of public policy are also liberal or conservative in other areas—a high proportion of the general public still harbor liberal and conservative attitudes side by side. Thus many people who are liberal on questions of government spending to reduce unemployment are conservative on issues relating to race or pornography or foreign policy, and vice versa.

Earlier (see Table 3-2), we looked at some evidence which suggested that the differences between activists and others have diminished. Between 1956 and 1973, we saw a clear tendency for opinion in the country to polarize. However, it should be noted from that table that, although the center lost ground, the combination of *moderate* leftists and rightists together with the centrists still clearly outnumbered the people at the left and right of the spectrum.

Moreover, it could be that the weakening of the center indicated in the 1973 figures is already being reversed. If the attitudes of college freshmen give us a clue to the politics of the future, the trend is toward moderation. In the fall of each year a questionnaire is distributed to all students entering colleges and universities in the United States[8] and responses number close to 200,000 each year. Among the questions is one that asks students to identify themselves along an ideological spectrum. The results for the years 1970, 1972, and 1976 are shown in Table 3–3.

TABLE 3–3   Percentage Ideological Self-identification of Freshmen Students (percentages rounded to the nearest whole number)

Year	Far Left	Liberal	Middle of the Road	Conservative	Far Right
1970	3	38	42	16	1
1972	2	33	48	16	1
1976	2	29	53	16	1

According to these figures, then, there is a significant increase in the strength of the middle-of-the-road position—mostly at the expense of the liberal position.

In any case, most candidates for national public office persist in the view that they must make their appeal primarily to the people in the middle. This assumption is reinforced by the two presidential elections in recent history when one of the parties came to grief by departing from the safe middle ground.

Two case studies in leaving the safe middle ground: Goldwater and McGovern.   The first notable failure was the 1964 presidential campaign of conservative Republican Barry Goldwater against Lyndon Johnson. In making the case for nominating Goldwater, the conservatives in the party claimed that the Republicans had lost so many times in the past because they had repeatedly selected as their standard-bearer spokesmen for the eastern liberal establishment for whom conservative voters had refused to turn out. The Goldwater nomination, they said, would bring back into the system these disenchanted conservatives, and there would be a great outpouring at the polls of ideologically committed people who at last would have something to work and vote for. This did not happen. The conservatives were building their hopes on two false assumptions.

The first was that ideologically committed conservatives could only be brought to the polls by a candidate who clearly expressed their philosophy. But this is refuted by data from the 1952 presidential election. In that election conservatives had backed Senator Robert Taft of Ohio against the "establishment" candidate, Dwight Eisenhower. Taft had lost the nomination after a hard, close struggle. But Taft's conservative supporters did not stay home and sulk in November. In fact, 94 percent of the erstwhile Taft Republicans voted for Eisenhower in the final election, as against a voting turnout of only 84 percent of those who had been for Eisenhower from the beginning. The point is that the Taft supporters were more ideologically committed to their party than were their more centrist counterparts, and even though they were not enthusiastic about Eisenhower, they swallowed their reservations and turned out to vote for their party's nominee. The

Goldwater assumption that conservatives would rally only behind a staunchly conservative candidate was obviously mistaken.[9]

The second false assumption of the Goldwater campaign was built around his fundamental misreading of the mood of the electorate. He responded to criticisms that John Birchers and other right-wing extremists were among his chief supporters by declaring in his acceptance speech that "Extremism in the defense of liberty is no vice." He called for the sale to private interests of some of the Tennessee Valley Authority's power stations. Though he denied that he was against Social Security, he used language that aroused fears that he might weaken, if not dismantle, the program. His foreign policy statements made him vulnerable to charges that he was dangerously interested in force as a solution to international problems.

The result was that Goldwater got 27 million votes to Johnson's 43 million. Traditionally rock-ribbed Republican states such as Maine, Vermont, and the Dakotas defected. So did many voters even to the right of center—businessmen who had always voted Republican contributed instead to the Republicans for Johnson's campaign. And a considerable number of newspapers that had always endorsed a Republican for president came out for Johnson. Furthermore, Goldwater dragged down to defeat with him many other Republicans in congressional races and even in several state legislatures.

But, after all, that was back in 1964. Most of the erosion of middle-of-the-road opinion has taken place since that time. However, there is a more recent and equally disastrous effort by one of the parties to move away from the center in an election campaign. This was the McGovern fiasco in 1972. During his campaign to win the Democratic nomination George McGovern called for the heavily liberal programs of a guaranteed annual income of $1000 a person; limiting inheritances to $500,000; and a $30 billion cut in defense spending over a five-year period. It is true that, once nominated, he qualified these proposals, and that his acceptance speech was obviously designed to unify the party and to gain goodwill. Still, labor and other moderate elements in the party were seriously underrepresented at the national convention, which was packed with very liberal delegates; major powers in the Democratic party, such as Mayor Richard Daley of Chicago and labor leader George Meany, were enraged by the McGovern nomination; and McGovern was unsuccessful in changing the electorate's perception that he was identified almost entirely with the liberal (if not radical) wing of his party.

The result was that he received less than 38 percent of the vote to Nixon's 60.8 percent. He lost every state in the country except Massachusetts. Nixon won about half the blue-collar vote as compared with a third in 1968; around 37 percent of the Jewish vote (18 percent in 1968); and almost 60 percent of the Catholics. Even among the young, although McGovern won big margins in precincts inhabited mostly by students (94.5 percent at the University of California at Santa Cruz, 83.6 percent at Yale), he was supported by not much more than half the new voters.

Now there were factors affecting the 1964 and 1972 results other than the candidates' stands on the issues. Neither Goldwater nor McGovern was believed by the majority to be competent enough to be president, and both made serious mistakes in the handling of their campaigns. Moreover, it is highly unlikely that *any* Republican could have won the presidency against Lyndon Johnson in 1964, or *any* Democrat against Richard Nixon in 1972. Still, the lesson that both parties drew from these shattering defeats was that it was very dangerous to move too far away from the center.

Thus the Republicans nominated Richard Nixon, a more moderate conservative than Goldwater in 1968 and 1972. Then, in 1976, the very conservative people, who were in a substantial majority at the Republican National Convention, chose Gerald Ford over the more conservative Ronald Reagan. The result was breathtakingly close; Reagan was clearly more admired by the majority of delegates than Ford, and he was an accomplished campaigner. Yet the memory of 1964 was still sufficiently painful for some of the Reagan admirers that they reluctantly went with the safer Ford.

As for the Democrats the memory of the 1972 election was so vivid that the more liberal candidates for the nomination in 1976 avoided identifying themselves as liberals. Morris Udall, a congressman with a strongly liberal record, called himself a "populist" rather than a liberal. But it was to no avail. Jimmy Carter might advertise himself as an "outsider," but his policy positions were close to the mainstream of the Democratic party, which was clearly the right place to be to win the nomination and then the election.

So, despite all the data on heightened ideological awareness, increased issue consistency, and growing polarization, 1976 did nothing to shake the view of party leaders that they should choose centrist candidates, and that in their election campaigns the candidates should do everything possible to occupy the middle ground.

The Majority Lack Deep Party Loyalty

There have been times and places in American history when party loyalties ran very deep; but those loyalties are weakening. Thus, during the great waves of immigration, when masses of people poured off the boats into the cities of the East, unable to speak English, jobless, homeless, and often friendless, it was the city political "machine" that took them in hand, gave them food, helped them find a place to live and a job, asking only one thing in return—their support and their votes. Later the loyalties were sustained by the favors that the party machines performed for the people in their neighborhoods, giving them direct access to city hall. In time, however, personal favors gave way to regular welfare payments and services provided by large, impersonal bureaucracies; many of those who had grown up in the machine's orbit moved out into the suburbs; and the old loyalties weakened.

Then, too, the Democratic coalition that Franklin Roosevelt put together during the New Deal years is not as solid as it was. The combination of blue-collar workers, poor farmers, blacks, Jews, Catholics, the South, and intellectuals won

Roosevelt reelection three times; and enough of it held together to elect Harry Truman in 1948, when all the experts assumed that it would be a Republican year. However, this coalition was forged by the Great Depression and its massive unemployment. As the memory of that grim period receded, so did the gratitude to the Democratic party for its efforts to revive the economy. And we have already noted that the South's historical attachment to the Democratic party is slowly fading.

So today we have a situation in which only about a quarter of the electorate consider themselves strong supporters of a party; somewhat over a third are in a party camp, but not very enthusiastically; and almost two-fifths call themselves Independents. As we see from Figure 3-2, these proportions represent a significant change since 1964, particularly with respect to the decline of strong party attachments and the rise of the Independents.

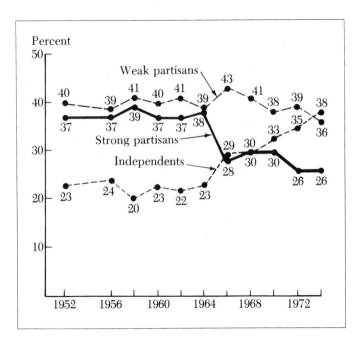

FIGURE 3-2   Partisan Affiliation,
1952–74   (Redrawn from Norman N. Nie, Sidney
Verba, and John R. Petrocik, *The Changing American
Voter* [Cambridge, Mass.: Harvard University Press,
© 1976, the Twentieth Century Fund], p. 49.)

The result is that the party has become a less important factor than it used to be in determining how people vote, and two other factors have become increasingly significant. The first is the personality and competence of the candidate. The response to a Gallup poll question—"Generally speaking, do you think it is better to vote for the man or the party?"—was 74 to 22 percent man before party in 1956. In 1968 the preference for man over party had grown to 84 to 12 percent. The second factor of increasing importance is the voters' response to issues. According to *The Changing American Voter,* "the American public has been entering the electoral arena since 1964 with quite a different mental set than was the case in the late 1950s and early 1960s. They have become more concerned with issues and less tied to parties."[10]

This emphasis on personal qualities and issues shows itself in a number of ways. There has been an increase in "ticket-splitting"—voting for a Democrat for one office and a Republican for another. A great many people, too, switch parties from one election to the next. The most obvious evidence of these tendencies is the fact that Republicans have occupied the White House for twice as many years as the Democrats between 1952 and 1976. If voters divided strictly along party lines, the Republicans, who have consistently been greatly outnumbered by those registered as Democrats, would never have a chance of winning the presidency. Yet in 1952, 1956, and 1972 they not only won—they overwhelmed the Democratic candidate.

This is not to suggest that party has become a totally irrelevant factor in voting. In congressional elections it remains the most important of all influences, and in most years Congress is firmly in Democratic hands by roughly the same margins by which registered Democrats outnumber registered Republicans in the country. Thus the "weak partisans" may defect from their party in presidential races, but they are still inclined to stay with their party in congressional races.

As for the Independents, two points must be stressed. The first is that the increase in the proportion of Independents is largely accounted for by new voters who have entered the electorate since the late 1960s. Thus there has not been a massive abandoning of parties by former loyalists. Instead almost half the children of these loyalists have declined to accept their parents' affiliation, opting instead for independence. But an even more significant point for our purposes here is that well over half these self-defined Independents are not completely liberated from party ties. They *lean* toward one party or the other, and more often than not they vote in the direction in which they are leaning.

So party is still very much alive in the minds and behavior of a high proportion of the electorate. But it has lost some of its potency. And as party leaders and candidates look at the tendency of a great many voters to fluctuate between the parties and to split their tickets, they are likely to play down those aspects which set their party off sharply from the other. They know that people in the opposite camp can be won over to their side, and that people in their own camp can be lost to the opposition. As for the Independents, some of these—perhaps an increasing number—are strongly ideological, and may be looking for bolder policies than the parties have proposed till now. But a majority of the Independents, both the pure kind and the "leaners," are more likely to be found in the middle of the political spectrum. So, again, to attract their votes, most candidates avoid giving an impression of undue militancy or harshness on the issues.

Government Weakens the Parties

Earlier we saw that parties are integral elements in democratic governments. Yet certain features of American government tend to weaken parties and to undermine their ability to present clear policy alternatives to the people. First is the extraordinary power that the American system has vested in the presidency. A president needs his party's support to help him get elected, especially the first time (though a presidential candidate typically sets up a campaign organization separate from the party structure). Once he is elected, however, the party can do very little if a president decides to pursue policies contrary to the promises of the platform. And in the sources of advice sought out by a president, the national committee of his party is rarely among his inner circle.

As for Congress, party is an important factor in its decision-making process, but much less so than in the legislatures of other countries. Power in Congress is heavily concentrated in its committees and committee chairpersons. The party leadership in each house can make proposals and do its best to persuade the committees to accept a given policy. But it has few sanctions to enforce its will. And the separation of powers gives the Congress a good deal of independence from presidential will—even when (as is not always the case) the president and the majority in Congress are of the same party.

Finally, certain imperatives go with the exercise of power that detract from the willingness or ability of an officeholder at any level to carry out party platforms. Once he is elected, he must speak not only for the members of his own party but for the entire constituency. And sometimes he discovers that, desirable though his party's platform may be, he cannot find the political support to put it through. So he will be accused of reneging on his party's principles; and this accusation will be leveled sooner or later at *every* elected official—liberal, conservative, and even radical. For at some point the responsibilities that go with power must come into conflict with ideologies and subject them to compromise and dilution.

In summary, the differences between the parties are muted because both parties are very broad coalitions, because they are not tightly organized, because the electorate still tends toward the center in elections, because the majority of the people are not strongly partisan, and because some of the elements in our governmental system weaken the ability of parties to control the policies of officeholders.

However, along the way we have observed that some changes are in progress, including indications of a possible trend toward polarization of the electorate and the gradual emergence of a two-party system in the South. So far these changes have not altered in any fundamental sense the workings of the party system in America. Whether they will and whether they *should* are subjects for debate among our five perspectives.

Five Perspectives
on Political Parties

The Liberals: Realign and Restructure

As the liberals see it, much of the contemporary apathy and cynicism toward politics results from the inadequate distinctions between the Democratic and Republican parties. Where the party programs do not offer real choices, and where government succeeds government without major changes in direction, the public at large is bound to see politics as a charade, a game of musical chairs, profitable for the participants but tedious and irrelevant for everyone else. Liberals have been making this point for many years.[11] But they believe it to be especially applicable today. For, on the one hand, we see the increase in ideological levels, in issue awareness and consistency, and in polarization—all factors that point to an electorate ready to perceive and make real choices. But, on the other hand, we see a decline in partisanship, a falling away of identification with party. The conclusion liberals draw is that the people are ready for clearer alternatives but the parties won't provide them. Accordingly, the liberals propose that we reform our party system in two ways: ideological realignment and structural reorganization.

Realignment.   If the people are ever to have a chance to choose true liberalism, rather than the mildly reformist centrism which has passed for liberalism till now, the parties must be realigned. One should become more liberal, the other more conservative. Actually, say the liberals, the Republican party does not have to change very much. It is already a predominately conservative party, and if the few liberal Republicans would recognize that they belong in the Democratic party and act accordingly, the Republicans would have as much internal consistency as is needed.

The problem is with the Democrats. And to the liberals even this more substantial problem could be taken care of in large measure by one basic shift—the movement of conservative southerners out of the Democratic into the Republican party. This would remove the albatross around the liberal Democrats' necks. One drastic and rather simple piece of surgery would release the Democratic body politic of its most intolerable tensions.

The realignment proposed by the liberals would not constitute a total polarization of the parties, with only the liberals and some radicals of the left glaring across a great centrist no-man's land at the conservatives and some radicals of the right, as in Figure 3–3. Rather, they are suggesting a moderate or limited realignment, in which the Democratic party would be composed of liberals joined by a few left radicals and a large body of centrists, and the Republican party would combine conservatives, some radical rightists, and centrists, as seen in

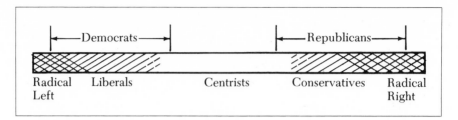

FIGURE 3–3   Polarized Realignment of Parties

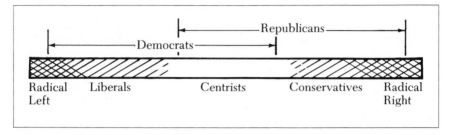

FIGURE 3–4   Limited Realignment of Parties

Figure 3–4. There would still be some overlapping in the appeal of the parties: both would be broad coalitions; both would have to go after the middle-of-the-road vote. But the more absurd contradictions within each party, especially within the Democratic party, would have been resolved, and the voters would have a reasonably clear choice between one party that consistently stood for fairly liberal policies and another that represented a considerably more conservative approach to government.

However, this liberal strategy seems to be very risky. Liberals like to win. They want to see their policies put into effect, and this cannot happen unless they get their candidates elected. Yet they are ready to exclude the southern conservatives, who have helped the Democrats win many elections, from the Democratic party. Their answer is that, if southern conservatives leave the Democratic party, there are others who could take their place. First, there are the blacks, Chicanos, and other minorities who are disproportionately poor. These groups are already heavily Democratic. The only problem is that all too many of them do not vote. The liberals' solution is to simplify registration and voting procedures, and to conduct more effective get-out-the-vote drives among these groups.

Next, there are the young. As we have seen, young voters tend to be considerably more liberal than their elders. This is especially true among college students; we saw this in the figures on college freshmen (Table 3–3), and other surveys show that the liberalism grows more marked as students move from their freshman to their senior year. But even among the under-25 voters who are not in college (almost three-quarters of that entire age group) there are trends at work that the liberals believe are favorable to them. Thus, according to studies undertaken in 1969 and 1973 by pollster Daniel Yankelovich, although there had been a wide gap in the values of college and noncollege youth in the 1960s, this gap had narrowed sharply by 1973.

With the young, too, the task is to get them to the polls by making voting easier. But there is a second, equally important, problem with this group—the very high proportion of Independents. Between 1952 and 1972 the percentage of the under-25 electorate calling themselves Independents rose from about a quarter to more than half. In the liberals' view, the major reason for this is that the idealism of the young is turned into a corrosive cynicism by the substitution of political maneuver for principled policies. If the parties start to represent clear alternatives, the young will respond—and heavily in the liberal Democratic direction.

Then, too, liberals see good prospects for winning over to a reformed Democratic party a good number of affluent suburbanites. Their income level and status would seem to put them in the conservative camp. But liberals believe that college-educated professional and technical people are disgusted by the corruption, waste, and selfishness that they see all around them, in business no less than in government. This makes them ready to respond to a party that puts the public interest before special interests, protecting the environment before exploitative gain, and honest and rational government in place of conflicts of interest and outmoded procedures. As evidence that this is no pipe dream, liberals point to the several congressional seats that the Democrats won in 1974 in traditionally Republican suburbs; and the Democrats held onto most of those seats two years later.

Liberals also see opportunities for attracting women as adherents to a revitalized Democratic party. To the extent that the Democrats identify themselves clearly and strongly with women's liberation and the Equal Rights Amendment—ideas that are appealing especially to younger women—the Democratic party can become the party of the future among the more than half of the electorate that is female.

So the liberals see plenty of sources from which they can recruit replacements for the departing southern conservatives. But now the liberals come up against another objection. These were the very groups in the population that the Democratic party appealed to so enthusiastically in 1972. At the Democratic convention that year, young people, blacks, women, upper-middle-class lawyers, and other professionals were very much on display in the televised coverage of the convention. Yet the Democratic nominee went down to massive defeat. This was hardly a good omen for the liberals' proposed strategy for the Democratic party.

The liberals' response to the Democrats' 1972 defeat is threefold. First, McGovern ran a poor campaign; a better candidate would have run more strongly. Second, against an incumbent president who had scored heavily with the public by his foreign policy, no Democrat could win. Third, the kind of realignment the liberals call for must involve *both* parties. If only one departs from the middle-of-the-road and the other then moves to the center, the latter party will probably win. In the 1972 campaign Nixon played the centrist, coming out in his conservative colors *after* the election was over. So for the liberals the real test will not come until the Democrats nominate an attractive candidate of liberal principles, running in a year when the Democrats have a reasonable prospect of winning against a Republican who stands unashamedly for conservative principles.

But when such a showdown takes place, what makes the liberals think they can win? Opinion polls do not bode well for them. Whereas in the mid-1950s there were slightly more people left of center than right of center in the electorate, those who see themselves as conservatives now outnumber the liberals by 4 to 3. And a May 1974 Gallup poll asked people in the event the parties were realigned: "Which party would you, personally, prefer—the conservative or the liberal party?" The responses: 26 percent the liberal party, 38 percent the conservative party, 36 percent undecided. Liberals contend that these figures are not conclusive. When people use the word "conservative," they are often using it in the context of lifestyles and attitudes toward sex, marijuana, and other social and cultural questions rather than the traditional economic issues. As these anxieties about changing mores fade and the perennial economic questions become dominant again, the pendulum could well swing back to liberalism. In any case, say the liberals, they are prepared to take their chances. A liberalized Democratic party might lose some elections, but it could win some, too. And the liberals would rather put up with periodic conservative administrations as long as liberals had a chance to show what they could do from time to time. At least the people would be able to see the alternatives clearly spelled out and put into practice. This would be vastly preferable to the present minor variations in policy which submerge the possibilities for genuine reform of the American system.

Structural changes.   Realignment is not enough for the liberals. If the parties are to be effective, they must not only represent contrasting interests and policies. They must also be able to hold together as organizations, providing enough strength in the party leadership to be able to speak with authority for the membership, yet giving the rank-and-file members an influential voice.

Thus the national party organizations should follow through on the party platforms and be given authority to discipline state and local units that refuse to abide by the national party positions or support the party's national candidates. National party conferences should be held every year, or at least every other year, rather than once in four years as at present, so that policy can be constantly reexamined and debated. Then, supporters of each party should be given a sense of active participation both locally and nationally. They should be asked to join a local party organization that is a unit within a national structure; membership dues should be charged by the local group, and a portion of these assigned to the national committees, which would then be in a better position than now to underwrite the campaigns of party nominees.

Along with these structural changes in the party organizations should come a stronger party role in Congress, whose committee chairmen should surrender much of their power to the congressional party leaders, who in turn would work closely with the national committee of the party.

It was precisely this kind of reorganization that was proposed by the Commission on Party Structure and Delegate Selection appointed by the Democratic party after the 1968 convention, and of which the first chairman was George McGovern. What the reformers on the commission called for was, as James MacGregor Burns put it, "a national membership base for the party, an invigorated leadership system at the top, and annual policy-making conferences." They wanted to "create something the Democrats have never had—a centrally led, nationally responsible, programmatic party with extensive grass-roots involvement in its ruling councils and policy statements."[12]

In line with these proposals the Democrats convened a national party conference in the fall of 1974 to draft policies for the selection of delegates to the 1976 convention, and also to discuss national and international policy issues. They finally succeeded in drafting guidelines for selecting candidates (to be described in the next chapter) after a heated debate between the party's liberals and centrists. But the conference did very little about the other purpose of the liberals, to take firm stands on some key policy issues. All that emerged was a consensus statement on economic policy that captured few headlines.

Nonetheless, political scientist Gerald Pomper sees considerable significance in the Democrats' organizational changes. He noted the strengthening of national rules governing delegate selection, and sees this and other developments as indications that the Democrats are "altering their character, sometimes deliberately, sometimes unknowingly, into a coherent organization" which is undermining "the position of the established local baronies and islands of power."[13] He even suggests that the Democrats "may soon follow with a national definition of party membership and a supportive financial structure of individual dues."[14]

This cannot happen fast enough for the liberals. As they see it, the parties are lagging behind the public sentiment in bringing about policy and organizational changes. A noted political researcher has supported the liberals' charge:

> Investigation of the data has demonstrated that people lack confidence in the ability of the existing parties to bring about responsive government. The great dissatisfaction with the policies of both parties implies that conditions are highly conducive to party realignment and reformation or a third-party movement. What appears necessary to reestablish confidence in the parties is a wave of populism and party reforms which will allow those who normally lack access to legitimate power, but want change, to bring about desired modifications.[15]

Note that this statement concludes that the time is ripe either for realignment and reform "*or a third-party movement.*" From time to time liberals toy with this option. Whenever the prospects for Democratic party reform grow particularly remote, some liberals threaten to bolt the party and start a new one. Occasionally, they do precisely this, as when Henry Wallace ran as a Progressive in 1948, claiming that Harry Truman's foreign policy was too belligerent. Then Eugene McCarthy offered himself as an Independent in 1976, alleging that there was no real difference between Carter and Ford. But the liberals' general preference for working within the Democratic party was reinforced by the fact that neither Henry Wallace nor Eugene McCarthy—both running on third-party tickets—got many votes (Wallace about 1,100,000, McCarthy about 700,000).

The Conservatives: Realignment—Or a New Third Party?

Conservatives are as dissatisfied with the present party system as the liberals are. They, too, believe that the people are not offered genuine alternatives, and that the Republican and Democratic parties persistently sacrifice principle to expediency.

Conservatives have worked hard to persuade the Republican party to adopt their doctrine. However, repeatedly from the 1940s the Republican party rebuffed the conservatives in the choice of candidates for the presidency. Wendell Wilkie in 1940, Thomas Dewey in 1948, and Dwight Eisenhower in 1952 and 1956 were seen by the conservatives as the spokesmen for the hated liberal establishment, repeatedly foisted on the Republicans over the claims to recognition of authentic conservatives such as Senator Robert Taft. At last in 1964 Senator Barry Goldwater, a real conservative, was chosen by the Republicans. Although he was heavily defeated in the final election, the conservative activists who had won him his nomination held on to key positions in the national party machinery. They were not delighted with the selection of Richard Nixon as the Republican standard-bearer in 1968, but he had accumulated some credit with them. And once he was in the White House, conservatives began to consider how a Republican presidency might be turned into a long-term advantage for the cause of conservatism.

In 1969 this thought was developed in a book by Kevin Phillips, who for a while was an aide to Attorney General John Mitchell in the first Nixon administration. In *The Emerging Republican Majority*[16] Phillips argued that it was time for the Republican party to break the throttlehold of the liberal establishment. No longer should the Republican party build its strategy on trying to sound as much like the Democrats as possible and thus hoping to win the big northern cities. Political power was moving away from the northern cities and away from liberalism. Population was shifting to the suburbs; and except in a few establishment strongholds around New York, San Francisco, and the college towns, the suburbanites (blue-collar as well as white-collar) were reacting with growing conservatism to rising taxes, increasing crime, and the general deterioration of traditional social values. The other big population trend that could help the conservative cause was away from the Northeast toward the "Sunbelt" states of the South and West—areas that are considerably more conservative than the Northeast and potentially Republican territory. And the South was finally and predictably turning against the civil rights and other liberal policies of the national Democratic party, a revolt that had been successfully channeled into the candidacy of George Wallace for the presidency in 1968. The Republican party's job was to capture the Wallace constituency (which included blue-collar workers in some border and midwestern states as well as southerners), not by emulating Wallace's racism but by being more sympathetic to the concerns of the white majority than the Democrats were.

So the Republican party, by following a conservative strategy, could add the South to its traditional strongholds in the mountain and plains states and in the Midwest. In fact, with polls showing a clear conservative trend nationally no part of the country need by written off by the Republicans except New York and New England. In Phillips's analysis we had come to the end of the long era of Democratic dominance, which started in 1932 and lasted, with only one eight-year break, until 1968. We were on the verge of a·new "conservative cycle." He concluded that if the Republicans followed a strategy of conservatism they could create a lasting Republican majority in the country.

Subsequently, the Nixon administration followed a strategy that incorporated some of the themes proposed by Phillips. There was close liaison with such southern Republicans as Senator Strom Thurmond of South Carolina; requests to the Supreme Court to give the South more time to carry out the federally mandated school desegregation; repeated sounding of the theme of "law and order"; and slashing attacks by Vice-President Agnew on the media as tools of a liberal elite. However, when this approach was given its first test in the 1970 midterm elections, the electorate apparently found it too harsh, for the Republicans made only minor gains in congressional races in the South, and in the rest of the country the result was a standoff. The main lesson of 1970 for the Nixon administration was that, if they were to win a big majority in 1972, they must move back toward the center.

Still, having moved to the center and won their landslide victory, the way was clear for the implementation of conservative policies. Indeed, in a newspaper interview Nixon explained that it was his firm intention to move in a more conservative direction. At last it seemed possible to conservatives that their hopes would be realized. Since Nixon could not be elected for another term, he could free himself of those short-term pressures that pulled parties and candidates toward the center and concentrate on building a long-term conservative future for the country and for the Republican party.

Those hopes were quickly dashed. Today more and more conservatives, including Kevin Phillips, are expressing doubts that their programs can be achieved through the Republican party. Three major factors are cited in their disillusionment with the party. First, of course, there was Watergate. The great scandal that enveloped the Nixon administration wreaked havoc on the Republican party. The southern Republican gains in Congress were halted and reversed in the 1974 elections. Several midwestern congressmen who had loyally stood by their president during the impeachment debate were turned out of office by Democrats. Many of the suburbs that had been counted on by Phillips for his emerging Republican majority fell to the Democrats—and stayed with the Democrats in 1976.

Then the polls were depressing news for the Republicans. The Democrats had lost some ground over the years, but the shift was to the Independents, not to the Republicans. Starting from a low base in the early 1950s the Republicans had slipped even further. By the mid-1970s they constituted little more than a fifth of the electorate; one poll taken for the Republican party in late 1974 indicated that only 18 percent of the people called themselves Republicans. The same poll showed that only about a quarter of the electorate regarded the Republican party as trustworthy or competent, and the general image that it conveyed was that of the party of big business and the wealthy. The loss of the White House in 1976 and the continuance of the Democrats' huge majorities in Congress were further indications of the serious weakness of the Republican party.

Finally, there is the constant sense among conservatives that, no matter how hard they try to keep the Republican party on a conservative course, and however great their majorities in the inner counsels of the party, the liberal establishment will always be there to undermine their efforts. As William Rusher puts it:

> it is the ineradicable presence in the Republican party of a liberal minority . . . —a minority unable to dominate the GOP itself, but always able to force it to compromise *toward* the liberal positions rather than away from them—that makes the Republican party, all else aside, so spectacularly unfitted to be the political vector of the conservative majority in the American society.

According to Rusher, in Congress and in national conventions "the recent history of the Republican party is little more than a record of the compromises made by conservative majorities, who know instinctively how victory could be fashioned, to appease a liberal minority whose sole effective function has been to insure the defeat of conservatism."[17]

Nothing could have confirmed this view more convincingly for conservatives than the events of 1976. According to polls of delegate commitments, Ronald Reagan came to the Republican convention only a few votes behind Gerald Ford. The outcome was to be determined by some still uncommitted delegates. The sentiment in the convention was clearly pro-Reagan. Yet the liberal minority, more intent on stopping the conservatives than beating the Democrats in November, filled the air with talk about Reagan's being too conservative for the electorate, suggesting that if he were nominated it would be 1964 all over again. But, said the conservatives, the two situations were not analogous. No Republican could have won in 1964. The polls showed a conservative tide in the country in 1976 that was not there in 1964. Moreover, Goldwater was not an effective candidate: Reagan, in sharp contrast, was a masterful campaigner and the most impressive exponent of the art of televised politics the medium had yet produced. Yet the old argument prevailed, Reagan fell short, and the Republicans lost in November.

What is to be done next? The conservatives, citing the polls mentioned earlier, are convinced that the country is basically conservative. But the more conservative of the two major parties, the Republicans, is very much a minority party. As noted earlier, it represents only about a fifth of the electorate. It is outnumbered two to one in Congress. In 1977 there were only 12 Republican governors, and the Republicans controlled both houses in only five state legislatures. In late 1976 conservatives pondered their future in a Conservative Caucus, formed after

Watergate to provide a framework in which conservatives could develop programs, raise funds to finance lobbying for those programs, and train political activists. Not surprisingly there was no unanimity in the caucus. Some, like William Rusher, called for a new party to supersede the Republicans. This was not to be just another little group of dedicated ideologists but a major party: "a party like the Democratic and Republican parties, consisting of a nationwide *coalition* of interests and capable of capturing both the presidency and the Congress."[18] In Rusher's view the time is ripe for a new party to take over from the Republicans just as the Republicans took over from the Whigs.

A Gallup poll published in April 1975 suggested that there might be considerable support in the country for Rusher's proposition. The poll asked people whether they would be likely to vote for a new party that "would support policies that are more conservative—that is, more to the right—than those of the Republican Party today." The answers: 25 percent yes, 51 percent no, 24 percent no opinion; and the affirmative responses were as frequent among Democrats as among Republicans, and even more so among Independents.

Just the same, others in the Conservative Caucus, impressed by the vast difficulties our electoral system puts in the way of any new party, prefer to continue working within the Republican party, or to try to turn both the Democratic and Republican parties in more conservative directions and thus elect more conservatives to Congress.

In addition to this lack of consensus behind Rusher's proposal, it faces another immediate difficulty. A new party could hope to establish itself quickly only if it were headed by an extremely impressive presidential candidate. Rusher's first choice in his 1975 book was Ronald Reagan. But Reagan's reputation among conservatives was tarnished somewhat in 1976, when, in a last bid for delegate support just before the Republican convention, he announced that he was selecting Senator Richard Schweiker of Pennsylvania as his vice-presidential running mate. Schweiker's voting record was intolerably liberal for conservative tastes; and many conservatives were greatly distressed by what, in their view, was one more example of the kind of expedient game playing that was so deeply entrenched in the two-party system—and which they had looked to Reagan to change.

But even if this episode were to be forgiven (and most conservatives were eventually ready to do so), Reagan did not encourage those who wanted him to head a new party (though, like many conservatives, he was ready to consider changing the party's name). He told interviewers that he still felt there was hope for a party that had lost the presidency by such a narrow margin in 1976. And he was pleased with the 1976 Republican platform, which he and his supporters had so heavily influenced. He argued for the Republicans to do what the Democrats had done in 1974; convene a "miniconvention" without waiting for the next presidential election. If the Republicans did this, they could reconfirm their 1976 platform as a continuing statement of Republican policy; and they could consider a realignment of the parties that would draw conservatives away from the Democratic party and from among the Independents.

Conservatives made another move toward keeping their position constantly before the public when, in February 1977, they formed a "shadow Cabinet," comprising a conservative counterpart to each member of Jimmy Carter's official Cabinet. Through this shadow Cabinet, conservatives explained, they intended "to provide the American people with a vision of where Conservatives hope the nation will go and with a definite plan as to how we move from here to there." However, there was no consensus within this group on whether a new conservative party should be formed.

Thus the diagnosis of our party system among conservatives is similar to the liberals' assessment but more fragmented. Conservatives, too, would like to see a realignment (though conservatives, who emphasize decentralization, are much less prone than the liberals to talk about restructuring the parties' organization to concentrate more power in the national leadership). However, since the Republican party has been doing so poorly in elections and polls, there is a greater tendency among conservatives than among Democrats to talk about a new party or at least a renaming of the Republican party in the hope that a new label, combined with new policies, will make it more appealing to the people.

The Radical Left:
Alternatives to the Property Party

To the radical left the kind of realignment proposed by liberals and conservatives would still offer no basic alternatives to the present system. It would not really change the fact that, as William Domhoff puts it, there is only one political party in the United States—the Property party, with two wings, Democratic and Republican.[19] Domhoff does not deny that there are differences between the parties which run along liberal–conservative lines. But these differences do not challenge the basic assumptions of capitalism, private property, and imperialism.

That even a realigned Democratic party would not produce any basic change is clear to the left from the evidence of 1972, when the Democrats tried realignment with George McGovern. McGovern had a long record of backing and filling on the issues. Although he was among the first in the Senate to speak out against Vietnam and march in an antiwar demonstration organized by left activists, he was never to be relied on by the left. He moved very slowly toward the demand for total withdrawal from Vietnam; and after his participation in the antiwar march he proceeded to attack bitterly such radicals as Huey Newton, Tom Hayden, Jerry Rubin, and Abbie Hoffman.[20] In 1972 he won the nomination by moving to the left—for this was the only way he could get the enthusiastic backing of the young people without whom he had no chance. But in the fall, acting under the pressures of the two-party system, he backed away from his earlier positions and showed himself to be just another Democratic party politician.

This does not mean that there are no Democratic candidates at the congressional level who qualify for support from the left. In fact, occasionally a radical enters the Democratic primaries. For example, Tom Hayden, one of the founders of the radical Students for a Democratic Society in the 1960s, put up a strong fight for the Democratic nomination for U.S. senator in 1976. But this led many radicals to question his continued credibility as a leader of their movement. And, generally speaking, if the radicals of the left are to engage in party politics at all (and most of them prefer other kinds of action), they must create their own parties—Communist, Socialist, Socialist Labor, Peace and Freedom, the People's party, and so on. They know that, for many years at least, these parties cannot win. But they can serve three purposes. First, they provide organizations within which radicals can take clear and unequivocal positions, avoiding the dilution, compromise, and expediency that are an inevitable aspect of the major parties. Second, they can influence the programs of the bigger parties. The small Socialist party had no chance of winning in 1932, but its ideas had an important impact on the Democratic party during the formulation of the New Deal. Third, they provide a means of educating the public, especially during election campaigns, and thus preparing the way for the ultimate awakening of the American people to the state of exploitation under which they live.

The Radical Right: The Need for a Leader

On the radical right there is slightly more affinity for the Republican party than the radical left feels for the Democrats. As we have noted, a few members of the John Birch Society have become Republican congressmen; and the Birch Society was actively engaged in support of Barry Goldwater in 1964. However, no matter how conservative the Republican party might become, as a major party it must include too many positions to satisfy the demand for ideological purity that characterizes radicals. Ronald Reagan enraged the right wing by the size of his budgets when he was governor of California and by the selection of the liberal Schweiker in 1976. And Barry Goldwater was not far enough to the right to win the approval of the radicals once the 1964 election was over.

So on the right, as on the left, there are political parties to challenge the dominance of the two big ones. In recent years one of these has been of special significance—the American Independent party. This party was especially strong in the years when it was headed by Alabama Governor George Wallace, who had the ability through his oratory to arouse the enthusiastic support of large numbers of southern whites, and then to extend his following into border and midwestern states. He mounted his strongest challenge to the Republicans and Democrats when he ran for the presidency in 1968, declaring, "There's not a dime's worth of difference" between the two major parties. Although there was no prospect that he would win the presidency, the polls indicated that there was a strong possibility of his winning enough southern states to prevent either of the major candidates from getting the needed clear majority in the electoral college. Had Wallace captured enough southern states, the election would have been thrown into the House of Representatives (see Chapter 4). There, one or both of the other candidates, in an effort to get the votes of Wallace's delegates, might have accepted parts of Wallace's programs and perhaps allowed him a veto over key administration appointments.

As it turned out, Wallace's strength fell short of some of the earlier predictions, and he never got his opportunity to play president maker in the House of Representatives. Still, both the major parties were deeply aware of the threat represented by Wallace during the election; and the Republican party in particular moved to head off this threat by adopting conservative postures in their platform and their campaign strategy. Even after the 1968 election the Nixon administration showed continuing concern about the threat represented by Wallace, for the polls showed that Wallace remained the favorite of at least one-eighth of the nation's voters until he was shot and seriously wounded in May 1972.

After that, paralyzed, his political impact declined, and his presidential fortunes were finally shattered when Jimmy Carter beat him in some key Democratic primaries in the South in 1976. But, in his prime, he had articulated the anger of many people who believed that the country was being run by a leftist elite that favored blacks over whites, welfare indigents over working people, criminals over their victims, atheists over believers, and pacifists over patriots.

In giving voice to these themes he had aroused the enthusiasm of radical right groups all over the country; and his choice of General Curtis LeMay, an exponent of a belligerently anticommunist foreign policy, as his vice-presidential running mate in 1968 confirmed Wallace's identification with the right wing. Yet we have already observed that the Wallace phenomenon was a complicated one, drawing its strength from sources beyond the radical right itself. Moreover, Wallace abandoned the American Independent party after 1968; and, as the 1976 campaign approached, Wallace began to move toward the center and dropped the overt racism that had been his hallmark.

Without Wallace the American Independent party moved further right. Its standard-bearer in 1972 was a John Birch Society member, John Schmitz, who gained over a million votes nationwide. In 1976 Lester Maddox, a former governor and lieutenant governor of Georgia, won the party's nomination. Maddox had been propelled into politics when, as the owner of a small restaurant, he fought an attempt to integrate it by threatening blacks with a pickax (subsequently making an ax handle his political symbol). The American Independent party's program under Maddox opposed gun control, national health insurance, the ERA, a guaranteed annual income, abortion, school busing, a Vietnam amnesty, and the 55-mph speed limit, whereas it supported segregation, school prayers, capital punishment, higher defense spending, and the white regimes of Rhodesia and South Africa. A rival right-wing group entered the 1976 election battle as the American party, headed by Tom Anderson, with a program that included support for constitutional amendments to prohibit school busing and budget deficits. Together the two parties could not muster one-half of 1 percent of the total votes cast. There is still a good deal of latent support for a populist right-wing party that appeals to resentments against both the poor and the rich, as the American Independent party did in its heyday in the 1960s. But it is apparent that such a party cannot hope to capture electoral votes in the absence of a charismatic leader.

The Centrists: In Defense of the Party System

A number of scholars and political commentators have developed rebuttals to the various attacks on the present two-party system.[21] They believe that whatever its defects these are far outweighed by its advantages.

Two is the right number.   First, the centrists argue, two is the best number for a party system. One-party systems go with dictatorships; there are no choices. Multiparty systems are often found in democracies, but they tend to cause instability. Elections under these conditions do not usually settle the key question—who will form the government? Typically in multiparty elections no one party emerges with enough strength to form a majority, so two or more parties have to get together and form a coalition government. But since they have no real organizational commitment to each other, one or more of them may withdraw from the alliance as soon as it no longer serves their purpose, which starts the process of forming a government all over again. Furthermore, this system requires just as much bargaining, compromise, and coalition building as under the American two-party system. The major difference is that in our system the compromises take place *within* the parties *before* an election, and under the multiparty system they occur *among* the parties *after* the election. So the critics' complaint that there is too much compromise in American party politics is foolish. Compromise is inevitable in all democratic politics. The only question is when and how the compromises will be worked out.

Our parties provide alternatives.   It is not true, as liberals, conservatives, and radicals allege, that the choice between Democrats and Republicans is almost meaningless, that they are merely Tweedledum and Tweedledee. At the very least, our two-party system provides for one of the essential conditions for democracy—a choice between a party of the "ins" and a party of the "outs." The party that forms the government is made constantly aware of the fact that, should it lose its hold on the affections of the electorate, another group is ready and able to take over as soon as the next election comes along. To some extent the alternation between the two governing groups is the result of the electorate's growing bored with the incumbent administration or dubious about its integrity. Yet the alternatives provided are not based merely on the relative vitality and honesty of the two parties. There are, as we have seen, differences between them with regard to programs and policies.

We do not need wider differences. The differences, it is true, are not wide. But the very narrowness of the ideological gap between the parties is a profound virtue. The social and economic factors that divide Americans are numerous and deep. Tensions and conflicts are part of our normal condition, and violence is all too likely to erupt at any time. Our two parties, because they are such large and diverse coalitions, are forced to emphasize compromise and conciliation as a condition of their holding together. In doing this, they perform a vital function—that of building a certain level of consensus among competing groups and reducing the amount of divisiveness which is so much a part of our culture. To sharpen the distinctions between the parties on liberal–conservative lines would thus promote not consensus but more conflict, which we do not need at this stage of our history.

More centralization of parties is undesirable.   The liberals' proposal to reorganize our parties to make them more centralized and more disciplined is alien to the American tradition. It may be appropriate in Europe, but it will not work here. Local party organizations are not about to take orders from national committees. And legislative leaders will certainly not follow instructions given them by national party organizations. Previous attempts to build closer links between national party committees and congressional leaders have failed dismally. Thus in the 1950s the chairman of the Democratic National Committee created a Democratic Advisory Council to develop policy alternatives to the Eisenhower administration. The council was all but ignored by the Senate majority leader, Lyndon Johnson. Again, after its defeat in 1968 the Democratic party set up a Democratic Policy Council in an effort to reform its structures and procedures. The council included representation of various strands of opinion in the party, but none of the official leaders of the Senate or the House participated.

The people don't want realignment.   Ideological leaders call for sharper divisions between the parties, but this is not what the people want. Polls indicate that large majorities believe that the parties stir up conflict where none really exists. In fact, the contentiousness and divisiveness of parties is the principal reason for the general dislike and distrust of parties.

What do the centrists make of the data indicating an increase in polarization among the electorate? They are concerned about it, but they doubt that it calls for drastic changes in our party system. The largest single body of opinion is still to be found in the moderate ranges of the spectrum; and they believe that today, with Vietnam and the other tensions of the sixties and early seventies behind us, the trend is again toward the center.[22]

In any case, whatever the research studies suggest about polarization on issues, the ultimate test comes when people cast their ballots. And, say the centrists, most voters who take very strong, even extreme positions on issues will still not accept candidates who are outside the mainstream. The evidence seems clear: parties that desert the center lose elections. This is the lesson of 1964 and 1972, and no matter how the conservatives and liberals try to explain those disasters away, the conclusion is inescapable that major parties cannot win with candidates who stray from the middle ground.

Surely there should be no question about this in the minds of the leaders of the Republican party. A party that claims the allegiance of such a small minority of the electorate dare not repeat the experiment of 1964. They came very close to doing so in 1976; but Ronald Reagan, for all his personal attractiveness and lucidity, was too deeply committed to a hard conservative doctrine to have a chance of winning over enough Independents and Democrats to make victory in November possible. Barry Goldwater, himself, had learned the lesson of 1964; though still a conservative and an admirer of Reagan's philosophy, he came out for Ford. Even Reagan was aware of his problem, as was indicated by his desperation move in selecting Schweiker as his more liberal running mate. Of course, Ford lost in the final election. But Ford, though quite conservative in his views, was widely perceived to be a reasonable, practical man rather than a dogmatic type. As a result he appealed to many moderates, and won 48 percent of the vote—far more than the number of registered Republicans.

As for the Democrats, they wisely showed in 1976 that they were very much aware of the meaning of 1972. They could have avoided their 1972 disaster if they had taken note of a 1970 book called *The Real Majority*,[23] which argued that no party could win unless it appealed to the "Middle Voters." The most typical Middle Voter, according to the authors, was a "forty-seven-year-old housewife from the outskirts of Dayton, Ohio, whose husband is a machinist."[24] To speak persuasively to Middle Voters, the Democrats should emphasize economic issues, particularly the federal government's responsibility to combat unemployment. They should also recognize a fundamental reality about the mores and attitudes of Middle Voters: they are profoundly hostile to the elements that have become associated with the youth culture, and with the liberals' tolerant attitudes toward departures from sexual and social norms of behavior. Thus the Democrats should not allow the Republicans to preempt the "Social Issue"—the majority's concern with "racial problems, crime as an issue, student disruption, marijuana, pornography, morals, school integration, and raucous dissent."[25] Although Democrats should not advocate racist policies, they should split off the race issue from the rest and come out strongly against crime, disorder, and immorality. This advice was followed by several Democratic congressional candidates in their 1970 election campaigns—apparently with a good deal of success.

But it was not followed by McGovern. Quite the contrary. The result, as we have seen, was wholesale defections from among traditional Democratic sources of strength, such as labor unions, ethnic groups, and the South, and the general alienation of the Middle Voters. Nor did the hoped-for huge margins of young voters materialize to fill the gap. Even if they had voted overwhelmingly for McGovern, it would not have been enough. For the young constituted a small minority of the electorate. The median age of the voting population in November 1972 was 43. A Gallup survey in 1971 concluded that, with teenagers a declining proportion of the population, "the youth cult" was almost over, and that the youth vote did "not presage a drastic convulsion for the American political system."[26] Certainly no such convulsion occurred in November 1972.

By 1976 the "social issue" had receded considerably, and the Democrats could once again emphasize the economic issues that have been their strong suit.

It was even possible for the Democrats to speak about pardoning Vietnam defectors and decriminalizing marijuana, without being punished for it at the polls. But their language on these issues was suitably moderate; and it was made more acceptable when uttered by Jimmy Carter, a Southern Baptist, clearly located in the political center and certainly no idol of the vanguard of the cultural revolution.

Now, say the centrists, we badly need a period of moderate policies competently executed. For in large part the declining support for the parties is merely one dimension of the general deterioration of trust in government that has resulted from the failings of government over the past decade. An improvement in government's performance will not make our parties popular, for it is their fate in a democracy to be the butt of a great deal of abuse. But, for all that, their condition will be healthy enough so that we need not engage in ill-conceived changes that are out of place in the American scheme of things.

Conclusion

Three major topics have surfaced repeatedly throughout this chapter: party realignment, with particular reference to the Democratic party; the deteriorating prospects of the Republican party; and the general public decline in identification with political parties. In each of these problem areas the future is shrouded in uncertainties. Speculations in the recent scholarly studies of parties are full of qualifying clauses: "It seems possible that . . . ," "on the other hand," "the unpredictability is made greater by . . . ," and so on. The reason for this is not simply the reluctance of academics to make unequivocal statements. With party ties weakening, the electorate's moorings are coming adrift, and there are fewer fixed elements in the situation to help us make confident assertions. So as we offer our concluding comments here on the key questions of the chapter, we cannot dispense with qualifications and admissions of uncertainty.

Will the major parties realign?   Probably yes, but slowly, and only in limited degree. Limited realignment is likely to come about not because of any surging demand on the part of the electorate or because of firm decisions by party leaders, but mostly because the South will proceed gradually toward the establishment of a two-party system. That process was slowed, as we have seen, by Watergate and the Jimmy Carter victory. But even in 1976 Carter won only about half the southern white vote; he won some key southern states because of the lopsided margins given him by black voters. There is a reasonable prospect that white southern voters will continue to leave the Democratic party. So far most of the ex-Democrats have declared themselves Independents. But with more and more votes cast for Republican candidates the Republican party should be able to build an organizational base from which to win more congressional, state, and local elections. Once this happens, the one crucial change needed for a limited party realignment—moving southern conservatives out of the Democratic party—will have been accomplished.

Will the Republican party die?   Probably not. For one thing, the emerging changes in the South will add to the number of registered Republicans and to the strength of the Republicans in Congress. For another, more people see themselves as conservatives than as liberals, and the Republican party is the more conservative of the two major parties. Then, with the Democrats in control of both White House and Congress, the Republicans stand to gain from anything that government does wrong. Finally, the party's 1976 standard-bearer, Gerald Ford, still won 48 percent of the vote and almost all the western states, even in the aftermath of Watergate. These facts do not quite square with Kevin Phillips's statement to the Conservative Caucus in December 1976 that the GOP is like "a turned-over turtle which has aged so much that its life expectancy is questionable."

However, the question of the life expectancy of the GOP cannot be resolved without considering a final question.

Is the American party system about to disappear?   Probably not, but it may grow still weaker than it is now. Parties will not become extinct in America for the reasons suggested earlier: as long as people are free to organize anything, they will organize parties. However, it is growing increasingly difficult to contain all the political impulses of the American electorate within a stable two-party framework, even if this framework is realigned. So we may well see the emergence of either or both of the following trends.

First, there could be a proliferation of new parties. Given the nature of our electoral institutions, none of these is likely to grow strong enough to overtake the major parties. Taken together, however, they could be a source of increased confusion in elections.

Second, there could be an acceleration of the tendency for voters to attach themselves to candidates on the basis of personality and issues with little or no preference to party. This is the prospect that led Walter Dean Burnham to the prediction cited at the beginning of this chapter, that political parties might disappear, leaving us with a volatile, unpredictable, unanchored electorate. We are not yet at that point, for, as we have seen, party is still an important factor in electoral decisions, and conceivably the parties have already hit the lowest point of their fortunes. But we had better suspend judgment on this question until we have taken a closer look at what happens in elections. This we shall do in the next chapter.

Notes and References

1.   See Jack Dennis, "Trends in Public Support in the American Political Party System," *British Journal of Political Science*, July 1975.

2.   Walter Dean Burnham, *Critical Elections and the Mainsprings of American Politics* (New York: W.W. Norton & Company, Inc., 1970), p. 132.

3.   David S. Broder, *The Party's Over: The Failure of Politics in America* (New York: Harper & Row, Publishers, 1971), p. 245.

4.   Gerald M. Pomper, *Elections in America* (New York: Dodd, Mead & Company, 1968), pp. 185–87.

5.   See Everett Carl Ladd, Jr., with Charley D. Hadley, *Transformations of the American Party System: Political Conditions from the New Deal to the 1970s* (New York: W. W. Norton & Company, Inc., 1975); and Gerald Pomper, *Voter's Choice, Varieties of American Electoral Behavior* (New York: Dodd, Mead & Company, 1975).

6.   Angus Campbell, Philip E. Converse, Warren E. Miller, and Donald E. Stokes, *The American Voter* (New York: John Wiley & Sons, Inc., 1960), pp. 179–87.

7.   Arthur H. Miller, "Political Issues and Trust in Government," *The American Political Science Review*, September 1974, p. 963.

8.   The survey is directed by Alexander Astin of the University of California at Los Angeles on behalf of the American Council on Education.

9.   See Philip E. Converse, Aage R. Clausen, and Warren E. Miller, "Electoral Myth and Reality: The 1964 Election," *The American Political Science Review*, Vol. 59, No. 2 (June 1965), pp. 321–36.

10.   Norman H. Nie, Sidney Verba, and John R. Petrocik, *The Changing American Voter* (Cambridge, Mass.: Harvard University Press for the Twentieth Century Fund, 1976), p. 166. See also Arthur H. Miller, Warren E. Miller, Alden S. Raine, and Thad A. Brown, "A Majority Party in Disarray: Policy Polarization in the 1972 Election," *The American Political Science Review*, Vol. 70, No. 3 (September 1976), pp. 753–78, and Comments and Rejoinder in the same issue, pp. 779–849.

11.   See James MacGregor Burns, *The Deadlock of Democracy* (Englewood Cliffs, N.J.: Prentice-Hall, Inc. [Spectrum Books], 1963); American Political Science Association Committee on Political Parties, *Toward a More Responsible Two-Party System* (New York: Rinehart & Company, Inc., 1950); Elmer Eric Schattschneider, *Party Government* (New York: Farrar & Rinehart, Inc., 1942).

12.   James MacGregor Burns, "The Democrats on the Eve," *The New Republic*, July 1, 1972, p. 19.

13.   Gerald M. Pomper, Ross K. Baker, Charles E. Jacob, Wilson Carey McWilliams, and Henry A. Plotkin, *The Election of 1976: Reports and Interpretations* (New York: David McKay Company, Inc., 1977), p. 7.

14.   Ibid., p. 34.

15.   Miller, "Political Issues," p. 971.

16.   Kevin Phillips, *The Emerging Republican Majority* (New Rochelle, N.Y.: Arlington House, Inc., 1969).

17.   William A. Rusher, *The Making of the New Majority Party* (New York: Sheed and Ward, Inc., 1975), p. xxii.

18. Ibid., p. 96.

19. See G. William Domhoff, *Fat Cats and Democrats: The Role of the Rich in the Party of the Common Man* (Englewood Cliffs, N.J.: Prentice-Hall, Inc., 1972).

20. See Robert Sam Anson, *McGovern: A Biography* (New York: Holt, Rinehart and Winston, Inc., 1972), p. 174.

21. See, for example, Arthur N. Holcombe, *Our More Perfect Union* (Cambridge, Mass.: Harvard University Press, 1950); Herbert Agar, *The Price of Union*, 2nd ed. (Boston: Houghton Mifflin Company, 1966); Pendleton Herring, *The Politics of Democracy* (New York: W. W. Norton & Company, Inc., 1940).

22. See Jack Citrin, "Comment: The Political Relevance of Trust in Government," *The American Political Science Review*, September 1974, pp. 973–88.

23. Richard M. Scammon and Ben J. Wattenberg, *The Real Majority* (New York: Coward, McCann & Geoghegan, Inc., 1970). Scammon is the director of the Elections Research Center in Washington, D.C., and Wattenberg was a White House aide to Lyndon Johnson and a campaign aide to Senator Henry Jackson in 1972.

24. Ibid., pp. 69–70.

25. Ibid., p. 282.

26. *Newsweek*, October 25, 1971.

Elections:

Majorities, Media, and Money

In the United States, the election process offers a choice of candidates for most public offices, awards each office to whoever gets the most votes, and thus builds the principle of majority rule into the governmental system. However, there is a great deal of debate on the extent to which our elections truly provide a choice and whether they register the authentic will of the majority. To set up the terms of that debate we shall discuss the various elements that go into nominating and electing candidates for office in America. Although we shall have something to say about elections at all levels, most of our examples will be drawn from presidential elections.

For a people who do not vote very much, we are called upon to vote a great deal. A much greater number of public offices are contended for in elections in this country than in other countries. Every fourth November we elect a president, and at the same time we fill all the seats in the House of Representatives and one-third of the seats in the Senate. Two years later we go through the same process for the House and the Senate. Then, as we shall see in Chapter 10, we are also called upon to choose among candidates for a great array of state and local government jobs—governors and lieutenant governors, state senators and assemblymen, mayors and city council members, sheriffs and judges, commissioners and tax assessors, and more. In addition, we have laws that establish elections of state and local officials of political parties. And, large numbers of state and local issues are placed on the ballot to be disposed of by decision of the voters at large.

Nominating Our Presidential Candidates

Primaries

We are not content with subjecting more offices to the election process than is the case elsewhere. We also bring the general public into the process of choosing—directly or indirectly—the candidates whom political parties put forward for election. In other democracies only the active, subscribing members of the parties are involved in deciding who their candidates will be. Here we have adopted the system of direct primaries, in which rank-and-file voters can participate. In most states each party's primary is "closed"—that is, reserved for those rank-and-file voters who register ahead of time with that party. Thus, in a state holding a closed primary, registered Republicans may vote for only Republican candidates. But there are some "open primary" states where this qualification is not imposed, and a voter can decide on the day of the primary in which party's primary he will participate. Primary elections are held for congressional and most partisan state offices, are official occasions, paid for out of public funds, and are administered under legally authorized procedures in the same way as general elections.

Primaries have also become a major factor in nominating the parties' candidates for the presidency. Each party's presidential candidate is selected by a majority vote of the delegates to the party's national convention, which is held in July or August before the November election. The precise number of delegates needed to nominate a candidate varies from party to party and year to year; but both parties apportion delegates among the states mostly on the basis of population, with a bonus of additional delegates going to states that did well for the parties' candidates in the previous election. Given the power to nominate a presidential candidate vested in these delegates, how they are chosen becomes a crucial question.

Historically, delegates were chosen at state conventions or committees —political assemblies to which delegates were elected from the ranks of the local party organizations. But in recent years more and more states have adopted presidential primaries as their means of selecting delegates to the national conventions, and the delegates' names have appeared on the voter's ballot along with various candidates for public office. The extent to which delegates are committed to supporting a particular candidate at the national convention varies according to the laws of the states. Some of the primaries bind the delegates to a candidate, whereas other states permit the delegates to express their individual preferences, leaving the delegates unpledged. However, the trend has been toward securing commitments to specific candidates based on the votes in the primaries of the party's rank and file.

John F. Kennedy was the first presidential candidate to depend heavily on the primaries to secure his nomination. As Theodore White tells it, Kennedy "clubbed the big city bosses into submission"[1] after winning some key victories in the early primaries. But Kennedy still needed those big city bosses, and his success did not establish conclusively that candidates must depend principally on primaries to gain the nomination. Thus, in 1964, Barry Goldwater won some primaries but lost others by big margins; he received only 25 percent of the votes cast in the primaries he entered; and he was clearly not the first choice of Republican rank-and-file voters in the opinion polls. But he won the nomination because in 1964 56 percent of the delegates to the national convention were picked at state conventions, and Goldwater was popular among the conservative Republican party leaders who were influential at those conventions. Then, in 1968, Vice-President Humphrey won the Democratic nomination without entering a single primary. Robert Kennedy's bid had been brought to a tragic end by an assassin's bullet; and, since only 15 states held presidential primaries in 1968, none of the other candidates had amassed enough delegates to prevent the established party leaders from choosing one of their own at the national convention.

By 1972, however, the number of states holding presidential primaries had been increased from 15 to 23, and this was crucial to George McGovern's success in mounting a liberal challenge to the candidates preferred by the Democratic party leadership. But even McGovern's victory was dependent to some extent on the efforts of his liberal supporters at state conventions; for he won only 10 of the 23 primaries he entered, some by narrow margins.

The number of presidential primary states increased to 30 by 1976; and this was the essential factor in Jimmy Carter's nomination. He was very much the outsider, challenging the established party leadership structures. But he won the opening primary in New Hampshire; put an end to George Wallace's flickering hopes of getting to the White House with primary victories in the South; and confounded the skeptics who said he would not carry any major industrial states by winning in Pennsylvania, Michigan, and Ohio. This is not to say that Carter's progress was an unbroken triumphal march. Some of his critical primary victories were by tiny margins. In the last part of the primary season he lost to California's governor Jerry Brown in four states and to Senator Frank Church of Idaho in three. Moreover, Carter first began to be taken seriously as a candidate because of his success in a convention state, Iowa. Before the primary season started, Carter received more votes than any other candidate in Iowa: 27 percent of the 10 percent of the state's Democrats who participated in the convention voting. The attention lavished by the media on that 2.7 percent of Iowa's Democrats made Jimmy Carter a candidate to be taken seriously. Just the same, unlike his Democratic opponents, Carter entered every primary, and more than any other nominee before him was a product of the primaries.

Even Gerald Ford, though an incumbent president, had to undergo a grueling ordeal in the 1976 primaries and only just came through. In the early going, Ford built up what appeared to be a commanding delegate lead. But a series of primary victories by Ronald Reagan in Texas, the South, and the West reduced Ford's margin to the point at which the struggle focused on 10 states, with a total of 283 delegates, which made their selection through state conventions. There Ford just held on to his narrow advantage. But the final, intense struggles in the state conventions, followed by the quest for support, one person at a time, among the uncommitted delegates at the convention, should not distract us from the central fact of the Republican nominating process of 1976: the bulk of the delegates came from the primary process, and the primaries were easily the largest factor in the outcome.

Deficiencies in the primary process.   As the number of primaries has increased, so has the chorus of criticism about the primary process. For one thing, the turnout at primaries is usually low; less than 18 percent of the voting-age population voted in the 1976 primaries. Moreover, the minority that does participate in the primaries tends not to be a cross section of the party's rank and file, but rather, as we saw in Chapters 2 and 3, the more committed, more ideological members of the public. Then, too, the primaries are spread out from March through June, sometimes taking place in one state at a time, sometimes a few on the same day, so they are registering the will of different voters at different periods. One result of this is that a disproportionate emphasis has been placed on small numbers of voters in the early primaries. New Hampshire is always the first state to hold its primary. Lyndon Johnson's prospects were destroyed there in 1968 because he did not win by a big enough margin. And McGovern, Carter, and Ford made much of their New Hampshire victories. Yet New Hampshire has less than 0.4 percent of the nation's population, and in 1976 it accounted for only 17 of the Democrats' national convention delegates, and 21 of the Republicans'

Moreover, the primaries place a tremendous burden on the candidates, who must be in perpetual motion, flying from state to state, winding up the current primary while campaigning for the next and laying the groundwork for the ones after that. The process is confusing to the candidates and bewildering to the public. It is also very expensive.

So it has been suggested that we carry the logic of the primaries to its ultimate conclusion and establish national presidential primaries, conducted by the states but held on the same day everywhere. One proposal considered by Congress provides for a runoff election between the two leading candidates if no one receives more than 40 percent of the vote. National conventions would still be held, but their job would be limited to choosing the vice-presidential candidates and writing the platform. A Gallup poll in 1972 found 72 percent of the public in favor of this idea, and only 18 percent opposed.

However, a number of objections have been voiced. Such a reform would reduce the jealously guarded role of the states. It would weaken the role of the national convention and thus of the political parties. It would cost candidates at least as much money as the present system. And it would all but eliminate the route to the nomination available now to "outsiders" such as McGovern and Carter. McGovern began 1972 with only 2 percent of the Democratic vote in the polls; by mid-March he was up to only 5 percent. Then, although he did well in New Hampshire, he still lost the primary. If that had been the only test, he would have been finished. But the present system allowed him to build his strength cumulatively, choosing those primaries in which he was likely to do well and bypassing the rest. Carter, too, began as an unknown. The December 1974 Gallup poll of prospective Democratic candidates mentioned on page 46 did not even list Carter. He had hardly any more name recognition by the beginning of 1976. But the Iowa caucuses followed by New Hampshire propelled him from an unknown into a front-runner. After that, he entered all the primaries, even those in which his chances were poor, and succeeded in forcing his nomination on reluctant party leaders. If we consider it a virtue to provide a route to the presidency to those out-side the established national leadership ranks, then a change to simultaneous nationwide primaries would undermine this advantage.

Among the other proposals that have been offered to make reform more palatable to its critics is the establishment of regional primaries. Five of these might be held, one a month from March to July. They would serve the purpose of rationalizing and coordinating the state primaries, yet leave the final choice of candidates to the national conventions by delegates elected at the regional pri-maries. A variation of this idea would leave it to the states whether or not they wanted to hold presidential primaries, but would limit them to a choice among a few dates on which all primaries must be held. There was movement in this direc-tion in 1976, when some neighboring states coordinated the scheduling of their primaries, and there will undoubtedly be further consideration of this approach before 1980.

The National Conventions

The character of the national conventions has been transformed by the growing use of presidential primaries. Earlier in our history the conventions were the setting for maneuvering by party leaders and decision making behind closed doors. Thus, in 1920, Harry Daugherty went to the Republican convention in Washington as a representative of the undistinguished claims of Senator Warren Gamaliel Harding. He explained his scenario to some reporters:

> There will be no nomination on the early ballots. After the other candidates have failed, after they have gone their limit, the leaders, worn out and wishing to do the very best thing, will get together in some hotel room about 2:11 in the morning. Some fifteen men, bleary-eyed with lack of sleep, and perspiring profusely with the excessive heat, will sit down around a big table. I will be with them and present the name of Senator Harding. When that time comes, Harding will be selected, because he fits in perfectly with every need of the party and nation.[2]

Events followed this program closely. There was a deadlock among the major candidates; at around two o'clock in the morning before the last day of the con-vention, a small group of men, after long discussion in the "smoke-filled room" of the convention hotel, wearily gave up on the possibility of nominating anyone but Harding. He was nominated the next day on the tenth ballot. As Harding put it: "We drew to a pair of deuces, and filled."

Nobody draws to a pair of deuces and wins a presidential nomination anymore. Successful candidates have to arrive at the convention with a very **strong** hand indeed. In fact, it has to be strong enough to overwhelm the opposition very quickly, for conventions now do not go to the 10 ballots required before Harding could get his majority (or the 103 ballots the Democrats took to nominate John Davis in 1924). Every Republican presidential nominee has won on the first ballot since 1948, and every Democratic nominee since 1956.

Sometimes there have been hard-fought struggles at the conventions to win on that first ballot. However, since Dwight Eisenhower narrowly defeated Robert Taft for the Republican nomination in 1952, there has been only one real cliff-hanger—Gerald Ford's win over Ronald Reagan in 1976. It had been the conventional wisdom before 1976 that nobody could come into a Republican national convention with anything close to 1000 votes and fail to win the nomination. Reagan had more than that, finishing with 1070 votes of the 1130 needed. But Ford got 1187. And, close though the contest was, there was little doubt by the time the convention began that Reagan had lost.

Thus even the 1976 Republican convention did not contradict the general rule that the national conventions have now become forums to ratify previously made decisions on the naming of presidential candidates. Certainly, this was also the case on the Democratic side in 1976. Until well into the spring, political experts were still speculating that no candidate could possibly arrive at the convention with anything close to a majority. So, it was assumed, there would be a deadlock, and there would be backroom dealing and maneuvering as there had been in 1920, and the party would turn again to Hubert Humphrey. Yet, well before the convention, it became clear that its main business would be the ceremonial confirmation of Jimmy Carter's nomination.

This is not to say that the national conventions have become nothing but ritualistic occasions. Often there are dramatic struggles on various matters—for instance, contests over delegates' *credentials*. Thus the 1972 Democratic convention refused to seat a delegation headed by one of the great powers in the party, Chicago's Mayor Daley, because the Credentials Committee found that they had not complied with new delegate rules requiring proper representation of women, young people, and minorities. The party *platform* can also generate fireworks. Although Reagan lost in 1972, he was able to force through planks in the Republican platform that were implicitly critical of some key elements in the Ford–Kissinger foreign policy. And the nomination for the candidate for *vice-president* can also cause conflicts. With the exception of 1956, when Democratic presidential nominee Adlai Stevenson let the convention choose the vice-presidential nominee (Tennessee Senator Estes Kefauver beat John Kennedy), conventions have endorsed the presidential nominee's choice of running mate. However, in most cases the decision is made during the convention after a great deal of pressure from competing forces in the party. Thus Ford chose conservative Senator Robert Dole to placate the Reaganites in 1976, and Carter selected liberal Senator Walter Mondale to mollify the liberals in the party who were unhappy with the Carter candidacy.

Finally, arguments over procedural *rules* at the parties' national conventions can determine much larger questions. For example, Reagan's managers in 1976 forced a showdown on the procedure by which vice-presidential nominees are selected. They demanded a change in the rules that would compel Ford to follow Reagan's example and announce his selection for running mate before the vote on the presidential nominee. (It was hoped that the proposal might, on its merits, appeal to some of the Ford supporters; and then, if Ford had to announce his choice ahead of time, he would antagonize those who preferred someone else, and thus lose some votes for his own candidacy.) The Reaganites' proposal was rejected, and its rejection foretold the final outcome on the Ford–Reagan struggle.

All these conflicts over credentials, platforms, vice-presidential running mates, and rules serve to focus public attention on politics. The long, noisy demonstrations for the candidates are of little interest to anyone not participating in them. And most of the speeches are full of predictable denunciations of the opposite party and repeated references to the party's own glorious achievements under past leaders (though references to Richard Nixon at the 1976 Republican convention were conspicuous by their absence). However, to the annoyance of party leaders, most of these speeches are interrupted or ignored by the television networks, which concentrate on trying to find out what is going on behind the scenes to resolve the conflicts facing the convention. Although some of these controversies are blown up beyond their true significance by the media, others are of great importance, and the media's instinct in concentrating on them rather than on the formal business of the conventions is sound.

The delegates and fair representation.   Traditionally, the delegates to national conventions were representative of party leaders rather than of the electorate generally. In 1968 this was challenged by liberals, who claimed that the riots that erupted in the streets of Chicago during the Democratic convention would not have occurred if representatives of the people involved in the riots had been at the convention rather than in the streets. Liberals pointed out that 18 states had sent delegates to the convention without a single person under 30, and that blacks, Chicanos, and women were grossly underrepresented. So a commission was appointed, first under George McGovern, then under Congressman Donald Fraser, to draw up new guidelines for representation at the 1972 convention. Under the ensuing guidelines the delegate selection process was to be open to all registered party members, and public or party officials would no longer automatically be delegates. The state delegations must also include representatives of minorities, women, and young people "in reasonable proportion to their representation in the party as a whole in the state." The result at the 1972 convention was that many top officials were excluded, and there was a massive increase in the number of minorities, women, and youth.

Now it was the turn of the newly excluded groups to complain. They said that the 1972 delegations were at least as unrepresentative of rank-and-file Democrats as the previous composition of conventions. There were few blue-collar workers and labor union leaders—the most important of all Democratic constituencies. Many Democratic congressmen and state and local government officers, all elected by vote of the people, were denied the opportunity to attend their national conclave. Instead "quotas" had been set for the delegations; and the quotas, based on race, sex, and age, had to be filled whether or not any of the delegates selected had any political experience and could speak for anyone but themselves. Thus Mayor Daley's Illinois slate of delegates, elected by 900,000 people in the primaries, was rejected as unrepresentative because it lacked the approved quotas, and it was replaced by a reform slate hastily pulled together by a small pro-McGovern group and subjected to no election process whatsoever.

The crushing McGovern defeat in November 1972 strengthened the force of these criticisms, and there was a further revision of the rules when the Democratic party held its midterm national conference in 1974. After a clash between liberals and centrists a compromise was reached. An "affirmative action" program was adopted that moved away from the notion of quotas but admonished the states to encourage participation by the young, blacks, and women. The result was that at the 1976 convention there were considerably more people in these categories than there had been in 1968 but fewer than in 1972, and the union leaders and elected officials were back again in force. Less has been done in the Republican party to ensure the representation of minorities, women, and the young, though it is the announced intention of the party to take steps in this direction.

Candidates and Their Qualifications

With respect to both the election machinery and the selection of delegates, we have seen a trend toward making the nomination process less exclusive. To a limited extent this trend can also be seen in relation to the candidates themselves. What qualifications must a candidate have in order to be seriously considered as a presidential nominee? Here we must look at the candidate's personal origins and background, experience in public office, and character.

Personal origins and background.   It used to be assumed that a presidential candidate should be a white male Protestant of north European extraction in his fifties. John Kennedy, a Catholic in his early forties, changed two of these requirements. And Barry Goldwater's ancestry was of eastern European rather than northern European extraction. However, Carter and Ford in 1976 both fitted the earlier profile. Polls indicate that fewer and fewer Americans say that they would not vote for a women or a black for president. Yet no woman or black has been seriously considered by a Democratic or Republican convention for the presidency.

From the Civil War until 1976 it was assumed that a major party candidate must come from outside the South. The states below the Mason–Dixon line were considered to be outside the national mainstream because they were relatively backward economically and also because of their history of racial discrimination. But, as we have seen, the South has undergone major changes, and Jimmy Carter demonstrated in 1976 that a southerner can indeed by acceptable to a national constituency. In fact, to the Democrats in 1976 the fact that Carter was a southerner was an asset, for it enabled them to win back a part of the country that had deserted them in recent presidential elections.

The educational requirements for a presidential candidacy have been growing more demanding. Generally speaking, delegates expect a viable candidate now to have a college education. In fact, since 1968 all the candidates put forward by the two parties have gone on to graduate work—Nixon and Ford in law, McGovern in theology, Humphrey in political science, and Carter in engineering and physics.

Political experience.   A candidate is expected to have substantial experience in public office. Wendell Wilkie, the Republican nominee in 1940, was a corporate executive with no experience in government, and Dwight Eisenhower had held no elective office, though as leader of the Allied Forces in World War II he was deeply involved in public decision making with political leaders. After Eisenhower all candidates for the presidency have had the experience of serving in a public office to which they had been elected.

What public offices are best suited for this purpose? In the past state governors were preferred, for a governorship provided executive experience. However, this requirement has changed. A governorship is still a good background, as Carter's nomination proves. But the examples of Goldwater, Humphrey, Nixon, and McGovern suggest that the United States Senate, which exposes its members to great national and international issues and also gives them excellent opportunities for exposure in the media, is a springboard to the presidency.

However, to win a presidential nomination the best kind of public experience is to be president already. Harry Truman said that any president who wanted the nomination of his party and didn't get it was a damned fool. For a party to refuse to renominate its own president is to repudiate the performance of its own administration and to confess failure to the electorate. Still, incumbency can be a liability. Lyndon Johnson's identification with the Vietnam war had become a grave political drawback and led to his decision not to seek his party's nomination again. And Gerald Ford, who had not himself been elected to the presidency, suffered from criticisms of his performance in the office. Nonetheless, the fact that Ford managed to get his party's nomination, however narrowly, against such an effective campaigner as Ronald Reagan, is in part a tribute to the power of incumbency. As a political tactic, before some of the crucial state primaries in 1976, the White House would announce a federal grant or some other benefit to the state for which the candidates were contending. And during the last, close-fought struggle for the allegiance of the uncommitted delegates the president had the advantage. Obscure local party leaders would be deluged with calls and invitations from the rival camps. A luncheon with Ronald Reagan in person was an occasion to be long remembered. But it was not quite the same as an invitation to a banquet for a foreign dignitary at the White House and a personal chat with the president and his wife.

Next to the presidency the best prior experience for a presidential nomination is the vice-presidency, as it indicated by the experience of Richard Nixon and

Hubert Humphrey. And the vice-presidency was also the means of getting the top job in the cases of Harry Truman, Lyndon Johnson, and Gerald Ford. In some cases the vice-presidential nominees have been men of sufficient caliber to be considered prime presidential possibilities themselves, as was the case with Lyndon Johnson in 1960, Hubert Humphrey in 1968, and Walter Mondale in 1976. In other cases, however, the prime consideration has not been impressive performance in public office, but rather the desire to balance the presidential ticket geographically and ideologically. This was the case with William Miller, Barry Goldwater's running mate in 1964, and Spiro Agnew, Nixon's choice in 1972.

One other kind of experience is enormously important—service to the party. Gaining the support of delegates requires the cultivation of local party leaders and activists all around the country. Thus Barry Goldwater did well in the state conventions because from 1960 onward he had addressed fund-raising dinners that brought in large amounts of money for Republican candidates and he had gotten to know state and local leaders personally. Although George McGovern devoted less time to regular party functions than Goldwater and much more to college campuses, he, too, traveled the country after his party's defeat in 1968, making speeches and working for various Democratic candidates.

Jimmy Carter, though unknown to the general public, was personally acquainted with large numbers of local political leaders well before the 1976 campaign started. He started his quest for the presidency in 1974 after his tenure as governor of Georgia was over. Working for local candidates wherever he went, he stayed at the homes of party activists. (There were about 800 of these hosts, and all were invited to a special White House reception the day after Carter was inaugurated in 1977.) And in this respect Carter (like Ronald Reagan, who came so close to getting a nomination) had an important advantage over his rivals. The others still had to attend to their jobs in the Senate and House. In addition to having the time to travel around the country, his private business provided him with enough money to do so. So, at least for a challenger from the outside, it may be that the best experience is *past* experience, with nothing to distract him from active pursuit of the presidency.

Character.   Although much has been written about the qualities of temperament and character needed to win a presidential nomination, we shall concentrate on three essential attributes. First, a candidate must have stamina. Thirty primaries plus several state conventions impose enormous physical and emotional stress on a candidate. For many months, even years, he must be incessantly on the move, snatching sleep whenever he can, alternating snacks with monotonous political dinners, shaking hands, making speech after speech (or making the same speech over and over again), trying to project spontaneity, vitality, and individual concern at all hours of the day or night to people he has never met and knows little or nothing about. Physical endurance, then, the capacity to survive, is the first, indispensable requirement.

Second, under all this pressure a candidate must remain sufficiently cool and self-possessed to avoid blunders. Wherever he goes, he is bombarded with questions by the media, some sensible, some foolish. In dealing with these questions he knows that one serious mistake could end his candidacy. Thus, George Romney, the governor of Michigan, was widely assumed to be the front-runner for the Republican nomination in 1964. But in a radio interview on a local station he explained his shift away from support of the Vietnam war by declaring that the first time he had gone to Vietnam he had been "brainwashed" by the military. The phrase was picked up by the national media and proved fatal to his candidacy. It destroyed the image he had created of a highly competent, aggressive executive and replaced it with that of a vacillator who was easily brainwashed. Similarly, Maine Senator Edmund Muskie was thought to be easily in the lead for the 1972 Democratic nomination. But during the New Hampshire primary television cameras caught him weeping publicly as he denounced a right-wing local newspaper that had printed a harsh criticism of his wife. This shattered his image of a cool, imperturbable leader, and his candidacy never recovered.

Some mistakes can be survived. Carter, for example, told *The New York Daily News* during his primary campaign that he saw nothing wrong with communities of Polish, Czech, French-Canadian, or black Americans trying to "maintain the ethnic purity of their neighborhoods." The "ethnic purity" phrase infuriated blacks, Jews, and liberals generally, and Carter made matters worse when, under pressure from the press to clarify his point, he said that, although opposed to housing discrimination, he would not use government power to promote "the intrusion of alien groups," or "black intrusion," into a neighborhood simply to bring about integration. Under a storm of protest, including a complaint from Carter's chief black supporter, Andrew Young, that "ethnic purity" was a "Hitlerian" term, Carter apologized, saying that his words were "ill-chosen" and "unfortunate." The apology helped, and the Reverend Martin Luther King, Sr., gave Carter his continued blessing. But if the error was not fatal, it continued to plague Carter throughout the battle for the nomination, confirming the liberals in their belief that his views were unacceptable to them.

The final essential attribute of anyone who aspires to be a presidential nominee is ambition. He must want the nomination with an all-consuming passion. Walter Mondale was the liberals' favorite candidate for the presidency during 1974; but after traveling around the country in search of campaign funds and supporters, he said in November of that year, "I did not have the overwhelming desire to be President that is essential for the kind of campaign that is required." He lacked the burning ambition to sustain him through the ordeal of the primary campaigns. As one of his aides put it, he "didn't want to spend the next two years in Holiday Inns."

Another, though more remote, prospect for consideration by the Democrats was Illinois Senator Adlai Stevenson III, whose father had been nominated for the presidency by the Democrats in 1952 and 1956. But Senator Stevenson took himself out of the race in November 1975, declaring the nomination process "a tragically degrading experience for those who participate in it." A candidate, he said, must plunge into "a welter of endless, draining detail . . . into a morass of unintelligible regulations and dervish-like activity, all largely beyond his control and comprehension." So, to gain a nomination, a candidate must be possessed by the certainty that this is what he wants in life above all else. And some of the time, at least, he must find it satisfying and stimulating rather than degrading. Otherwise, he will lose the zest that is essential to sustain his supporters as well as himself, and to convince the voters that he above all others is best suited for the job.

General Election Strategies

Once nominated, a presidential candidate must move on to the final test in November—the general election. As the standard-bearer of a major party he will be guided by two main considerations. The first is that to win an election he cannot rely only on the enthusiasts who carried his campaign for the nomination. He must build a broad enough coalition to gain the 40 million or more votes needed for victory. So he must bind up the wounds in his own party if the nomination campaign was strongly contested, and he must begin the process of reaching out to independents and those members of the opposition whose commitment to their party is weak.

But there is another important fact to bear in mind. People do not elect a president directly. The results of a presidential election are not determined until 538 electors in the *electoral college* have cast their ballots. This was part of the design of the Founding Fathers, who, cautious about the wisdom of people in the mass, preferred to have the president chosen by delegations from each state, the total number "equal to the whole number of Senators and Representatives to which the state may be entitled in the Congress." The framers' assumption was that the delegates would vote on the basis of their independent judgments. In fact, as the two-party system evolved, electors cast their ballots mostly along party lines. Today voters in each state are presented a choice between lists or slates of electors selected by the state parties and pledged to the parties' candidates; and the slate that gets more popular votes than any other slate, no matter how small the margin, wins *all* the state's electoral votes. With this in mind the candidates set out to win 270 or more electoral college votes, a majority of the total 538 from the fifty states.

The 1976 Election

We can best understand candidate strategies for winning the necessary 270 votes by looking at a specific election. The 1976 election provides a good example for our purposes. Both Carter and Ford worked to build coalitions drawn from a range of constituencies; to take issue stands that would attract those constituencies; and to design a winning electoral college strategy.

The Carter campaign was addressed in the first place to the basic Democratic majority in registered voters. As we saw in Chapter 3, Democrats are found most heavily in the South; in the inner cities; among lower-income groups, blacks, and Spanish-surname groups; Catholics and the ethnic groups that are most heavily Catholic; Jews; and the young. But Carter did not limit his efforts to these traditionally Democratic groups. As a fundamentalist, "born-again" Christian he could hope to make inroads in the usually Republican Protestant vote. And as a Washington outsider, crusading against corruption in government, he could appeal to affluent suburbanites sickened by the Watergate scandals.

Carter spoke to a broad range of issues during the campaign. But he placed particular stress on the unemployment problem for the lower-income people, who constitute a high proportion of the traditional Democratic votes. And for his other constituencies he placed heavy emphasis on the need to restore trust in government.

Translating all this into an electoral college strategy, the Carter people started with the South, which could be brought back to the Democratic camp by one of its native sons. The border states, those between North and South, were also generally Democratic in registration, and might well ally themselves with their neighbor states to the South. Then there were the industrial states of the Northeast, with large blocs of electoral votes and big-city populations of typically Democratic voters. If all the normally Democratic states of the South, the border region, and the Northeast went for Carter, he would gain 237 of his needed 270 electoral votes. Another 10 could be counted on from Walter Mondale's home state, Minnesota. Then Oregon and Hawaii, with 10 votes between them, were listed as probable Carter states. And either Ohio (25) or Texas (26) would take the total over 270. Though this left no margin of error, it also did not allow for hopeful prospects in California, Illinois, Indiana, and Wisconsin.

Ford, on the other hand, saw his natural constituencies in the groups who traditionally voted Republican: middle- to upper-income earners, college-educated business and professional people, farmers, suburbanites, residents of small towns and rural areas, and Protestants. From this base the Ford appeal would be directed to the many moderate conservatives among the Independents and Democrats. And the Republican platform support for a constitutional amendment banning abortion could give Ford an advantage among Catholics over Carter, who, like his party, had come out against such an amendment. Ford's key issues would be the record of his administration in maintaining peace in the world, in bringing inflation under control, and in restoring the integrity of the presidency.

To garner the necessary electoral votes, Ford needed to sweep the mountain states of the West (34 votes), the far West (61), the Midwest (98), the traditionally Republican portions of New England (11), and to wrest 37 votes from Carter in the South and border states. This would give a total of 241. Ohio and Texas would put Ford over the top, and there was also the possibility of up to 28 votes in the East.

Of the two, the Ford strategy seemed much the more difficult. He started from a much smaller party base than Carter. The Ford electoral college plan was built on winning in a large number of states, several of which had small popula-

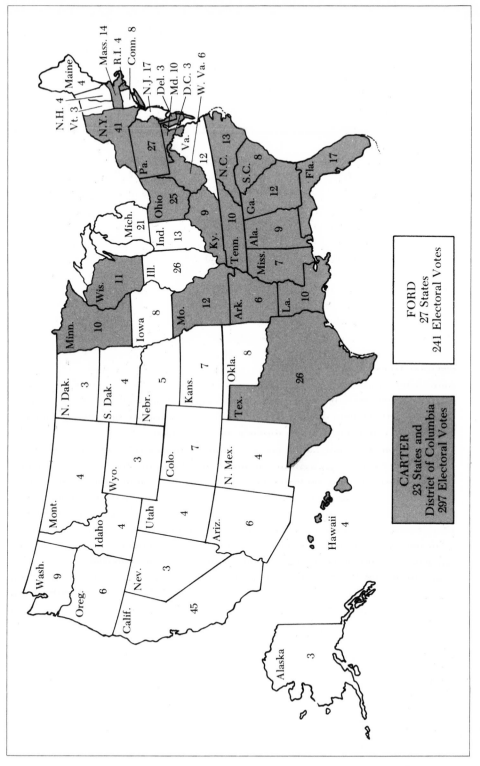

CARTER
23 States and
District of Columbia
297 Electoral Votes

FORD
27 States
241 Electoral Votes

FIGURE 4–1   1976 Electoral Vote

tions and few electoral votes. And most of the preelection forecasts in news magazines gave Carter a much bigger base of assured and probable states than Ford. Yet the Ford plan did not fall far short. Ford got almost 38,600,000 popular votes (48 percent) to Carter's 40,300,000 (51 percent). In the electoral college Carter prevailed by only 297 to 241. As the map in Figure 4–1 indicates, Ford took the entire West except Hawaii, much of the Midwest, the hoped-for New England states, *plus* Connecticut, New Jersey, and Virginia. He fell short because Carter carried all but one southern state, most of the border states, just enough of the eastern industrial states, both Ohio and Texas, and Wisconsin as well as Minnesota. So close was the vote in several states that a switch of fewer than 8000 votes in Ohio and in Hawaii would have given Ford 270 votes in the electoral college; conversely a total shift of 70,000 votes in eight other states would have made Carter's winning margin 337 to 201.

Ford came as close to winning as he did for a number of reasons. As the leader of the more conservative of the two parties he was able to capture a majority of business and professional people, higher-income groups, suburbanites, college graduates, older voters, and farmers outside the South. He held Carter to only 55 percent of the Catholic vote. In an October 1976 Gallup poll he scored better than Carter in handling foreign policy, and in holding down government spending. In the same poll twice as many people picked Ford over Carter on "leadership qualities and experience." And on questions relating to stability of personality and forthrightness of character, far more doubts were expressed about Carter than about Ford.

One other factor that helped Ford was the Independent candidacy of Eugene McCarthy. Although McCarthy won no states, in Iowa, Maine, Oklahoma, and Oregon he won more votes than Ford's margin over Carter. Since a substantial share of those votes would probably have gone to Carter had McCarthy not been running, McCarthy clearly cost Carter some electoral votes, perhaps as many as 26.

Still, enough of Carter's strategy prevailed to enable him to win. He won in the first place because he was a Democrat, and he gained majorities among those groups who traditionally vote for the Democratic party. Thus Carter received over 60 percent of the low-income vote, as well as slightly over half the middle-income vote. Close to 60 percent of blue-collar workers, especially union members and their families, and big-city residents went for him. He did moderately well among the young. Among Catholics he slipped well below the percentages who had turned out 16 years earlier for John Kennedy, but he kept the majority with him. In addition, he won about 46 percent of the Protestant vote. Over two-thirds of the Jewish voters kept their traditional Democratic allegiance. And over 80 percent of black and Spanish-speaking people supported Carter. In fact, black people turned out in sufficient numbers to make the difference for Carter in some crucial states, especially in the South, where a lopsided black vote combined with an almost even split of the whites to give Carter his indispensable bloc of southern electoral votes. Thus Carter was able to revive a semblance of the old coalition that Franklin Roosevelt had pieced together—the New Deal coalition of labor, minorities, intellectuals, the northern cities, and the South. The liberal elements in that coalition were less than enchanted with Carter. But he wooed them with, among other things, the selection of Walter Mondale as his fellow campaigner. And Mondale proved an asset to the ticket; polls showed that he was preferred over Ford's running mate, Robert Dole, by a substantial majority of the electorate.

Surveys of how the public saw the candidates in relation to the issues showed that Carter was strongly favored over Ford on reducing unemployment, and Carter had a smaller but clear margin on the question of "building trust in government," for Ford had never fully overcome the resentment aroused by his pardoning Richard Nixon.

There were other factors influencing Carter's victory and the narrowness of his margin. Both candidates committed blunders during the campaign, as we shall see shortly, though Ford's were probably more damaging than Carter's. On the other hand, Carter's lead in the polls immediately after his nomination was over 30 points; after Ford's nomination in August, Carter was still ahead by 10 to 12 points; yet he won by only 3 points. This suggests that in itself the Ford campaign was more effective than the Carter campaign. It was not quite enough, however, to overcome the basic strategic advantages from which Carter started.

The Electoral College: Abolish or Reform It?

In 1976 Carter's margin of victory in the electoral college was not very different from his margin in the popular vote. More commonly, however, there is a fairly wide disparity between the two votes. Thus in 1972 McGovern got almost 40 percent of the popular vote, but was awarded only 17 electoral votes. In 1960 Kennedy beat Nixon by only 119,000 popular votes, but in the electoral college he prevailed by 303 to 209. The reasons for these disparities between popular and electoral votes are of two kinds. First, the electoral college gives an advantage to the small states, since the Constitution assigns each state a minimum of three electoral college votes no matter how small its population. Far more significantly, another advantage goes to the most populous states, since tiny margins in the popular votes, by winning all of those states' large number of electoral votes, may more than offset large majorities for the opposition in smaller states, which have very few electoral votes. The consequence could conceivably be that a candidate would be elected after receiving fewer popular votes than his rival. This actually happened in 1824, 1867, and 1888, when Andrew Jackson, Samuel Tilden, and Grover Cleveland led in the popular balloting but were denied the presidency. Furthermore, Harry Truman's popular vote lead of over 2 million in 1948 could have gone for naught had there been a shift of 30,000 votes in California, Illinois, and Ohio—states that awarded him large numbers of electoral votes.

A further problem with the electoral college is the procedure for breaking a deadlock should no candidate receive the required majority of 270 votes. In such a case the decision is thrown into the House of Representatives, where each state

TWO

receives only one vote, and a majority of the states is required to elect a president, the House choosing from the three top electoral college presidential candidates.

Only twice in our history, in 1800 and 1824, has the House been called upon to settle the issue because no candidate won a majority of the electoral votes. However, the election campaign of 1968 was haunted by the possibility that it could happen again. The early opinion polls indicated a very strong showing by George Wallace, and it seemed very possible indeed that neither Nixon nor Humphrey would get a majority in the electoral college and that the Wallace delegations from the South would hold the balance of power in the House. As it happened, the Wallace vote declined by election day, and Nixon emerged with 301 electoral votes to Humphrey's 191 and Wallace's 46. Even so, Nixon's popular vote margin over Humphrey was very small, and it was so close in several states that the possibility of the election's being decided in the House was not disposed of until the small hours of the morning after the polls closed.

A third problem with the electoral college is that the requirement that an elector vote according to the instructions of the voters is not completely binding. Some states have passed laws to tie the electors' hands, and there are very few examples of electors kicking over the traces. Nonetheless, in 1960 an Oklahoma Republican elector refused to vote the party line; in 1968 a North Carolina Republican bolted to George Wallace; and in 1972 a Virginia Republican decided that he had "reached the end of the line with the Nixon administration" and voted for the Libertarian party candidates.

This last problem is a minor one, but the first two—the possibility of a president's being elected even though he has fewer popular votes than another candidate, and the danger of the elections being thrown into the House of Representatives—have been the cause of great concern from time to time. This was particularly true when the great Wallace scare of 1968, coming only two elections after the razor-thin margin of the 1960 Kennedy–Nixon race, brought to a head demands for a basic change in the system. In 1969 an overwhelming majority of the House of Representatives approved a constitutional amendment that would replace the electoral college with direct popular election of president and vice-president. The winner would be the candidate with the largest number of votes, so long as he secured no less than 40 percent of the total. If no candidate received 40 percent, there would be a runoff between the top two. A Harris survey had already revealed public approval for the abolition of the electoral college by 79 percent to 11. After some hesitation President Nixon came out in favor of the proposal.

However, the issue did not come to a vote in the Senate. Among the reasons was the fear that it would weaken the two-party system. Under direct election a large number of candidates would probably enter the fray, hoping that there would be enough minor party votes to prevent anyone from getting the required 40 percent and thus providing all kinds of bargaining opportunities for the ensuing runoff. So the effort to eliminate the danger of minor party candidates such as George Wallace might actually lead to an increase in their number and influence.

With the possible consequences uncertain and the immediate dangers removed, the pressure for abolition or reform of the electoral college dissipated. So it fell to the Carter administration to try to revive interest in the issue; and in March 1977 Carter proposed that the electoral college be abolished.

Campaign Tactics

Candidates for public office in America must get out and meet the people. They must be seen by as much of the public as possible, preferably with their wives and children; they must "press the flesh"—shake hands with thousands upon thousands of voters; they must eat ethnic dishes, hold babies, and smile until their faces ache. This is true of candidates for almost all offices, but most can concentrate on a single community, district, or state. Only the presidential and vice-presidential candidates have to try to make contact with the entire nation.

In the past the campaign train was the most effective means of doing this. In 1948 Harry Truman took his case to the people in a "whistle-stop" transcontinental train trip, making speeches from the rear platform in large and small communities across the country. Ford and Carter used the same device in 1976, but only for short distances. The jet plane, met at airports by a motorcade, has vastly increased the number of places a candidate can get to during a campaign.

Yet even with the jet there is a limit to the personal appearances a presidential or vice-presidential candidate can make between Labor Day, the traditional kickoff for the campaigns, and the first Tuesday after the first Monday in November, election day. In 1960 Richard Nixon made the mistake of promising to visit all 50 states during his campaign. The effort exhausted him, hurt his performance, and possibly cost him the election. So the focus has shifted away from showing the candidates to the people in the flesh to projecting them over the media. The radio was an essential campaign tool in the 1930s and 1940s. But since the 1950s television has predominated. Candidates still jet from city to city. Newspapers continue to play a vital role in their campaign coverage and advertisements. Radio, billboards, and direct mailings have their place. Volunteers in local campaign organizations are essential in making personal contacts and telephone calls, particularly during the last, crucial effort to get voters to the polls on election day. But for the candidates, their staffs, and the public, television is the focal point of political campaigning today.

Television: The
Focal Point of Campaigning

Presidential candidates appear on television in various formats: news programs, spot announcements, longer commercials, telethons, and televised debates. An incumbent president has a considerable advantage over the challenger in the news format, since he and his administration can *make* news by proposing new programs or announcing dramatic developments in international affairs. Thus whatever slim hopes George McGovern might have cherished in the closing stages of the 1972 campaign were wiped out by Henry Kissinger's televised news conference just before the election declaring (prematurely) that "peace is at hand" in Vietnam.

Commercial spots were first used extensively in a presidential campaign in 1952. The Rosser Reeves advertising agency made a series of 20-second television commercials. A typical spot had an announcer saying: "Mr. Eisenhower, what about the high cost of living?" The reply: "My wife, Mamie, worries about the same thing. I tell her it's our job to change that on November 4." "To think," said Eisenhower as they were putting on his makeup for one of these commercials, "an old soldier should come to this."

Adlai Stevenson, too, found this style of campaigning intensely distasteful. In his 1956 acceptance speech he told the Democratic party: "This idea that you can merchandise candidates for high office like breakfast cereal—that you can gather votes like box tops—is, I think, the ultimate indignity to the democratic process." Yet, in 1956, the Democratic National Committee prepared a publicity manual for candidates for office in which they offered advice on how to present issues on television. The central admonition was, "Make it short and simple." Spot announcements, said the manual, should be in the form of "a simple slogan or message that is memorable and lends itself to repetition." All subsequent presidential campaigns, as well as a great many campaigns at the state level, have made heavy use of brief commercials as a means of conveying a candidate's position on the issues.

Toward the end of a campaign it is customary to supplement the commercials with longer presentations, in which candidates buy periods of half an hour on each of the networks. A typical show will consist of a documentary-style account of the candidate's life, shots of the candidate with his family, interviews with people from different backgrounds explaining why they will vote for the candidate, and some comments from the candidate on what he will bring to the presidency.

Then there is the telethon. Richard Nixon made skillful use of this device in 1968. In a series of live, regional programs, Nixon would appear on an unadorned stage, without a lectern, without notes, ready to respond to unrehearsed questions from a selected panel of local citizens. However, the dangers of this format were much less great than appeared to the television audience. In fact, most of the panelists were selected with a view to their not causing any embarrassment; the audiences were carefully chosen to ensure a response so approving as to make every answer appear the ultimate word in wisdom; and the candidate developed bland, formula answers that did not begin to come to grips with the complexity of the problems he was addressing.

The financing of the 1968 Humphrey campaign could not support the number of programs presented by Nixon, but a telethon was beamed from Los Angeles the night before polling day. This presented Humphrey and Muskie in a format that was more open and spontaneous than the Nixon series. Yet those who organized the program were not pinning their hopes only on the way the issues were covered. "The Vice President's advisers said they were confident the Humphrey format with its large number of popular entertainment personalities provided a more lively program than Nixon's telethon."[3]

Finally, there are televised debates. These have become commonplace in races for the Senate and for the governorship in some states. The first set of televised debates for the presidency took place between Kennedy and Nixon in 1960. Kennedy's effectiveness in these "Great Debates" was probably a major factor in his victory. Though there were televised debates in the primary races between Robert Kennedy and Eugene McCarthy during the 1968 primaries, there were no further general election debates between presidential candidates until 1976, when Ford challenged Carter to debate in his acceptance speech at the Republican convention, and Carter immediately accepted. Polls and pundits alike generally gave the edge to Ford in the first debate, whereas Carter was thought to have come out well ahead in the second and slightly ahead in the third debate.

Selling the Image:
The Personal Factor

When we looked at political parties in the last chapter and at the election strategies of presidential candidates in this chapter, we emphasized party and issues as the basis for the voters' decisions on election day. But voters are also extremely interested in the personal characteristics of the candidates. Campaign managers are acutely aware of this fact, and they work assiduously to build up in the public mind a favorable image of their candidates and an unfavorable view of their opponents. The effort to produce favorable perceptions of a candidate was overwhelmingly successful in the case of Eisenhower. When he said, "I will go to Korea," he did not explain what he would do when he got there. But people trusted him to do what was necessary. They had faith in the man, in the image of authority, benevolence, and integrity that he radiated.

A principal purpose of the 1960 Kennedy campaign was to convey the picture of a man of great attractiveness, vitality, and drive. Television news coverage of his campaign helped accomplish this. But the Great Debates were especially important. The issue content of the debates was rather thin. But Kennedy projected a sense of excitement, whereas Nixon, part of the existing administration, was on the defensive. The contrast of styles and appearance was particularly apparent in the first debate, for Nixon was at a severe disadvantage through fatigue and a poor makeup job. (It is interesting to note that, for the majority of listeners on radio, Nixon won the debate, whereas the opposite verdict came from those who watched on television.)

Again in 1968, a prime concern of the organizers of the campaigns of both presidential candidates was to counteract unfavorable aspects of their candidates' images. Each, it is true, had his assets: Humphrey—open, outgoing, energetic, enthusiastic, knowledgeable; Nixon—competent, controlled, well-informed, experienced. Nonetheless, certain aspects of each candidate's personality made him vulnerable, and a considerable part of each campaign was devoted to warding off the efforts of the other side to exploit the areas of vulnerability.

Humphrey's advisers were hampered by his tendency to be overly talkative and impulsive. As for Nixon, his problem was stated by Roger Ailes, a television executive producer who organized the Nixon telethons: "Let's face it, a lot of people think Nixon is dull. Think he's a bore . . . a funny-looking guy . . . ," a man who conveyed the impression that he had never had any other interest all his life but to work to become president. "That's why these shows are important. To make them forget all that."[4]

By 1972 the campaign managers' difficulty in formulating a suitable image for Nixon had vanished, for he was the incumbent president. Now he could be portrayed as the candidate of experience and proven competence—a man above the fray, attending to great affairs of state, building peace in the world—while his opponent indulged in partisan politics. And McGovern made it easy for them to draw the contrast. Soon after he had selected Thomas Eagleton as his running mate, the press uncovered the fact that Eagleton had, some years earlier, received shock treatments for attacks of depression. McGovern's staff issued an announcement that Eagleton would remain on the ticket, that McGovern was behind him "1000 percent." Subjected to intense pressure from within the Democratic party, McGovern wavered, then got Eagleton to withdraw. This incident, combined with McGovern's backing away from some of the strong issue positions he had taken during the primaries, conveyed to the voters the impression of indecision and unreliability. The damage to McGovern's candidacy, according to opinion surveys,[5] was enormous. Nixon scored considerably higher than McGovern on survey questions dealing with competence. And even with respect to trustworthiness, Nixon, whose career had been dogged by an aura of slipperiness (captured in the nickname "Tricky Dick"), came out ahead of McGovern, a Methodist preacher, the representative of "new politics" that was to replace the old, discredited, sleazy brand of politics.

Assessment of personal qualities was an important factor again in 1976. The Carter forces stressed two principal features about their candidate. First, there was his integrity, his refusal to compromise, his role as an outsider coming in to clean up the mess in Washington. Ford, they implied, was a decent man, but one who was part of the system that had to be cleaned up. Ford's pardon of Nixon helped support the Carter campaign organization in this approach.

Second, Carter was presented as a man of high intelligence, trained as a scientist–technologist, qualified by experience and intellect as a problem solver. Ford, on the other hand, was a man fumbling with problems he did not understand. Here they were assisted by the media's diligent reporting over a two-year period of Ford's proneness to slips of the tongue and to stumbling or banging his head when getting out of a jet or a limousine. And Ford reinforced this image of ineptness when, in the second televised debate, he declared, "There is no Soviet domination of Eastern Europe," and stubbornly refused to retract the statement for days afterward, until at last he bowed to the storm of protest from people of East European extraction.

Yet Carter did not win the battle of personalities. He had set an extraordinarily high standard for himself, promising during the primaries that, during the election and in his presidency, he would "never tell a lie, or make a misleading statement, or avoid a controversial issue." He also offered a message of love, of bringing people together in their commonality of interests in contrast to the divisiveness of the past. These themes, together with his much discussed religious beliefs, made him an irresistible target not only to the Ford campaigners but also to the press; for in the post-Watergate era nothing could be more pleasing to journalists than the opportunity to puncture an aura of sanctimoniousness. So they drew attention to any Carter statement that appeared to contradict his earlier positions, or could be construed as misleading or fuzzy. And Carter was hurt when, in an effort to dispel the sense that he was claiming to a degree of virtue amounting to saintliness, he gave a long interview to *Playboy* magazine on sex and morality. In this interview he explained that he did not believe in condemning sinners too easily:

> Christ said, "I tell you that anyone who looks on a woman with lust has in his heart already committed adultery." I've looked on a lot of women with lust. I've committed adultery in my heart many times. . . . God forgives me for it. . . . But that doesn't mean that I condemn someone who not only looks on a woman with lust but who leaves his wife and shacks up with somebody out of wedlock.[6]

Carter was widely criticized for this interview by the very fundamentalist religious groups who shared his own "born-again" Christianity.

So, in a preelection Gallup poll we find the following responses of the voters to the candidates:

	Percentage for	
Statements about Candidates	*Carter*	*Ford*
He is a man I'm not sure I understand.	51	26
He may be promising more than he can deliver.	59	17
He leaves me with questions about the way he really feels about things.	54	30
He has a sound, stable personality.	30	52

SOURCE: *Newsweek,* November 1, 1976, pp. 20—21.

And, by large margins, Ford, the alleged bumbler, came out ahead of Carter, the problem solver, on questions relating to "good judgment in a time of crisis" and "good leadership qualities and experience." Evidently, the sharp decline in Carter's margin in the polls from the beginning of the campaign to the end was at least partly attributable to the uneasiness that many people felt about his personal qualities. It was also further testimony to the increasing emphasis that the electorate has been placing on those personal qualities. As we saw in Chapter 3, voters are demonstrating a growing tendency to attach themselves to a candidate on the basis of issues, while the importance of party affiliation has been steadily declining. But alongside the importance of issues, the public's reaction to a candidate's image, or personality, has been looming larger and larger in presidential elections.

Campaign Tricks and Smears

Most campaigns are marred by charges and countercharges of deliberate efforts to deceive the electorate or disrupt the opposition. In many cases slander or libel suits are filed in the heat of the campaign, usually to be dropped when the election is over.

The 1962 race for the governorship of California was particularly notable for the use of disruptive devices on both sides. Thus a political prankster named Richard Tuck infiltrated the Nixon gubernatorial campaign and gave out instructions that wrought considerable confusion. For example, Tuck told a locomotive engineer to start up the train while Nixon was still in the middle of a speech from the platform. In turn, the Republicans in that campaign, led by H. R. Haldeman and John Ehrlichman (and others later implicated in the Watergate affair), were accused of using eavesdropping and other illegal tactics against the campaign of the incumbent, Governor "Pat" Brown.

The most systematic and elaborate use of "dirty" campaign tricks came in the course of the 1972 Nixon reelection campaign. There was the abortive Watergate break-in. And Donald Segretti confessed to heading up a group that used a variety of methods, some illegal, to cause dissension among Democratic contenders during the presidential primaries. Among these was sending out pamphlets containing fabricated charges of sexual misbehavior by Senators Humphrey and Jackson.

Most candidates for the presidency, Congress, or governorships have signed a Code of Fair Campaign Practices, and since 1954 the nonpartisan Fair Campaign Practices Committee has investigated and publicized candidates' complaints about their opponents' campaign behavior. A record for grievances registered was set in 1972: 39 filed by Republicans for various offices, 43 by Democrats, and 2 by Independents. Of the total of 84 complaints filed, however, only 12 went to the arbitration procedure provided, and only 6 went through the entire process.

The 1976 presidential campaign showed a marked improvement in this respect. Although both Ford and Carter protested that the other had made unfounded charges and allegations, the Fair Campaign Practices Committee reported that it had received fewer complaints than in any previous election. Apparently the reaction against Watergate was having a salutary effect on campaigners.

Managing Campaigns

The management of a presidential campaign today has become such an incredibly complex affair that a candidate must surround himself with a large staff of specialists in such fields as public relations and press services, media advertising, mailing, fund raising, budget control, travel arrangements, relations with ethnic groups, polling, computer data processing, and issue research. Similar staffs are appointed on a smaller scale for senatorial, congressional, gubernatorial, and other races. When a candidate cannot afford to cover all the bases by direct staff appointments, he can contract with one of the several public relations and advertising firms that specialize in providing campaign services, sometimes even to the extent of taking on the entire management of a campaign.

The Polls: Their Accuracy and Influence

The use of political polls has become an important element in campaign tactics. When Gallup, Harris, or Roper—the three major polling organizations—indicate that a candidate is ahead, he will use that poll to argue that an irresistible momentum has been established in his favor. If the polls show him falling behind, he will cite the fact that Harry Truman won in 1948 against the evidence of all the polls; or he will hire a pollster to conduct his own private survey, from which data will be culled selectively to prove that the other polls are wrong.

Two major questions are constantly raised about the polls. First, how accurate are they? Second, how much influence do they have?

Since their unhappy experience in 1948 the major polling agencies have done quite well with respect to their final preelection analyses (which they insist are not predictions, but merely readings of public attitudes on the day the poll was taken). Gallup and Harris were close to the mark in 1972, as shown in Table 4–1.

TABLE 4–1   Polls of Voters for 1972 Presidential Candidates (percent)

Candidate	Gallup	Harris	Actual Vote
Nixon	59	59	61
McGovern	36	35	38
Others, undecided	5	6	1

Of course, 1972 was not a very difficult year in which to gauge the electorate's intentions. The 1976 election was much more volatile, with a large number of people not making up their minds until the last moment. Consequently, the pollsters, Harris in particular, were more reluctant than usual to guess who the undecided were likely to go for; and only the Roper poll was very close to the mark, as you can see from Table 4-2.

Still, even in 1976 all the polls were correct in seeing the election as close, and all were within the 3 percent margin of error which they admit their sampling

TABLE 4–2   Polls of Voters for 1976 Presidential
Candidates (percent)

Candidate	Gallup	Harris	Roper	Actual Vote
Carter	48	46	51	51
Ford	49	45	47	48
Others, undecided	3	9	2	1

method contains. However, when their readings of opinion are taken at other times than just before an election, we have no conclusive way of testing their findings. And doubts have been raised about their accuracy by discrepancies between Gallup and Harris that appear from time to time. Thus in late 1975 Gallup and Harris conducted "trial heats"—Ford or Reagan against Humphrey—and came up with sharply differing results (Table 4–3).

TABLE 4–3   "Trial Heats" of Potential Presidential
Candidates (percent)

Poll	Ford	Humphrey	Reagan	Humphrey
Gallup	51	39	50	42
Harris	41	52	43	50

It is true that Harris took his sampling just before Ford went on a visit to China and that the Gallup survey was conducted just after he got back. However, the Ford trip did not receive the kind of sustained media attention that had accompanied the Nixon visit in 1972, and it is doubtful that it could account for the sharp differences between the two polls. Moreover, Reagan did nothing between the two polls that could account for the discrepancy.

Whatever doubts may exist about the accuracy of the polls (and what we have said does not detract from their validity as at least crude indices of general trends in opinion), there is no question about the attention their findings command. It is sometimes suggested, in fact, that these readings of opinion actually become shapers of opinion, that they create a "bandwagon" effect that carries along with it voters who want to be on the winning side. However, this is not supported by Harry Truman's victory despite the findings of the polls, or by the extent to which both Hubert Humphrey and Gerald Ford closed the large gaps indicated by all the polls at the start of the 1968 and 1976 campaigns. Perhaps, then, the opposite of the "bandwagon" effect is true—that the polls create a groundswell of sympathy for the underdog. But this clearly did not happen in 1964 and 1972, when the Johnson and Nixon landslides were indicated by the polls from start to finish. Where the polls are most influential is on the conduct of the campaign itself. The candidates and their staffs are buoyed by a favorable poll, and, in contrast, may come close to giving up if a poll shows them far behind. The polls are also critical factors in fund raising. Big contributors like to invest in a winner and clearly do not want to throw their money away on a candidate the polls suggest has little chance of winning.

Money and Elections

There was one very significant respect in which the 1976 presidential campaign differed from previous campaigns: it was publicly funded. This resulted from the passage of the 1974 Campaign Reform Act, which grew out of a widespread sense that election costs were getting out of hand, that candidates were becoming excessively dependent on large private contributions, and that these factors had given rise to serious abuses.

Once media advertising and polling became such integral parts of campaigns, elections became extraordinarily expensive. Campaigns for governor or senator in a large state can rarely be conducted for less than a million dollars. In 1970 Congressman Richard Ottinger of New York spent about $4,500,000 in a losing effort to be elected senator. In presidential election races these figures are multiplied many times over. The total cost of the presidential primaries and general election in 1968 was about $100 million, which rose to about $110 million by 1972. The total cost for all elections in America rose from $140 million in 1952 to $300 million in 1968 to $425 million by 1972.

This money came from a number of sources. First there were *organized interest groups.* The Taft–Hartley Act of 1947 forbade corporations from spending corporate funds and labor unions from spending their members' dues on national campaigns. However, there were many ways of evading these restrictions.

Thus corporations could encourage their executives and their families to contribute, even giving them pay raises and expense accounts with the understanding that these would be used for political purposes. Some of them also provided free services to candidates—company cars and planes; office space, equipment, and postage stamps; public relations, advertising, and legal services. They loaned officials and secretaries to campaign staffs while keeping them on the corporate payroll; bought tickets at fund-raising dinners for $100 and even $1000 a plate; purchased advertising space in national convention books; and helped underwrite the costs to the cities that hosted national conventions.

Labor unions, forbidden to levy compulsory assessments on their members for political purposes, undertook energetic campaigns for voluntary contributions to such organizations as the AFL–CIO's Committee on Political Organization (COPE), which played an active role in elections at all levels. Individual unions used the same kind of device to get money into the campaigns of potential legislators who would be sympathetic to the unions' interests. For example, in 1974 the maritime unions donated money to the campaigns of 141 members of Congress, all but four of whom supported a bill requiring that a larger portion of

America's oil imports be shipped in U.S. tankers manned by U.S. crews. Moreover, the Taft–Hartley law did not prevent unions from using their members' dues for voter registration drives and for the expression of partisan views in union papers and union-sponsored radio programs. And perhaps the most important of labor's contributions to campaigns was providing union officials and members to manage campaigns and carry out precinct work.

Some agricultural organizations contributed heavily to campaigns. Associations of milk producers put large amounts of money into presidential election campaigns, and into the campaigns of 85 members of Congress, mostly members of committees concerned with dairy prices and marketing. And professional organizations such as the American Medical Association have donated to many campaigns at the state as well as the federal level. In 1974 the AMA gave money to help reelect 10 members of the House Ways and Means Committee, which deals with legislation in the field of health insurance.

Next, *wealthy individuals* have made enormous contributions to campaigns, most particularly presidential campaigns. W. Clement Stone, a Chicago insurance man worth perhaps $400 million, has reported that he contributed nearly $7 million to Republican campaigns between 1968 and 1972 in gifts and loans, including $2,800,000 to the Nixon campaign in 1968, and over $2 million to the Nixon reelection drive in 1972. Other contributions to the Nixon 1972 campaign included $1 million from Richard Scaife of the Mellon banking family of Pittsburgh; $600,000 from John Mulcahy, whose fortune had come from the development of a steel blast furnace; $300,000 from Arthur Watson, then ambassador to France; $250,000 from Walter Annenberg, ambassador to England; and $310,000 from five Rockefellers.

Democratic candidates, too, have their wealthy patrons. Stewart Mott, of the General Motors family, gave $210,000 to Eugene McCarthy in 1968, and during the 1972 primaries pledged $350,000 to McGovern. Max Palevsky, who founded a computer company in Los Angeles and then sold out to Xerox, has been a heavy contributor to liberal candidates and causes and provided $320,000 for the McGovern campaign. Hubert Humphrey in 1968 received one donation of over $100,000, and six others of $50,000 or more.

Special recognition is given by candidates to the larger contributors. Thus Lyndon Johnson had his "President's Club," for supporters who contributed $1000. This was much criticized by Republicans—until, with Richard Nixon in the White House, the Republicans rewarded their $1000 donors with membership in "RN Associates."

Wealthy candidates and their families have also drawn upon their own resources to finance their campaigns. The Kennedy money helped build John Kennedy's political career. Nelson Rockefeller put a good deal of his own money into his campaigns for the New York governorship; and his stepmother, Mrs. Martha Baird Rockefeller, provided almost $1.5 million for his bid for the presidency in 1968.

In contrast, some candidates made a special effort to solicit a very large number of *small contributions* from ordinary people. Barry Goldwater broke all prior records when, in his quest for the nomination, he received more than 300,000 contributions. In 1968, 150,000 people contributed to Eugene McCarthy's campaign. This number, however, was easily surpassed by George Wallace, whose third-party bid was supported by 750,000 contributors. Then in 1972 George McGovern's campaign included a massive effort to get small contributions through a computerized mass mailing system, inserts in Sunday newspapers, telephone convassing, and television appeals. During the primaries 110,000 people gave almost $4 million, the largest proportion coming in $5, $10, and $25 gifts.

Reforming Campaign Finance

Despite the importance of small contributions in some instances, it was clear that big money was eagerly sought and very much in evidence in major campaigns. Obviously the purposes of earlier legislation in this field were not achieved. The 1925 Corrupt Practices Act limited a congressional candidate's spending to $2500, a senatorial candidate to $10,000; or, 3 cents per vote cast for all candidates for office at the previous election, with a maximum of $5000 for a representative and $25,000 for a senator. The 1939 Hatch Act and its later amendments set a limit of $3 million a year for any political committee. Individual contributions were legally limited to $5000 a year. However, ways of evading these restrictions were quickly found. For instance, several committees could be created, each of which could spend up to $3 million a year. Thus, when Clement Stone made his contributions to the Nixon campaign in 1972, it was made in the form of 700 $3000 checks made payable to such dummy organizations as Americans United for a Moral Society, Americans United for a Lawful Society, Americans United for Political Moderation, Responsible Leaders for a Balanced Society, Responsible Leaders for a Stable Society, and Responsible Leaders for Reform in Society. (This also served Stone's personal income tax purposes, for the tax code allowed big donors to make huge contributions without paying gift tax by splitting their donations into multiple gifts of no more than $3000 each.)

This was the situation until 1971, when the increase in the size and number of large contributions and the escalating costs of campaigns finally led Congress to pass new legislation. First, in the Revenue Act of 1971 political contributors could claim a tax credit for half of any contribution up to $12.50 ($25 on a joint return) or take a deduction for up to $50 ($100 on a joint return). Another provision, not applicable until after the 1972 campaign, has allowed each taxpayer to earmark $1 of his taxes for a fund to subsidize presidential campaigns. Second, the Federal Elections Campaign Act of 1971 set spending limits and required full disclosure of income, outlay, and debts. On the expenditure side, a limit was set of 10 cents per voter in any presidential or congressional campaign for the various uses of media—television, radio, newspapers, magazines, billboards, and automatic telephone equipment. Of this no more than 60 percent could be used for television and radio. Then, all committees spending or receiving more than $1000 in any year on behalf of federal candidates must report the names and addresses of all persons making contributions or loans over $100 and all persons to whom payments of over $100 are made.

Watergate and Other Abuses

The 1971 legislation might have satisfied the reform impetus for some time had it not been for the astonishing revelations brought out by the Watergate investigations. Key figures in the Committee for the Reelection of the President (CREEP or CRP), together with two White House aides, had engaged in dubious financial transactions with respect to both fund raising and expenditures.

On the revenue side the committee's official or unofficial agents were involved in a variety of "fund-raising" activities. Thus a strong drive was made to raise funds before April 7, 1972, thereby beating the deadline for the disclosure requirements of the 1971 act. In the four weeks before the deadline over $11 million came in. Maurice Stans, the CRP finance chairman; Herbert Kalmbach, President Nixon's personal lawyer; and others met with top corporation executives to ask for contributions. In itself this was not unusual. But there was resentment at what some executives took to be excessive pressure and an effort to impose quotas related to the resources of various corporations. In some cases the results were confessedly illegal contributions. George Spater, the chairman of American Airlines, admitted in July 1973 that Kalmbach told him in 1971 that a $100,000 donation "was expected." American Airlines then had a proposed merger with Western Airlines pending before the Civil Aeronautics Board, and Spater knew that Kalmbach was counsel to United Airlines, which opposed the merger. "I concluded," said Spater, "that a substantial response was called for." The response was $75,000 in cash—$55,000 of it in corporate funds. Other large corporate contributions came from Occidental Petroleum, Braniff International Airways, and the Security National Bank of Long Island. These were clear violations of the existing federal laws on campaign funding.

Millions of dollars were raised in cash. In addition, over $1,700,000 left over from the 1968 presidential primaries was entrusted to Kalmbach, and placed in safe deposit boxes in several cities for later campaign use.

The monies thus raised were used for several purposes beyond the presidential campaign itself. There were the outlays for the men and materials involved in the Watergate burglaries and buggings. Then for the indicted men—for their legal defense, for support of their families, and, allegedly, for their silence—came parcels and briefcases of cash, surreptitiously passed along from messenger to messenger with code words and aliases reminiscent of a grade B spy movie.

Large sums were also provided to Donald Segretti and others for their "dirty tricks"—political sabotage aimed at various Democratic presidential aspirants during 1972. And $400,000 was allegedly sent into Alabama in 1970 in an abortive effort to thwart George Wallace's bid for the governorship.

Nor were Republicans the only ones to be guilty of receiving illegal campaign contributions. In the 1972 California primary Hubert Humphrey's campaign received $300,000 from Walter Duncan, a real estate speculator from Texas. At the time Duncan was in financial difficulties that resulted in his defaulting on loans and his being named defendant in a $2.27 million lawsuit brought partly on behalf of a government agency, the Federal Deposit Insurance Corporation, after investigations by the FBI, the IRS, and federal and state grand juries. And some of the businesses that illegally donated corporate funds to the Nixon campaign had also donated to the Johnson campaign in 1964 and to the campaigns of a number of Democratic members of Congress.

Some of the more flagrant examples of illegal contributions led to indictments and convictions. Braniff was fined $300,000, and a number of other companies were fined lesser amounts. And in 1974 two former executives of a milk producer's association were sentenced to jail terms for illegal contributions to the campaigns of Nixon, Humphrey, Democratic Senator Edmund Muskie, and Democratic Representative Wilbur Mills.

However, more and more voices were raised protesting that enforcement of the existing laws was insufficient, that mere disclosure of contributions and expenditures was not enough. Something had to be done to free campaigns from their dependence on large contributions. An intense lobbying effort was mounted in Congress by Common Cause, some labor unions, the League of Women Voters, and a philanthropic organization, the Center for Public Financing. Spearheading the drive within Congress were Representative Morris Udall and other more or less liberal members of the two houses. Opposed to them were the United States Chamber of Commerce, the Democratic leaders in the House, and President Nixon. In the climate created by Watergate, the reformers prevailed and the 1974 Federal Election Campaign Act was passed and signed by the president.

The Federal Election Campaign Act of 1974

The act contained four main provisions. First, it imposed limits on candidates' spending for presidential and congressional primary and general elections. Second, it set limits to the amounts that could be contributed to campaigns by individuals, by candidates and their families, and by organizations. Third, it authorized the funding of presidential campaigns from public funds (specifically the dollar that people could check off on their income tax form) for primaries, conventions, and general elections. Finally, it created a Federal Elections Commission to supervise and monitor the other provisions of the act.

In January 1975 an appeal against the law's constitutionality was filed by a group ranging across the political spectrum from James Buckley, a New York senator bearing both the Conservative and Republican party labels, the conservative periodical *Human Events*, Democratic Senator Eugene McCarthy of Minnesota, and the New York Civil Liberties Union. A U.S. Court of Appeals upheld all of the law's major provisions in August 1975, but on January 30, 1976, as the candidates were already embarking on their quest for convention delegates, the

Supreme Court handed down a complicated decision striking down some of the law's provisions and upholding others.

Two key sections were found unconstitutional. First, the spending limits were struck down. Second, the structure of the Federal Election Commission was found to be in violation of the separation of powers, for some of its members were appointed by Congress, and the Court said that the legislative branch cannot make appointments to an executive body.

However, the Court left intact three essential features of the law. First, it accepted the limits on contributions by individuals and organizations. Even though these might interfere in some degree with freedom of political expression, said the Court, the interference was relatively minor and not to be compared with the spending ceilings. Second, the Court found nothing unconstitutional in the principle of public financing of campaigns. Third, the Court declared that its prohibition of spending limits did not apply if the candidate accepted public funds for his campaign. After all, the candidate did not have to take the government money; and if he accepted it, he must also accept the strings attached to it. The result was that in 1976 every presidential candidate in the general election requested public financing, and thus agreed to limit his spending. But since the 1974 law did not include public financing for congressional races, the spending limits that the 1974 act had imposed on congressional campaigns ($70,000 for a House seat, and for the Senate 8 cents a voter in the primaries and 12 cents a voter in the general election) did not apply.

The Court gave the election commission only till March 22, 1976, to hand out primary funds. So, unless the commission could be reconstituted by then without infringing the constitutional separation of powers, no more public funds could be distributed to candidates. In fact, there was a hiatus, for the commission was not reconstituted until May 21 (with all the members appointed by the president subject to confirmation by the Senate). As a result, no federal money was available for some key primaries.

The Federal Election Campaign Act Amendments of 1976 reestablished the Federal Election Commission. The results of the 1974 act, the Supreme Court decision, and the 1976 Amendments are given in Table 4–4.

Financing the 1976 Presidential Campaign

During the primaries every candidate who made a substantial bid for the nomination of either of the major parties asked for and received public funding. On the Republican side Ronald Reagan received the largest amount, close to $5 million, while Jimmy Carter received more than any other Democrat, $3.4 million. These public monies were matched by small private contributions, and candidates also actively pursued larger contributions of amounts up to the permissible limits of $1000 from individuals and $5000 from organizations. Once the parties' candidates were selected, public financing took over entirely from private contribu-

TABLE 4–4   *Final Provisions of the Federal Election Campaign Acts*

Contribution Limits per Candidate

	Primaries	General Election	Total for All Candidates
Individuals	$1000	$1000	$25,000 (plus $5000 a year to a political action committee and $20,000 to a national committee of a party)
Organizations	$5000	$5000	No limit to the number of candidates
			No more than $100 in cash

Spending Limits per Candidate (presidential campaigns only)

Primaries	General Election
$10,000,000	$20,000,000
	plus 20% for fund-raising costs
	plus 2¢ per voter by national party organization
	plus unlimited amounts in "independent expenditures" by individuals or committees who swear that the expenditures were not made in collusion with the candidate

Public Financing per Candidate (presidential campaigns only)

Primaries	General Election
Matching funds from $100,000 up to $5,000,000 for contributions of $250 or less; to qualify for minimum $100,000, candidate must obtain $5000 from at least 20 states	$20,000,000 for major party candidates; proportional amount for minor party candidate who received 5% or more of total vote in previous presidential election (or available retroactively if 5% obtained in current election)

Other Provisions

Allows $2,000,000 public financing per major party national convention.

Requires candidates to establish a single central campaign committee (no more multiple committees).

Permits business corporations and labor unions to maintain separate political funds. But company committees are generally limited to stockholders and executive and administrative personnel and families, and unions to union members and families.

TABLE 4–4   (continued)

Limits presidential candidate's personal or family contribution to own campaign to $50,000 if candidate accepts public financing.

Sets limits to speaking and writing honoraria that members of Congress and federal employees may receive.

Puts the administration and monitoring of this statute in the hands of a six-member Federal Election Commission empowered to issue regulations, seek court injunctions, and refer criminal cases to the Justice Department.

Provides for fines and jail sentences for substantial and deliberate violations of the law.

---

tions, and both Carter and Ford spent close to the legal limit of about $25 million. These figures compare with the $61 million spent by Nixon and the $30 million by McGovern in 1972, when costs were lower. Clearly, the 1974 reform law has had a major impact on the way presidential elections are financed.

Five Perspectives on Elections

The Liberals: We Need Still More Election Reforms

Liberals make three basic criticisms of the electoral system in America. It does not help the people understand the issues or help them make choices on the basis of the issues. Second, it does not adequately express the clear will of the majority. Third, it is heavily influenced by private contributions of money.

Liberals contend that the issues are obscured and distorted in election campaigns. It is obvious that 20-second television commercials cannot possibly present the issues properly. The whole emphasis of the modern election process is on packaging personalities. And, since packaging is a highly intricate task, the conduct of campaigns is no longer in the hands of candidates and parties but instead managed by media specialists and technicians. The mentality of these people was revealed in the statement of Roger Ailes, the producer of the Nixon telethons in 1968: "This is the beginning of a whole new concept. This is it. This is the way they'll be elected forevermore. The next guys will have to be performers."[7] So the medium is the message, and the packagers produce a message that is totally misleading. How else could the electorate have been induced to conclude that Richard Nixon was more trustworthy than George McGovern?

Even presidential debates are not devices for clarifying the issues but carefully rehearsed efforts to present the candidate's personality, presence of mind, and debating skill. We look for winners; and the winner is the person who comes across most attractively and avoids making mistakes. Thus Ford was said to win the first of his debates with Carter because Carter seemed nervous at the beginning. And Ford lost the second debate because, in the heat of the confrontation, he made a statement on Eastern Europe and the Soviet Union that obviously did not convey his real beliefs. Then Carter was hurt in the campaign because of a huge media uproar about an interview on morality and sex, as though his view of adulterers was a matter of major concern to the future of America.

Moreover, the determined effort of candidates as they approach election day to avoid saying anything controversial produces a middle-of-the-road blurring of the issues. So, despite the majority's growing interest in the issues and readiness to be educated about them, our elections serve only to distract attention from the issues or to present them in distorted form.

The failure to clarify the issues makes it difficult to read the results of an election as a clear expression of the majority will, for the majority have not been asked to decide anything important. And there is another respect in which the majority will is not properly articulated. As we saw in Chapter 2, almost half the voting age population does not go to the polls even in presidential elections. We speak of majority rule as an essential condition of democracy. Yet our leaders are chosen only by minorities.

However, when we come to look at the mechanics of elections, we find the liberals, normally the champions of majorities and participation, caught in some apparent self-contradictions. First, primaries are efforts to involve the electorate at large in choosing nominees for election. It would seem to follow that liberals would press for a change to national primaries, so that the voice of the majority can be expressed in the nomination process. In fact, most of them are unenthusiastic about this prospect. The reason is that liberals are also advocates of stronger parties, and primaries, especially national primaries, tend to deprive parties of one of their most important roles: selecting candidates for public office.

Then again, the electoral college would seem, from a liberal's point of view, to be an absurd vestige of an eighteenth-century effort to place an impediment in the way of direct majority rule. Yet liberals have not pressed very hard for its abolition, for its existence pushes candidates into strategies that overemphasize the big industrial states, where liberals find their greatest strength.

With respect to money in elections, however, liberals have provided a strong impetus for reform. In their arguments that led to the passage of the 1971 and 1974 campaign finance acts, they declared that allowing wealthy individuals to buy personal influence in Washington through huge donations was a gross denial of the democratic spirit. They insisted that the big companies which, either illegally out of corporate funds or legally from the pockets of their executives, contributed heavily to campaigns were not doing it from pure altruism but because they wanted something in return: government contracts, tax advantages, or the prevention of legislation unfavorable to their businesses. The candidates who received those donations had to feel beholden to their contributors; and it was this fact more than any other that led to the corruption of the political process. Watergate was the most flagrant example of how this method of campaign funding corrupts. In fact, it was the availability of so much money to the Nixon campaign in 1972—a result of the disgraceful pressure of the CRP on corporate executives and other sources of campaign funds—that helped create the Watergate mentality. With money as no object and large quantities of it in cash sitting around in safe deposit boxes and White House offices, all kinds of harebrained schemes—such as the Watergate break-in—could be hatched and approved. But liberals do not dwell only on Watergate. They deplore the extent to which Democrats as well as Republicans have been dependent on large contributors.

They do draw a distinction between the parties, however. They argue that the system greatly favors the Republican party, the party of big business, over the Democrats. Nixon spent more than twice as much as Humphrey in 1968. Humphrey's campaign was in desperate straits all the way and had to be financed in large measure by loans. Given the closeness of the result in 1968, it is quite conceivable that if Humphrey had received enough money early in the campaign he would have won the election. Again in 1972 the Republican advantage was demonstrated. In one closed-circuit, television speech to dinner functions all around the country Nixon raised $6 million.

So the liberals were pleased with the changes brought about by the 1974 act, and, although they were unhappy with the Supreme Court's action in striking down the expenditure limits for congressional campaigns, they felt that the Court's upholding the contribution limits and the provision for public financing of presidential campaigns left them with a substantial improvement over the pre-1974 situation. As for the first test of the new law in 1976, the liberals feel that it came through very well. While the bill was being debated in Congress, a barrage of criticisms was leveled at it, which continued long after the act was passed. The opponents and the skeptics said that it was unworkable and that it would provide so little money for presidential candidates that they could not properly present their case to the people. In fact, despite a number of problems caused by lack of experience with the new laws and the temporary disruption created by the Supreme Court's intervention, public money was made available to several candidates in the primaries, to parties for their national conventions, and to the presidential nominees in the general election.

The contest between Carter and Ford was defective in many respects, but the fact that they spent less money than went into the 1972 campaign did not prevent their receiving plenty of exposure to the electorate. Moreover, there was no repetition of the 1972 $2 million donation of Clement Stone. The "fat cats" were no longer catered to. And big business money did not weigh heavily in the outcome. Moreover, the 1974 act's provision for additional sums to be raised and spent by national party organizations pleased the liberals, for it helped the parties, who had generally been pushed into a subordinate role by the candidate's personal organization, to build a more significant place for themselves in campaigns.

What needs to be done now, say the liberals, is to build on the experience of 1976 by correcting certain deficiencies in the 1974 act. First, the amount of public money to conduct presidential campaigns should be increased, *while ensuring that the increase is not spent on media advertising.* Second, minor party candidates should be able to get public funding more easily. Third, and most important, public financing should be extended to congressional campaigns. Its omission in 1974 was no simple oversight. The law was written by the incumbents, the people who held the congressional seats. Incumbents generally have little difficulty raising campaign funds, so they were not anxious to have the government take care of the fund-raising problems of their opponents.

To make their positions doubly secure the members of the House proceeded to write into the law a provision setting a limit of $70,000 in allowable campaign spending for an election campaign for a House seat. This item fell before the Supreme Court ruling; but its intent is worth noting. Normally it takes at least $100,000 to give a challenger a chance of upsetting an established member of the House. Moreover, the "equality" of spending permitted all candidates was an illusion, since incumbent congressmen can use their congressional printing and mailing privileges to send "newsletters" to all their constituents. This tactic keeps their names and their efforts on behalf of their district continually in the minds of the voters. So, the liberals say, the only way to give challengers a chance and to free members of Congress of their servitude to the big contributors is to provide financing for congressional campaigns, an idea that Jimmy Carter endorsed in March 1977.

The Conservatives: Improve the Campaigns, but Don't Tinker with the Machinery

Like the liberals, conservatives generally deplore the tone and style of contemporary election campaigns. They admire the high seriousness of the debates in which the men who founded the Republic engaged, and they believe that the vulgarity and superficiality of campaigns today are symptomatic of the general debasement of the quality of our national life. This has resulted from our becoming a mass society in which politicians appeal to the lowest common denominator in a frantic effort to engage the attention of the least qualified members of the electorate. The media dominate the electoral process, and the liberal establishment, which controls the media, distracts the people with trivia and irrelevances rather than presenting them with the clear alternatives that would help them reject the establishment's ideas.

With respect to the machinery of elections conservatives are disturbed by the trend toward placing all the decisions in the hands of the masses. They dislike proposals, for example, that would abolish the electoral college. Although they do not ask for a return to the original intent of the framers—that the college's electors make their own independent decisions on the choice of a president—they are not disposed to favor the complete abandonment of an institution that has been with us for so long. To do away with the electoral college, says the conservative analyst M. Stanton Evans, "would clearly diminish the authority of the states in the federal balance . . . and transform the presidency even more decisively into a 'national' plebiscitary executive."[8] The idea of the president as the product of a national "plebiscite," or the direct expression of the will of the mass electorate, is antithetical to the entire spirit of the Constitution, according to the conservatives. Conservatives are not opposed to making the system fairer than the present method of giving all the electoral votes of a state to the candidate who gets slightly more votes than any of his rivals. The reform they suggest is a "district" plan, whereby the electoral college and the role of the states would be preserved, but the electors would be chosen within congressional districts rather than statewide. This would preserve the conservatives' principle of preferring local constituencies to the national, mass public.

Conservatives take strong issue with liberals over money in elections. They oppose the limits on contributions and spending and the idea of public financing. They argue that interfering with the right of individuals to give as much money as they want to a candidate is a clear denial of the freedom of expression guaranteed by the First Amendment. Although they were pleased with the Supreme Court's striking down of the spending limits in the 1974 act, they do not understand how the Court could then find that, while it is unconstitutional to limit expenditures, there is no constitutional barrier to controlling contributions.

Moreover, contribution limits do not bring equity to the system. They merely make the present inequities worse. As Patrick Buchanan put it:

> If Republicans are prohibited from contributing their savings to conservative presidential candidates, who will prevent George Meany's Committee on Political Education from making its quadrennial contribution of $10 million in manpower and time to the candidate of the Democratic Party? And what requirements are to be imposed upon the nation's dominant networks which, in the estimation of many conservatives, annually provide millions in free publicity for liberal candidates and liberal causes?[9]

Public financing of campaigns is another dreadful idea, say the conservatives. They do not see why the taxpayer should foot the bill for the monstrously wasteful folly that goes into political campaigns. Although public opinion polls show strong majority support for public financing, the answer might be very different, says Buchanan, if the question the pollsters ask is: "Do you believe political campaigns should be funded with voluntary contributions, or with your tax dollars?"

This is not to say that conservatives are unconcerned with the conflicts of interest and outright corruption that has resulted from the dependence of candidates on private contributions. Conservative spokespersons expressed outrage at the financial manipulations of the CRP. But their solution is not to tinker with the machinery or tamper with our constitutional rights. Instead we should attack the root cause of the problem—the growing entanglement of business in government. When businessmen allow themselves to become dependent on government contracts, or seek special tax breaks, or submit to government regulation, it is difficult for them to avoid pressures from elected officials to contribute to campaign chests. So the most effective means of cleaning up politics is to get government out of business, for businessmen will then have no need and no inducement to make political contributions.

"Let me know who you're voting for so I can cancel out your vote."

Leo Garel

The Radical Left: Elections are Meaningless Rituals

As we saw in Chapters 1 and 2, the left sees elections in America primarily as contests between rival wings of the ruling elite. Thus it is absurd to suggest that meaningful choices based on reasoned analyses can be provided. The machinery of elections, notably the electoral college, is also calculated to prevent true alternatives from emerging by squeezing out minority parties and candidates. In 1960 and 1976 the presidential debates excluded all but two candidates, and the media make little or no reference to the existence of any other competitors in campaigns. (One Peace and Freedom party candidate for governor of California in 1974 did discover a way of getting a large group of newsmen to follow her around. She campaigned on a nude bathing beach without any clothes.)

Liberal proposals to change the system by reform of campaign financing are futile. The capitalist system concentrates enormous amounts of money in a few hands, and there is no way of preventing this money from influencing the political process. As loopholes are closed, new ones will be opened up by the armies of lawyers retained by the rich to protect their privileges. In fact, some aspects of the reforms can actually further discriminate against dissenting opinions. Public funding goes only to the campaigns of the established parties. Furthermore, the requirement of the 1971 law for full disclosure of campaign contributions makes it harder for candidates to the left to raise money. Publication of donations to radical candidates can lead to the contributor's name being fed into the files of the FBI and state and local police forces, thus making him vulnerable to years of harassment.

The Radical Right:
How Can the Patriots Be Heard?

In large measure the criticisms of the election process put forward by the radical left are also subscribed to on the right. They, too, believe that the system is controlled by a dominant elite, that alternative programs and leaders are given almost no hearing by the media and are discriminated against by the machinery of elections.

Beyond this the radical right is strenuously opposed to the type of campaign reform laws imposed by the 1971 and 1974 laws. They want no limitations placed on the right of patriots to give their money to save the country from subversive men and doctrines. Some right-wing candidates have, in fact, received large donations from wealthy businessmen in the Southwest, particularly Texas. However, the obstacles that the election system imposes has inclined the large donors of the radical right to contribute to the advancement of causes and educational programs rather than the election of candidates.

The Centrists:
The People Are Not Fooled

On the whole, the centrists argue, elections in America have served well enough to enable the people to make significant choices among candidates. They recognize that the mass media, especially television, have changed the style of elections, and that there is a great deal of irrelevant nonsense in our campaigns today. But they demur from the complaints of the various critics in several aspects.

First, they doubt that all the defects of the process can be blamed on the media. Oversimplification and distortion of the issues have been present in all campaigns in recorded history. So has the emphasis on images and personalities. People with attractive, salable personalities have always been sought after as candidates. The difference is simply that today the media require a special technique for projecting personality.

Moreover, the fact that the public has become very much concerned with the personal qualities of candidates is not an indication of the triviality of our political process. If we learned anything from the Johnson and Nixon presidencies it is that we had better look very closely at the characters of our leaders as well as their professed policies. And in the final analysis the people have been able to see through the advertising agencies' and media's images to the realities of character underneath. In the prolonged ordeal that constitutes a presidential campaign, a candidate is seen so many times, in so many different contexts, that the majority of people—even those who are not particularly interested in the campaign—should be able to form fairly effective judgments about what kind of a person he actually is. Thus the impression of great vigor that John Kennedy conveyed in the 1960 campaign was not simply the consequence of successful mass media packaging. Kennedy had a genuine vitality that proved to be of great importance in his conduct of the presidency. Conversely, despite all the efforts of the image makers, television has pitilessly revealed the shortcomings of the men who have offered themselves for the presidency.

This is not contradicted by the fact that Richard Nixon was given an enormous majority in 1972. The people were not expressing strong approval of Nixon the man. In fact, his opinion poll ratings on various personal qualities were not very high. It was just that McGovern had behaved so ineptly that he was rated lower than Nixon.

Critics may argue that the election process is demeaning and is not a true test of the kinds of qualities needed by a president. Yet our long election ordeal is a test of a number of qualities: stamina, organizational skills, diplomatic finesse, judgment in the selection of staff, the ability to handle crisis after crisis, coolness under fire, and the capacity to attract the support of various segments of the people. Every one of these is vital to effective performance in the White House.

Nor is it true that this emphasis on personal qualities and character has come at the expense of concern with issues. As we saw in Chapters 2 and 3, the majority show considerable awareness of the issues. This awareness is applied to elections and results in choices based very largely on perceived differences between the candidates on the issues. Thus, in 1972, there was little to support the claim that media executive Roger Ailes had made in 1968: "The next guys will have to be performers." Neither Nixon nor McGovern was a charismatic personality or the embodiment of telegenic charm. Nixon won partly because McGovern's competence and trustworthiness were in question, but also because of the issues. On Vietnam, the economy, and other issues that the majority can understand clearly enough—despite all the campaign mumbo jumbo—Nixon was strongly preferred over McGovern.[10] As for 1976 it is clear that the issues were powerful factors in the minds of the electorate, for with respect to most personal traits the majority very much preferred Ford over Carter.

On the machinery of elections the centrists doubt that the problems the liberals and others complain of are particularly serious. Some changes may be in order, and perhaps it is time to establish regional primaries and abolish the electoral college. But the primaries generally produce the candidate who has more support than any other within his party. And in this century the candidate with the most popular votes has been elected. So the alleged risks of a denial of the majority will—either in the primaries or the electoral college—are apparently overstated.

With respect to money in elections centrists have expressed serious concerns about the 1974 reforms. First, they suggest that too much is made of the allegedly heavy burden of campaign expenditures. We are staggered by the fact that $300 million was spent on elections in America in 1968. Yet in that same year Proctor and Gamble spent $270 million for advertising. Although the cost of campaigns was up to $425 million in 1972, this was little more than $3 for each of the 140 million Americans of voting age, or about $5 for each actual vote.

Then, although centrists recognize the importance of money in elections, they doubt that it is the dominant consideration. For all his wealth, Rockefeller did not win the Republican nomination for the presidency in 1964 or 1968. And although Democratic presidential candidates have usually been outspent by their rivals, Democrats have spent more years in the White House since 1932 than Republicans. While Nixon did raise large sums easily in 1972, McGovern's problem was not money. He spent about as much on broadcasting as Nixon did. In fact, McGovern's campaign (like Goldwater's in 1964) finished in the black.

Of course, it is helpful for a candidate to have plenty of money at the outset. But once a candidate can inspire enthusiasm—and especially if he seems to have a reasonable chance of success—the money will come. It should also be noted that a principal avenue to the presidency is the vice-presidency; and the examples of Harry Truman and Richard Nixon made it clear that it is not necessary to have a personal fortune in order to become vice-president.

Moreover, to the extent that campaign contributions are made as financial investments, a skillful politician knows how to handle matters so that he takes the money but still goes his own way. In any case, wealthy people tend to donate to campaigns not to make more money but rather to have access to the prestige and the social opportunities which come from hobnobbing with presidents and other high officials.

Centrists recognize that the financial abuses connected with Watergate are intolerable. However, the most important reform of campaign financing, the requirement that sources of funds be fully disclosed, was accomplished by the 1971 legislation. The secret funds used in Watergate would not have been available had the 1971 act been in operation earlier. As it was, the CRP applied tremendous pressure on contributors to get their money in before the deadline for disclosure of sources went into effect. After disclosure, the only additional reform that was called for by the Watergate mess was to prevent large amounts of cash from coming into campaigns.

But centrists were highly dubious about the other elements that made up the 1974 law. They worried in particular about two things. First, there was the difficulty of challenging incumbents. Incumbents are overwhelmingly reelected to Congress. Of all members of Congress who run for reelection, 90 to 95 percent are successful. This results not only from their newsletter mailing privileges but also from the name recognition that their office brings and the fact that they have staffs on the public payroll who become campaigners for their reelection. It takes organization and media exposure to overcome such advantages, and these require a great deal of money. The liberals are correct in stating that incumbents usually find it easier to raise money than do challengers. But the fact remains that some challengers are in a position to attract enough money to give the incumbents serious competition. Now their opportunity to do so is seriously impeded by the limitations on contributions imposed by the 1974 act. Fortunately, the Supreme

Court struck down the patently self-serving limits on spending in congressional campaigns. However, although challengers can now spend as much as they raise, it is much more difficult than it used to be to raise money.

The second major problem with the 1974 act in the centrists' view is that public financing of presidential campaigns, and the consequent holding down of spending, sharply reduces the opportunity of the candidates to get their messages across to the public. In 1976, with the help of the free air time made available for the debates, Ford and Carter were able to get a reasonable amount of exposure on television. But there are other aspects to a campaign than television; and in 1976 much less money was available than in the past for local campaign organizations, for bumper stickers and campaign buttons, and for all those elements that lend color to a campaign and provide ways for volunteers to be actively engaged. Moreover, both camps were inhibited by having to constantly watch their expenditures to make sure that they did not exceed their permitted limits and thus make themselves vulnerable to prosecution.

In the aftermath of the election centrists admitted that their worst fears were not realized in 1976. However, this does not incline most of them to support the liberals' proposal to extend public financing to congressional races. What might be tolerable and manageable in presidential elections would not be so if applied to hundreds of congressional elections. Policing so many elections would be an enormous task. And the difficulties in the way of unseating incumbents would become even greater than they are now, for public funding would never provide enough money to overcome the incumbents' natural advantages or to enable the rival candidates to do an adequate job of presenting the issues to the electorate. In the quest for an impossible degree of purity in politics we could cripple the electoral process and seriously detract from the people's opportunity to make effective choices.

Conclusion

We have been discussing in this chapter perhaps the most involved and complicated electoral system the world has ever seen. Somehow the procedures work, and vast numbers of public offices are filled on schedule. Yet the anomalies and complexities are so numerous that we are constantly considering proposals to reform the system.

Some of these proposals, though strongly supported in public opinion polls, are debated periodically and then shelved. Abolition of the electoral college is a case in point, though Jimmy Carter's endorsement of the proposal in 1977 brought the issue to life again. In other cases we make changes—only to find that the changes have complicated the situation even more. Thus the increase in the number of primaries leaves candidates and public more harried than ever and steps up the pressure to move toward regional primaries. If campaign finance reform has cleared up parts of the problem, it is difficult to understand the rational principles behind providing public funds for presidential but not congressional campaigns and limiting contributions but not expenditures (except in presidential campaigns).

Then there is the overriding question that people have been raising with increasing insistence and anxiety about presidential elections. For at least three elections in a row there has been a noticeable lack of enthusiasm about either of the major parties' nominees. Nixon, Humphrey, McGovern, Ford, Carter—as candidates none has been admired by the majority. And a high proportion of the people voting for the victor in each case have expressed strong reservations about the personal qualities of the man they have made president. Why is it, people ask, that from all the extraordinary talent so abundantly available in America we cannot produce candidates who win not only the votes of the electorate but also their trust and esteem? How is it that from a population of less than 4 million in the 1780s America produced such a marvelous array of leaders, whereas from more than 215 million people today we can find nobody who even remotely compares with those remarkable men?

It is important to set these harsh questions in context. For one thing, as historian Henry Steele Commager reminds us, 200 years ago the top talent in America inevitably gravitated toward politics, for there was very little else in those days that required leadership on a large scale. Today many areas attract people of high caliber: business (which pays much more than politics at the top levels), science, law, medicine, and so on. Moreover, we have become so suspicious of politicians that many people of integrity and ability will not subject themselves to the abuse heaped on everyone who enters politics. In fact, our standards have become so high, particularly in the wake of Watergate, that we find fault with almost everything that political leaders say and do. No doubt Jimmy Carter set himself up for the doubts we examined earlier by inviting the people to judge him by criteria that few human beings can ever live up to. Still, Carter, Ford, and other candidates in 1976 were subjected by press and public to a merciless scrutiny that was bound to damage their credibility. So part of the problem may be that, in making unreasonable comparisons with the Founding Fathers and in establishing impossibly high standards, we cannot possibly find candidates who will measure up to our expectations.

Even if we have set up unreasonable expectations, few would maintain that our leaders have consistently been the best qualified among us. It may be that a substantial part of the reason for this lack of excellence is that our procedures for nominating and electing presidents are effectively ruling out some people who would be extraordinarily well qualified to be president. We have looked at the argument that there is no necessary contradiction between the qualities needed to *win* the presidency and the qualities needed to *be* a president. But the argument is clearly debatable. We may be in a better position to examine that issue when we have reviewed more fully the nature of the presidency in Chapter 6.

Notes and References

1.   Theodore H. White, *The Making of the President, 1960* (New York: Atheneum Publishers, 1961), p. 166.

2.   Mark Sullivan, *Our Times: The United States 1900–1925*, Vol. 6, *The Twenties*, (New York: Charles Scribner's Sons, 1935), p. 37.

3.   *The Los Angeles Times*, November 5, 1968.

4.   Joe McGinniss, *The Selling of the President, 1968* (New York: Trident Press, 1969), p. 103.

5.   See David E. Repass, "Comment: Political Methodologies in Disarray: Some Alternative Interpretations of the 1972 Election," *The American Political Science Review*, Vol. 70, No. 3 (September 1976), p. 822.

6.   *Playboy*, November 1976. The article was released to the press and TV in late September 1976.

7.   McGinniss, *The Selling of the President 1968*, p. 103.

8.   M. Stanton Evans, *Clear and Present Dangers: A Conservative View of America's Government* (New York: Harcourt Brace Jovanovich, Inc., 1975), p. 67.

9.   *The Los Angeles Times*, December 3, 1973.

10.   See Arthur H. Miller, Warren E. Miller, Alden S. Raine, and Thad A. Brown, "A Majority Party is Disarray: Policy Polarization in the 1972 Election," *The American Political Science Review*, Vol. 70, No. 3 (September 1976), pp. 753–778.

Interest Groups

and the Public Interest

Thus far we have talked about public opinion, political parties, and elections—the various means by which government is connected with the will of the people. But we have already noted that it is deceptive to describe the people as simply a great number of totally separate individuals. For people congregate into groups, and we are all, in various ways, group members. There are the smallest group units, face-to-face primary groups—families, friendships, work teams—to which, at various stages of our lives, we all belong. We also fall into categories of sex, age, race, ethnic background, education, and so on which fasten different kinds of group identification upon us.

But beyond these group linkages which come by inheritance or the mere fact of social existence, America has an abundance of organizations—groups created to achieve specific ends. Although membership in organizations can sometimes be gained by inheritance, it normally requires an act of joining. And America is a nation of joiners, more than half the population being members of one or more organized groups. From almost any idea or interest, an organization springs forth; and in time that organization may spin off other organizations in all directions.

Some of these have a specifically political purpose and range from the John Birch Society on the far right through the liberal Americans for Democratic Action to the Weather Underground on the far left. They are not political parties as such, but their prime purpose is to influence public policies in a particular ideological direction.

Then there are quasi-political organizations—citizen action groups such as Common Cause, founded in 1970 by John Gardner (former secretary of health, education and welfare) to press for reforms in the political process, and achieving a membership of almost 300,000 by 1976.

In addition, there are religious denominations and sects; nationality and ethnic organizations; fraternal associations and service clubs; civic groups and women's groups, and groups speaking for the young and the aged; groups, too, for the cultivation of the arts and for almost every conceivable hobby, cult, cause, or preference.

Each profession is elaborately organized to establish entrance requirements to maintain and improve its standards—and sometimes to advance its economic interests; for doctors, lawyers, dentists, and others are mostly self-employed businesspeople as well as professionals, and teachers negotiate for salary increases as well as improved schools.

Economic Interest Groups

Finally, there are the organizations that spring directly from economic interests. Among these are business associations, labor unions, agricultural organizations, and consumer-oriented groups. Since these are of particular importance in this chapter, we shall not only list them but also provide a brief assessment of their strength and of their relationship with government.

Business Associations

A multiplicity of organizations speak for business. At the national level the most prominent have been the Chamber of Commerce of the United States and the National Association of Manufacturers (NAM), the latter made up of member companies; the two are now merging into the Association of Commerce and Industry. Every field of economic activity embraces many kinds of businesses, each brought together in appropriate trade associations. For example, the construction, financing, and sale of housing engages the efforts of the National Association of Realtors (over 100,000 members), the National Association of Home Builders (with over 50,000 home-building companies), the United States Savings and Loan League (close to 5000 savings and loan associations), as well as the Mortgage Bankers Association of America, the American Bankers Association, the National Apartment Owners Association, the Producers' Guild, the National Association of Retail Lumber Dealers, the National Association of Lumber Manufacturers, the Associated General Contractors of America, the Building Products Institute, and many others.

At the level of formulating policy, business leaders speak through such organizations as the Business Roundtable, consisting of presidents of 160 major corporations, and the Committee for Economic Development, which publishes studies of major issues in trade and economic policy.

Competition is a cardinal principle of the private business system. However, the extent of competition varies considerably from industry to industry, and there has been a trend toward the combination of resources in very large companies. Thus one official study in 1955 showed that 43 percent of the nation's manufacturing and mining assets were owned by 200 corporations, and the percentage has increased since then. Moreover, nearly half the nation's total deposits of money are held by the 50 largest commercial banks. Public policy in America has opposed excessive concentrations of industrial and financial power, and a number of federal laws have been enacted to combat the growth of monopoly and other practices that interfere with competition between firms. Early in this century the Sherman and Clayton Anti-Trust Acts were passed to deal with this problem, and the Anti-Trust Division of the Department of Justice is charged with enforcing these laws.

Labor Unions

In 1935 the Wagner Labor Relations Act gave workers in most industries involved in interstate commerce the right to organize and bargain collectively, and since then labor unions have grown from a membership of about 3½ million in the mid-1930s to over 20 million in the mid-1970s. Of these, 14 million are organized in the American Federation of Labor–Congress of Industrial Organizations, a fusion of two former rivals. Independent of the AFL–CIO are the Teamsters Union (now combined with the International Longshoremen and Warehousemen's Union) and the United Auto Workers.

Although these gains in the number of organized workers appear impressive, they have not kept up with the growth of the work force. Thus union membership represented about a third of the total work force in 1955. By 1976 the proportion was down to barely a quarter. A prime reason for this is that major technological and industrial changes are working against the interests of the unions. As a result of increased automation, old industries in which unions have been strongest—automobiles, steel, mining, and so on—need a declining number of workers, whereas the labor force is expanding in such industries as computers, which have been difficult to unionize. Moreover, as we saw in Chapter 2, there is a shift away from blue-collar and production-line workers to white-collar, technical and professional staffs. Only partially offsetting these unfavorable factors for organized labor is the increasing unionization among government workers and teachers.

Then, too, the mandate that the unions received from the Wagner Act of 1935 has been somewhat limited by laws passed since the late 1940s. The Taft–Hartley Act of 1947 restricted their position in a number of ways, most significantly in outlawing the closed shop (a contract permitting the hiring only of union members) and permitting the union shop (which compels newly employed workers to join the union within a given period) only under certain conditions.

Most obnoxious to the unions was Section 14(b) of the act, which allowed states to outlaw the union shop—a section that was seized upon by a number of states, especially in the South, to pass "right-to-work" laws. The unions fought bitterly for repeal of Section 14(b); but even Lyndon Johnson's backing in 1965 and 1966 and the huge Democratic majority in Congress of that session were unable to give the unions what they wanted.

In addition the Landrum–Griffin Act of 1959 imposed restrictions on the internal workings of the unions as a result of revelations of corruption and dictatorial rule in some of them.

Agricultural Federations

Agriculture is represented by a number of diverse organizations. Middle-sized to large enterprises join together in the American Farm Bureau Federation, the National Grange, and/or the American National Cattlemen's Association, among others. Speaking for small farmers and for farm workers are the National Farmers Organization, the National Farmers Union, and Cesar Chavez's United Farm Workers' Union.

However, the current trend in agriculture is toward the reduction of the number of small farmers and of the people working and living on the land. In 1925 there were about 6.5 million farms in America. By 1970 the number was down to little more than 3 million. By 1980 it may well fall to around 2 million. Of those that remain, a relatively small number of big farming enterprises produce a high proportion of all agricultural output.

Since the Great Depression of the 1930s, which wiped out many small farmers, agriculture has tended to look to the federal government for help. The government has been responsive and has provided billions of dollars a year in subsidies to provide stable prices for the farmer. Sometimes, in fact, to prevent huge surpluses from inundating the market and sending prices plummeting, the federal government has actually paid farmers not to plant certain crops. Then, as world food shortages emerged in the 1970s, policies designed to limit production gave way to encouragement to expand output to the maximum possible. However, whenever international shortages recede, pressures mount again for government intervention, the regulation of output, and subsidies to compensate for holding output down.

Consumer-oriented Groups

Consumers constitute the broadest of all economic interests and are represented by an increasing number of organizations. There is a long tradition of cooperative societies whose purpose is to sell foods and other goods to members on a nonprofit basis. And since the 1960s consumers have had a potent representative of their interests in Ralph Nader, a lawyer who began with a solitary crusade for auto safety and then institutionalized his efforts on behalf of the consumer by establishing the Center for Auto Safety, the Public Interest Research Group, the Center for the Study of Responsive Law, the Corporate Accountability Project, Congress Watch, Tax Reform Research Group, and several others. These activities are financed by Nader's lecture fees, foundation grants, and a direct-mail campaign for contributions to Public Citizen, Inc.

The Public
Functions of Private Groups

These "interest groups," though part of the "private sector," are important contributors to the governmental and political system. First, they provide a training ground for political leadership. Being active in one or more of these groups is among the most common ways for individuals to get into politics. The group offers an opportunity to learn the skills of leadership. It also provides a constituency and a source of money, campaign workers, and votes. It is, in other words, a potential power base. For people who lack personal wealth, unusual eloquence, or charisma, hard and patient work in private organizations may yet provide a way to break into political life.

Second, since these groups are organized for the purpose of furthering their shared interest, they play a major role in shaping public policy. Although only a small proportion of voluntary organizations are primarily political in purpose, at one time or another most groups will be affected by some aspects of public policy and will as a result become politically active to voice their support or objections.

Interest groups operate at all levels of government—national, state, and local. Their representatives follow the workings of legislatures. Their lobbyists maintain close contact with executive agencies, from the lowest-level bureaucrat to Cabinet members and possibly even to the president himself. National interest groups may retain lawyers in Washington to argue their causes in court. They try to influence the programs of political parties. They seek to inform, educate, and persuade the general public and members of other groups. Furthermore, interest groups seek to educate their own membership, for many people look to their organizations for guidance on what to think about politics and how to vote on candidates and issues.

Political Tactics

Organizations use a great variety of tactics in their efforts to influence government's decisions. Many of them hire professional *lobbyists*, who specialize in trying to induce legislation that will further the interests of the group they represent. These professionals employ three kinds of resources: *knowledge, money,* and *constituency power.*

Specialized knowledge.   In making public policy, government agencies and legislatures must draw on expertise wherever it exists. Interest groups represent special kinds of experience and are a prime source of expertise. Inevitably, then, government bodies turn to these organizations for detailed information on the content of proposed programs, and for predictions on how these programs will affect the lives and fortunes of the memberships represented by the organizations.

Money.   Money is one of the wellsprings of politics, and organizations are a principal source of political money. In earlier periods of American history the tactic of directly bribing public officials was commonplace. Even now periodic scandals reveal that bribes are still offered and accepted. Such crudely illegal tactics are less common today, however, than they were in the past, at least at the national level.

Nonetheless, organizations have found a number of other ways to give funds to politicians—in the form of lucrative speaking engagements, appointments to paid directorships of savings and loan leagues, retaining law firms whose partners are members of state or federal legislatures, and contributions to election campaigns. Campaign contributions to congressional campaigns for 1974 and 1976 are shown in Table 5–1.

TABLE 5–1   Congressional Campaign Contributions by Interest Groups (millions of dollars, rounded to the nearest $100,000)

Group	1974	1976
Labor	6.3	8.2
Business	2.5	7.1
Health	1.9	2.7
Agriculture	.4	1.5
Ideological	.7	1.5
Miscellaneous	.7	1.5
Total	12.5	22.5

SOURCE: Figures compiled by Common Cause from reports filed with the Federal Election Commission.

Constituency power.   The power inherent in a particular group's membership must be reckoned with by government decision makers. Thus a lobbyist's ability to bring the national leaders of his organization to Washington can exert a potent influence on Congress and on executive agencies. Moreover, most national organizations are made up of local units. Since members of Congress are generally very sensitive to opinion in their own districts, Washington lobbyists work hard at marshaling pressure from the folks back home. Whenever a decision point is approached in the legislative process, an organization's Washington staff can send the word around the country, and congressmen in the areas affected may find themselves inundated with letters, telegrams, and phone calls from constituents.

There is a good deal of debate about the usefulness of this technique. Some legislators say that they refuse to be stampeded by a sudden barrage of messages that they know have been orchestrated by a lobbyist, for these are not genuine expressions of constituents' concerns but artificially engineered pressure campaigns. This is especially obvious when the letters coming in are all identical. Many legislators insist that they are not impressed even when the lobbyists take pains to ensure that every communication is individualized.

Still, most members of Congress have to be impressed by the ability of a national organization to produce an avalanche of comments from its members. Typically, a congressman will use the comments for his purposes if they endorse his own position. If they do not, he will sometimes send out urgent pleas for mail from his sympathizers. To the legislator who is wavering on an issue, a deluge of letters and wires from a particular interest group, supplemented by individual contacts from influential group members in his district, may sway him to make a decision in their favor.

Lobbying Reforms

From time to time public concern builds that private organizations are exercising too much influence on public policy, and that this influence is exerted through secret deals hidden from public scrutiny. In response to this concern legislation has been passed to set limits on the influence of "pressure groups" and lobbyists and to open their activities to full public view. The most notable of the laws addressing this problem is the 1946 Federal Regulation of Lobbying Act, which requires paid lobbyists, who are usually individual staff members of public relations or law firms, to register and file quarterly reports on all receipts and expenditures for lobbying purposes. For the year 1973 these reports produced the information given in Table 5–2 on declared spending totals.

TABLE 5–2   Lobby Spending by Category in 1973

Category	Amount Reported
Business	$3,287,561.89
Professional	732,633.35
Labor	1,886,793.86
Agriculture	672,838.74
Military and veteran	249,899.74
Miscellaneous	2,634,095.69
Total	$9,463,823.27

SOURCE: Data from Congressional Quarterly, *The Washington Lobby*, 2nd ed., September 1974, p. 43.

The top 25 organizations in reported spending for 1973 are listed in Table 5–3. However, these figures fall far short of telling the full story of spending by lobbyists, for the 1946 act was full of loopholes.

Although the Supreme Court sustained the constitutionality of the act in the *Harriss* case in 1954, it was held to apply only to groups and individuals who

TABLE 5–3   *Twenty-five Top Spenders in 1973*

Organizations	Amount
Common Cause	$934,835
International Union, United Automobile,	
Aerospace and Agricultural Implement Workers	460,992
American Postal Workers Union (AFL–CIO)	393,399
American Federation of Labor–Congress of	
Industrial Organizations (AFL–CIO)	240,800
American Trucking Associations, Inc.	226,157
American Nurses Association, Inc.	218,354
United States Savings and Loan League	204,221
Gas Supply Committee	195,537
Disabled American Veterans	193,168
The Committee of Publicly Owned Companies	180,493
American Farm Bureau Federation	170,472
National Education Association	162,755
National Association of Letter Carriers	160,597
National Association of Home Builders	
of the United States	152,177
Recording Industry Association of America, Inc.	141,111
National Council of Farmer Cooperatives	140,560
American Insurance Association	139,395
The Farmers' Educational and Co-operative	
Union of America	138,403
Committee of Copyright Owners	135,095
National Housing Conference, Inc.	125,726
American Petroleum Institute	121,276
American Medical Association	114,859
Citizens for Control of Federal Spending	113,659
American Civil Liberties Union	102,595
National Association of Insurance Agents, Inc.	87,422

SOURCE: Data from Congressional Quarterly, *The Washington Lobby,*
2nd ed., September 1974, p. 38.

solicited, received, or collected money for the "principal purpose" of influencing legislation through direct contacts with members of Congress. Groups that spent their funds to influence legislation without hiring a lobbyist, as many of them did, or groups that could claim that their principal purpose was not legislative, as most of them could, were able to avoid disclosing the extent of their lobbying outlays. Moreover, the costs of indirect pressures on Congress through such methods as mass mailings were not covered by the act.

As we saw in Chapter 4, controls have also been set on the ability of organizations to contribute to campaigns. Business corporations, in particular, have been prohibited from contributing corporate money. However, as we noted, there were loopholes here, too, and the law has sometimes been ignored by business concerns and politicians. Further, in many states the federal ban on corporate campaign contributions does not apply to state and local offices.

A further limitation on interest groups' efforts to influence Congress was contained in a provision of the 1974 Campaign Finance Reform Law (amended in 1976 and 1977) imposing limits on the lecture and writing fees paid to members of Congress by private organizations.

Five Perspectives
on Interest Groups

The Liberals:
Groups versus Democracy

The way in which organized groups influence the American political process offends the liberals' concept of democracy in several ways: the disproportionate influence of business groups, the pressure tactics they use, and their neglect of the public interest.

The business bias.   To the liberals business groups easily comprise the most formidable source of private power. Corporations are where most of the resources are concentrated and where the financial rewards to individuals are greatest. The liberals do not suggest that business is all-powerful. Nor do they believe that it represents a unified power bloc. They concede that each firm is concerned with its own survival and profits, which can lead to intense rivalries with other firms. Just the same, they see in the business sector common interests that increasingly override the factors that make for competition.

First, the growth of monopolies has stifled competition. The antitrust laws have failed dismally to prevent mergers of individual companies into industrial and financial giants. Moreover, these giant firms are linked by the fact that the largest stockholders in some of the biggest manufacturing corporations—Ford, Chrysler, General Electric, and Mobil, for example—are banks and other financial institutions. The growth of "conglomerate" empires, such as Litton, which are able to absorb many firms from totally different fields into a single fiscal framework, results in a still further concentration of industrial resources. Nor does the trend toward concentrated business power stop at the water's edge. Firms such as IBM, ITT, Ford, General Foods, and Singer are, in fact, huge "multinational corporations," which own plants and whole companies abroad.

Another factor that binds the separate entities of the business world together is a shared ideology. Liberals do not deny that there are considerable differences between the doctrines expressed by the conservative National Association of Manufacturers, on the one hand, and the more moderate Committee for

Economic Development, on the other. Moreover, there is an increasingly important group of "technocrats" within industry—experts whose values are molded more by their scientific and technical interests than by economic and political ideologies inherited from an earlier era. Still, the liberals insist that there is a rhetoric and a creed of free enterprise which most business leaders subscribe to and that tend to unite them against proposals for governmental controls—unless these serve their own interests.

In the liberals' view, the impact on politics of this vast and increasingly concentrated business power is enormous. Government and politics never operate in a vacuum. It is highly unlikely that huge private resources would not affect governmental decisions. In fact, business is heavily involved in the task of shaping public policies.

Business is involved, in the first place, through lobbying. Two-thirds of the groups listed on the Lobby Index, the register of those organizations which admit to maintaining a legislative representative in Washington, represent business, and the greater part of the lobbying funds spent comes from business. Then, as we shall see in Chapter 8, business maintains close links with the federal agencies that are supposed to be regulating them. Many business leaders hold high public office, particularly in the executive branch. And the general climate of ideas in the country is permeated with beliefs that are generally favorable to business, establishing a framework that can be challenged only with great difficulty.

There are, the liberals recognize, many other kinds of private groups—Common Cause, the Nader groups, labor, and so on—that oppose business power. Sometimes they win significant victories against business, and the liberals strive

"Marge! You must meet Roger Ditlow. Roger has been endorsed as a Person by Common Cause."

By permission of Mort Gerberg, from *TOPPIX* (1–8–77, Chicago Tribune-New York News Syndicate).

constantly and hopefully to increase the ability of these groups to stand against business. Yet they believe that on the larger number of issues business strength is greater than that of any other combination of forces affecting governmental policy making. This becomes clear as we compare the power of other interest groups with business. Thus labor unions have fought for the kinds of programs that liberals support, providing the most important backing for most of the legislation since the 1930s that favors the less privileged groups in society. Just the same, in general terms liberals do not see labor as a match for business. A Gallup Poll in August 1968 showed that the power of big labor was regarded as a threat to the future of the country by twice as many people as were alarmed by big business. This, say the liberals, reveals a vast overestimate of labor's strength.

The relegation of unions to less than the top echelons of power is apparent in several respects. To begin with, labor officials, unlike business leaders, have not been appointed to any of the highest positions in the executive branch. Even the secretary of labor—not one of the central figures in any administration—has usually come from outside the ranks of labor. Labor leaders such as George Meany sometimes have been consulted by presidents on foreign policy questions when their views are known to be compatible with the president's; but they have not been among the inner circle of presidential advisers. Men and women with a background in organized labor constitute only about 1 percent of the membership of Congress. Moreover, the weakness of the unions' political position is revealed by the passage of such antilabor legislation as the Taft–Hartley Act of 1947 and the Landrum–Griffin Act of 1959. Again in 1977, the unions, with a Democrat in the White House and large Democratic margins in Congress, failed to gain passage of legislation ("the common situs picketing" bill) which would have given a labor union the right to close a construction site in a dispute with one subcontractor. Organizations which, however impressive their legislative record on general issues, are unable to get their own legislation through Congress or even to protect themselves from the passing of laws directly hostile to their own interests can hardly be regarded as sources of towering strength in the political system. As one labor lobbyist put it: "I'm still looking for the first piece of pure labor legislation to be enacted into law. If we've got that kind of power, we must be terrible lobbyists."[1] Finally, liberals point to the declining proportion of the work force that is organized into unions as evidence that labor's power is overrated.

Nor do liberals look to agriculture as an effective countervailing force to business. Cultivators of the land were the dominant interest group in the early stages of the American Republic, but their influence has steadily decreased as their numbers have declined. Moreover, with the big farms turning to mechanization on a large scale, their owners need working capital in the millions. So agriculture is fast becoming merely another branch of business—"agribusiness"—competing for power with other forms of business but no longer the focus of a separate lifestyle and set of values.

As for the consumer, liberals contend that this broadest of economic interests has been treated shamefully. The notion that the consumer is all-powerful is an illusion. It is the corporation that is dominant, limiting consumer choice by monopoly and various kinds of collusion; deceiving the consumer by manipulative advertising and deceptive packaging; defrauding through short weight, shoddiness, and overpricing; endangering health and safety by recklessly selling faulty or insufficiently tested goods.

In their efforts to check these abuses consumer organizations have suffered from a basic difficulty. The consumer interest is diffuse: we are all consumers. And when a category includes everyone, it is difficult to give it any meaning. It is the other categories of our lives that are more easily segmented, to which we tend to attach more intense and sustained feelings, and to which, therefore, we are more likely to make an organizational commitment. This gives business groups, which have clearly defined interests as well as massive resources, great advantages over consumer groups.

Thus, as the liberals see it, business power is much greater than that of labor, small farmers, consumers, and other organized interest groups. And they believe that this contradicts the idea of democracy, which vests power in the people at large, and not in any particular segment of the community.

Pressure politics.   The advantages of business over other groups is also manifested for the liberals in the superior resources that business brings to the task of influencing political decisions. Thus business organizations have the largest and best-paid staffs for the purpose of presenting information to governmental agencies and congressional committees. In fact, government depends heavily on industry for information in such highly technical fields as energy sources and air pollution, and liberals suggest that, on such technical issues, whoever controls the information controls the decisions.

Then liberals contend that business has far more of that vital political resource, money, than does any other group, as is clear from the role played by business in contributing to political campaigns. Certainly there has been no campaign chest in the history of American politics that approaches the scale of the funds contributed by business leaders to the Committee to Reelect the President in 1972.

Further, business groups are best equipped to provide members of Congress with lucrative speaking engagements at their national conferences; or to curry favor by retaining the services of the legislators' law firms; or to provide them with stipends for serving on boards of directors. And only big business and financial corporations can afford to have their interests represented by the celebrated Washington law firms that have strong contacts in the upper circles of government.

Business is also particularly skillful at organizing constituency power to influence legislation, and at arranging for messages to be sent to Washington in such a way that the concerns of a small segment of the population are made to seem like the interests of the mass of the people. The United States Chamber of

Commerce is adept at orchestrating pressure from local units in every sizable community in the country, as are many of the national trade associations that represent particular industries.

As an example, some of the most effective organizations in marshaling power from back home are those representing the private housing industry. They have been successful in pressuring for laws providing federal guarantees to those loans which are essential to the buying, selling, and renting of homes. They have applied the same pressures to attack proposals for federal underwriting of housing for the poor, which they have condemned as socialistic.

Thus when President Truman in 1945 suggested the expansion of the public housing program—government-owned and subsidized housing for the poor—the private housing industry lobbied Congress to defeat it. They succeeded until 1949, when a housing act, which supplied federal aid to private housing, also included funds for 810,000 units of public housing to be completed by 1955.

Defeated on this issue in Washington, the national housing organizations sent word out to their local units—real estate boards, home builders, and savings and loan associations—to fight the program in the communities and to let their congressional representatives know of their opposition. Vast quantities of mail poured into Washington, much of it directed at the committees of the House and Senate that dealt with the housing issue, and carefully timed for maximum impact. This mail campaign was supplemented by calls from "special contacts" in the communities—close friends of congressmen, large campaign contributors, newspaper publishers, and so on.

Year after year the organized attacks on the program continued. The result was that by 1955, instead of the proposed 810,000 units of public housing, only 200,000 units had been completed. It took until 1960 to build 300,000 units. And the full allocation was not constructed until some 20 years after the passage of the 1949 law.

The public housing battle provides an excellent illustration of the argument that special interests are able to work their will by lobbying Congress. But the private housing groups represent mostly small and middle-sized businesses. When we move beyond the level of real estate and home-building companies to the great business corporations, we enter another dimension of the liberals' case against pressure politics. In that dimension the people at the top talk to the people at the top.

A case in point is the successful effort of International Telephone and Telegraph in 1970–71 to preserve its merger with the Hartford Fire Insurance Company. ITT, planning to expand its conglomerate empire, moved to take over three corporations: Hartford, Canteen Corporation (a frozen meals and vending company), and Grinnell Corporation, the biggest fire protection business in the United States. The move was challenged in the courts by the Anti-Trust Division of the Justice Department, headed by Richard McClaren.

In November 1970 ITT offered to negotiate. They would get rid of Canteen and most of Grinnell. To sweeten the deal they would even divest themselves of

Levitt, a home-building company. They would do all this if only they were allowed to keep Hartford, for Hartford took in $1 billion a year in insurance premiums. This represented the kind of cash flow, or liquidity, that ITT very much wanted. McClaren refused, insisting that he wanted to take the matter to the Supreme Court as a test case that could be used against expansion by other conglomerates.

Six months later, in June 1971, McClaren changed his mind. If ITT would give up Canteen, part of Grinnell, Levitt, plus Avis, the auto rental firm, and if they would agree not to acquire any other large companies without special approval, they could keep Hartford. The offer was accepted.

What had happened between November 1970 and June 1971 to change McClaren's mind? The answer, say the liberals, was a tremendous lobbying campaign. This was not traditional, behind-the-scenes lobbying in Congress, since the decisions were not being made there. The pressure had to reach McClaren and the Justice Department. This required going to the people above McClaren in the executive hierarchy. So ITT's president, Harold Geneen, and some of his vice-presidents met with Vice-President Spiro Agnew; White House staff members, including John Ehrlichman; two successive secretaries of the treasury; the secretary of commerce (later head of the Committee to Reelect the President), Maurice Stans; Attorney General John Mitchell; and the assistant attorney general, Richard Kleindienst, the official directly responsible for handling the issue. Geneen also arranged for an approach to Kleindienst by one of the partners in the New York banking concern that had put the ITT mergers together, who made a presentation to the staff of the Anti-Trust Division in which he warned that, if ITT had to dispose of Hartford, this would represent a grave threat not only to ITT but also to the stock market and the entire U.S. balance of payments.

Still one more high official pressured Kleindienst on the problem—President Nixon himself, who told Kleindienst that McClaren was not working within administration policy, and ordered the case dropped. This order, however, was withdrawn in face of a threat by Kleindienst to resign.

One further element entering the picture was a pledge made by the Sheraton Corporation, another ITT subsidiary, to help finance the forthcoming 1972 Republican convention. Nixon wanted the convention held in San Diego; the city was reluctant to put up the necessary money; ITT's Geneen offered to put up $400,000 toward convention costs, in the event, the Republicans held their convention in Miami Beach, and the pledge did not have to be redeemed. But some ITT officials, including the company's chief Washington lobbyist, believed that the pledge had been helpful in influencing the Hartford decision.

Whether this was a factor or not, the contacts with the White House and the Cabinet were instrumental in getting McClaren to reopen the case. He called for a new study by an independent investment analyst. The analyst's report on this complex matter took two days, for which he charged a fee of $242. His conclusion was that splitting off Hartford from ITT would indeed be damaging to the stock market and the economy.

McClaren found the report persuasive. He had not, he said, previously understood the harmful consequences of his proposal. Liberals, however, were skeptical that he had been persuaded by $242 worth of facts and logic.

Reasserting the public interest.   If the liberals are dissatisfied with the group process, it is not only because it is unbalanced in favor of business and because business is more successful than other groups in playing the game of pressure politics. They also complain that when organized groups get into politics they work for their narrow, selfish interest against the public interest—the interest of the people at large, the concept on which the American political system is based.

Certainly, they allege, this is true of business, which operates with very little sense of public responsibility. Driven by the desire to make profits, it is accountable only to itself and its shareholders. It cares little for the consumer, and the public has to pay for its reckless disregard of the human and physical environment. Its conduct in politics reflects this preoccupation with its own concerns rather than the good of the society.

But the way business operates in politics is characteristic of the way most groups behave in our system. Each fights hard for its special concerns. The American Medical Association worries little about the doctor's Hippocratic oath of service to patients and lobbies furiously against program after program designed to help those who cannot afford the escalating costs of medical care. The National Rifle Association, in the face of public opinion polls showing clear majorities in favor of gun controls, uses every kind of pressure tactic to intimidate Congress and prevent legislation that would curb the ownership of guns.

Of course any group, no matter how small, must have the right to organize to express its ideas and interests, and must have access to the decision makers in government. But this freedom does not extend to the right of self-interested minorities to impose their will persistently over the well-being of the public in general through concentrated pressures and behind-the-scenes deals. And all too often, maintain the liberals, this is the result of the group process in America.

How is the power of business and of other narrowly based special-interest groups to be kept in line and their public responsibility asserted? The liberals offer a number of proposals.

1.   Tighten the lobbying laws to force more public disclosure of lobbyists' activities. For example, lobbyist registration requirements should apply at much lower levels of expenditure than is now the case. Lobbyists should publicly disclose who employs them, for what purposes, and with how much money. People who are not employed as full-time lobbyists but who communicate frequently with members or employees of Congress or the executive branch should be brought under the provisions of the law. This would include many corporate presidents and vice-presidents who devote only a small proportion of their time to lobbying.

2.   Attack monopoly and the biggest concentrations of economic power by one or more of the following means:

Splitting monstrous organizations such as General Motors and Standard Oil into smaller firms.

Nationalizing companies where, as in the case of armaments and aerospace firms, they work mostly under contract to the federal government.

Establishing publicly owned companies in such fields as energy production to force the big corporations to be competitive.

Placing representatives of the public and of the consumer on the boards of directors of the corporations.

Subjecting corporations to federal chartering. Currently, corporations are registered by individual states, which rarely impose the kind of controls needed for public accountability. Passing legislation that would force major corporations to apply to the federal government for their right to operate would give the federal government the opportunity to compel the corporations to act in the public interest.

Ensuring that the governmental agencies which are supposed to regulate private business do their jobs properly. As we shall see in Chapter 8, regulatory agencies have been all too willing to serve the interests of the businesses they are supposed to be regulating.

Putting an end to government underwriting of industry through tax advantages, tariffs, and subsidies.

3.   Build the power of those groups which are presently underrepresented in the group process, particularly the poor, racial and ethnic minorities, and women.

4.   Build the power of those organizations which speak for the public interest in general, such as Common Cause and the Nader groups. These draw upon the reservoir of enthusiastic public spiritedness among large numbers of educated people in America who are concerned about the environment, open and honest government, and the quality of life in general.

5.   Strengthen the political parties. This would cut down on the leverage of private interests, for lobbyists would find it harder to deal with the individual legislator if he were expected to follow the general party positions.

6.   Extend the reform of campaign financing to reduce still further the influence exerted by pressure groups through campaign contributions.

By these means, say the liberals, business power would be counterbalanced by other sources of power, political decisions would be made in the open where everyone could see what influences were being brought to bear, and the public interest would prevail over selfish interests.

The Radical Left: Corporations versus the People

Much of the liberal critique of the power of business is echoed by the radical left. However, the radicals complain once again that the liberals' analysis is too timid and does not go to the heart of the matter. For the left, corporate capitalism is the central source of power in America. This holds true whether we are talking about private power or governmental power, since, the left argues, the distinctions between the two kinds of power are meaningless. The two form a seamless web. Decisions made in the privacy of the corporate board rooms become public policy.

There are no important rival sources of power in the system. Organized labor is puny by comparison. In any case, with few exceptions labor is part of the business system. Many unions participate in the management of vast pension funds, a considerable portion of which has been invested in stocks and land development projects. Some of the most prominent labor leaders subscribe to the values of capitalism, bitterly attack the habits and beliefs of young people, and make belligerent foreign policy statements.

Middle-class organizations such as Common Cause and the Nader groups are no match for the corporations. The poor and the blacks, lacking money and the other resources needed to be effective, are able to muster only weak pressures.

The liberals' proposals for reform fall far short of what is needed. The regulation of lobbying, the strengthening of the two-party system, and so on do not get at the roots of the problem. Antimonopoly laws have been a dismal failure; in fact, they are counterproductive, for they create the illusion that effective action is being taken to check the power of the corporations. Nothing will do short of replacing the principle of private ownership and operation of economic resources with the ethic of cooperation and community.

The cure: mass participation and common ownership.   As we have noted, the old left sees government as the agent of this transfer of power. To the new left this may merely replace one kind of servitude with another. What is needed is democratization of power relationships not only *between* groups but also *within* groups. Democracy in every sphere is a central concern of the new left. They want participation of the people as a whole. The fact that over half the population belongs to at least one organization is not sufficient. A high proportion of these belong to organizations for purely social reasons. Membership in labor unions is simply something that goes with the job. Only a small proportion of the joiners belong to a civic or political organization. And the "activists"—those who belong to four or more organizations—come predominantly from business and professional groups and thus from the more affluent part of the community. Further, most of the decisions within these organizations are made by a small number of leaders, some of them career officials, others elected by the small proportion of the members who bother to vote.

Leaders of corporations make no pretense of speaking for the wishes or best interests of the masses of the workers they employ, say the left. Concessions are made in face of the demands of organized labor. But negotiations between the bureaucracies of industry and labor do not constitute any real sharing of power. The rulers of the corporations have almost unlimited, autocratic power and always put their own selfish interests before those of the people. So private ownership must give way to common ownership, and corporate oligarchy—or government by the few—must be replaced by workers' control of industry.

The Conservatives: The Invisible Hand

The liberal–left attack on business is angrily rejected by conservatives. From their perspective business is not the dominant power in the economy.

The relative unimportance of business monopoly.   It is true that monopoly exists and that it is undesirable. But its extent has been vastly exaggerated. As Milton Friedman puts it, "The most important fact about enterprise monopoly is its relative unimportance from the point of view of the economy as a whole."[2] There are millions of separate businesses in America. Hundreds of thousands of companies are born, and a somewhat smaller number die, each year. Almost a fifth of the working population is self-employed.

In almost any industry that one can mention there are giant corporations and tiny firms side by side. IBM is far and away the biggest company in the computer field. But new firms, generated by the imagination and energy of inventive individuals, bring out new products and successfully capture a corner of the computer market.

To the extent that monopoly does exist in America, its greatest single cause is government intervention. Government regulation of industries is often nothing more than using public authority to "support and enforce cartel and monopoly arrangements among private producers."[3] Tariffs, special tax breaks, and subsidies of various kinds all enable inefficient industries to survive and grow, thus diminishing the impact of competition.

The conservatives will admit that the blame for this cannot all be placed on government. Too many business leaders have turned to the government to protect them rather than take the painful steps necessary to enable them to prosper under the spur of competition. Some of these leaders regard themselves as conservatives and contribute to the campaigns of conservative candidates. In truth, any businessperson who seeks artificial aids from government is forsaking the true principles of conservatism, which are based on private initiative, not government handouts.

Labor—the real monopoly.   The truest monopolies in America are the great labor unions. They apply every kind of pressure available to them, including the force of law, to compel workers to join them. They control the labor force not just in individual firms but in whole industries. In fact, some unions, such as the Teamsters, reach across industrial lines and dominate wide segments of the economy.

Liberals complain that big businesses sometimes act in restraint of trade. But there is no restraint of trade that can compare with a strike. In the hands of the Teamsters (many of whose locals are riddled with corruption and are in collusion with organized crime), the power to strike can paralyze whole sectors of the economy. As manipulated by local unions, the strike weapon can bring entire cities to a standstill. This is monopoly power that no business concern can match. Yet labor is not covered by the antitrust laws, which are directed only at business corporations.

Organized labor's economic power has not even done very much for the workers. The unions have increased the wages of a minority of the total work force while reducing employment opportunities for unorganized workers by pushing wages up to the point at which employers turn to machines rather than people. Strikes demonstrate the power of the union leaders; but even where they are "successful," strikes may cost the workers more in lost earnings than they gain by the eventual settlements.

The dominance of government.   The single, most important source of economic power in America today, however, is government. This is true not only because it interferes massively with the natural flow of market forces through taxation, budget deficits, and a never-ending barrage of rules and regulations. It also directly employs a substantial section of the work force. From the conservatives' viewpoint, business economic power is now greatly outweighed by government economic power. (We shall explore this claim further in Chapter 8.)

Pressure politics.   As they look at the tactics used by groups to achieve their political purposes, conservatives insist that every one of the devices used by business is also used by groups hostile to business. And as conservatives read the record, the opposition has been more effective than business. *Labor* is an extraordinarily potent lobbying force. It uses its political funds to contribute heavily to campaigns. In the 1974 and 1976 congressional elections, for example, labor contributed more than $14 million mostly to Democratic, prounion candidates. Unions also provide the manpower needed to get out the vote for their favored candidates.

The AFL–CIO maintains a staff of full-time lobbyists in Washington (there were seven of them in 1976) who are skillful in the arts of backroom lobbying. They have close relationships with the key congressional committees and subcommittees that deal with legislation of concern to labor. Thus the labor subcommittee of the House Committee on Education and Labor is chaired by a longtime friend of the unions, Frank Thompson, a Democrat from New Jersey. In the Senate the Labor and Public Welfare Committee has been generally supportive of labor causes; and what particularly annoys business groups is that the two senior Republicans on the committee, Javits of New York and Schweiker of Pennsylvania, have repeatedly sided with the Democrats in favoring labor. Furthermore, when it comes to providing Congress with specialized information, the AFL–CIO is very well equipped. Its lobbying team is backed by research groups in economics, social security, education, and so on, capable of producing fact sheets and position papers almost at a moment's notice.

As for the use of grass-roots pressures, no group is better situated than labor for letting the lawmakers in Washington hear from the folks back home. It is not at all difficult for the heads of union locals to get their memberships to deluge Congress with letters and telegrams. And when the national lobby wants to reach a senator, they often arrange for him to be visited by the head of the AFL–CIO from his own state.

The legislative product of all this is regarded with dismay by conservatives. They believe that the vast array of liberally oriented legislation has resulted largely from labor's lobbying. They point to the fact that labor remains exempt from antitrust laws, despite the big unions' obvious status as a monopoly.

Nor are conservatives impressed with the argument that labor's failure to repeal the "right-to-work laws" of Section 14(b) of the Taft–Hartley Act is proof of its political weakness. After all, that clause does no more than allow states to sanction a nonunion shop. Business groups, working through the National Right-to-Work Committee, would like to see a federal law permitting the nonunion shop, so that unions will everywhere be deprived of the power to force workers to join unions against their will. But, under pressure from the labor lobby, inclusive right-to-work bills have never been given a hearing by Congress. The regulatory agencies of *the federal government* are also highly effective manipulators of the arts of lobbying. They provide much of the expertise needed by congressional committees. And they know how to encourage pressure on Congress from the constituencies who benefit from federal government subsidies.

Then there is the *education* lobby. At every level of education there are groups demanding more and more federal money. For elementary and high schools there are the National Education Association (1.5 million members) and the American Federation of Teachers (400,000 members); organizations of school administrators and boards of education; and the National Congress of Parents and Teachers (over 8 million members). Then there is higher education, with organizations speaking for professors, students, and administrators; public and private universities; four-year colleges and junior colleges; graduate schools; continuing education, vocational education, libraries, and educational broadcasters. *All* of them want federal money. All of them work hand in glove with the Office of Education in the federal government's Department of Health, Education and Welfare.

They lobby. Since they are knowledge producers, they are prime and prestigious sources of the information that government agencies and legislatures need; some of them put money into political campaigns; and with their millions of members they far outdistance General Motors, Standard Oil, and all the other "devils" in the liberals' cast of evil characters when it comes to constituency power. With this in mind, it is hardly surprising that federal outlays for education at all levels have reached such massive proportions.

Along with the professional educators, social workers, and others whose salaries and power grow as federal programs expand, a great many "*do-gooders*"—self-appointed protectors of the public welfare—join the pressure for more government spending. These include the social action committees of churches, women's organizations such as the League of Women Voters and the American Association of University Women; and others claiming to represent minority groups, senior citizens, consumers, and the environment.

Many of these groups are extraordinarily adept at applying the arts of pressure politics on government. Notably successful have been Common Cause—rated by many legislators as the most effective of Washington lobbies today—and the several "Public Interest Centers" identified with Ralph Nader. These groups have made a close study of the vulnerable points in the system. They organize mass mailing campaigns to create the illusion of widespread support for their programs. They know how to use television and other mass communications media to inflame public opinion against business.

So in contrast with the liberals' picture of a system that produces results overwhelmingly favorable to business, the conservatives' view is that the pressures from labor, government, education, and "do-good" groups have repeatedly damaged the interests of business. In the face of huge federal budget deficits, more and more governmental controls, and constantly rising minimum wage laws, how can it be argued that in the group struggle business overwhelms its opposition? Throughout this book there are examples of what conservatives see as the superior lobbying power of antibusiness organizations. In Chapter 4, for example, we saw how Common Cause prevailed over business in passing the election finance law. In later chapters we shall see how business people are harassed and frustrated, according to conservative observers, by a multiplying profusion of impractical laws forced through by the pressure politics of consumer and environmental groups.

Business and the public interest.   Whereas liberals believe that election finance, minimum wage, consumer protection, and other such laws represent the public interest, conservatives reject this assertion on two grounds. First, who are these groups that claim to speak for the public? Labor bosses claim to speak for their memberships when they issue platforms and manifestos and candidate endorsements. But opinion polls and election results show that the rank and file frequently think differently from their official spokesmen. The church groups that claim to articulate the political concerns of tens of millions of church members actually consist of small, unrepresentative social action committees. Organizations of women voters often take positions contrary to the way women actually vote. Common Cause is made up of a few hundred thousand affluent people—hardly a cross section of America. As for Ralph Nader, despite his popularity nobody has elected him to speak for the American people. His organizations are dominated by Nader's own, driven personality; and their staffs consist mostly of young people, students and recent graduates, who constitute an elite far different in their tastes and beliefs from the great majority of the American public.

Second, conservatives protest the claim of these various groups that only what they stand for can be defined as the "public good." In calling his organizations "Public Interest Centers," Nader is making an arrogant assertion. What these liberals are doing is identifying the public interest exclusively with liberalism and the attack on business. In fact, business can make a much better claim to represent the public interest than all the groups that have tried to copyright the idea with such titles as Common Cause, Public Citizen, and so on.

Conservatives agree with liberals that, to a considerable extent, the public interest is the interest of the consumer. But it is precisely in this respect that conservatives believe that business has been most effective. As they see it, Nader and others are attacking the system at its strongest point—its treatment of the consumer.

This is not to suggest that consumers are always supremely satisfied with their purchases. But instead of focusing on the individual complaints that we all have from time to time, we should consider how consumers are treated in most other countries in the world. That comparison produces an assessment of the American business system as a brilliant success story. It has poured out an incredible abundance and variety of goods of generally high quality. Nowhere, in other words, are the interests of the people at large better served.

Hence the conservatives argue that the proposals of the liberals and the radical left are the very opposite of what is needed. We should move in the direction of getting government out of business. We should even avoid pious pleas to business to fulfill its "social responsibility." In a free economy "there is one and only one social responsibility of business—to use its resources and engage in activities designed to increase its profit so long as it stays within the rules of the game, which is to say, engages in open and free competition, without deception or fraud."[4]

The framework of law must be there, of course. The honest businessperson, as well as the public at large, must be protected against crooked practices. But other restraints, imposed or self-imposed, are undesirable. The best thing we can all do is pursue our own interests rather than pretend to be looking out for the good of others. Selfish though this may seem, the result will be for the benefit of all—so long as we are operating in a genuinely competitive economy. For that kind of economy has a built-in genius first described by the father of the discipline of economics, Adam Smith. As Smith studied the play of competition in a free market, he concluded that a competitive market, though apparently chaotic, in fact was governed by a kind of natural law. Without benefit of government control, it was as though "an invisible hand" produced the good of the society as a whole out of the competing interests of individuals.

To conservatives, in other words, the public interest is served not by accepting the presumptuous claims of self-anointed leaders, but through the full, though fair, pursuit of private gain and by the competition between private economic interests.

The Radical Right:
Groups versus America

With the radical right we come to a still harsher indictment of those aspects of the system of interest groups criticized by the conservatives. Government intervention in the economy is equated with socialism, which is akin to communism. The growth of government has been brought about by pressures by labor unions, and by organizations claiming to speak for minority races, churches, and the public interest—all of them, wittingly or unwittingly, serving the cause of the left-wing conspiracy.

Certain organizations still win the praise of the radical right for trying to preserve whatever is left of the American system. A number of patriotic groups—the American Legion, the Daughters of the American Revolution, and others—are heard from in the halls of Congress, though rarely do they have access to the White House. And some business groups, fortunately, persist in opposing the spread of the welfare state and the takeover of the economy by government.

Like all groups that attack pressure politics as subversive of the common good, radical right organizations also use lobbying tactics when it serves their purposes. Thus they pressure Congress to abolish the income tax and to reduce and eventually do away with the national debt. And various right-wing groups, including the John Birch Society, participate in the antigun control movement. They are active, for example, in a coalition called the Gun Owners of America, which set up a campaign committee in 1976 to collect funds for candidates opposed to gun control legislation.

In a field such as gun control the radical right has been able to feel that it has contributed effectively to saving America from subversive proposals. In general, however, the right wing believes that the system of pressure politics is dominated by groups aiming at the destruction of the American system, and that it is fighting a desperate, rearguard action against overwhelming forces.

The Centrists:
Pluralism and the Group Balance

To the centrists the group process is a key element in their explanation and defense of the American system. They see the existence of a large number of private groups as an essential guarantee of a free and open society. By fighting for their respective causes, groups contribute a great diversity of ideas, values, and interests, thus ensuring the availability of choices on which our democratic system thrives.

They reject the criticisms we have discussed from the other positions on the spectrum, making the following counterarguments.

Pressure politics.   In the public mind terms such as *lobbying* and *pressure tactics* have assumed covert, even sinister overtones. Two points need to be made to correct the most common misconceptions. First, there is very little that is mysterious about lobbying. Anyone who takes the trouble to follow what is going on can discover which groups are applying pressure on which side of an issue. Of course, the precise details of each stage of discussion are not necessarily known immediately to the public. But group politics is very largely a process of quiet bargaining between competing organizations and public officials. It is impossible to conduct delicate negotiations in the full glare of publicity. In any case, few secrets are kept for very long in Washington. There are too many suspicious (and publicity-seeking) opposition groups, members of Congress, and investigative journalists to allow very much to remain off the record indefinitely.

Undoubtedly, there are still abuses. Some tightening of the lobbying disclosure laws might be desirable. Yet there are limits to how far regulation can be pushed without interfering with the First Amendment guarantee of free speech and the right of the people "to petition the Government for a redress of grievances." Moreover, on this issue of regulating lobbying, the more extreme proposals of Common Cause have isolated it from other citizen action groups and labor. For example, Ralph Nader does not want to see the effectiveness of his organizations reduced by the kind of detailed registration requirements that would cost them an enormous outlay of time and money in filling out forms. Similarly, the AFL–CIO complains that the legislation backed by Common Cause would be impossibly burdensome. On one day in 1975, for example, one AFL–CIO lobbyist logged 17 contacts on Capitol Hill, 8 with outside groups, and 4 with union groups, each of which would have to be duly recorded if Common Cause had its way. It is one thing, say the centrists, to require openness and honesty in government. It is quite another to destroy constitutional rights by attaching to them intolerable quantities of bureaucratic paperwork.

Second, the power of private lobbyists is vastly exaggerated in the liberal ideology and the popular imagination. Political scientist Lester Milbrath, who conducted extensive interviews with members of Congress, their staffs, and lobbyists, came to this conclusion: "The weight of the evidence that this study brings to bear suggests that there is relatively little influence or power in lobbying *per se.*"[5] Congressmen, according to Milbrath, make up their minds on the basis of many different factors. Lobbying is but one of these—and far and away the most potent lobbyist is the president himself. Then, legislators are very much concerned with the climate of opinion in their districts and in the country as a whole. They are also affected by what their staffs and other members of Congress think of them.

And, naturally, legislators have their own beliefs. If Frank Thompson of the House Committee on Education and Labor generally sides with labor, this is not because he is lobbied by labor and gets campaign contributions from them. "It happens that I'm philosophically in agreement with labor," he says. And when he is not, he votes the other way.

The group balance.   Critics left of center declare that business and conservative groups dominate. Right of center the diagnosis is that labor and liberal groups are the most potent pressures. Nothing could provide clearer evidence to the centrists that there is a rough-and-ready balance of power between the competing forces. In fact, centrists find it more useful to talk about specific issues than about the group system as a whole. And on specific issues sometimes business groups win, sometimes the antibusiness forces prevail, and sometimes the contending parties have to settle for a compromise—more evidence that pluralism is at work.

Indeed, compromise is by far the most common outcome. To prove this, centrists point to the very cases that liberals and conservatives use to make their respective arguments. The public housing struggle, for example, did not end in a clear-cut victory for the private housing industry. Arrayed against the realtors, home builders, and mortgage lenders were labor groups, church and civic organizations, public housing offficials, and federal government agencies. They lobbied hard, as did the opposition to the program. The opponents did succeed in slowing the progress of the program considerably; but eventually the program reached its original target. Moreover, the delays resulted in considerable improvements in the structure of the program.

Although the ITT case did include some behind-the-scenes pressures that centrists might criticize, the result was not as one-sided as the liberals suggest. In order to keep Hartford, ITT had to get rid of several major, profitable companies. Future plans for taking over other major companies would be inhibited, for these required approval by the Justice Department. Doubts about the invincibility of ITT as a political force are also raised by the fact that ITT had previously been thwarted in a merger attempt. Back in 1965 ITT had proposed a merger with ABC Television. The Federal Trade Commission gave its approval. Had this merger gone through, the combined power of the new enterprise might have been awesome indeed. But the Justice Department intervened and took the matter to court. The case dragged on; the shares of ABC fell; exasperated, ITT's president called the merger off.

Similarly, the controversy over the union shop shows that the rival estimates of labor's political influence are both wrong. The right-to-work struggle does not demonstrate either the conservatives' allegations of labor's control of Congress or the liberals' argument that on questions concerning its most vital interests the unions are weak. Labor has proved itself sufficiently powerful to prevent any damaging federal laws dealing with union affairs since the 1947 Taft–Hartley Act and the 1959 Landrum–Griffin Act. On the other hand, they have not been able to change their major provisions despite repeated efforts to get Congress to repeal Section 14(b) of Taft–Hartley, which permits states to outlaw the union shop. The result is a reasonable compromise.

The restraints on the power of any one group to dominate the system include not only the power of opposition groups, but also the disunity within each of the groups themselves.

Not one of these groups is a united political force. In the case of business, the oil companies' proposals that government approve increases in the price of oil are not received enthusiastically by the automobile manufacturers in Detroit. And when Lockheed turned to the federal government for a loan to prevent its going into bankruptcy, some business leaders protested the idea. Labor is also a much divided force. Within the AFL–CIO there are 110 unions with widely diverging interests and spread across the political spectrum, ranging from the increasingly militant teachers and government workers on the left to the more conservative craftsmen's unions that represent the building trades. The "education lobby," too, is a combination of groups with often sharp internal disagreements. Public school organizations generally resist the request of Catholic schools for federal aid. Public universities oppose the diversion of government funds to students of private universities. Teachers and administrators do not always see eye to eye. And the position of student organizations may differ from both of these.

Therefore, once we look beneath the surface of these vague categories called business, labor, education, and so on, we discover that we must discard the myth of single-minded, monolithic group forces in America. And if groups cannot hold themselves together, they are not likely to be in a position to exercise complete sway over the entire system.

Defining the public interest.   No single group can define for everyone what the public interest is. All groups claim to be acting for the common good. Thus drug companies defend the very large gap between their production costs and their price lists as being necessary to supply the research funds from which new, life-saving drugs can be generated. The National Rifle Association claims to be concerned not only with the rights of sportsmen but also with the defense of individual liberties and the implementation of the constitutional right to bear arms. The automobile industry contends that its profits are necessary not only to its shareholders but also to the health of the nation's economy. Business groups in general rest their case not on their right to make money but rather on the merits of the free enterprise system, which guarantees not only our prosperity but also our essential liberties. Labor unions speak not merely of wages and fringe benefits but of the need to stimulate the economy and to protect human rights.

The only resolution of this dilemma is to define the public interest as the result of group pressures. "What may be called public policy," says Earl Latham, "is actually the equilibrium reached in the group struggle at any given moment. . . ."[6] The same definition can serve for the public interest, which emerges out of the process of negotiation and mutual accommodation between groups that is characteristic of democracy.

In suggesting this, the centrists are not taking quite the same position as the conservatives. They do not contend that government should play only a minimal role. Government has a major contribution to make in determining the public interest. But government has to be seen not as a source of ultimate and impartial wisdom, above the petty clamor of group pressures, but rather as a large number of institutions that are themselves very much a part of the group struggle, striving to inject their ideas along with the private groups.

Moreover, while centrists tend to be irritated with people such as Ralph Nader as being inaccurate and unnecessarily abrasive in tone and tactics, they incorporate such rebels into their analysis. By drawing attention to overlooked and underrepresented interests, the "muckrakers" help establish a new equilibrium and a revised definition of the public interest.

So the centrists defend the group process against its critics and argue that it provides a vital supplement to the constitutional checks and balances by establishing an informal balance between a great number of power centers. It ensures, in other words, a pluralistic arrangement of power.

Groups represent the people.   The other perspectives overlook another great virtue of our system of interest groups. It provides an important means of representing the people. Public officials are elected to represent people geographically, where they live. But people are not only residents. They are workers, businesspeople, farmers, consumers, artlovers, collectors, believers in causes, and so on. And the organized groups to which so many of them belong speak for them so that these other aspects of their lives can be properly considered when public policy is made.

No doubt the representation is not perfect. Organizations, as the left complain, are run by the few. But this is not peculiar to American culture. The sociologist Robert Michels, after studying European socialist parties in the early part of this century, concluded that an "iron law of oligarchy" operated, placing power in the hands of small minorities. But, as we noted in earlier chapters, centrists do not think that this is necessarily harmful. And to the extent that it may be undesirable, we live, after all, in an imperfect world. There is no such thing as perfect representativeness. There is no such thing, either, as a perfect group balance. But the system that we have serves our purposes reasonably well; for, in contradiction to the allegations of the critics, no group or combination of groups dominates the rest, lobbying tactics are mostly legitimate and are used effectively by all groups, and the prevailing balance produces a reasonable definition of the public interest.

Conclusion

We have reviewed in this chapter the range of interest groups in America, the purposes they serve, and the methods they use to influence political decisions. We have also examined five rival interpretations of how well the interest group system is working, and the extent to which it represents a balance between contending forces.

Throughout this discussion the question has recurred: What is the public interest? We cannot hope to resolve it completely here. It has been a perennial subject of debate among political and legal philosophers. Does the public interest emerge, as though by an "invisible hand," from everyone's pursuing his personal interest? Or is it simply the point at which the interests of competing groups intersect at a given moment? Or is there a public interest over and above the sum of private interests?

To liberals it is impossible to shape the common good by sanctifying an ethic of dog-eat-dog. There has to be a public interest that transcends all the separate interests. We should not accept the doctrine associated with Charles F. Wilson, president of General Motors before he became secretary of defense under Eisenhower, that "what is good for General Motors is good for the country." (What he actually said was: "What is good for the country is good for General Motors and vice versa." But liberals are inclined to think that this distortion by the press of what he said revealed what he really felt.)

There is, as Grant McConnell suggests, "a constituency of the entire nation." It may be that "at many points narrow, and even personal, interests should be preferred to general interests."[7] Just the same, there are such things as public values, and these can be expressed only by organizations speaking for very large constituencies—political parties, for example, rather than pressure groups. McConnell admits that we cannot finally prove this idea. He also suggests that we should not try to establish the concept of an absolute common good that will apply to all societies for all time. Still, he argues that we cannot plan public policy rationally unless we have in mind what will best serve the entire national constituency.

Centrists are skeptical of this view. How are we to judge between the rival claims when *every* group says that it is acting in the national interest? The only safe thing to do is to define the public interest as a constantly changing notion that comes out of the interplay of the group process. Any other approach is not only misleading but dangerous. Centrists remind us that the idea of a common good higher than that of the individuals and groups who make up the society is a mystical notion that provides totalitarian governments with a convenient rationale; in the twentieth century a succession of dictators have claimed that they, and they alone, spoke for an abstract common good.

In American political practice it might seem that the centrists would have the best of this argument. Most American politicians fit into the centrist category, and few of them are attracted by abstractions and totalitarian concepts. And yet practical politics is not conducted entirely without reference to the idea of a public interest. Even the most constituency-minded congressman will at least occasionally respond to appeals to the broad national interest. The most intensely dedicated organization leaders will, from time to time, put their group loyalty second to their concept of themselves as citizens of the nation.

There are two facets that go into the popular notion of the public interest. The first is that of numbers—of the larger constituency against the smaller. The second is that of time—concern with the future as against present gratification. Gradually, topic by topic, consensus develops on what constitutes the public good. Thus dangerous goods and drugs should be kept off the market; debate may continue over the birth control pill but not over thalidomide (a drug prescribed as a sedative for pregnant women, which resulted in many babies' being born with terrible deformations). Children should not be allowed to work in the mines. Cornices should not extrude from buildings in new construction in earthquake country. The public interest on these matters has been settled and incorporated into law, even though, in each case, some private interests were hurt.

Today the effort to incorporate more areas into the public interest extends beyond questions of public health and safety to issues affecting the quality of life, particularly the protection of the consumer and the physical environment. As we shall see in later chapters, the issues in those fields become immensely complicated. And the formulation we have suggested here—large numbers against small, the future against the present—will not always offer a sufficient guide to legislators trying to make policies protecting the public interest. Moreover, the balance between the majority and the minority cannot be determined only in terms of numbers but also must allow for the intensity of people's feelings. So it is not surprising that scholars cannot agree on the meaning of the public interest,[8] and some have even recommended that a notion so vague had better be abandoned altogether.

Yet in the practice of politics it cannot be abandoned. So we shall come back to the dilemma of the public interest in later chapters to see how it is dealt with in various contexts.

Notes and References

1.   Congressional Quarterly, *Guide to Current American Government*, Spring 1976, p. 107.

2.   Milton Friedman, *Capitalism and Freedom* (Chicago: The University of Chicago Press, 1962), p. 12.

3.   Ibid., p. 125.

4.   Ibid., p. 133.

5.   Lester W. Milbrath, *The Washington Lobbyists* (Chicago: Rand McNally & Company, 1963), p. 354.

6.   "The Group Basis of Politics: Notes for a Theory," *The American Political Science Review*, Vol. 46, No. 2 (June 1952), p. 390.

7.   Grant McConnell, *Private Power and American Democracy* (New York: Alfred A. Knopf, Inc., 1966), pp. 367–68.

8.   See Carl J. Friedrich, ed., *The Public Interest* (New York: Atherton Press, 1962).

2 Part Two 2

The Institutions of Government

NOW WE TURN

from the forces that influence the decisions of government to the institutions where the decisions are formally made. These institutions operate within a constitutional framework of checks and balances, which is designed to separate, divide, and share power among the three branches of government. In large measure this part of the book discusses whether the constitutional balance of power still holds or whether events have created an imbalance.

Thus in Chapter 6 on the presidency we describe the enormous growth of the power vested in the White House; we examine the misuse of power represented by the Watergate scandal; and we ask whether a similar crisis could recur. In the discussion of Congress in Chapter 7 we review the national legislature's deterioration of status in relation to the presidency and the efforts that both houses have been making to improve their performance and recover their reputation. Chapter 8 on the federal bureaucracies covers a more recent concentration of power, which now amounts to virtually a fourth branch of government. We encounter the criticisms that have been heaped on the bureaucracies from all sides of the political spectrum and we debate their validity. In Chapter 9 we examine the powers and functions of the U.S. Supreme Court, exploring the tension between its judicial and its political roles. Finally, in Chapter 10 we shift the focus away from Washington to the states and the cities, assessing the federal principle of division of powers among the different levels of government—national, state, and local—and asking how much strength and vitality exists in the subnational units of government.

Throughout Part Two we come again and again to the debate among our five perspectives on the questions: *Is the system of checks and balances a good idea? Is it working today?*

The Presidency:

A New Despotism?

The controversies that swirl around American governmental institutions reach their greatest intensity over the presidency. For the White House is the center of the policy-making process. More decisions of massive weight must be resolved there than at any other location of political power.

So the issues of liberty and the distribution of power raised in Chapter 1 are brought into sharp focus by the nature of the modern presidency. The question comes from all sides: Is the power vested in the presidency becoming so great that it might override all restraints? Could we be heading for a new despotism?

The Scope of the Presidency

"The history of the Presidency," says one of the leading scholars of the institution, "has been a history of aggrandizement."[1] We can see how enormously the office has grown by looking first at the functions of the president and then at the machinery of the government that he directs.

The Functions of the President

The wording of the Constitution (see Appendix 1) seems to suggest a rather limited range of functions for the president. Article II makes the president the chief executive officer. As such he is designated commander in chief of the armed services. He has the authority to "require the Opinion in writing, of the Principal Officer in each of the executive Departments, upon any subject relating to the

Duties of their respective Offices." He has the power to pardon for offenses against the United States.

He has the power to make treaties, subject to the concurrency of two-thirds of the Senate; and to make appointments, subject to Senate approval, of ambassadors, Supreme Court justices, and heads of Cabinet departments. He is required to report to the Congress periodically on "the State of the Union," and to "recommend to their Consideration such measures as he shall judge necessary and expedient." He is furthermore instructed to "take Care that the Laws be faithfully executed."

There is not much more than this on the president's functions, as you can quickly see by reading the very brief Article II in Appendix 1. But there is very much more to be said after nearly two centuries of experience with the presidential office. Today the president has an extraordinary range of responsibilities.

To begin with, the president has symbolic functions. He is our chief of state, the ceremonial leader of America in his dealings with other countries. He embodies the mystique of the American system, and the continuity of the nation.

The young child's first perception of government is typically centered on the president.[2] And the horror that swept the nation after the assassination of John F. Kennedy was elicited not only by his personal popularity, but also by the fact that the president, the symbolic leader, had been killed. Even when Warren Harding, an inept leader who was surrounded by corruption, died in office, there was a deep and widespread sense of personal loss in the country.[3]

But the president is, of course, much more than the symbolic leader. He is the head of the government, the top policy maker.

As chief diplomat he is the principal shaper of foreign policy. The armed services and our entire machinery of diplomacy report to him as commander in chief. He is expected to preserve the security of the nation, maintain the peace, or, failing that, win the war. Since the atom bomb was dropped on Hiroshima in 1945, the president's role in foreign and defense policy has become a matter of life and death not merely for large numbers of individuals, but for whole nations, possibly the entire world. The president has many others to help him make his decisions; but only the president is followed everywhere he goes by a military aide carrying the coded instructions that could unleash a thermonuclear war.

In domestic affairs the president, more than anyone else, is expected to maintain harmony among socioeconomic groups and among races, protect the environment, and prevent a recurrence of the Great Depression of the 1930s. He must work for high economic growth and low unemployment while still keeping prices from rising too rapidly.

To carry out these responsibilities he exercises leadership in many directions. He influences public opinion by speaking to the people at large about his policies. He legislates. The Constitution talks only of his suggesting ideas to Congress; but not much major legislation gets through Congress unless the White House proposes it and works hard for its enactment. Then, as head of his political party, he is actively engaged in partisan politics.

Finally, he is chief executive, which means that he must direct a vast machinery of government to help him shape and carry out his legislative program, determine and control the federal budget, and administer his foreign policy.

The Machinery of the Executive Branch

As the responsibilities of the president have grown, so has the size of the federal government staff that works under him. As we shall see in Chapter 8 on the federal bureaucracy, there are currently over 2,800,000 federal employees, spread over a vast panoply of institutions. Among these are 12 Cabinet departments—State; Defense; Treasury; Justice; Commerce; Labor; Agriculture; Transportation; Interior; Housing and Urban Development; Health, Education and Welfare; and Energy—and the many administrative and regulatory agencies which will be discussed in detail in Chapter 8.

The vice-president.   The vice-president is the next highest ranking officer of the executive branch. He sits in the Cabinet and the National Security Council, is nominally the president of the Senate, and is given a variety of executive, political, and ceremonial assignments. Yet, despite the assurances of each incoming president that his vice-president will take on functions of vast importance, the promises have never been fulfilled. Presidents have not allowed their vice-presidents to build up the vice-presidency as a source of independent power. Consequently, the office has been a frustrating, often a humiliating experience, for most of its incumbents. Energetic men such as Hubert Humphrey and Nelson Rockefeller found that their extensive backgrounds in public service were hardly drawn upon once they were appointed to the second highest post in the land.

Perhaps all this will be changed by Jimmy Carter's insistence at the beginning of his administration that Walter Mondale would play a much more important role than any previous vice-president. However, until now there has been only one really important function for the vice-president—to understudy the president. The significance of this lies in the fact that out of the 35 men elected to the presidency, eight have died or been killed in office, and one has resigned. In this century Theodore Roosevelt, Calvin Coolidge, Harry Truman, Lyndon Johnson, and Gerald Ford came to the presidency following the death or resignation of a president. And both major party candidates in 1968 had been vice-president.

The Executive Office.   Far more crucial to the carrying out of the president's purposes are the people he appoints to the Executive Office of the President. This office includes several agencies, the number varying with the changing needs of each president. In the Nixon administration, for example, the number of Executive Office agencies went down from 16 to 10 and then up to 13. Among the most important of the Executive Office agencies have been:

The National Security Council, established by Congress in 1947 to help the president pull together the foreign policy planning of the Departments of State and Defense and the Central Intelligence Agency.

The Domestic Council, created by President Nixon in 1970 to act as the counterpart of the National Security Council in coordinating domestic policies.

The Office of Management and Budget, also established by President Nixon in 1970, rides herd on the sprawling bureaucracies of the federal government. The OMB absorbed the Bureau of the Budget, set up by Congress in 1921 to act as the president's instrument for shaping the federal budget out of the proposals of hundreds of agencies and for scrutinizing the performance of those agencies.

The Council of Economic Advisers, brought into being under the terms of the Employment Act of 1946, which declared as public policy the maintenance of a high level of employment and a flourishing and stable economy. The council consists of three people with substantial standing in the field of economics.

In recent years the Executive Office has also included councils and offices on environmental quality, energy, telecommunications policy, wage and price controls, international economic policy, and drug abuse.

The White House staff.   Closest of all to the president within the Executive Office is the White House staff. They provide informal channels of information and ideas, undertake political negotiations, carry out liaisons with Congress, help write the president's speeches, handle press relations, and monitor his appointments. Among these, the senior staff members (some of them with top Executive Office positions) have a great deal of authority. Such men as Theodore Sorenson during the Kennedy administration and Bill Moyers during the Johnson years were White House staff members whose advice was sought on a daily basis by the president.

In foreign policy the president's assistant for National Security Affairs has, in some cases, superseded the secretary of state as the president's chief adviser on foreign affairs. This was the case with McGeorge Bundy under both Kennedy and Johnson, and with Bundy's successor in the Johnson era, W. W. Rostow. In the same job Henry Kissinger was Nixon's top foreign affairs aide even before he became secretary of state; once appointed secretary of state he continued to hold the White House staff post until he reluctantly gave it up during the Ford presidency.

The power of the White House staff was especially great during Richard Nixon's presidency. John Ehrlichman and H. R. Haldeman were the two top "assistants to the president." Ehrlichman was responsible for supervising domestic affairs machinery, including several Cabinet departments. Haldeman was the White House chief of staff, in charge of the president's appointments list. He was present at most of the president's meetings, and responsible for following through on decisions reached at those meetings. The shock waves set off when Watergate toppled these two from power was a measure of the authority that they exercised.

This is not to suggest that the only people a president listens to are the members of his immediate White House staff. Some Cabinet members continue to exert great influence. This was certainly true of President Kennedy's brother, Attorney General Robert Kennedy; of Robert McNamara, secretary of defense under Kennedy and Johnson; of George Schultz, Nixon's secretary of the treasury; and of Secretary of State Kissinger even after he lost his White House staff position.

Still, the White House staff enjoys the advantage of being close to the president physically, and thereby of seeing him regularly. There is also a special kind of power that accrues to a presidential aide when he can telephone a senator or a corporation president and have the operator say, "White House calling!"

Constraints on Presidential Power

With such a vast expansion of their functions and staff resources, presidents, it would seem, must feel enormously powerful. However, many of them complain that their power does not match their responsibilities. On all sides they have the sense of being hedged in by constraints. Some of these are built into the Constitution. Others result from political and social realities.

The Congress and its traditional jealousy of the president is the first major constraint on presidential power. The two houses of the legislature have at their disposal an armory of devices which give them a good deal of independence from the president and a considerable capacity to thwart his policies. A second constraint built into the Constitution is the court system. An object lesson to presidents was the successful challenge to Harry Truman laid down by the courts in 1952. Confronted by a steel strike when fighting was still going on in Korea and the United States desperately needed steel products, Truman seized control of the industry. The workers, now government employees, went back to work. The companies took their case to court, the Supreme Court upheld a district court verdict in their favor, and the president had to give up his hold on the industry. For seven weeks the strike continued. The president's judgment that the national security was threatened had been set aside by the Supreme Court. Third, the doctrine of federalism, or the constitutional division of powers between the federal government and the states, reserves some powers to the states that are thereby not available to the president.

National elections are another political reality that sets limits on presidential power. The president knows that every four years his policies must be submitted to the electorate for their approval. This constraint has been weakened by the Twenty-second Amendment to the Constitution, ratified in 1951, which prevents a president's running for more than two terms of office. Even so, presidents want to have their own party win the next election, perhaps with their personal choice of nominee. Otherwise they must face the knowledge that they have been repudiated by the people.

Between elections, too, presidents nervously watch their ratings in the public opinion polls. The wide fluctuations experienced by all presidents are revealed by the following readings by Gallup surveys on the percentages of people who felt that the president was doing a good job:

President	High	Low	Average
Roosevelt	84	54	68
Truman	87	23	46
Eisenhower	79	49	66
Kennedy	83	57	70
Johnson	80	39	54
Nixon	68	24	48
Ford	71	37	46

Generally speaking, presidents have hit their high points at the beginning of their administrations. But they have seen their popularity, and their influence, plummet after severe setbacks to their policies. Thus Truman hit his low point in the polls because of Korea. For Johnson the damage was done by Vietnam; for Nixon, Watergate; for Ford, his pardoning of Nixon.

Next, there are the political parties. Although the president is leader of his party, American political parties are loose and undisciplined bodies, and not very reliable instruments of the president's will. Members of his own party in Congress often refuse to go along with his legislative program. And his problems are compounded when Congress is in the hands of the opposition party, as happened for all or part of the terms of Truman, Eisenhower, Nixon, and Ford. Then, too, the Cabinet, though selected by the president to carry out his programs, can also include people of independent will who may not see things the president's way and thus limit his power. This is even more true of some members of the permanent bureaucracies of the departments and agencies of the federal government. Harry Truman made the point when Eisenhower, a long-time general, was about to take over the presidency: "He'll sit here, and he'll say, 'Do this! Do that!' *And nothing will happen.*"

Even when nobody is trying to thwart the president, his power may be limited by faulty information or incompetent execution. A prime example is the Bay of Pigs fiasco of 1961. On orders from the Eisenhower administration the CIA had trained some exiles from Fidel Castro's Cuba for a small-scale invasion of the country, intended to set off a revolt of the masses of the Cuban people. Soon after Kennedy became president, he gave the go-ahead for the invasion. But the plan failed ignominiously. The invaders were met by withering fire from a much larger force of Castro's troops. Furthermore, there was no indication of widespread support for a general uprising against Castro. Clearly, it is not enough for a president to decide that he wants something done. If he does not have accurate information or fails to carry out his plans effectively and thoroughly, his show of strength will be revealed as hollow.

A further limitation on presidential power is that all of America's money, technology, prestige, and military force do not necessarily prevail in other parts of the world. The closest of allies, even those dependent on our support for their survival, can prove to be infuriatingly balky. No president can harbor any longer what the British scholar D. W. Brogan called "the illusion of American omnipotence."

Finally, both at home and abroad, great social forces are in motion, and science and technology unleash sweeping transformations of our world—all with hardly a bow to the power of the presidency. So, if people outside the White House view the presidency as a center of awesome power, presidents tend to see themselves as surrounded by a myriad of constraints on their freedom of action.

Presidents and
Their Approaches to Power

The extent to which presidential power has expanded has varied with the incumbents. The administrations of Grant, Tyler, Taylor, Fillmore, Pierce, Buchanan, Harding, and Coolidge were hardly imaginative, nor were they associated with great accomplishments or the restless accumulation of power. In some cases these men were simply out of their depth or content to accept the constraints of the presidency as proper to the role assigned by the Founding Fathers. As President William Howard Taft saw it, the Constitution does not give the president many functions, and the president would be exceeding his authority if he tried to exercise powers that were not clearly indicated by the words of the Constitution or by appropriate statutes passed by Congress.

But there were other men who took a much broader view of their responsibilities. The presidents after Washington whom children hear about from grade school onward—Jefferson, Jackson, and Lincoln—were leaders whose actions could not be explained by a strict construction of the language of the Constitution. Early in the twentieth century Theodore Roosevelt provided a rationale for their vigorous conduct of the office. The Constitution, in his view, was deliberately written in general terms to provide the flexibility needed for growth of the office. Thus Section III of Article II instructed the president to take "such measures as he shall deem necessary and appropriate," and to "take care that the Laws be faithfully executed." This gives the president plenty of scope; and it was the president's duty, said Roosevelt, "to do anything that the needs of the Nation demanded unless such action was forbidden by the Constitution or by the laws." If he did not act in this way, he would find himself overwhelmed by the countless potential limits on presidential power and thus would fail to carry out his constitutional responsibilities.

In the debate over the powers of the modern presidency, Theodore Roosevelt's interpretation has prevailed. Franklin Roosevelt, Truman, Kennedy, Johnson, and Nixon, each in his own way, saw the need to reach out for power and overcome the constraints in order to respond to the needs of their time. However, the growth of the office has not been steady. With the election of Eisenhower after Truman, and the succession of Ford after Nixon, the nation turned to leaders who slowed down the pace of presidential action. The world had changed too much for Eisenhower and Ford to go back to Taft's doctrine of the limited presidency. But each represented at least a pause, a modest shift away from Theodore Roosevelt's concept of the aggressive presidency. So, as we turn to a brief analysis of presidencies since the 1930s, we see two great periods of *expanding power,* each followed by a shorter interval of *consolidation.*

The Presidency Expands

Franklin Roosevelt, 1933–1945.   We date the history of the modern presidency from the administrations of Franklin Roosevelt not simply because he had an expansive view of his responsibilities. In this century Woodrow Wilson as well as Theodore Roosevelt took an energetic view of their responsibilities and fought to provide strong leadership in domestic and foreign affairs. But during the successive administrations of Franklin Roosevelt the scope of the federal government and the power of the presidency itself took a leap in magnitude that could never be fully retraced.

What made this enormous change possible was a crisis more serious than any that had afflicted the country since the Civil War—the collapse of the economy known as the Great Depression. Roosevelt was elected to do what his predecessor Herbert Hoover had not been able to accomplish, to rescue the drowning economy. He had no program to do this at the outset, so he and his associates improvised a series of bold and unprecedented programs known as the New Deal. Industry, banking, and agriculture were brought under federal regulation and given subsidies. New rules were established for the operation of the stock market. The right of labor unions to organize was protected. Large numbers of jobs were created by special government projects. Money and services were provided to the poor. As a result, to administer all these services, government agencies proliferated in all directions. To pay for the programs, the federal government spent far more than it took in, and large budget deficits were incurred.

Of course, so many changes could not be brought about without opposition. To overcome this, Roosevelt could not simply issue commands. Although he had many powers granted him by laws that he had initiated as well as those stemming from the Constitution itself, these could not prevail unless he made effective use of the most important power of the presidency—what Richard Neustadt has called "the power to persuade."[4] And Roosevelt was a superb persuader. He had an air of authority tempered by enormous charm. He was a master of the arts of maneuvering and bargaining. He could be understanding and compassionate, but he could also be ruthless. And his ability to persuade in face-to-face discussion was more than matched by his talent for mass persuasion. Using public speeches, informal press conferences, and, most effective of all, "fireside chats" over the radio, he was able to project his ideas and his personality with charismatic impact on the public at large.

He was not always successful. For example, he ran into difficulties with the Supreme Court, as we shall see in Chapter 9 in our discussion of the court system. Some of his early programs for industry and agriculture were administrative monstrosities and had to be abandoned or completely overhauled. Others continued to be riddled with defects. He never really solved the unemployment problem until the time came to prepare for World War II. Still, the New Deal brought the federal government deeply and irreversibly into the economy.

Then America's entry into World War II in 1941 brought the centralized planning that accompanies all major wars and vested even greater power in the national government. That war placed Roosevelt in the one presidential role he had not fully played until then—commander in chief of the armed services. For almost 13 years, through more than three terms in the White House, the people came to identify the institution of the presidency with the ideas, character, and personality of Franklin Roosevelt. Through his political and legislative skills and through his expert use of the media, Roosevelt projected the presidency into the consciousness of the nation with an impact that was to have a lasting effect on the nature of the institution.

Harry Truman, 1945–1953.   Truman came to the presidency on the death of Roosevelt less than a year after Roosevelt's reelection for a fourth term. He could not hope to match the charismatic leadership style of his predecessor, and at first he was somewhat overawed by his enormous responsibilities. Nonetheless, he quickly concluded that some major decisions had to be made; that only the president could make them; and that "the buck stops here," in the Oval Office of the White House. So he did not shrink from the need to exercise power and developed a brisk self-confidence in making big decisions without much agonizing.

Thus he gave the order to drop the atomic bombs on Hiroshima and Nagasaki to force a quick end to the war against Japan—a decision that changed the character of foreign policy as profoundly as the New Deal had changed domestic policy. He played a major role in shaping the Marshall Plan, a program of billions of dollars in aid to help rebuild war-shattered Western Europe. Although the constitutional authority to declare war is vested in Congress, Truman led the nation into a war in Korea, getting congressional approval *after* he had acted. In the course of that war he fired (after a good deal of vacillation) a magnetically popular military leader, General Douglas MacArthur. In the domestic field he worked hard for his "Fair Deal," a series of programs in housing, health, education, and so on, which were intended to be the next wave of social reform after the New Deal.

Unfortunately for Truman the electorate was growing tired of so many years of activism by government at home and abroad. Although Truman managed to win reelection in 1948 against apparently overwhelming odds, he won acceptance for only a few of his Fair Deal proposals. And as the Korean war dragged on and on, with no victory in sight and tens of thousands of American troops killed, Truman's popularity dropped to incredibly low levels. He had lost his ability to lead. The potency of the presidency was gone.

Consolidation

Dwight Eisenhower, 1953–1961.   The election of Eisenhower reflected the end of an era of social change and wars. The mood of the people seemed to favor a pause, a time for consolidation, a reluctance to respond to challenges from vigorous presidential leadership.

Eisenhower fitted the mood of the time perfectly. Although he had none of the eloquence and the vivid, almost theatrical style of a Franklin Roosevelt, vast numbers of people found his sincerity, warmth, and geniality immensely appealing, and few presidents have matched his personal popularity. Yet he did not use this to muster support for bold new programs. A moderate conservative, he believed in slowing the pace of change.

His style of leadership reflected this approach. He delegated much more responsibility than had Roosevelt or Truman. He vested extensive authority in Sherman Adams, the assistant to the president, who acted as a kind of chief of staff, organizing the material sent to the president so that it reached him in the briefest possible form and with the smallest range of alternatives for his final choice. Eisenhower liked to stay within channels, relied heavily on the advice of the Cabinet and the National Security Council, and established greater formality in their procedures.

This is not to say that nothing much happened under Eisenhower, or that he left all the decisions to others. He contributed to the expansion of the federal highway and Social Security programs. Despite delays and obvious reluctance he finally made the decision to send National Guard troops to Little Rock, Arkansas, to enforce the Supreme Court's decisions on school desegregation. In foreign affairs, though he leaned very heavily on the advice of his secretary of state, John Foster Dulles, he played a major role personally in ending the Korean war. He also made the crucial decision not to give military support to the French during their last stand in Indochina despite the urgings of the majority of his advisers. And after Dulles's death he tried to soften the bitterly anti-Soviet tone of U.S. foreign policy by bringing Soviet premier Nikita Khrushchev to this country for a visit.

Clearly, he was not a Grant or a Harding or a Coolidge. After the New Deal and the emergence of the United States as the greatest military power ever, no president could again be guided by William Howard Taft's view of the presidency. Just the same, Eisenhower did no more in the presidency than he felt was absolutely necessary.

The Imperial Presidency

By the end of Eisenhower's second term in office there was a widespread sense that we had consolidated long enough. The economy was in the doldrums, unemployment was high, and the Soviet Union dealt a blow to U.S. prestige and self-respect when it beat us at our own technological game by being the first to put a satellite ("Sputnik") into orbit around the earth.

John Kennedy, 1961–1963.   John Kennedy built his 1960 presidential campaign around this sense of restlessness in the country. The nation, he argued, had lost its momentum. It was time to get things moving again across "The New Frontier." We needed a president who would challenge events, not merely respond to them, and who would provide bold, imaginative leadership. The narrowness of his election victory limited his ability to produce on his promises, but he set about the task of revitalizing national policies at home and abroad with immense enthusiasm.

He presented new legislative programs in such fields as education, health care, housing, and space exploration. When Congress did not act fast enough on his proposals, the president used televised press conferences to build up support for his positions. When the U.S. Steel Company raised its prices after Kennedy had negotiated with industry and labor to keep the prices down, he forced the company to cancel the increase by using all the persuasive powers of his office. In foreign affairs his feeble performance at the Bay of Pigs was followed by a strong and effective handling of the Cuban missile crisis. As we shall see in Chapter 14, he also checked Soviet efforts to undermine the Western position in Europe, particularly in relation to Berlin. At the same time dramatic efforts were made to reduce the tensions between the Soviet Union and the United States, including the signing of a treaty between the two nations to ban the testing of nuclear weapons in the atmosphere.

Kennedy's perception of the purposes of the presidency was reflected in the way he organized the office. He was much less inclined to delegate authority than Eisenhower. He did not wait for issues to work their way through various departments, reaching his desk only in their last, refined stages. He wanted to know not merely the eventual alternatives, but the information and reasoning that went into shaping these alternatives. To get at this he did not care much about the proper channels, but would get in touch directly with anyone who might shed some light on an issue, even though this might be a middle-level member of an agency. He was impatient with the Cabinet and the other institutions that comprise the formal machinery of government, and created whatever institutions he needed, sometimes on an ad hoc basis. Thus for the life-and-death decisions made during the Cuban missile crisis he pulled together a crisis team, journalistically dubbed the "Excomm," since it acted as an executive committee of the National Security Council. His brother Robert and his chief White House assistant, Theodore Sorenson, were his closest confidants, but neither was given a chief of staff role.

Kennedy's administrative style did not always work as well as it did in the

Cuban missile crisis. Sometimes it created uncertainties and confusion. Still, Kennedy's methods reflected his personality, his view that the governmental machinery ought to be forced out of its tendency to inertia, and his expansive view of the responsibilities vested in the presidency. And Kennedy did succeed in capturing the public imagination. People were captivated by his vitality, his wit, his lucidity, and his mastery of information. His wife Jacqueline was on the cover of women's magazines week after week. The Kennedy children became public favorites. The large Kennedy clan and their friends became the center of a revitalized Washington and New York social life. The media spoke of a new "Camelot," conveying a promise of an exciting, more colorful, more fulfilled life for America. And the source of this promise was the energy generated by the White House.

When the president was struck down by an assassin's bullet in Dallas on November 22, 1963, the sense of loss in the nation seemed irreparable.

Lyndon Johnson, 1963–1969.   There was no way that Lyndon Johnson, whose television style tended to lack force and conviction and who was not an appealing personality to the public, could match the youthful attractiveness of Kennedy. Nonetheless, where Kennedy brought zest to the tasks of presidential leadership, Johnson applied himself with compulsive energy. "Presidents," he said, "deal with power." Johnson sought it and dealt with it. This was clear from his decision-making structures. He called Cabinet meetings, but they were little more than evangelical assemblies in which Cabinet members and their staffs were exhorted to work ever more effectively for the president's programs. The National Security Council was consulted periodically, but Johnson worked primarily through small groups of advisers. For foreign policy he looked to the secretaries of state and defense and his White House national security aide. On domestic affairs his confidants were members of the White House staff.

But always at the center of the decision-making process was Lyndon Johnson himself—restless, constantly inquiring, talking, working, subjecting senators, congressmen, governors, party leaders, journalists, and others to the "Johnson treatment." This consisted of an overwhelming array of techniques, including flattery, cajolery, humility, and threats, as well as appeals to conscience and party, all directed toward getting his legislation through Congress and receiving favorable treatment in the press.

The results in domestic policy were prodigious. The years 1964 and 1965 saw a dazzling succession of presidential triumphs in Congress. Where Kennedy had not been able to get much action out of Congress, Johnson put through new and innovative laws in the fields of civil rights, housing, health, education, and poverty—all building blocks in the construction of "The Great Society." Nothing like it had happened since the New Deal years, and this time there was no great national economic emergency to spur things on as there had been in the 1930s.

Reelected in 1964 with a huge majority, Lyndon Johnson seemed unassailable, and, as the Great Society legislation poured out of Congress at Johnson's instigation, the presidency appeared to be the key to the creation of a better life for the great majority of Americans. But then came Vietnam, which dealt an even more savage blow to Johnson's popularity and prestige than Korea had inflicted on Truman.

Johnson and Vietnam: "military intervention," not war.   Johnson inherited the Vietnam problem from his predecessors, particularly Kennedy. The government of South Vietnam had received help from the Kennedy administration in trying to put down a persistent rebellion aimed at its overthrow which was backed by communist North Vietnam. Kennedy had sent South Vietnam large quantities of arms and growing numbers of so-called military "advisers"—men who trained the South Vietnamese troops and helped to lead them in combat.

After his reelection in 1964 Johnson decided to expand our intervention. He sent substantial numbers of troops with air support, then more, and more again. This looked very much like war, and the Constitution says that the president cannot declare war without congressional approval. So Johnson refused to call it a war. It was merely a military intervention. In any case he claimed that he had already received congressional sanction for his actions. In August 1964, North Vietnamese PT boats twice attacked American destroyers in the Gulf of Tonkin, off Vietnam. The circumstances of the attacks were murky, and it was never really clear who had started the fighting. But when a president tells the Congress that American servicemen have been the victims of unprovoked aggression, Congress finds it difficult not to give him what he wants. So Congress passed a joint resolution—known as the Tonkin Gulf resolution—authorizing him to "take all necessary measures to stop aggression in Southeast Asia." This, said the administration later, was the "functional equivalent" of a declaration of war.

Johnson could also find backing for his policy in the public opinion polls, for international crises tend to rally the people behind the president. After the Bay of Pigs incident President Kennedy was brought the news of an opinion poll that showed 82 percent supporting him. "It's just like Eisenhower," he said in exasperation. "The worse I do, the more popular I get." Similarly, after each major escalation in Vietnam Johnson's ratings in the polls went up.

Now it seemed that presidential power had reached its zenith. In both domestic and foreign affairs the presidency had achieved a clear dominance over all other aspects of the system. Few kings or emperors in the past, said some commentators, could match the power of the American president. We had produced, said Arthur Schlesinger, Jr., "the imperial Presidency."

But, of course, Vietnam did not prove to be the final proof of the aggrandizement of presidential power. On the contrary, it broke the power and the reputation of Lyndon Johnson. Each escalation only produced a counterescalation. No matter how much money, manpower, and ingenuity the United States threw into the war, the promised "light at the end of the tunnel" remained as distant as ever.

The president found himself attacked persistently and ferociously in the Senate. His hold on mass opinion declined, at first gradually, then with a rush; for, even though his rating improved briefly after each escalation (and after each peace overture we made), he discovered that a president can only control public opinion over the long run if his policy works. But Vietnam did not respond to the Johnson treatment. His frustration became intense. "Power?" he said bitterly. "The only power I've got is nuclear and I can't use that."[5]

As support for the war dwindled, Johnson's chief national security aide, McGeorge Bundy and Defense Secretary Robert McNamara, who had initially urged escalation upon him, changed their minds and left his administration. Facing hostility on all sides, this formerly gregarious man drew more and more into isolation. He listened only to the dwindling few—particularly Secretary of State Dean Rusk, and W. W. Rostow, Bundy's successor—who still agreed with his Vietnam policy. Deviousness and distrust of those who would not respond to his blandishments became his dominant traits and increased his isolation.

At last, faced with the ultimate testing ground of presidential power, a presidential election campaign, he gave up. On March 31, 1968, he announced his decision to change course on Vietnam and not to run for another term of office.

The Abuse of Presidential Power

Richard Nixon, 1969–1974.   Once again a pause was indicated. It seemed time to assimilate the enormous quantity of social legislation passed during the Johnson administration, to scale down our overseas involvements, and to deemphasize the power of the presidency. So the general expectation was that just as Eisenhower had cooled things down after the New Deal, the Fair Deal, and Korea, so Richard Nixon would follow the New Frontier, the Great Society, and Vietnam with a period of restraint.

Indeed, during his 1968 presidential campaign Nixon made a strong effort to show that he did not share Lyndon Johnson's expansive view of the presidency. The president, he said, "should not delude himself into thinking he can do everything himself or even make all the decisions himself."

Once elected, Nixon did not try to match Johnson's early record of legislation. Very little emerged during Nixon's first hundred days in office, the traditional "honeymoon period," which a new president is expected to exploit to the full before his popularity begins to slip. When Nixon finally sent his proposals to Congress, they did not break much new ground, and were full of reminders that "making working proposals takes time" and that we must take a "careful approach" rather than "hasty action." Language of this kind prompted commentators to suggest comparisons with the Eisenhower era. They noted Nixon's repeated reorganizations of the Executive Office, which indicated a concern, similar to Eisenhower's, with organizational tidiness.

It soon became clear, however, that the Eisenhower analogy was inappropriate. It did not square with some of the other things Nixon had said about the presidency during the 1968 campaign. "The days of a passive Presidency," he argued, "belong to a simpler past. . . . The next President must take an activist view of his office. He must activate the nation's values, define its goals, and marshall its will. . . . The President's chief function is to lead, not to administer." This was the tone, not of William Howard Taft, but of Theodore Roosevelt.

Nixon's methods of organizing his administration reflected his view that he could not depend on many allies outside his own immediate orbit. Congress was in the hands of the opposition party. The bureaucracies and their programs had grown mostly during the terms of his Democratic predecessors, and it was difficult to bring them into line behind new policies.

In his view the media were controlled by the liberal establishment. He used television and radio to explain his policies to the people, but mostly in the form of addresses that did not allow for cross-examination. He held fewer press conferences than his predecessors. He saw his administration as a beleaguered group of carefully chosen men who would ensure him of the advice and support he could not get from anywhere else. So he gave unprecedented power to the top members of his White House staff, particularly to assistants to the president, H. R. Haldeman and John Ehrlichman, who were dubbed by a hostile press "the palace guard."

The long-run purposes espoused by Nixon and his administration were to reduce the massive involvements of the American federal government in solving the problems of the world in general and the American system in particular. His strategies for achieving these purposes were built on the vigorous display of presidential power.

Thus in foreign policy he and his secretary of state, Henry Kissinger, finally ended the involvement of U.S. troops in the Vietnam war. Moreover, by making a historic visit to the People's Republic of China, then going on to the Soviet Union, they instituted the policy of détente, the reduction of tensions with the communist powers. At the same time Nixon was determined that his actions not be read as an indication of weakness. Thus he took four years to accomplish the withdrawal from Vietnam and, along the way, ordered the invasion of Cambodia and Laos, the mining of North Vietnamese harbors, and massive bombing of North Vietnam. These attacks provoked bitter criticism in Congress and upheavals on college campuses. But Nixon refused to be deterred from his resolve.

In domestic affairs Nixon's basic purpose was to halt the expansion of the role of the federal government in economic and social affairs. This did not mean the dismantling of all the programs introduced since the New Deal. In some respects, indeed, Nixon sought to achieve bold social reforms, as in his unsuccessful effort to replace the existing welfare programs with a Family Assistance Plan (see Chapter 11). He also presided over enormous federal spending programs, which involved a series of large budgetary deficits. And, in his attempts to get inflation under control, he twice imposed federal government controls over wages and prices. Nonetheless, during his first term of office he fought to hold down some of the spending plans of the Democratic Congress that he believed would ruin the economy. He used his veto power to block congressional appropriations in a number of fields. When Congress overrode some of his vetoes, he declared that he would not spend the money, come what may. He would "impound" it, hold it in abeyance, releasing it later or perhaps never.

Once reelected for his second term, Nixon made it clear that he was going to do more than merely impound appropriations. He intended to go over to the offensive. In an interview given to *The Washington Star-News* in November 1972, Nixon declared that it was time to bring to an end the philosophy of the social welfare programs of the 1960s, the philosophy of "throwing money at problems."

The enormous majority by which he won the 1972 election he took to be a mandate for his policies. His triumph, however, was short-lived. He was able to do very little about his policies in his second term, which was cut short by his resignation. The basic reason for his downfall was that, although his avowed policies called for lessening the role of the federal government, he did not connect this with a reduction of the power of the presidency. On the contrary, he and the men he chose to work with him built their power enormously and abused it. Their abuse of power came to be symbolized by the word "Watergate"; and just as Johnson's authority was destroyed by Vietnam, so was Nixon's by Watergate.

The Watergate scandal.   On the evening of June 17, 1972, five men were arrested for breaking into the headquarters of the Democratic National Committee (DNC) in the Watergate office and apartment building in Washington, apparently to place a bug in the telephone of DNC chairperson Lawrence O'Brien. Among the five was the director of security for the Committee to Reelect the President, James McCord. Another carried an address book containing the name and White House address of an E. Howard Hunt.

In response to inquiries the president's press secretary dismissed the break-in as "a third-rate burglary." As the story unfolded piece by agonizing piece over a period of over two years, there was much more to it than that. It was a small part of a much larger pattern of action by top officials that was to force the first resignation ever of a president of the United States. The major elements in the story were as follows.

The Watergate break-in was planned by leading members of the administration and of the Committee to Reelect the President. These included Attorney General, later CRP director, John Mitchell; Jeb McGruder, who became CRP director after Mitchell resigned; and Charles Colson, a top aide to Nixon and Haldeman. Heading up the break-in itself were CRP counsel, G. Gordon Liddy and E. Howard Hunt, both of whom were former CIA men who had carried out various investigative assignments for the White House.

The break-in was one incident among several aimed at opponents of the Nixon administration. Thus:

In July 1970, the president gave his approval to a plan (the "Huston plan," after its chairperson, Tom Huston) for extensive domestic intelligence operations, including breaking and entering premises without warrants. This plan was drawn up by a committee representing the FBI, the CIA, the Defense Intelligence Agency, and the National Security Agency. The plan was aborted by the disapproval of FBI director J. Edgar Hoover, who was jealous of the threat to his own power that the plan implied. However, the president then endorsed the establishment in June 1971 of a Special Investigations Unit, known as "the plumbers," for their purpose was to stop national security leaks. Hunt and Liddy were members of this unit.

At the direction of John Ehrlichman, members of the plumber's unit burglarized the office of Daniel Ellsberg's psychiatrist, Dr. Lewis Fielding, in a fruitless effort to find Ellsberg's medical records. Ellsberg was facing criminal charges of leaking Defense Department documents (the "Pentagon Papers") to the press.

The phones of suspected subversives were tapped at the order of the Justice Department, a practice that was stopped when the Supreme Court found it illegal. However, the FBI subsequently resorted to illegal breaking and entering on a number of occasions.

The president's official counsel, John Dean, compiled an "enemies list" of people targeted for harassment by Internal Revenue Service tax audits and other means.

Donald Segretti and others carried out a series of "dirty tricks" during election campaigns under White House direction.

The president personally participated in an illegal "cover-up" of the Watergate break-in. Once the burglars were caught, Nixon and his top aides decided that the links to the White House must not become known—especially before the election in November 1972. So Nixon asserted, and continued to assert, that he knew nothing about the involvement of his associates in perpetrating the break-in and then covering it up until John Dean revealed some of the story to him in March 1973. From the beginning, Nixon insisted, he had instructed everyone in his administration to tell the truth to FBI agents investigating the matter. However, he said, this did not mean that he and his associates could give Congress and the courts all the information they were seeking. Some conversations and documents could not be revealed for reasons of national security and the separation of powers; they were protected by the doctrine of "executive privilege," which gives the president the right to keep confidential communications within his official family. Nonetheless he was determined, he said, to get at the truth and to make it known to the public.

There was widespread skepticism that this was his intention. Criticism of the White House widened and deepened, and, on April 30, 1973, Ehrlichman, Haldeman, Dean, and Attorney General Richard Kleindienst resigned. Still the president insisted that, even if his top aides had tried to cover up, he had known nothing about it.

Then John Dean told a Senate committee that he believed the president had known about the complicity of the White House in the Watergate burglary at an early stage and that the president had probably engaged in the cover-up with them. It was Dean's word against the president's. However, the ability of the president to maintain his story was threatened when in July 1973 a White House aide revealed that, ever since 1970, Nixon had taped most of his conversations and phone calls at the White House and at the presidential retreat, Camp David. Repeatedly, Nixon used executive privilege to withhold the tapes from congressional or judicial scrutiny. But under intense pressure he finally produced transcripts of some of the tapes. Although heavily edited, they revealed clear indications that Nixon, Haldeman, Ehrlichman, Dean, and others had discussed how the staff should commit perjury, and how to arrange for payments and promises of pardons to keep the Watergate burglars from revealing what they knew about the involvement of the higher-ups.

The final proof of the president's culpability came in July 1974, when the Supreme Court forced him to produce some of the key tapes. One of them dated back to June 23, 1972, six days after the Watergate break-in. The decisive passage went as follows:

> H. [Haldeman] You know the Democratic break-in thing. We're back in the problem area because the FBI is not under control. . . . The way to handle this now is to have [deputy CIA director] Walters call [acting FBI director] Gray and just say, "Stay to hell out of this—this is, ah, business we don't want you to go any further on it."
>
> P. [President] What about Pat Gray? You mean Pat Gray doesn't want to?
>
> H. Pat does want to. He doesn't know how to, and he doesn't have any basis for doing it.
>
>   o   o   o
>
> H. And you seem to think the thing to do is get them [the FBI] to stop?
>
> P. Right, Fine.

Here was the "smoking gun," the final proof that the president had lied when he said repeatedly that he had known nothing about the complicity of his subordinates and their effort to cover up the truth until nine months after the break-in, and that he had tried aggressively to get the truth out. Here was the evidence that he himself had conspired illegally to try to use the CIA to suppress the facts, and that he had lied repeatedly in a series of public statements, some of them in reports to the people on television.

Who broke the story?   Several institutions participated in getting at the truth about Watergate. The principal parties were the press, the courts, the special prosecutor, and Congress.

The initial credit for breaking the story goes to two young reporters assigned by *The Washington Post* to cover the trial of the Watergate burglars. Robert Woodward and Carl Bernstein wrote a series of articles showing the links between the burglars, the CRP, and the White House. Other newspapers were slow to pick up on the *Post's* lead, but eventually *The New York Times, The Los Angeles Times, Time,* and *Newsweek* unearthed different pieces of the story, and kept up a drumfire of comment and criticism that made it impossible for the administration to divert public attention from the issue.

At first, the prosecutors in the break-in trial did not press questions that would establish a relationship between the accused and the administration. However, federal district court judge John Sirica, who presided over the trial, was not satisfied with the prosecution's efforts, and took over the questioning himself. When the accused were found guilty, he imposed harsh sentences, offering to soften them if the defendants told what they knew. This resulted in a confession by John McCord, the CRP security man, that perjury had been committed at the trial. Later Sirica worked with a federal grand jury investigation of Watergate. When the jury asked for some of the White House tapes, Sirica ordered the White House to turn them over to him for his private inspection. Eventually, the president's lawyers agreed to do so (though two of the tapes turned out not to exist, and another contained a gap of 18½ minutes, which electronic experts declared had probably been deliberately erased).

If the courts' role was crucial at the beginning, it was even more so at the end. The "smoking gun" tape was produced as a result of a unanimous decision by the Supreme Court, which the president, after a short hesitation, accepted.

In May 1973, under intense pressure from Congress, press, and public to get the facts out, the president appointed Archibald Cox, a Harvard law professor, as special prosecutor in the Department of Justice for Watergate-related crimes. Cox issued a subpoena for several of the tapes and sued in court for its enforcement. Nixon ordered Cox to stop the court action, but Cox refused. Nixon wanted Cox fired. But Attorney General Elliot Richardson resigned rather than do so, Assistant Attorney General William Ruckelshaus was fired when he supported Richardson's position, and Nixon had to turn to the third-ranking man in the Justice Department to get the job done. This "Saturday night massacre" (it took place on Saturday, October 20, 1973) of highly regarded men in an obvious effort to keep the truth from coming out provoked a "fire-storm" of protest from Congress and the public. Nixon bowed to the pressure by appointing a new special prosecutor, Texas lawyer Leon Jaworski. It was in response to Jaworski's subpoenas that the Supreme Court handed down its decision that brought forth the incriminating tape.

Although Congress was slow to get into the act, first the Senate, then the House played vital roles in bringing about Nixon's downfall. In the summer of 1973 a U.S. Senate Select Committee on Presidential Campaign Activities, under the chairmanship of Sam Ervin of North Carolina, conducted televised hearings on Watergate. In the course of those hearings, various degrees of complicity were admitted by the top White House and CRP staff members who were interrogated, John Dean making easily the greatest impact with his confessions and accusations. It was also to this committee that White House aide Alexander Butterfield revealed the existence of the White House tapes.

As the evidence against the president mounted, the spotlight shifted to the House. There was growing sentiment for impeachment, the means that the Constitution provides to force the removal of a president for offenses covered by the phrase "treason, bribery, and other high crimes or misdemeanors." The procedure for impeachment includes a vote by the Judiciary Committee of the House to recommend articles of impeachment; their approval by a majority of the House; and a trial by the Senate. Conviction, requiring a two-thirds vote by the Senate, leads to the removal of the president from office, and his exposure to possible criminal and civil charges in the courts.

After an extensive staff study during the spring of 1974 the 38-member committee conducted a televised debate on the various charges, grouped under five articles of impeachment. Nixon's supporters on the Judiciary Committee claimed that by "high crimes and misdemeanors" the Founding Fathers were referring only to clearly criminal conduct, and that this had not been proven against the president. Nixon's opponents replied that when the framers used the words "misdemeanors" they had in mind not its modern meaning of illegal offenses short of felony, but gross abuses of the public trust even where these were not palpably criminal.

Following an eloquent televised debate the accusers prevailed on three articles of impeachment. Article I dealt with "obstruction of justice"—the various efforts by the president to cover up the Watergate affair by withholding and falsifying evidence and by encouraging others to do the same. Article II covered the alleged "abuses of power" by the president—his violation of his oath of office to protect the Constitution, his invasion of the constitutional rights of citizens. Specifically he was accused of setting up the plumbers unit to engage in illegal activities, including the break-in of Dr. Fielding's office and of the Watergate; of the misuse of the IRS, the FBI, and the CIA; and of his approving CRP's illegal fund-raising activities. Article III dealt with Nixon's refusal to honor a subpoena that the Judiciary Committee had sent him for some of the tapes. The first two articles passed by large margins, with first six and then seven Republicans joining all the committee's Democrats in voting against the president. Approval of the third article was by a much narrower margin. Two other articles were defeated. One charged the president with invading Cambodia illegally and lying to Congress about our previous military attacks there. The other dealt with charges of tax evasion: Nixon's tax accountant had altered the dates on a contribution of Nixon's vice-presidential papers to the National Archives to make them qualify for a huge tax reduction. (Subsequently, Nixon agreed to pay a substantial amount to set this straight.)

The resignation.   The subsequent publication of the "smoking gun" tape demolished much of the case made by the president's defenders on the Judiciary Committee. Most of them declared that, had they known of that tape earlier, they would have voted in favor of Article I, the obstruction of justice charges. Faced with the certainty that impeachment proceedings would be overwhelmingly approved by the House, and the near-certainty of a vote for conviction in the Senate, Richard Nixon, on August 8, 1974, became the first president of the United States to resign his office.

During 1974 various members of the Nixon administration were tried and convicted on charges related to the Watergate cover-up and other illegal activities. They included Mitchell, Haldeman, Ehrlichman, Dean, Magruder, Colson, and Dwight Chapin, Nixon's former appointments secretary, and all served jail sentences.

Nor were these the only members of the Nixon administration to suffer disgrace. In October 1973, Vice-President Spiro Agnew was accused of taking bribes from Maryland businessmen in return for government contracts, payments that had started when he was in state politics and had continued while he was in the White House. He avoided a trial by pleading "no contest"—essentially a plea that implies guilt on some charges but eliminates the process of presenting and proving these or other charges. He was fined and put on probation on a charge of income tax evasion, and several other charges against him were dropped on condition that he resign from the vice-presidency. Nixon then nominated Gerald Ford to fill the vacancy under the terms of the Twenty-fifth Amendment to the Constitution, which provides for the president to nominate a new vice-president subject to confirmation by the Senate. The nominee received the Senate's endorsement. Less than a year later Ford was president of the United States.

Cooling Off the Presidency

Gerald Ford, 1974–1977.   Gerald Ford saw his presidency as having two basic functions. The first was to restore the integrity of his office by putting a stop to the abuses to which it had been subjected. George Reedy, who was Lyndon Johnson's press aide, had described these abuses even before Watergate. The president, said Reedy, has become "a reigning monarch rather than an elected administrator. . . . The White House is a court," and a court is the setting for courtiers who tell the monarch not what he needs to know, but what he wants to hear. Accordingly, presidents were allowing themselves to be sealed off from reality and from alternative sources of information and ideas.[6] So it was Gerald Ford's task to open up the presidency and end the practices of deceit, guile, and secretiveness. His second purpose was to continue the general direction of Nixon's policies—reducing the role of the federal government in economic affairs and combining military and diplomatic strength with a lowering of tensions in international affairs.

Ford was well suited to perform both these functions. His open, unpretentious manner contrasted sharply with the deviousness of Nixon and Johnson. No one could imagine Ford's trying to emulate Nixon's brief attempt to dress up the White House guard in resplendent, slightly absurd uniforms. Ford's lifestyle and that of his family were disarmingly simple. Nor did he isolate himself as Nixon had done. He maintained a large White House staff and there were power struggles within it and between the staff and Cabinet members. But none of his top assistants had the power or the personal style of H. R. Haldeman. The president himself was often in the public eye, and he held a reasonable number of press conferences. He took action to put an end to the illegal actions of the CIA and the FBI and restore their tarnished reputations. He signed the "Sunshine Act," which opened the proceedings of federal regulatory agencies to the public on all matters except those pertaining to national defense or security, trade secrets, criminal proceedings, or personal privacy. And he approved legislation that phased out an accumulation of "emergency powers" granted the president, some originating during the New Deal, others established in World Wars I and II, providing executive authority for sweeping controls over the economy.

The act that somewhat damaged Ford's image of integrity was his granting Richard Nixon a month after he took office a "full, free and absolute pardon . . . for all offenses against the United States which he . . . has committed or may have committed during his tenure as President." There were accusations that a "deal" had been worked out, that the pardon was set up earlier as Nixon's condition for agreeing to resign. Ford denied this, said there had been no bargaining. His only motive, he said, was to get an ugly episode in our national life behind us once and for all.

As for his policies, Ford's views were close to Nixon's in both national and domestic affairs. Although he presided over the expenditure of vast sums of money and accepted huge budgetary deficits, he followed Nixon's example in fighting Congress's desire to spend even more, and vetoed a total of 56 bills. In foreign affairs he supported Henry Kissinger's continuation of the policy of détente, visiting Peking himself, putting the United States' signature to a treaty growing out of a conference at Helsinki that recognized Soviet control over Eastern Europe, and pursuing arms limitations talks with the Soviets. At the same time Ford pushed for higher spending on defense, and he took strong action against a communist country in May 1975, when he dispatched marines to recapture the American merchant ship *Mayaguez*, which had been seized by Cambodia.

Although Ford won a good deal of public approval for his style and his policies, the overwhelming support that greeted him when he began his presidency eroded before long. First, the granting of a pardon for Nixon was extremely unpopular. Then came a growing sense in the country that he lacked the competence and decisiveness needed in a president. A considerable part of his difficulty was that Congress was in the hands of the opposition party, and the Democrats were eager to make a strong record of accomplishment. Thus he was forced onto the defensive and had to make his arguments not through his own initiatives but through the use of his negative power, the veto. Even there Congress overrode his vetoes 11 times, exceeded only by the 15 vetoes overridden during the presidency of Andrew Jackson and the 12 inflicted on Harry Truman. Finally, the Ford administration was roundly criticized for not being able to bring unemployment down below 7½ percent.

The mood of the country seemed to favor a cooling-off period after the Kennedy, Johnson, and Nixon eras. But Ford discovered that to provide a respite is not sufficient. A president must also convey a sense of competence and decisiveness. Ford fell short in this crucial respect and, as a result, he encountered increasing political difficulties. The leadership of his political party is normally one source of a president's power. But even there Ford was not securely entrenched. Although his nominee for vice-president, Nelson Rockefeller, was confirmed by the Senate after an intensive and embarrassing investigation of the Rockefeller family finances, Ford did not have the sway in his own party to keep Rockefeller on his ticket in his 1976 reelection bid. And he was barely able to ward off Ronald Reagan's challenge for the Republican nomination. At last, when he sought the endorsement of the national constituency in November 1976, he could not quite convince enough people that what he stood for was what the country needed for the next four years.

The Open Presidency?

Jimmy Carter, 1977–.   During his quest for the Democratic nomination for the presidency Jimmy Carter was the anti-Washington candidate. He attacked the federal government as overblown, unwieldy, and remote from the people and their needs. But he also insisted—and with increasing emphasis as the November election approached—that he was not attacking the office of the presidency itself. He was against the inefficiency and waste of the federal bureaucracy; and his second target was the kinds of abuses of presidential power associated with Richard Nixon. The right type of presidential leadership, on the other hand, was sorely needed.

Although Carter began his inaugural address by thanking Gerald Ford "for all he has done to heal our land," this did not contradict Carter's campaign appeals to put an end to Ford's negativism, his "government by veto." It was time, Carter said repeatedly, to meet the needs of the people more adequately, and this could not be done without strong initiatives on the part of the president. Of course, the president and the government generally could not do everything. "We have learned," he said at his inaugural, "that 'more' is not necessarily 'better,' that even our great nation has its recognized limits, and that we can neither answer all questions nor solve all problems." Still, he had offered a program of cutting unemployment and inflation, reforming the tax system, reducing our dependence on foreign oil, reorganizing the federal government, providing a broad program of health insurance, giving more aid to the cities, and bringing the arms race under control. Even though Carter warned that he could not achieve all these purposes at once and that increased spending must not jeopardize the goal of a balanced budget by 1980, he had nonetheless set forth an extremely ambitious agenda. And making good on his promises would require a vigorous use of presidential power.

As Carter began his term of office, the polls indicated that the majority of the electorate expected that he would take steps to make good on his promises. The polls also showed that the widespread doubts about his personal qualities which, as we said in Chapter 4, had plagued his campaign were giving way after his election to a favorable assessment of the way he was approaching his new job.

But this posed the old dilemma about presidential power once again. We had a president who, while warning against excessive expectations, had raised rather high expectations. He planned to be a strong president, and, at the outset at least, he had considerable public support for his proposals. The signs pointed to accelerating momentum, to another period of stepped-up government action. What, then, would protect us against the dangers implicit in another supercharged presidency? How could we avoid being plunged into another period of excessive aggrandizement of presidential power before we had fully recovered from the last?

Carter was not unaware of this dilemma, and he proposed to undertake some changes in the way the presidency operated so that past disasters would not be repeated. Before we examine his ideas, we must review a number of proposals that have been considered to reform the presidency.

Proposals to Reform the Presidency

Although Gerald Ford's term in office reduced some of the public's fears of the "imperial presidency," it did not stop the demands from political scientists, members of Congress, and other political observers for the reform of the institution.

For one thing, once Nixon had gone, revelations began to pour forth which showed that the kinds of abuses of power for which he had been indicted by the Judiciary Committee had not all been invented by him. The public was to learn that, during the Kennedy administration, the FBI, acting on orders from the White House, had bugged the telephones of civil rights leader Martin Luther King and collected a dossier on his sex life—in order, it was said, to check on the possibility of his being mixed up with subversive, left-wing elements. During the Kennedy era, too, the CIA had prepared assassination plots against Cuban Premier Fidel Castro and other foreign leaders. Still more of the gloss rubbed off the Kennedys' "Camelot" legend when documentation appeared of many White House phone calls between President Kennedy and Judith Exner, with whom the president was apparently having an affair. In itself this might not have been viewed as much worse than imprudent. But it was revealed that she had also been the mistress of a leader of organized crime, with whom she was still in touch. She had also played a part in one of the abortive efforts to kill Castro through a plan in which the CIA had worked with leaders of the syndicate (see Chapter 14).

As for Lyndon Johnson, he had enjoyed salacious tidbits about the sex lives of various politicians fed to him by FBI director, J. Edgar Hoover, from the agency's files. And there was speculation that Johnson, too, had used the Internal Revenue Service to harass his political opponents. So, if Richard Nixon had abused his power more systematically and thoroughly than his predecessors (and had also engaged in illegal actions to cover up his abuses), the problem of the corruption of presidential power did not begin with Nixon, nor even with Johnson. Consequently, these abuses represent a danger that may be inherent in the institution itself, not just in one or two men, and there seems nothing to guarantee that future presidents will not revert to the earlier patterns.

The second concern of those who propose reform is that the sudden alternations of approach from president to president is no way to run a government. The presidency is the governmental system's prime source of energy, acting as a great generator of power. Instead of keeping it going at a more or less steady pace, with reasonable variations, we have lurched between overheating the system, subjecting it to almost intolerable strains, and then suddenly relapsing into a pace so slow that the needed energy is no longer supplied.

A number of proposals have been offered to counter the dangers of abuses of power and excessive variations in the degree to which power has been used.

Adopting Elements of the Parliamentary System

First, there are proposals to adopt certain elements of the parliamentary, or cabinet, system of government. Under this system the chief executive (the prime minister) is not elected separately for a fixed term, but comes to office by virtue of being the leader of the biggest party in the legislature. Since parliamentary systems do not use the principle of separation of powers, the prime minister and his cabinet continue to hold their seats in the legislature. In fact, they remain in office only as long as they command majority support in the legislature. If they lose this support, they must either call a new election (since elections can be held any time they are needed, and are not subject to the fixed terms established by our Constitution), or the prime minister can be replaced with any other party leader who can get majority support in the legislature. Thus it is possible under this system to get rid of a chief executive who, for whatever reason, has lost his ability to lead without having to go through the arduous, lengthy, and uncertain process of impeachment.

Whether or not such a parliamentary system would be better equipped to prevent or quickly uncover a Watergate (and there is some question about this), there is no prospect that our constitutional structure of separation of powers will be abandoned. Thus proposals for reforming the presidency have been concerned not with going over entirely to the parliamentary system, but with borrowing and adopting certain of its features. Thus Democratic congressman Henry Reuss of Wisconsin has suggested a constitutional amendment that would separate the functions of chief of state and head of government, as is the case in all the parliamentary systems. In Reuss's view a primary source of our troubles with presidents is that we have vested too much of the aura of monarchy in the presidency by combining the governmental and political responsibilities with the ceremonial and ritualistic functions. Thus in the British system the queen embodies the myths and rituals of the nation as a whole, while the prime minister and his cabinet get on with the job of running the country. So Reuss suggests creating a chief of state, nominated by the president and confirmed by the Senate, who would handle all ceremonial functions.

Another adaptation from the parliamentary system would be the establishment of regular question periods in the Congress, when the president and the top members of his administration would be compelled to answer for their policies in detail. Currently, the only devices for forcing the president to account for his policies are the State of the Union and other major presidential addresses to Congress; appearances by administration officials (but not the president) before congressional hearings; and press conferences, which are convened only at the president's pleasure, and are fairly easily manipulated by a skillful president.

Restructuring the Presidency

The next set of proposals to reform the presidency involves changes within the president's office and in the terms by which he holds that office. One obvious target is the concentration of power within the White House staff. Suggestions for change include a requirement for ratification of the top White House positions by the Senate, and giving back to Cabinet members some of the authority they have lost to White House staff members.

Reducing the ability of the president to use the FBI, the CIA, and other intelligence agencies for his own political purposes is also proposed. Another suggestion—the permanent establishment of a special prosecutor's office—has already been acted upon. In 1976 a special prosecutor's office in the Department of Justice was created by Congress. The prosecutor is limited to a single three-year term, and he can be fired only for committing a felony or a gross breach of ethics. He is employed to investigate and prosecute crimes committed by the president, other top officials of the executive branch, federal judges, and members of Congress.

Another proposal for constraining presidential power is to limit the president to a single six-year term. This would carry still further the logic of the Twenty-second Amendment to the Constitution, which limits a president to two terms.

Building the Effectiveness of Congress and Political Parties

Another group of ideas for reform are responses to the fact that the growth in the power of the presidency has been matched by a decline in the power of Congress and political parties. It is therefore suggested that Congress reorganize itself and increase its vigilance so that it can perform its constitutional function of constraining presidential power more effectively.

As for political parties, it has been recommended that presidential candidates stop bypassing their party machinery in favor of their own personal campaign organization—a tendency that reached its zenith in 1972, when the Republican campaign was vested in CRP, and the Republican National Committee all but ignored.

Screening Personal Qualities

Political scientist James Barber[7] has argued that institutional changes come too slowly and that we must put more emphasis on selecting people for the White House who are free from the personality defects that lead to abuses of power.

Thus a fourth area for reform concentrates on the personal qualities of presidential candidates. Barber uses two criteria for testing candidates' qualifications for the presidency. The first is their view of presidential leadership, ranging from *active* to *passive*. The second is their basic personality structure, their view of themselves and of their relationship to other people, ranging from *positive* to *negative*.

In Barber's view the two Roosevelts, Truman, and Kennedy were active–positive types—confident, flexible, striving for results through "rational mastery." Eisenhower (and later Ford) was a passive–positive type—a secure, well-adjusted personality who, however, did not seek to use presidential power aggressively. But both Johnson and Nixon were the worst possible combination—active–negative types, combining an assertive view of presidential power with a conviction that people did not like or accept them personally.

So we should set up mechanisms, says Barber, for selecting out the potential active–negative types before they get their party's nomination. For this purpose candidates should be screened by a panel of experts drawn from psychology and psychiatry, political science, journalism, and other appropriate fields. The panel would have no power beyond presenting its findings to the public. It would not presume to make the final selection and would almost certainly not arrive at

"Page one"

Drawing by Don Hesse, © 1976, *St. Louis Globe Democrat.*
Reprinted with permission, L.A. Times Syndicate.

unanimous conclusions. But it could reasonably hope to issue effective warnings against those people whose personality structure renders them profoundly unfit to be president.

Thus we have had an abundance of proposals to correct the defects that have been associated with presidential government in recent years. These are adaptations from the parliamentary system, proposals for restructuring the presidency within the existing model, suggestions for controlling presidential power by building the strength of other parts of the system, and the recommendation that we worry less about institutional reform and more about the character of the people we choose for the presidency.

Carter and the Reform of the Presidency

In considering these various possibilities, it was obvious that Jimmy Carter would not choose to abandon the presidential system in favor of the parliamentary–cabinet system of government. But he has been influenced by some of the less drastic proposals for change designed to resolve the dilemma of how to provide strong leadership without endangering the constitutional structure. What he has promised is a presidency that is less neurotic, less concentrated, less pretentious, and less belligerent, while being more cooperative, more honest, and more open.

His would be a *less neurotic* presidency, he said, because, having read James Barber's book about presidential character before his election, Carter decided that he fitted precisely the specifications of the active–positive type of president—the first since John Kennedy. Then he proposed a *less concentrated* presidency, to be accomplished by restoring the status and authority of the Cabinet. The White House staff was to be reduced, and no member of that staff was to try to tell a Cabinet member how to run his department or deny him periodic access to the president (a change, incidentally, that had already taken place under Ford). Carter promised, too, that he would be a *less pretentious* president than some of his predecessors and would try to make the office human again by removing the pomp and the imperial trappings that had grown up around it. He symbolized this at the very beginning by walking down Pennsylvania Avenue in his inaugural parade instead of riding in the presidential limousine, by wearing a sweater instead of a formal business suit in his first televised address from the White House, and by sharply cutting the number of cars and chauffeurs available to the White House staff. Next, Carter's early foreign policy statements suggested that internationally his administration would be *less belligerent*, less inclined to involve us in the kind of tragic mess represented by Vietnam. Moreover, there would be much tighter controls over the CIA and far fewer of those covert efforts to upset foreign governments or assassinate their leaders that have come to light in recent years.

Conversely, his administration, Carter indicated, would be *more cooperative* with Congress than was the case with most of his predecessors. He gave evidence of this by preparing his first set of economic proposals in close cooperation with congressional leaders, and withdrawing his nomination of Theodore Sorenson, a former aide to President Kennedy, to be director of the CIA when strong congressional opposition appeared. Next Carter promised a *more honest* presidency than the country had experienced under Johnson and Nixon. Unlike them he would not lie to the people, he said, and he drew up a new code of ethics for himself and his top officials.

Finally, Carter offered a *more open* presidency. There were more press conferences and informal talks on radio and television; two-way live radio and television programs during which Carter fielded questions phoned in by people around the country; and presidential participation in "town hall" meetings in small communities—all with the avowed purpose of restoring the people's declining trust in their president and their government.

Whether this can be achieved will be, of course, one of the prime tests by which Carter's administration will be judged. And the widespread approval of Carter's commitment to an open, honest and responsive presidency soon mingled with some harsh criticisms. His White House staff, it was said, was inexperienced and disorganized. He suffered embarrassment at the hands of Congress. Moreover, the critics asked, if the Carter administration was to be so much more open and more honest, why had the president been so reluctant to dispense with the services of OMB Director Bert Lance after the revelations in the summer of 1977 that Lance's career as a banker had been marked by a careless disregard for proper banking procedures?

So the Carter administration is caught up in the nearly inevitable problem of the presidency after Vietnam and Watergate. The people continue to invest their hopes in the presidency. But hand in hand with their expectations go suspicions and anxieties about the institution and the power it contains.

Five Perspectives on the Presidency

The Liberals

Historically, the liberals have been the great champions of presidential power. The presidency seemed the most likely institution for achieving far-reaching economic and social change. This was the one office elected by the people as a whole and equipped with the authority to move decisively.

It might be thought that liberals, as devout believers in the free society, would worry about the potential threat to our liberties in the enormous growth of presidential responsibilities. But they dismissed such fears as alarmist. After all, there were all those restraints on presidential power mentioned earlier—limits imposed by the Constitution, political practice, and so on. Wherever the president looked, there were limits on this power. Those presidents who worked vigorously to use their "power to persuade" were successful; those who had not were failing to carry out their constitutional responsibilities.

This was the test implicit in the judgment of 75 political scientists and historians who were asked in 1962 by Harvard professor Arthur Schlesinger, Sr., to rate the past presidents. The results appear in Table 6–1. To satisfy the liberals a

TABLE 6–1   *Poll of Presidential Greatness*

Great	Average	Below Average
1. Lincoln	12. Madison	24. Taylor
2. Washington	13. J. Q. Adams	25. Tyler
3. F. D. Roosevelt	14. Hayes	26. Fillmore
4. Wilson	15. McKinley	27. Coolidge
5. Jefferson	16. Taft	28. Pierce
Near Great	17. Van Buren	29. Buchanan
6. Jackson	18. Monroe	*Failure*
7. T. Roosevelt	19. Hoover	30. Grant
8. Polk ⎱ tie	20. Harrison	31. Harding
9. Truman ⎰	21. Arthur	
10. John Adams	22. Eisenhower ⎱ tie	
11. Cleveland	23. A. Johnson ⎰	

SOURCE: Adapted from Arthur Meier Schlesinger, "Our Presidents: A Rating by 75 Historians," *New York Times Magazine,* July 29, 1962, pp. 12–14+ ©1962 by the New York Times Company. Reprinted by permission.

president must aspire to greatness. None has achieved that accolade since Franklin Roosevelt, though Truman measured up reasonable well by their standards. Although Kennedy was not included in the 1962 list, liberals rated him considerably higher than Eisenhower. They liked the flexibility of Kennedy's decision-making methods, and condemned Eisenhower's as too rigid for the dynamic requirements of the modern presidency. They appreciated Kennedy's enthusiasm for his job, and accused Eisenhower of being a part-time president.

When political scientist Richard Neustadt's book *Presidential Power* appeared in 1960, it took the Eisenhower presidency as an example of how not to realize the potential of the office. Neustadt's prescription was to reach out for and use power aggressively. Otherwise, the president would be unable to get anything done because of the constraints on his power. Later Neustadt was to give high praise for the way Kennedy carried out his responsibilities during his brief term of office.[8]

In the last year or so of the Kennedy administration, liberals grew restless, for Kennedy's popularity and effectiveness on television were not being translated into very much legislation. Still, he had been elected by the slimmest of margins. His support in Congress was tenuous. He could do little more in his first term than prepare the ground. Later, when his popularity would lead to his election for a second term with a much larger margin in the Congress, liberals hoped that he would use the mandate to press forward.

The liberals on Johnson: personal style and Vietnam.   The liberals' hopes were shattered by the assassination of President Kennedy, and they saw Lyndon Johnson as a southerner with a background as a power broker in the Senate and a scornful attitude toward liberal reformers.

Soon, however, they observed with delight that Johnson was the very model of the president as described by Neustadt, who would seek and use power aggressively. And his achievements in producing the great flood of Great Society legislation were far beyond anything they had hoped for.

This early assessment was soon to be revised. First a few, then a rapidly increasing number of liberals became deeply hostile to the Lyndon Johnson presidency. There were two principal causes for their displeasure: his crude personal style and his foreign policy. Initially, the liberals had tended to overlook the crudities of Johnson's manner. But as time went on they found him overbearing and boorish. They objected to his notorious fury at unfavorable comments in the press. They criticized the way he treated his staff, from whom it was said he demanded total subservience and adulation. (Apparently he got it from Jack Valenti, his first appointments secretary, who described Johnson in a speech in 1965 as "a sensitive man, a cultivated man, a warmhearted man. . . . I sleep each night a little better because Lyndon Johnson is my President.")

Then there was what came to be known as the "credibility gap," a chasm of

Happy days on the old plantation

L.B.J. is "A sensitive man, a
cultivated man,
A warm-hearted
man. . .
I sleep each night a
little better,
A little more con-
fidently because
Lyndon Johnson is
my President."
—speech by Jack
Valenti.

The Herblock Gallery (Simon & Schuster, 1968)

distrust between people and president. There was a widespread sense that Johnson managed and manipulated the news, withholding from the public any facts that might be unfavorable to his image. Suspicions of the president in this area grew out of the impression he gave of deviousness.

In part this was a product of his unimpressive television style. But it was also related to suspicions of his ethical standards. During his years in the Senate his wife's modest family inheritance had grown into a several million dollar fortune, encompassing ownership of the only television franchise in Austin, Texas, and a considerable amount of land and bank stock. While in the Senate, too, he was closely associated with Bobby Baker, the Senate majority leader's secretary, who, as we shall see in Chapter 7, became embroiled in a particularly venal financial scandal.

And yet, if Johnson's problems had been solely matters of style and personality, most liberals might have found excuses for him. In fact, for his first year or so in office, they did. What changed their response was not further examples of uncouth behavior but Johnson's foreign policy, especially in Southeast Asia. As the Vietnam war escalated, so did the liberals' bitterness; and they began to use language that in the past had belonged to conservatives.

The president's power, they proclaimed, had grown dangerously, and with a passive Congress passing the Tonkin Gulf resolution, discussed earlier, there were no apparent checks on that power. Previously, they had been impatient with the checks and balances of the constitutional system. Now they began to ask: What have we done? Are these the fruits of the philosophy we have expounded? How do we control the Frankenstein's monster we have created? So the repudiation of the Lyndon Johnson policies had forced a reappraisal of the liberal view of the presidency itself.

Nixon and Watergate.   The Nixon presidency forced the liberals to intensify their reappraisal. In Watergate they found confirmation of all the charges they had made against Nixon since he had first appeared on the political scene.

To begin with, they had always accused him of unprincipled conservatism. They would not have found conservatism as such reprehensible, but they complained that he was a conservative without compassion, always exploiting those themes that appealed to the people's fears and hostilities, especially anticommunism. His earliest election campaigns, they said, had been built on smearing his liberal Democratic opponents with false charges that they were linked with communists. As vice-president he had claimed that the nation's leading Democrats were covering up for "communism in high places." Now, they said, he was justifying his illegal conduct by the alleged need to protect the national security from subversive left-wing elements. This was the reason he and his men gave for their complete disregard for constitutional liberties, for wiretapping without warrants, and for ordering the mass arrests without formal charges of antiwar demonstrators who gathered in Washington (Almost all of those arrested were freed by the courts.)

Next, the White House tapes, revealing the rehearsals of plans to twist the truth and throw the investigation off the track, gave the liberals new evidence for their allegation that Nixon had always been thoroughly dishonest. They recalled with particular anger his 1952 election campaign, when he had stood in danger of being jettisoned as Eisenhower's running mate because of charges that his political career was backed by a "slush fund" of secret contributions from a group of businesspeople. He saved himself by talking past the issues with a television address of maudlin sentimentality in which he cited his little dog Checkers and his wife's "Republican cloth coat."

The people had not recognized the man's basic dishonesty then. They were less forgiving later when they heard about CRP's slush funds; and money moving in and out of White House safes after passing through the hands of the president's close friend, businessman Bebe Rebozo; and the mixture of personal and public funds that went into the management of the president's estate in San Clemente.

Finally, the liberals had always seen in Richard Nixon a deeply neurotic personality, a man with great personal insecurities who found it extremely difficult to relate to others. Out of this difficulty, said the liberals, came his contrived gestures, his awkwardness of manner, and his tendency to withdraw into isolation. They were reflections of the fact that he was unsure of himself, that he was not comfortable with and did not trust people.

So it was natural for him to believe that he was surrounded by enemies. High on his enemies list were the media, against whom he conducted a vendetta throughout his career. (He told them in his farewell-to-politics pronouncement after his defeat for the California governorship in 1962, "You won't have Dick Nixon to kick around any more.") Other enemies were the Democrats, the bureaucracies—the entire liberal establishment.

Thus, said the liberals, it would not be enough merely to win in 1972. His victory had to be overwhelming—otherwise, he would not receive the reassurance of the people's support that he apparently so desperately needed. The Watergate break-in was part of the plan to ensure that he would win by a landslide. Even when the landslide came, he still could not stand the thought of opposition, and pursued a course calculated to stamp it out. As the Watergate investigation intensified, his defects of personality led him to see conspiracies on all sides. The only way to deal with the conspiracies was to suppress them, which meant that he must drive relentlessly for more and more power. This drive was shared by his subordinates, men selected because they would serve Nixon's purposes without question. Mitchell, Haldeman, Ehrlichman, and the rest were all dedicated not only to Nixon's brand of conservatism but also to protecting and enlarging his power.

At last, these men felt that the power of the presidency was so great that nothing could touch them. They could arrange to burglarize offices with impunity. (John Ehrlichman claimed that, under the doctrine of "inherent powers," the president had the right to order an otherwise illegal break-in if the national security were clearly threatened.) There seemed to be no sense of what kind of conduct was appropriate for a president and his staff. They had set themselves above the proprieties, above accountability, and above the law.

Fortunately, the worst did not happen. The danger of a police state was checked. The top men in the administration had fallen. Those who had ruthlessly abused power were indicted and found guilty—all but one: the president himself. The liberals were angry that he had been pardoned. But at least he had been brought down and abjectly humiliated.

It was a great vindication for the liberals. Everything they had said about Nixon for all those years was finally accepted by the great mass of the people. But the liberals were in no position to gloat over their triumph.

First, as they saw it, America had been lucky. If the burglars had not been bunglers, if they had not taped a door open in such a way as to lead to its discovery by a security guard, they might not have been caught. Or, if the federal judge in the break-in case had not been John Sirica, the tough and persistent search for the truth might not have been made. Or, if *The Washington Post* had assigned their regular political writers to the case, rather than two young men eager to make their reputations and able to work around the clock, the story might not have been so diligently pursued. Or, if Nixon had not had his conversations taped, there would not have been enough hard evidence to ensure his ouster. Or, if he had ordered the tapes destroyed as soon as their existence came to light, claiming the needs of national security, he could probably have ridden out the storm. The country was saved, then, by accidents and miscalculations.

Second, the corruption of presidential power had not started with Nixon. We had had two presidents in a row, acting furtively and deviously, treating their opponents as conspirators, and inflicting terrible damage on the political system. And the evidence of eavesdropping on Martin Luther King and others during the Kennedy years caused further dismay among the liberals.

The liberals' conclusion: still the favored institution.   For a time the liberals' belief in a strong presidency was shaken. They debated the merits of various proposals to check the power of the office. They favored steps to prevent the reappearance of the Nixon kind of "palace guard" in the White House. They even found new virtues in Congress, which had been long out of favor with liberals. Congress had been instrumental in bringing Nixon down, and might have limited the damage earlier if it had fulfilled its obligations more diligently.

Despite everything, the presidency still remains the liberals' favorite institution of the federal government. Its effectiveness from their point of view will vary according to who holds the office; Jimmy Carter, for example, had been the target of a great deal of liberal criticism for not pushing liberal programs aggressively enough. Still, for liberals the presidency is more likely than any other institution over the long run to take the lead toward equality and social progress.

How, then, do liberals deal with the tremendous dangers of presidential power brought home to them by Vietnam and Watergate? Their answer is that we cannot rely on the presidency alone. A strong presidency need not be a threat to our liberties if we also do something about the other proposals that liberals believe essential for a free society—a revitalized two-party system, an informed and active electorate, more effective controls on lobbying, and the reduction of the political power of money.

These are the real checks on presidential power, the best assurances of an open presidency, the only real guarantees against future Vietnams and Watergates.

The Conservatives

Historically, the conservative view of the presidency[9] favored a strictly limited role for the office. The very attributes of Franklin Roosevelt and Harry Truman that liberals praised were condemned by conservatives. Although Eisenhower was not a hero to the conservatives (he had denied the Republican nomination in 1952 to their beloved Senator Robert Taft), his presidency was much preferred by conservatives to that of Kennedy. They approved of precisely those aspects of Eisenhower's style—his reluctance to provide aggressive leadership, his highly structured mode of decision making—that liberals criticized. These methods were good in themselves and in the fact that they limited the federal government's role in economic and social affairs.

A president's constituency is the mass national electorate. He is much too likely to respond to demands to limit property rights and interfere with business. The traditional cry of conservatives has been to check the power of the president by bolstering the authority of Congress and by keeping as much of the action at the state and local level rather than in Washington, the president's domain.

Lyndon Johnson's Great Society programs gave them further evidence of the trend toward the federal takeover of the economy. More and more of the functions that people ought to be able to exercise for themselves were being assumed by government.

And yet, when it came to Johnson's foreign policy, conservatives took a different view of the uses of presidential authority. When he deployed American military power in the Dominican Republic, conservatives dismissed the liberals' complaints as unrealistic squeamishness. On Vietnam the conservative criticism was not that Johnson had exceeded his authority, but that he had let himself be intimidated by Congress and public opinion into stopping short of the steps needed to win the war.

Conservatives on Nixon.   The conservative ambivalence that had thus shown itself in the Johnson years deepened into a near-schizoid attitude during the Nixon presidency.

Conservatives made a number of points in Nixon's favor. First, they admired him for many of the policies and actions that had aroused the ire of liberals. There was much to approve in his career before he entered the White House. While a congressman, he had conducted a successful investigation of Alger Hiss, a former State Department official who became president of the Carnegie Endowment for International Peace. Nixon charged that, while in government service, he had passed American secrets to the Soviets, and the outcome was that Hiss was sent to jail on perjury charges. Hiss had been the darling of the liberals. Most of them never quite believed he was guilty, and they never forgave Nixon for unmasking him. Conservatives also approved of Nixon's anticommunist posture and his generally conservative congressional votes on economic and national security issues.

During his presidency they applauded the Cambodian incursion and the stepped-up bombing of Vietnam. They liked the impounding of funds to keep down the federal budget. When he won his second term, they were delighted with his promise to stop the kind of programs that "threw money at people."

Thus, when the attack on Watergate first developed, conservatives tended to see the charges as a desperate effort by the liberal establishment to overturn the mandate of 1972 and to stop Nixon from moving in the conservative direction he had signaled.

Second, conservatives held that Watergate grew out of a justifiable concern for the national security. They were impressed by the president's reminder that, when he set up the special machinery that led (without his intent, he said) to the Watergate, he was acting to deal with serious problems of domestic and international security. In a statement made on May 23, 1973, Nixon warned the nation:

> In the spring and summer of 1970, another security problem reached critical proportions. In March a wave of bombing and explosions struck college campuses and cities. There were 400 bomb threats in one 24-hour period in New York City. Rioting and violence on college campuses reached a new peak after the Cambodian operation and the tragedies at Kent State and Jackson State. The 1969–70 school year brought nearly 1800 campus demonstrations and nearly 250 cases of arson on campus. Many colleges closed. Gun battles between guerrilla-style groups and police were taking place. Some of the disruptive activities were receiving foreign support.

As for the Daniel Ellsberg case, conservatives disagreed with the liberals' charge that he was an innocent victim of administration persecution. The Pentagon Papers, which he had illegally taken, constituted a massive, secret study of the history of decision making in the Vietnam war *before Richard Nixon was president*. Ellsberg had the documents copied and gave them to *The New York Times* and *The Washington Post*, which published them, and to Senator Gravel of Alaska, who read a portion of them on the Senate floor. This breached the confidentiality of our entire defense system; it was the biggest leak of military information in our history; and, as the president pointed out:

> It created a situation in which the ability of the government to carry on foreign relations even in the best of circumstances could have been severely compromised. Other governments no longer knew whether they could deal with the United States in confidence. Against the background of the delicate negotiations that the United States was then involved in on a number of fronts—with regard to Vietnam, China, the Middle East, nuclear arms limitations, U.S.–Soviet relations and others—in which the utmost degree of confidentiality was vital, it posed a threat so grave as to require extraordinary actions. [10]

It was not surprising, then, that the president, as commander in chief, would do everything in his power to carry out his responsibility to protect the national security; that he would order a thorough investigation to find out how this had happened; and that he would move to set up machinery ("the plumbers" and the rest) that would plug the leaks and bring about better coordination among the several intelligence agencies, which obviously had not been doing their job adequately.

Third, conservatives suggest that the liberals have a double standard. Liberals claim to be great defenders of the rights of the accused. Yet only a few of them protested when Judge Sirica gave three of the Watergate burglary defendants 35-year sentences as a bludgeon with which to get them to talk. A typical burglary penalty for a first offender is a three-month suspended sentence or perhaps a year's probation. Yet Sirica was applauded for his stern commitment to justice.

Finally, according to the conservatives, Watergate was nothing new. Nixon differed from previous presidents, not in that he sanctioned illegal acts but in that he was caught. The FBI and the CIA had long been engaged in practices that went beyond their legislative mandate. Dirty campaign tricks, including the bugging of the opposition, had been practiced before by both sides. Probably Democratic presidents had approved their own Watergates; but they had been more successful than Nixon in covering up their misdeeds.

These points were made enthusiastically by a hard core of Nixon supporters headed by Rabbi Baruch Korff, who raised money for Nixon's legal defense, and urged that he be brought back into public life, perhaps as an ambassador. Other conservatives, while subscribing in whole or in part to the pro-Nixon arguments, were nonetheless far from enchanted with him.

These conservatives made the following criticisms of Nixon and his tactics.

First, throughout his political career he had shown himself to be an expedient politician. Perhaps his basic ideological leanings were conservative. But he was ready to qualify his conservatism whenever that was to his advantage. This became very clear during his first term in the presidency. Nixon's administration turned away from conservative doctrine by incurring huge budgetary deficits, imposing wage–price controls, and proposing a welfare reform that would be tantamount to giving people a guaranteed annual income. In foreign policy he reached an agreement in Strategic Arms Limitation Talks that conservatives believed would make us fall behind the Russians. Worst of all were his trips to Communist China and the Soviet Union, which made nonsense of our continuing involvement against communism in Vietnam.

He surrounded himself with power-driven pragmatists. As an expedient politician, more concerned with power than principles, it is not surprising that Nixon chose as his aides men like Haldeman and Ehrlichman. Conservatives had long been bitterly resentful of these men, whom they considered to be high-handed and arrogant, keeping the president from contact with Congress, with conservative supporters, and with political reality.

Under the guidance of Haldeman, who had been an advertising executive, Nixon and his assistants had replaced politics with public relations. To Haldeman, Ehrlichman, and the men they appointed power was all that mattered. They were the ultimate, hard-boiled pragmatists who had no use for issues or people who cared about issues.

Nixon's personality was unsuited to leadership under pressure. His sense that he was surrounded by enemies had a solid foundation in fact. As a Republican president he faced hostile forces in many directions. But a leader who wants to produce change must be able to deal with hostility. Nixon was temperamentally unable to do so. Opposition of any kind became an obsession. So, instead of keeping his eye on the main task, he allowed himself to become involved with people whose trivial mischief-making projects would ultimately prove ruinous.

He misled his own supporters. He lied not only to the people at large but to his most devoted supporters. Questioned closely by conservatives in Congress as to whether he was holding anything back, he repeatedly reassured them. This was the case right up to the surrender of the "smoking gun" tape. Thus, as revelation followed revelation, his supporters' credibility was damaged almost as much as his own, for he made them look like fools. This did great harm to the cause of conservatism.

He was a bungler. Entangled by incompetents, he lacked the ability to extricate himself. Had he, at the outset, admitted White House involvement in the Watergate break-in, denied personal knowledge, and fired a few staff members, he would have suffered only a minor setback. Or had he ordered the tapes destroyed, there would have been a great furor, but he would have survived. He lacked the judgment to see that, once the cover-up was started and as long as the tapes existed, executive privilege could not finally protect him.

To conservatives, the reelection of Richard Nixon had brought them their supreme opportunity to undo the damage caused by 40 years of liberalism. His public statements gave conservatives cause to hope that at last he would rise above expediency and act on conservative principle. However, the lust for power of the people around him, and his own shortcomings of character and performance, destroyed the glittering prospect that had beckoned to them. And so great was the havoc caused by Watergate that conservatives feared it would be many years before such a chance to reassert conservatism would come again.

Conservatives on Ford.   In Gerald Ford the conservatives saw their hopes flicker again; for he was a man of solid, midwestern conservative credentials. But he, too, was a politician; and though he was to be commended for vetoing the more outrageous of the Democrats' spending proposals, he could not escape responsibility for the federal budget's reaching $400 billion.

Consequently, Ronald Reagan became the candidate of the larger number of conservatives in 1976 (though Barry Goldwater finally came out for Ford). Reagan's narrow defeat at the convention in Kansas City was one more sharp disappointment for conservatives and for their hope of making the presidency into an effective instrument of conservatism.

The conservatives' proposal: reduce the scope of the presidency. Watergate, say the conservatives, was the natural result of the overgrown presidency, which was itself an instrument of the monstrously inflated federal government. Given the enormous amount of power that has been concentrated in

Washington and in the White House, it was inevitable that sooner or later that power would be grossly abused.

To prevent any recurrence it will be necessary to reorganize the White House office so that never again will so much power gravitate to a small group of staff members who can cut the president off from the world. More important than this or any other institutional rearrangements, however, is to cut down the size of government and its bureaucracies, thereby making possible the reduction of the scope of the presidency. Thus the basic conservative preference is still to reduce the power of the presidency and restore the dwindled authority of Congress.

However, this basic preference is subject to two important reservations. The first is that Congress is not as conservative as it was, and in some years cannot be relied on to check liberal power in the White House. The second is that, from time to time, the prospect arises of electing a conservative to the White House, or at least a person with whom conservatives would have significant influence. In such a case conservatives reserve the right to call for a lively display of presidential power, as indeed they did early in 1973 before their hopes were destroyed in the quagmire of Watergate.

The Radical Left

Radical groups on both left and right see the president as little more than a servant of a small group of men who rule America. In the eyes of the left, the liberals' dismay at the abuses of presidential power is absurd. For the left has never accepted the position that their purposes can be achieved by an expanding presidency. For one thing, it is inconceivable to them that an institution so remote from the control of the people, operating through vast bureaucracies that render popular participation in executive decisions impossible, can serve the interests of the people. Nixon's isolated decision making was the ultimate expression of the extent to which power has been removed from the people at large.

Second, the presidency to them is but one element in a power elite and can only produce the policies the power elite want. They note that the men appointed by presidents to key positions of power fitted perfectly the characteristics set forth in power elite theory. Eisenhower's secretary of defense was Charles Wilson of General Motors; Johnson's was Robert McNamara of Ford. A succession of investment bankers occupied the post of secretary of the treasury. Roy Ash, president of Litton Industries, was appointed director of the Office of Management and Budget. H. R. Haldeman, and several other members of the White House staff, came from big advertising and public relations agencies—a very appropriate background for Nixon's purposes. The top foreign policy jobs in the State Department and the White House went to corporate lawyers (John Foster Dulles, William Rogers) and foundation and Harvard–M.I.T. men (McGeorge Bundy, Walt Rostow, Henry Kissinger).

Moreover, since World War II a succession of presidents had called on certain types of men from outside their administrations for advice and help in times of crisis—and these men were typically power-elite members. A perfect example was the ever-present corporate lawyer John McCloy. At the time of the 1962 Cuban missile crisis *The New York Times* reported:

> In Frankfort John J. McCloy was about to go into a big private business conference when he got a call from President Kennedy. He told the waiting businessmen, "Sorry, boys, I hate to drop names, but the President needs me." He took the next plane home. [11]

Once home, he sat at Adlai Stevenson's elbow at the United Nations while crucial negotiations were conducted. And throughout the decision making on Vietnam, Lyndon Johnson consulted with a "Senior Advisory Group" drawn from men of this kind, including McCloy, corporate lawyers Dean Acheson and Abe Fortas, and investment banker Douglas Dillon.

Nor can the power-elite interpretation of the presidency be dismissed by pointing to the fact that among recent presidents only Kennedy was born into wealth and a big business background. The humble origins of Eisenhower, Johnson, Ford, and Carter did not produce in them any basic antagonism to the values of corporate capitalism.

Eisenhower loved to consort with big businessmen. As for Nixon, he was a particularly interesting case in point. He was born poor. As a boy he used to get up early to go to market before school to buy the fruits and vegetables for the grocery shelves in his father's filling station. He studied diligently at such non-Ivy League institutions as Whittier College and Duke, where he was president of the student bar association. He tried and failed to get a job in a big New York law firm and then in the FBI; he became an assistant city attorney in Whittier, worked in Washington as a lawyer in the Office of Price Administration, and was a lieutenant in the Navy. This was his background when he was elected to the House in 1946. And when he ran for president in 1960, he still had very little money.

By the time he was nominated in 1968, however, it was a very different story. He was a member of the New York law firm of Nixon, Mudge, Rose, Guthrie, Alexander, and Mitchell; he was also on the board of directors of several companies; he belonged to exclusive clubs; and he lived in a very expensive 10-room cooperative apartment on Fifth Avenue.

Is the Nixon saga, then, a perfect illustration of the Horatio Alger syndrome? Not for the left. For them it is an example of the way a man can make it in America by being useful to the power elite. From the beginning he was a candidate of the business interests. The Dana Smith Fund—the one that came to light in 1952 and which would have cost him the vice-presidency but for the Checkers speech on television—was made up of contributions from realtors, manufacturers, and oil and gas interests.

Once in the presidency his dependence on big business and wealthy individuals for campaign contributions continued, but on a much larger scale. And his choice of friends indicated where his values lay. His closest friend was Bebe Rebozo, the land developer, with whom he spent much of his time when he went to Florida. Another was Robert Abplanalp, the multimillionaire inventor of the aerosol spray-can valve. Both of them helped the president with personal investments, including the purchase of the western White House at San Clemente.

According to the left, though the Watergate uproar uncovered the financial greed of Nixon and his associates, it dealt only with those transgressions which even the power elite found to be in bad taste. Certain forms must be preserved if the power of the elite is not to be shaken. Nixon was too crude and too insecure to work within the approved norms of behavior. But the investigations never went beyond uncovering the grossest excesses. The Ervin and Rodino Committee debates, said Sheldon Wolin, responded to "an unrelenting pressure to confine the issues to legal categories, the hearings to courtroom norms, and the abuses to the standards of the criminal law."[12] The Nixon pardon was a further effort to contain the damage and prevent exposure of the real problem—the perpetuation and expansion of the power of the ruling class.

Even within the context of illegal conduct the investigators made much more fuss about the withholding of tapes, and the use of the IRS to harass a few rich liberals, than about the revelations of the habitual use by the FBI of flagrantly illegal methods to infiltrate and break up dissident left groups and the Black Panthers. For years the left complained of their being subjected to official repression. Now everything they alleged was publicly documented. But the revelations evoked only mild interest, nothing like the "firestorm" of protest set off by the "Saturday night massacre"—a journalistic catchphrase for a couple of firings and a resignation of men whose careers in the long run would only be advanced by the incident.

In its essence Watergate was merely one more expression of the corruption and power mania that permeate the presidency, the power elite, and the entire governmental system. It was so crudely managed that those responsible for it had to be removed. But nothing has happened to prevent the presidency from serving the interests of corporate capitalism in the future.

The Radical Right

To the radical right, the presidency is an office that is almost bound to serve undesirable ends. "Those who control the President indirectly gain control of the whole country," says Gary Allen.[13] Woodrow Wilson was controlled by Colonel House, who worked with Wall Street to get us into World War I and bankroll the Bolshevik revolution of 1917. Nelson Rockefeller controlled Richard Nixon. He was then chosen by Ford as his vice-president, and was successful in placing his men in key positions in Ford's White House staff, especially the Domestic Council. Although conservatives forced Rockefeller off the 1976 Republican ticket, he would continue to be a dominant force behind the scenes as long as people such as Ford—or any of the Democrats—were president.

Foreign policy under Nixon and Ford was in the hands of Kissinger, who was a Rockefeller man *and* a Harvard man—the most undesirable possible combination from the perspective of the right.

The proof of the dominance of the Rockefellers and the Kissingers was in the policies themselves. Nixon openly admitted that he was a Keynesian, a disciple of the British economist John Maynard Keynes, who was the prophet of deficit spending, of the socialist New Deal, and the welfare state. Even while the debate about impounding went on, giving the illusion of Nixon's conservatism, the national debt rose, inflation ran rampant, and the dollar depreciated abroad.

What was happening in America was merely part of the preparation for a world federation. As Robert Welch explained it in a John Birch Society newsletter in 1971, Nixon (who had publicly criticized the society for several years) was using the presidency as a stepping stone to becoming ruler of the world. This he could only do with the approval and even the support of the communist powers. Welch came to this conclusion as a result of Nixon's announced trip to China, his monetary policy, and his appointing "left-wingers" to his administration.

Not all right-wingers saw Nixon in this light. For a time the liberals' attacks on him aroused sympathy for him on the right. But the right wing generally could never find much to approve of in Richard Nixon. Although he took some steps in a conservative direction, his general posture was to undermine the country's security and prestige.

He was forever trying to secure a place in history for which the standards were set by leftist academics who gave Franklin Roosevelt the ultimate accolade of greatness. Franklin Roosevelt started this country on the road to its decline and fall. Richard Nixon, with minor variations, used Roosevelt's main themes from the time he entered the White House. Gerald Ford, Nixon's choice, continued those themes. There might have been some improvement had Ronald Reagan made it to the White House. But as governor of California he, too, had not matched his rhetoric with his actions, and had presided over massive spending programs.

Whether the White House is occupied by Democrats or Republicans seems to make little difference. The left-wing establishment continues to rule.

The Centrists

Centrist scholars have been among the great admirers of the presidency. They saw the growth of the responsibilities and authority in the office as a demonstration of the flexibility of the constitutional system established by the Founding Fathers, allowing every generation to deal with contemporary problems without destroying the original framework.

With the Johnson and Nixon presidencies, however, centrists grew uncomfortable. Although they were attached to the presidency as an institution, their basic analysis called for a balance between the different branches of government. For a while it seemed that the enlargement of presidential power was throwing the system out of balance.

Then the mounting evidence of improper and illegal conduct in the presidency was acutely unsettling to the centrists. They were deeply reluctant to face up to the prospect of impeachment. They shrank from the thought of plunging the country into a long drawn-out constitutional crisis and of taking a measure that had only been tried once in the country's history. And that one example was a poor model, for the effort to impeach Andrew Johnson, which had fallen short by only one vote in the Senate, had been inspired not by malfeasance in office but solely by disagreement with his policies.

So there was a sense of relief among centrists when Nixon's resignation came. And the way it came about reinforced their belief in the efficacy of the American system.

Restoring the balance.   What happened to the two presidents who had gone beyond reasonable bounds in their use of presidential power is immensely reassuring. Vietnam, which had driven Lyndon Johnson to mishandle power, destroyed his power. The inability to overcome the resistance of a small country, and opposition in the Congress and in the country, clearly demonstrated the limits on presidential power and forced his withdrawal from politics.

As for Watergate, nothing could show more plainly that the plan of the Founding Fathers was as effectively relevant as ever. The Congress, the courts, the free press, and public opinion all came into play to check the undoubted excesses of presidential power.

Liberals argued that the outcome was in large part the result of sheer luck. But to centrists it was the system itself that had prevailed. The president and the men around him had overreached themselves in so many directions that somewhere along the line it was inevitable that a judge, a reporter, or a congressional committee would have sounded the alarm. But for the lucky breaks, it might have taken a little longer. But in the American system there are just too many people in too many places with a vested interest in challenging the White House to allow power to get completely out of hand.

The imperatives of the office.   Centrists do not accept the accusations from the radicals of left and right that the presidency is merely a captive of powerful outside groups. No matter to whom a president is beholden for campaign money and support he has to answer to two imperatives. The first is the electorate; and there is no group or business that can offer a president a greater reward than reelection to the presidency. So presidents repeatedly disappoint influential supporters by acting expediently, that is, in response to the prevailing wishes of the people at large.

The second imperative is the institution of the presidency itself. No matter what their class or background or socioeconomic affiliations, presidents become deeply aware of the history and mystique of the office. They think of presidents who came before them; they want to measure up to the best of them; they are concerned with the verdict of history.

Thus when Kennedy forced U.S. Steel to rescind its price increase, he was not simply dealing with an economic problem. He felt that the corporation's president, Roger Blough, had betrayed him: he had not kept the implied steel industry promise that if the president persuaded labor not to ask for large wage increases the industry would hold the line on prices. Moreover, Blough had come to the White House to tell the president of his decision *after* it had been released to the press. Kennedy took this as an affront to the presidency itself. So here was a confrontation between two centers of power. The presidency was not an agent of outside forces but an institution in its own right, and the holder of the office must defend it.

Centrists, who voted for Richard Nixon in large numbers in 1972, are no longer eager to find favorable things to say about him. He tarnished the office that they venerate and inflicted grave damage on the political system before it found ways of stopping him. Some of his predecessors had abused their powers, too, but not as comprehensively and systematically as he had done.

Still, centrists note that, even in the last, convulsive throes of his tenure he held back from doing his worst. He did not burn the tapes. He accepted (apparently after some hesitation) the decision of the Supreme Court that he must deliver the tapes. He did not respond to the desperate pleas of his associates to pardon them before he resigned. Some degree of decency remained, along with a continued concern with the verdict of history. Although it is unlikely that history will do well by him, he could still hope that his foreign policy would ultimately loom larger than Watergate. But there could be no such hope if he had abandoned all shreds of ethics and morality at the end.

We still need a strong presidency.   Some reforms are needed within the presidency, say the centrists. We do not need to incorporate any of the elements of the parliamentary system into our own. Our system has grown according to the nature of American society; it will reject efforts to transplant organs that have grown in other cultural settings.

Still, a more open presidency than those of Johnson and Nixon is clearly desirable. The president should be more accessible, not allow his staff to isolate him, and hold more press conferences. However, there is a limit to the extent to which the president can conduct the affairs of the country in full view of the cameras. Nixon used executive privilege to cover up illegal acts. But executive privilege for legitimate purposes is a perfectly reasonable doctrine.

In a different context, the case for executive privilege that Nixon presented in a statement issued on March 12, 1973, would have been sound. It was rooted, he said, in the Constitution's vesting of executive power solely in the president. Consequently, it is necessary

> to protect communications within the executive branch in a variety of circumstances. . . . Without such protection, our military security, our relations with other countries, our law enforcement procedures and many other aspects of the national interest could be significantly damaged and the decision-making process of the executive branch could be impaired.

Under the doctrine of the separation of powers, "the manner in which the president personally exercises his executive powers is not subject to questioning by another branch of government." What applies to the president must apply to members of his staff, "for their roles are in effect an extension of the Presidency." He must be able to trust his staff and trust the confidentiality of his discussions with them. They "must not be inhibited by the possibility that their advice and assistance will ever become a matter of public debate, either during their tenure in government or at a later date." Otherwise, they'd hardly be likely to speak their minds freely to him. The doctrine, he said, must not be used "as a shield to prevent embarrassing information from being made available" but only "in the most compelling circumstances" and where the public interest is directly threatened.

In its 1974 decision in the case of *United States* v. *Nixon* the Supreme Court found that Nixon had in fact used the concept "as a shield to prevent embarrassing information being made available" and ordered him to provide the necessary information. But the Court also said that the rest of his reasoning was valid, and that executive privilege was implicit in the Constitution.

As the centrists see it, then, the president must be able to act decisively, and sometimes out of the public view. We must have a strong presidency. But we also have need of a strong Congress, a strong Supreme Court, a strong system of state and local governments, as well as a potent public opinion, press, and interest group system. We must maintain a balance, the kind of balance that emerges not from inertia and weakness on all sides, but from the interplay of strong forces, sometimes cooperating, sometimes competing with each other.

Conclusion

Two main points emerge from this chapter. The first is that the debate over the institution of the presidency that has occurred since the mid-1960s has been useful and healthy. Until then the office was enveloped in a mystique that carried it beyond human scope to realms normally inhabited by supermen or gods. It was not only the courtiers in the White House who invested their presidents with the mysteries and rights of monarchs. The scholars who wrote the college textbooks extolled the presidency in exalted terms. Theodore White, who wrote chronicles of each presidential election from 1960 to 1972, described Kennedy and Nixon as if they had become mystic figures in some great poetic drama. It is time, says Thomas Cronin, to deflate our rhetoric and see the presidency for what it is—a human institution, occupied by fallible men. The responsibility that has gravitated there is great. But the power of the office is not unlimited; and it is absurd to burden this single office with all the hopes and aspirations of the total society.[14]

Thus the chastening of the liberals and the centrists that has taken place in the last few years has been all to the good. Watergate, despite the trauma that it generated, will at least reduce the danger of another bid for excessive power and deflate some of the more grandiose self-perceptions that the occupants of the White House may develop.

The second conclusion from this chapter is that, despite the deflation and debunking that has occurred, the presidency will remain an institution of substantial power no matter who occupies the office. For one thing, there is little prospect that we will separate the functions of chief of state and head of government. The president will continue to be our ceremonial leader, and the media will continue to lavish attention on every move of his family and himself, treating them as if they were a kind of royal family. This was true even of the unpretentious Jerry Ford. And when Jimmy Carter and his family chose to walk the inaugural parade route rather than ride in the presidential limousine, the media went into paroxysms of delight, as though he were a king who was deigning to walk.

So much awe has been invested in the presidency, in fact, that a president, by the very act of trying to break through the mystique to establish contact with the people, could thereby augment his power and status. A president who was highly successful at broadcast, two-way conversations with the public could very well endow himself with more power, deliberately or despite himself, than any of his predecessors. Openness, in other words, does not in itself guarantee constraints on power.

Then, too, presidents (and the people who write about them) will inevitably test their actions against the judgment of history. In fact, concern with the verdict of posterity may well, as the centrists argue, have a desirable restraining effect on the conduct of the president. Yet, the opposite could result. The appeal to history, like the appeal to conscience or creed, can move men to either moderation or impatience with the restraints of politics and public opinion.

As Lyndon Johnson got into deeper and deeper trouble in Vietnam and as his political instincts told him how much damage he was doing to his reelection prospects, he plunged forward, reassuring himself with the belief that history would vindicate him. Richard Nixon was similarly convinced that his actions must be seen in the long context of time. After his reelection he told an interviewer:

> Now when Henry [Kissinger] comes in here in the morning and brings up what Scotty Reston and the other columnists are saying, I tell him, "Henry, all that matters is that it comes out right. Six months from now, nobody will remember what the columnists wrote." Decision makers can't be affected by current opinion, by TV barking at you and commentators banging away with the ideas that World War III is coming because of the mining of Haiphong. Nor can decisions be affected by the demonstrators outside.[15]

Certainly decision makers should not allow the commentators to unnerve them or to make their decisions for them. Presidents must sometimes take actions that run counter to the majority wishes in the hope that the majority will later see that the decisons were right. Yet the danger persists that future presidents may regard themselves as figures in a great historical panorama, responsible never to the present but only to their conception of the future.

Still, even the most modest of presidents can no longer take William Howard Taft's advice on how to do his job. With the federal government so inextricably caught up in the economy, with great stockpiles of thermonuclear weapons guarding the national security, presidents have massive responsibilities and will inevitably have the power that goes with such responsibilities. Some, like the Roosevelts, Kennedy, and Johnson, will exercise their power with enthusiasm and work constantly to overcome the constraints that confront them. Others, like Eisenhower and Ford, will adopt a somewhat more subdued role. But whether we like it or not, the prospect is that the White House will continue to be easily the most potent source of power in the American national government.

Notes and References

1.   See Edward S. Corwin, *The President: Office and Powers*, 3rd ed. (New York: New York University Press, 1948), p. 38.

2.   David Easton and Jack Dennis, "The Child's Image of Government," *The Annals*, Vol. 361 (September 1965), pp. 40–57.

3.   See Fred I. Greenstein, "The Psychologic Functions of the Presidency for Citizens," in *The American Presidency: Vital Center*, Elmer E. Cornwell, ed. (Glenview, Ill.: Scott, Foresman and Company, 1966), pp. 31–32.

4.   Richard E. Neustadt, *Presidential Power* (New York: John Wiley & Sons, Inc., 1960), p. 10.

5.   Johnson claimed subsequently that he had never intended to run for another term anyway. However, incumbent presidents who are eligible for another term are likely to find it difficult to resist pressure on them to run again—if they are popular.

6.   George E. Reedy, *The Twilight of the Presidency* (New York: The World Publishing Company, 1970).

7.   James Barber, *The Presidential Character* (Englewood Cliffs, N.J.: Prentice-Hall, Inc., 1972), and "President Nixon and Richard Nixon: Character Trap," *Psychology Today*, October 1974, pp. 112–14.

8.   Richard E. Neustadt, "Kennedy in the Presidency," *Political Science Quarterly*, Vol. 79, No. 3 (September 1964), pp. 321–34.

9.   See, for example, Amaury de Riencourt, *The Coming Caesars* (New York: Coward, McCann & Geoghegan, Inc., 1957); and Willmoore Kendall, *The Conservative Affirmation* (Chicago: Henry Regnery Company, 1963).

10.   Statement of the President, May 23, 1973.

11.   *The New York Times*, November 3, 1962.

12.   Sheldon S. Wolin, "From Jamestown to San Clemente," *The New York Review of Books*, September 19, 1974, p. 6.

13.   Gary Allen, *None Dare Call It Conspiracy* (Rossmoor, Calif.: Concord Press, 1971), p. 34.

14. Thomas E. Cronin, "Superman, Our Textbook President," *The Washington Monthly,* Vol. 2 (October 1970), and *The State of the Presidency* (Boston: Little, Brown and Company, 1975).

15. Interview with Associated Press writer Saul Pelt, December 20, 1972.

Chapter 7

The Congress: How Much Has It Changed?

In the current debate over Congress we find almost a mirror image of the controversy over the presidency. Traditionally, left-of-center spokesmen criticized Congress as a tiresome institution—unrepresentative, obstructionist, corrupt, tyrannical, unresponsive to the needs of the age and thus obsolete. To the right of center, Congress was typically seen as the most important defender of the values of American life. Centrists, while admirers of the presidency, have regarded Congress as *their* institution, a source of endless study and fascination and the epitome of most of the virtues that they prize in political life.

But Vietnam unsettled these assessments. Moreover, Congress has been in the throes of change for the past few years, and these changes have caused reevaluations by our various perspectives. Before we examine some rival perspectives on our national legislature, let us begin by describing the major functions and characteristics of Congress.

The Functions of Congress

Congress is assigned three major functions under the Constitution: to legislate, to represent the people, and to play its part in the system of checks and balances (see Appendix 1). To begin with, Congress is defined as the lawmaking, or legislative, arm of the government. According to Article I, Section 1, "All legislative Powers herein granted shall be vested in a Congress of the United States, which shall consist of a Senate and House of Representatives." The lawmaking powers specified in Article I relate to establishing and maintaining armed forces, raising and spending money, controlling commerce between the states, as well as those laws which are "necessary and proper" to carrying out its other powers.

Then, it is Congress's job to represent the people. But it represents them differently in each of its two houses. The House of Representatives speaks for the people at large. Members of the House are elected from 435 districts of more or less equal population, with each district electing one representative. Thus less populated rural districts may spread over a much wider area than the smaller, densely populated inner-city districts. Further, the Constitution guarantees each state a minimum of one representative. As a result, Alaska, Delaware, Nevada, Vermont, and Wyoming—because of their low populations—have only the minimum of one representative in the House. The current number of representatives for each state is indicated in Figure 7–1. This distribution of House seats changes every 10 years in accordance with population shifts indicated by the census.

Senators, on the other hand, speak for the people in their states. Each state elects two senators, regardless of the size of its population. Thus in 1976 Wyoming's two senators represented a population of around 350,000, whereas California's represented close to 21 million people.

Since there are over four times as many representatives as senators and they are more equally distributed among the population, the House claims that it is the more representative of the two legislative bodies, and closer to the people. This claim is reinforced by the fact that representatives must stand for election every two years, while senators serve for six years, with a third of their seats being subject to the election process every two years. Senators, on the other hand, argue that they speak for large, diverse areas that include cities, suburbs, and rural areas, whereas each representative typically speaks for a much more limited constituency.

Finally, the Constitution assigns Congress a key role in the system of checks and balances. The Founding Fathers were afraid of concentrating too much power in any one branch of the government. Accordingly, they divided the legislative power between the two houses of Congress, requiring that laws must be ratified by both, and they assigned both houses differing constituencies and differing terms of office to ensure that their power bases and assessments of the people's needs would not be identical. Furthermore, the two houses' constituencies and terms of office differed not only from each other's but also from those of the executive branch. Thus Congress and the president would limit each other's power. And the framers spelled out these mutual limitations by requiring that the president's top appointments and treaty-making power be subject to approval by the Senate; that he could spend no money not specifically appropriated by Congress; and that in turn he could veto a congressional bill, but that his veto could be overridden by a two-thirds vote of both houses of Congress. As we saw in Chapter 6, these mutual limitations have not always prevented a greater accumulation of power than the framers intended, particularly in the executive branch. Still, in comparison with most other democratic systems in the world today, the U.S. Congress is a remarkably strong rival to executive power.

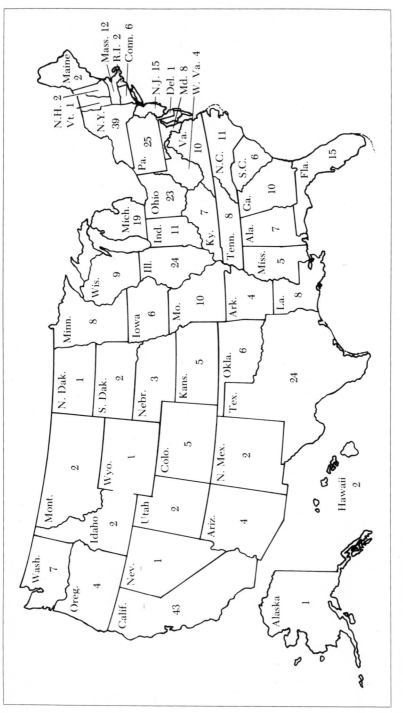

FIGURE 7–1   Membership in the House of Representatives by States, Based on 1970 Census (Data from U.S. Bureau of the Census, *Statistical Abstract of the United States* [Washington, D.C.: Government Printing Office, 1976], p. 458.)

The Major
Characteristics of Congress

Six major characteristics of Congress need to be discussed before we can get into our debate between the perspectives. These are its composition; its orientation toward the local constituency; its diffusion of leadership; the elaborate nature of its procedures; its power to investigate; and the way it handles its ethical problems.

Composition

As is clear from Table 7-1, Congress is made up of people from a great diversity of backgrounds. It is also clear that they do not constitute a precise cross section of the American electorate. The typical member of Congress is a white, Protestant male, lawyer or businessman, around 51 years old.

Localism

The president is elected by a national constituency. Since members of Congress are given their office by a district or state, their political roots are deeply embedded in the community. The money and manpower for their campaigns, their organizational strength, and their power bases are in their home districts. Therefore, they must take care of the requests and grievances of individual constituents and organized groups in their districts.

TABLE 7-1   95th Congress, 1977–78

Characteristic	House (435)	Senate (100)
Occupation		
Law	215	65
Business and banking	81	13
Education	45	6
Agriculture	14	6
Career government service	22	0
Journalism and media management	24	4
Medicine	3	1
Geology	0	2
Labor	6	0
Other	25	3
Sex		
Men	418	100
Women	17	0

TABLE 7–1   (continued)

Characteristic	House (435)	Senate (100)
Race and Ethnicity		
Whites	412	96
Blacks	16	1
Orientals	2	3
Spanish surnames	5	0
Religion		
Protestant	255	69
Catholic	107	12
Jewish	18	5
Mormon	4	3
Other	51	11
Average age	49	54

SOURCE: Adapted from "Congressional Directory," National Democratic and Republican Congressional Committees, Associated Press, and U.S. News and World Report, January 10, 1977, p. 29.

Until recent years the difference in congressional and presidential constituencies was not simply a matter of local versus national electorates. As we saw in Chapter 4, the electoral college arithmetic produced a presidential bias toward urban, industrial areas; Congress, on the other hand, tended to look out for the interests of the small town and the farm. This was especially true of the House of Representatives. Even the most rural states contained at least one sizable city, so Senators could not easily ignore urban interests. The House, on the other hand, still spoke for a disproportionately large number of districts outside the major urban centers. This was because the state legislatures, which were supposed to redraw the boundary lines between congressional districts every 10 years, often ignored the surge of population away from the small towns and farms toward the cities and continued to give small numbers of rural people the same representation in Congress as large numbers of urban and suburban dwellers.

Gradually, however, the big population centers gained ground in Congress, and their position improved still further in 1964 with the Supreme Court's decision in *Wesberry* v. *Sanders*. Wide disparities in the populations of congressional districts, said the Court, were unconstitutional. Subsequently, the states redrew their district lines under persistent prodding from the Supreme Court, which insisted in 1969 that the states must justify any significant variations in the populations of congressional districts. Since the 1960s there has been a substantial shift in the population base of congressional districts, with a decline of predominately rural districts and an increase in predominately suburban districts. Both kinds of district now number about 130—which constitutes a decrease of about 50 for the rural areas, and a gain of close to 40 for the suburban districts.

Despite the removal of the rural bias in the composition of Congress, president and Congress still report to different power bases and must sometimes come into conflict. A president may appeal to Congress on grounds of party or national interest, and he has some powerful resources to back up his appeal. But in the final analysis the member of Congress must build a case for reelection on the relations with the district or the state rather than with the White House.

Dispersal of Leadership

Power in Congress is distributed in several directions, which often rival each other. The political party, the congressional committees, the committee chairpersons, and seniority determine the power bases in both houses.

Political party—its importance and its limitations.   In most national legislatures the political party is a principal means of providing leadership. This is especially true in parliamentary systems. Under those systems the executive branch of the government is not elected directly by the people but by the legislature from among the members of the party or combination of parties that constitute a majority in the legislature. And the chosen members of the executive branch continue to constitute the government only so long as their party or parties in the legislature continue to support them.

The power of party is much less in the United States, but it is not insignificant. Party plays an important role in the organization and leadership of Congress. Almost all members of Congress run for office under one of the two main party labels; and they stay with their party affiliation faithfully during the first votes of every new session of the House and Senate. Those first votes determine which party will hold the official leadership positions. These positions for the 95th Congress and the legislators elected to them are shown in Table 7-2 in descending order of importance for each house.

TABLE 7–2   *Elective Leadership Positions,*
95th Congress, 1977–78

	Majority Leadership (Democrats)	Minority Leadership (Republicans)
House of Representatives	Speaker: Thomas ("Tip") O'Neill, Massachusetts	
	Majority leader: Jim Wright, Texas	Minority leader: John Rhodes, Arizona
	Majority whip: John Brademas, Indiana	Minority whip: Robert Michel, Illinois
Senate	Majority leader: Robert Byrd, West Virginia	Minority leader: Howard Baker, Tennessee
	Majority whip: Alan Cranston, California	Minority whip: Ted Stevens, Alaska

The House leadership includes a position not paralleled in the Senate, that of the Speaker, who is the leader of his party, official spokesman for the House, and next in line for succession to the president after the vice-president. Thus the majority leader in the House is the second spot, whereas in the Senate it is the top position. The job of the majority and minority whips is to provide liaison between party leadership and rank-and-file members and also to try to achieve as much party unity in voting as possible.

Party considerations also prevail in the selection of the chairpersons of the several committees which, as we shall see shortly, do a large part of the work of both houses of Congress.

Since 1932 the Democrats have been the majority party in both houses of Congress in every year except 1947–48 and 1953–54. In 1977–78 their margins over the Republicans were exceptionally large: 292 to 143 in the House and 61 to 38 (with one Independent) in the Senate. Consequently, in most years the Democrats have held the top positions in the Congress, whereas Republican elections in Congress have determined only who would lead the minority, or opposition, party. This has been the case in the committees, too. To be a Republican in most years since 1932 meant being deprived of the chance to run a committee and being able to rise no higher than ranking minority member of a committee.

Also contributing to the party spirit in Congress are the various groups and committees that bring together party members in each house. At the broadest level, there are conferences of all members of the party (the Democrats in the House calling their conference the party "caucus"); and each party conference has a steering committee. There are also policy committees of party leaders. Finally, within each party there are factional groups—informal associations of members who are to the left or the right of the prevailing consensus within their party in the Congress. The most potent of these associations is the Democratic Study Group in the House, which comprises about 170 of the Democrats' more liberal members.

The result of all this party machinery, both formal and informal, is that more often than not members vote with a majority of their party. Moreover, the trend toward party-line voting appears to be gaining ground. Thus in the 90th Congress of 1967–68, on those issues that clearly separated Democrats from Republicans (that is, a majority of voting Democrats opposing a majority of voting Republicans), the average Democrat voted with the majority of his party 62 percent of the time—57 percent in the Senate, 63 percent in the House. By the 94th Congress of 1975–76 there was more party unity among Democrats in the House. In the first half of 1975 Democrats were sticking together 72 percent of the time whenever there was a confrontation with the Republicans; and the figure for the newly elected Democrats was 79 percent.

On the Republican side there has been a slightly higher tendency to hold together with close to two-thirds of the senators and more than 70 percent of the representatives uniting on party-line votes.[1]

Although these figures suggest a certain degree of party cohesion, they also reveal a much higher incidence of crossing party lines than is true in legislatures in most other democratic countries. Elsewhere it is most unusual to find from a quarter to a third of the members of a party voting against the proposals of their party leadership.

The reason for this relative weakness of party structure in Congress is closely related to the point made earlier—the importance of the local constituency to the congressman. In practice, the national parties, like the president, rarely control the congressman's relationships with his own district. The larger part of his campaign funds will usually have to be raised at home, and his political organization, though identifying itself with the national party label, is essentially a local structure. Consequently, when the party leaders in Congress ask for the member's vote, they may be refused if their position is contrary to what the congressman perceives to be the wishes of a vital segment of opinion in his home district. Thus the party whip, whose job it is to try to get the members to vote with the leadership, does not give orders. He conveys the wishes of the leaders, but often those wishes are ignored.

In 1968, for example, there were six Democrats in the House who voted against their own party's majority more than 70 percent of the time, two as often as 83 percent—yet they continued to call themselves Democrats, and there was no suggestion that they be cast out of the party. Nor did the Democratic party do anything about the fact that in 1977 four southern Democratic senators—James Eastland of Mississippi, John McClellan of Arkansas, Herman Talmadge of Georgia, and James Allen of Alabama—helped sponsor a fund-raising event for the 1978 reelection campaign of Strom Thurmond, a Republican senator from South Carolina.

On very rare occasions, punishment has been inflicted on members who come out flagrantly against their own party. In 1965 two Democratic representatives, one from Mississippi, the other from South Carolina, were deprived of their seniority for openly supporting Barry Goldwater in the previous year's presidential election. Even then both of them continued to call themselves Democrats.

The committees. Legislatures, like all other large decision-making bodies, must do some of their work in committees. National assemblies are too big to handle details expeditiously. Moreover, mechanisms have to be provided to divide up the members so that they can specialize in one or more of a vast multitude of complex problems.

In Congress the power of committees emerges not only from these logistical requirements but also from the relative weakness of other sources of leadership. In consequence, the permanent, or standing, committees of Congress have become small legislatures in their own right.

Their power is not absolute, for their recommendations may be overruled or modified by the majority of the House or Senate. Still, the committees' conclusions carry great weight; and committees are often able to overcome potential opposition by entering into agreements with other committees for mutual support.

There is a hierarchy of power among the standing committees. In the House, members value positions on Appropriations, Ways and Means, and Rules. In the

Senate the committees on Foreign Relations, Appropriations, and Finance are the most prestigious. In both chambers, members also vie for assignment to the new Budget committees, created in 1974 to bring federal expenditures into line with revenues. However, even less important committees such as Public Works, Interior, Government Operations, or Labor may provide valuable opportunities for bringing benefits to constituents, or for gaining national publicity if they can capture an issue of public concern.

The pressure to specialize has led Congress to go even further in splitting up decision-making responsibilities, for most of the standing committees are divided into subcommittees. And when the 1946 Reorganization Act cut down the number of standing committees, the result was a considerable increase in the number of subcommittees, some of which have a good deal of responsibility and status. This is especially true of the subcommittees of the Appropriation committees.

A further problem with the committee structure both in the House and the Senate is that of overlapping and competing jurisdictions. Thus several committees each claim that they have total or at least partial jurisdiction in such fields as energy, transportation, health, and research and development. In 1973 a select committee of the House under the chairmanship of Richard Bolling of Missouri undertook a study of this problem. After two years and an expenditure of $1.5 million, the Bolling committee brought in proposals for a substantial reorganization of committee assignments and responsibilities. However, almost all the recommendations were rejected by leaders of the House Democrats, who did not want their various committees to lose any of their power. The Senate, on the other hand, has put through a major reorganization of its committee system. In February 1977, the Senate voted 89 to 1 (the dissenting vote coming from a member who was in line to become chairperson of a committee abolished by the reorganization) to reduce its number of committees from 31 to 25, and a still further reduction in the number of committees to 22 was under active consideration. Moreover, the new system limited the number of committees and subcommittees on which a senator may serve to 11 in most cases (previously some had served on 28 to 30) and restricted each senator to chairing one committee and three subcommittees.

No discussion of congressional committees is complete without mention of the professional staffs they appoint to help them to do their work. Some of these staff members are specialists in the legal and procedural matters involved in drafting legislation, others in the technical substance of policy issues. Although some of these staff members come and go according to the political fortunes of particular congressmen, others become indispensable to committee work, and build lifetime careers with a particular committee. They become, essentially, permanent bureaucrats. As we shall see in Chapter 8, bureaucracies have a life of their own, and congressional staffs are often as important as their elected chiefs in affecting decisions in Congress.

The committee chairpersons.   For many years the power of committees and subcommittees was almost synonymous with the power of their chairpersons.

The chair, if sufficiently determined and adept, could usually be the decisive voice on such pivotal matters as selecting and assigning committee staff, appointing subcommittee chairpersons, allocating funds, and deciding whether and when committee hearings should be held and votes taken. In extreme cases (and there were more than a few of these) the chair used these powers arbitrarily and despotically, ignoring the wishes of the majority of their committees.

This is much less the case today as a result of reforms that began around 1972. In the House, Democrats weakened the power of committee chairpersons over the subcommittees; they barred congressmen from chairing more than one committee or subcommittee, thus giving junior members a chance to chair a subcommittee. And meetings of congressional committees have been opened to the public except where the committee specifically votes to close them on a particular day. House Democrats have also taken steps to increase the influence of their caucus, so that committee chairpersons will take account of the sentiment of the entire Democratic membership and not only their own and the committees' preferences.

Seniority.   In 1910 the House revolted against the power of the Speaker, "Uncle" Joe Cannon, and stripped him of the power to decide who would chair House committees. After that both House and Senate resorted to the practice of promotion through seniority. This operates simply through the process of political survival. A member is appointed to a committee, and is then reelected and reelected to Congress until other committee members who were there before him die or retire or move over to other committees. At that point he takes over the chair if he is of the majority party in the Congress, or becomes the ranking minority member on the committee.

This law seemed sacrosanct until change came in the 1970s. First, the Republicans in the House made the minority leadership of each committee subject to election by all Republicans on the committee. Then the Democrats required that the selection of chairpersons be decided by secret ballot of the entire caucus.

At first the reforms seemed to be matters of form only, for all the challenges to senior committee leaders were rejected, and seniority prevailed. However, with the impetus provided by a surge of Democratic freshmen elected in 1974, some senior members were removed from the chair at the beginning of 1975. F. Edward Hebert of Louisiana, aged 73, lost the top position on Armed Services, by vote in the Democratic caucus. The same happened to W. R. Poage, Texas, aged 75, on Agriculture; and Wright Patman, Texas, aged 81, on Banking and Currency.

We should also remember two other limiting factors on seniority. It counts toward leadership once a member is on a committee, but in itself it does not determine which committees a member gets on in the first place. Second, the principle applies only to the committees themselves, and not to the party leadership positions—Speaker of the House, Senate majority leader, the party whips, and so on.

A further shift of power is indicated by the decline in the seniority of southern members. The South had gained great strength in the Congress because its Democratic senators and representatives faced little Republican opposition, were reelected term after term, built up decades of seniority, and succeeded to the chair of many key committees. Consequently, in the House in 1964 the South held 53 percent of the important committee and subcommittee chairmanships. But this is changing. By 1975 the proportions of southern chairmanships were down to 39 percent for committees, and 32 percent for subcommittees. The trend in the Senate has been similar.

And worse is yet to come for the South. In the Senate in 1975 five southerners and five northerners had 20 or more years of seniority. But among those who had been in the Senate for 10 to 19 years—the next generation of committee leaders—there was only one southerner to 19 northerners.

In addition, a series of sex scandals that rocked Congress in 1974 and 1975 toppled other congressional giants from power. Wilbur Mills, chairperson of the Ways and Means Committee, whose authority over vital social and economic legislation had sometimes seemed greater than the president's, ran into trouble in the fall of 1974. Long regarded as a man devoted only to his work and family, Mills amazed Washington and his Arkansas constituents by becoming publicly involved with a burlesque dancer known as "Fanne Fox, the Argentine Firecracker." His escapades ended in his being hospitalized and his issuing a statement that his erratic behavior had been caused by alcoholism. He vowed to stop drinking and wanted to continue as committee chairperson. However, under pressure from House leaders, he conceded that this would no longer be possible, and he gave up the chairmanship and his power. Another sex scandal, this one involving a misuse of congressional funds, forced the resignation of Wayne Hays from the House Administration Committee in 1977.

Procedures: How a Bill Becomes Law

In most parliamentary systems legislation is introduced by the executive branch, and the legislature is expected to examine, debate, and sometimes amend it. However, the final form is usually not fundamentally different from the original proposal. Nor is the process a very lengthy one. In the U.S. Congress, however, a proposed bill must pass through many stages and be subjected to intensive and prolonged scrutiny; thus it stands a high risk of either being killed or altered beyond recognition. The following is a description of the procedure by which a bill becomes law.

The House.   A bill is first introduced in one or both houses. Assuming in this case that it begins in the House, the Speaker refers it to a standing committee. If the committee chairperson supports the proposal, he may get the committee staff to work on preparing it for public hearings, or he may refer it to a subcommittee for preliminary discussion and hearings. The hearings themselves may prove to be a substitute for action and may end with the conclusion that more study is needed. However, the hearings may be followed by subcommittee and committee discussion and voting; and if the vote is favorable at both stages, the bill, usually amended, will have passed through the standing committee stage.

There is still another House committee to traverse. Of the 10,000 or so bills introduced into Congress each session, several hundred are approved by the standing committees. Most of these do not raise large issues and proceed routinely to the floor of the House for action. Still, there are enough bills of substance emerging from the standing committees to require that priorities be assigned. That is the Rules Committee's job. Except for money bills no important legislation proceeds to the floor of the House without procedural instructions assigned by Rules.

Deciding when a bill will be presented for a vote places a great potential for power in the Rules Committee. For years this potential was exploited to the full by Judge Howard Smith of Virginia. Chairing a committee which then consisted of 12 members, he could often find five others—a conservative southern Democrat and four Republicans—to join him in opposing legislation he disapproved of; and without a majority no bill could advance. Sometimes, where it appeared that he could not keep all his allies in line, he would avoid a vote by going home.

This situation changed in three stages. First, under pressure from President Kennedy, the membership of the Rules Committee was increased from 12 to 15, so a bill could no longer be defeated by a tie vote. Then Judge Smith retired. He was succeeded by a conservative southern Democrat, who was forced by the committee majority to agree that the committee would hold regular weekly meetings and establish a written set of procedures. When that chairperson retired in 1972, a more liberal northern Democrat took his place, and he was joined by enough new members to ensure a moderate-to-liberal majority on the committee. Since then the Rules Committee has no longer been a graveyard for large numbers of bills. Even so, the standing committees of the House cannot ignore the power of the Rules Committee, and there are still times when a bill that emerges from a standing committee with a strong endorsement is stalled by lack of support in Rules.

If a bill passes through these stages, it will be reported to the floor of the House. Generally, the House respects the work of its committees and provides the simple majority vote needed for final approval. Even so—and especially where the vote in standing committee has been close—some bills are rejected on the floor and others subjected to substantial amendment.

The Senate.   After passage in the House, action still must be taken by the Senate, which has its own network of committees. The standing committees of the Senate often hold extensive hearings that in considerable measure duplicate those of the House.

The Senate's Rules Committee does not have the veto authority of its counterpart in the House. Most bills are taken up on the floor in the order in which they came out of the committees unless they are accepted for immediate consideration by unanimous consent. On the other hand, there are three ways of veto-ing or delaying action that are the special preserve of the Senate.

First, the president's top *appointments* must be ratified by the Senate. This was a hurdle that defeated Johnson when he wanted to appoint Abe Fortas as chief justice and Nixon when he wanted to appoint Clement Haynsworth and Harrold Carswell to the Supreme Court and L. Patrick Gray as FBI director.

Second, a two-thirds vote of the Senate is required to ratify any *treaties* with foreign governments the president may enter into. He has ways of bypassing this requirement in some cases through the use of the Executive Agreement—an agreement ostensibly of too limited and technical a nature to be dignified as a treaty, yet sometimes dealing with matters of considerable importance. None-theless, if his treatment of the Foreign Relations Committee is too cavalier, the committee might find ways of retaliating later.

Third, there is the device of the *filibuster,* a tactic that takes advantage of the Senate's rules permitting unlimited debate and allowing a flow or oratory that can be ended only if its participants drop from exhaustion or if "cloture" is voted. Cloture, the closing of debate, used to require the support of two-thirds of the members present and voting, and this was for many years very difficult to secure. Consequently, the Senate tolerated a solo, continuous oration of 15½ hours by Huey Long of Louisiana, and another of 22 hours by Wayne Morse of Oregon in 1953. Other filibusters, conducted by relays of Senators, went on much longer and succeeded in killing many civil rights bills by preventing the Senate from doing any other business until their proponents agreed to drop the bills.

However, the filibuster was finally broken on the two most important civil rights bills ever considered: the Civil Rights Act of 1964 and the Voting Rights Act of 1965. Then, in 1975, the number needed to apply cloture was reduced to 60, thus making the filibuster a much less formidable obstacle than it used to be.

Conference committees.   When a bill passes the Senate, it may differ from the product that emerges from the House. If the House is unwilling to ac-cept the Senate's version, as is typically the case on important measures, a con-ference committee is convened. This committee is usually comprised of senior members of the appropriate House and Senate standing committees or subcom-mittees.

Occasionally, the differences between the two chambers cannot be recon-ciled, and a bill having survived the rigors of the two houses separately, dies none-theless in the conference. In other cases agreement is reached only after sections in dispute have been referred to both the House and the Senate for further in-structions. When the conference committee manages to arrive at an acceptable compromise, a conference report is drawn up and submitted to both houses for ap-proval—on a take-it or leave-it basis, for further amendment is not allowed. If ap-proval is obtained, the bill goes to the president for his signature. However, under his constitutional authority the president may *veto* the bill by sending it back with his objections to the house that initiated it. If Congress is to prevail, it must override his veto by a two-thirds vote in both houses. A bill can become law without the president's signature if he neither signs nor vetoes it within 10 week-days after it reaches him. On the other hand, if Congress adjourns within those 10 weekdays, the president can kill the bill by taking no action, thereby exercising his *pocket veto.*

Appropriations.   Even if the president signs, the matter does not necessarily end there. Most legislation has little meaning unless funds are provided to implement it. But the process just described, though usually specifying the expenditure of funds, merely provides congressional *authorization* to spend the money once it is provided. The money cannot be provided until Congress has gone through the stage of *appropriation*, which will normally originate in the House and will be initiated in each chamber by the Appropriations committees.

Often this step is a mere formality. But sometimes it is the occasion for further discussion and debate, conducted first in the Appropriations committees and then on the House and Senate floors. The result more often than not is that the amount of money in the appropriations bill is less than the amount authorized in the bill establishing the program.

Figure 7-2 gives us a summary of the procedures for passing a bill we have just described.

Investigations

Congress does not limit itself to legislation. It is also an investigative body. The Constitution does not specifically say that Congress can conduct investigations. But it has been doing so since 1792. And in a 1972 case the Supreme Court said that investigations were a natural corollary of the Constitution's grant to Congress of "all legislative powers," for, without investigating, Congress cannot gather the information it needs to make wise laws.

Congress has ranged far and wide in its investigations, looking into charges of corruption in business and labor; of communist subversion; of presidential abuses of power; of illegal conduct by the CIA; and of the mishandling of foreign policy. The cutting edge of the investigative tool is the power to subpoena witnesses and compel them, under threat of imprisonment for contempt of Congress, to testify under oath (unless they take the Fifth Amendment).

In recent years the Supreme Court has set some limits to Congress's power to punish, insisting that Congress not "expose for the sake of exposure," and that it relate its questions to its legislative purposes. However, since almost every area of life can be the subject of legislation, it is not difficult to make a case for investigating almost anything.

Congress is eager to make this case, for a well-designed investigation can provide the drama the media loves; and televised hearings have helped to make

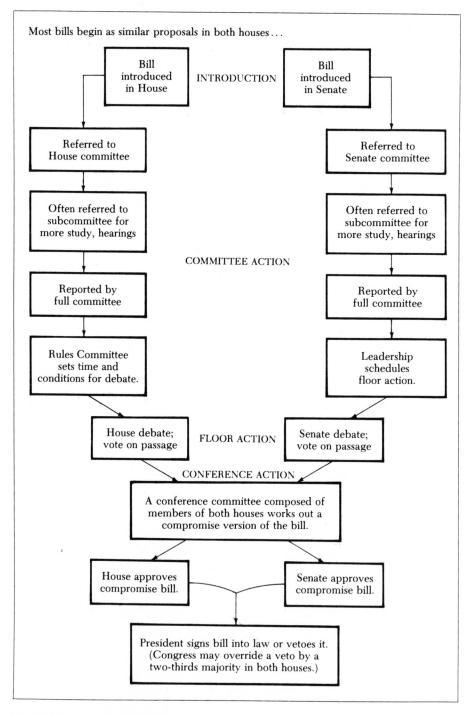

FIGURE 7–2   How a Bill Becomes Law

national figures out of such senators as Estes Kefauver of Tennessee (investigating organized crime), Joseph McCarthy of Wisconsin (communism), George McGovern of South Dakota (hunger in America), and Sam Ervin (Watergate).

Ethics

Congress, like other institutions, is more enthusiastic about criticizing the wrongdoing of others than of its own members. Yet, like other institutions, Congress includes people who are guilty of transgressions ranging from the merely unethical to the grossly criminal.

To begin with, Congress faces such ethical problems as small-scale corruption: placing friends or relatives on the payroll though they do little or no work; padding expense accounts; or going on junkets abroad that have only the vaguest relation to pending legislation. In 1976 Democratic congressman Wayne Hays of Ohio was accused by a former staff member, Elizabeth Ray, of having been put on Hays's payroll in exchange for sexual services rendered to him and others designated by him. Ray alleged that these were the only services she provided, since the typing skills for which she was paid were practically nonexistent and she spent very little time in the office. Hays resigned his positions as chairperson of the House Committee on Administration and of the House Democratic National Congressional Committee, which raised and dispensed funds for congressional candidates. Ray also alleged that six other women provided sex for members of Congress or their constituents as part of their government jobs.

The misuse of money raised for campaign purposes has been a more significant cause of ethical difficulties. Thus, Bobby Baker, a protégé of Lyndon Johnson, built a fortune of $2 million while secretary to the Senate majority leader. He was indicted by a federal grand jury and convicted on seven counts of tax evasion, theft, and conspiracy to defraud. One of the charges was that he had received almost $100,000 from California savings and loan association executives as campaign contributions, and that, instead of handing it all over to the Democratic Senatorial Campaign Committee, he had held on to about $80,000 himself. Then in 1967 Democratic senator Thomas Dodd of Connecticut was censured by the Senate for taking monies from campaign fund-raising dinners and using them for his private purposes.

Next, various members of Congress have been accused of such grossly illegal acts as bribery, extortion, kickbacks, and tax evasion. Between 1955 and 1975, 16 members were indicted for such activities and 12 were convicted. Among them were a Brooklyn Democrat convicted in 1974 of taking a bribe from a trucking company (allegedly controlled by the Mafia) for helping obtain a post office contract; a Texas Democratic representative convicted of perjury in 1972 in connection with an investigation of a $25,000 bribe from a Maryland construction firm; a Pennsylvania Republican congressman convicted of forcing his staff members to kick back part of their salaries to him; and a Maryland Democratic senator convicted on a charge of receiving a bribe from a mail-order firm that wanted to influence his vote on postal-rate bills.

Far more damaging to the reputation of Congress than these examples of individual corruption was a far-reaching scandal that blew up in 1976. Disclosures in the press revealed that Tongsun Park, a South Korean businessman, apparently acting on behalf of a branch of the South Korean government, had donated considerable sums of money and expensive gifts to several members of the House; and had thrown a series of lavish parties attended by congressmen. Among the recipients of his hospitality and donations were some high congressional leaders, including two successive Democratic whips. One received a total of $4650 in campaign gifts from Park, the other $4000, which he admitted to depositing in an unofficial office fund. The House, through its Ethics Committee, launched a probe into what appeared to be a sustained effort to buy influence on Capitol Hill that would lead to more military and economic aid for South Korea. Former Watergate prosecutor Leon Jaworski became special counsel for the investigation, and told the Ethics Committee in August 1977 that he believed there had been Watergate-type efforts to cover up the truth.

Congress has to be concerned not only about the conduct of its own members but also of its staffs. This was brought home painfully in 1970, when the top assistant to the Speaker of the House was indicted along with a lobbyist for trying to fix a case before the Securities and Exchange Commission (SEC). They had used the Speaker's office and phone, apparently without his knowledge, to put across a variety of schemes, including the SEC affair.

Apart from these obvious cases of betraying the public trust, there was the more subtle but nonetheless serious problem represented by conflicts of interest. Could legislators deal objectively with proposed legislation when they retained their association with law or business firms or have financial investments in a field affected by the legislation? For example, in 1974 official reports on the outside interests of members of the House indicated that:

> 86 members (51 Democrats, 35 Republicans) had an interest, usually stock ownership, in banks, bank holding companies, savings and loan associations, or finance companies. Four of these were on the House Banking and Currency Committee, and 10 were on the Ways and Means Committee, which deals with legislation affecting the income taxes paid by financial institutions.

> 48 members (24 from each party) had holdings in big defense companies. Two were on the Armed Services Committee.

> 37 members (18 Democrats, 19 Republicans) owned stock or had income from oil or gas companies. Nine of these were on the Science and Technology Committee or the Interior and Insular Affairs Committee.

> 53 members (26 Democrats, 27 Republicans) had a financial interest in real estate.

Among other fields in which more than 10 members reported a financial interest were pharmaceuticals, power and light, radio and television, farming or ranching, transportation, and insurance. In addition, 76 members (55 Democrats, 21 Republicans) said they were partners or former members of law firms, practiced law as individuals, or were corporate lawyers, and received $1000 or more income in 1974 from legal practice, 13 of them receiving more than $5000.

The danger was that, when members with these interests considered legislation in these fields, it might not always be easy for them to make dispassionate judgments. A flagrant example of the failure to separate a congressman's private interest from his public responsibility was that of Representative Robert Sikes, Democrat of Florida, and chairperson of the Appropriations subcommittee on military construction. Sikes was accused of not declaring his stock holdings in a major defense contractor and a bank in his district; of using his influence to obtain a state charter and federal deposit insurance for the bank (which was located at a

"*NEWS ITEM: Tip O'Neill will forgive House members for past sins but in the future the 'gates of mercy are closed.'*"
Paul Szep; The Boston Globe.

naval air station); and of sponsoring legislation to remove restrictions on Florida land parcels without disclosing that he had a financial interest in the land. In 1976 the House voted a formal censure of Sikes; and in January 1977, despite Sikes's protestations that he was guilty of nothing more than mere "oversights" and despite support from the chairperson of the House Ethics Committee, the House Democrats stripped Sikes of his subcommittee chairmanship.

Reform

In the aftermath of the scandals surrounding the Baker and Dodd campaign fund frauds mentioned above, Congress set up new codes of conduct for members and employees of both houses. Both houses required disclosure of all substantial business interests and sources of outside income. This produced a considerable amount of financial information about members of the House. In the case of the Senate, however, much of the most significant data merely had to be placed on file with the Congress and could be opened to the public only in case of investigation of charges of unethical conduct.

Then in 1976 the Commission on Executive, Legislative, and Judicial Salaries recommended an increase in congressional salaries from $44,600 to $57,500. But this recommendation was accompanied by a proposal for a sweeping reform of congressional ethics. After much agonized debate, in 1977 both houses passed new codes of ethics to accompany the salary increase. The principal provisions of the new codes were:

Tightened requirements for disclosure by members of Congress and their top aides of all earned income and financial holdings.

A limit on members' outside earnings from speaking engagements, articles, and other sources of 15 percent of their annual salary, or $8625. (Investment income, copyright royalties, pension benefits, and family business earnings where these are not generated by the lawmaker are exempted from the limit, though they must be disclosed.)

A restriction on gifts from individual lobbyists to $100 a year.

Limits on the use of the free-mailing privilege for constituency newsletters to six a year, and prohibition of any franked mass mailing sent less than 60 days before an election.

Tightened control of office and foreign travel expenses.

Five Perspectives on Congress

The Liberals

Liberals have long been unhappy with Congress. Some of the changes of recent years have mollified them to a certain extent. They approve of the weakening of some of Congress's most sacred institutions—seniority, the filibuster, the Rules Committee, and the like. They are pleased that most committee meetings are at last open to press and public.

Very little is heard any more of the old liberal complaint that Congress, instead of carrying out the intent of the framers of the Constitution—that Congress be a defender of the liberties of the people—had instead become an instrument of oppression. In the 1940s and 1950s liberals were indignant at the tactics employed in some of Congress's investigations, particularly those of the Un-American Activities Committee in the House and of Joseph McCarthy in the Senate. But McCarthy is long gone, and so is the HUAC (replaced by the Internal Security Committee, which was abolished in 1975). In fact, liberals were delighted with congressional inquiries into Vietnam and Cambodia, the CIA, the big oil companies, and Watergate.

Still, if the complaint of congressional oppression has almost disappeared, and others have been softened by congressional reforms, liberals continue to express strong dissatisfaction with some of the basic features of Congress, charging that it is unrepresentative, it is obstructionist, it thwarts the majority will, and it is tainted by corruption.

Unrepresentativeness.   In a number of respects, liberals find that Congress overstates some interests at the expense of others. First, Congress gives local interests priority over national concerns. This is no longer a matter, as we have seen, of giving the rural and small town localities a great advantage over urban areas, for reapportionment has largely corrected this. Some vestiges of this bias remain, for, despite Supreme Court rulings, it is not possible to eliminate completely the practice of *gerrymandering*—the process by which a state legislature manipulates congressional boundary lines to protect the seats of incumbents or to give an advantage to the majority party.

However, if the liberals no longer complain about a rural bias, they still worry about the overrepresentation of local interests in general. The members' preoccupation with district and state matters gives them a parochial outlook. Thus members from California and Texas fight for space and defense contracts. Spokespersons from sheep and cattle states argue for import quotas on meat. The Michigan representatives are not enthusiastic about smog and safety controls on automobiles. And senators and representatives wage war against the growth of the federal budget while demanding more spending for their own states and districts.

Liberals note with satisfaction the weakening of the South's throttlehold on committee chairmanships. But preponderantly the older southerners in both chambers incline to the conservative side. So liberals feel that the South is still overrepresented in positions of congressional power and wait impatiently for the South's advantage in seniority to disappear.

Almost 70 percent of the members of Congress are lawyers, businessmen, and bankers, and most come from middle- and upper-middle-class families. Blacks, constituting about 12 percent of the people, had 17 members in the House out of 435 in 1977, and one senator out of 100. Spanish-speaking Americans fared even worse; with 5 percent of the population, there were only five Hispanic members of the House, and none in the Senate. Well over half the American electorate are women. But in 1977 there were 17 women in the House, not one in the Senate. Thus Congress, one of whose prime functions is to represent the people, cannot adequately represent the interests of the poor, the racial and ethnic minorities, women, and the less advantaged generally, for it is made up overwhelmingly of white middle- and upper-middle-class men.

With respect to age, liberals are pleased with a trend toward better representation of younger people. Congress used to be an old man's institution, for incumbents are hard to beat, and constituents are reluctant to give up the advantages that seniority brings to their districts. In 1967 a proposal by Senator Joseph Clark to set an age limit of 70 for committee chairpersons received one vote—his own. At that time six of the Senate chairpersons were over 70, including Carl Hayden of Arizona, who was 89, and there were several others in their sixties. In the House the average age of chairpersons was 66, as compared with 64 in the Senate.

However, there has been a trend in the last few years toward earlier retirement in the Congress, partly because of generous pension benefits. This trend accelerated in the 94th Congress, for the 1974 elections brought in 92 new members to the House and 11 to the Senate. The average age of House members in 1975 fell below 50 for the first time since World War II. Eighty-seven members of the House were 40 or under, and six were under 30. The result was that over 1000 years of seniority were lost in the House; and over a third of the House members had two years or less seniority. Moreover, most of the entering class of 1975 were reelected in 1976.

Liberals are not yet convinced, however, that the young are taking over. Even in 1975, when there were 92 newcomers to the House, 170 members had 10 or more years of seniority, 52 had 20 or more years. In the Senate the 12 new members had to deal with 45 Senators with 10 or more years seniority, 14 with at least 20 years.

Then the liberals complain that the excessive responsiveness of Congress to the interests of business stems from not only the number of businesspeople (and lawyers who work for business) in the Congress, but also the greater ability of businesspeople to impress their case effectively on Congress. Businesspeople are the chief source of campaign funds, and they are better organized and financed than others in pursuing the techniques of lobbying. Thus other important groups comprising the mass of the population are left underrepresented.

These various elements in the malrepresentation of Congress—the biases in favor of the local as against the national, the South against the North, high-status and affluent groups against ethnic and racial minorities and the poor, business against the rest—conspire to produce a general distortion in congressional representation: the conservative is favored against the liberal position, the status quo against the forces of change.

Defects of leadership, organization, and procedures.   In the liberals' view the conservative bias in the composition of Congress is reinforced by its patterns of leadership, its organizational structure, and its procedures. Liberals recognize that some significant changes have been taking place with respect to seniority, the filibuster, and so on, which they believe point in the right direction. Yet they persist in their belief that the way Congress operates prevents it from providing the decisive, forward-looking policy making that liberals call for.

To begin with, they dislike the diffusion of leadership resulting from the lack of party cohesion. Without strong party structures in the Congress, liberals do not see how they can put their programs through. They recognize that there is a good deal of party-line voting, but they do not find its extent very impressive. They see little point in members of Congress identifying with a party if they can feel free to join the opposition party on a vital issue whenever they choose—and on the average they choose to do so at least a quarter of the time.

This might not be so damaging to liberal causes if in fact the crossing of party lines occurred purely in relation to the individual needs of each constituency. But this is not so. There are certain consistencies of behavior on the part of some of the most frequent offenders. One pattern, in particular, emerges with some frequency—a *conservative coalition* in which a majority of the southern Democrats desert their party to vote with most of the Republicans. This coalition is not formally organized, and the frequency with which it appears varies from year to year. However, when it shows itself it can be a potent force, in most years winning between half and two-thirds of its battles.

Against the conservative coalition the northern Democrats can usually find only a small number of Republicans to join them in a liberal coalition. And the unreliability of the southern Democrats means that, just because there is a Democratic majority in both houses, this is no guarantee of the success of liberal programs.

To pass a substantial amount of legislation, liberals complain that they need a very large Democratic margin indeed. This is made clear, they suggest, by a comparison between the situations confronting Presidents Kennedy and Johnson. When Kennedy was elected, the Democratic margin in the House was 89, and it went down to 83 as a result of the 1962 elections. With southern defections this was not enough to put much of his program through. In 1965, on the other hand, Johnson had a Democratic majority in the House of 145, enough to get him most of what he wanted. But when the 1966 election reduced the Democratic margin in the House to 61, Johnson's domestic legislation was in trouble again.

Moreover, unless the White House is in Democratic hands, overwhelming margins in the Congress may not help liberal programs very much. The 1974 elections brought to the House 291 Democrats to 144 Republicans; but with Gerald

Ford in the White House there was no prospect of a new surge toward liberalism.

Liberals go on to complain about the consequence of weak party leadership—the independent strength of committees, the often arbitrary power of the committee chair, seniority as the sole qualification for the chair—for more often than not each of these factors hurts their cause. For example, liberals were critical of the sway long exercised over the House Ways and Means Committee, and thus over the House of Representatives, by Wilbur Mills of Arkansas. This committee deals with policy areas of vast importance; and so completely did Mills dominate the committee that a succession of presidents went to him cap in hand, negotiating with him to get favorable Ways and Means treatment in such fields as taxes, international trade, the national debt, unemployment compensation, and health insurance. And Mills, being a rather conservative man, did not blaze many liberal trails. Then there was Carl Vinson of Georgia, for many years chairperson of the House Armed Services Committee, and a strong advocate of the military. Although he recognized that the president and the secretary of defense had certain responsibilities in the military field, Vinson used to say, "I'd rather run the Pentagon from up here." Of course, this was an overstatement, but Vinson was not simply bragging.

As we have seen, a number of changes have taken place in the direction pointed to by the liberals. Step by step, the power of the committee chairpersons has weakened. The first of the titans to fall was Wilbur Mills; but Mills brought himself down. Of greater long-run significance for the liberals was the stepped-up assault on seniority at the beginning of the 94th Congress in 1975. There was the unprecedented spectacle of old, powerful men parading before the freshmen asking for their support; and then came the defeat of three of the longtime committee chairpersons.

Liberals had to be impressed, too, with the other reductions in the power of chairpersons referred to earlier: the requirement that they follow rules limiting the arbitrary use of their authority, and the strengthening of the House Democratic caucus by giving it the power of election of chairmanships, and making it into a forum in which votes are taken to give guidance to committees on policy issues.

Further, there were reductions in the powers of particular committees. The Rules Committee was no longer a reliable bastion of conservatism. The potency of Ways and Means was weakened by two changes. It used to be the Democratic "committee on committees," controlling all assignments of members to committees; this role has been given to the House leadership. Ways and Means' recommendations always went to the House floor with a "closed rule," that is, they had to be voted up or down, with no amendments permitted except by agreement with Ways and Means; this is no longer the case.

Finally, the requirement that committee meetings be held publicly unless a committee specifically votes to conduct a particular day's business in closed session has reduced the opportunity for chairpersons to act despotically and for special interests to exert their behind-the-scenes leverage.

Still, the liberals insist that all these changes constitute only the first tentative steps toward reform, and that very much more is needed. For one thing, the downfall of the various committee chairpersons did not represent a massive swing toward liberalism in the House. Only on the Agricultural Committee did the unseating of the old guard bring a clear change from a very conservative to a quite liberal chairperson. On Banking and Currency a liberal replaced an older liberal. On Armed Services an elderly southern supporter of the military gave way to an elderly backer of the Pentagon from Illinois. The new chairperson of Ways and Means was more liberal than Wilbur Mills, but still very much the moderate. And when Wayne Hays of the Administration Committee lost his chairmanship, it was not because the freshmen members were outraged by his having fought against such reforms as the 1974 campaign finance law, nor even his high-handed, arrogant, and sometimes cruel manner (he had ordered the operators' seats taken out of the House elevators, for it was unfitting for elevator operators to sit in the presence of members of Congress). On the contrary, the freshmen had voted for him to continue as chairperson. They were impressed by his knowledge and competence—and the fact that as chairperson of the Administration Committee he could be helpful to them with respect to the assignment of office staff and space, expenses, and travel. So it was certainly not the surge of liberalism represented by the freshman class of 1975 that caused Wayne Hays's undoing, but his own venal indiscretions.

Thus the liberals interpret the changes in chairmanships as merely a reaction against the most obvious examples of extreme age and infirmity, rather than a rejection of the conservative policy positions taken by chairpersons. A number of reactionaries remain in the top positions in committees and subcommittees. They are confirmed as long as they meet minimal requirements of competence. Seniority, in other words, is still very much alive.

Then, too, the efforts of liberals to move power from the committees to the Democratic caucus has had useful but only limited results. When California's Phillip Burton, former chairperson of the Democratic Study Group, became chairperson of the Democratic caucus, he and other liberal members of the House hoped to commit Democrats in committee and on the floor to the positions taken by the majority of the caucus. This notion ran hard up against the cherished independence of committees and of individual members. Burton retreated. "Some people," he said, "were steamed. We have to lay off using the caucus for a while."

It was the same story with the Bolling committee's efforts to bring about major changes in the committee structure of the House. The established committee chairpersons shot down almost all of its major recommendations, thus leaving intact most of the ridiculously wasteful competition between committees for control of key issues.

The only substantial structural reform the House has put into effect was the creation of the Budget committees. Liberals have always argued for more rationality in congressional procedures, and they can hardly object to the idea of trying to establish a conscious relationship between income and outlay. But they have some misgivings about the fact that the only area in which a major change of committee responsibility has been made is in the budgetary area, for they are afraid that the result will be to provide conservatives in Congress with the weapon they need to hold down spending on liberal programs.

Thwarting the majority will.   In the interpretation of the liberals, the diffusion of leadership and the endlessly complicated procedures are perfectly suited to perpetuating private, selfish interests, rather than the majority will and the public interest. The congressional system particularly serves the purposes of organized interest groups and associations, which can present a unified front to the fragmented system of congressional power and play one power center off another. The mysterious, subterranean windings of bills through Congress also provides repeated opportunities for skilled lobbyists to inject their ideas at various stages and to work out quiet, unpublicized understandings with friendly legislators. The congressional system offers no such advantages for the kinds of social legislation favored by the liberals. On the contrary, Congress becomes a hazardous obstacle course; and the process of getting programs that the people want through the two houses of the Congress can take years, even decades.

For example, it took 20 years to get anything done in the field of *health insurance.* President Harry Truman proposed the idea of compulsory national health insurance in 1945. In face of opposition by the American Medical Association (AMA) the proposal did not get a serious hearing in Congress until 1958, when the House Ways and Means Committee held hearings on a bill that provided benefits only to people over 65. Even this limited proposal was voted down in Ways and Means by 17 to 8. This was not surprising for three reasons. First, the conservative Wilbur Mills was the committee chairperson. Second, the committee membership was not inclined toward social innovation. Great care was taken in the selection of members to ensure that only "moderate" and "responsible" types would be appointed to it. As one of its members said: "We don't want any screwballs and since I've been a member we haven't had any screwballs. These men are pretty carefully selected you know, so we won't get any radicals."[2] Third, the AMA was lobbying heavily against the bill and contributed a good deal of money to the 1958 congressional election campaigns.

However, by 1960 pressure for the proposal was mounting. For a time Mills headed it off by getting together with Senator Robert Kerr and putting through the Kerr–Mills bill, which provided federal support for state programs of medical assistance for the aged poor. This was not enough to satisfy the new administration of President Kennedy, which drafted a new bill, the King–Anderson proposal for Medicare. Again Mills resisted, delaying action while more and more hearings were held. Every year from 1958 there had been hearings on the issue. By 1964, 13 volumes of testimony had appeared totaling 14,000 pages.

By 1964, however, Mills knew that he could not hold out indefinitely. The Kennedy administration, working through House leaders, had influenced the appointment of new Ways and Means Committee members to ensure that they would not be opposed to Medicare. Twelve of the 25 members of the committee in 1964 were known to be in favor of the program. The rest was taken care of by the 1964 elections—the Johnson landslide, the very large Democratic majority in the House, and the resulting appointment to Ways and Means of 17 Democrats and 8 Republicans, establishing a clear pro-Medicare majority. At last, Mills, faced with inevitability, undertook the leadership to enact Medicare; and on July 30, 1965, Lyndon Johnson signed Medicare into law.

The liberals were pleased. But they could not regard this achievement as a triumph of the democratic process. Twenty years was a ridiculously long time for Congress to respond to what the polls had repeatedly shown to be the will of the majority. And what had finally emerged from this arduous process was, by the standards of other countries, quite inadequate to the needs of the people. As Theodore Marmor has pointed out: "No industrialized country in the world has begun its government health insurance program with the aged."[3] Moreover, the coverage provided was far from complete. So the battle for comprehensive national health insurance was only just beginning. The opposition of the AMA, combined with the obstructive machinery of Congress, indicated that the battle would not be quickly won.

Nor was Medicare the only legislation that took 20 years to get through the congressional labyrinth after being proposed by Harry Truman. *Federal aid to education* suffered the same kind of ordeal. Introduced into Congress in 1945, and persistently supported in public opinion polls, the proposal fell afoul of one legislative technicality after another until it was approved in 1965 within the rubric of Lyndon Johnson's War on Poverty. Here again, a full generation had passed before the will of the majority had prevailed.

A third case, that of *public housing*, tells us that 20 years can pass even *after* legislation has been approved before a program is fully implemented. We saw in Chapter 5 in our discussion of interest groups that the private housing lobby was a major factor in delaying the construction of the 810,000 units of public housing provided for in the 1949 Housing Act. Instead of the original schedule of 6 years, close to 20 years were needed to complete the program. And the reason the lobbyists were so effective was the readiness of Congress and the committees to respond to their pressures.

One more example cited by liberals of Congress's unwillingness to represent the majority will in face of pressure from a determined minority is that of *gun control*. The National Rifle Association (NRA) has been particularly skillful over the years in harnessing constituency pressure and the money of gun manufacturers and distributors in lobbying against proposals either to ban or require registration of firearms or to control their sales. The tide of opinion appeared to turn against the NRA in 1968, when the shooting of Robert Kennedy on June 5, soon after the assassination of Martin Luther King, set off a massive and largely spontaneous letter-writing campaign from all over the country demanding tighter controls on the sale and ownership of guns. President Johnson responded by calling for national registration of every firearm and a license for every gun owner. At first the NRA seemed overwhelmed. Before long, however, the letters from the general public dwindled, and the NRA launched its counterattack. By the end of June members of Congress reported that their mail was running against controls. Finally, a bill did pass, prohibiting the interstate sale or shipment of rifles, shotguns, and ammunition to individuals (earlier in the year Congress had done the same for handguns), and imposing a few other restrictions. But the president's more sweeping proposals were rejected.

The story was repeated in 1972, when the shooting of George Wallace was followed by efforts to tighten the gun laws. The Senate passed a bill banning the sale of "Saturday night specials"—cheap handguns said to be instruments of half the murders in the country. Seventy-one percent of the people supported the proposal, according to a Gallup poll, and President Nixon came out in favor of it. But after intensive lobbying by the NRA, the bill died in the House Judiciary Committee.

The new Congress?   But these long delays took place before reform came to Congress. Has the era of reform, accompanied by the influx of new, young members, brought into being a new, vigorous spirit in Congress, which would be more responsive to the liberals' purposes? Liberals had hoped this was the case, but they are not entirely convinced. The years 1975 and 1976 should have been vintage years for liberal legislation if we are to judge by the size of the Democratic majority and the number of liberally inclined freshmen. There were some useful results. Legislation passed on education, child nutrition, jobs, and other areas benefiting the poor and working people. Ford's frequent vetoes were overridden more times than was true of any president since Andrew Johnson. Yet liberals wanted much more. There should have been effective tax reform, for example. Yet very little of any significance got through Ways and Means. There should have been a comprehensive energy program. But Congress could not agree on a viable alternative to President Ford's ill-conceived proposals.

And there should have been gun control legislation. Yet the National Rifle Association was able to continue its record of success in opposing controls even after there had been two unsuccessful attempts to shoot President Ford. Again there was strong popular support for controls, two-thirds of the public expressing approval of registration of all firearms in a Gallup poll. And, as had happened each time before, religious, educational, professional, labor, and public interest organizations joined forces to fight for control legislation. But the "new," "revitalized," and "reformed" Congress produced nothing.

Nor did the liberals find very much to encourage them at the outset of the 95th Congress in 1977. "Tip" O'Neill was moderately liberal, and likely to be a more vigorous leader than his predecessor as Speaker, Carl Albert. But the narrow defeat of the very liberal John Burton by the moderately conservative Jim Wright for House majority leader did not augur well for the liberals. Similarly, the Senate selected the quite conservative Robert Byrd as majority leader instead of Hubert Humphrey. Perhaps these were the kind of leaders who would put efficiency and party loyalty ahead of their own ideology and help deliver the votes for Jimmy Carter's programs. But liberals had to believe that their selection raised grave doubts that even a reformed and heavily Democratic Congress has much appetite for charting bold new policy directions.

As the liberals perceive it, then, Congress is rarely galvanized into action without the spur of strong presidential leadership. Even this must be aided by some exceptional circumstances—the collapse of the economy that made the New Deal possible, or the collapse of the Republican party in 1964, which gave Lyndon Johnson his huge majority in Congress. Once the full impact of these unusual conditions passes, Congress tends to get back to business as usual—which is not enough business to bring about new directions in policy.

Corruption.   After the Wayne Hays–Elizabeth Ray and Wilbur Mills–Fanne Fox scandals, the press eagerly looked for other examples of members of Congress's straying from the paths of sexual rectitude. Jack Anderson and other investigative journalists unearthed fulsome accounts of legislators consorting with prostitutes, keeping mistresses, and seducing constituents in their offices. This, however, is not the kind of thing liberals have in mind when they allege that Congress is tainted by corruption. Their complaint is not the human nature of representatives and senators, whom they believe to be no more sinful than the rest of us. The liberals' concern is with the nature of the institution. Given the way the congressional system works, they believe it inevitable that its members will constantly be caught up in ethical dilemmas.

One perennial target of the liberals' attack on congressional ethics has been financial conflicts of interest—the refusal of members of Congress to disqualify themselves from acting or voting on issues in which they stand to gain personally. In this respect liberals are impressed by the provision of the 1977 ethics codes that severely limits outside income. However, they are not convinced that members of Congress will henceforth be entirely uninfluenced by their previous (or prospective) business connections. And they note that independently wealthy members are not much affected by this provision, since (unlike members of the executive branch) they do not have to divest themselves of investment income from such sources as stocks and bonds.

In any case, another source of ethical conflict is still very much with us—campaign financing from private sources. As long as campaigns are expensive to conduct, and as long as the money must come from private sources, most members of Congress inevitably seek money from affluent individuals or organizations. This means that, to some degree at least, they will be beholden to those contributors, and to the lobbyists who arrange contributions.

The fact that Bobby Baker went to jail and Thomas Dodd was censured by the Senate for misappropriating campaign money does not in any way convince the liberals that the system was correcting its abuses in any fundamental way. If Baker had handed over the money received from savings and loan companies for use in Democratic campaigns instead of keeping some of it, he would have been applauded by Democrats in the Senate. Yet the intent of the contributions was to influence legislation in favor of the savings and loan industry. No complaint would have been heard about Senator Dodd had he not diverted campaign funds to his personal account. Yet the money had come from campaign fund-raising dinners; and those who bought blocs of tickets for the dinners must have thought that they were making a useful investment and that they might look to the senator for some favors in return.

Liberals are pleased that an important step to correct such abuses was taken in the 1974 campaign finance reform law, with the limitation on contributions of $1000 for an individual and $5000 for an organization. Even so, congressmen must still spend much of their time seeking the support of the $1000 and $5000 contributors, and cultivating the wealthy people who, although forbidden from putting up $10,000 of their own money, can get together 10 of their friends who will produce $1000 apiece. In the absence of public financing of congressional campaigns, say the liberals, this problem will persist.

More reforms.   Liberals call for considerably more far-reaching reforms of Congress than have yet been undertaken. However, among the liberals there are two streams of thought on precisely what kind of reforms are needed which sometimes flow together, sometimes diverge. On the one hand, there are proposals designed to make Congress a more effective rival to the presidency. A Nader team study of Congress by Green, Fallows, and Zwick speaks of Congress as "the broken branch of government," because it has abdicated its power to the president and to special interest groups. "Congress has its problems, but the only way to restore balance to the government is for it to stand up for the rights it retains—and to fight for the return of those that have been taken from it."[4] Congress must therefore reform its procedures—abolishing seniority, ending autocratic committee-chairperson rule, opening all committee and subcommittee meetings to the public, compelling disclosure of all outside financial interests, forbidding members to serve on committees that have jurisdiction over matters in which they have a personal financial interest, and reforming election finance laws. Congress must also provide itself with the research capacity and information it needs instead of depending on the administration or on lobbyists.

The purpose of the various reforms that this group of liberals propose is to make Congress more efficient, more open, more honest, and more responsive so that it can acquire the capacity and moral standing it must have if it is to recapture the position accorded it by the Constitution.

There are still some observers, however, who, with certain modifications, restate the classical liberal position on Congress: that the primary leadership must come from the president, with Congress providing a careful review of presidential proposals and a check on possible abuses of power. Like the first group of liberals, they argue for a better-informed and more efficient legislature, for an end to conflicts of interest, and for changes in campaign financing. But James MacGregor Burns, for example, is more concerned with helping Congress to withstand the claims of special interest groups than setting it up as an effective instrument for thwarting presidential power.[5]

Burns continues to emphasize the need for strengthening the parties as the principal means of bringing president and Congress together and helping Congress work with the president on national problems instead of being preoccupied with its narrow, provincial concerns. Moreover, says Burns, Congress should end its obstructionist ways. Instead of attacking a president's proposals with interminable delays and crippling amendments, Congress should select certain issues for priority attention, then grant the president broad powers to take action on those issues, subject only to congressional veto within a specified period. On other less vital issues Congress would continue to have a full partnership role. It would also debate programs and policies, conduct investigations, expose failures of the administration, and serve as the spokesperson for individuals in their dealings with federal agencies.

These roles, while significant, would still leave the main initiative and power in the White House. Burns recognizes that this power has been dangerously abused by some presidents. But he and other liberals like him prefer to take their chances with the clearer presentation of alternative policies, allowing those policies to be played out fully so the people can judge them and, in time, choose liberal policies when they see their merit. It is true that in the short run, with liberals on the defensive, Congress can provide them with a sanctuary, and Burns does not disdain this. But in the long run Burns points out that liberals cannot achieve their purposes merely by resisting proposals they dislike. They are advocates of rapid economic and social change. The presidency is the most likely institution for achieving this. They would be better served by working hard to elect liberal presidents rather than by sapping the powers of the office and undermining its ability to serve the people when it is in friendly hands.

The Centrists

The long decline of congressional power as presidential power expanded in the twentieth century was a source of considerable concern among centrists. Consequently, by the 1970s they were ready to accept some reforms of the institution. However, the reforms they support are designed to help Congress fulfill its traditional roles in the constitutional structure of checks and balances more effectively. In large measure, those reforms have now been accomplished and, in some cases, may have gone a little too far for the centrists.

In any case, centrists bridle at the harshness of liberal criticism of Congress, criticisms that ignore the basic strengths of the congressional system. These strengths can be explained in rebuttal to each of the charges made by the liberals.

Is Congress unrepresentative?   Centrists do not accept the various liberal criticisms about Congress's inability to represent the people adequately.

It is true that Congress is sensitive to local community concerns. So it should be. Local interests are being overwhelmed by mass communications, giant industry, and big government. A prime function of a national legislature in a country as large as the United States is to protect the local constituency, to speak for diversity against standardization.

Another function is to respond to the requests and grievances of individual constituents. Sometimes this may involve no more than sending material to students seeking information for high school themes. More significantly, it is a matter of helping people who need someone to speak for them in dealing with the vast bureaucracies of the federal government. The issue may be a pension, a tax bill, a job, or a prison sentence. In each case the member of Congress is looked to as a person with influence who can intercede on behalf of the ordinary individual.

There is nothing wrong, then, with legislators' spending a good deal of their time dealing with the concerns of individual constituents and local communities. This does not prevent members of Congress from attending to national and international issues. Nor, in dealing with those issues, are they necessarily limited by the views of their constituents—partly because they may not be able to determine the views of their constituents, partly because most of the time their constituents know very little about what positions their members of Congress are taking. Thus, as long as they are careful to voice the wishes of their constituents on matters of local concern, members of Congress may often vote their own consciences (or their party line) on major policy questions.

As to the matter of whether or not Congress accurately represents the geographic distribution of the population, the old liberal complaints have now been laid to rest. Reapportionment has corrected the bias against the urban centers. However, it should be noted that the great shift has been not to the center of the cities, but toward the suburbs; and greater suburban representation in the Congress will not always be to the advantage of liberals.

The South, too, has been losing ground steadily in Congress. Reapportionment has taken away some of the House seats that used to go to the deep South. And liberals have ignored the fact that the South does not have a monopoly on the one-party districts that make it easier to build up seniority. All over the country there are growing numbers of districts in which one party has established a firm grip on local politics; and this is demonstrated in the figures given earlier which indicate that the South will not be disproportionately represented in the next generation of committee chairpersons.

Centrists do not try to refute completely the liberals' charge that Congress fails to provide a faithful cross section of the electorate. Some segments of the public, particularly women and minority groups, are insufficiently represented. Yet the prospect is that there will be a steady increase in the numbers coming from these groups. Even now the membership of Congress comes from a diverse range of backgrounds. There are considerable numbers of lawyers, of course, but this is always the case with legislatures, which need and attract people who can deal with the intricate work that goes into drafting statutes. It is also true that the educational level of Congress is well above that of the general population, which is as it should be.

Nor is it surprising that the average age should be above that of the population at large. It takes time to acquire the experience and reputation that qualify a person to be a representative leader in a national legislature. As for seniority's giving the top roles to older people, this is by no means disastrous. Long years of service have made committee chairpersons masters of specialized areas and highly skilled at scrutinizing legislative proposals and surveying executive performance. Naturally, seniority, like any other system of selecting leaders, has placed some incompetents in positions of authority. But it has also produced some extraordinarily able men.

In any case, we have an unreasonable prejudice against age in this country. Some of the greatest executive leaders of the modern era—France's de Gaulle, Germany's Adenauer, China's Mao Tse-tung, and others—were in their prime in their seventies and eighties. So it is not inappropriate that the top men in the deliberative branch of the United States government should be seasoned elders.

Liberals contend that business interests are excessively represented in Congress and that business groups have easier access to Congress than any other groups. As we saw in our earlier discussion of the group process, centrists do not agree that business dominates the American system. This view applies to Congress, too. Many groups are represented in Congress and bring pressure to bear on Congress. Since these groups are often in conflict with each other, the member of Congress must mediate between them, working out solutions that are at least tolerable to as many of the parties in conflict as possible. The results sometimes favor business, but by no means always; and the liberals' argument that Congress is overly responsive to the conservative interests in the nation is not accepted by centrists.

Can Congress act?   The liberals complain that Congress's diffusion of leadership, overelaborate organization, and endless procedures prevent its being effective—that is to say, effective in producing programs that the liberals believe the majority of the people want.

Now, say the centrists, it is quite true that the way Congress operates puts obstacles in the way of new proposals. But this is as it should be. For one thing, Congress is charged by the Constitution with acting as a check on presidential power, and it would be ignoring its obligations if it did not subject every proposal coming from the White House to the most meticulous scrutiny. Moreover, since legislation often has an enormous impact on large numbers of people, it is essential that every law proposed be examined very carefully, and that every interest likely to be affected by a piece of proposed legislation be given every opportunity to express its reaction.

So it is wise to require that any proposal for change win the approval of standing committees, usually after extensive hearings designed to ensure that the relevant information is brought forth and all points of view are heard. It is essential that full provision be made for debate on the floor, that both chambers be fully involved, that differences between the two be reconciled in conference committees. Moreover, with hundreds of billions of dollars being spent it makes sense to have to submit every proposal to the Appropriations committees. Clearly the Founding Fathers intended that Congress should be a deliberative body, should make haste slowly. Congress's structures and procedures, although always subject to modification, are within the spirit of the Constitution.

The filibuster, though not specifically established by the Constitution, is also within that spirit. The framers were acutely sensitive to the need to protect minorities against majority tyranny. The filibuster serves that end by holding up action until the concerns of the minority have been attended to. For years the filibuster served the purposes of southern segregationists and acquired the onus of that association. But it has stopped serving those purposes since the filibusters against civil rights bills were broken in 1964 and 1965.

Today liberals, too, resort to the filibuster. Thus liberal senators filibustered in September 1971 to force extended debate on the draft and on an amendment to end the Vietnam war. The Senate voted cloture, and Senator Alan Cranston, formerly an advocate of efforts to make it easier to shut off a filibuster, was annoyed. "When our dislike of filibusters," he said, "becomes more important than our distrust of the draft or our revulsion with Vietnam, it's time we took another look at the filibuster. I look upon the filibuster as a means, not an end. When it can be used to good purpose, I support it. When it is used against ends that I favor, I shall oppose it."[6] In any case, the filibuster, despite the fact that it is used by all factions in the Senate, is only resorted to occasionally. Conservatives have voted for cloture; in fact, every senator in the 94th Congress had voted at some time to put an end to a filibuster. Cloture is even easier to accomplish since the votes needed for this purpose have been reduced to 60. So the filibuster remains as a protection for minority rights, but not as a constant threat to the orderly conduct of Senate business.

In any case, centrists do not argue that Congress is merely there to veto proposals for action. It is a legislature, and it does legislate. In fact, Congress has greater responsibilities and wields more power than any other legislature in the world. Its procedures have evolved over a long period of time to enable a large body of people to handle its tasks as effectively as possible. Thus the structure of committees and subcommittees was not developed to provide bastions of power for a few obstinate old men but to provide specialized institutions that could examine an enormous number of proposals with some degree of understanding and sophistication. Even seniority expedites action; for if this principle did not exist, a considerable part of each session (and each session lasts only two years) could well be lost in bitter struggles over the top leadership positions.

The proof of the argument that Congress is a productive institution is its output. A large number of important statutes emerge from Congress every year. Although few years match the frenetic pace of 1964 and 1965—the aftermaths of a presidential assassination and then of an overwhelming election victory—even the normal pace is impressive enough. Thus in 1968, a year in which it was thought that Congress might draw back from its earlier strenuous labors, laws were passed in the field of fair housing and consumer protection, along with a tax increase and approval of an unprecedentedly ambitious low-cost housing program. In 1969 a sweeping reform of the tax laws was passed. Even during the Eisenhower years, a period of consolidation and retrenchment, substantial programs in housing, highway construction, and Social Security were approved.

Of course, not everything the liberals propose is accepted by Congress, and it does not move as fast as they would like. But this does not prove that Congress is inefficient, nor even that it is acting against the majority wishes. This becomes clear if we look again at some of the examples given by liberals to make their case that congressional legislation usually lags far behind the will of the people.

In the case of federal aid to education, for example, it is true that polls indicated that a clear majority of the electorate supported the idea in principle. But the large percentages in favor began to break up to some degree when people were asked whether they favored federal aid to parochial schools and whether they were ready to support higher taxes to pay for the federal aid.[7] Even the most representative legislatures have to go beyond generalities to deal with specific conflicts, and, in doing so, they do not find it easy to register the majority will precisely.

The same may well have been true in the health insurance field. Exactly what kind of program did the majority want? And how intensely did they want it? Until the 1960s, at any rate, congressmen's soundings in their constituencies did not tell them that here was an overwhelming demand. In the American context we do well to move cautiously and deliberately before advancing into major new areas of social legislation. Congress should probe and test the atmosphere, acting when the majority will has gelled and become insistent and not before; and then making sure that the product is well conceived and technically sound.

This is precisely what happened in the case of Medicare. Wilbur Mills was an extraordinarily competent and knowledgeable legislator. He was also a very careful chairperson. He was reluctant to make proposals that the House might reject. His committee was made up of representatives selected not because they were conservative but because they were responsible and capable of dealing with the highly complex and technical legislation that came before the committee.

Mills and his committee demonstrated their abilities to the full in the health insurance field. When it was clear that the demand for action was irresistible, Mills first tried a program (Kerr–Mills) that established the principle of federal involvement while giving the states a chance to show their effectiveness. When this proved insufficient, and when in 1965 the majority for further intervention was unmistakably present, Mills showed his mastery.

Before his committee were three bills. There was the administration's proposal for compulsory insurance, King–Anderson, which provided hospital care for everyone over 65 who was on Social Security. The AMA offered a program, Eldercare, which was essentially an expansion of Kerr–Mills. And the Republicans proposed a bill covering doctor and drug care for elderly people to be financed on a voluntary basis by pensioners plus some government subsidy.

Mills got to work on these proposals. Now he was the technician, intent on producing a workable bill. At the hearings the AMA spokesperson made more speeches against "socialized medicine." Mills was furious. The time for ideology was past. He refused to permit AMA representatives to attend any further hearings on the bills.

What he came up with astounded the Johnson administration, for he had gone beyond King–Anderson to combine the best of all three bills. Liberal editorial writers were ecstatic. What had happened was that Mills, having accepted the inevitability of Medicare, had expanded it to make it *his* proposal, reflecting credit on his committee and himself. By doing so, Mills, the responsible legislative craftsman, had made sure that what emerged was technically and financially sound.

It was not the final word on the subject, of course. There will be further legislation in the field of health insurance. But if we are still far short of anything like the all-encompassing British National Health program, it is because we are not sure that this would be workable or popular in America.

Finally, the liberal argument that Congress is insufficiently responsive to the majority is based on the premise that the electorate at large is more liberal than the Congress. But this is an affluent nation, in which the majority have a stake in the established order. Such a nation is not likely to clamor for social and economic change. Congress reflects this fact, though there are distortions in the reflection. If the distortions were removed by the reforms proposed by the liberals and Congress became a true mirror of society, the reality might well be disconcerting to liberals. That is, they might find the country (and thus its representatives) much more conservative than they had hoped or imagined.

Is Congress corrupt?   Centrists take strong objection to liberals' charges that Congress as an institution is tainted by corruption. They concede that such examples as the Baker, Dodd, Hays, and South Korean cases bring Congress into disrepute. But they see these cases as exceptions, and they believe that to read too much into them is unjust and does grave damage to the credibility of our entire system.

Centrists recognize that the cost of elections may confront a candidate with ethical problems. But they doubt that the problems are as serious as the liberals allege. Members of Congress are only as beholden to their financial contributors as they choose to be. As we saw in Chapter 4, a skillful politician knows how to get money from people on both sides of an issue, for each side is afraid that not to contribute will give an advantage to the other side. Then, once funds have come in from both sides, the officeholder is obligated to neither and is free to vote the way he wants. Whatever disadvantages the present system entails are outweighed by the dangers of the system proposed by the liberals—federal funding for congressional races.

As for conflicts of interests stemming from legislators' outside earnings, centrists contend these have always been exaggerated. The 1977 ethics codes, though well-intentioned, may have gone too far. After all, the majority of congressmen's political careers are insecure. Why should a person who is chosen to represent a constituency for two years and may then not have his appointment renewed sever all contact with his alternative career? Cutting off all such avenues when a man runs for office gives the advantage to people who are independently wealthy or assured by a big organization of a job on their return. Most members of Congress have not allowed their outside affiliations to influence their voting in Congress. It is difficult to prove this, for only the abuses fill the columns of journalists who make their living by innuendo and by alleging guilt by association. But those who have studied Congress most closely, say the centrists, do not accept the muckrakers' view of the institution as corrupt.

The only thing that can be demonstrated is that when people come to Congress they bring with them their preconceptions and predispositions to be sympathetic to various kinds of interests. But these inclinations are held by 535 different people who, in the aggregate, voice the concerns of the full range of interests present in the society. It is also true that legislators are eager to do what they can for the individuals and organizations who make up their constituencies. But this is exactly what they should do. That is what representation is all about.

Reforms.   The centrists' high regard for Congress does not rule out their acceptance of the need for reform. Despite their contention that Congress has performed much better than the liberals give it credit for, the growth of presidential power has led centrists to believe in the need for important changes to help Congress reassert its authority vis-a-vis the executive branch.

Centrists recognize that the legislative initiative lies with the presidency—though they point out that many of the programs for which presidents have claimed credit have been adopted by the White House after long study by committees of Congress. But centrists do not feel that the active legislative role of the president in itself destroys the viability of Congress. What is needed, they believe, is for Congress to improve its ability to assert its own standing in three respects.

First, they would like to see Congress propose long-range public policy of its own, thereby lessening the president's dependence on the federal bureaucracies for the design of policy. Second, they want Congress to equip itself better to scrutinize the legislative proposals coming from the administration, and to do a more effective job of amending and improving them. Third, they urge Congress to improve its performance in the essential field of "legislative oversight"—reviewing the implementation of programs by administrative agencies to ensure that the intent of the legislation is being carried out and to protect the public against abuses of governmental power.

In general, they think that the kinds of changes that have come about in recent years will help in these respects. Modifying the seniority rule, for example, prevents the type of arbitrary behavior of which some chairpersons were guilty in the past.

But we do not need drastic new departures in the leadership structure of the Congress. Seniority, having been made accountable, should be preserved. Certainly we should avoid the liberals' prescription, which is to replace the traditional procedures and leadership styles with centralized party organization. Tight party discipline, backed by the power to expel a dissenter from the party, has no place in our scheme of things. It is not what the voters want. It could not be imposed on the 535 individuals who make up the U.S. Congress.

Persuasive guidance from party leaders in Congress is appropriate. But this can be achieved, not by abandoning our present structures, but by Congress's choosing effective party leaders. Lyndon Johnson as Senate majority leader and Sam Rayburn as Speaker of the House demonstrated the authority that resided in their offices. There has been an unfortunate decline since their time. But with "Tip" O' Neill as the new Speaker of the House, and the competent Robert Byrd as Senate majority leader, there is a good prospect of the restoration of as much party leadership as is needed.

One reform that centrists have considered essential has already come about. Both the Senate and the House have a Budget Committee that sets an upper limit for total federal expenditures early in the year, relating this ceiling to the tax programs needed to produce the agreed-upon expenditures. Then it reviews the spending recommendations coming out of each committee in the course of the year, and applies pressure on the committees to ensure that the total of these recommendations does not exceed the budgeted expenditure ceiling. This procedure has been working very effectively and has freed Congress from the accusation that only the executive branch of government is concerned with fiscal responsibility.

What remains to be done is to move somewhat further in the direction of rational management. The Bolling committee's recommendations for reorganization of the House committee structure should be considered again and steps taken to reduce overlapping responsibilities and jurisdictional squabbling between committees. And Congress's ability to obtain and interpret information on policy issues must be greatly improved through computerization and the appointment of more research staff. Today power goes with access to information; and Congress must make itself less dependent on the executive branch for this vital resource.

The Conservatives

In considerable measure conservatives agree with the centrists' rebuttal of the criticism that liberals level at Congress, so we need not repeat those rebuttals under this heading. Despite these areas of agreement the conservatives have their own distinctive appraisal of Congress.

Traditionally, conservatives have much preferred Congress to the presidency. Congress was a representative body in a fuller sense than the presidency. Thus Willmoore Kendall spoke of the presidency as an institution responding to the national mass electorate, "a *plebiscitary* political system, capable of carrying through *popular mandates*," whereas Congress represented the electorate in all its complexity and diversity. Against the liberalizing dynamic of the presidency, Congress was an institution that could serve conservative purposes—supporting the reduction of government spending, strong measures against internal subversion, large military forces, and vigorous nationalism.[8]

In the last few years, however, conservative enthusiasm for Congress has dimmed for two reasons. First, Congress is less reliable than it used to be in defending the nation against the trend toward the welfare state. Although it imposed some delays, it eventually caved in to the pressures for federal instrusion in such fields as education and health care. Thus the centrists' admiration for the process that created Medicare is not shared by the conservatives. Wilbur Mills could not be a conservative hero when he had insisted on going even further than the very liberal King–Anderson bill in 1965.

The trouble with Congress is that the factors that combined to protect its conservatism are vanishing. There is the decline of rural, small town, and southern influence; the breaking of the filibuster; the undermining of seniority; and the reduced role of the Rules Committee. There are the efforts to make Congress more modern and efficient. For those attributes, said the conservative analyst James Burnham, look to "Hitler's Reichstag, the Kremlin's Supreme Soviet, Franco's Cortes, Mao's and Mussolini's and Trujillo's Chambers."[9] There is also the fact that Congress is less and less likely to protect the country against unnecessary federal spending when it is feeding so hungrily at the public trough itself. Thus our representatives have been voting themselves large salaries as well as an array of fringe benefits. Even the 1977 ethics codes have not deprived them of their grossly expanding staffs, excessive travel expenses to and from their districts, frivolous overseas junkets, and free mailing privileges. Amid so much socially approved greed, it is inevitable that some of them should step over the line that separates the immoral from the illegal, and bring Congress into public disrepute.

The second reason for the conservatives' diminished reliance on Congress is that sometimes the president has taken a more conservative stand than Congress. Thus William Buckley sided with President Nixon's use of executive privilege against efforts to make members of his administration testify before the Senate Foreign Relations Committee in January 1973 on the renewed bombing of Vietnam. "On the whole," said Buckley, "it is sensible to take the side of Congress against the executive. . . ." It was "the operative presumption that the White House has entirely too much power." In this case, however, the president was right. His policy and reasoning were clear, and there was no need to give his opponents a forum in which to harass him.[10]

Conservatives are prepared to make other exceptions in favor of the president. Whenever Congress is heavily under the influence of liberal Democrats, and especially whenever the president is at least moderately conservative, the choice between institutions may have to give way to a choice between people.

Still, the natural affinity of conservatives over the long term tends to be with Congress rather than the president. Despite its general deterioration, Congress contains a considerable number of very conservative members, and Capitol Hill is usually more accessible to conservatives than is the White House. Sometimes the president should be given his head in an international crisis; but in the view of some conservative scholars this should apply only to clearly specified circumstances and subject to congressional ratification after a specified time.[11]

The Radical Left

In the radical left analysis, Congress is not one of the central decision-making institutions in America. They see it essentially as a source of secondary influence. The real power is in the corporate board rooms and the White House, not on

Capitol Hill. "More and more of the fundamental issues never come to any point of decision before the Congress, or before its most powerful committees . . . ," said the radical sociologist C. Wright Mills. The member of Congress operates at the "middle levels of power."[12] Mostly nothing much gets done in Congress. But whatever it produces is biased in favor of business, for Congress is full of people with a background in small and middle-sized business and the law firms that serve business's purposes. The periodic cases of corruption that come to light are merely the more bungled examples of how Congress normally operates. There is nothing surprising about this corruption, for it is a direct and inevitable reflection of the greed and dishonesty that drive the American business system.

Still, the left recognizes that Congress can occasionally have a useful nuisance value. Its preference for obstruction rather than action can be used to get in the way of the ruling elite's programs when the elite overplays its hand. Thus Congress played an important, though sadly belated, role in the struggle against Vietnam and in uncovering Watergate.

So the left found it worth its while to support some peace candidates during the Vietnam war even though they were liberals. And here and there leaders of the left, notably Tom Hayden in 1976, worked hard to win a seat in the Congress. As Hayden saw it, gaining a seat in the Senate would not have brought him much of the reality of power. But he would have gained a superb vantage point from which to project, via the media, a different view of the potential of life in America than the people hear from anyone else in public office.

The Radical Right

In the eyes of the radical right, Congress must be given much of the blame for the disastrous course the American system has been taking toward socialism. In some periods, when the Democrats have huge majorities, the pace is headlong, whereas at other times the damage is done more slowly. But inexorably, and usually in step with the White House, Congress passes avalanches of laws that are burying the people in rules and regulations. Without those laws presidents would not become glutted with power, the bureaucracies would not grow, and businesses would not be strangled in red tape.

There are, of course, some very conservative members of Congress who resist the passage of these laws, and who are respected by the radical right, including two members of the John Birch Society. They and their conservative colleagues do their best to oppose the liberal–left elites who dominate Congress, and they keep the ideas of Americanism alive by persistently introducing bills for the repeal of the income tax, the abolition of some of the federal regulatory agencies, and so on. But although they receive the backing of right-wing organizations, they feel that they are outmanned and outlobbied by such organizations as Common Cause, the Ralph Nader groups, labor unions, and others, who can work with their allies in the media to apply irresistible pressures on Congress.

Conclusion

We have reviewed the functions, composition, organization, and procedures of Congress and have discovered a number of problems that have brought its standing among the public to abysmally low levels. The legislative branch has not performed adequately as a counterbalance to presidential usurpations of power; its structure and procedures have resulted in failures to produce decisions on urgent policy issues like energy; it has been beset with notorious publicity over the unethical conduct of some of its members. These complaints are voiced with particular intensity by critics to the left and right of center. But even the centrists, who have generally regarded Congress as their favorite institution, have recognized the need for some reforms.

So, at last, have the majority of the members of Congress. In consequence, Congress is changing. Reforms have been introduced that point toward greater integrity, openness, and efficiency. However significant these reforms may be, it is unlikely that they will lead quickly to a total transformation of power relationships in the American federal government.

First, the reforms will take time to work out, and they will be limited by compromises of various kinds. Hallowed procedures will not be easily abandoned. Any practice that has existed for a considerable period builds vested interests. Thus new members of Congress are inclined to be frustrated by the seniority principle. But when they have been reelected once or twice, they begin to develop a reluctance to give up their accumulating seniority. The very fact that congressional leaders have been giving better committee assignments to newcomers and have now greatly enlarged the number of members with subcommittee chairmanships could reduce the zeal for reform.

Second, even if the current wave of reform is carried out to the full, it will not take the prime legislative initiative away from the presidency. Certainly, Congress can become a more potent counterbalance to the presidency—a fact which was clearly demonstrated during Jimmy Carter's first year in the White House.

Still, this is an age of executives rather than of legislatures. Given the enormous scale and complexity of the policy-planning process and the speed with which many economic and foreign policies must be made, Congress can only establish parity of power with the White House if the presidency falls into particularly inept hands.

Notes and References

1.   Congressional Quarterly, *Guide to Current American Government*, Spring 1976 (Washington, D.C., 1976), pp. 17–20.

2.   John F. Manley, "The House Committee on Ways and Means: Conflict

Management in a Congressional Committee," *The American Political Science Review*, Vol. 59, No. 4 (December 1965), p. 934.

3.   Theodore R. Marmor, "The Congress: Medicare Politics and Policy," in *American Political Institutions and Public Policy*, Allan P. Sindler, ed. (Boston: Little, Brown and Company, 1969), p. 15.

4.   Mark J. Green, James M. Fallows, and David R. Zwick, *Who Runs Congress?* (New York: Bantam Books, Inc., 1972), p. 130.

5.   James MacGregor Burns, *Uncommon Sense* (New York: Harper and Row Publishers, 1972), pp. 124–126.

6.   Alan Cranston, "A Liberal's View: Why We Need the Filibuster," *The Los Angeles Times*, October 10, 1971.

7.   See Frank Munger and Richard Fenno, Jr., *National Politics and Federal Aid to Education* (Syracuse, N.Y.: Syracuse University Press, 1962), pp. 93–94.

8.   Willmoore Kendall, *The Conservative Affirmation* (Chicago: Henry Regnery Company, 1963), pp. 22–24.

9.   James Burnham, *Congress and the American Tradition* (Chicago: Henry Regnery Company, 1959), p. 266.

10.   William Buckley, *The National Review*, February 2, 1973, p. 167.

11.   Burnham, *Congress and the American Tradition*, p. 266.

12.   C. Wright Mills, *The Power Elite* (New York: Oxford University Press, 1956), p. 255.

Chapter 8

The Federal

Bureaucracy: A Fourth Branch

Perhaps no aspect of government in America arouses more controversy and is the target of more hostility than the huge institutions in Washington that employ large numbers of federal employees. This national bureaucracy has been a traditional target of the conservatives and the radical right. From the mid-1960s the federal bureaucracy has received pungent criticism from the new left. Then in the mid-1970s a number of politicians of the center joined the assault on the bureaucracy and made it a prime political issue.

It was easy to turn the federal bureaucracy into a political issue because of a growing resentment of federal agencies among the public at large. In polls asking people what they regard as "the biggest threat to the country in the future," big government is mentioned more often than either big business or big labor. And in 1976 a Louis Harris poll indicated that 72 percent of the public "no longer feel they get good value" for their tax dollars.

The Dimensions
of the Bureaucracy

In 1800 the federal government employed about 5000 people, and the total federal budget was under $6 million. By 1977 the number of civilian employees had risen to about 2.8 million, and the budget was over $400 billion.

The staffs of the federal government work for a number of different types of organizations: the White House, the Cabinet departments, a variety of more or less independent agencies, and government corporations.

The Executive Office of the President

Immediately serving the president himself is a core group in the White House—the president's top advisers, key staff members, and their subordinates. In recent years this White House staff has numbered some 300 to 500 people. The top members of Jimmy Carter's White House staff in 1977 comprised five assistants to the president (Hamilton Jordan—almost but not quite a chief of staff; Stuart Eizenstat, domestic affairs; Jack Watson, Jr., intergovernmental relations and Cabinet secretary; Margaret Costanza, public liaison—contacts with special interest groups; Frank Moore, congressional liaison), press secretary Jody Powell, and presidential counsel, Robert Lipshutz. Immediately below this group were five special assistants to the president with responsibilities in such fields as appointments, personnel, and drug abuse.

This White House staff is part of the larger Executive Office of the President, the size of which has varied over the years according to the councils and offices which each president has decided to include, but which has lately numbered around 4000 to 5000. Key agencies in the Executive Office include the Office of Management and Budget (directed in 1977 by Bert Lance, until his resignation under pressure in September, 1977);the National Security Council (Zbigniew Brzezinski); and the Council of Economic Advisers (Charles Schultze).

The Cabinet

Then there are the Cabinet departments. These, too, have changed in recent years through the consolidation of old functions and the addition of new. Thus since World War II the Cabinet departments have included the Department of Defense (supervising the former separate departments for each branch of the military), the Department of Health, Education and Welfare, the Department of Housing and Urban Development, and the Department of Transportation. On the other hand, the Post Office Department was abolished in 1970, to be replaced by the U.S. Postal Service. Further reorganizations are considered by each administration. Carter, for example, established a Cabinet department to focus on the energy problem. As of late 1977 the Carter Cabinet consisted of the following 12 positions and people:

Position	Officeholder
Secretary of State	Cyrus Vance
Secretary of Defense	Harold Brown
Secretary of the Treasury	Michael Blumenthal
Attorney General (Justice Department)	Griffin Bell
Secretary of Labor	F. Ray Marshall
Secretary of Commerce	Juanita Kreps
Secretary of Agriculture	Robert Bergland

Position	Officeholder
Secretary of Health, Education and Welfare	Joseph Califano
Secretary of Housing and Urban Development	Patricia Roberts Harris
Secretary of the Interior	Cecil Andrus
Secretary of Transportation	Brock Adams
Secretary of Energy	James Schlesinger

The size of the Cabinet departments varies considerably, the Department of Defense being by far the largest, with over a million employees in 1976. Next came the Department of Health, Education and Welfare with about 150,000 employees, Treasury with 136,000, and Agriculture with more than 100,000.

Heading each Cabinet department is the secretary (the attorney general in the case of the Justice Department), who is appointed by the president, subject to confirmation by the Senate. The secretary reports directly to the president (though some presidents, notably Richard Nixon, have used their White House staff as intermediaries between them and their Cabinet chiefs). The secretaries' top aides hold the title of undersecretary or deputy secretary, according to the department, and there are assistant secretaries at the next level. The structure of the Department of Defense is more elaborate, for the secretaries of the Army, Navy, and Air Force report to the secretary of defense, not to the president.

Within the departments are various bureaus, offices, services, and administrations. Thus the Justice Department includes the Federal Bureau of Investigation and the Immigration and Naturalization Service; the Department of Health, Education and Welfare (HEW) includes the Office of Education, the Social Security Administration, and the Food and Drug Administration; and the Department of Commerce includes the Bureau of the Census. As for the Department of State, its multiplicity of functions is illustrated by Figure 8-1, which consists of the department's organizational chart in 1976.

The Independent Agencies

Next there are a number of "independent" agencies, so-called because they are not directly under the supervision of a Cabinet department nor part of the Executive Office of the President. The extent to which they are independent of direct control by the president, however, varies considerably, as we shall indicate when considering each category of independent agency.

Regulatory agencies.   Regulatory agencies include the Federal Communications Commission, the Federal Trade Commission, the Interstate Commerce Commission, and the National Labor Relations Board. Their jobs are to

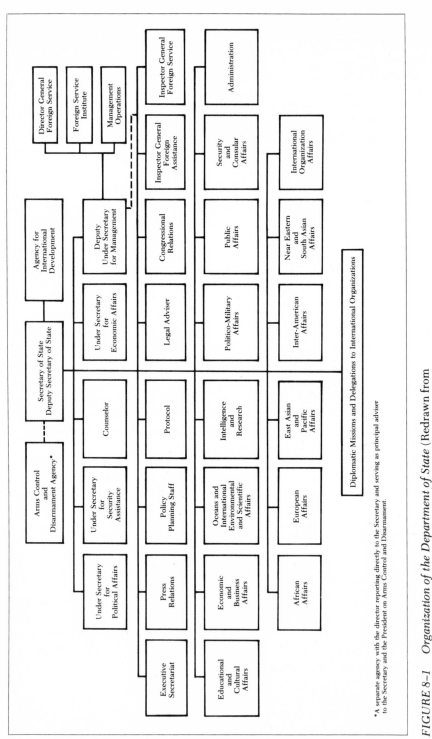

*A separate agency with the director reporting directly to the Secretary and serving as principal adviser to the Secretary and the President on Arms Control and Disarmament.

FIGURE 8-1 Organization of the Department of State (Redrawn from Office of the Federal Register, *United States Government Manual* 1977–78 [Washington, D.C.: Government Printing Office, 1976], p. 388.)

regulate the practices of business, labor, and other private economic organizations in accordance with principles established by federal legislation. The commissioners of these agencies are appointed by the president, subject to Senate approval, but are provided by law with a good deal of autonomy, for their appointments are for fixed terms, and the president cannot fire them as he can a member of the Cabinet or White House staff. Each agency is run by three or more commissioners with overlapping terms of office, and in some cases Congress has established the requirement that their membership be bipartisan to keep the agencies free of political bias.

Administrative or executive agencies.   Another group of agencies is directly involved in operating or supervising governmental programs, unlike the regulatory agencies, which intervene in the affairs of private businesses, although they do not try to run them directly. Agencies in this category include the Federal Reserve Board, the National Aeronautics and Space Administration (NASA), the Selective Service System, and the Veterans Administration. The degree of independence of these agencies ranges widely. Whereas the Veterans Administration reports directly to the White House, the Federal Reserve Board exercises a high degree of autonomy, for its chairperson is appointed by the president for a four-year term and cannot be fired by the president, even though he has great power to determine the flow of money into the economy and has sometimes exercised that power in ways that have infuriated presidents (as we shall see in Chapter 11).

Government corporations.   Finally, there are government-owned agencies that directly operate major services to the public. These include the Tennessee Valley Authority, created in the 1930s to provide hydroelectric power, irrigation, and flood control; and the U.S. Postal Service, the successor to the Post Office Department. Although these corporations are public agencies, owned by the government, they have a good deal more flexibility than Cabinet departments and are not subject to the degree of detailed administrative and financial controls that the White House and the Congress impose on the departments.

The Range of Functions

The functions of these various federal governmental agencies cover almost every kind of responsibility of modern government, including administering and implementing programs; drawing up specific rules or legislation; adjudicating, or settling disputes; and enforcing legislation.

Administration

First, in various degrees many federal agencies administer programs. Thus the Postal Service, the Tennessee Valley Authority, and the Veterans Administration directly manage enormous enterprises, with very large staffs and budgets running into the billions of dollars. In other cases, such as the public housing program or the unemployment services, detailed administration is in the hands of state or local agencies, but the federal agency retains ultimate administrative control by establishing national policies and guidelines, and then checking to ensure that these policies are adhered to as a condition of the local agencies' receiving funds.

Legislation

Federal governmental agencies are not limited to the administration or execution of the laws. In many cases, they actually legislate. When Congress passes laws, it usually couches them in rather general terms. This leaves it up to the Cabinet departments and the independent regulatory agencies to draw up the rules—that is, the legislation—which apply the laws' generalities to specific situations.

There is no escaping this need to delegate responsibility for legislation to departments and agencies. Even where Congress tries hard to set out its wishes in detail, it cannot anticipate every eventuality. For example, Congress simply does not have time to become involved in setting up the specific regulations that determine who will receive a license to operate a television channel or under what terms that license will be renewed. This power has to be left to the Federal Communications Commission (FCC). Congress retains the right to overrule the FCC's decisions; but it has had to surrender the authority to initiate important legislation to the FCC.

The FTC.   The work of the Federal Trade Commission provides a particularly interesting example of the delegation of legislative responsibility by Congress. The FTC was originally established to protect *businesses* from practices by other businesses that impeded fair competition, but Congress subsequently gave the FTC broad authority to protect *consumers* also against unfair business practices. The FTC has used this power to establish regulations on advertising, regulations that require manufacturers either to prove their claims or change their ads.

When Norelco claimed that its product shaved "up to 50 percent faster"; when General Electric declared that its air conditioners reproduced the "clean freshness of clear, cool mountain air"; when Smith, Kline and French told people that "a summer cold is a different animal," requiring a different medication from a winter cold; the FTC demanded that they prove it. Although the FTC did not challenge Profile Bread's assertion that it contained fewer calories per slice, the commission pointed out that this was only because Profile's slices were thinner, and it required future advertising to make this clear. Similarly, Lysol's claim that it "kills germs on environmental surfaces" was true enough. But, said the FTC, this meant very little, since communicable diseases are transmitted by airborne germs.

The FTC also issued guidelines governing the use of celebrities in advertising. Unless they actually used the product, the FTC would challenge the ads as an unfair trade practice. So former baseball stars Whitey Ford and Mickey Mantle could not be shown drinking Lite Beer on television commercials unless they also drank it off-screen. The same applied to Joe Namath's commercials for the breakfast food Maypo. (However, an ad that showed Namath wearing pantyhose could be considered "fanciful" under the guidelines, so he did not have to wear them regularly.)

The FTC's authority over false and misleading advertising was also used to limit cigarette advertising. In 1955 the FTC issued guidelines banning claims that cigarettes were good for you. (Kool cigarettes offered "extra protection" in the winter months, and Julep cigarettes were touted as a remedy for coughs.) Then the FTC took action on a 1964 report of a Surgeon-General's Advisory Commission on Smoking and Health. The agency began a series of steps that led eventually to the inclusion of a health warning on all cigarette packages and advertisments, and the banning of all cigarette commercials from television and radio.

The FDA.   The Food and Drug Administration provides further examples of the vigorous use of legislative power by administrative agencies. Using the authority that Congress gave it to protect the consumer against harmful foods and drugs, it has ordered many drugs off the market or insisted that they be sold by prescription only. Cyclamates, a synthetic sugar substitute, when found to cause cancer in rats, could no longer be used by the makers of dietetic drinks or foods; and in 1977 an order was issued to limit the sale of saccharin on the same grounds. Furthermore, FDA regulations now require that labels on food products must identify nutrients, vitamins, fat, and cholesterol content.

Adjudication

In addition to administering and legislating, some federal agencies adjudicate, that is, they settle conflicts between contending parties much as courts do.

Over the years Congress has passed a flood of legislation aimed at regulating and controlling business, labor, agricultural, and professional groups. Laws of that kind inevitably give rise to disputes, sometimes between the affected groups and government, sometimes among the groups themselves. These disputes have become so frequent and complex that the regular courts of law have neither the time nor the expertise to handle them. Consequently, federal regulatory agencies have been assigned a judicial, or quasi-judicial, function. In some cases this has led to their establishing hearing procedures which, though not as formal as the courts themselves, are nonetheless rigorous and quite elaborate.

The National Labor Relations Board (NLRB) is a good example of a federal agency that spends much of its time adjudicating disputes. Congress has passed laws forbidding unfair labor practices, and in a general way the legislation indicates the criteria for what constitutes an unfair practice. But whether or not management or labor has acted unfairly will depend on the very specific circumstances of a labor dispute, and this will often be settled by the NLRB after full-scale hearings between the parties to the conflict.

Enforcement

Yet another responsibility of federal agencies is enforcement. Although most of the law enforcement activity in the country is carried out at the state and local levels, many federal statutes include provisions for criminal penalties. For example, penalties were included in federal laws dealing with kidnapping, forgery, unauthorized wiretapping or electronic bugging, income tax evasion, violating the election finance code of 1974, or engaging in consumer fraud in any business that crosses state lines. Several agencies employ staffs to investigate, apprehend, and prosecute persons suspected of breaking such laws, most notably the FBI and U.S. attorneys in the Department of Justice, and the enforcement officers of the Treasury Department.

Sometimes all these functions—administration, legislation, adjudication, and enforcement—are exercised by the same agency. For example, the Interstate Commerce Commission *legislates* when it makes rules regulating the rates charged by railroads and trucks; it *adjudicates* when it sits as a tribunal to determine if its regulations have been violated; it enters the realm of *enforcement* when it investigates complaints and initiates proceedings against alleged violators.

So the constitutional principle of the separation of powers does not seem to set bounds to the work of the federal agencies. In this respect, they are not unique. As we have seen, the president is also a legislator, and congressional investigations sometimes take on the aura usually associated with the judiciary. Still, the federal agencies are even less bound by the separation of powers than any of the traditional three branches of government.

Taken together, federal government agencies spend vast sums of money, employ very large staffs, and make great numbers of decisions, some of enormous significance to the lives and fortunes of millions of people. There is power here—enough to suggest that the federal bureaucracy has become what amounts to a fourth branch of government.

Presidential and Congressional Supervision of the Federal Bureaucracy

Nominally this "fourth branch" is subordinate to the executive and legislative branches, and the president and Congress have a number of specific devices available to them to assert their power over the bureaucracy.

Presidential Influence

First, the president can place the stamp of his policies on the bureaucracy by appointing his people in the top positions. A new president has about 5000 jobs at his disposal, of which some 2000 are the key policy-making roles in executive agencies. In an effort to bring in people whose political attitudes are consistent with the president's, the appointees of Democratic presidents are predominately Democrats, whereas Republican presidents place mostly Republicans in the top spots.

Then presidents have ways of checking on the work of the departments and agencies. In the Executive Office the president has advisers who can give him detailed information on economic, national security, and many other problems, so that he does not have to rely only on the information submitted by the various departments and agencies, who may be trying to push forward their own ideas and interests. Then the budget proposals of every department have to be cleared and coordinated through the Office of Management and Budget (OMB—part of the Executive Office of the President).

Finally, presidents themselves have an expert interest in a number of fields and can have a powerful impact whenever they decide to concentrate their efforts in any of these fields. For example, Jimmy Carter's experience as governor in reorganizing the administration of the state of Georgia led to a personal commitment to reorganize the administration of the government. Wherever the president displays this type of personal interest, the Cabinet departments and their staffs can expect strong direction from the White House.

Congressional Influence

The bureaucracies must also reckon with Congress. In Chapter 7 we saw that one of a congressman's functions is to intervene with the bureaucracies on behalf of

© 1977 Dick Wright; Providence Journal-Bulletin.

his constituents. But we should not picture representatives as going cap in hand to beg for favors. After all, most members of the bureaucracy maintain a healthy respect for the wishes of Congress, since a department's requests for funds and proposals for legislation must be scrutinized by congressional committees and sub-committees whose staff and senior members will probably have acquired close knowledge of the department's activities and a special insight into the agency's patterns of spending. Another check on federal bureaucracies are reports to the Congress by the head of its General Accounting Office, the U.S. comptroller general, which frequently point out the failures in existing programs, thereby giving Congress a warning signal against approving similar proposals for the future. Congress can also investigate government programs through its Government Operations Committee or any of its standing committees or its special investigation subcommittees.

Finally, Congress has established precise rules governing the procedures of the regulatory agencies, and in many cases it has reserved the right to overrule a proposed agency regulation. This right was exercised in the cigarette advertising case. When the Federal Trade Commission in 1964 proposed a strong health warning on advertisements as well as on packages, Congress intervened and passed a law that softened the warning on packages; removed the requirement for the warning on advertising; and forbade any further FTC action until 1969.

Nothing more happened until 1970, by which time a large body of research had accumulated linking cigarette smoking with cancer. Congress passed the Public Health Cigarette Smoking Act, which strengthened the warning on packages, and banned all cigarette advertising from the airwaves. It was a strong measure. But it was not as strong as the rule that the FTC would have issued had Congress allowed it to act independently.

Then, too, the proposed FDA ban on saccharin in 1977 was delayed by Congress pending further research.

Bureaucratic Autonomy

In many ways, then, the federal bureaucracies are directed, supervised, checked on, and sometimes harassed by president and Congress. Yet it would not be correct to see them as merely instruments of the elected branches of government. Each bureaucracy has a life and a will of its own, and it is difficult, sometimes impossible, to bring it completely under control.

The president, as we have seen, appoints the top policy makers in each department and agency. But this accounts for only about 2000 out of 2,800,000 federal civilian employees. Most of the rest are protected by Civil Service rules, which were designed to cut down on the corruption in government commonly associated with a *spoils system*, a system under which appointments go to political allies, friends, or relatives. Civil Service also increases the attractiveness of federal careers by providing security of employment.

As for the independent regulatory agencies, the president's control is even more limited than over the regular Cabinet departments, since the commissioners who run the agencies serve long, staggered terms, and the president's right to remove them has been severely restricted by Congress.

The fact that the agencies are staffed mostly with people making a lifetime career in the bureaucracy means that each agency develops its own continuing identity and long-range purposes, which are not easy to change. The president's appointees fill the top positions, but they do not reach far down into the administrative hierarchy. The existing staff have to be persuaded to accept proposals for change.

Specialized Information

However, the staff may be able to show that newly proposed ideas cannot work. The staff members, after all, have built up years of experience and practical knowledge. They can draw immediately upon a staggering array of data of which a new director at the top is relatively ignorant. They can command the kind of technical and scientific competence that is increasingly necessary in making effective decisions and that is not usually part of the preparation of presidents (other than Herbert Hoover and Jimmy Carter, who were trained as engineers) or most of their top advisers.

Even though presidents have been trying to offset the bureaucracies' informational advantage by building up their personal staffs of technical advisers in the White House and the Executive Office, and, though Congress, too, has steadily improved its facilities for gathering data, they cannot possibly keep up with everything for which they are responsible. With over 1000 federal programs to deal with, the informational resources of president and Congress must be spread so thin that most programs can receive only occasional and perfunctory review.

Inertia

Even when an incoming administration is determined to produce major changes and refuses to accept the bureaucracy's expert arguments as to why the changes will not work, new policies may be slow in coming. Although the secretary can pass the word down the line that this is what the president wants and that the matter is urgent and must be given top priority, the response from the permanent staff may be one of inertia, an unwillingness to move and to accept change: "We're working on it, Mr. Secretary. We're moving as fast as we can. But these things take time. A great many people will be affected by the change, and they have to be consulted. There are statutes and legal problems and congressional sensitivities to take into account. It may cost more money than is available." And so on.

Only persistent, energetic pressure from the top can overcome this kind of resistance. And at the top all too many responsibilities and pressures divert attention from the issue at hand.

Constituencies

Bureaucracies do not operate in a vacuum. Over the years they build their own constituencies around the country. Agencies develop close ties with big and small business, professional groups, labor unions, farmers, veterans, minority groups, and consumer organizations. Thus the Federal Housing Administration works with home builders' organizations, the Department of Agriculture with farmers, the Air Force with the aerospace industry and the Air Force Association. As a result the agencies can muster outside support for their policies, which may or may not coincide with the policies of president and Congress.

Maneuvering between President and Congress

Federal agencies can also advance their programs by playing the executive and legislative branches off against each other. Any high departmental official who knows his job will try to establish close relationships with key congressional committee and subcommittee chairpersons. The president expects those relationships to be used for his own ends, and he demands that his appointed officials present and defend his policies before Congress. Often this will be the case, and federal agencies can be among the most effective lobbies for a president's program.

But it may not always be so. Suppose that the official is a general who is appearing before Congress to explain the administration's position that a new weapons system should be cut from the budget. He loyally presents the policy of the president and the secretary of defense. But then a member of the Armed Services Committee (who may possibly have discussed this ahead of time with the general) presses him hard on whether or not he really agrees with the policy. By some turn of phrase or intonation he may then let slip the possibility that he harbors doubts about the wisdom of that policy. This would hardly present his civilian chiefs with sufficient grounds for punishing him. But the doubts he has raised may well have damaged the chances that the president will have his way.

Thus the federal bureaucracies, by protecting their programs with specialized knowledge and inertia, by cultivating organized constituencies, and by maneuvering between Congress and president, have become much more than an instrument of presidential and congressional power. They have become a power in their own right. And power on this scale, with large numbers of people in vast institutions and impressive financial resources, will attract many critics. We shall review their arguments from various points on the spectrum, concentrating on the conservatives' strong criticisms and the liberals' defense of the bureaucracy.

Five Perspectives on the Federal Bureaucracy

The Conservatives: The Threat to Liberty

To the conservatives the greatest menace to the American constitutional system is the enormous growth of government. To them it is potentially the death-knell of our freedoms, taking us at an ever faster pace toward state socialism.

Concentrated power—people and money.   The sheer size of the resources—both in personnel and in money—accumulated in government represents a concentration of power of staggering dimensions. In addition to the 2,800,000 civilians who work for the federal government (plus 2 million in the military services), state and local governments employ over 12 million people. Thus there are about 15 million civilians who work for government in America, which is more than one-sixth of the total civilian work force. Then, too, the number of people on welfare has increased prodigiously to about 11 million by 1976. So we have about 26 million who are on the public payroll. There are millions more who work on research grants funded by the federal government, who get farm or other federal subsidies, or who receive help from Washington in the form of reduced interest rates or guarantees of loans, as in the housing industry.

When so many people are dependent, directly or indirectly, on the public exchequer, it becomes increasingly difficult to avoid governmental control of our entire society. Moreover, the danger is reinforced by the fact that the expansion of governmental employment has been far exceeded by the growth of governmental spending. In the 25 years from Truman to Nixon the federal budget went up tenfold, from $30 billion to $300 billion, then on to more than $400 billion under Ford, and, under Carter, it continues to rise. This rate of increase in federal spending has far exceeded the rates of inflation and of population growth. In addition, state and local government spending and employment has been increasing at a reckless pace.

In part this rise is because of the proliferation of programs providing financial help to almost every imaginable constituency. For the rest it results from the growth of the government payrolls. Of all the groups that benefit from larger government budgets none can compare with the employees of government.

Until recently a career in government was regarded as secure but relatively low-paid. The protection of civil service was accepted as a justification for rather modest salaries. But now, as the demand for government services has grown, and government employees have banded together in militant unions, there has been strong upward pressure on salaries. Between 1955 and 1973, for example, the average paycheck for federal workers rose 183 percent as against 129 percent for workers outside of government. The result was that federal government workers in

1973 earned an average of $13,000 per year, while in the private sector the average was $8900. With generous pension plans, vacations, and sick leaves, government employees are clearly doing better than workers in private industry.

Given the growing numbers joining the unions and the sympathetic attitudes of that other group of public employees, the members of Congress, the outlook for the taxpayer, who ultimately must support all these employees, is gloomy indeed.

Big government limits individual freedom.   This colossus of government interferes with our lives and liberties in many ways. First, big government *imposes an intolerable tax burden.* When so much of our money is taken in taxes, it denies us the right to make our own choices on how to spend it and substitutes the decisions of bureaucrats.

Second, *when government bureaucrats make decisions on our behalf, they assume that they know better than we do.* This assumption underlies the banning of cigarette advertising on television and radio, which we discussed earlier in the chapter. It may be that government has a duty to encourage research into the relationship between smoking and disease and to publicize the results of that research. But even if a relationship between cigarettes and cancer has been proved (and there is still some question as to whether the statistics conclusively prove a causal relationship), it does not follow that government should interfere with the right of citizens to make their own decisions.

As the conservative columnist George Will puts it: "The principle is that government has a duty to protect grown men and women from their own foolish habits. . . . The assumption is that Americans are such manipulable dolts that television commercials can cozen them into drastic behavior changes, turning nonsmokers into smokers." This is a foolish assumption, for advertising does not create smokers but merely gets some of them to switch brands. "The law banning cigarette commercials is a monument to the government's belief that Americans are manipulable, and the belief that the government can treat Americans that way and get away with it."[1]

The Food and Drug Administration is another agency determined to protect us from ourselves, especially since stringent new guidelines for the agency were adopted in 1962. Thus they banned cyclamates as a sugar substitute when research showed that rats who are fed massive doses of the chemical sometimes develop cancer. But if rats are fed massive doses of anything—far beyond the dosage likely to be ingested over several years by people—some ill effects will show up. When later research threw doubt on the earlier results, the FDA was unmoved. In fact, they proceeded to take action against saccharin. Who will protect obese people from the FDA?

Conservatives now question whether the FDA should exist. The agency has approved far fewer drugs than it used to before 1962 and it has taken longer to give its approval. Admittedly, this has kept some dangerous drugs off the market and prevented a recurrence of the thalidomide episode, when thousands of children (mostly in West Germany, England, and Japan) were born horribly deformed because the drug was prescribed as a sedative for pregnant women.

But, argues Milton Friedman, the tougher standards have also, by slowing down the rate of innovation, prevented or delayed the appearance of drugs that might have saved many lives or alleviated many ailments. On balance, much more has been lost than gained.[2]

We are being forced, say the conservatives, into a national hypochondria. Hidden dangers lurk in every commodity. Whatever was once wholesome and life-giving is now a deadly poison. It is true that there is a degree of danger in everything we do or use. But we cannot find total safety except in death.

As James Kilpatrick puts it: "Do Americans truly desire a society that is perfectly safe, a society purged of every trace of smog, germs, rough places and sharp edges? Do we want to live in a beautiful cocoon, padded in styrofoam layers of bureaucratic protection?"[3]

Third, big government has all but *deprived business people of the freedom to run their firms in the interests of themselves, their stockholders, and their customers.* Goodyear Tire and Rubber Company reported that it spent $30 million in 1974 complying with federal regulations on such matters as the environment, occupational safety and health, and motor vehicle safety. These costs may be supportable for big corporations (though the consumer ultimately pays). But for many small entrepreneurs the cost of complying with the regulations has been ruinous.

Bureaucratic waste and incompetence.   Pell-mell, say the conservatives, we are moving toward a centralized autocracy. And conservatives have no use for the argument that, even if centralized autocracies are unpleasant, they are more efficient than loosely organized, diffuse systems such as capitalism. In fact, conservatives insist, all the evidence points to the fact that our national bureaucracies are appallingly wasteful and incompetent. The very word *bureaucracy* is synonymous for conservatives with rigidity, extreme caution, confusion, duplication, evasion of responsibility, and lack of sensitivity and imagination.

Without the lash of competition or the lure of profits, and protected by Civil Service security, federal bureaucracies lack the incentives that inspire private business to perform well. As Peter Drucker suggests:

> The best we get from government in the welfare state is competent mediocrity. More often we do not get even that: we get incompetence such as we would not tolerate in an insurance company. In every country, there are big areas of government administration where there is no performance whatsoever—only costs. . . . And the more we expand the welfare state, the less capable even of routine mediocrity does it seem to become.[4]

It is no wonder that, when called upon to manage large enterprises, such as the Post Office, the performance of government agencies is pathetically inferior to that of private business. Even when Congress changed the Post Office Department into the U.S. Postal Service, freed from detailed supervision by Congress and run by a board empowered to set rates and sell bonds to finance capital outlays and operating costs, the mail service continued to grow more expensive and less adequate. For it was still a public monopoly, not a private competitive business, and the traditional inefficiencies of government-controlled organizations remained.

There is only one kind of activity in which federal government output is truly impressive—the production of paperwork. The government generates annually 10 billion sheets of forms, applications, and reports. More than 200,000 federal employees are kept busy sorting and filing this mountain of paper in 25 million cubic feet of files. Countless hours of form filling for government also prevents businesses from going about their business. Standard Oil of Indiana annually sends the government about 250 required final reports totaling 24,000 pages, plus 20,000 supplementary documents. Altogether, calculates the Office of Management and Budget, business spends over 35 million person-hours a year filling out federal government forms.

That so much time is spent this way results not only from the sheer number of forms but also from the difficulty of finding out what they mean. Obscurity in written communication is a persistent problem in the federal bureaucracy. Lyndon Johnson's secretary of labor, Willard Wirtz, was often baffled by the memos sent to him:

> Most sentences are long. Three or four ideas are loaded in to increase the odds that one will be impressive and that if another is wrong it will get lost. Paragraphs are built like sandwiches, the meat in the middle. . . . The Department's effectiveness would be doubled if its prose were cut in half, if those who initialled documents read them, and if those who signed them wrote some of them. In none of this is the Department of Labor in any way exceptional.[5]

Confusion is further compounded by the constant changes in federal regulations. In 1976 the state of California complained in a suit against the U.S. Department of Agriculture that the food-stamp manual had been rewritten annually from 1965 through 1968, then again in 1972; modified 89 times in the next two years; rewritten again in 1975; and further amended after that. No detail is overlooked in these regulations, one of which prescribed when paper clips should be used on food stamp files and when they should be stapled.

The bureaucratic passion for minutely detailed interference with business is further illustrated in the great potato chip controversy of 1975. This debate[6] was occasioned by a complaint of the rival potato chip manufacturers when Procter and Gamble brought out their Pringles. These chips were neatly and uniformly packaged in cylinders rather than the traditional bags, thus saving space and protecting them from breaking until eaten. The basis of the complaint was that Pringles were not true potato chips, since they were made from dried potato granules.

The Food and Drug Administration was sympathetic. It wanted full and accurate disclosure. On the other hand, Pringles were undoubtedly chips made from potatoes. So the FDA compromised, informing Procter and Gamble that they must describe Pringles not simply as potato chips but as "potato chips made from dried potatoes." This instruction was made official in the following regulation:

Part 102 of Chapter I of Title 21 of the Code of Federal Regulations is amended . . . as follows . . . . :

(a) The common or usual name of the food product that resembles and is of the same composition as potato chips, except that it is composed of dehydrated potatoes (buds, flakes, granules, or other form), shall be "potato chips made from dried potatoes."

(b) The words "made from dried potatoes" shall immediately follow or appear on a line(s) immediately below the words "potato chips" in easily legible boldface print or type in distinct contrast to other printed or graphic matter, and in a height not less than the larger of the following alternatives:

(1) Not less than one-sixteenth inch in height on packages having a principal display panel with an area of 5 square inches or less and not less than one-eighth inch in height if the area of the principal display panel is greater than 5 square inches; or

(2) Not less than one-half the height of the largest type used in the words "potato chips."

"Briefly the problem is this: The State Department has five million to stabilize their government, and the CIA has ten million to overthrow it."

From *HERE IT COMES* (Bobbs-Merrill). © 1958 Lee Lorenz.

Another cause of massive waste is the duplication and overlapping of effort that results from the great size and diversity of the federal establishment. It presents an intolerably unwieldy mass that cannot possibly be properly supervised and coordinated.

Resources are given to the bureaucracies not on the basis of rational allocation but as a result of presidential fiat and constituency pressures. And, once a program is established, it is extraordinarily difficult to put an end to it. "Of all our institutions," says Peter Drucker, "*business is the only one that society will permit to disappear.*"[7] Government agencies and programs, by contrast, survive long after they have outlived their usefulness. For example, during World War II, school districts that received a sudden influx of defense workers or service personnel were designated as "impacted areas" and were given federal aid. In the mid-1970s $300 million a year was still going from Washington to impacted areas, though many had become high-income communities.

Not only do federal agencies survive; most of them expand. Once a program has been started, there are always impressive reasons for its growth. Government agencies can show with great conviction and plausibility why they ought to have more money and staff. However small the first appropriation for a program may be, the camel's nose is under the tent, and soon the rest of the beast will follow.

Thus the Social Security program has grown prodigiously, supplemented by Medicare, which has been complemented by federally supported state programs of medical care for the aged (Medicaid). The Department of Health, Education and Welfare was started in 1953 with a budget of $1.7 billion. By 1970 it had passed $50 billion, and by 1976 $161 billion. And the urban renewal program has multiplied by more than four times since its creation in 1960.

A new department, or a new bureau within a department, or a new office within a bureau becomes a pressure group for its own enlargement. To be effective it must build a large staff. It must also develop outside constituencies—farmers for the Department of Agriculture, hospital administrators, professors, and social workers for the Department of Health, Education and Welfare, and so on. It nourishes those constituencies with grants and subsidies of all kinds. Here again, conservatives can point to evidence from outside their own ranks. Democratic Senator William Proxmire of Wisconsin has uncovered a mind-boggling series of federally funded research projects, including the following:

$84,000 to find out why people fall in love.

$58,000 for a study on the "Anthropometry of Airline Stewardesses" (the measurements of their noses, buttocks, and so on).

$120,000 to determine how smoking marijuana affects the sexual arousal of male college students.

These are small-scale examples of federal study grants and applied research projects that amount, in the aggregate, to billions of dollars a year. In the words of Jeffrey Hart, editor of the conservative *National Review:*

Since 1965 a large and powerful new class has grown up, drawing liberally upon the federal treasury. This new class is devoted to the application of academic social science theory to supposed social problems. This racket, for this is what it largely is, involves a huge and growing federal bureaucracy linked to assorted research groups, think tanks, academic empires, social workers, planners, lawyers and manufacturers with an eye for the main chance.[8]

At best, these projects have been expensive and frivolous wastes of taypayers' money. At worst, in Hart's words, "the racket is responsible for outright disasters: busing, urban 'renewal' schemes, proliferating regulations and guidelines of all sorts."

Damage to business and the economy.   Not only is government inefficient in itself. It is the cause of inefficiency in others. As noted in Chapter 5 in our portrayal of the conservatives' view of interest groups, when government protects business with subsidies, tariff barriers, and special tax breaks, it does grave damage to the efficiency of the economy by cushioning the impact of competition, and thus enabling incompetent business people to flourish. By some estimates government rate setting and regulations in the trucking industry may add $2 billion a year to the country's transportation costs. The Civil Aeronautics Board (CAB) provides another prime example of an agency that, until recently at least, was overzealous in its protection of an industry—to the detriment of the industry as well as to the consumer. As the conservative writer M. Stanton Evans sees it: "The principal activities of this agency [the CAB] have been to restrict entry into the field of commercial aviation, provide route monopolies, and prevent competitive pricing."[9]

Worst of all is the impact of the growth of government on the economy as a whole. With taxes taking a large bite of all personal income, incentives are all but destroyed for both businesses and individuals. The average American cannot help being discouraged when he hears of the U.S. Chamber of Commerce's calculation in 1971 that he has to work more than four months of the year (from January 1 to May 10) simply to pay his taxes.

Finally, the conservatives believe that huge federal budgets and deficits year after year are the principal source of inflation. And nothing is more demoralizing and more damaging to the economy than inflation.

The conservatives' proposals for reform.   To deal with these problems conservatives propose the following reforms.

First, we should *sharply reduce federal spending and federal staffs.* Government is needed only to perform certain essential functions, notably protecting the public health and safety; preserving the national security from external threats; and controlling the supply of money.

Beyond these necessary functions of government we should reduce and eventually do away with massive giveaway programs that do little more than provide funds for professional researchers, make business inefficient, and justify the existence of the bureaucracies; and we must do away with all interference in the relationship between business and the consumer designed to protect the consumer from himself. As James Kilpatrick puts it: "I hold to this simple proposition: that the government has no business passing laws to prevent a man from making a durned fool of himself—so long as his conduct harms no one else."[10] Thus we should cut down the regulatory powers of the Federal Trade Commission and curtail or abolish the Food and Drug Administration.

Certainly we should resist the proposal sponsored by liberals to establish a consumer protection agency that would ride herd on the other federal regulatory agencies. This is a typical example of the poverty of liberal thought. Confronted with the shortcomings of federal agencies, their remedy is to create yet another federal agency.

Second, we should *adopt businesslike practices* in the operation of the federal government. This means bringing more businesspeople into government and freeing them to use the methods they have applied so successfully in industry. It also means undertaking a determined new effort to reorganize, streamline, and simplify the federal bureaucracies. There have been a number of attempts to accomplish reorganization in the past, following various studies, of which the most notable was the Hoover Commission on Organization of the Executive Branch in 1949. Although the various reorganizations have produced some savings, they have not succeeded in overcoming the enormous waste and duplication in the federal government. The reason is that they have dealt with reorganization in the context of massively overgrown government. Reorganization can only be effective when it accompanies a reduction of the federal government that brings it down to manageable proportions.

Third, we should *decentralize*. As many functions as possible should be moved from the federal government to other management units. Some services would be run more efficiently by private industry—for example, the power-producing plants of the Tennessee Valley Authority. And government should abandon its monopoly of first-class mail, allowing private companies to enter the field and provide the type of healthy competition that is now limited to parcel delivery and to second- and third-class mail. In other cases, responsibility should be shifted to state and local governments. Although such a shift does not necessarily remove the taint of socialism from governmental activities, at least it lessens the huge, inefficient concentration of power in Washington.

Conservatives know that it will not be easy to bring these changes about. For the federal bureaucracies are supported by—are, in fact, an integral part of—the liberal establishment. The policies of the bureaucracies perpetuate the beliefs of a succession of Democratic presidents and Congresses from the New Deal on. The liberal slant of the bureaucracies was precisely the problem that Richard Nixon started to attack at the beginning of his second term in office. Although interested mainly in achieving his own ends and unlikely even to adopt consistent conservative principles, Nixon had apparently decided that he wanted to cut out some federal programs, reorganize the governmental structure, and shift many federal responsibilities to state and local levels.

Unfortunately, Nixon's desire to cut down on federal power was matched by the hunger to increase his own power. His mistakes—Watergate, the Ellsberg break-in, the cover-up, and the rest—were seized upon eagerly by the bureaucracy; and, in large part, the Watergate story broke not because of a vigilant Congress and free press but because of calculated leaks from hostile bureaucrats, eager to destroy the man who threatened their policies and privileges.

What conservatives must work for, then, is the election of a president who sees even more clearly than Nixon the need to reduce the federal establishment and who would not be handicapped by Nixon's personality defects and drive for personal power.

The Radical Right: The Bureaucratic Conspiracy

Where the conservatives are angry with the growth of the federal bureaucracies, the radical right are enraged. Where conservatives see the expansion of the welfare state as leading eventually toward socialism, the radicals see the danger as going deeper and farther: "There are many stages of welfarism, socialism, and collectivism in general, but communism is the ultimate state of them all, and they all lead inevitably in that direction."[11]

Moreover, conservatives see the trend toward socialism as being accomplished by people who, though often well-meaning, do not understand that their policies are leading us toward the end of our freedoms. The radical right, on the other hand, believe that the advance toward socialism–communism is a carefully planned operation, conducted by people who know exactly what they are doing. These conspirators include elected leaders who have brainwashed the people into choosing them. But they also include large numbers of career officials, bureaucrats who, year after year, are working away at building their power and subverting American institutions.

These bureaucrats, some of them communists, others close allies of the communists, are heavily entrenched in the State Department, and have been largely instrumental in controlling the policies that have allowed Soviet imperialism to extend its sway over so much of the world. Others are found in the civilian staff of the Defense Department, where they hamstring and overrule the military. Others again control our monetary policies from their positions on the Federal Reserve Board. Still more agents of the conspiracy are in key posts in monstrously large agencies such as the Departments of Health, Education and Welfare and Housing and Urban Development, which direct tens of billions of dollars taken from ordinary taxpayers into the pockets of social workers, university researchers, and community troublemakers; or they are in the Federal Trade Commission and the Food and Drug Administration, which are used as bases for the constant harassment of businesspeople.

These bureaucrats are able to exercise their power almost without restraint.

They have devised a Civil Service system that makes it well-nigh impossible to get rid of them. Their command of information and their ability to build their own constituencies to support them makes it difficult for their political chiefs to resist their proposals. In any case, the possibility of resistance from the top rarely arises, for most of our political leaders agree with the programs that the bureaucrats devise and administer.

Thus, in the radical right analysis, our gigantic bureaucracies represent one more, particularly pernicious, dimension of the ruling elite that is engaged in a carefully planned operation to destroy the American system.

The Radical Left: Decentralization, Participation, and Spontaneity

In the classical Marxist–Leninist analysis adhered to by the old left, government is essentially the instrument of the ruling class of monopoly capitalists. Even so, it can be tactically useful to join other groups in forcing concessions out of the capitalists in the form of federal government programs such as public housing and other programs for the poor. Moreover, the communists look to the central government as the machinery through which they must achieve their revolution, and which will persist until, in the ultimate communist society, it withers away.

From the 1960s, however, this view was challenged by the new left. Big government is big bureaucracy. And big bureaucracies are monstrous, remote, impersonal institutions that reduce the people to a sense of helplessness. Political scientists Sheldon Wolin and John Schaar picked up this theme in their analysis of the seizure by students at Berkeley of a piece of land owned by the University of California. The university wanted to use the land for its own housing purposes. The students demanded it be made into a "People's Park." University officials called in the police, and a pitched battle ensued.

The university officials, said Wolin and Schaar, were not wicked people. They were bureaucrats, who believed that everything must be done in a regular, standardized way according to established rules. The students were asking for a response different from the norm. They were expressing human needs that did not fit in with the university's carefully laid, rationally developed plans. The officials simply did not understand what the students were talking about. Baffled, confronted by defiance of their benevolent authority, university officials turned to the repressive machinery of the state to affirm their power.[12]

Ultimately, says the new left, this passion of well-meaning people for rationality, order, and central planning will lead us to the fascist state. A symptom of this trend is the increasingly insistent proposal for a national data center, which would amalgamate the records of several government agencies into a single data bank containing legal, tax, credit, educational, employment, medical, and security information on every citizen. The left is not convinced by the claims that access to the files would be protected by rigid rules. Once established, the data center would become the perfect instrument through which the power elite, using an all-knowing bureaucracy, would establish final and complete control over the people.

The new left's alternative to bureaucracy has included three principal elements: decentralization of government, participation of the people, and spontaneity of individual expression.

Decentralization.   The new left's approach to decentralization is quite different from the conservatives'. The left certainly does not want to see government programs handed over to private business. The corporations themselves are run by great, impersonal bureaucracies, which are even less concerned with the interests of the people than are the government bureaucracies.

As for state and local governments, the left perceives them to be controlled generally by the same kind of forces who are in control in Washington. However, in the 1970s left radicals began to run for state and local offices. For one thing, they had a much better chance of winning there than in national elections, and they did, in fact, have some successes, as we shall see when we discuss state and local government in Chapter 10. Furthermore, the local scene is precisely the context in which the left want to demonstrate their ideas. Their major concern is to bring the decision-making process down to the neighborhood and the work place. There people can get a sense of accomplishment, since they are dealing with problems on a human scale, they can see the impact of their actions, and they can thereby overcome their feelings of helplessness and dependency on faceless, impersonal institutions.

Participation.   Decentralization of policy making will give people a chance for active participation. Without this there is no meaning to democracy. As things now stand, the federal government discourages the involvement of people in the decisions that directly affect their lives. Only in the "maximum feasible participation" clause of the 1964–65 War on Poverty legislation, which stipulated that there must be representatives of the poor on the boards that ran the community antipoverty programs, was this idea given official approval. And, as we shall see in Chapter 11, in which we discuss political responses to poverty, government officials were furious when the mandated participation of the poor led to challenges to existing power structures.

Spontaneity.   In the 1960s the new left counterculture poured scorn on our rationally planned, regimented lives, and called for creative, spontaneous expression by individuals and small groups. This was seen as the purest way to fulfill the democratic value of free choice, for it nourished diversity and freed us from being "programmed" instruments of someone else's purposes.

As we shall see in Chapter 10 on state and local government, by the mid-70s a growing number of new left leaders criticized the tendency toward impulse as against rationality, and they prepared programs and proposals for change requiring organization and planning. Still, hostility to forcing people into large-scale bureaucratic structures remains a central motif of the new left.

The Centrists: Joining the Attack

From the 1970s the onslaught on the federal government, which had started with the conservatives and the radical right and had been joined by the new left, found reinforcements among the centrists. Although some centrist politicians, such as Hubert Humphrey, continued unabated in their support of bigger government, others, such as Jimmy Carter, expressed doubts that government could solve all our problems. In fact, in his quest for the 1976 Democratic presidential nomination, Carter took as a central issue "the horrible, bloated, confused, overlapping, wasteful, insensitive, unmanageable, bureaucratic mess in Washington."

Another influential centrist source that criticized the federal bureaucracy were the scholars and writers associated with the journals *The Public Interest* and *Commentary*. Most of them were long considered somewhat left of center, and they still see a substantial role for the federal government in the economy. Irving Kristol, co-editor of *The Public Interest*, rejected the conservatives' proposals for deregulation of industry, arguing that unrestricted competition would lead to the elimination of smaller firms and the total dominance of the biggest corporations—which would lead to new demands for government intervention.

Yet, if Kristol and his associates have significant differences with the conservatives, the type of criticisms they level at the federal government clearly places them on the conservative side of our centrist band of opinion. Indeed, they have been dubbed "neo-conservatives," for they insist that, even though we need a good deal of federal intervention, we now have far too much of it. We have placed an intolerable strain on the government machinery by asking that it take on too many functions. Instead of limiting government to those tasks which it is well equipped to perform, we are giving it more and more "problems that are insoluble precisely because people demand of government what government cannot do."[13]

What government cannot do is to produce magic solutions to deep-rooted social problems such as poverty and race discrimination. And especially useless, if not harmful, are the kinds of solutions offered by the liberals, which run counter to the wishes of the majority of the people, such as school busing. We shall come back to this argument at some length in later discussions of urban problems, poverty, and race.

The Liberals: Defending Big Government

The liberals have been shaken by these attacks on the federal government and bureaucracy from all fronts. They recognize, in James MacGregor Burns's words, that "no part of our system has appeared to sink so swiftly in popular esteem as the executive branch in recent years."[14] They concede that the criticisms cannot be dismissed out of hand, and they have themselves expressed unhappiness with certain features of the federal bureaucracies.

As we review the major points of the critics through the liberals' eyes, we shall see that, although the liberals have given some ground, they still look to the federal government and the bureaucracies to put their programs into effect.

Liberty and the growth of government.   Liberals worry much more than they used to about the threats to freedom represented by the growth of government. The revelations about the Nixon administration, which we discussed in Chapter 6, brought home the dangers that could result if the president gained complete control of the bureaucracy. Had Nixon succeeded in placing his own people in all the key positions in the bureaucracy, it would have been very difficult indeed to limit his power.

Moreover, a flood of stories in the press from 1975 revealed the abuses of FBI power during the Kennedy and Johnson administrations. The dangers of bureaucratic power, it seems, were well advanced long before Richard Nixon entered the White House.

Still, the liberals' dislike of certain kinds of bureaucratic actions does not imply a renunciation of their basic beliefs. As we saw in Chapter 1, the liberals' definition of liberty focuses on *civil* liberty. If part of the federal bureaucracy, such as the FBI, attacks civil liberty, liberals will attack that part of the federal bureaucracy. But the great expansion of the federal bureaucracy, after all, has resulted from economic policies. Liberals, we have seen, are tough-minded when it comes to the liberties of business. They are enthusiastic supporters of government intervention in economic and business decisions. In their view, this kind of government intervention increases rather than diminishes freedom.

First, without federal interference to reduce gross inequalities, freedom would be the monopoly of the affluent. Those at the bottom of the income scale would lack that minimal degree of security without which the concept of freedom is meaningless rhetoric. Devoid of resources we have no ability to make choices; without choices there is no liberty.

Second, without the power of big government, who would set limits to the power of the massive business corporations? As Henry Fairlie, a contributor to the liberal *New Republic* puts it: "When the private power—of the barons, of the corporations—is necessarily as great as it is in modern society, it can be checked only by a dynamic assertion of the public power."[15]

But even if government power is needed to offset business power, how do the liberals answer the conservatives' charge that government has now become so much bigger than business that it represents the principal threat to our freedoms? The liberals' response is to contend that the growth of the federal government has been exaggerated.

To begin with, the number of federal employees has not grown very much in recent years. The increase in civilian employees was from 2.1 million in 1947 to 2.8 million in 1975, less proportionately than the growth of population. The big jump is in state and local employment, which went up by two-thirds in the last decade. But this does not represent a concentration of power in Washington. On the contrary, it represents a trend toward decentralization which conservatives ought to be pleased with.

It is true that the federal budget and the federal payroll have grown at a rapid rate. But part of the budgetary increase is attributable to inflation and the growth of population. *As a proportion of the gross national product* (the nation's total output of goods and services), the federal budget has increased only from 17 to 20 percent in the last 20 years.

As for the higher earnings of federal as against private employees, in considerable measure this is due to a shift in the composition of the federal work force. Increasingly, the federal government employs professional, scientific, and technical people. There has been a sharp decline in the proportion of unskilled and semiskilled workers, so that today the types of positions that make up federal employment require on the average a considerably higher level of qualifications than is true of the average employment outside the federal government. The inevitable consequence is a higher average paycheck.

Even then, the advantage in federal salaries does not extend to the top jobs. There are not many people earning $50,000 a year in federal agencies. Salaries at that level are commonplace among executives in industry. The salary of the president of the United States is $200,000 a year. Table 8-1 is a list of corporation executives who earned $500,000 or more, exclusive of stock options and expense accounts, in 1976.

There is little public outcry against these large rewards for people whose levels of responsibility and contributions to society are much less than those of executives in charge of large federal agencies. We apply a double standard. Government salaries are regarded as, at best, a necessary evil, excessive payments to people feeding at the public trough. Private salaries and fringe benefits, no matter how enormous, are not considered a matter for public concern—even though in many cases the taxpayer is contributing to them heavily because they are written off by companies as business expenses on their tax forms.

To the conservatives' charge that the expansion of federal activities represents a mad rush toward socialism, liberals reply that we have accepted a much smaller dose of socialism here than in almost any other industralized country in the world. Socialism cannot be separated from the Marxist notion of government operation of the means of production and distribution. Clearly we have not gone far in that direction.

The governments of most other economically advanced, democratic countries have nationalized their railroads and airlines, their postal services, their coal, gas, and electric industries. They own and operate at least one television and radio network, and build a great deal of public housing.

In the United States federal ownership and operation is much more limited. We have the Postal Service, the Tennessee Valley Authority (a public water and power-generating corporation that works closely with farmers and private business), a relatively small public housing program (administered by local housing authorities). Then, through the Corporation for Public Broadcasting, we funnel federal money to meet part of the costs of the seriously underfunded public television and radio networks. In addition, at the state and local levels there are extensive programs of public education and several municipally owned gas, elec-

TABLE 8–1   *Earnings of Corporate*
Executives, 1976

Company	Chief Executive	Total Remuneration [a] ($000)
Halliburton	John P. Harbin	1593
J. Ray McDermott	Charles L. Graves	1233
Rapid-American	Meshulam Riklis	966
Intl. Tel. & Tel.	Harold S. Geneen	782
White Consolidated	Edward S. Reddig	706
Texaco	Maurice F. Granville	672
Amer Home Products	William F. Laporte	660
Atlantic Richfield	Robert O. Anderson	639
Mobil Oil	Rawleigh Warner Jr.	639
Norton Simon	David J. Mahoney	624
International Paper	J. Stanford Smith	619
Gulf & Western Inds.	Charles G. Bluhdorn	593
General Motors	Thomas A. Murphy	590
Tenneco	Wilton E. Scott	575
United Technologies	Harry J. Gray	569
Dow Chemical	Charles B. Branch	567
Johnson & Johnson	Richard B. Sellars	566
American Brands	Robert K. Helmann	562
H. J. Heinz	R. Burt Gookin	554
Exxon	Clifton C. Garvin Jr.	538
IBM	Frank T. Cary	538
American Express	Howard L. Clark	530
Intl. Minerals & Chem.	Richard A. Lenon	525
Burroughs	Ray W. Macdonald	525
Standard Oil Ind.	John E. Swearingen	517
Fluor	J. Robert Fluor	515
General Electric	Reginald H. Jones	500

[a] Salary, bonus, director's fees, and deferred compensation; excludes stock options.
SOURCE: "Who Gets the Most Pay," *Forbes* (May 15, 1976), p. 225.

tric, and transportation services. But all these taken together constitute a much smaller segment of public ownership and operation than is found elsewhere. So if socialism involves government ownership, we have much less socialism here than in other countries.

Even if we follow the trend of several Western European socialist parties and define socialism not in terms of nationalization but of the expansion of welfare services, we have been very timid in America. We do have a major Social Security program, which provides for unemployment and retirement benefits, and some medical care for the aged. But in the field of health insurance we still lack the comprehensive program of national health insurance that is standard fare in almost all other advanced economies.

What we do have is an enormous amount of government underwriting of private enterprises. The American way is not to take over an industry but to subsidize it, give it government contracts, or protect it with tariffs or special tax advantages. Our system provides socialism for the rich, private enterprise for the poor.

Liberals do not propose wholesale nationalization of American industry. But they do suggest that, where an industry or a company exists solely or primarily because of federal government support, we should give up the pretense that free enterprise prevails, and transform private concerns into public corporations. This might be the case with such firms as Lockheed, for example, which have to run to the government to bail them out with loans that private banks refuse to extend.

Effective government regulation of business.   The American way is not only to subsidize private business, but also to control it through government regulatory agencies, which are supposed to protect the public interest. Liberals have generally supported the notion of regulation of business—so long as the public interest is, in fact, protected. The trouble is that, all too often, federal regulating agencies have served the purposes of industry rather than of the public.

Typically, a regulatory agency is created against a background of public protest against abuses of private power, such as monopolistic practices and exploitation of the consumer by business. After a period of crusading zeal, the agency tends to become established and routinized, and the spotlight moves on to other issues. Then comes a stage at which the business or other leaders who are the objects of regulation begin to work closely and sympathetically with the regulating agency. This stage is usually associated with movements of personnel between government and industry. A governmental agency, looking for expertise in a given industrial field, quite naturally hires people from that industry. Thus more than 100 Food and Drug Administration officials once worked for drug and chemical companies.

Conversely, government employment is an excellent jumping-off point for lucrative positions in private industry. When Burke Marshall, one of Kennedy's appointees in the Justice Department, left government, he became vice-president and general counsel for International Business Machines (IBM), whose vast size invites periodic government antitrust suits initiated by the Justice Department. Marshall's successor in the IBM job was another man with top-level Justice Department experience, Nicholas Katzenbach. Similarly, when Nixon Cabinet members Caspar Weinberger and George Schultz left government, they joined Bechtel Corporation, which is actively engaged in the promotion of atomic energy, a field in which federal agencies are deeply involved. At the Federal Power Commission (FPC), 90 percent of the lawyers arguing cases before the agency on behalf of private companies once worked for the FPC. And so on. It is not surprising, then, that as political scientist Grant McConnell says, "the outstanding political fact about the independent regulatory commissions is that they have in general become promoters and protectors of the industries they have been established to regulate.[16]

It might appear that liberals agree with the conservative critics of government regulation as a means of providing undesirable protection to industry. Indeed, a number of liberals have joined with conservatives to demand that the Civil Aeronautics Board allow airlines to compete with each other by cutting fares. But liberals are against only the kind of regulation that puts government on the side of industry in gouging the consumer. What liberals want to see generally is not less regulation but more effective regulation. They find cause for encouragement in the actions of some regulatory agencies in recent years. They point, for example, to the change in the Federal Trade Commission.

When a Nader team had investigated the FTC in 1968, they concluded that, under Paul Rand Dixon, chairperson since 1961, the commission had not discharged its statutory responsibility to act against "unfair and deceptive trade practices." On the contrary, it had become "a patterned and intricate deceptive practice unto itself."[17]

Even so, it was the FTC that had taken on the powerful tobacco industry, and forced a reluctant Congress to get cigarette advertising off the air. To the conservatives' argument related to this issue—that government has no business trying to protect people against themselves—liberals answer that government cannot escape the responsibility of protecting the health of the people. Earlier we cited James Kilpatrick's dictum that a person should be allowed to make a fool of himself "so long as his conduct harms no one else." But cigarette smoking harms not only the smoker. It harms his family. It irritates, perhaps even damages the health, of nonsmokers. And the cost of treating cancer is borne by government-supported hospitals and by all the participants in health insurance programs. So private foolishness often has far-reaching public consequences.

With President Nixon in the White House from 1969, the liberals could not dare hope that the cigarette advertising case would be expanded into a broad-scale defense of the consumer by an FTC which stood accused by a Ralph Nader study team of sloth and incompetence. Yet it was under a succession of Nixon-appointed chairpersons that a revitalized FTC shifted the burden of proof about advertising claims from the government to the advertiser, embarked on its campaign against false and deceptive advertising, and gained wider authority to define and take court action against unfair business practices.

Liberals have also found cause for satisfaction in some of the efforts of the Food and Drug Administration to protect the consumer against harmful substances. Even the Commerce Department, which has generally been the principal voice of business in the Cabinet, has taken action against dangerous products. And liberals were pleased by the creation in 1972 of the U.S. Consumer Product Safety Commission, which has forced manufacturers to eliminate hazards to children in toys, sleepwear, and household poisons such as drugs and caustics.

If all this could happen under a probusiness administration such as Richard Nixon's, liberals could see real possibilities of serving the consumer and the public interest through federal agencies. Still, the FTC and FDA efforts were not enough to satisfy the liberals. Most regulatory agencies still tended to look after the interests of business rather than those of the consumer. The FTC, after all, was not tied to the interests of a particular industry but was established instead to regulate all trade. Other agencies such as the Civil Aeronautics Board and the Federal Communications Commission were associated with a single industry, and that association was much too cosy for the consumer's welfare.

So the liberals proposed the establishment of a new consumer protection agency to make the other regulatory agencies do their jobs properly by taking cases to court and by representing the consumer in the public hearings of the agencies. After prolonged struggles in Congress the creation of the agency was finally approved—only to be vetoed by President Ford in 1976. President Carter tried again in 1977 with a bill for an Agency for Consumer Protection; but this ran into trouble in Congress through intense opposition by business groups.

The question of inefficiency.   Liberals have two responses to the conservatives' charge that the federal government is awesomely incompetent. First, they believe it to be a gross overstatement. They draw attention to the many remarkable achievements of the federal government, for example:

The Social Security program is extremely well run. In 1967, with less than a year to make the arrangements, the Social Security Administration enrolled 19 million people in Medicare and set up machinery in 50 states to pay their hospital and doctor bills, all with so little dislocation that the operation deserves to be rated as one of the masterpieces of contemporary management.

The Internal Revenue Service does an extremely efficient job given the incredible complexities and inequities built into the income tax laws (and the tendency of some recent presidents to interfere in its operations to punish offenders).

The greatest organizational achievement of the 1960s, the flight to the moon, while involving many private companies, was ultimately the accomplishment of a government agency, the National Aeronautics and Space Administration.

Much impressive research in health, agriculture, and other fields has been conducted by federal agencies.

A University of Michigan survey of people's responses to services in the fields of employment, workmen's compensation, welfare, and social security indicated that only one in 10 thought that the administrators were very inefficient, while another 10 percent thought that they were rather inefficient. The great majority said their problems were handled quickly and efficiently.[18]

Second, liberals concede that, despite these accomplishments, there is a great deal of inefficiency and waste in the federal bureaucracy; but they contend that the reasons are not to be found in any natural mediocrity of government bureaucrats and the welfare state. Instead, they point to four factors: limitations on the president's ability to direct the bureaucracies, congressional interference, the difficulty of the problems assigned to federal agencies, and the inefficiency of bigness.

First, then, the president lacks adequate managerial power over the executive branch. Congress vies with him for authority over departments and agencies. In many instances, Congress intervenes constantly and inserts conditions in the establishing legislation that limit the president's role and enhance its own. The president, as has already been observed, is also hampered in the exercise of his executive functions by the vested powers within the bureaucracy and by the clientele groups in the private sector that support various segments of the bureaucracy.

Second, Congress is constantly looking over the shoulders of public officials, and there is always a committee or an individual member of Congress who is ready to pounce upon any failure or dereliction of duty. To prevent mistakes and especially to avoid the danger of misuse and misappropriation of public funds, most legislation imposes stringent rules and elaborate reporting requirements. Much of the bureaucratic paperwork thus stems not from the agencies' own appetite for routines but from the demands of Congress. And a good deal of the timidity and cautiousness that characterizes so many federal programs can be traced to the strictures of the legislation and the constant overseeing of the conduct of the programs by the 535-person board of directors that Congress comprises.

Third, many of the problems that government agencies are asked to deal with are intrinsically more difficult and complex than those which most other institutions must manage. These are problems, after all, that have been thrust upon government because no one else has been able to cope with them. They include the great social issues, which arouse the most intense pressures and resistances from many parties. They do not respond easily to simple notions of managerial efficiency. And the Postal Service, which has been the butt of so many caustic criticisms, has run deficits not so much because of inefficiency as because it deliberately provides some uneconomical services, such as maintaining services in communities in rural areas where the costs are inevitably high.

Fourth, inefficiency is not unique to government. In every kind of human activity a large part of the time and energy expended is wasted. Corporations are certainly not exempt from this rule. Big business suffers from much the same problems as big government. Like government, big business must employ huge bureaucracies—staffs that work within a framework of standardized procedures. Big business, too, is capable of massive failures, such as Ford's Edsel, the vast numbers of automobiles recalled after sale for dangerous defects, and the massive cost overruns of defense companies.

As for the argument that businesses, unlike government agencies, go under when they are not performing, this is true only of small businesses. Once a company reaches a certain size, it stays alive no matter how many disasters its incompetence brings down upon it. Too many banks have lent it money; too many congressmen worry about the loss of jobs and income in their district, to allow it to go under. The big corporation is sustained by the same life-giving principle as the big government agency: it survives because it exists.

The liberals' proposals for reform.   Liberals persist in their belief that there is still room to expand the roles of the federal government. It must do more to keep the economy healthy and to reduce unemployment. This, in their view, requires more spending in most areas except defense, and, although they agree that this might exert some inflationary pressure, they dispute the conservatives' charge that government spending is the prime cause of inflation, putting much of the blame instead on price fixing by business corporations. Then, too, government should bear down harder in its efforts to regulate business; and in some cases companies should actually be taken over by the government.

All this is likely to produce still bigger bureaucracies; and, although liberals tend to be defensive even about the bureaucracies' failures, they do not deny that with government growing ever larger, something must be done to improve its performance. So they propose various kinds of reforms.

First, Common Cause has suggested that, both at the federal and state levels, bureaucracies cannot be kept up to the mark unless they are subject to regular, searching review. This can be achieved by "sunset laws," which would impose a requirement for regular, five- to ten-year reevaluations of each program; and any program failing to establish that it served a useful purpose would be eliminated. This principle was adopted as part of the 1976 Democratic party platform, and backed by Jimmy Carter.

Second, more must be done to protect the public against conflicts of interest in the executive branch. Thus liberals welcomed the new code of ethics introduced by Jimmy Carter for the policy-level officials appointed by him. First, they were required to place on file statements of net worth and income for themselves, their spouses, and their minor children. Then they must divest themselves of any interests that would "more than rarely" cause them to disqualify themselves from being involved in a decision affecting that interest. Finally, these officials had to agree that after leaving the government they would not act as agent or attorney for a period of two years in any matter in which they had been involved while in the government, instead of the previously required one year. In addition, to discourage officials from jumping from government posts into lucrative private jobs, they were required by Carter to sign an agreement to serve in their government posts for the full term of appointment, unless fired by the president. The president also proposed legislation to require detailed financial disclosure by about 13,000 top government officials. Finally, liberals welcomed the passage in 1976 of the "Sunshine Act," which required all regulatory agencies to hold most of their meetings in public. This would help to cut down on the quietly arranged understandings between federal agencies and industry which, in the liberals' view, put private gain before the public interest. Although these changes would not solve all the ethical problems that concerned the liberals, they saw them as steps in the right direction.

Then there is the prescription offered by James MacGregor Burns. The great weakness that he believes must be addressed is the inability of the president to maintain control over the bureaucracy. Consequently, Burns, a liberal, even has some kind words to say about President Nixon's proposal to regroup several federal agencies into a smaller number of superagencies with which the president would be able to work more effectively than with the present multiplicity of institutions.

But mere reshuffling is only the beginning for Burns. "The line of command between the White House and action agencies in the field must be drawn taut . . . ," and "the mutual protection of agency, congressional subcommittee, and beneficiary interests" must be dissolved.[19] In addition, new flexible instruments are needed—for example, "administrative task forces" to get things done without regard to jurisdictional lines, and agency officials who see themselves as "presidential agents" charged with accomplishing missions rather than defending established departmental interests.

This is a projection, in other words, of Burns's argument that, despite the dangers of abuse that lurk in presidential power, we cannot create a better America without a strong president. And a president cannot be strong unless he can get the federal bureaucracies to carry out his policies efficiently.

Finally, liberals have taken note of the new left's criticism of bureaucracy as producing a sense of alienation and helplessness among the people. So liberals have given greater recognition than in the past to the idea of decentralization as a means of reducing the decision-making process to a scale people can understand and deal with.

However, their acceptance of this idea falls far short of the enthusiasm of the new left. And they are generally unimpressed by the new left's love of spontaneous expression and action. Industrial societies, in the liberals' views, cannot function without a high degree of rational planning and organized behavior. More than 210 million people cannot be governed, cannot govern themselves, by the methods that led to the creation of the Berkeley People's Park.

Conclusion

President Carter has established as one of his administration's highest priorities an effort to attack the major problems we have discussed in this chapter—the waste, inefficiencies, duplication of effort, lack of responsiveness, and conflicts of interest which, in varying degrees, all five of our perspectives associate with the executive agencies of the federal government. When he was governor of Georgia, Carter abolished several departments and regrouped state services into a small number of superagencies, and in his campaign for the presidency he indicated that at the federal level, too, great improvements could be accomplished by pruning and the drastic consolidation of the more than 2000 federal agencies. In 1977 Congress gave him authority (subject to congressional review) to proceed with the task of reorganization.

Liberals expressed grave reservations both about Carter's reorganization ideas and about his hostility to the federal bureaucracies. Reorganizing the government of Georgia was one thing, they said. Trying to impose a similar kind of simplicity and symmetry on the enormous structures of the federal government, which served such a vast array of purposes, was quite another. Moreover, liberals doubted that the hostility Carter directed at the bureaucracies really expressed the attitude of the people at large. Although everyone complains about the bloated size of government, they are usually talking about services government provides to *other* people, rather than the obviously necessary services that they themselves are receiving.

The liberals are on strong ground here. Big government, like the strong presidency, is here to stay. It is too attractive a mechanism for too many constituencies to allow even a conservative president to cut it back drastically. And some of the programs advocated by Jimmy Carter, such as national health insurance, could bring further additions to the federal bureaucracies.

Nonetheless, as the liberals concede, reorganization and change in the federal government structure must be undertaken. The deficiencies are too great, and their consequences too damaging, for them to be ignored. Moreover, it is most unlikely that expanding government will again be as popular as it was during Roosevelt's New Deal or Johnson's Great Society eras. Huge federal bureaucracies may be necessary, but they will continue to be resented. The problem is not so much the impersonality of bureaucrats and the overlapping of federal jurisdictions, which impinge very little on the lives of ordinary citizens. The problem is the cost.

Liberals may contend that government services (except for the military) are a bargain; that the federal bureaucracy has not grown very much in recent years; that, if we want a high quality of public servants, we must pay them good salaries; that federal income taxes have been reduced in the last few years to the point at which the provision of much needed services is jeopardized; and that the tax burden in this country is less than in many Western European countries.

Just the same, Americans will continue to resent high federal taxes, and to believe that there is less virtue in the spending of money by government than by private business or the individual consumer. Nor will they approve of federal employees' receiving both higher salaries and more security than private workers.

In sum, the conservatives are unlikely to be politically successful in achieving sharp reductions of government spending and employment. But hostile conservative attitudes toward the federal bureaucracies will continue to be widespread among the population, and will keep the liberals on the defensive in their efforts to use government to achieve their ends.

Notes and References

1.   George F. Will, the *Los Angeles Times*, January 30, 1974.

2.   Milton Friedman, "Frustrating Drug Advancement," *Newsweek*, January 8, 1973, p. 49. Friedman quoted a paper presented by Sam Peltzman of UCLA.

3.   James Kilpatrick, the *Los Angeles Times*, September 12, 1973.

4.   Peter F. Drucker, *The Age of Discontinuity* (New York: Harper & Row, Publishers, 1969), pp. 212–20.

5.   U.S. Department of Labor, *56th Annual Report: Fiscal Year 1968* (Washington, D.C.: Government Printing Office), p. 7.

6.   See George F. Will, the *Los Angeles Times*, December 16, 1975.

7.   Drucker, the *Age of Discontinuity*, p. 221.

8.   Jeffrey Hart, the *Los Angeles Times*, June 20, 1976.

9.   M. Stanton Evans, *Clear and Present Dangers: A Conservative View of America's Government* (New York: Harcourt Brace Jovanovich, 1975), p. 169.

10.   James Kilpatrick, the *Los Angeles Times*, December 7, 1975.

11.   Robert Welch, *The Blue Book of the John Birch Society* (Belmont, Mass.: John Birch Society, 1961), p. 142.

12.   Sheldon Wolin and John Schaar, "Berkeley: The Battle of People's Park," *The New York Review of Books*, June 19, 1969, pp. 29–30.

13.   Aaron Wildavsky, "Government and the People," *Commentary* (August 1973), pp. 25–32.

14.   James MacGregor Burns, *Uncommon Sense* (New York: Harper & Row, Publishers, 1972), p. 126.

15.   Henry Fairlie, "In Defense of Big Government," *The New Republic*, March 13, 1976, p. 27.

16.   Grant McConnell, *Private Power and American Democracy* (Alfred A. Knopf, Inc., 1966), p. 287.

17.   Edward F. Cox, Robert G. Fellmeth, and John E. Schulz, *The Nader Report on the Federal Trade Commission* (New York: Baron Publishing Co., 1969), p. 170.

18.   Robert L. Kahn, Barbara A. Gutek, Eugenia Barton, and Daniel Katz, "Americans Love Their Bureaucrats," *Psychology Today*, June 1975, pp. 66–71.

19.   Burns, *Uncommon Sense*, p. 127.

The Supreme Court

and Constitutional Rights

All governmental systems must include not only institutions for writing laws (legislatures) and for carrying them out (executives) but also for adjudicating or resolving conflicts that arise under the laws. So, in addition to the Congress and the presidency, the Founding Fathers established a *judicial* branch of government, a structure of courts and judges. The courts were to deal with a wide range of conflicts, some between individuals, others between individuals and various units of government, others again between the states or between state and federal governments.

This judicial branch, said Alexander Hamilton in *The Federalist*, would be "beyond comparison the weakest of the three departments" in the new federal government. It would have "no influence over either the sword or the purse, no direction either of the strength or of the wealth of the society." Hamilton was right only up to a point. The judiciary has not had much influence over "the sword" in the sense that determining foreign and military policy has been pretty much in the hands of the presidency. But in some periods the courts have been heavily involved in questions of economic policy. And, especially in recent years, the judiciary has been a major participant in decisions concerning the rights of individuals under the Constitution.

So, in areas of great importance to many people, the courts have exercised significant power; and where there is power there will be controversy. In this chapter, after briefly describing the structure of the system of courts in the United States, we shall examine the different contexts in which the courts have used their power and show how their use of power has varied from one period to another according to changing conceptions of the purpose of the highest court in the land, the Supreme Court of the United States. Then we shall set forth the contrasting views of our five perspectives on the proper role of the courts, particularly in the area of constitutional rights, and on whether the courts have used their power wisely or abused it.

The Structure of the U.S. Court System

Article III, Section 1, of the U.S. Constitution declares that: "The judicial Power of the United States, shall be vested in one Supreme Court, and in such inferior Courts as the Congress may from time to time ordain and establish" (see Appendix 1). Congress acted quickly to set up the federal court system through the Judiciary Act of 1789. At the lowest level of the federal court system, cases were to be dealt with by district courts; appeals from their decisions were to go to circuit courts, and from there to the U.S. Supreme Court. As the population and the business of the courts expanded, Congress increased the number of federal courts. Today there are 97 district courts and 11 circuit courts of appeal.

In addition, each of the states has established its own court system, starting with city, county, and state trial courts, then moving up to courts of appeal, and finally to a state supreme court. Anyone accused of violating a state law may appeal to the federal courts, but only after the case has been heard in the state courts and only when it can be shown that an issue in the case has implications for the federal Constitution or a federal statute.

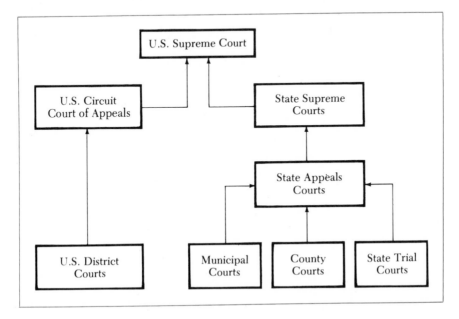

FIGURE 9-1   Paths to the Supreme Court

Some 90 percent of the cases coming to the U.S. Supreme Court do so as a result of a *writ of certiorari*—an order issued by the Supreme Court to a lower court calling for the records of a case to be sent up for review. An alternative path for a case to reach the Supreme Court is by the *writ of appeal*, which covers certain categories of cases as defined by statute. *Certification* is another device, rarely used, by which lower courts ask the Supreme Court for instructions and interpretations on questions of law.

In simplified form, Figure 9-1 shows us the various stages that most cases must traverse before coming to the U.S. Supreme Court for decision. In addition to the *appellate jurisdiction* of the Supreme Court—its authority to take cases on appeal from lower courts—the Court has *original jurisdiction*—the authority to receive a case directly without its going through the lower courts—where the parties to the case are states or foreign diplomats. Moreover, where the Supreme Court decides that a matter is of great public importance and urgency, it can bypass the appeals courts and take a case directly.

The Supreme Court and Judicial Review

Most of the discussion in this chapter will focus on the U.S. Supreme Court, for this is where the great constitutional issues are determined. The Supreme Court has the last word on what the Constitution means, despite the fact that the Constitution does not explicitly give the Court this authority. Although it is reasonably clear that the framers intended the Supreme Court to be able to declare state legislation unconstitutional, the authority to strike down acts of Congress can only be inferred from general provisions of the Constitution.

If the Court in its early years had not had a strong chief justice, it might never have attained its powerful stature. But John Marshall was a very strong chief justice; and his Court's decision in *Marbury* v. *Madison* (1803), by finding a section of the Judiciary Act of 1789 unconstitutional, went a long way toward establishing the principle that congressional statutes could be ruled invalid by the Supreme Court. An accumulation of later cases confirmed the principle that Marshall had built into *Marbury* v. *Madison*—that the court had the power of *judicial review*, the power to examine federal as well as state legislation, and declare it null and void if it conflicted with the Court's interpretation of the U.S. Constitution.

In our preoccupation here with the Supreme Court and its constitutional authority, we should not lose sight of three important facts about the judicial system in America. First, only a tiny proportion of all cases that are tried in the United States ever reach the Supreme Court. The vast majority are settled in local and state courts, mostly at the lowest levels of the judicial hierarchy; and of those cases that do come before the federal courts most are disposed of in the district courts.

Second, the larger number of cases that reach the Supreme Court do not involve interpretation of the Constitution. Instead, the question before the Court will be whether a state or local law conflicts with a federal statute, or whether a federal government agency has acted contrary to the terms of a congressional law. Moreover the Court will usually deal with the constitutional issues raised by a case only if it cannot dispose of the case on more limited grounds.

Third, the Supreme Court, when it raises constitutional issues, does so only in relation to the specific case which is before it. The Court does not offer advisory opinions to the president or the Congress or anyone else who wants to know whether a proposed law or action would conform to the Constitution. The Supreme Court will not act until the proposal has been acted upon, and until somebody feels that he has been harmed by the action (brings a suit against another party) an individual, a group, or the government, is dissatisfied with the decision of the lower courts, and appeals to the Supreme Court. Then, if the Supreme Court feels that this case is important enough for it to review (and it declines to review most of the cases that are sent to it), and if the case cannot be resolved on any grounds but constitutional ones, the Court will provide an interpretation of the Constitution. But that interpretation is binding on the lower courts only in situations very similar to those involved in the particular case; and plenty of room is left for further suits and further constitutional interpretations where the circumstances vary to a sufficient degree from the case in question.

Despite these qualifications, the Supreme Court's responsibility to declare whether or not federal and state laws and executive actions are constitutional makes it an extremely powerful institution. And since it is reviewing public policies made by political bodies—the president, Congress, state and local executives and legislatures—its role cannot help being a part of the public policy-making process and thus have direct political implications.

The Supreme Court, then, is part of our political system. Yet it is more than just another political institution. It is also a court, a judicial body. And this makes it act differently in some very significant ways from legislative and executive bodies. The central theme of this chapter is the tension between the political and the judicial characteristics of the Supreme Court. We shall look first at the political context of the Court's work, then at the judicial considerations.

The Court as an Instrument of the Political System

Since the nine members of the Supreme Court are not elected but appointed for life by the president with the concurrence of two-thirds of the Senate, they are not as influenced by every shift in the political wind as are the members of the elected branches of government. Still, the Court is made up of people who are products of their time and who are not totally oblivious to what is going on in the political world. Evidence for this is to be found in the fact that periodically the Court has changed the tenor of its decisions as the political environment has altered.

In the modern era there have been three major changes of direction by the Supreme Court: the first in the 1930s, in the struggle over the New Deal; the second, under Chief Justice Earl Warren in the 1950s and 1960s; and the third in the 1970s under Chief Justice Warren Burger.

The Court and the New Deal

Through a large part of America's history the Supreme Court had protected the individual's right to do whatever he wanted with his money, property, or business without governmental interference. Thus the Court struck down as unconstitutional the first statutes establishing a federal income tax in 1895 and prohibiting child labor in 1918. So it was not surprising that when Franklin Roosevelt gained overwhelming congressional approval for proposals to impose detailed regulation of manufacturing, industry, and agriculture, the Supreme Court found the legislation unacceptable. In *Schechter Poultry Corporation* v. *United States* (1935) and six other cases in 1935 and 1936, much of the early New Deal legislation was struck down. The statutes, said the Court majority, represented an unconstitutional invasion of the power of the states by the federal government and an unconstitutional delegation of power to the president by the Congress. Angrily, the president, labor, and liberal groups attacked this usurpation of power by "nine old men," appointed for life by Republican presidents in the 1920s. "The Court," said the president, "has been acting not as a judicial body, but as a policy-making body"; and its policies were oriented toward preserving entrenched propertied interests.

But then, from 1937, the Court backed away from its confrontation with president and Congress. In that year the Wagner Labor Relations Act of 1935 was reviewed by the Court. The same Court that had voted by margins of 5 to 4 or 6 to 3 against the National Industrial Relations Act, Agricultural Adjustment Act, and other New Deal legislation now found in favor of the Wagner Act by a 5 to 4 margin. The difference was that Chief Justice Hughes and Justice Owen Roberts had voted against Roosevelt's programs in 1935 and 1936 and for them in 1937.

Two events had intervened to change their stance. The first was a request by President Roosevelt in 1936 for authority to add one justice for each member who reached the age of 70, had served 10 years, and refused to retire within six months, subject to a maximum Court membership of 15. The purpose of this was either to force some of the elderly judges who were opposing Roosevelt's programs to retire or to add enough sympathetic new members to the Court to outvote the old guard. The Senate vetoed this plan to "pack" the Court. Nonetheless, the Court could not ignore this reminder that it was vulnerable to attack from other branches of government. The second event of great significance in 1936 was a massive victory at the polls for Franklin Roosevelt and the Democratic party in Congress, enabling the president to claim that he had obtained a clear mandate for his policies.

Hughes and Roberts denied that these events had anything to do with their verdicts in the 1937 case. They had not changed their minds, they insisted. The circumstances were different from those of the earlier cases. Yet fundamentally the same issues—the right of the federal government to intervene in the economy, to interfere with business—were involved. And in 1937 the Social Security Act was upheld by the same vote of 5 to 4. After that, in Roosevelt's and subsequent administrations, the Court supported with few exceptions the steady enlargement of the role of the federal government in economic affairs.

But the relationship between government and the individual is not limited only to economic issues, and courts must deal with a great range of questions concerning the rights and liberties of individuals and groups. These rights became the subject of the next great change in direction of the Supreme Court, that which took place under Chief Justice Earl Warren in the 1950s and 1960s.

The Warren Court

From the time that Earl Warren became chief justice in 1953, the Supreme Court, at first slowly and then with increasing momentum, handed down a series of decisions in the areas of the First Amendment freedoms of speech, assembly, press, and religion; the rights of the accused in criminal cases; the reapportionment of legislatures; and the rights of racial minorities. The thrust of these various decisions was to favor the rights of individuals and minorities against the power of government. And the protection provided was not only against the federal government. The Constitution, and especially the Bill of Rights, said the Warren Court, guaranteed certain liberties to the people, and these liberties could not be taken away by *any* level of government. So, by a process of "incorporation," the rights afforded by the U.S. Constitution must be assured not only against the federal government but also against the actions of state and local governments. In other words, the process of incorporation makes the prohibitions and guarantees of the Bill of Rights applicable to all levels of government and governmental officials.

First Amendment rights.   The First Amendment to the U.S. Constitution, a crucial component in the Bill of Rights, declares: "Congress shall make no law respecting an establishment of religion, or prohibiting the free exercise thereof; or abridging the freedom of speech, or of the press; or the right of the people peaceably to assemble, and to petition the Government for a redress of grievances." But these statements are subject to interpretation; and the question the Warren Court, like every U.S. Supreme Court, had to consider was: What is the proper balance between these First Amendment freedoms and the needs of society for order and stability? Generally speaking, the Warren Court reversed the trend of earlier Courts, which had tended to emphasize the need for order as the necessary condition for individual liberties.

Free speech and the Communist party.   A classic statement of the right of government to impose limits on free speech had been made in 1919 by Justice Oliver Wendell Holmes, Jr.:

> The most stringent protection of free speech would not protect a man in falsely shouting fire in a theater and causing a panic. . . . The question in every case is whether the words are used in such circumstances and are of such a nature as to create a clear and present danger that they will bring about the substantive evils that Congress has a right to prevent.[1]

An even broader limitation on the right of free speech was contained in a 1925 case in which the Supreme Court found that speech could be banned if it represented a "dangerous tendency."[2]

In the post-World War II period in the United States, the great test of these doctrines was the extent to which the Communist party was to be allowed to organize and speak freely. Hostility to the Soviet Union ran high during this era, and the prevailing sentiment in Congress and the country was that the Communist party of the United States and its advocacy of the Soviet system constituted not only a "dangerous tendency" but also a "clear and present danger" to the survival of the American system. In this context the Supreme Court, under the leadership of Chief Justice Fred Vinson, considered the appeal of 11 leaders of the Communist party against their conviction under the 1940 Smith Act, which had made it illegal to advocate "overthrowing or destroying any government in the United States by force or violence." In *Dennis* v. *United States* (1951) the Court upheld the convictions and the constitutionality of the Smith Act. Subsequently, during the era of anticommunist investigations by Senator Joseph McCarthy and the House Un-American Activities Committee, the Vinson Court rejected appeals against the congressional committees' tactics. The Court also upheld the right of state governments to require "loyalty oaths" from public employees—sworn declarations that they would uphold the Constitution of the United States and of their own state and were not members of the Communist party. Only two members of the Vinson Court, Justices Hugo Black and William O. Douglas, consistently argued against these positions, protesting that the Bill of Rights was being abandoned.

This was the climate when President Eisenhower appointed Earl Warren chief justice in 1953. In a number of key free-speech cases Warren sided with Justices Black and Douglas, and their position gradually became the majority view on the Court. The conviction of a number of second-string Communist party leaders by lower courts was overturned in 1957. Further rulings relating to the Smith Act limited its applicability so severely that it became virtually unenforceable. The Court also overruled legislation denying passports to communists and excluding them from jobs in defense industries or from leadership positions in labor unions; and it overturned a number of contempt of Congress convictions on the grounds that the procedures of congressional investigating committees were unfair and arbitrary.

Free speech and obscenity.   Does the First Amendment guarantee of free speech and press extend to the publication of works that are allegedly obscene or pornographic? On this question the Warren Court at first said that obscenity did not have the same privileged position under the Constitution as political expression, but then the Court shifted its stand to give broader protection against sexual censorship.

In two 1957 cases, *Roth* v. *United States* and *Alberts* v. *California*, the Warren Court established a test for deciding whether a work was obscene and thus not worthy of protection under the First Amendment. The criterion was: "Whether to the average person, applying contemporary community standards, the dominant theme of the material taken as a whole appeals to prurient interests." In *Ginzburg* v. *United States* (1966), the Warren Court added another test—the intent of the purveyor. In upholding publisher Ralph Ginzburg's five-year prison sentence for sending allegedly obscene materials through the U.S. mails, Justice William Brennan delivered a Court opinion in which he said that Ginzburg's publications were "originated or sold as stock in trade of the sordid business of pandering." Ginzburg had deliberately represented the publications as "erotically arousing," which "stimulated the reader to accept them as prurient." Among the evidence on which Brennan based his conclusion was that Ginzburg had tried to get mailing privileges (which would place the name of the town on the envelopes) for one of his publications from Intercourse, Pennsylvania; rejected there, he settled for Middlesex, New York.

In a 1968 case, *Ginsberg* v. *New York*, the Court also upheld the right of government to protect minors against obscenity. Ginsberg sold four "girlie" magazines to a 16-year-old boy, thereby running afoul of a state law regulating the sale of harmful books and magazines to anyone under 17.

But then in 1966 the Court changed its stance on obscenity. In *Memoirs* v. *Massachusetts* it dealt with the banning of a new edition of *Fanny Hill*, a detailed account of the sexual adventures of a country girl in the big city, written in 1749. The Court produced some new guidelines. Now for a work to be found obscene it must be established that

(a) the dominant theme of the material taken as a whole appeals to a prurient interest in sex; (b) the material is patently offensive because it affronts contemporary community standards relating to the description or representation of sexual matters; and (c) the material is utterly without redeeming social value.

Literary critics testified that *Fanny Hill* had literary significance. The Court was impressed and found that the book had "redeeming social value" and could not be banned. The *Fanny Hill* case represented a sharp departure from the 1957 *Roth* case, in which the Court formulated its earlier test of "obscenity," and it would be much more difficult to secure indictments under the new criteria.

Prayer in the public schools.   In the 1940s the Supreme Court had handed down decisions building what Justice Black called "a wall of separation between Church and State."[3] This was an interpretation of the First Amendment's declaration that: "Congress shall make no law respecting an establishment of religion, or prohibiting the free exercise thereof." These earlier cases forbade the spending of public funds to help church schools. In 1962, in the case of *Engel* v. *Vitale*, the Court went a step further. A daily school prayer could not be required even if it was entirely nondenominational. Even if dissenters are allowed to leave the room, said the Court in *Abington Township School District* v. *Schempp* (1963), public schools may not open with a prayer or Bible reading, for a subtle kind of compulsion would be impossible to avoid. Thus the Court insisted that school prayers constituted an "establishment of religion"—the creation of an official form of worship—because the power of the state was used to compel attendance at religious worship; and this was in defiance of the Constitution.

Rights of the accused.   The Warren Court did not limit its concern for the rights of the individual to those covered under the First Amendment. It gave a great deal of attention to the requirement established by the Fifth Amendment—and extended by the Fourteenth Amendment to include actions by state governments—that no person may be "deprived of life, liberty or property without due process of law." So the Warren Court overturned a number of convictions in criminal cases which, the Court said, had been obtained without giving the accused "due process of law." Of particular significance were:

Mallory v. *United States* (1957), in which the Court held that confessions obtained during any "unnecessary delay" in bringing an accused person before a magistrate were not admissible.

Escobedo v. *Illinois* (1964), which established that a suspect had the right to consult a lawyer when a police interrogation moved from "the exploratory to the accusatory stage."

Miranda v. *Arizona* (1966), in which Chief Justice Warren declared that a suspect "must be warned prior to any questioning that he has the right to remain silent, that anything he says can be used against him in a court of law, that he has the right to the presence of an attorney, and that if he cannot afford an attorney, one will be appointed for him prior to any questioning if he so desires."

Other decisions in the field of criminal law rejected police lineup tactics that the Court found to be deliberately biased and set stringent limits to the types of searches police can conduct without a warrant. This is not to say that the Warren Court always decided against the wishes of law enforcement authorities. The right of police to frisk citizens on the street without probable cause for arrest was upheld. Electronic eavesdropping was approved as long as a warrant was obtained; this, said the Court, did not conflict with the Fourth Amendment's prohibition of "unreasonable searches and seizures."

On the whole, however, the Warren Court extended the protection provided by the Constitution to people accused of crimes. In particular, the Court established an "exclusionary rule," according to which any evidence obtained without scrupulous attention to the constitutional rights of the accused must be excluded from the accused's trial.

Reapportionment.   A further provision of the Fourteenth Amendment led the Warren Court into another field of great political importance—legislative reapportionment. Previous Supreme Courts had refused to accept suits that complained that the boundaries between legislative districts were deliberately drawn in such a way that some districts had much greater populations than others. This, said the plaintiffs, conflicted with the Fourteenth Amendment's instruction that no state shall "deny to any person within its jurisdiction the equal protection of the laws," for, if people are unequally represented, they are unlikely to get equal protection. However, the courts had repeatedly said that this was a political matter to be decided by legislatures, not by the judiciary. But in *Baker* v. *Carr* (1962) and *Reynolds* v. *Sims* (1964) the Warren Court moved boldly into the reapportionment issue. Legislatures must stop justifying wide disparities in the populations of districts on extraneous grounds such as the need to protect the interests of rural areas. "Legislators," said Chief Justice Warren in *Reynolds* v. *Sims*, "represent people, not trees or acres. Legislators are elected by voters, not farms or cities or economic interests." Boundaries must be drawn to contain equal numbers of voters. "One man, one vote" was the principle to follow, or there could be no "equal protection of the laws."

Desegregation.   The "equal protection" clause was applied by the Warren Court in yet one more policy field of surpassing importance—the segregation of the races. In *Plessy* v. *Ferguson* (1896) the Supreme Court had found that separate railroad facilities for white and black people were constitutional as long as the accommodations were of equal quality. This was overruled in its application to public schools in the case of *Brown* v. *Board of Education of Topeka, Kansas,* in 1954. Black children did not have the equal protection of the laws as provided for by the Fourteenth Amendment, said the Warren Court, if the laws forbade them to go to the same schools as white children. In subsequent decisions the Court applied this principle to all public facilities. By definition, separate could not be equal, since implicit in laws requiring segregation of the races was the assumption that one race was inferior to the other.

Why the Warren Court was different from its predecessors.   These decisions of the Warren Court represented a major change in direction from its predecessors in areas related to the protection of the rights of individuals and minorities against government. The key factor in producing this sharp shift in the Court's attitudes was the change in the Court's membership that began with Eisenhower's appointment of Earl Warren as chief justice and William Brennan as associate justice. Together with Hugo Black and William Douglas they had to pick only one more vote to gain a majority oriented toward a liberal approach to the rights of individuals. When Lyndon Johnson appointed Arthur Goldberg, this majority was assured. Goldberg resigned from the Court to become ambassador to the United Nations, and Johnson replaced him with the fairly liberal Abe Fortas. Then Thurgood Marshall, the first black justice, was appointed, which strengthened the liberally oriented bloc further. Against this group the more conservative members dwindled in number. In the last years of the Warren Court they included only Tom Clark (until he was replaced by Thurgood Marshall) and John Marshall Harlan, with Potter Stewart and Byron White joining sometimes with the more liberal group, sometimes the more conservative members.

The attack on the Warren Court.   Now the Warren Court was subjected to angry demands for change. A movement was launched, led in Congress by Senator Everett Dirksen of Illinois, to repeal the Court's reapportionment decisions by a constitutional amendment. In the Omnibus Crime Control and Safe Streets Act of 1968 Congress laid down challenges to the *Miranda* and *Mallory* rulings on confessions and the right to remain silent. A Harris survey in November 1966 indicated that, although almost two-thirds of those polled agreed with the Warren Court's antisegregation rulings and three-quarters supported the reapportionment decisions, two-thirds disagreed with the Court's disallowing confessions without counsel, 70 percent were opposed to the outlawing of prayers in the classroom, and there was an even division on the question of letting communists have passports.

In themselves these critical reactions might have influenced the Warren Court in time to be somewhat more cautious in its decisions. But no major alteration of course was likely as long as the membership stayed as it was. Lyndon Johnson saw this clearly when, in 1968, Earl Warren announced his intention to retire. Johnson jumped at the chance to appoint a new chief justice before he left the White House and nominated Abe Fortas. However, Fortas failed to get the consent of the Senate. Most Republicans opposed him; and a number of Democrats became disenchanted, despite the fact that Fortas was a brilliant lawyer, when they learned that Fortas, while on the Court, had continued to act as an adviser to President Johnson on a number of matters, including Vietnam. Fortas's position became untenable when certain revelations about Fortas's financial affairs suggested possible conflicts of interest. Fortas protested his innocence; but faced with widespread criticism he withdrew his name from nomination.

Now the way was open for a new president to appoint the chief justice. In his 1968 campaign for the presidency, Richard Nixon made it clear that he would take care to avoid appointing people to the Court who would continue the direction charted by Earl Warren and his colleagues. This was confirmed by his first appointment, that of Warren Burger, a Republican from the U.S. Court of Appeals, as chief justice of the United States.

The Burger Court

Soon after the appointment of Burger there was another vacancy on the Court. The press had uncovered additional indiscretions in Fortas's finances. Again, Fortas insisted he had done nothing wrong; but he resigned from the Court.

Nixon ran into difficulties in replacing him, for the Senate rejected his nominations first of Judge Clement Haynsworth of South Carolina and then of Judge Harrold Carswell of Florida. In May 1970, however, the Senate accepted the appointment of Judge Harry Blackmun of Minnesota.

Now the Court headed by Chief Justice Burger began to moderate its liberal tendencies somewhat, particularly in the field of criminal law. However, the holdovers from the Warren days were still able to muster a majority on a number of issues, with Burger, frequently joined by Blackmun, in vigorous dissent.

This, too, changed when, in September 1971, Justices Hugo Black and John Marshall Harlan resigned because of ill health. In their places Nixon proposed and the Senate accepted Lewis Powell of Virginia and William Rehnquist of Arizona, the assistant attorney general under John Mitchell. Both were known to be conservative in their leanings, particularly Rehnquist, who had been a strong supporter of Barry Goldwater in his 1964 bid for the presidency.

These were the last of the Nixon appointees. However, President Ford had his opportunity to appoint to the Court when Justice William O. Douglas, the unreconstructed liberal on the Court, retired because of ill health in 1975. His successor was Judge John Paul Stevens, who had served for five years on the U.S. Court of Appeals in Chicago. Now only four justices remained from the Warren Court—Marshall, Brennan, White, and Stewart; and of these only Marshall and Brennan had been more or less consistently on the side of the majority that had forged the liberal direction of the Warren years.

This does not mean that the Warren decisions were to be totally repudiated. The picture, in fact, was a very mixed one. There were fields in which the Burger Court kept to the course charted by the Warren Court. In other areas the Warren Court's positions were modified, but by no means abandoned. And even on those issues in which there was a clear departure from the earlier Court, some vestiges of the previous doctrines persisted.

Reapportionment.   Reapportionment was an area in which the changes wrought by the Warren Court remained essentially intact. After his retirement Chief Justice Earl Warren declared that his Court's reapportionment decisions were perhaps its most important achievement. Even if the next Court had wanted to undo that achievement, it could have had little effect. Legislatures were reapportioned in the years following *Baker* v. *Carr* and *Sims* v. *Reynolds*, and the eggs could not be unscrambled.

Abortion.   The Burger Court handed down some bold decisions on the fiercely controversial subject of abortion. In *Roe* v. *Wade* (1973) Justice Blackmun read the majority decision of the Court that states could forbid abortions only dur-

© 1977 Jules Feiffer; Dist. Field Newspaper Syndicate.
Richard Rice

ing the last three months of pregnancy, could do so only to protect the mother's health in the second three months, and not at all during the first three months. Blackmun based his decision primarily on the right of privacy. No such right is mentioned in the Constitution, but the notion has evolved in Court decisions over the years as a combination of First Amendment freedoms, Fifth and Fourteenth Amendment due process, and the Ninth Amendment rights "retained by the people."

Then in 1976 the Court struck down a state requirement for approval of an abortion by a husband or parent.[4] However, in 1977 the Court ruled that neither the Constitution nor the federal Medicaid law required the government to provide free abortions for indigents if not medically necessary.[5]

Desegregation.   The Nixon Administration failed in its appeal to the Court under Chief Justice Burger to give the South more time to carry through with school desegregation. The Court insisted that "the equal protection of the laws" meant desegregation *now.* The Court then proceeded to uphold lower court decisions requiring desegregation not only in the South but also in northern cities, even though this sometimes involved the hotly contested device of school busing. However, as we shall see in our discussion of the racial issue in Chapter 12, the Burger Court gradually began to qualify the extent to which desegregation was required. It turned down a proposal, for example, to force the suburban school districts outside Detroit to join with the Detroit city schools in a plan for racial integration; and in other cases the Court indicated that desegregation was required only where segregation had been deliberately contrived by governmental bodies.

Sex discrimination.   The Burger Court ventured further into the field of the rights of women than had previous Courts. In some cases the decisions insisted on equal protection of the sexes. Thus the Court found that exclusion of women from juries deprived defendants of their right to a fair trial; that the Fourteenth Amendment's guarantee of equal protection of the laws invalidated Idaho's laws giving preference to fathers over mothers in the administration of their children's estates; that widowers must be given the same survivors' benefits under Social Security as women; and that an Oklahoma law that allowed women to buy beer when they were 18 but made men wait till they were 21 was another denial of the equal protection clause. In the Oklahoma case the Court declared that, henceforth, laws that differentiated on grounds of gender would be found invalid unless they "serve important governmental objectives and [are] substantially related to achievement of those objectives."[6]

However, in allowing exceptions based on "important governmental objectives," the Court was establishing a less rigid standard for judging the acceptability of sex-based laws than of laws based on race. Thus employers were allowed to exclude pregnancy from sickness and disability insurance programs without running afoul either of the Fourteenth Amendment or of Title VII of the Civil Rights Acts of 1964, which forbade job discrimination based on gender. Said Justice William Rehnquist for the Court: "Pregnancy is, of course, confined to women. But it is in other ways significantly different from the typical covered disease or disability," and "gender-based discrimination does not result simply because an employer's disability benefits program is less than all-inclusive."[7]

First Amendment rights.   In the area of the First Amendment freedoms, the Burger Court handed down some decisions that strongly sustained the liberties of speech, assembly, and press. Thus in 1972 the Court overturned the banning of a chapter of the left-wing Students for a Democratic Society from a college campus. In 1973 it struck down the conviction of a man for wearing an American flag patch on the seat of his pants. And in a landmark case, it repudiated the efforts of the Nixon administration to prevent the publication of the Pentagon Papers, which, as we saw in Chapter 6, Daniel Ellsberg had leaked to *The New York Times*.[8]

However, in other cases the Burger Court sided with government against the claims of individuals to speak their minds. The Court agreed in 1972 that the State Department did not have to give a visa to a Belgian scholar who was a member of the Communist party so he could speak at American University. In the same year a Massachusetts loyalty oath requiring all state employees to swear to uphold the laws and Constitution of their state was upheld. Also in 1972 the Court dismissed a suit against the army for compiling dossiers on civilians it considered potentially subversive on the grounds that the plaintiffs had failed to show that they themselves were directly harmed.

Free speech and obscenity.   In the area of obscenity the Burger Court gave a much narrower reading of the First Amendment freedoms than the Warren Court had provided in the *Fanny Hill* case. By a 5 to 4 margin in the 1973 case of

Miller v. *California* the Burger Court turned away from the criterion of "redeeming social value" set in *Fanny Hill*. Miller was a California bookseller who mailed unsolicited advertising brochures for such books as *Sex Orgies Illustrated*. The Court went back to the earlier *Roth* doctrine—that obscenity is not protected by the First Amendment. Then it went on to provide new guidelines for what constituted obscenity or pornography. They were:

> (a) whether the average person, applying contemporary community standards, would find that the work, taken as a whole, appeals to the prurient interest; (b) whether the work depicts or describes, in a patently offensive way, sexual conduct specifically defined by the applicable state law; and (c) whether the work, taken as a whole, lacks serious literary, artistic, political, or scientific value.

Chief Justice Burger elaborated on what the Court meant under guideline (b). It included "patently offensive representations or descriptions of ultimate sexual acts, normal or perverted, actual or simulated," and "patently offensive representations or descriptions of masturbation, excretory functions and lewd exhibitions of the genitals." Guideline (c) replaced the "utterly without redeeming social value" test, and insisted that the First Amendment could not apply without a clear showing of "serious literary, artistic, political, or scientific value."

Now, said Burger, it was a matter for local communities to take whatever action they saw fit—so long as it stayed within the new guidelines. No one, he said, would suffer under these rules, except hard-core "pornographers." This promise was kept in subsequent cases, when Chattanooga was told that it could not ban the rock musical *Hair*,[9] and an Albany, Georgia, jury was overruled when it held the movie *Carnal Knowledge* obscene.[10] As Rehnquist made clear in the *Carnal Knowledge* case, the Court would not "uphold an obscenity conviction based upon a defendant's depiction of a woman with a bare midriff." Even nudity was not sufficient grounds for censorship; not even the simulation of the sex act, so long as it was not actually conducted in full view and in graphic detail.

Still, pornography, as the Court defined it, could be banned by a community, under the "contemporary community standards" clause of the opinion. Thus the Court sustained a local law requiring "adult" bookstores and theaters to locate themselves a certain distance apart; and it upheld the conviction of a man accused of sending obscene materials to adults who requested them.

Rights of the accused.   It is in the area of the rights of the accused in criminal cases that the Burger Court has made its most significant departures from the Warren years. Here again, the change has not been total. The Burger Court has not scrapped the constitutional rights of individuals to a fair trial and to protection from arbitrary government action. Thus it rejected an administration claim that the Crime Control Act of 1968 gave the president authority to wiretap domestic subversives without a warrant.[11] Government wiretaps of 600 people, used in 60 cases, were invalidated because Attorney General John Mitchell had not followed the letter of the law, which required that the orders must be signed by himself or by a specific assistant attorney general.[12]

In other cases the Court found that no person may be sentenced to jail, even for a day, without representation by a lawyer or unless the right to be represented has been specifically waived (upholding the "due process" clauses of the Fifth and Fourteenth Amendments, and the Sixth Amendment's guarantee of the "Assistance of Counsel"); and that the Fourth Amendment prohibition "against unreasonable searches and seizures" prohibits the Internal Revenue Service from entering a taxpayer's business office without a search warrant to seize assets or documents to satisfy a tax debt.

But there were plenty of other Burger Court decisions to make it clear that the majority felt the balance had swung too far in the direction of the rights of the accused and against the security of society. Thus the Court has found that a policeman arresting a motorist can conduct as complete a search of the suspect as he deems necessary, even without a warrant; that the right of indigents to free legal counsel does not continue to apply if they want to appeal their cases to higher courts; and that defendants convicted in a state court cannot appeal the verdict to a federal court on the ground that evidence used against them was illegally obtained.

Then, although the Burger Court did not overturn the *Miranda* rule setting limits on the use of confessions in trials,[13] the rule was modified in a number of cases. For example, testimony by a witness whose name was learned by police during the illegal questioning of a suspect did not have to be thrown out; police were given permission to resume an interrogation after a suspect had exercised his right to remain silent as long as they stopped if he renewed his protests; and suspects must be advised of their constitutional rights only if they are taken into custody, and not if they go voluntarily to a police station and confess under questioning.

Finally there were the capital punishment decisions. In 1972 the Supreme Court, by a majority of 5 to 4, found that the death penalty, as then administered by the states, constituted a violation of the Eighth Amendment ban on "cruel and unusual punishments."[14] But two members of the majority indicated that their decision was based on the argument that capital punishment was meted out randomly and unpredictably. This suggested that, if state legislatures passed new laws setting forth clear standards for judges and juries, or defining capital crimes more precisely, the death penalty might still be found constitutional in some future cases. Subsequently, many states and the federal government wrote new statutes designed to meet the Supreme Court's standard by making capital punishment less capricious. Some states, for example, made death mandatory for certain specific crimes, such as murder by an already convicted killer; and the federal government declared that murder during an air highjacking was a capital offense.

At last in July 1976 the Supreme Court found, by 7 to 2, that some of these new laws were constitutional.[15] "There is no question" said Justice Potter Stewart for the majority, "that death as punishment is unique in its severity and irrevocability. But . . . it is an extreme sanction suitable to the most extreme crimes." But the decision was qualified when the Court found the mandatory death penalties in two other states unconstitutional, because they took away the discretion of judges and juries to reduce the penalty despite mitigating circumstances. And in 1977 the Court declared that it was unconstitutional to impose the death penalty for rape.[16] "Rape is without doubt deserving of serious punishment," said Justice Byron White, "but in terms of moral depravity and of the injury to the person and the public, it does not compare with murder."

Hence the Court was still setting stringent limits to the states' authority to sentence people to death, and there would be grounds to continue to appeal the sentences of many of the several hundreds of prisoners who had already been waiting for months or years on death row. However, in January 1977 a convicted murderer, Gary Gilmore, who had long been pleading to be put to death by a firing squad, was granted his request in a Utah prison. He was the first person to be executed in the United States since 1967.

Thus by 1976 the Burger Court had moved to the view that concern for the rights of the accused must be balanced and sometimes outweighed by the need to protect society. As Burger saw it, the Warren Court's exclusionary rule, excluding from a trial any evidence seized illegally, had been applied so rigidly that it had become an intolerable handicap for law enforcement. So in relaxing restrictions on searches and seizures, expanding the power of arrest, and accepting more confessions, the Burger Court gave the police more leeway and served notice that only flagrant misconduct by law enforcement agencies would result in the overturning of a conviction. The net impact of all these changes can be measured by the declining proportion of cases won by the American Civil Liberties Union (ACLU), a liberal organization that fights, mostly in the courts, for the unqualified upholding of the Bill of Rights. In 1968–69, the last of the Warren years, the ACLU won 90 percent of the appeals it took to the Supreme Court. By 1974–75 the proportion had fallen below 50 percent.

Political Influences on the Court's Decisions

This account of the way the Supreme Court has changed its positions over time suggests that its nine justices are very much influenced by political considerations. The changes in the Court's attitudes seem to have been brought about by two factors: public opinion and the men appointed to the bench. In the 1930s the majority of the people welcomed the efforts of the federal government to save the economy. At first the Court resisted the New Deal, but Roosevelt's landslide reelection in 1936 gave the Court an unmistakable signal, to which they responded. In the 1940s and early 1950s the anticommunist fervor personified by Senator Joe McCarthy was reflected in the Court's decisions. When McCarthy's power was broken, the Court protected the rights of communists. As public concern about crime grew, the Burger Court reflected the prevailing mood in the country by modifying the Warren Court's decisions protecting the rights of the accused.

Second, there is little question that presidents have political considerations seriously in mind when they make their nominations to the Supreme Court.

Mostly, presidents look for people who share their political philosophy in order to bring the Court into line with their own policies. When Roosevelt failed to change the composition of the Court by statute, he succeeded in creating a desirable climate by making appointments of supporters to replace opponents who retired from the Court. Nixon, too, set out to make the kind of appointments that would alter the Court's direction, and we have seen that, in considerable measure, he was successful.

Much of the same political considerations go into making appointments of federal judges generally. Overwhelmingly, presidents appoint people of their own party to the bench—and usually people who have been actively engaged in partisan politics. Given the great importance of the Supreme Court, it would be most surprising if presidents failed to use their nominating power to propose people of their own party and of their own general outlook.

Voting blocs.   Reinforcing the impression that the Supreme Court is a political body is the tendency, as we have observed, for the Court to form itself into factions, or blocs, that rather consistently vote together on important decisions. We have noted a more or less liberal group of justices opposed to a more or less conservative group, with some others acting as "swing men," sometimes tipping the balance on the liberal side, sometimes on the conservative side. For example, in the 1974–75 term of the Supreme Court we can line up the justices along our spectrum as shown in Figure 9–2. There was Douglas, the liberal, and Rehnquist, the conservative. Marshall and Brennan can be identified as liberal centrists; and Burger, Blackmun, and Powell as conservative centrists (Burger being the most conservative of the three). White and Stewart hovered around the middle of the road, on the whole perhaps slightly to the right of center, but sometimes siding with the liberal bloc. The result was a high proportion of split votes—6 to 3 when White and Stewart sided with the conservative group, 5 to 4 when one or both of them joined the more liberal members. Evidence that Douglas and Rehnquist were outside the centrist mainstream is found in the fact that these two were more likely than any of the others to take a solitary stand against the majority of the Court. When Douglas left the Court in 1975, his successor, John Paul Stevens, came to be viewed as a moderate rather than a conservative. Still, the Court had lost its only clearly liberal member, and its rightward tilt appeared to be confirmed.

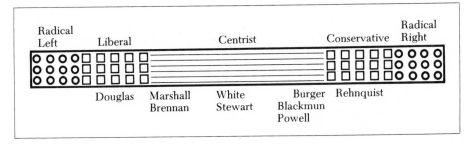

FIGURE 9–2   *U.S. Supreme Court, 1974–75 Term*

So we may well ask the following question. If a principal criterion for selecting justices of the Supreme Court is their political affiliation; and if their decisions fit into a pattern based on their political and ideological outlook; and if they split into voting blocs that can be identified on our political spectrum—isn't the Court just another political institution, exercising political power according to political criteria? The answer is that, although the Supreme Court is a part of our political system, it is also a distinctly judicial body, whose procedures and decision-making criteria are very much those of a court.

The Court as a Judicial Body

Procedures

In a number of ways the Supreme Court functions very differently from the other branches of government. Its procedures illustrate this very clearly. The Court does its own work. Its staff is limited to nine justices and 19 law clerks—two for each associate justice and three for the chief justice. The justices do not delegate any of their work to committees or task forces. All nine are involved in every case (unless any disqualify themselves for having been associated with one of the parties to a case). In the discussion of each case the chief justice speaks first, followed by others who wish to speak, in descending order of seniority. The reverse order is followed for voting, however, to avoid the psychological pressure that might be exerted by the senior members over the newer justices.

Since there are no committees, there are no separate bastions of power within the Court. Power in the Court derives from prestige, which tends to flow from ability. The chief justice, as chairman of the Court's conferences, does have an advantage, for he can formulate the issues and determine how long debate will continue. How great an advantage this is depends on the man and on his colleagues. But however strong the character of the chief justice, his power is not that of a congressional committee chairperson over his committee, nor that of a president over his staff and Cabinet.

Of course, the Court, in the conduct of its business, cannot be entirely free of politics, of the process of bargaining and accommodation among the justices. A certain amount of judicial logrolling occurs. Still, the whole structure and mode of operation are very different from the legislative or executive process.

Then, too, the Supreme Court operates in secrecy. Even when the press is excluded from deliberations of Congress and the administration, columnists are able to extract detailed, if varying, accounts of what went on behind closed doors. Very little of the Court's private discussions ever becomes public knowledge. The Court is unique among our institutions in that, most of the time, it shuns publicity.

All these factors help protect the Court from the immediate pressures of the political world. Although it cannot be isolated from the society of which it is a part, it can preserve through its procedures a greater degree of autonomy from the demands of specific groups and interests than can the legislative and executive branches. Faced with the confidentiality of the justices' conferences, pressure groups lack the knowledge they need as to when and how to apply pressure. Although individual judges have their own acquaintances and contacts and frequently go out into the world, the Court is generally not accessible to Washington lobbyists who might try to work on the justices and arrange for pressure from the folks back home. Of course, organized groups often turn to the courts to protect their interests when other branches of government are not giving them what they want.[17] However, since the justices have lifetime tenure, they are immune to direct constituency pressures.

Judicial Criteria

Nor are the Court's differences from other governmental agencies limited to matters of procedure. Its criteria for testing issues are by no means identical with those of legislative and executive agencies. Thus it is very much concerned with the facts of a case. Of course, so is Congress, which accumulates data massively; but in the legislative process facts tend to be mutilated under the bombardment of competing statements and special pleading. Although the Supreme Court, like any other human institution, cannot claim complete objectivity in its identification and selection of facts, it may still be true that, as Justice Jackson claimed, "most contentions of law are won or lost on the facts." Logic is another powerful consideration. As they interrogate the attorneys who appear before them to argue cases, the justices will often pursue the logic of an argument even though it leads them in a direction contrary to their own preconceptions; rarely is this paralleled in congressional committee hearings. Next, the justices are sensitive to professional opinion, especially as this is expressed in the law journals, which assess the performance of justices not only in relation to the validity of their conclusions but also the legal quality of the opinions they deliver.

Then there is the necessity of considering precedent. A fundamental principle of Anglo-American law is *stare decisis:* to stand by what has been decided. The assumption is that the courts will generally follow what they have said in the past, and the Court is careful to quote precedents extensively in its decisions and to avoid overruling precedents casually.

The Court also exercises judicial restraint in its dealings with other branches of government. In recent years it has rarely overturned congressional statutes. It has ruled against a number of state and local laws and local police actions. But even there it has tried to avoid handing down rulings that would create administrative chaos or a threat to public safety. Thus it has usually not made its criminal law rulings retroactive. For it is one thing to overturn a conviction because, according to the rules defined by the present Court, the evidence was obtained illegally. It is quite another to declare that thousands of people now in prison who were convicted years ago when the Court's requirements were different should have the right to a new trial or even to be set free.

Finally, and most important, there is the Constitution itself. "We must never forget," said Chief Justice John Marshall, "that it is a Constitution we are expounding." The Court has taken this for its doctrine and has established itself as *the* authoritative interpreter of the Founding Fathers' document. Congress and the president, too, see themselves as defenders and interpreters of the Constitution; but there are times when, under the spur of events, they override protests that their proposals may be unconstitutional with the answer that, if that be so, the courts will take care of it.

Nonpolitical Influences on the Court's Decisions

The result of these important differences in procedure and in criteria between the Supreme Court and the other branches of government is that, although the Court is very much a part of the political system, many of its decisions cannot be predicted simply by projecting each justice's partisan and ideological leanings. Innumerable cases prove this point. Thus in *Wallace* v. *Ohio* (1968) the Court found, 6 to 3, that Ohio had no right to keep George Wallace off the presidential ballot. Among the majority were men who were obviously hostile to George Wallace's politics—Douglas, Black, Brennan, Fortas, and Thurgood Marshall, a black man.

Street v. *New York* (1969) provides another illustration of the justices' rendering opinions that seem to contradict their ideological bias. In June 1966, Sidney Street, a black man, hearing that a black student, James Meredith, had been shot by a sniper in Mississippi, went down to a street corner in Brooklyn and burned his American flag, announcing, "If they let that happen to Meredith, we don't need no American flag." Street was convicted in a New York City Criminal Court of the crime of "malicious mischief" in that he "did willfully and unlawfully defile, cast contempt upon and burn an American flag" in violation of the New York penal law. On appeal Justice Harlan spoke for the majority of the Court in overturning the conviction. Street was protected by the Constitution, said Harlan, because his words were part of the reason for his conviction. If he had merely burned the flag, he would have been culpable under the law. But ". . . his words were an essential element, for without them no one would have known the object of his protest." The words alone were not unlawful, and "the Fourteenth Amendment prohibits the States from imposing criminal punishment for public advocacy of peaceful change in our institutions." Flag burning was abhorrent to Harlan; yet "we are unable to sustain a conviction that may have rested on a form of expression, however distasteful, which the Constitution tolerates and protects." Chief Justice Warren thought this ridiculous. The man had burned the flag in defiance of a perfectly constitutional New York law. He could not be exonerated merely because he had accompanied the act with some words. He had the right to say what he did, but not to do what he did.

Justice Black agreed with Warren. He was the passionate defender of individual liberties and the rights of the accused, the great dissenter with Justice

Douglas during the McCarthy era. He had always taken the position that the First Amendment means what it says, that Congress shall make *no* law abridging the guaranteed freedoms. It was his view, he explained, "without deviation, without exception, without any ifs, buts or whereases, that freedom of speech means that you shall not do something to people either for the views they have or the views they express or the words they speak or write."[18] However, the right he had in mind was free speech. The First Amendment, he said, does not give people the right to shout "Fire!" in a crowded theater, for shouting is not speaking, and creating a disorder in a theater is not an expression of free speech. And burning a flag is not an expression of free speech.

Black's process of reasoning, then, stems from a lawyer's preoccupation with the words of the Constitution, and it cannot easily be fitted into clear-cut liberal–conservative categories. Many others on the Court have also moved away from political preconceptions as they examined the facts in a specific case, the precedents relating to it, the acts of executive and legislative bodies that might bear upon it, and their reading of its relationship to the relevant sections of the Constitution. This becomes clear not only from the actual votes cast by the justices, but also from the elaborate legal reasoning they set forth in their written opinions to support their conclusions. It also helps to explain the large number of *concurring opinions*—opinions that support the majority view, but that provide different or additional reasons. It is not enough for the writers of these opinions to cast their vote; they must offer their own special legal reasoning to show exactly how they have arrived at their decision, and how their reasoning differs even from those whose vote they are supporting. The same is true of minority or dissenting opinions, for sometimes there are several of these in a single case.

The difficulty of making predictions of how justices will vote has been particularly exasperating for presidents. Thus Eisenhower called the appointment of Earl Warren "the biggest damn fool mistake I ever made."

As for Nixon, all his appointees did prove to be somewhat more conservative then the majority of the Warren Court. But these same men presented him with some painful surprises. As we have seen, Chief Justice Burger rejected the appeals of the Nixon administration for further delays in the carrying out of *Brown* v. *Board of Education*. It was Justice Blackmun who delivered the decision upholding abortions—a decision very much against Nixon's own position.

And then there was *United States* v. *Nixon* (1974), in which the Supreme Court told the president that he must comply with the special prosecutor's subpoena of the crucial Watergate tapes. The vote was 8 to 0 (with Justice Rehnquist disqualifying himself because he had served in the Nixon administration as assistant attorney general under a Watergate defendant, John Mitchell). In this case the president's counsel, James St. Clair, implicitly challenged the Supreme Court's authority as an institution. When he was pressed to assure the Court that, if its decision went against the president, the president would comply, St. Clair was evasive. He assumed that the president would comply but could not give a categorical assurance. This was not good enough for the Court. The challenge had been made. *Marbury* v. *Madison*, which established the principle of judicial review and said that the Supreme Court was the final arbiter of the Constitution, was being brought in question. Though Warren Burger was Richard Nixon's appointee, he was chief justice of the Supreme Court, and his institution must be defended.

But it was not just the Supreme Court as an institution that was being tested. It was the rule of law. It was true, said Burger's decision, that the president has a special role under the Constitution, and his position must therefore be considered with even greater care than anyone else's. It was also true that there was such a thing as executive privilege—the right of the president to confidential communication within the executive branch. Ultimately, however, where there is sufficient evidence of criminal behavior as attested to in this case by a valid grand jury indictment, executive privilege cannot prevail. Accordingly, Burger, Blackmun, and Powell decided against the man who had put them on the Supreme Court, and joined with the others in the verdict that led to the surrender of the crucial tapes, which sealed Richard Nixon's fate.

There is one final point to be made in establishing the fact that the Court is very much a legal body. The split decisions on the Court that we have described represent only a small proportion of the 3000 or so cases that come before the Court each year. Most of them do not involve major constitutional issues; they are settled without dissension on technical legal considerations. So the political–ideological dimension of the Court's work, though of very considerable importance in some key policy areas, does not enter most of the cases disposed of by the Court.

Five Perspectives
on the Supreme Court

The Conservatives:
Against Judicial Activism

Although the Supreme Court is not always predictable, the reactions of political leaders to its decisions offer few surprises. This is certainly true of conservatives. When the Court struck down New Deal legislation, they applauded its decisions to the echo. When Franklin Roosevelt proposed to "pack" the Court, they accused him of wanting to establish a dictatorship in America. They lauded the Vinson Court's refusal to prevent Communist party leaders from being sent to jail. They were outraged by the Warren Court's liberal positions. In 1956, 19 senators and 74 representatives from the South issued a "Southern Manifesto" in which they protested the Brown and other school desegregation decisions "as a clear abuse of judicial power" resting not on judicial reasoning but on liberal sociology. Conservatives from other parts of the country joined the southerners in protest against Supreme Court decisions in such fields as communist activities, congressional investigations, and federal–state relations. In 1958 two attempts were made in Congress to limit the Court's jurisdiction to strike down state laws because they were "preempted" by federal legislation, and to prevent government action against communism and subversion. Both moves lost, but by narrow margins. In the 1960s Senator Everett Dirksen led widely supported though unsuccessful efforts to amend the Constitution and thus overrule the Court's rulings against school prayers and legislative reapportionment.

Then Richard Nixon won conservative plaudits by his criticisms of the courts in his 1968 presidential campaign for going too far "in weakening the peace forces as against the criminal forces in this country." Subsequently, conservative sentiments were expressed by Nixon speech writer Patrick Buchanan, who blamed the Court for not protecting the people against the rampaging crime wave:

> Criminal trials were more and more taking on the appearance of investigations to discover police error rather than arrive at the truth and achieve justice. If justice dictates not only that the innocent go free, but that the guilty be punished, less and less was justice being done in the American criminal courts. [19]

In general, conservative politicians were pleased with the Nixon appointments to the Court and the trend against the Warren Court's positions in the fields of criminal law and obscenity. They were perplexed and disappointed, however, by the abortion decision, and by the Burger Court's pursuing the logic of *Brown* v. *Board of Education* from the South into the North with only limited indications of softening the zeal of its predecessor. Altogether, then, conservative politicians and activists interpreted the Court's decisions primarily from the viewpoint of whether or not these agreed with the conservative political positions of the movement.

Some conservative scholars, however, provide a more fundamental analysis of the institutional role of the Supreme Court than the extent to which it satisfies ephemeral political needs. The laws of men, they argue, must operate within the constraints of a higher law—a law based on fundamental principles of man and God. Our Constitution represents the attempt of the Founding Fathers to capture in an approximate way the principles of that higher law. If the executive or legislative branches of government breach the principles of the Constitution, they must be held to account. The body that does this, that exercises restraint over the elected representatives of the people, and prevents their exercising uncontrolled power, is the Supreme Court. The Court is an essential element in the principle of checks and balances. Perhaps more than any other part of the system in fact, it is the balance wheel of the constitutional structure.

But suppose that, instead of acting as a balance wheel, it assumes an unhealthy degree of power itself? This was very much the case with the Court under Earl Warren. Whenever the Warren Court concluded that the elected representatives of the people were not acting with sufficient vigor, it sprang into action itself. As M. Stanton Evans puts it, the courts decided to take on themselves the task of projecting affirmative policy, ordering that certain things be done, commanding actions and expenditures, assuming control of prisons and schools and asylums . . . in order to achieve legislative effects that have been rejected by the legislatures themselves.[20]

It did this on reapportionment and abortion. It forced the pace of the school integration far beyond what the people and the legislatures wanted. In the case of the Boston schools a federal judge, furious because his integration orders had not been carried out, actually took over the decision-making process from the local school district, and forced upon the district a busing plan that generated persistent violence and drove many of the white parents to keep their children out of school, send them to private schools, or move out of the neighborhood. And the Supreme Court refused even to consider a review of the case, for the district judge had been acting within policies that it had laid down. Here was unchecked power in the courts, indeed.

A strict construction of the Constitution.   What, then, is the proper role of the Supreme Court? It should construe the Constitution strictly. Although this is not an easy matter given the brevity of the document, the spirit of the Constitution is clear. It calls for limited government. The framers did not want the powers of government to be expanded by great leaps. Thus the Courts should not read anything into the document that is not there in order to justify more and more government.

All parts of the Constitution should be given equal importance. Some justices have argued that the Bill of Rights is more fundamental than the rest, that the First Amendment must be given a "preferred position." This idea was articulated by Chief Justice Harlan Stone in 1942, and it was the constant position of the liberals' favorite justice, William O. Douglas. To conservatives, there is nothing in the language of the Constitution that gives some rights preference over others. In any case, as we saw in Chapter 1, conservatives believe that property rights are as essential as any other kind of rights. M. Stanton Evans puts it this way:

> As for the notion that rights of free speech and press are logically prior to rights of property, this is not in the least self-evident. Indeed, it may be plausibly argued that the true relationship is all the other way: Only to the extent that one enjoys property rights and some sort of economic base of operations can First Amendment rights become effective. . . . If I can control the economic aspects of your life, then I can control whether you live or die, or what you say in print.[21]

Judicial restraint.   The Court should exercise great restraint in reviewing the claims of the federal government to override the decisions of state governments. Section 8 of Article I of the Constitution gives Congress the power "to regulate Commerce . . . among the several states." This has been construed by the Supreme Court over the years to allow the federal government to reach deeper and deeper into the conduct of businesses within the various states. Again, the Warren Court's process of "incorporation" applied most of the provisions that the

Bill of Rights established at the federal level to the states, declaring that this was required by the language of the Fourteenth Amendment forbidding the states to interfere with the rights of citizens of the United States. This interpretation blithely ignores the language of the Tenth Amendment, which reserves to the states or to the people those powers not delegated to the federal government.

Conservatives were pleased to note that Chief Justice Burger was anxious to avoid having his Court usurp the functions of the states. Repeatedly, he warned against the tendency to move cases out of the states into the federal courts. He warned that the burden this imposed on the federal court system was becoming intolerable. In the course of these warnings he sounded another note that fell pleasingly on conservative ears: not only the federal courts, but the state systems were being overloaded. Suddenly it seemed that everyone was demanding his rights, and almost everyone was litigating—turning to the courts to handle conflicts that used to be resolved by private bargaining or through political bodies. Blacks and women, in particular, were flooding the courts with demands for equal access to jobs, to higher education, and every other kind of opportunity; and this was generating an avalanche of legal counterattacks by white males. The overreliance on courts of law, said the conservatives, was the inevitable result of the impossible expectations raised by the liberals' rhetoric and the Warren Court's encouragement of unreasonable claims.

"As I see it, your problem is that you've become a 'glutton for precedent.'"

Richard Rice

Precedent.   Next, since conservatives believe in preserving the values of the past, it is natural that they should have great respect for precedent. The Warren Court, they insist, was all too ready to abandon the rulings of previous courts to make way for their own preferences. Inevitably, over a long period of time, some earlier cases may come to be overruled. But this should be an exceptional practice. Where precedents are easily ignored, there can be no stable body of law. And without legal stability, there can be no rule of law.

Appointments to the Court.   Thus the conservatives want to see on the Supreme Court people who will construe the Constitution strictly, will respect the acts of state governments, and will value precedent. The type of people who will do this are people of substantial legal training and judicious temperament. They are most likely to be found on the bench; and conservatives approved the announced intention of Richard Nixon when he became president to prefer people with substantial judicial experience in making appointments to the Supreme Court. This has not been the general rule. All Supreme Court justices have been attorneys (though even this is not specified in the Constitution). Some have been prosecuting attorneys in the lower courts, defense counsel, practitioners of corporate law, or law professors. Although several others have actually served on the bench, at least on the police court level, only about a quarter of the total have had really extensive judicial careers. Conservatives would like to see this proportion raised.

Conservatives recognize that their prescription for the Court may, from time to time, have to be adjusted. Given the rampant activism of the Warren Court, it may be necessary for a time to be activist in the opposite direction. Thus some of the Warren precedents may need to be overturned in order to repair the damage they have inflicted on the constitutional system.

In general, however, conservatives declare themselves to be opposed to judicial activism. We have more than enough legislatures in this country already. We do not need the Supreme Court to legislate for us. Certainly we do not need it as our supreme legislature.

The Liberals: For Judicial Activism

To the extent that the conservatives detested the Warren Court, the liberals loved it. Here and there a decision of the Court might not please them. But on the whole they found it the one institution of American government whose product they could endorse with enthusiasm.

The reapportionment decisions corrected a defect of federal, state, and local legislatures that had long been one of their main grievances. Racial integration is one of the central tenets of the liberal creed; and until *Brown* v. *Board of Education* in 1954 no branch of government had done much about it except utter pious platitudes. Although opposed to the policies and tactics of communists and other radical left groups, liberals believe that they should be free to present their case as long as they do not resort to violence. Liberals, therefore, were bitterly opposed to the Smith Act and the *Dennis* decision upholding it, and welcomed the Warren Court's decisions that supported their view.

On obscenity, they agreed with the finding of a Presidential Commission on Obscenity and Pornography, which, in 1970, recommended the repeal of all laws intended to interfere with "the right of adults who wish to do so to read, obtain or view explicit sexual material."

In criminal law they have been principally concerned to see that police power is not abused, and they would rather see a guilty person go free than take a chance on an innocent person's being wrongfully convicted. Thus they share Earl Warren's indignation when, in explaining the *Miranda* decision, he quoted from several police manuals on interrogation. One of these suggested that questioning take place in a police station, where "the investigator possesses all the advantages" rather than in the suspect's home. The same manual advised the questioner to "interrogate without relent, leaving the subject no prospect of surcease." Various devices were suggested to encourage a confession, including the mention of other unrelated crimes and a lineup with coached witnesses, in the hope that "the subject will become desperate and confess to the offense under investigation in order to escape from the false accusations."

So liberals were unhappy with the extent to which the Burger Court weakened the Warren Court's positions, but were as pleased as the conservatives were disappointed by the Burger Court's upholding the constitutionality of abortion.

Yet, as we have already observed, the conservative's perspective on the Court is not argued solely in terms of its product. They also present an analysis of the Court as an institution in the American governmental structure. They ask that the Court adopt a strict construction of the Constitution; use restraint in dealing with the states; and venerate precedent. And they believe that the Court should consist of people of judicious temperament and judicial experience. What is the liberals' response to these positions?

A flexible interpretation of the Constitution.   In most areas liberals favor a more flexible interpretation of the Constitution than do the conservatives. Since the document is brief, it must be cast in general terms; and generality breeds ambiguity.

Thus it is absurd to suggest that the Warren Court went far beyond the Constitution in its decisions on the right of the accused to counsel. The Fourteenth Amendment says that no state shall "deprive any person of life, liberty, or property, without due process of law." The Sixth Amendment says that an accused person shall have the right to "have the Assistance of Counsel for his defense," and for some time the Supreme Court has found that this is a necessary part of "due process." But the Constitution does not tell us when the right to counsel begins and under what conditions. So in *Escobedo* and *Miranda* the Warren Court said that the right is meaningless unless it begins early in the investigative process, and that, if the accused cannot afford an attorney, the Court will appoint one for him free. This is not in the language of the Sixth Amendment. But can there be due process without these protections? Given the kind of police practices Warren described in the *Miranda* decision, liberals do not think there can be. They believe that the Court must go beyond the words of the Constitution to apply their intent to contemporary situations.

Similarly, the Constitution makes no specific mention of abortion, or school segregation, or pornography. But individuals and groups bring the grievances to the courts. The Supreme Court has no alternative but to search the language of the Constitution to see what guidance it can find in the general principles of the document that can apply to the issues of our contemporary world. Moreover, the intent of the framers must be construed in a twentieth-century not an eighteenth-century context. The genius of the Constitution is that it provides general principles that are amenable to flexible and evolving interpretations. The Warren Court was not going beyond its charter in accepting the opportunity for broad interpretation.

Liberals, however, take a much less flexible view of the First Amendment freedoms. Here, they contend, we are dealing with those liberties without which all the other rights of a constitutional system become meaningless. So the rights of freedom of speech, the press, and assembly must be "preferred rights." They may not be absolute—they can be limited by laws of libel and slander, for example—but they should generally be given a preferred status over property rights, for example.

On the whole, liberals have sided with the federal government as against state governments. For one thing, they believe that more and more of our social problems are national in scope and cannot be handled by smaller units of government. Thus it has been necessary to adopt an expansive view of the interstate commerce clause of the Constitution.

For another, most of the infringements against the liberties and rights of the individual that come before the courts are imposed by state legislatures and local law enforcement agencies. The Tenth Amendment reserves to the states all the powers that the Constitution does not give to the federal government or deny to the states. But the Fourteenth Amendment *does* deny to the states the power to "make or enforce any law which shall abridge the privileges or immunities of citizens of the United States," or to "deprive any person of life, liberty or property without due process of law," or to "deny any person within its jurisdiction the equal protection of the laws." Since this is part of the federal Constitution, is it not reasonable that the federal Supreme Court, should apply the protections guaranteed by the Bill of Rights to individuals threatened by the actions of state and local jurisdictions? Does the doctrine of judicial restraint mean that the Supreme Court should restrain itself from enforcing the Constitution?

Precedents cannot always rule.   Liberals do not deny that judges should treat precedents seriously. However, they are not as reluctant as conservatives to depart from past rulings. They like Justice Oliver Wendell Holmes's statement to the effect that: "It is revolting to have no better reason for a rule of law than that so it was laid down in the time of Henry IV. It is still more revolting if the grounds upon which it was laid down have vanished long since, and the rule simply persists from blind imitation of the past." In fact, the Court has overruled its own prior decisions more than 100 times in its history. And Justices Felix Frankfurter and John Marshall Harlan, who were among the Court's principal advocates of judicial restraint and of adhering to precedent, have both participated in the overturning of precedents.

Frankfurter joined in the unanimous decision on *Brown* v. *Board of Education* (1954), which, in essence reversed the finding of *Plessy* v. *Ferguson* (1896) that separate could be equal. And in *Gideon* v. *Wainwright* (1963), which found that a state could not send an indigent defendant to prison unless he were provided full counsel, Harlan supported the overruling of *Betts* v. *Brady* (1942), which had rejected this interpretation of the Constitution.

A major difficulty in seeking guidance in precedents is that, though there are vast bodies of previous decisions in the areas covered by each case, no case is identical with any other that has come before it. So the determination must be made as to which earlier cases might indeed be considered as precedents; and that determination will be especially difficult where there are several possible precedents and these contradict one another. Thus we typically find the majority and the minority opinions backed by equally imposing arrays of precedents, with both sides claiming that *their* precedents should be accepted as the ones most relevant to the present case.

Justices need not have judicial experience.   Liberals are not overly impressed with the argument that the people appointed to the Supreme Court should be experienced judges. Some of the greatest, most "judicial" members of the Supreme Court have not come from the lower courts. The first great chief justice, John Marshall, did not. Nor had Chief Justices Taney, Hughes, and Stone, or such eminent associate justices as Louis Brandeis and Felix Frankfurter.

Liberals are unconvinced that coming from a lower court increases the likelihood that a Supreme Court justice will be free from political preconceptions. Politics plays an important role in appointment to the lower courts. Thus when Warren Burger was selected as chief justice, Nixon was mindful of the fact that Burger had been active in Minnesota politics; went to the 1952 Republican convention as floor manager for presidential candidate Harold Stassen; spoke for the Minnesota delegation in announcing the switch from Stassen to Eisenhower that gave Eisenhower his majority; was appointed by Eisenhower as an assistant attorney general; and was appointed by Eisenhower in 1956 to the U.S. Court of Appeals in Washington.

Politics is very much a factor, then, in getting onto and moving up the judicial ladder. Liberals believe this to be inevitable. The law is interwoven with politics. The Supreme Court, more than any other court, deals with political issues. The Constitution is our fundamental political document, and there is no escaping political considerations in its interpretation.

Liberals, however, are concerned about the criteria for appointments to the

Supreme Court; but their complaint is that the Court is unrepresentative of the population. Mostly the justices have come from upper-middle- to upper-class families, and have been predominately white Anglo-Saxon Protestants. Thurgood Marshall, appointed in 1967, was the first black on the Court. There is always a Catholic on the Court today; and for years there was a Jew, though there has been none since Abe Fortas resigned. But there have been no women. It is time, say the liberals, to make the Court, which deals in great issues of public policy that affect the future of the entire population, more representative of that population.

The liberals' dilemma.   This brings us squarely up against an acute liberal dilemma. Here is a body consisting of nine mostly elderly, mostly well-to-do, mostly white men. They have lifetime appointments. They have the power to render null and void the decisions of legislative and executive bodies duly elected by the majority will of the people.

And here are the liberals, devout advocates of majority will, offering an elaborate structure of reasoning why the decisions of these nine unelected men should outweigh the acts of the representative branches of government. Of course, they did not always take this position. In the 1930s the liberals were able to take up their natural stance of opposing the "nine old men" who were thwarting the will of the majority. But they seemed to be in a hopelessly incongruous position when they became devout defenders of the Warren Court against its critics.

No longer was it the liberals who made the case for majority rule. Instead, it was two justices usually associated with the more or less conservative side of issues, Felix Frankfurter and John Marshall Harlan. Frankfurter, one of the great jurists of modern times, consistently presented the view that, unless a federal or state law is flagrantly in conflict with the Constitution, the Supreme Court should restrain itself from overturning legislation. The assumption of democracy, he argued, is that the people, acting through a representative system, must be left to make their own mistakes and to learn from them. The Court should stay as far as possible out of the political process.

Justice Harlan made the same point in a 1964 reapportionment case: "What is done today saps the political process. The promise of judicial intervention in matters of this sort cannot but encourage popular inertia in efforts for political reform through the political process with the inevitable result that the process itself is weakened." This sounds like liberal doctrine, for the liberals claim to be advocates of majority rule; yet the liberals applauded the Court's decisions that rejected these arguments.

How do the liberals handle this dilemma? How, if they support majority rule, do they deal with the fact that in the 1940s and 1950s the majority did not believe that communists had the right to propagate their ideas? Or that in the 1960s the majority were much more concerned with the rights of the victim than the rights of the accused, and were strongly against the Supreme Court's ban on school prayers?

To this the liberals' response is that democracy is concerned not only with majority rule but also with individual and minority rights. It is one thing to ask that the majority be allowed to make its own mistakes. But in the area of free expression those mistakes may involve the suppression of rights. If dissenting opinions are suppressed, an essential condition of democracy—the free play of ideas through which alternative policies are presented—may disappear. It is an unfortunate fact for liberals that the majority of people do not always have a deep commitment to the values that underpin a free society.[22] But in their view this results from the disproportionate influence on majority attitudes exercised by propertied, conservative interests, who place such high value on law and order, nationalism, and militarism. Until the power of those interests in constrained more effectively, political dissenters, blacks, and other minorities will have to look to any place in the system—including the courts—to defend their rights. Of course, it would be better if elected executives and legislatures did their job of preserving and advancing our rights and freedoms. But on school desegregation, on reapportionment, and so on, president, Congress, and state governments had failed to act. There was a gaping void, and there was nothing for it but for the Supreme Court to move into the void.

Although the liberals make this case, they are still not entirely comfortable with it. And at least some liberal scholars, including James MacGregor Burns, doubt that they should rely on the Supreme Court to do their work for them in any area except the freedoms guaranteed in the Bill of Rights. On such issues as school desegregation and reapportionment they worry about the liberals' having looked to the Warren Court to bail them out rather than getting action from the executive and legislative branches of government. Judicial activism in the hands of the Warren Court produced highly desirable results for the liberals. But judicial activism can be a two-edged sword. The Warren Court has established the precedent of having the Court intervene vigorously in many issues. What will the liberals, who applauded the Warren Court's activism so enthusiastically in the 1960s, have to say if a later, much more conservative Supreme Court decides to intervene vigorously on the conservative side in social, economic, and sexual issues? No doubt the liberals will set up a great outcry, as they did in the 1930s. But their opponents will be able to turn against them the arguments for activism that the liberals used so passionately in the 1960s.

The Radical Right: How the Supreme Court Has Subverted American Values

The far right has not found much comfort in the decisions of the Supreme Court since 1936. The brief effort by the Court to stop the New Deal's advance to socialism was abandoned in 1937. For a while in the late forties and early fifties the Court took a stand against communism, but the Warren Court put an end to that. The entire Warren era was a disaster from the radical right perspective. To the John Birch Society it was clear that the Warren Court was working not merely for a domestic but for a foreign dictatorship.[23] The answer was given by Robert Welch: ". . . Warren will simply have to be impeached, as a warning to other judges of the lower courts as well as of the Supreme Court, before we can ever return this country to a rule of law instead of the rule of men."[24]

The Birch Society launched a campaign to "Impeach Earl Warren" that included the sale of large billboard posters and packages of pamphlets by Robert Welch and Mississippi senator James O. Eastland. Others who joined in the demand for Warren's impeachment included the right-wing radio–television commentator Dan Smoot, and the fundamentalist preacher Billy James Hargis, who was particularly incensed by the school prayer decisions, and who was not satisfied with the demand that Warren alone be impeached. Hargis demanded that every Supreme Court member "who either voted to outlaw prayer in the public schools, or was a party to this decision by silence should be impeached."[25]

The passing from the scene of Earl Warren did little to mollify the radical right. The Burger Court's decisions in the criminal law area took some of the steam out of the widespread hostility that the Warren Court had aroused, and this made it harder for the right to find allies on the "law and order" and "support your local police" movement. But they could work with local groups which, though not part of the radical right, were enraged by Supreme Court decisions on abortion and school desegregation.

The Radical Left: The Myth of Equality under the Law

For the radical left the Supreme Court is the apex of a rule of law designed to protect the interests of the ruling elite. They see equality before the law as a myth. Law enforcement is applied overwhelmingly against the poor, minorities, and political activists. White-collar criminals, those who subvert the law by swindling the masses and manipulating huge amounts of money through a variety of crooked schemes, are usually untouched by the criminal law. And, on the rare occasions when they are brought to trial, white-collar defendants are treated very gently, in contrast with the poor, who are treated like faceless rabble.[26]

Although the Warren Court made an effort to restrain the methods by which the police harass blacks and the young and political dissidents and trick them into convicting themselves, the police have learned how to go through the motions, protect themselves technically, and still employ brutal tactics. And the Burger Court has steadily eroded even the thin protections demanded by the Warren majority.

This is not to say that the courts can never produce justice for the oppressed. Juries have acquitted the "Chicago Seven"—seven leaders of the left accused of conspiracy to incite riots at the Democratic National Convention of 1968; 21 Black Panthers accused of acts of violence against the police in 1971; and, in 1972, 28 Catholic antiwar activists in Camden, New Jersey, and the Veterans against the War in Gainesville, Florida, accused of engaging in disruptive demonstrations.

These acquittals were achieved by a new generation of lawyers, dedicating themselves to service to the people rather than to the big business corporations. Their courtroom tactics are unconventional to the point of bringing down on their heads charges of disruption, which have in some instances led to their being held in contempt of court.

William Kunstler is the most prominent of this brand of lawyer. He has aroused the ire of Chief Justice Burger. "There are some few lawyers," said Burger, "who scoff at the idea that manners and etiquette form any part of the necessary equipment of the courtroom advocate." According to Burger, the performance of the greatest courtroom lawyers has always been characterized by "coolness, poise and graphic clarity, without shouting or ranting, without baiting witnesses, opponents or the judge."[27] Kunstler (who was convicted with three of the defendants on contempt-of-court charges arising out of the Chicago Seven trial, then released without penalty) saw in this argument an effort to intimidate attorneys like himself: "Like the now thoroughly-discredited cry of 'law and order' the clamor against a mythical 'disorder in the courts' must not be permitted to cloak another vicious attack on personal freedom."[28]

The Centrists: Sound Judgment and Good Craftsmanship

To centrists there is a recognizable, though steadily changing, position between the conservative and liberal versions of the Court's proper role offered in this chapter. This middle ground takes essentially no account of the extreme arguments of the radicals. No consideration should be given to proposals to impeach justices who are doing their duty in good faith, whether or not one agrees with their decisions. The tactics of a William Kunstler, sometimes reducing the courtroom to a shambles in a frenetic attempt to provoke the judge into losing his temper and thus laying the ground for an appeal from an inevitable conviction, cannot be condoned.

Putting aside the radicals' doctrines, then, the centrists take their stand between the liberal and conservative viewpoints. Thus the Court in the 1930s was too stubborn in its rejection of the New Deal legislation (though some of that legislation was atrocious and had to be abandoned as unworkable). On the other hand, Franklin Roosevelt went too far in trying to "pack" the Court, and it was fortunate that he was forced to retreat.

Then the Warren Court was too adventurous. Many of its decisions were necessary. But it moved on too many fronts at once, and made itself vulnerable to attack from several directions. This damaged not only the reputation of the Supreme Court but also respect for the law. Centrists may differ on the merit of particular decisions of the Burger Court, but they believe that it has served the necessary function of swinging the pendulum back toward the center. There may be a danger that the pendulum will now swing too far; but in time this, in turn, would lead to motion in the opposite direction.

Centrists recognize, then, the political context in which the Supreme Court works. Although the Court should not allow itself to be governed by opinion polls, neither should it set too great a distance between the trend of its decisions and the long-range climate of opinion in the country. It should fall neither too far behind the mood of the people as in the 1930s, nor get too far ahead of it, as in the 1960s. Otherwise, instead of being a force for stability and moderation—the traditional role of the law—it becomes a source of tension and hostility.

In addition to sensible political judgment by the justices, the centrists look for good craftsmanship in their decisions. The public at large may look only at the outcome of a decision. But lawyers study the reasoning behind an opinion. And if that reasoning is sound and well crafted, lawyers, even if they disagree with the conclusions, respect it. And lawyers, being influential people, may win broad public respect in time for the opinion. Generally speaking, then, the best and most enduring decisions are based on sound logic and a thorough grasp of the techniques of the law.

In this respect centrist scholars have not been impressed with the Court's work in the last few years. Much of the Warren Court's product they regard as shoddily wrought—in part because that Court tried to do too much.

However, centrist scholars do not assume that, because a Court becomes more conservative, it therefore improves its quality. The decisions of the Burger Court have included some of great importance, such as the abortion and capital punishment decisions, but none that was destined to become a legal classic.

Conclusion

In this chapter we have reviewed the two dimensions of the Supreme Court's work, the political and the judicial. The Court, we have seen, is no metaphysical abstraction, detached from the ways of the world. It is a human institution, and the individuals who make up its membership cannot separate their actions completely from the way they perceive the world. As Judge Jerome Frank pointed out: "Much harm is done by the myth that, merely by putting on a black robe and taking the oath of office as a judge, a man ceases to be human and strips himself of all predilections, becomes a passionless thinking machine."[29] Ours, it is often said, is a government of laws, not men. Yet the laws must be interpreted by men. There is no way that those men can be completely insulated from the currents of political opinion that have shaped their own experience and that move in the society at large.

Moreover, the Supreme Court has responsibilities that go beyond the merely legal. It is charged with the task of testing the actions of other branches and levels of government against the Constitution. So it cannot help engaging in policy making. Even if it refuses to overturn acts of Congress and state legislatures, it may thereby be making a judgment on their constitutionality and thus participating in the making of policy. Doing nothing, in effect, is doing a great deal. So the battle over the Court today, as it has always been, is over how it exercises its power in broad fields of public policy.

At the same time, the Supreme Court is also a judicial body, a legal institution. We saw in our discussions of the presidency, Congress, and the bureaucracies that, although these are all deeply engaged in the political process, each of them has particular institutional characteristics that powerfully affect the way they operate. This is even more the case with the Supreme Court, which must attach great weight to the Constitution, to the acts of executives and legislatures, and to precedent. Further, the criteria and procedures of the Supreme Court are very different from the other branches of government.

It is these judicial considerations that make it difficult to predict how each justice will vote on a given issue. And it is these same considerations that cause conservatives and liberals alike to be caught up in self-contradictions. Conservatives, who believe in strict construction of the Constitution, respect for state legislatures, and deference to precedent, sometimes call for decisions that stretch the wording of the Constitution to the utmost, overturn state government actions, and overrule precedents. But the liberals' inconsistencies are greater still. Believers in majority rule, they are unwilling on some issues to abide by the majority will, and turn to the most unrepresentative body in the federal government to protect them from the majority.

This is not to suggest that conservatives and liberals are cynically playing with symbols, and using whatever arguments come to hand to serve their unbending purposes. The point is simply that, try though they will to address themselves to the debate over institutions, they cannot lose sight of the fact that institutions are not ends in themselves, but human creations to serve human purposes.

Notes and References

1. *Schenck* v. *United States*, 1919.

2. *Gitlow* v. *New York*, 1925.

3. *Everson* v. *Board of Education*, 1947; *Illinois* ex. rel. *McCollum* v. *Board of Education*, 1948.

4. *Planned Parenthood of Central Missouri* v. *Danforth*, 1976.

5. *Beal* v. *Doe*, 1977; *Maher* v. *Roe*, 1977; *Poelker* v. *Doe*, 1977.

6. *Craig* v. *Boren*, 1976.

7. *General Electric Co.* v. *Gilbert*, 1976.

8. *New York Times Co.* v. *United States*, 1971.

9. *Southeastern Promotions, Ltd.* v. *Conrad*, 1975.

10. *Jenkins* v. *Georgia*, 1974.

11. *United States* v. *U.S. District Court*, 1972.

12. *United States* v. *Giordani*, 1974.

13. See *Brewer* v. *Williams*, 1977.

14. *Furman* v. *Georgia,* 1972; *Jackson* v. *Georgia,* 1972; *Branch* v. *Texas,* 1972.

15. *Gregg* v. *Georgia,* 1976; *Proffitt* v. *Florida,* 1976; *Jurek* v. *Texas,* 1976.

16. *Coker* v. *Georgia,* 1977.

17. Clement E. Vose, "Litigation as a Form of Pressure Group Activity," *Annals of the American Academy of Political and Social Science,* Vol. 319 (September 1958), pp. 20–31.

18. Edmond Cahn, "Mr. Justice Black and the First Amendment 'Absolutes': A Public Interview," *New York University Law Review,* Vol. 37 (June 1962), pp. 549–63.

19. Patrick J. Buchanan, *The New Majority* (Philadelphia: Girard Bank, 1973), p. 28.

20. M. Stanton Evans, *Clear and Present Dangers: A Conservative View of America's Government* (New York: Harcourt Brace Jovanovich, Inc., 1975), p. 104.

21. Ibid., p. 267.

22. See Herbert McClosky, "Consensus and Ideology in American Politics," *The American Political Science Review,* Vol. 58, No. 2 (1964), pp. 366–67.

23. *American Opinion,* July–August 1965.

24. *Bulletin of the John Birch Society,* November 1965.

25. Pamphlet, "Six Men against God," 1965, quoted in Benjamin R. Epstein and Arnold Forster, *The Radical Right* (New York: Vintage Books, 1967), p. 22.

26. See Robert Lefcourt, "Law against the People," from *Law against the People: Essays to Demystify Law, Order and the Courts,* Robert Lefcourt, ed. (New York: Random House, Inc., 1971).

27. Warren Burger, address at Fordham University Law School, November 1973.

28. *The Los Angeles Times,* December 28, 1973.

29. Jerome Frank, *Law and the Modern Mind* (New York: Coward, McCann & Geoghegan, Inc., 1949), preface to 6th ed., p. xx.

Chapter
10

Chapter
10

Federalism:

States and Cities

The Tenth Amendment to the Constitution of the United States says:

> The powers not delegated to the United States by the Constitution, nor prohibited by it to the States, are reserved to the States respectively, or to the people.

Thus the fundamental law of the land reserved for the states an important share of the powers they had exercised before they formed the new nation. This was a necessary precondition if the United States was to be established, for the states were intensely jealous of their prerogatives. After independence had been won from the British, the states had at first agreed only to cooperate under the Articles of Confederation. A confederation is merely a loose association of essentially separate, "sovereign" states—sovereign because they are free to run their affairs without being subject to any higher authority. It soon became clear, however, that 13 separate states could not prevent monetary chaos (for each could print its own currency), assure order and security, or adequately represent the common interests of the several states in their dealings with foreign powers. So the states eventually agreed that confederation was not enough and that they must join together to form a single nation.

Still, given the great diversity of traditions, religions, and economic and political interests, the states would never agree to surrender all their authority to a *unitary* system—one in which all the ultimate sovereignty is vested in a central national government. Resistance to a unitary government was especially strong among the small states, which feared that their interests would be overwhelmed by the big states if they all joined together. At last the 13 states settled on a *federal* system, a type of government in which some powers are assigned to the central, or federal, government and the rest to the subnational governments.

Today the 50 states continue to be important elements in the system of power and politics in America. Moreover, the state governments have delegated much of their authority to other governmental units still closer to where the people live. Thus today there are over 3000 counties, 18,500 municipalities, and 17,000 towns and townships. In addition to these general-purpose units of government, there are nearly 16,000 school districts and 24,000 special districts for such matters as water supply, fire protection, smog control, and public transportation. Thus we have a grand total of over 78,000 units of government within the United States. The domain of these governmental units ranges from small villages to great metropolitan areas with populations and budgets larger than those of many states and, indeed, of many nations.

Characteristics of State and Local Governments

The States

There are a number of similarities between the governments of the various states and the federal government. Each of the states has a written constitution. And each of them has adopted the principle of separation of powers. There is an executive branch headed by a governor; state legislatures, all of which have two houses except Nebraska, which has only one; and a hierarchy of courts, beginning with local police courts and moving up through courts of appeal to a supreme court.

However, there are also important differences between state and federal government. To begin with, the state constitutions tend to be much longer than the U.S. Constitution. Although a constitution is supposed to be the underlying or fundamental law, many of the state constitutions have become cluttered up with immense masses of technical detail. Moreover, constitutions tend to grow longer in several of the western states because, in addition to the most common method for amending state constitutions—a two-thirds vote of the state legislature followed by a vote of the general electorate—provision has been made for amendment through the *initiative*. This procedure allows a proposal to be placed on the ballot by securing a sufficient number of voters' signatures on petitions even if the state legislature has not voted on the matter.

Then there are significant differences between the power of state and federal executives. Whatever we have said about the frustrations of presidents is even more true of governors. For one thing, they are held accountable for many problems, such as the increase in unemployment and in welfare costs, which can only be handled at the national level. Then in most states a number of members of the executive branch—for example, the lieutenant governor, the attorney general, the secretary of state, the state treasurer, the superintendent of education—are elected separately from the governor, and thus have their independent bases of power, which effectively limits the power of the governor. Most governors, however, wield a weapon that the president lacks: the *item veto*, the authority to trim items from the budget proposed by the legislature rather than take or leave the whole thing.

As for the legislatures they differ from Congress in a number of important respects. For the most part, their members serve part-time, and in all but a few of the largest states the legislators are paid far too little for them to consider their legislative office their principal occupation. Salaries are increasing, however, and the larger number of state legislatures now hold annual sessions rather than the former practice of meeting every other year. Unlike the U.S. Congress, in which the upper chamber represents the widely varying populations of the fifty states, both chambers of each state legislature now draw their members from districts having roughly equal populations (though state senators are drawn from fewer and larger districts than are the representatives of the lower house). This is the result of the U.S. Supreme Court's reapportionment decisions, *Baker* v. *Carr* (1962) and *Reynolds* v. *Sims* (1964). Before these decisions, the upper chambers were generally modeled on the U.S. Senate, in that state senators represented counties, even though some counties had much larger populations than others, just as U.S. senators represent states of widely differing populations.

As is the case in the federal system, state courts may strike down any state law that conflicts with the state's constitution. However, whereas the U.S. Supreme Court has the final word on the interpretation of the U.S. Constitution (unless the Constitution is amended), state and local court decisions may be appealed to the federal courts, *so long as there is a federal issue involved.* If the existence of the constitutional issue can be demonstrated to the federal courts' satisfaction, the issue will be resolved by the principles established in the federal Constitution or statutes, and the state law or state court decision may be overruled accordingly.

And a notable difference between state and federal judges is that the latter are appointed for life, whereas most local and state judges have to face the judgment of the electorate from time to time. A high proportion become judges in the first place by running for election. In other cases they are appointed by the governor after nomination by a nonpartisan commission, and then have to stand for election after they have served their first term.

The Localities

Governments in the communities vary more widely even than state governments. Most of the larger cities—those with a half million or more population—and about half the smaller cities, have a mayor and a city council, usually elected independently from each other. However, the relative strength of mayor and council varies enormously. In some cities, especially in the West, departments of city government may be headed by commissions, whose members are appointed by the mayor and ratified by the council but which may have a good deal of independence from both. These commissions deal with special fields such as airports, harbors, and fire and police services. About a third of the middle-sized cities have adopted a council–manager form of government, in which the elected council hires a professional city manager to run the city government subject to general policy direction by the council.

The counties usually include less densely populated areas than the cities, though population growth in some formerly rural areas has made some counties, such as Los Angeles, very populous indeed. Counties are usually run by elected boards of commissioners or supervisors, and there are a number of other elective offices such as sheriff, county prosecutor or district attorney, and county coroner. The smallest units of American government are the towns and townships, which are either villages or subdivisions of counties.

Cutting across various units of local government are the special districts, set up to deal with problems or services that reach across governmental boundaries and that need a tax base broader than a single governmental unit. In some cases the boards running these special districts are directly elected, as is true of most school boards. In other cases, where the problems are particularly complex, as with rapid transit or smog control, the members are usually appointed by the elected leaders of the communities participating in the special district.

Elections and Political Parties

Elections to these various units of state and local government are by the same franchise that prevails in federal elections—anyone from age 18 who registers to vote. In some parts of the country the voters have the power to do more than elect representatives. New England has its tradition of the town meeting, in which local issues are settled by vote of the entire citizenry, though interest in the town meetings has fallen off considerably. Then a number of states in the West use the referendum and the initiative, which enable voters to decide issues directly through the ballot box.

In state elections political parties are still important devices for nominating and electing candidates, though the weakness of the Republican party in several of the southern states has deprived state politics in that region of much of the competition that makes the party system useful. At the local level parties are a less important factor than statewide, and their significance is diminishing fast.

Political bosses are a dying breed, as we saw in Chapter 3. In fact, the crudities and corruption of the political machines of the eastern cities started a reaction against parties in local government that began in the early part of this century and persists to this day. The reaction has been especially strong in the West, where most cities require that the election of the mayor, the city councilmen, and other officeholders be at least nominally nonpartisan.

Sharing the Power

This multitude of state and local governments touches the lives of ordinary citizens in more ways even than the federal government. They are charged with the responsibility of protecting the people's safety, health, morals, and general welfare. They regulate and administer schools and colleges; provide police and fire protection; run transportation systems; build and maintain roads and parks; supply water, electricity, and gas, or regulate those who do; help the poor with money and social and health services; control the use of land by zoning and other methods; establish laws on marriage and divorce; and levy taxes to pay for all these and a myriad of other services.

The Federal Role

At the same time, the federal government's actions have an impact on the lives of citizens in their states and communities, and the respective roles of the different levels of government must therefore constantly be redefined. Some tasks, such as making foreign policy, are assigned exclusively by the U.S. Constitution to the federal government. The Fourteenth Amendment to the U.S. Constitution instructs the states to provide the individual due process and the equal protection of the laws. As we saw in Chapter 9, the U.S. Supreme Court has extended the guarantees of the Bill of Rights to protection against state and local government as well as federal action. Further, the Supreme Court has construed the constitutional authority given to Congress to regulate commerce between the states, to allow the federal government to regulate businesses that are locally based but that send a portion of their product across state lines or provide a service to interstate travelers.

Then, too, the federal government has been drawn more and more into state and local affairs by virtue of its financial contributions. Federal "grants-in-aid" to states and communities—funds to support programs in education, health, welfare, transportation, and many other fields—amounted to about $3 billion in 1955. By 1969 they had passed $20 billion, and they were over the $50 billion mark by 1975—over a fifth of all state and local revenues. Since it is always difficult to separate power from the source of funds, the contribution of $50 billion a year has involved the federal government heavily in decision making at the state and local level.

Thus the state employment services are run by state officials; but many of the rules for the administration of the program are written in Washington. Failure to go by those rules could mean denial of unemployment checks and the virtual elimination of the employment service staff. Even in such fields as education, which would appear to be among the powers that the Constitution reserves to the states, local school districts have to abide by federal guidelines if they want to receive the federal aid that most of them regard as indispensable.

The Local Impetus

Substantial though the role of the federal government is in the affairs of states and communities, there is still a strong local impetus in the American system. As we saw in Chapter 8, the expansion of the federal government since the 1930s has not resulted in a reduction in the scale of state and local government activity. Instead, the demand for public services has increased so prodigiously that it has produced a vast expansion of the role of government at *all* levels. Total state and local expenditures increased from less than $50 billion in 1959 to about $230 billion in 1975. State and local outlays for education, health services, highways, welfare, and police and fire protection are still much greater than federal expenditures in those areas. The number of people employed at the state and local levels—over 12 million in 1977—was more than four times the number working for federal agencies.

Moreover, the example of the state employment services, which are dominated by Washington, is not typical of state and local programs, even of those which receive financial help from the federal government. In some of them, decision making is a joint endeavor, with federal, state, and local officials all participating significantly. In others, the local people dominate. Thus the respective roles of the different units of government vary from program to program and are interwoven in many patterns. Federalism in America, then, cannot be described in terms of clearly separated strata or layers of responsibility, but is better expressed as "a marblecake,"[1] in which the state and local ingredients lend essential elements of substance and flavor to the whole.

Contemporary Problems of State and Local Government

There are many advantages to this system of shared powers we call federalism. It expresses the diversity of the country and the people while providing for national action where this is needed. It offers opportunities to experiment with programs and policies community by community, state by state, long before a national consensus has taken shape. It reduces the danger that power will become excessively concentrated.

Yet the federal system in America is beset with problems. Chief among these are citizen apathy, jurisdictional conflicts, corrupt officials, and a chronic shortage of funds. And all these come together in their most acute form in the great metropolitan areas to constitute what is commonly called "the urban crisis."

Voter Apathy

In Chapter 2 we saw that a smaller proportion of people bother to vote in our national elections than is the case in most other industrialized countries. But it is sometimes argued that this is true because what happens in Washington is remote from the interests of most people in their daily lives. It ought to follow, then, that the closer we get to home the more people are likely to be involved in government and politics. The unhappy fact is that as we move from national government to state and then to local government we tend to find smaller and smaller proportions of the people going to the polls. Thus for presidential elections we get voting turnouts in the 50 to 60 percent range, and for Congress somewhat less than this. But races for a governorship or a state legislature often attract less than 40 percent of the potential electorate (unless candidates for president appear on the same ballot). And in some local elections less than 20 percent cast their votes.

Jurisdictional Conflicts

Both the states and the localities encounter difficulties because their geographical areas of jurisdiction are often inappropriate to the social and human needs they are intended to serve. The state boundaries were drawn long ago. They may have corresponded initially to the major groupings of population; but populations have shifted, whereas boundaries have not. Moreover, there are many problems that refuse to stop conveniently at the state line. There is a good deal of cooperation between the states, and in the form of *interstate compacts* this cooperation has been formalized to deal with such concerns as water pollution, flood control, port operations, recreation and parks, and conservation. However, members of interstate compact commissions are appointed by state governors, feel their first loyalty to their respective states, and can embark on new activities only if they are unanimously agreed on. So interstate cooperation continues to face severe limitations—which gives us another reason for the massive intrusion of the federal government into state affairs.

In the communities the problem of governmental boundaries is even more acute. The large majority of local units are far too small to be able to deal effectively with many contemporary problems. Over half of the more than 38,000 territorial governments—counties, municipalities, townships, towns—contain populations of under 1000; less than 10 percent have more than 10,000 inhabitants; less than 1 percent have over 100,000. Then there are complicated and confusing layers of government. Los Angeles County, for example, is one solid metropolitan area (which is itself part of an even larger metropolitan region). Yet within that one county there are 77 cities. There is a good deal of cooperation among those cities, and the county provides services by contract to most of the smaller ones. However, because there is no single, comprehensive unit of government, a variety of special districts has sprung up to supply water, develop parks and sanitation facilities, or control floods and air pollution. Some of these are countywide, others operate within single cities, still others cut across political boundaries. So, in addition to 77 cities, Los Angeles County contains more than 100 school districts and almost 350 other special districts and taxing jurisdictions, producing a grand total of more than 520 units of government. Nor is this situation unique. The metropolitan area around New York City includes almost 1500 distinct political entities.

The resulting system has been criticized for fragmenting responsibility, confusing the voter, and hindering the prospects of achieving economies of scale. Scholars of local government have for years urged the consolidation of governmental units, especially in the metropolitan areas, into regional governments corresponding to large concentrations of population, industry, and resources. Although a certain amount of consolidation has been achieved through the reduction in the number of school and other special districts, Dade County, Florida, remains the only example of consolidated metropolitan government in the nation. In 1970 Indianapolis moved in this direction also by incorporating the surrounding suburbs of Marion County and establishing a governmental scheme known locally as "Unigov."

Corruption of Public Officials

In the chapters on interest groups and Congress we looked at breaches of integrity ranging from conflicts of interest to outright bribery. We encounter the same problem in state and local units of government. At the state level matters have improved since the period in the nineteenth century when railroads would "buy" entire state legislatures. Nonetheless, flagrantly corrupt behavior by state politicians has persisted in a number of states. For example, when Spiro Agnew resigned from the vice-presidency in 1973, he admitted that, while governor of Maryland, he had accepted payments from contractors who wanted business from the state; had used some of the money for private purposes; and had not paid taxes on the income. He explained: "My acceptance of contributions was part of a long-established pattern of political fund raising in the state."[2] Apparently the pattern persisted, for in 1977 Maryland governor Marvin Mandel was convicted of mail fraud and racketeering for helping friends with legislation favorable to a racetrack they owned. Similar practices have surfaced from time to time in the Illinois legislature, and in 1969 evidence was uncovered of illegal conflicts of interest involving members of the state supreme court. Many other states have gone through periodic scandals because legislatures have received payoffs from lobbyists, or because state officials have connived with business interests to give them favorable tax treatment.

Examples of dubious practices are found in profusion at the local level. Here, again, matters are not as bad as they used to be. The old political party machines in the big cities were lubricated by graft. George Washington Plunkett, the boss of the New York City political organization known as Tammany Hall, saw nothing wrong with this as long as it was "honest" as against "dishonest" graft. Honest graft provided a profit to the politician but no loss to the public, since the issue was which among equally competent and equally priced companies or banks would handle the city's business. Dishonest graft involved paying a politician for an arrangement that cost the city more than it should spend.

Today there is not much left of the party machines, the indulgent attitude toward honest graft is gone, and the prevailing ethos calls for honesty and efficiency in government rather than the system of personal favors on which the old machines flourished. Even so, in many cities, large and small, elected and appointed officials have been convicted of receiving money for awarding a city contract or for supporting legislation favoring a particular business. In some instances the pattern of graft has extended into the very agencies that are mandated to enforce the laws—the police departments—and communities have been wracked periodically with scandals indicating that a high proportion of the police are taking bribes.

Why are conflicts of interest and unqualified corruption even more serious problems at the state and local levels than in the federal government? The answer is to be found in a combination of low pay, high expenses, and strong temptation. Running for office costs money, sometimes a great deal of money. And the people who hold local offices are called upon to make decisions that may make the difference between large profits and bankruptcy for private interests.

This opens the way for a number of possible scenarios. For example, the owner of a new enterprise that needs governmental approval, such as a race track, approaches a legislator and offers to set aside some stock in the enterprise—to be held anonymously for the official and issued at a price much lower than it will be worth when sold to the public. Or a member of a city council or zoning board approves a land development and is given an opportunity to buy into the development on highly advantageous terms—that is, if the public official is not already a part of the business.

Then, too, since public officials generally cannot afford to give up their regular profession or business, and since all but a few state legislatures and local councils have very small staffs, the expertise of the members must be used to the full. The result is that banking committees are made up mostly of bankers, insurance committees of insurance agents, agricultural committees of farmers, and so on. This means that legislators must sometimes pass judgment on matters in which they or their companies have a direct interest—and commonly they do not disqualify themselves because of their special interest.

The consequence of all this is that in many states and communities, giving public officials a piece of the action has become part of the normal cost of doing business. Some businesspeople resent this, wish they could operate differently, but feel compelled to go along with the prevailing practice. Others feel no compunction, and have refined the art of corrupting government as their means of getting ahead of the competition. Within the latter group are organized criminal elements that use government to provide an entree into legitimate businesses in which funds obtained through illegal activities can be invested. In 1967 a federal Task Force on Organized Crime declared that this represented a problem of great seriousness for government in America. While admitting that it was impossible to determine precisely the extent of the corruption of public officials by organized crime, the Task Force insisted that "in recent years some local governments have been dominated by criminal groups. Today, no large city is completely controlled by organized crime, but in many there is a considerable degree of corruption."[3] Evidently Newark was one of these, for in 1970 a former mayor of the city was convicted of extortion and conspiring to extort money from an engineering firm doing business with the city while he was mayor; and among those convicted with him were two men reputed to be leaders of an organized crime syndicate. There was also considerable evidence suggesting that in New Jersey organized criminal activities were not limited to the municipalities but reached all the way up to the state legislature.

This is not to say that all or most of the decisions made by state and local governments are tainted. Vast numbers of contracts are awarded by scrupulously conducted competitive bidding. Elaborate procedures are established for the auditing of public funds; and rules and regulations to guard against improper expenditures are often so rigorous that they promote inefficiency and long delays. Nor does the fact that legislators take campaign contributions from lobbyists necessarily mean they will accept that lobbyist's advice.

Moreover, the national revulsion against Watergate has produced a wave of reform in state government. Since 1972 over 20 states have passed new laws requiring lobbyists to disclose their activities and their contributions. The model in this respect is California's Political Reform Act of 1974, approved by the voters in a referendum by more than two to one. This law not only requires disclosure by lobbyists but sharply restricts their spending. Although their organizations may make campaign contributions, the lobbyists themselves may not. Even more drastic is the requirement that lobbyists not make gifts, including food and drink, to any one state official totaling more than $10 a month—enough for "two hamburgers and a coke"—in place of the more sumptuous lunches and dinners over which many legislators frequently conducted their business with lobbyists.

The Fiscal Squeeze

It has become increasingly difficult for state and local governments to find the money to pay for the job they are expected to do. People in the communities ask for more services at constantly rising levels of quality and sophistication. Yet the tax base has not been expanding proportionately.

In the communities the prime source of revenues is the property tax, much of which is levied on private residences. This tax has three shortcomings. First, it is a "regressive" tax: it tends to cost low- and middle-income people a higher proportion of their incomes than upper-income people. Second, it causes inequality not only between individuals but also between localities. In particular, the great disparities in the quality of school systems, which are funded in large part by property taxes, results in large measure from the fact that affluent communities have a much larger residential tax base than poor communities. Third, rising taxes on property—and the rate of increase in some parts of the country had become staggering by the mid-1970s—was forcing many people, especially the elderly, to sell their homes. As a result, there is deepening resistance to further increases in the property tax, and a high proportion of bond issues placed on the ballot to

ENTERING
BELLSVILLE
SETTLED   1762
INCORPORATED 1801
BANKRUPT   1975

Drawing by D. Fraden; © 1975 The New Yorker Magazine, Inc.

provide for expanded government services have been rejected by the voters because eventually they might lead to more taxes.

Cities, counties, and school districts have therefore searched for other kinds of revenues but have had only limited success because of voter resistance or because their communities simply do not have the resources. So they have turned to the state governments and demanded that the states assume a greater share of the costs of local schools, welfare, and other services traditionally associated with the communities. The states have responded up to a point out of their expanding revenues from sales taxes, income taxes, and a variety of other sources of income. But the states have their own ever-growing responsibilities, too, in such fields as highways, conservation, higher education, and so on; and state governors and legislatures have been reluctant to increase state taxes sufficiently to provide for substantial property tax relief at the local level.

So the states have joined the communities in looking to Washington for help. As we have seen, this help has been forthcoming in massive proportions. Yet, far from satisfying state and local officials, federal aid evoked from them two kinds of criticism. First, they argued that Washington's help was not nearly adequate. Second, they complained that too many strings were attached to it. Sometimes the money came in the form of *categorical* grants, limited to a very specific area and subject to tight regulation from Washington. Otherwise funds came as *block* grants, covering somewhat broader fields and less rigidly controlled. But whether categorical or block, the grants generated constant criticisms that getting and spending the money involved an enormous amount of red tape and that federal bureaucrats were always trying to tell people in the communities how to run their own affairs.

Revenue sharing.   In response to this criticism the federal government developed a program of *revenue sharing*—giving to the states and localities a proportion of federal tax revenues to be spent by them as they saw fit, essentially without strings. This idea was first given currency in Washington in the early 1960s by Walter Heller, President Kennedy's chairperson of the Council of Economic Advisers. However, no action was taken on it until Richard Nixon declared after his election in 1968 that one of the goals of his presidency was to shift as much power as possible from Washington to the states and communities, and that revenue sharing was to be a principal device for achieving this. In 1972 Congress accepted his proposal, and authorized the spending of $30 billion over a five-year period, two-thirds going to counties, cities, and towns, the other one-third to the states.

In 1976 President Ford worked out an agreement with Congress to extend the program until September 30, 1980, with a further $26 billion to be spent at the rate of about $6.8 billion a year. These monies are distributed to states and communities under complex formulas that favor the lowest-income areas and also those communities whose high tax rates indicate that they are making strong efforts to finance their own programs. Few strings are attached to the expenditure of the funds, other than the requirement that they may not be used in a way that discriminates against anyone on the basis of race, national origin, religion, sex, age, or a physical handicap.

Important though the revenue-sharing funds are, they fall far short of resolving the fiscal difficulties of the states and localities. The sum of $6.8 billion a year is a great deal of money. But per capita the contribution to the states ranges from $24.43 in Florida up to $42.86 in Mississippi, and in the cities the range is from $10.99 a person in San Diego to $43.34 in Chicago.

Trouble in metropolis.   All these problems come together in their most intense form in the nation's great metropolitan centers. The concentration of millions of people in a relatively small space has produced air and noise pollution, massive traffic tie-ups, overloaded recreational facilities, and a long catalogue of urban ailments.

But the metropolitan problem is not just a matter of numbers and congestion. A high proportion of the people who have migrated to the cities during the twentieth century have come from the poorest areas of the country—rural communities and the South—looking for jobs, the opportunities, and the services that their own communities lacked. Among these people were a great many black families. And as they moved into the heart of the cities in ever-increasing numbers, whites moved out into the suburbs. So great was the white exodus that the population of some of the biggest cities stopped increasing and by the late 1960s had actually begun to decline. Thus between 1970 and 1975 St. Louis and Cleveland lost a seventh of their population, and Minneapolis, Pittsburgh and Detroit declined by an eighth.

Those who remained included a disproportionate number of very low income people, whose needs and problems placed heavy demands on city services—welfare, health, law enforcement, and so on—but who were not able to contribute very much to the tax rolls that paid for these services. And many of those who could more easily afford to pay had moved out to the separately incorporated cities in the suburbs. Thus, even though many of these suburbanities continued to work in the city, they paid their property taxes elsewhere. The consequence of this combination of circumstances was a deterioration of the city centers, the spread of slums, the decline of investment in transportation and other city services, an increase in crime and delinquency, and, in the 1960s, the eruption of riots.

New York City: a case study.   In 1975 the accumulation of these problems brought the city of New York to the verge of bankruptcy. The city's expenses were enormous, for it provided welfare payments and an array of services to a large population of poor people—blacks, Puerto Ricans, and others; it offered a free university education on an open admissions basis; and its employee salaries and pension benefits were among the highest in the nation. Yet its revenues were depleted by the exodus of affluent families and business concerns from the city. So for years the city ran budgetary deficits, which were covered by short-term loans from whoever would lend the city money—banks, purchasers of bonds, even labor unions representing teachers and other city employees. This repeated borrowing, combined with the longer-term loans issued by the city for its construction projects, finally undermined the city's credit. New York could not borrow any more money, and for several months in 1975 the only question seemed to be exactly when the city would default on its obligations and declare bankruptcy.

The city turned to the state, and the state made it clear that any help it could give would be insufficient and that only the federal government has the resources needed to save the city. President Ford at first would have none of it. He would not consider federal aid unless New York went into bankruptcy (that is, the courts would have to declare that the city could not pay all its debts and establish how much could be paid to various creditors), and unless the city then took drastic steps to make itself solvent again. However, pressures began to build on the president and Congress to prevent bankruptcy. New York's fiscal collapse could have a grave impact on the standing of the billions of dollars invested in municipal bonds all over the country and make it difficult for cities to raise money for construction and other purposes. Moreover, New York City showed a willingness to undertake some drastic changes under the direction of the state. The Municipal Assistance Corporation ("Big Mac") was established with state backing to provide loans in the form of 10-year bonds in place of $1 billion worth of city bonds that were about to come due, and a moratorium was declared on the payment of the city bonds. New taxes were imposed on city residents by the state and the city. The city budget was cut, employees had to pick up a bigger share of pension contributions, a number of jobs were eliminated, the city university imposed tuition, and unions agreed to buy more of the city's bonds. When the city pledged to balance its budget within three years, the federal government agreed to lend it up to $2.3 billion a year through the middle of 1978 to help it meet its short-term credit needs. This seemed to resolve the problem for the time being—until in November

1976 New York's highest court declared that the moratorium on payment of the city's bonds was unconstitutional.

However, the state and the city set to work to devise an alternative plan; and the new Carter administration promised to help. So for the moment the city was saved from bankruptcy. But it is not clear that New York, still plagued by the social and economic problems that helped bring about the crisis in the first place, can put its affairs in order with a moderate amount of federal underwriting. Nor is it clear that other cities, faced with many of those same problems, can avoid stumbling into similar crises. At least seven other cities—Buffalo, Detroit, Newark, St. Louis, Boston, Cleveland, and Philadelphia—face severe financial difficulties for reasons similar to those afflicting New York.

Hope for the Future

In the long run the apparently desperate conditions of some of our major cities may take a turn for the better. The great immigration from the deprived regions of the country has almost run its course. The escalating costs of housing in the suburbs may encourage more people to stay in the cities, especially if the decaying areas of the cities can be rehabilitated through urban renewal and redevelopment, now underway in a number of communities. Since the early 1970s population growth has tended to occur in smaller and middle-sized towns rather than in the metropolitan areas, a trend that in time will relieve the big cities and suburbs of the congestion caused by population pressures. Not long ago it was customary for urbanologists to speculate that by the year 2000 half the total population of the country would be concentrated in three unbroken built-up areas: "Bos-Wash" (Boston to Washington), "Chi-Pitts" (Chicago to Pittsburgh), and "San–San" (San Francisco to San Diego). That appalling prospect now seems much less likely, and the fears that the present crises of metropolis would assume nightmarish proportions beyond all hope of solution have receded accordingly.

Just the same, the physical, social, economic, and political problems of New York, Detroit, and several other major cities are still very much with us, and the answers to their problems will not be easy to find.

Five Perspectives on Federalism

The Liberals: The Failure of Governments

Over the years the liberals have shown a general preference for federal as against state and local action. For one thing they believe that the types of programs they advocate—economic planning, national health insurance, welfare reform, and so on—can only be undertaken effectively on a national scale. Anything less must make for administrative fragmentation, excessive costs, and wide inequities from one area to another.

Second, they argue that the federal government was forced to take on more responsibilities because the states were too complacent, apathetic, and incompetent to act themselves. Liberals have been persistent critics of those deficiencies of state and local government described earlier—the archaic structures and procedures of state governments, the maze of local jurisdictions, the widespread corruption, and the failure to raise the funds to pay for needed services. And liberals believe that in considerable degree these shortcomings are the result of a failure of political will.

Governmental structures, say the liberals, are made by people and can be changed by people—if they want to urgently enough. The difficulty of producing sufficient revenues from local taxpayers is only partly a consequence of the large amounts siphoned off by the federal Internal Revenue Service. It is not indisputably true that state and local taxes cannot be increased significantly. Tax levels in the United States are still not as high as they are in some other industrialized countries. And it is absurd for the wealthier states, whose per capita income far exceeds that of any other part of the world, to cry poverty.

Although state and local government activity and spending has been increasing rapidly, there is a dearth of sound, long-range planning. State and local agencies, even more than the federal government, demonstrate the American governmental tendency to react to crises rather than to anticipate and prevent them. This syndrome is especially apparent in the cities. But the attack on the terrible and mutually reinforcing ailments that plague the cities is feeble. True, there are dazzling cultural complexes going up in some communities. Skylines are dramatically transformed by towering edifices. Shopping malls, free from the noise and threat of automobiles, are all the fashion. Some dilapidated areas are cleared by urban renewal and redevelopment plans. Yet the plight of the cities grows deeper, and the leaders of the cities' political life grow more helpless in the enveloping morass.

The central reason for this—more important than the structural and fiscal deficiencies of metropolitan government—is the fact that the desperate condition of the cities has not generated a sense of crises for the majority of the people who live in the metropolitan areas. Why is this so? Because very large numbers of people, including those who are the prime leaders of political and social opinion, do not live in the inner city but in the suburbs. There is no total sanctuary from the cities' problems, even in the suburbs, but the intensity is usually diminished as one moves away from the central city. Crime is everywhere; but the crimes of violence are mostly on the other side of town. Poor people and black people are more or less excluded from middle-class communities, and their children go to different schools than do those of the suburban whites. Public transportation systems have been deteriorating. But the majority in most cities use their own automobiles; and a system built around the automobile makes only feeble attempts to attract people to alternative forms of travel.

Consequently, there is no great dynamic for change among the great numbers of urban dwellers who live outside the inner cities. The suburban middle classes are provoked into involvement only when something threatens to change the "character of the neighborhood"—a zoning variance, a proposed park or highway, or a new housing development (especially where this might include low-income people, and thus racial and ethnic minorities). And when the crisis of the city finally forces itself into the consciousness of the middle class through riots and spreading crime, the reaction is not to deal with the causes of the crisis but to subordinate everything else to the restoration of "law and order."

To a degree, this liberal dissatisfaction with the performance of state and local government has been modified in the last few years. They note that a number of states have been improving their governmental structures and taking steps to combat corruption. They are pleased that in some cases states and localities have moved ahead of the federal government in protecting the environment, in legalizing abortion, in asserting the rights of homosexuals, and so on. And faced with the increasing conservatism of the Supreme Court under Chief Justice Burger, liberal groups have turned increasingly to the state courts for redress of their grievances.

Yet, on balance, the liberals' judgment is that the states and localities have failed to undertake imaginative social experimentation. On the contrary, conservatives long used the slogan "states' rights" to preserve racial segregation in the South and business privileges everywhere against pressures for change from the federal government. If some states led the way in legitimizing abortion, others spearheaded the attack on the Supreme Court's decision upholding the right to abortion. And the most pernicious examples of censorship and persecution of unpopular views are to be found in local communities. Generally speaking, then, liberals have tended to see the states as supporting narrow, provincial attitudes against the forces of progress.

Remedies.   Liberals offer a number of proposals for improving the performance of the states and communities. First, they favor strengthening the executive branch of government. States and localities, they believe, have made a fetish of reproducing the separation of powers and checks and balances of the federal government. Liberals argue that there is less need locally for constraints on powers, for there is much less power to abuse than at the national level. And when the governmental structures become too divided, the results are inertia instead of action and confused instead of clear lines of responsibility. So liberals would like to see governors and mayors given more authority to provide effective leadership.

Next, liberals advocate a revival of the two-party system in local politics. They do not propose that we go back to the old party machines, for essentially these ran one-party systems. But the nonpartisan politics of the West is unacceptable to them, and they advocate two-party competition as the best means of presenting clear alternatives and securing broader participation—for voting turnout tends to be highest in those states where the two parties are both strong.

They urge, too, the consolidation of jurisdictions, leading toward metropolitan, county, and even regional government in place of the present chaos of overlapping and fragmented governing bodies.

Beyond this, there are two contrasting strands in liberal thought. James MacGregor Burns argues for regional agencies of the federal government, which would work directly under the supervision of the president's office and be charged with the task of integrating all governmental policies in such priority areas as poverty and the environment. Each regional agency would be headed by one person, representing the president, and given the power to get the job done. Existing agencies would continue to operate, handling important administrative responsibilities for the regional agencies and maintaining their role in nonpriority areas. But "the task of the federal agency would be, through leadership, management, persuasion, cajolery, financial inducements, and legal authority, to mass all the local agencies behind clearly defined goals."[4] What Burns is arguing for, in other words, is "the localization of federal power."

Other liberals, still traumatized by the abuses of presidential power and the unresponsiveness of the federal bureaucracy, give more attention to the cultivation of a sense of local community and neighborhood control. They have been impressed by the demands of blacks, Chicanos, and other minorities for a decentralization of power that would give them a larger role in the local decision-making process.

Still, lending support to such proposals catches liberals in a conflict of values. Local control of schools, for example, a key demand of some black organizations, could reinforce and legitimize racial separation. And decentralization would bring still further fragmentation of government, thereby making rational area-wide planning impossible.

So liberals are groping toward a reconciliation of these two contrasting strands and they believe that the answer is to have much larger units of government for some services, such as the control of air and water pollution, and smaller units for services whose impact is primarily at the neighborhood level.

The liberals' solutions to the fiscal problems of state and local governments include stepped-up federal aid and a more vigorous and equitable effort by the state and local units to raise more money themselves. With respect to federal support, liberals have been less than enthusiastic about revenue sharing. From the beginning they were afraid that disbursing funds without conditions to state and local governments would shield them from the consequences of their failings and help them escape the need for reform. Moreover, much of the money might be wasted through inefficiency, duplication, and corruption. As revenue sharing went into effect, some of these fears were confirmed. Many of the smaller communities and suburban areas were devoting their windfalls to such projects as building city hall offices and even remodeling a golf course. And this was money that might have gone to the areas of greatest need, the big cities, which complained that whatever they gained in revenue sharing was offset by cuts in other federal grants imposed by the Nixon administration.

As time went on, the number of examples of frivolous uses of revenue-sharing funds declined, and with the mayors of the big cities applying pressure for a major increase in revenue sharing, the liberals slowly came around to a grudging acceptance of the program. However, it is still not their preferred approach.

They would rather see a two-pronged strategy of federal help to the states and cities. First, some services now within the domain of state and local government should be wholly or partially federalized. The patchwork welfare program, for example, should be replaced by a federally guaranteed minimum income. This might be supplemented from state and local sources, but a large part of the welfare burden should be lifted from the homeowner and made a charge against the federal budget. Second, grants-in-aid should be increased. Education, health, transportation, housing, and other problem areas are all in desperate need of further infusions of federal funds.

As for the strings attached to federal funds, these are not always harmful. Certainly we should get rid of the red tape resulting from excessive congressional caution or bureaucratic fussiness. But sometimes federal conditions for receiving money may be the means by which local officials are forced to face up to the shortcomings of their governmental structures and practices. For example, local governments have been organizing regional planning associations because federal agencies refused to give them funding for various urban programs unless they demonstrated their ability to cooperate across their boundary lines.

By using this combination of federalizing some services and providing grants to states and cities to achieve specific purposes, the liberals believe that it is possible to restore New York and other major cities to solvency. In the liberals' view there is no question but that the federal government has a responsibility to come to the aid of the cities. Each of them has had to carry enormous burdens not of their own making but the result of great national forces. In the case of New York this is especially true. New York City has been the refuge of successive waves of immigrants, mostly poor, from Europe, from the American South, from Puerto Rico. Its alleged extravagances have consisted of trying to provide schooling, higher education, welfare, and other public services to needy people who could not possibly afford to pay enough in taxes to cover them.

So increased federal aid to the cities is one of the liberals' top priorities. However, liberals also believe that state and local governments should be doing much more to expand revenues from their own populations. The income tax can be used much more fully at the subnational levels of government. Business corporations should be required to pay their fair share of local services. The practice of underassessing large landholders should be stopped. In sum, the liberals are suggesting that state and local governments must show much more imagination and initiative in expanding their revenue base, even though in so doing they will face the entrenched opposition of powerful interests—business corporations, large landowners, and so on.

The Radical Left: More Power Elites

As we saw in our discussion of the federal bureaucracies, the old, communist left focuses on the need for highly centralized power until the revolution has been fully accomplished and the power is taken by the masses. It is the new left that argues for the greatest possible degree of decentralization to the smallest possible unit of government. However, the new left does not want merely to shift power to the existing structures of state and local government. They believe that these structures are just as repressive as the federal government, for they replicate, many times over, the national power elite.

Thus in Montana, Anaconda, the great copper-producing corporation, dominates the economic life of the state. Delaware has been described as being almost completely controlled by the du Ponts,[5] and this view was reinforced when Pierre du Pont was elected governor of the state in 1976. Few Texas politicians challenge the claims of oil. In many other states business is ranked higher than other interests in its ability to put its stamp on public policy by lobbying legislatures, working closely with regulatory agencies, financing election campaigns, and so on.

As for the cities, C. Wright Mills argued that an upper social class, a monied aristocracy, was very much in evidence there. Floyd Hunter, in his study of Atlanta, Georgia, found that business and financial leaders made most of the key policy decisions for the community, leaving these to be communicated and implemented by a second level drawn from government, education, the professions, church, and civil groups.[6] Business leaders were found to be the dominant figures in a study of decision making in Dallas.[7] And many towns with populations ranging from 20,000 to 50,000 are dominated by "non-political persons or coalitions between such persons and elected officials," businesspeople being the most common of the "non-political persons."[8]

Of course, the big corporations do not always bother with the relatively petty affairs of local communities. Although their leaders live and their headquarters are located in the communities, their interests are elsewhere. All they are concerned about locally is to secure the best possible tax situation for themselves and their corporations and the maximum services from state and local government at the least possible outlay.

Remedies.   What can be done to change this bleak situation? The new left sees no hope in the liberals' proposals. The liberals call for stronger mayors and governors, but there is too much power there already for the left. Revitalizing the two-party system merely gives a bigger role to institutions that offer no real alternatives to the present power structures and policies. Federal aid is mostly controlled at the state and local levels by groups that use it to reinforce their own position. Instead, say the left, we must move the action to the grass roots. Power must go to the people; and this means that the people must be brought together in groups small enough to make possible effective participation by everyone. The answer, then, is community control, exercised through the smallest units of the community, the neighborhoods.

The process must begin by getting people together on issues of concern to the neighborhood—the quality of the schools, the placing of street lights, and so on. This will give people practice at the art of civic dialogue; and out of this experience the people can go on to the task of transforming mere discussion into decision-making procedures. From a network of these neighborhood forums and structures can come a consideration of broader local and regional issues. In fact, says Marcus Raskin, "there is no reason . . . why national budgets could not be voted locally in assemblies, or why the people should not demand that the largest corporations begin a transformation toward control by communities of workers and consumers."[9]

Some steps have already been taken to build popular participation in the communities to challenge the existing order. Poor people have been organized in some cities to apply pressure for better housing, improved health facilities, and more jobs. Blacks and others have demanded, and sometimes achieved, a shift of power over local schools from citywide boards to community groups. In some cases candidates of the left have won local offices. In 1971 three radical left candidates won election to the Berkeley, California, city council. And, although the left lost ground in subsequent Berkeley elections, they did have some measure of success in making the police more sensitive to the concerns of students and minorities in their communities.

Others who were leaders of the peace and civil rights movement in the 1960s, and still hold more or less radical views, have been successful in electoral politics. Two have been mayors of university towns—Austin, Texas, and Madison, Wisconsin. Another sixties leftist leader was the principal mover behind ACORN (Association of Community Organizations for Reform Now), which started in Arkansas by organizing poor people to deal with such problems as public housing conditions, school lunches, and street lights; next successfully backed several candidates for city councils and school boards; and then expanded its work into other states. A Chicano group, La Raza Unida, gained control of Zavala County, Texas, in 1975 after organizing Chicano families in weekly town-meeting gatherings and winning city council and school board elections. There were enough of these people, in fact, to lead to the formation of the National Conference on Alternative State and Local Public Policies, whose third annual meeting in 1977 attracted about 450 people from all over the country.

The left recognize that there are strong resistances to their ideas, and that they face a long, slow, uphill struggle. But they believe that they must begin among the people in their neighborhoods if the present remote, depersonalized institutions are to be replaced by a society built upon the principle of community.

The Conservatives:
Federalism and Limited Government

Support of state and local governments as against the federal government is an essential part of the conservatives' creed. There are three reasons for this. First, the power of state and local governments sets limits to the power of the central government. This was what the Founding Fathers intended. The division of powers between the national and state governments was as important to the framers in preventing a dangerous concentration of authority as was the separation of powers among the branches of the federal government.

Second, the federal system encourages diversity, the varying expressions of regional and local interests and cultures, as against the kind of bureaucratized uniformity the federal government seeks to impose nationwide.

Third, conservatives find the most receptivity for their values in local communities. It is there that private property is most solidly established in the form of home ownership. Nothing contributes more effectively to conservative attitudes than ownership of a home. The local community also provides the focal point for church, for ethnic identity, for family; and along with these go the values that protect against the peddlars of pornography and other debauchers of our traditions. These are the attitudes that the liberals scorn as narrow, provincial, and unsophisticated; to conservatives they are the core values of Western civilization.

Conservatives fear, however, that the virtues inherent in the states and localities are being overwhelmed by federal money and power. As James Kilpatrick puts it:

> If the central government can aid our disabled, and pension our old people, and succour our illegitimate children; if it can fill our fish ponds and level our slums; if it can build our highways and lay our sewers and vaccinate our children and finance our college students, it can dominate our lives in such a way that freedom is lost altogether.[10]

But this is exactly what is happening. On the one hand, there is the expansion of the power of the presidency and the federal bureaucracy. On the other, we have suffered from the tortured constructions of the Supreme Court that "incorporated" federal power into the sphere of the states and interpreted the interstate commerce clause to cover almost every kind of business activity in blithe disregard of the clear meaning of the Tenth Amendment to the Constitution. So the intent of the framers that federal power be limited by state power has been ignored. "Only power restrains power," says Russell Kirk, "and impotent state and local 'governments' that have been deprived, over the years, of effective decision-making must end unable to hold in check the force of the total state."[11]

Consequently, conservatives were pleased when President Nixon in 1969 called for a redistribution of power between the federal government and the states: "After a third of a century of power flowing from the people and the states to Washington, it is time for a new Federalism in which power, funds, and responsibility will flow from Washington to the states and the people." This new federalism, he said, was to be an essential aspect of his redirecting of government and power in America.

On the face of it, then, his revenue-sharing plan should have been received enthusiastically by conservatives. In fact, their response was lukewarm. They conceded that it was superior to categorical grants because it placed the authority to spend money closer to the people from whom it came, and it reduced the power of the swollen bureaucracies in Washington. But what conservatives are looking for is not a mere reshuffling of governmental authority to spend tax money but a sharp reduction of government spending and taxing. And during the past 30 years or so, state and local spending has increased at an even faster rate than federal spending. Altogether close to a third of the total output of the economy is now going through the hands of one agency of government or another. So the real issue is not how to achieve a proper distribution between federal and other levels of government but how to scale the total down before we are all working for the government.

Ronald Reagan confronted this issue squarely when he was governor of California. In 1973 he proposed an amendment to the state constitution which, in addition to offering an immediate substantial cut in the state income tax, would have placed an arbitrary limit on the total amount of revenue that the state could raise in taxes each year, setting this limit at a slightly smaller percentage of the state's income from individual taxes each year. The governor claimed that his proposal would save Californians $118 billion in the next 15 years. The proposal was rejected by the voters by 54 to 46 percent. Still, large numbers of people had expressed support for a major change in policy, and conservatives would like to see this kind of change adopted by states throughout the country—and, even more important, in Washington.

Implicit in this approach is the assumption that the liberals' assessment of the job that government needs to do is fundamentally wrong. In the eyes of the liberals, more, not less, money needs to be spent, and their principal evidence for this is the terrible plight of our urban communities. As the conservatives look at the urban communities, they recognize that they contain serious problems and that the existence of huge, segregated ghettos represents a danger to the health of the society. But they are skeptical of the "urban crisis" rhetoric beloved by the liberals.

First, the conditions of the poor generally, and the blacks specifically, are not as bad as is often assumed. Segregation is partly a result of free choice and self-selection. Many poor people find community, support, or excitement in the slum. Nor is it true that the ghettos consist primarily of slums; they contain a wide range of living standards, some of them very attractive. Moreover, there is a steady trend toward the improvement of living conditions among the poor and throughout the ghettos. The problem is that regardless of how much conditions improve, they cannot keep up with the reckless increase in expectations encouraged by the liberals.

Second, when we shift our gaze from the ghettos, we find that for most urban dwellers life is far from intolerable. In fact, says Edward C. Banfield:

By any conceivable measure of material welfare the present generation of urban Americans is, on the whole, better off than any other large group of people has ever been anywhere. What is more, there is every reason to expect that the general level of comfort and convenience will continue to rise at an even more rapid rate through the foreseeable future.[12]

So it is entirely understandable if the suburbs fail to become galvanized into action by proposals to change the character of their communities. People who find the quality of their lives satisfying will usually resist having change imposed upon them. This is true even in the ghettos, where there is growing resistance to the kind of urban renewal programs which, in the name of progress, move people out of the communities they know and have become attached to.[13]

Thus, although conservatives recognize that all is not well in our urban communities, they argue that the liberals' prescriptions for changes in governmental structures cannot make much difference. Government is not the key, and we should stop experimenting with the kind of programs—urban renewal, public housing, antipoverty projects, and so on—that arouse expectations that cannot be fulfilled and encourage militant demands for change. We should respect the patterns of suburban and ghetto life. We should allow the workings of the economic system to continue the process of raising the standard of living for most of the people. For those whose cultural or intellectual handicaps prevent their participating in the general advancement, we should, perhaps, provide a minimum income. And to cope with the persistent threat to the peace of the community (the black as well as the white community) represented by high crime rates, we should give the police and the courts the authority they need to act firmly.[14]

The conservatives and the crisis of New York.   But what do conservatives say when these general concepts come up against a specific, apparently desperate crisis such as the threatened bankruptcy of New York City in 1975? Their answer is that the city should have been compelled to face the consequences of its disastrous policies. One New York City administration after another has tried to win votes by giving in to the demands of powerful municipal unions, minority groups, and others for more and more money. New York City outlays in every field—police and fire, health and hospitals, education, welfare, pensions, debt interest—have been greater, in some cases several times greater, than those of other major cities. Total outlays per capita in 1973–74 were:[15]

New York	$1446
Los Angeles	875
Philadelphia	731
Chicago	715
Detroit	693
Atlanta	650

Year after year the resulting deficits were hidden by financial sleight of hand. At last, there was no more room for manipulation, and bankruptcy loomed. President Ford was right when he told the city that it would be a mistake for the federal government to bail it out. He was wrong when, fearing widespread financial repercussions from a default, he changed his mind, rationalizing his action on the basis of some inadequate promises by the city. "Some individuals and institutions would of course be seriously hurt by New York's default . . . ," said Milton Friedman. "But the overall effect would be small, and there is no chance that it would cause a serious financial panic." Default would finally shock the city into the needed reforms. Nothing else would work. Every other proposal "founders on the very fallacy that has brought New York to its present condition—the belief that it is desirable to do good with someone else's money—in this case, that of taxpayers outside New York. The rest of us deserve the same fate if we do not learn this lesson from New York's experience."[16]

The Radical Right

As we saw in Chapter 8 in discussing the federal bureaucracy, the radical right has been passionately opposed to the expansion of the federal government, seeing in it the all-but-final transformation of the United States into a left-wing dictatorship. Yet even at the state and local levels they see the same trends toward socialism. New York is only the most vicious example of the combination of ruinous government action and the collapse of traditional values associated with big city life. Other major eastern cities are embarked on the same course of trying to do for people what they should be doing for themselves, and leading the way to socialism by a spineless surrender to the demands of big labor, minorities, the media, and the intellectual establishment.

Only in the South, the Southwest, parts of the West, and in smaller communities in the Midwest is there still hope of building pockets of resistance. There the right can lead campaigns against the selection of subversive or obscene textbooks by state and local boards of education; against pornographic movies, performances, and books; against the fluoridation of water; and so on.

There, too, the battle against high taxes can be waged most effectively. This, to the radical right, is the most crucial battle of all. Revenue sharing is not the answer. As the right-wing commentator, Gary Allen, sees it, revenue sharing is an instrument of further centralization.

> The money must first go from the states to Washington before it can be shared. . . . As soon as the states and local governments get hooked on the federal funds, the controls will be put on just as they were in education and agriculture. Every field the government takes over it first subsidizes. You can't decentralize government by centralizing the tax collections.[17]

The Reagan plan in California was attractive to the right as far as it went. But they felt that it did not go far enough, for the governor claimed that, even with his proposed limits, the state budget could well expand in the next 15 years from its 1973–74 level of $9.3 billion to about $27 billion a year. To the radical right, a $27-billion-a-year state government is no alternative to socialism. So the right has supported a variety of propositions on the ballot in various states to freeze state spending, limit employment in state government, require a majority of all registered voters for any state or local action that would lead to an increase in taxes, limit the tax rate by constitutional mandate, and reject federal aid.

The radical right, too, know that their struggle is uphill, for control of the system by the federal government, working as the agent of the Rockefellers and other "insiders," is already far advanced. But successes in local communities here and there can be used as bridgeheads from which the counterattack can be launched.

The Centrists

Essays on federalism by centrist writers are usually cast in glowing terms. They speak with great admiration of the Founding Fathers' prescription for assigning sufficient authority at the center while still maintaining sources of initiative and independence at other locations in the system. This does not mean that centrists are complacent about the performance of state and local government in America. Like the liberals, they express concern about the multiplication of jurisdictions, the confusion of decision-making responsibility, the inefficiency and corruption found in many units of state and local government, and the fiscal dilemma of the subnational governments. Still, their prognosis of state and city government is much less gloomy than that of the liberals.

As centrists see it, the shortcomings of state and local governments do not prevent them from performing quite well in a number of respects. They provide a vast array of excellent public services. The special districts may be confusing to voters, but they supply clean water, prevent floods, and develop parklands, usually with a high degree of efficiency. State governments have funded fine systems of higher education, developed impressive water and highway systems, and given local governments indispensable financial help. Moreover, they are improving their structures and performance. State legislatures have become more representative since the Supreme Court's reapportionment decisions. They are modernizing their constitutions, and increasing their expertise by hiring skilled staffs and consultants; similar trends are operating in the cities.

As for the alleged public apathy about local government, surveys indicate that, on the contrary, there is a greater understanding of policy matters and more of a sense of being able to make an impact on local decisions than on national affairs.[18] It is true that this is not reflected in voting figures, for local elections usually produce rather poor turnouts. However, low levels of voting locally might be an indication not that voters are turned off by the system but rather that they are reasonably well satisfied with the services provided and cannot become excited about efforts to stir up controversy in election campaigns.

The centrists concede that the biggest problem faced by state and localities is the difficulty of raising enough money to pay for government services. Centrists sympathize with the resistance of taxpayers to the heavy increases in the property and other taxes resulting from the expansion of state and local government spending, and they see New York City as providing a timely warning of the dangers resulting from imprudence and irresponsibility at any level of government. Still, centrists do not support the proposals of conservatives and radical rightists to set harsh, arbitrary limits to taxes and government spending.

Remedies and a defense of federalism.   The centrist solutions to the fiscal problem of state and local governments are more moderate than these conservative proposals. Thus they look for reforms that would shift some of the burden from property taxes to income, sales, and other kinds of taxes.

Centrists also recognize the need for a moderate expansion of federal aid to states and cities; and they particularly like revenue sharing. In the centrist's view, the acceptance of revenue sharing represented the triumph of reason and moderation over established interests. When Nixon first presented the proposal to Congress, it encountered strong opposition. Many members of Congress disliked the idea of having to bear the onus of imposing taxes on constituents but giving the credit for spending the money to other units of government. Big city mayors were afraid that, if the money were channeled through the state houses, not much of it would get to the cities. Civil rights groups pointed out that, if no strings whatever were attached, the money could be used by southern states for segregated facilities in contravention of federal civil rights laws.

The problems were worked out by the process of negotiation and compromise that characterizes the American system. The fears of the mayors were allayed by establishing a formula that ensured that two-thirds of the money would go to counties, cities, and towns. The provisions of the civil rights laws were made a requirement of revenue sharing. The reluctance of members of Congress was overcome by the sheer logic of the plan and by the pressure of state and local officials who were desperate for a supplement to their funds and frustrated by the endless red tape and haggling involved in categorical grants-in-aid. It was time for some devolution of responsibility from the federal bureaucracies to state and local agencies, and revenue sharing was a creative means of setting this process in motion. Despite the complaints of the liberals and another extended debate in Congress in 1976, the extension of the program until 1980 was a clear recognition of its merits as a constructive solution to the problems facing the federal system.

Finally, the centrists defend federalism against the charge of the radical left that the federal division of powers has become meaningless because a power elite operates at every level of American government. Centrists agree that in the second half of the nineteenth century some state governments were almost totally controlled by railroad and other business interests. But no state government in America today can be accurately described as a mere appendage of one or more business corporations. Even in Delaware the power of the du Ponts has not prevented the senators and congressmen from voting against the high tariffs that presumably would be advocated by du Pont to protect its products from foreign competition.[19] And in Montana it has been possible for a politician to build a political career out of opposition to Anaconda, which in recent years has limited its intervention in politics to those matters of direct concern to its economic interests.[20] Strong competition to business interests is provided by labor in some states, especially in Michigan. And in states whose economy is not dependent on one or a small number of industries, competition among business groups to influence public policy is more common than a united business coalition.

Among studies of power structures in cities the finding of concentrated power seems to be the exception. Dahl found a highly diverse system of decision making with leadership shifting with the issue. Business and finance, "far from being a ruling group, are simply one of the many groups out of which individuals sporadically emerge to influence the politics and acts of city officials."[21] As for the big cities, it appears that most of them are ruled "not by a sinister power elite lurking behind the arras, but by the men who [hold] formal political office and power."[22] It may be that, if the business and financial leaders of the cities made up their minds to run their communities, they would be able to do so. But for a variety of reasons—their policies are nationally rather than locally determined; they live in the suburbs rather than in the cities; they do not want to attract community hostility by the heavyhanded exercise of influence—they have rarely chosen to transform their potential power into actual control. Thus, in Chicago, business leaders have been criticized not for running the city but for not accepting their civic responsibilities fully enough, leaving power in the hands of the late Mayor Daley's machine.[23]

This evidence fails to support a generalization that state and local governments are firmly in the grip of power elites. There are examples of business and financial interests being the prime force in some areas; and in most sizable communities their interests are not strongly represented in the policy-making councils. Still, the patterns of power below the federal level seem to be varied and in many states and communities come much closer to the pluralistic than the power-elite model.[24]

Conclusion

Despite the fact that most of this book is concerned with our national government, this chapter has reminded us that it would be a mistake to identify government in America with Washington, D.C. The decisions made by more than 38,000 territorial governments, and 40,000 special districts in our states and localities, touch the lives of our people in innumerable ways. Where there are so many governments making so many decisions, there are bound to be problems. In the case of the states and cities the main problems relate to citizen apathy, jurisdictional complexity, corruption, and finances. With respect to most of these problems some improvements have been made in recent years. The centrists find these improvements impressive—more so than the other four perspectives do.

Even the centrists, however, do not claim that there is no trouble ahead. There are two areas that continue to give cause for concern, both rooted in the problems of the big cities. The first is race relations. Since 1968 there have been no major riots. But tensions persist and sometimes erupt into violence (as in the orgy of looting that broke out during a New York City blackout in 1977). This topic we shall defer for much fuller treatment in Chapter 12, but its importance in relation to the future of the cities and of the federal system cannot be overstated.

The other ominous problem of the cities is, as we have emphasized, the growing danger of running out of money, so vividly illustrated by the case of New York City. As a result of strenuous efforts by city, state, and then federal governments, the incredible question of what would happen if a giant city declared bankruptcy was at least postponed, and President Carter (whose election margin of 675,000 votes in New York City secured his victory in the state, and thus in the country) promised to be more forthcoming than Gerald Ford had been. Still, there are several other cities that might get into line behind New York City asking for the same kind of help; and Carter has promised to balance the federal budget by 1981.

Maybe it will all work out. In the early 1970s some studies suggested that deficits in state and local budgets might soon disappear. This happy prospect would be brought about by a reduction in spending on education because of the declining birth rate and the leveling off of welfare expenditures. Now the predictions have become gloomy again, and the experts emphasize inflation, the rising costs of energy, the enormous financial burden of public employees' pension plans, and the incessant demand for more and better public services. With fashions in predictions changing so drastically and so rapidly, it is possible that the great New York City bankruptcy scare will soon be looked back on as a vastly overblown problem. But it is also possible that the 1975 incident will come to be seen as the prelude to a disaster engulfing a number of major cities, deeply affecting the total national economy, and thus constituting a great crisis of American federalism. So the question still looms: Can states and cities govern themselves, or will their dependence on Washington become so complete as to reduce the principle of the federal division of powers to an empty slogan?

Notes and References

1.   See Morton Grodzins, "The Federal System" in *Goals for Americans: Report of the President's Commission on National Goals* (Englewood Cliffs, N.J.: Prentice-Hall, Inc., 1960).

2.   Statement by Spiro T. Agnew, October 10, 1973.

3.   *Organized Crime*, Task Force on Organized Crime, The President's Commission

on Law Enforcement and Administration of Justice (Washington, D.C.: Government Printing Office, 1967), p. 6.

4.   James MacGregor Burns, *Uncommon Sense* (New York: Harper & Row, Publishers, 1972), p. 134.

5.   John Gunther, *Inside USA* (New York: Harper & Row, Publishers, 1951), p. 678.

6.   Floyd Hunter, *Community Power Structure* (Chapel Hill, N.C.: University of North Carolina Press, 1953).

7.   Carol Estes Thometz, *The Decision-Makers: The Power Structure of Dallas*, rev. ed. (Dallas, Tex.: Southern Methodist University Press, 1963).

8.   Scott Greer, "The Shaky Future of Local Government," *Psychology Today*, August 1968, p. 66.

9.   Marcus Raskin, *Notes on the Old System: To Transform American Politics* (New York: David McKay Company, Inc., 1974), pp. 148–49.

10.   James Jackson Kilpatrick, "The Case for 'States' Rights," in Robert A. Goldwin, *A Nation of States* (Chicago: Rand McNally & Company, 1961), p. 103.

11.   Russell Kirk, "The Prospects for Territorial Democracy in America," in Goldwin, *A Nation of States*, p. 52.

12.   Edward C. Banfield, *The Unheavenly City* (Boston: Little, Brown and Company, 1970), pp. 3–4.

13.   See Martin Anderson, *The Federal Bulldozer: A Critical Analysis of Urban Renewal* (Cambridge, Mass.: The MIT Press, 1965).

14.   See Banfield, *The Unheavenly City*, pp. 245–246.

15.   Adapted from *Newsweek,* August 4, 1975, p. 24, and U.S. Bureau of the Census: Department of Commerce.

16.   *Newsweek*, November 17, 1975, p. 90.

17.   Gary Allen, *None Dare Call It Conspiracy* (Rossmoor, Calif.: Concord Press, 1971), p. 117.

18.   See Robert A. Dahl, *Pluralist Democracy in the United States* (Chicago: Rand McNally and Company, 1967), pp. 198–201.

19.   Raymond A. Bauer, Ithiel de Sola Pool, and Lewis A. Dexter, *American Business and Public Policy* (New York: Atherton Press, 1963), pp. 265–76.

20.   Thomas R. Dye and L. Harmon Zeigler, *The Irony of Democracy*, (Belmont, Calif.: Wadsworth Publishing Co., Inc., 1970), p. 277.

21.   Robert Dahl, *Who Governs?* (New Haven, Conn.: Yale University Press, 1961), p. 72.

22.   Greer, "The Shaky Future of Local Government," p. 66.

23.   Edward Banfield, *Political Influence* (New York: The Free Press, 1961).

24.   Claire W. Gilbert, "Some Trends in Community Politics: A Secondary Analysis of Power Structure Data from 166 Communities," in Charles M. Bonjean et al., *Community Politics: A Behavioral Approach* (New York: Macmillan Publishing Co., Inc., 1971), p. 215.

3 Part Three 3

Issues in Public Policy

IN THIS FINAL

part of the book we turn our attention to some major issues in public policy: poverty in Chapter 11, race in Chapter 12, energy and the environment in Chapter 13, and foreign policy in Chapter 14. In each case we shall be interested in more than just the nature and causes of the problems. Because this is a text in the American political system and not in sociology, economics, or technology, we are concerned primarily with the *politics* of the issues, the ways they are handled by our policy makers and political institutions.

Thus this final part of the book pulls together the material dealing with the political processes and institutions covered in Parts One and Two and examines these processes and institutions in action, in the operational setting of contemporary issues. Each of the four chapters on public policy is divided into three sections. First, we provide historical, descriptive, and analytical background of the issue and some proposals for resolving it. Second, we describe how the relevant institutions of politics and government have tried to deal with the issue. Finally, each chapter presents a five-perspective debate on the most important of all the questions considered in this book: *Can the American political system deal effectively with the great issues facing the people today?*

Economic Policy:

Sharing the Wealth

By what principles should the goods and services produced by the economy be distributed among the population? This is a central question that all societies must confront. As we examine its application to the American system in this chapter, we shall focus on a particular aspect of the problem: Can we abolish poverty in America?

But we cannot understand this issue by concentrating only on public policy as it relates to the poor. We have to review the total context of economic policy. We must look at the size and growth of total economic output, for this will tell us how much is available to distribute among the people, including the poor; and we must examine the methods for maintaining economic stability, for, when economies suffer from sharp alternations of boom and slump, the poor fare particularly badly.

So our procedure will be to discuss first the growth of the American economy; next the devices used to maintain stability of growth; and then the policies that affect the distribution of wealth and income, with particular reference to efforts to reduce poverty. Next, we shall examine the roles of the various aspects of the American governmental and political system that have been involved in making policy on economic affairs in general and poverty in particular, focusing on the presidency, Congress, special advisers and bureaucrats, the interplay of the federal with the state and local governments, interest groups, and public opinion. With this as background we shall be ready to proceed to our five-perspective debate.

Economic Growth

The output of the American economic system has been prodigious. Partly this is because of an abundance of natural resources. The millions of people pouring in from Europe in the eighteenth and nineteenth centuries found everything needed for an incredibly productive agriculture, and, as the eastern lands were filled, there was the frontier always beckoning westward with the promise of more vast spaces. However, there was more to it than soil and climate. Extraordinary effort and inventiveness went first into that agricultural achievement and then into the creation of an industrial revolution that surpassed anything experienced in even the most technologically successful countries of the Old World. By 1975 the Gross National Product (GNP)—the total of all goods, services, and investments produced in this country—had reached a value of close to a trillion and a half dollars, almost 40 percent of the entire world GNP, produced by less than 6 percent of the world's population.

It is a remarkable record, which translates into a staggering supply of homes, automobiles, television sets, college educations, and an array of other goods and services. However, some economists have expressed concern that the rate of future growth may not be high enough to sustain the expectations aroused by past growth. Already we have lost the enormous lead over all other industrialized countries that we once had. The standard of living in Sweden and Switzerland is on a par with ours, and our economic growth rate is exceeded by those of West Germany and Japan. (The great pools of oil on which some of the Arab countries sit has catapulted their output per head of population well beyond ours; but they are special cases resulting from the sudden jump in the price of oil.)

Economic Stability

Our extraordinary economic expansion has not proceeded at a steady pace. Until recent times there have been great fluctuations, with booming prosperity giving way to stagnation and depression followed by good times again. This series of alternations, or *trade cycles*, has moderated considerably since the last massive downturn, the Great Depression of the 1930s; but we still experience alternating periods of expanding business activity and much slower periods, or "recessions."

Each phase of the cycle contains its own special problems. When the economy turns down, the rate of growth dips; profits decline; small business bankruptcies go up; and, most damaging of all, unemployment rises. All these problems lessen as the economy moves up, but usually another evil takes their place—inflation, a rising price level, which devalues people's incomes and damages our international trade balances by pushing up the prices of our goods abroad. Only in rare periods have we managed to achieve such a perfect balance that we have kept both unemployment and inflation down at the same time. Usually they have an inverse relationship to each other: when unemployment falls sharply, the rate of inflation tends to go up, and vice versa. However, as we shall see, there has been a growing tendency of late to get the worst of both worlds.

Ways of Combating Instability

Since both unemployment and inflation are unpopular, they generate political pressure on the federal government to do something about them. The government has responded with two kinds of devices. The first is *monetary policy*. The federal government prints the currency, and it can put more money or less money into the economy at any given time by a variety of methods. It can also influence the supply of credit by raising or lowering the interest rate. Thus, if the economy is slipping, the federal government may try to pick it up by injecting more money into the economy and encouraging businesses to borrow and invest by lowering the interest rate; and it can reverse its course when the economy seems to be moving ahead so fast as to be generating inflation.

Second, the government employs *fiscal policy*, which is concerned with public spending on the one hand and taxes on the other. Until the 1930s the government used common sense to deal with economic slumps. Since times were bad, and government revenue was falling, the federal budget was cut to keep the budget in balance. But common sense was not necessarily economic sense. Cutting the budget took money out of the economy and depressed still further the level of business activity and the number of jobs. So, as unemployment reached 25 percent of the work force in the Great Depression of the 1930s, the administration of Franklin Roosevelt began to adopt the principles put forward by the British economist John Maynard Keynes. The Keynesian theory said that, as the economy turned down, government should compensate for the decline in private investment by increasing its own spending. So, as part of the Roosevelt New Deal, the federal government launched a number of programs designed to stimulate business and create jobs, and deliberately ran deficits in the budget—that is, it spent more money than it raised in taxes and other sources of revenue. The deficits were covered by printing more money, and increasing the national debt—the money the government owes to private lenders.

Since that time Keynesian principles have prevailed. Even when Republican administrations took over the White House, spending exceeded income in periods of recession, though the tendency was to do this less enthusiastically than during Democratic administrations. In 1959–60 President Eisenhower did try to balance the budget. His attempt was followed by a sharp recession which helped to elect John Kennedy in 1960. Subsequently, Richard Nixon (who called himself a Keynesian) ran a series of substantial deficits—$23 billion in 1971 and again in 1972. The deficit came down in 1973 and was reduced to below $4 billion in 1974. But it turned up sharply again the next year, and the deficit under Gerald Ford in 1976 was over $66 billion. As Figure 11-1 shows us, from 1958 to 1976 there were budget deficits in all but two years from 1954 to 1976, producing a total national debt of over $600 billion.

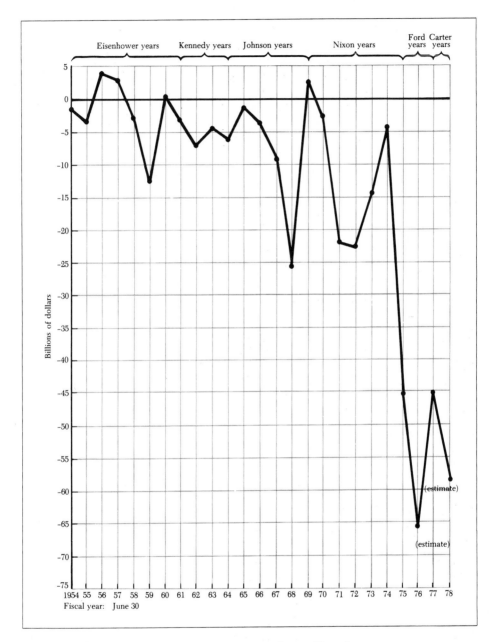

FIGURE 11–1   Deficit Budgeting, 1954–78 (Data from Office of Management and Budget.

If deficit spending succeeds in getting unemployment down, we do not have long to bask in our achievement, for we then have to start worrying about how to handle rising prices. The measures that the Keynesian analysis then calls for are the, reverse of those used to get us out of recession. We should pull money out of the economy and aim at a balanced budget or a surplus. This may require higher taxes. But tax increases are unpopular, and presidents and members of Congress are reluctant to propose them. Moreover, any policy whose purpose is to slow down the expansion of the economy raises the specter that it will be too successful and force the economy into a steep decline.

One other recourse is available for dealing with inflation—government-imposed controls on wages and prices. This technique is greatly disliked by business and labor, it is difficult to administer and enforce, and as soon as the controls are lifted, the pent-up pressures may produce another big surge of inflation. So government leaders prefer to use persuasion rather than compulsory controls, offering guidelines for acceptable price and wage increases and appealing to business and labor to stay within those guidelines for the good of the economy. However, pressures for controls have become greater since the early 1970s because the American economy has been afflicted with both ailments, high unemployment and high rates of inflation at the same time. This condition came to be known as "stagflation"—stagnation (a stagnating economy with very little growth, resulting in high unemployment) combined with inflation. This unholy combination of prices rising at the double-digit rate of close to 12 percent a year and unemployment hovering around 9 percent resulted in the imposition of a freeze on wages and prices in 1973.

The Distribution
of Wealth and Income

Enjoyment of the abundant wealth that the United States has produced has not been limited to a very small number of people. A high proportion of the population have achieved a standard of living undreamed of in most societies. By 1975 the median family income was approximately $13,700, which means that half of America's families earned more than $13,700 a year and the other half earned under $13,700. Altogether close to three-quarters of all families earned over $8,500. Moreover, by 1975 two-thirds of families owned their homes. Not surprisingly, then, a majority of the people view themselves as middle class or higher, according to a 1973 survey by the National Opinion Survey Research Center that asked people to say which social class they thought they belonged to; see Figure 11-2.

This represents a much higher proportion in the middle socioeconomic groups than has been true in most other countries. In part, this has come about because of the opportunities that the economic system has made available to the

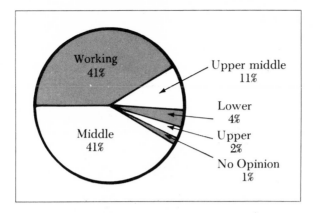

FIGURE 11–2   *Self-Perceptions of Social Class*

population at large, and because we have not had the rigid class and caste barriers found in so many other societies. But a number of government policies in the twentieth century have been designed to protect and advance the living standards of lower- and middle-class people: income tax, unemployment and retirement insurance, minimum wage laws, support for home ownership, and so on.

However, these government programs have not eliminated wide inequalities in America. The very rich and the very poor are still with us.

The Rich

The explosion of wealth that took place in the nineteenth century produced some great personal fortunes. Men who combined qualities of ingenuity, energy, organizational skill, and ruthless ambition were dubbed the "robber barons" and acquired fortunes surpassing those of most of the landed aristocracies of Europe. These fortunes created family dynasties, in which the heirs became leading bankers, industrialists, and occasionally philanthropists.

The income tax, combined with increasingly heavy inheritance taxes, has made it much more difficult to create or to inherit enormous personal wealth. Yet we still have a few billionaires, including shipping and real estate tycoon Daniel Ludwig, whose wealth has been estimated at close to $3 billion, and John Donald MacArthur, a real estate magnate worth perhaps $1 billion. Another 50 families are worth $100 million or more, including Ray Kroc, owner of the McDonald's hamburger chain; Paul Mellon, art patron, who has given away much of his family fortune but still retains between $500 million and a billion; and German immigrant Leonard Stern, manufacturer of pet supplies.[1] There are also some hundreds of families who own around $10 million, and about 100,000 in the millionaire class. If we look at stock ownership alone, 5000 Americans owned more than $5 million worth apiece in 1969, and another 50,000 had at least $1 million each. These 55,000 owned about 18 percent of all corporate stock. If we spread the net wider and look at the top 5 percent of the income group, we find that they own about 40 percent of all the nation's property. Altogether close to a third of total income received by people in America comes to them not as salaries or wages but as "unearned" income—dividends, interest, rent, and so on.

Now, income tax is a "progressive" tax in that it becomes progressively heavier as we move up the income scale; it calls for a higher proportion of upper incomes than of lower incomes. Accordingly, federal income tax rates go up to 50 percent on wages and salaries, and up to 70 percent on unearned income. How, then, do the very rich manage to hold on to such large fortunes? Why is wealth not more equally distributed than it is? Much of the answer lies in the loopholes in the tax laws. These laws allow a variety of deductions from gross income. Middle-income people claim some of these deductions—on property taxes and mortgage interest, for example—but the rich gain most from being able to write off business losses and from the use of "tax shelters" in the form of investments—which shelter or remove much of their income from tax liability—in such fields as real estate developments, oil, cattle, movies, and tax-free municipal bonds.

Some of the rich, in fact, drive their entire incomes through these loopholes. In 1974 five Americans with adjusted gross incomes (total incomes less certain business expenses and special allowances) of $1 million or more paid *no* federal income tax. The same was true of 244 people with adjusted gross incomes of at least $200,000, and of over 3000 people with adjusted incomes of $50,000 to $200,000. These were only small proportions of the total number of people in each of those income ranges. But they were extreme examples that revealed sharply that the published tax rates are not the true tax rates and that the progressive income tax does not redistribute income to nearly the extent that might be assumed from the tax tables. The percentage of their income that people in different brackets actually paid in 1973 as compared with the apparent or nominal rate is indicated by Table 11-1.

The Poor

There is another group of people in America who pay no federal income taxes, not because they claim business losses or receive income from nontaxable sources such as municipal bonds, but because their incomes are below the minimum levels on the tax scales. In 1976 about 12 percent of the people lived below the officially defined poverty line—an annual income of $5500 for a family of four. This proportion was a considerable reduction from earlier periods in our history.

In the nineteenth century many of the immigrants who had come to this country with visions of streets paved with gold were quickly disillusioned. Instead of enjoying affluence they endured great hardships. By the second generation conditions for the larger number had improved considerably; but a significant minority continued to struggle unsuccessfully against a hostile environment. There was grinding poverty on the land—not only among the slaves in the South,

TABLE 11–1   *Actual Taxes Paid as Compared to Nominal Tax Rate*

Total Income (dollars)	Nominal Tax (as % of total income)	Actual Tax Paid (as % of total income)
Under 1,000	14.2	a
1,000–2,000	15.1	a
2,000–3,000	16.2	1.4
3,000–4,000	17.0	3.4
4,000–5,000	17.8	5.0
5,000–6,000	18.6	6.3
6,000–7,000	19.3	7.2
7,000–8,000	20.0	7.9
8,000–9,000	20.8	8.6
9,000–10,000	21.6	9.3
10,000–15,000	23.9	10.3
15,000–20,000	28.0	12.4
20,000–25,000	32.0	14.2
25,000–50,000	38.4	17.4
50,000–100,000	49.0	25.2
100,000–150,000	57.0	29.6
150,000–200,000	60.6	30.2
200,000–500,000	63.8	30.4
500,000–1,000,000	66.9	30.7
1,000,000 and over	67.5	31.4

a Less than 0.05.

SOURCE: Derived from the Brookings 1970 Tax File (sample of about 95,000 returns). Rates and other provisions are those in effect in 1973. Cited in Richard Goode, *The Individual Income Tax*, rev. ed. (Washington, D.C.: The Brookings Institution, 1976), p. 309.

but also among dirt farmers and hired migrant laborers, who eked out their lives on the very edge of subsistence. In the factories and mines, too, long hours were worked for pitifully low wages by millions of men, women, and often children; and in periods of economic depression even these wages were not available.

Step by step these conditions improved. But in the 1930s Franklin Roosevelt could still speak of "one-third of a nation—ill-housed, ill-clad, ill-nourished."

From the late 1930s, however, the numbers living in poverty began to come down. The economic prosperity generated when World War II provided jobs for everybody made major inroads into the problem, and after the war the proportion of families living below the poverty line went down by about 1 percent a year until the end of the 1960s. There were occasional interruptions in the decline, as during the economic recessions of 1956 and 1958. But by 1965 the poverty group was down to 19 percent of the population, and to a little over 12 percent by 1969.

Then progress slowed to a halt. In 1975 there were still about 12 percent of the people officially designated as poor, and this was a slight increase over the previous year. That 12 percent represented almost 26 million people.

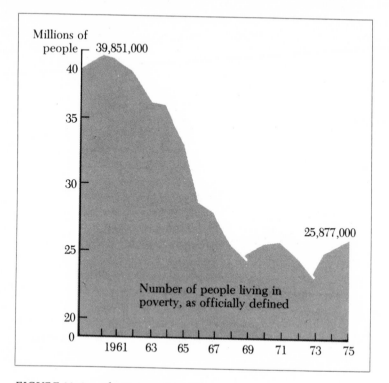

FIGURE 11–3   The Extent of Poverty
(Data from U.S. Census Bureau.)

We turn our attention now to who these people are, and what government has tried to do about their plight.

Who are the poor?   There are people living in poverty from almost every kind of background, from every ethnic, racial, and religious group. However, they are most likely to be found among the following categories. First, there are the racial and ethnic minorities: blacks, Mexican Americans, Puerto Ricans, and American Indians. About a quarter of the poor come from these groups. Then, the elderly. One American in 10 is now over 65, and there are a million over 85. Many of these did not earn enough money during their working lives to save very much, or had their savings wiped out by an illness and live on a small and inadequate pension. At the other end of the age scale are the teenage high school dropouts, without jobs or marketable skills. Unemployment among this group typically runs to a fifth or a quarter of the work force and much higher in some cities, especially among black and Spanish-surname groups.

Next come families headed by women. In 1973 there were 6.6 million such families, an increase of a million from 1970. The high rate of divorce, separations, desertions, and child-bearing out of wedlock has contributed to this large number. The rate of increase in female-headed families has been especially great among blacks. The median income of families in which there is no man around the house is less than half that of families in which the husband is present. Since this median figure is barely above the poverty level, close to half of the families headed by women are below the poverty line.

Geographically, the poor are concentrated in the inner cities; in such areas as the Appalachians, where the local industry has died; and in those parts of the Old South, particularly Mississippi, Alabama, and South Carolina, which are much less industrialized and urbanized than the rest of the country. And they are found in large numbers among small tenant farmers and migrant agricultural workers.

Thus the people most likely to be poor are elderly black people living in Mississippi; or black divorced mothers of large families in a central city of the North; or migrant Chicano farm workers. *Least* likely to be poor are middle-aged, white suburban families who are Jewish, Catholic, or Episcopalian. Table 11–2 gives us a more precise statistical picture of the groups who made up the poor in 1975.

The poor suffer from many disabilities, apart from their lack of money. They are below the national average in years of schooling. They are more likely than the average to be out of work, to live in squalid housing, to be in poor health, and to be the perpetrators—and the victims—of crimes of violence. Some sociologists and anthropologists have viewed these various deficiencies as being part of a vicious cycle of poverty: poor people are likely to get poor schooling, which leads to unemployment, which breeds poor health and antisocial attitudes, which reinforce the likelihood of remaining poor. And this cycle of poverty, say these scholars, reflects a *culture of poverty*, a way of life, which is found not only in this country but wherever there are significant numbers of people who are the inheritors of several generations of poverty.

According to anthropologist Oscar Lewis, the poverty culture is preoccupied with the present rather than the future; and it does not place much emphasis on the "work ethic" associated with the Puritans who helped to found this country, an ethic that holds work, punctuality, and thrift as high values. Lewis finds some positive aspects to the "poverty culture." For example, it gives people a certain amount of protection from a hostile environment by offering warmth and human contact; further, "living in the present may develop a capacity for spontaneity and adventure, for the enjoyment of the sensual, the indulgence of impulse, which is often blunted in the middle-class, future-oriented man." Yet Lewis does not romanticize the lifestyle of the poor. It is "a comparatively thin culture," containing "a great deal of pathos, suffering, and emptiness. . . . Its encouragement of mistrust magnifies individual helplessness and isolation." Thus many individuals who grow up in this culture have a strong feeling of fatalism, dependence, and inferiority.[2] Others, though recognizing that poverty can be severely damaging to the belief in self, doubt that there is a universally recognizable poverty culture or that the attitudes of the poor are actually different from the majority's. These

TABLE 11–2   Who Are the Poor?

Race: Nonwhites — 1 out of 3	Number	All Poor (%)
Whites	17,770,000	68.7
Nonwhites	8,107,000	31.3

| Age: Mostly children, teenagers, and elderly | | |
	Number	All Poor (%)
Under age 18	11,104,000	42.9
Aged 18–64	11,456,000	44.3
Over age 64	3,317,000	12.8

| Home: More in central cities, rural areas | | |
	Number	All Poor (%)
In central cities	9,090,000	35.1
In suburbs	6,259,000	24.2
Outside metropolitan areas	10,529,000	40.7

| Region: Largest number in South | | |
	Number of Families	All Poor (%)
South	2,343,000	43.0
North Central	1,152,000	21.1
Northeast	1,014,000	18.6
West	941,000	17.3

Education: Mainly those with less schooling Among Heads of Households over Age 25 with:	Poor Families (%)	Families Above Poverty Line (%)
1–8 years of schooling	41.8	18.6
9–11 years of schooling	24.3	14.4
High school diploma	23.7	34.5
College—1 year or more	10.2	32.5

SOURCE: Data from U.S. Census Bureau, as cited in U.S. News & World Report, Nov. 8, 1976.

sociologists suggest that the behavior of the impoverished would be changed quickly by dramatic changes in the social environment. Leonard Goodwin, after surveying more than 4000 people, concluded that "poor people—males and females, blacks and whites, youths and adults—identify their self-esteem with work as strongly as do the nonpoor." He agrees that people become discouraged after repeated failures to find work. But "even long-term welfare mothers and their teen-age sons, though the sons have spent virtually their entire lives on welfare, continue to have a strong work ethic and do not need to be taught the importance of work."[3]

Still, if there is disagreement about the existence of a deep-rooted poverty culture, there is little question but that millions of people in America today live in conditions of poverty; that a great many of the poor have developed a sense of defeat and low self-esteem; and that the various disabilities of life below the poverty line feed upon and reinforce each other.

Programs to Reduce Poverty

For a long period there was no general effort by government to attack poverty. In the latter part of the nineteenth century "social Darwinism" was the most influential doctrine. Darwin had told us that evolution was a process of natural selection based on survival of the fittest. And America's economic success has been based on the same principle, according to the social Darwinists. Therefore, we should not spend our time worrying about those who lag behind in the economic race, for the success of the system depends on the efforts of those who rise to the top. However, Christian beliefs would not let the poor starve, so the general sentiment was that the affluent should give some of their money away as charity. Private charity might be supplemented by government help to orphan children or the destitute elderly. But this was the job of local not national government, and it should be carried out parsimoniously and through Poor Laws that sometimes required the recipients of aid to be shut up in institutions.

In some of the big cities a different ethos began to take over. Political bosses and their machines met immigrants as they got off the boat, gave them food, found them housing and jobs, and asked only one thing in return—their votes.

Toward the end of the nineteenth century and increasingly in the twentieth century, some states, particularly in the populous, urbanized parts of the country, began to introduce pension programs for the elderly and, here and there, supplemented private funds with public monies to build housing for the very poor.

The federal government, however, was slow to intervene. After a long struggle, child labor laws were passed to prevent children from working in mines and to limit their hours in factories. The income tax was a step toward the redistribution of income from the richer toward the poorer segments of society and thus a challenge to the principle of social Darwinism. Nonetheless, the persistence of poverty was still regarded as a problem to be dealt with by private charity and local government, with occasional help from state government.

This situation changed dramatically when the stock market crashed in 1929, and the economy plunged into a cataclysmic breakdown. Franklin Roosevelt, whose election campaign was full of promises about balancing the budget, inaugurated a series of measures after he was elected that changed the way the economic system worked and took a different approach toward the poor than had ever been the case in the past. Since that time a vast number of programs have emerged that address the problem of poverty. Some of them are aimed at major segments of the American people, and help the poor together with many working- and middle-class people. Others are directed primarily or exclusively at the poor.

Broad Economic and Social Programs

We mentioned earlier in the chapter the monetary and fiscal policies that help keep growth high and unemployment low. These benefit the poor, for poor people, who are more likely to be unemployed than anyone else, are particularly hard hit in periods of recession when unemployment is high generally. Then, in the 1930s, a number of social welfare programs emerged and were subsequently expanded. These were designed to help the broad mass of the people, but they were enormously important to the lowest-income group. Among them were the "social security" programs, financed by compulsory assessments on employers and workers, to provide old-age pensions and payments to unemployed and disabled workers; and the establishment of minimum wages and maximum hours for employees of businesses engaged in interstate commerce. Poor people also benefited from such programs of the 1960s as Medicare, which pays part of the medical costs of retired people, and federal aid to education.

Programs for the Poor

The New Deal offered a number of programs designed particularly for the people at the lowest end of the income scale. These programs were continued and expanded under Harry Truman in the late 1940s and again in the early 1960s during the Kennedy administration, and new programs were added in the mid-1960s as part of the "War on Poverty" launched by the federal government under Lyndon Johnson. These various programs fell into the following principal categories.

Job creation and job training.   During the New Deal the great imperative was to get people back to work. The Works Projects Administration (WPA) and other programs created temporary jobs, some of them nothing more than busy-work to get people on a payroll, others much more imaginative, which made lasting creative contributions in the arts and in the conservation of natural resources. In the early sixties, under Kennedy, job training programs were developed by the federal government. Then the Johnson administration's Economic Opportunity Act of 1964 established the Job Corps, which trained young men and women for work in conservation camps and urban and rural residential centers.

Housing.   The New Deal programs included public housing—apartments for very low income people under a program of federal subsidies to specially created local housing authorities. The Housing Act of 1949 provided for 810,000 additional units of this low-rent public housing. Variations on this program were developed in the 1960s, including the rehabilitation of run-down housing. And the War on Poverty included the Model Cities program, which undertook a coordinated effort to upgrade the blighted areas of a number of urban communities.

Education.   When federal aid to education was finally approved in 1965, it came in under the rubric of the War on Poverty, and special attention was paid under the program to the needs of the schools in the poverty areas of the cities. Head Start, a program for preschool children in low-income areas, was launched in an effort to overcome the educational and cultural disadvantages associated with a poverty background. Financial aid programs were provided for low-income students in colleges and universities, together with work–study opportunities, which provided employers with federal money for offering part-time jobs to students.

Welfare.   The New Deal introduced the notion of federal grants to the states to help elderly people not covered under Social Security (or whose needs were still not fully provided for by Social Security benefits), the blind, and needy families with dependent children. All these programs grew under successive administrations, and were given a major new impetus under the War on Poverty. Medicare was supplemented at the state and local levels by Medicaid. And in 1961 the federal food stamp program was inaugurated; this entitled poor people to buy stamps that could be redeemed at markets for food worth considerably more than the price of the stamps. The scale of the food stamp program grew at a prodigious rate in the 1970s. By 1976, 5.8 million families were receiving the stamps at a cost to the federal government of nearly $6 billion a year. (However, the number of families receiving the stamps had fallen to 5.1 million by June 1977.)

A high proportion of these people were also receiving welfare payments, primarily under the Aid to Families with Dependent Children Program. Despite the decline in the proportion of people living in poverty that took place in the 1960s the numbers on AFDC soared. By 1976 over 11 million people in more than 3.5 million families were receiving AFDC funds. In large measure, this was the result of the migration of large numbers of poor people, especially blacks, from the South to the urban ghettos of the North and West. When they arrived, many of them found that the job opportunities they had hoped for were not available. As soon as they were eligible, they turned to the local relief programs. In addition, an increasing proportion of poor people were in families headed by black women. The children of these families thus came either from broken homes or were illegitimate.

The growth of AFDC and related welfare programs was the subject of widespread dissatisfaction. Critics complained that these programs encouraged the disintegration of family life, because the benefits went mostly to families in which the father was not present. Another defect cited by the critics of the program was that recipients were discouraged from working because their AFDC grant was reduced by the amount of their earnings. In 1969 President Nixon proposed that it be replaced by the Family Assistance Program (FAP), which would provide a federal foundation "under the income of every American family with dependent children that cannot care for itself." A basic federal payment would be provided, which the states were invited to supplement. Work, or job training, would be required of all recipients of the grants except the elderly, the incapacitated, and mothers of preschool children—and day-care centers would be set up to encourage these mothers to take a job. An incentive to work was built into the proposal, since people on FAP could keep over half their earnings and still receive benefits until their income reached the limit of almost $4000. FAP failed to pass Congress. However, other proposals to reorganize or replace the existing welfare program continue to receive vigorous support.

Community action.   The Johnson administration's 1964 Economic Opportunity Act introduced an innovative approach to the problem of poverty, the Community Action Programs (CAP), under the Office of Economic Opportunity. Instead of merely giving financial and other benefits to low-income people, CAP invited the "maximum feasible participation" of the poor in decisions affecting a wide range of community problems. The basic assumption of CAP was that poor people are afflicted by a sense of helplessness, of being passive objects of decisions which other people make for them. To increase their belief in themselves, CAP set out to give the poor a chance to participate actively in the decision-making process at the community level. Policy boards were set up in the communities to make decisions on the spending of federal poverty funds, and representatives of the poor were given a major voice on these boards.

Poverty, the Economy, and the Policy Makers

Efforts to reduce poverty in America provide an especially useful illustration of the way our governmental and political process works. Many of the concepts that were developed earlier in this book—particularly those related to the presidency, political parties, Congress, the federal bureaucracy, state and local government, interest groups, and public opinion—can be applied in the following discussion of how the policy makers deal with the issue of poverty and the distribution of wealth in America.

The Presidency

Our analysis in Chapter 6 would lead us to certain assumptions about the presidency, economic policy, and poverty. First, strong federal action favoring low-income groups would require presidential leadership. Second, this would be most likely to come from Democratic presidents, since the Democratic party's constituency is drawn more from the lower than the higher ranges of the income and status scales. Republican administrations, on the other hand, would be less likely to make the poverty issue a top priority because of their doubts about the effectiveness or desirability of federal government solutions, and because of their preoccupation with holding down taxes and inflation. However, they would not be able to ignore the dangers of recession and unemployment. In fact, these expectations are confirmed in the context of poverty and the distribution of wealth.

Without vigorous presidential leadership, programs designed to help the lower-income groups have never gotten off the ground. Typically this leadership has been provided during Democratic administrations. Thus, Roosevelt's New Deal represented an unpredecented thrust by the federal government into the nation's economic problems with particular attention to the problems of the unemployed and the poor.

With Kennedy there were two controlling factors. First, when he came to the White House, the economy was in a recession and unemployment was high. Second, a president who was eager to do something bold, innovative, and responsive to the needs of lower-income Democratic voters would be very likely to discover the poverty in America as a prime problem for political action. So Kennedy asked Walter Heller, chairman of the Council of Economic Advisers, to prepare the way for action on the subject, and in mid-November, a few days before his death, he decided to present a major legislative program aimed at attacking poverty.

Two days after the assassination Heller told Lyndon Johnson of Kennedy's decision. Reviewing the material presented to him by Heller, Johnson responded, "That's my kind of program. It will help people. I want you to move full speed ahead." So Johnson adapted and expanded Kennedy's proposal, and a draft of the Economic Opportunity Act was sent by the president to Congress, together with a message calling for "total victory" in the war on poverty.

Unfortunately for Johnson's place in history, the War on Poverty had to take second place to the war in Vietnam. Funds for antipoverty programs were held down in favor of money for troops, guns, and bombers. Moreover, the launching of the War on Poverty coincided with an income tax cut, and Johnson did nothing to restore the cut as spending on Vietnam expanded at a rapid rate. The result was to contribute substantially to the inflationary pressures which his successors had to face, and which increased the resistance to federal spending for social welfare programs.

On the Republican side, presidential policies have been more or less in line with our expectations. In other words, Republican presidents have not treated poverty as a top priority. Eisenhower, true to Republican form and in his reluctance to enlarge presidential power, was basically hostile to having the federal government protect people against economic misfortune. "If all Americans want is security," he said during his campaign for the presidency in 1952, "then they can go to prison. They'll have enough to eat, a bed and a roof over their heads." So he slowed down the public housing program and held down federal spending in 1959 and 1960 to the point at which it probably contributed to the onset of a fairly severe recession. However, his approach was to slow the expansion of the welfare state, not to scrap what already existed. He still ran budget deficits in some years, and Social Security benefits were increased under his leadership.

With Nixon as the chief executive, the picture becomes much more complicated, however. In his 1968 campaign he attacked Lyndon Johnson's War on

Poverty as wasteful and ineffective. Yet, once elected, he did not merely oppose programs. As Daniel Moynihan explained it:

> Nixon in office was beginning to change. The cautious, negative campaign was behind him. Ahead lay his reputation in American history. He had watched the near-sighted decisions of the Eisenhower years gradually close off his chances for the presidency in 1960; he was concerned that the same style should not now take over his own Administration.[4]

Nixon saw himself as a man who, precisely because he had conservative credentials, had the credibility to bring about important, compassionate changes. He increased the benefits under Social Security and the food stamp program. While changing the administrative structure of the antipoverty programs and redefining their purposes, he gave them $2 billion a year for two years. And it was Nixon who tried to get rid of the almost universally criticized Aid to Families with Dependent Children program and replace it with the Family Assistance Plan.

Then, too, Nixon's way of dealing with inflation did not fit the orthodox Republican mold. Inflationary pressures became severe first in 1971, largely as a result of years of spending on Vietnam, and again in 1973, when the Arab oil boycott forced a huge increase in oil and other prices. Traditional Republican policy would have called for drastic cuts in federal spending. But this could have brought on a recession. So, as an alternative to major spending cuts, he twice turned to wage and price controls. Nixon's rejection of a deliberate effort to dampen the economy was of considerable importance to the poor; for a depressed economy means rising unemployment, which would make it particularly difficult for the poor, who are mostly unskilled, to find jobs.

However, if the poor did better under Nixon than his 1968 campaign rhetoric might have suggested, they were not at the top of his list of priorities. After his first two years in office he proceeded to dismantle the antipoverty machinery and cut back on the Johnson era programs. When Congress overrode his vetoes of a number of appropriations, including some in the fields of health, housing, and education, he declared he could not accept so much inflationary pressure and impounded the funds. When the Family Assistance Plan stalled in the Senate, he expressed keen disappointment, but his efforts to revive the program were lackluster. Had his second term not been aborted, his declared intention to "stop throwing money after problems" did not augur well for federal funding for poverty programs.

Nor was Gerald Ford an ardent reformer. It is true that he, too, ran huge budgetary deficits, but to him the great enemy was inflation. So he fought hard against Congress's proposals for higher spending and vetoed several congressional appropriations. As he left office in January 1977, Ford proposed a budget calling again for spending reductions, including significant cuts in programs of great importance to the poor—Medicare, Medicaid, public service jobs, low-income housing, and food stamps.

Congress ignored the Ford budget, waiting instead for President Carter's proposals. And Carter, setting out to show that his would be an activist, energetic presidency, set forth a bold series of economic and social proposals in his first year in office. Among these were:

Reduction of unemployment by the end of 1979 to between 5 and 5½ percent.

Replacement of AFDC, special supplements for the aged, blind, and disabled, and food stamps with a new cash assistance program called the Program for Better Jobs and Income. This program would provide:

(a) A guaranteed minimum income for all very poor families and individuals judged unable to work.

(b) Payments to poor people judged able to work. Benefits would be reduced if they did not meet the work requirement; but they would be able to retain a substantial portion of their earnings and still receive benefits until their income exceeded $8400 (for a family of four).

(c) Allowances for child day-care costs for recipients of benefits who have children between the ages of 7 and 13. Parents of such children would be required to accept part-time jobs during school hours.

(d) Creation of 1.4 million public service work and training positions, including 300,000 part-time jobs for mothers with children between 7 and 13.

Interim reform of the food stamp program by removing the requirement for paying cash for the stamps. This would add some needy families to the program. However, others just above the poverty level would be removed from the food stamp rolls.

A substantial reform of the tax system to remove some of the present inequities.

However, Carter also made it clear that most of these programs, as well as any proposal for national health insurance, would be phased in slowly and carefully so as not to conflict with two other central goals of his administration: a balanced federal budget by 1981 and a reduction in the inflation rate to between 4 and 4½ percent by 1979.

Congress

As we saw in Chapter 7, major innovations in social legislation require not only leadership from Democratic presidents with a strong sense of mission but also very large Democratic majorities in both houses of Congress. This combination existed during Franklin Roosevelt's first two terms and in the first two years of Lyndon Johnson's presidency. These were precisely the two periods in modern history when public policy was heavily biased in the direction of the lower-income groups. Both Kennedy and Truman would have liked to have done more for these groups; but neither had those huge bodies of supporters in Congress that Roosevelt and Johnson could rely on—for a time at least. Thus, in the absence of overwhelming Democratic majorities, the tendency of Congress to deliberate at great length before acting, and sometimes not to act at all, was very much in evidence. As we saw in Chapter 7, this tendency was clearly illustrated in the cases of Medicare, federal aid to education, and public housing.

How much social welfare legislation comes out of those periods in which the Democrats have considerable margins in Congress but the White House occupant is a Republican? This was the situation that confronted Eisenhower after his first two years in office and Nixon and Ford throughout their presidencies. Invariably, these Congresses have wanted more social welfare spending and have been willing to tolerate larger budget deficits than the presidents. They have had some success in pushing through their policies.

However, without presidential initiatives, the Democratic Congresses produced no policy breakthroughs aimed at the lower-income groups. Very few congressional proposals to close tax loopholes favoring the rich became law. One reform to require wealthy people to pay at least *some* income tax went through in 1969; but this turned out to be full of loopholes, too. The overwhelming Democratic majorities of 1975–76 ended some tax shelters, but were not sufficient to force real tax reform through. If they passed the House, they came up against the implacable hostility of Senate Finance Committee chairperson Russell Long of Louisiana, and they died in his committee. It was Long's committee, too, that killed Richard Nixon's initiative in the field of welfare reform, the Family Assistance Plan; for FAP, with Wilbur Mills's support, had been approved by the House.

As a result of Congress's internal reforms in 1974 it is now better equipped than it used to be to shape sound and fiscally responsible social policies. The establishment in 1974 of House and Senate Budget Committees, along with a congressional Budget Office to provide the necessary expert staff, at last enabled Congress to set budgetary targets for the various standing committees and to see to it that the committees stay within their allocations. Consequently, Congress is much less vulnerable to the charge that its proposals for spending on the poor and other groups are made in reckless disregard of budgetary realities and are feeding the fires of inflation.

Even so, these reforms are not sufficient to transform Congress into an effective agent of innovative social programs. It appears that fundamental reform in a field like welfare can only be accomplished when a large congressional majority favoring change is matched by effective leadership from a president who gives high priority to reform; and even then action may be slow in coming.

Advisers and Bureaucrats

A president does not lack for advisers on economic policy. In his Executive Office he has an assistant for economic affairs, the Office of Management and Budget, and the Council of Economic Advisers, the three-person group of economists created by the Employment Act of 1946 to keep the economy moving at a healthy pace. In the Cabinet every department has a hand in economic matters, but the secretary of the treasury, who under both Democrats and Republicans comes from a banking or business background, outranks the rest. Among the independent government agencies the Federal Reserve Board has an especially important economic role, for its speciality is monetary policy, and it has at its disposal a variety of intricate mechanisms for influencing the supply of credit and the rate of interest.

Up to a point these various institutions serve the president's purposes and reflect his economic views. Thus under Kennedy and Johnson the chairperson of the Council of Economic Advisers was a moderately liberal academic economist, Walter Heller, and he and his associates on the council advocated policies to expand the economy and hold down unemployment. Republican presidents, on the other hand, have preferred as the chairperson of the Council of Economic Advisers a moderate conservative, such as Arthur Burns, who was chairperson under Eisenhower, or the very conservative Alan Greenspan, who served under Nixon and Ford. As for Cabinet members, though they are sometimes inclined to see things from the vantage point of their departmental constituencies, they are not often inclined to engage in frontal assaults on the economic policies of the president.

However, as we saw in our discussion of federal agencies in Chapter 8, presidents do not always enjoy unwavering allegiance within the executive branch. One recurrent source of frustration for presidents is the Federal Reserve Board (FRB). Members of the board serve terms of 14 years, and their chairperson is selected from among them for four years at a time. Neither the members nor the chairperson can be fired by the president simply because he dislikes their policies. Consequently, the man Nixon appointed as FRB chairperson in 1970 and reappointed in 1974, the highly respected and very independent Arthur Burns, took public issue with the economic policies first of Nixon, then of Carter, complaining that both were flirting dangerously with inflation.

As we also noted in Chapter 8, the lesser members of the bureaucracies can be another source of frustration to presidents by dragging their feet in the implementation of his policies, especially where these policies are designed to blaze trails with which the bureaucrats are unfamiliar. Knowing this in advance, Lyndon Johnson, when he wanted to launch some innovative approaches to solving the problem of poverty in America, decided to go outside existing channels. A large number of programs already existed to help the poor, spread throughout, among others, the Departments of Health, Education and Welfare; Housing and Urban Development; Labor; and Commerce. But the programs were not imaginative enough for Johnson and too much embroiled in regulations and standard procedures. So Johnson turned to Sargent Shriver, director of the Peace Corps under Kennedy, to propose a fresh approach. Shriver consulted with several Cabinet departments. But he also turned to a group of personal friends and advisers, mostly rather liberal people, and even two writers of the left, Michael Harrington, a socialist, and Paul Jacobs, a radical writer and editor. People from business, city government, the universities, local welfare agencies, and the Ford Foundation were called in for consultation.[5]

From their recommendations the Economic Opportunity Act emerged, and the Office of Economic Opportunity (OEO) was created to establish the Job Corps, the work–study programs, the projects aimed at rural poverty, and the Community Action Program. At Shriver's urging, OEO was set up as a separate agency reporting directly to the White House. The intent was to provide an agency that would not be limited by the bureaucratic inertia and rigidities of the old-line departments, but would provide a dynamic, flexible instrument to produce bold innovations. Unhampered by ties to existing constituencies and jurisdictional lines, it would work directly with cities and counties, public schools, universities, business corporations, community agencies—whoever could get the job done.

Indeed, there was a great deal of interesting experimentation. OEO was able quickly to initiate a number of projects that might never have found their way through the layer upon layer of decision making and non-decision-making of the existing federal agencies. Yet, as was bound to happen with a new, innovative agency, there was a great deal of confusion during the first years of OEO with a rapid turnover of top staff and a constant changing of administrative guidelines.

When Nixon came to office, he set about the task of straightening out some of the confusion. But this was mere prelude to the dismantling of OEO. It did not happen immediately, but eventually even a reorganized OEO would not suit a Richard Nixon or his successor, Gerald Ford. So, one by one, OEO's functions were spun off to other departments, such as the Department of Labor and HEW, and whatever was left was transferred in 1974 to a new, independent agency, the Community Services Administration. In some degree, then, the programs survived. But, as we shall see, their more controversial aspects, which represented a direct challenge to established ways of providing government services to the poor, were diluted or abandoned—and this might well have happened even if Lyndon Johnson had been elected president again.

Washington, the States and the Cities

Although state and local governments have a significant economic role to play through their patterns of spending and taxing, governors and mayors know that the crucial public decisions affecting economic growth, employment, prices, interest rates, and so on can be made only in Washington. This is often equally true with respect to social welfare programs. On the other hand, it was a different story with the Economic Opportunity Act. Most of the criticism that the OEO programs attracted revolved around the largest single component of OEO activities—the Community Action Program.

'Of all the projects included in the 1964 antipoverty package, CAP was the only one that was truly innovative or at least could not have been fitted reasonably comfortably into the existing federal agencies. Indeed, CAP was the cornerstone of the antipoverty program.

When the task force which had framed the OEO legislation moved on to set up guidelines for the local implementation of the program, the "maximum feasible participation" of the poor proved to be a cardinal principle. Representatives of the poor were to be included on the local policy boards, and local government bodies were told that their representation must include no more than one-third of the total membership of each board. Thus mayors and other local political officials were often unable to control the poverty agencies in their communities. Despite strenuous protests they failed to convince Washington of their right to appoint more than one-third of the members to the poverty boards.

Moreover, maximum feasible participation was not simply a matter of giving the poor a limited opportunity to share in the making of policies governing the use of poverty funds. As the program took shape, CAP often involved confrontations with established structures of local power. Thus, with money from the federal government, groups of poor people marched on city hall, organized to present demands to public housing authorities, fought for their *rights* as welfare recipients, and sued state and local government agencies which, they claimed, were not granting what was legally due them.

Once this began to happen, complaints about the program poured in from state and local officeholders. And it then became clear that the leaders of the administration and Congress who had approved CAP had never thought through its full implications. The community action in which the poor were supposed to participate meant many different things to the various groups that were proposing it. To some of the prophets of the community action field, it was essentially a radical notion. Poverty could be cured only if the poor themselves played a central role. And that role would have to be assertive, even abrasive, if the existing power structures were to be forced out of their complacency; and, if the poor were to gain the self-confidence they needed to break out of their characteristic fatalism and dependency. Thus the poor should be encouraged to fight for federal funds as their right, not as charity. There was to be no need to express gratitude, for this would negate the purpose of the program. Variations of this view were urged on the Shriver task force both by university scholars of social work and by Ford Foundation specialists on social welfare programs. All of them believed that the poor should be directly involved in challenging local power structures and transforming or replacing the established welfare agencies.

But most members of the Shriver task force were looking for "a program that would pass the Congress, help win the Presidential election, and eliminate poverty, in perhaps that order."[6] Maximum feasible participation seemed like a good idea to them as it related to black people in the South, for otherwise white politicians in the South might prevent the funds from reaching the black population. But the Shriver task force spent little if any time considering the implications of the participation of the poor in CAP in northern urban ghettos.[7] Had they done so, they might well have been very cool to the idea.

As for Johnson himself, there is no evidence that he accepted the doctrine of "power to the poor." The White House did not even get the point that the poor would help to shape and administer the program. The president, according to his closest aids, apparently believed that the local governments themselves would operate CAP rather than rely on separate corporations.

In Congress, the Community Action title of the antipoverty legislation and the "maximum feasible participation" clause were hardly discussed. After all, the phrase that was to become so controversial later looked innocuous enough in the proposed legislation. Section 202(a) (3) described a "community action program" as one "which is developed, conducted, and administered with the maximum feasible participation of residents of the areas and members of the groups served." Thus "the poor" as such were not even mentioned specifically.

It was precisely the haziness of the ideas of the political leaders in Washington that gave the advocates of CAP their opportunity. Politicians and bureaucrats who wanted a program but had only a vague notion of what it should be were susceptible to the influence of a group of innovators who knew their own minds and who were articulate, dedicated, and persistent.

But if this were enough to prevail at the outset, it would not suffice when the full implications of CAP appeared, and the troubles began in the communities. The angry protests of the poor against mayors and governors were soon matched by angry protests against the White House by those same mayors and governors.

When the situation became clear to the administration, steps were taken to give governors and mayors a greater degree of control over the local programs. The Nixon administration provided them with even further reassurance. Once this was done, most of the big city mayors and governors of urban states became advocates of OEO. After all, it brought desperately needed money into their communities. Consequently, there were strong protests from many of them when the Nixon administration started the process of dismantling OEO.

Nonetheless, to governors and mayors, CAP and the other OEO programs were not at the center of their concerns. Much more important to them was the escalating cost of welfare, especially AFDC, which seemed by the late 1960s to be the greatest threat to the fiscal viability of the states. So most of them supported some kind of national plan to guarantee a minimum income to every American family.

Interest Groups

Economic policy, particularly as it concerns the distribution of wealth among the various groups that make up American society, has been the focus of intense and continuous pressures from a great range of interest groups.

Business.   For many years representatives of American business fought against the enlargement of the welfare state. They protested the coming of income tax, deficit spending, Social Security, Medicare, and federally funded public housing. In time, however, many business leaders came to accept the inevitability, even the desirability, of these programs. If government action to counter recessions could raise profits and prevent bankruptcies, then there was something to be said for government action. If AFDC encouraged the existence of a permanent class of demoralized, dependent people, then perhaps it would be better to produce a more efficient, rational approach to the problem. So, although the U.S. Chamber of Commerce opposed FAP when it was first presented, the National Association of Manufacturers testified in its favor. And top leaders of such corporations as Xerox and Standard Oil of New Jersey spoke through the Committee for Economic Development in favor of FAP as a useful first step toward an even more generous program.

So business groups have tended to mellow in their approach to social legislation, and to move away from their earlier posture of diehard opposition. Nonetheless, most business representatives are usually to be found on the side of strong antiinflationary measures; holding down federal budget deficits; opposing increases in the minimum wage; pruning the number of people eligible for food stamps; favoring tax incentives for business; and resisting most other programs that increase federal spending and taxes.

The pro-welfare-state coalition.   On the other side is a large array of groups forming a loose coalition that gives top priority to fighting unemployment and redistributing income from the more to the less affluent. The most important of these are the labor unions. Then there are the "public interest" groups—the "do-gooders" as their opponents call them derisively—including Common Cause, the Ralph Nader organizations, religious social action groups, and associations speaking for racial minorities. The education lobby and the urban lobby (the National League of Cities and the U.S. Conference of Mayors) are usually to be found on this side of the interest group lineup. Social work professionals are also usually allied with these groups, though they had reservations about the Community Action Program, which challenged the methods of existing welfare agencies, and about the work provisions of FAP.

Then there are the poor themselves. Until recent years they had not been able to do very much in an organized way to improve their lot. Their position in the economic system was weak, for possessing few marketable skills they filled menial positions or none. Their pay was low, their jobs in many cases threatened by new technologies. Efforts to organize them into labor unions were sporadic and successful only in a few limited situations. And powerlessness in the economy was matched in the political arena. Political involvement and potency are, as we noted in Chapter 2, associated primarily with affluence and education. The poor tend to be apathetic, noninformed, and noninvolved. Most politicians view them as an inadequate and unreliable resource, for they are hard to get to the polls, they are not active in campaigns, and, by definition, they are no source of campaign funds.

Still, despite the general principle set forth in Chapter 5 that the poor are weakly represented in the interest group system, there were organizations speaking directly for large numbers of poor people whose potency was increasing rapidly. First, the organizations representing the elderly articulated the concerns of an increasing proportion of the population. There were a number of state and national associations in this field, and politicians were becoming increasingly attuned to the interests of their older constituents.

More important still, black people were becoming a force to be reckoned with politically. From the early 1960s a new urgency and effectiveness came to the civil rights movement. Previously, the leadership had been largely in the hands of white liberals. Then, out of the conflict in the South, came a remarkable group of black leaders, who presented their claims in a way that could no longer be ignored by national policy makers. More than anything else, it was the emergence of this new generation of civil rights leaders and the sense that, if they were not given something to show for their methods, they might be pushed aside by more militant contenders for leadership that changed the balance of group pressures in Washington in favor of the poor.

Then, once CAP had been inaugurated, organized pressures from poor people were increased by two kinds of groups, both brought into being by the OEO programs. One consisted of the local staffs of CAP, mostly people from the communities, essentially paraprofessionals working with (or sometimes against) the professionals employed by the traditional welfare agencies. The other group generated by the OEO ferment was the National Welfare Rights Organization (NWRO), an organization of welfare recipients. NWRO took the position that welfare recipients had rights and that they must fight in an organized, aggressive way for those rights. The benefits proposed in FAP, they argued, were utterly inadequate, and they demanded a guaranteed annual income of $5500.

Public Opinion

Generations after the Great Depression, its memory is still a crucial element in forming American political attitudes. As most politicians read their constituencies, recession and high rates of unemployment are regarded as intolerable, and the federal government is expected to take whatever action is necessary to sustain strong growth and keep unemployment down.

On the other hand, the coming of double-digit inflation to America also created deep anxieties among the mass of the public. In 1973, when prices were going up at 12 percent a year, the damage was widespread, for even the most powerful labor unions would have difficulty in negotiating wage increases greater than the rate of inflation, and most people were not members of powerful unions. This contributed to increased resistance to taxes and government spending. But if spending cuts went too deep, they might send the economy into a decline and cause a big jump in unemployment. So the electorate, like the political leadership, was torn between the two unpalatable alternatives of inflation or unemployment.

Unpleasant choices breed frustration and hostility. There were two directions in which the majority might vent their unhappiness. The first was toward the rich. As news stories broke about millionaires' paying little or no income tax, there was talk about a "taxpayer's revolt" against a system that bore more heavily on the middle and working classes than on many of those in the upper-income group.

There was also a growing resentment toward the poor. This was not an unqualified antipathy. Most people believe that government should see to it that poor people do not lack the necessities of life. Thus a Gallup poll in May 1966 indicated that 48 percent viewed the War on Poverty favorably as against 31 percent who looked at it critically. On FAP the public's response to the president's proposal was strongly favorable. A Gallup poll shortly after the president presented the program in August 1969 showed the division to be 65 to 20 in favor, and Gallup reported that "public opposition to the proposals stems mainly from the belief that the new system does not go far enough toward meeting the increased needs of the poor."

However, contrasting with this attitude was another view, often held by the same people who supported many government programs to help the poor. This was the traditional American position that people ought not to get something for nothing. This emphasis on self-reliance became less central as the farmer gave way to the urbanite, and it was severely shaken by the Great Depression. Still, as we have noted, the belief persisted that we are more worthy if we contribute to the economy, if we work for a living; and that dependence for survival on the support of the community makes us morally inferior. Accordingly, to large numbers of people the poor are a shiftless lot, lazy, apathetic, much given to antisocial behavior, including crime—and with no one to blame for their misfortune but themselves.

Generally speaking, the affluent have been the least prone to these unsympathetic attitudes. Hostility to the poor in recent years has been more commonly found among those who are little more than just above the poverty line. These are the people who were dubbed in the late 1960s as the Forgotten Americans or the Middle Americans. Typically they lived separately from the very poor—but not far removed. And they did not want their communities to be invaded by the poor, for this, they thought, would lead to a decline in their property values, deterioration of the standards of the neighborhood schools, and disruption of the public order.

There was one other dimension to the resentment of the poor—race prejudice, for many of those on welfare were black. But the resentment was also felt against poor whites. After all, many working-class and lower-middle-class whites had established only a precarious foothold on success. They were having great difficulty in sustaining what they regarded as a reasonable standard of living. They had to make payments on their mortgages and put some money aside, for they wanted to give their children a better start in life than they had had themselves. Higher taxes, to underwrite those who for lack of will or effort or morality (for this is what the majority believed) were perpetual failures, inevitably aroused resentments.

These attitudes were brought sharply into focus by proposals for a guaranteed annual income. Among experts and intellectuals a consensus in favor of this idea had been developing. In June 1968, more than 200 economists at 143 institutions of higher learning endorsed a statement calling for "a national system of income guarantees and supplements." But if experts and intellectuals are generally among the nation's opinion leaders, they were not leading the majority on this subject. In a 1968 Gallup poll on a proposal to provide a guaranteed annual income of $3200 to a family of four, the division was 58 to 36 percent against. Not surprisingly, a frequent comment was that "nobody should get something for nothing."

So there were two competing pulls within majority attitudes toward the poor—the one benign and charitable, the other grudging and resentful. Which of them dominated varied with the circumstances of the time. During the Great Depression a majority were poor, related to someone poor, or afraid of imminently becoming poor. So poverty was no stigma but a socially produced calamity. But later, when the majority had been able to take advantage of the opportunities opened to them by the system, they tended to assume of those who had not been able to "make it" that something must be wrong with them as individuals, some defect of will or character that made them unwilling to work for a living.

The poor should not be left to starve. The majority still maintained that government must do something about them. And the majority's benevolence could be especially expansive in the case of the War on Poverty, for the declaration of this war closely followed a federal income tax cut of $11.5 billion.

But these circumstances changed quickly. Inflation, fueled by the Vietnam war, began to impose severe strains on the economy. More and more claims were made on the federal budget, and some of them had to be rejected. Expenditures on antipoverty programs were going up. Moreover, under CAP the poor were encouraged not to feel grateful for federal funding. The middle and lower-middle classes were asked to contribute their taxes to help the poor and were receiving in return not gratitude but militant demands for more.

Then there was the frustrating fact that, despite all the money that was being spent on so many antipoverty programs, the number of people on welfare in several states and cities was actually increasing. The Aid to Families with Dependent Children program became the most rapidly growing part of relief outlays. And, although there was general support for the view that government must help children, there was also growing resentment at what was felt to be irresponsible behavior by the parents—behavior which placed a heavy tax burden on the rest of the population.

Throughout all this, ironically, the fundamental political problem of the poor in the post-World War II era has been the fact that their numbers have been reduced to a minority, a decreasing minority, of the population. This very accomplishment has made the position of the poor weak, tending to isolate them from the rest of the society. Prospects for programs helpful to the poor have improved when these programs have also offered benefits to much broader segments of the population. This was true of Social Security, for example, and of Medicare. But support for programs that are seen by the majority to be designed specifically and exclusively for the poor—public housing, the War on Poverty—has generally been lukewarm at best. An increasingly aggrieved middle class has come to complain: the rich can afford their luxuries; the poor get all kinds of assistance from the government. But who, asks the middle class, cares about us?

Five Perspectives on
the Distribution of Wealth

The Liberals: Inequality in America

Equality is one of the prime values of liberals. As they see it, the disparities of property and income between the top and the bottom of the scale in America to-day are unacceptable. According to U.S. Census Bureau figures, in 1975 the richest 5 percent of the population, those with earnings of more than $34,000, had 15.5 percent of all income in the country; the top 20 percent had 41.1 percent of all income; while the poorest 20 percent, those with incomes below $6900, had 5.4 percent of all income.

Despite income and inheritance taxes, and all the other devices of the federal government that are supposed to redistribute income, the concentration of wealth at the top has changed very little since World War II. The old family fortunes are still there, and enormous new ones have been made in oil and in land development in the Southeast and Southwest. In earlier chapters we noted the consequences of these concentrations of wealth for our political system, as we described the corrupting influence of big campaign contributions on the political process.

When liberals look at the tax structure, they are not surprised that people in the middle and lower-middle income brackets feel discriminated against. They cannot turn to tax shelters in land or cattle or oil or movies. The "progressive" income tax is actually progressive up to the middle levels, and not very much more beyond that. Moreover, the income tax is only part of the total tax picture. Social Security is actually a "regressive" tax, for it is levied at the same rate at all income levels and thus takes a larger share of the income of the poor than of the rich. And Social Security taxes have been rising rapidly, and may increase even faster in the future. When various other regressive taxes are added to the picture—state sales taxes, the increasingly unpopular local property taxes, and so on—it becomes clear that the proportionate spread indicated in Table 11–1 is very much reduced, and that the tax burden on the middle class is considerably greater than on the wealthy. Unfortunately, although there is widespread antagonism toward the tax loopholes of the rich, more of the frustration of the middle-income groups is directed at the poor.

Now the liberals agree that poverty in America has been significantly reduced in the past half century. In large measure, they claim, this achievement should be credited to ideas generated by liberals and eventually accepted by political leaders. This is true whether we are talking about the willingness to accept deficit budgeting, Social Security, Medicare, public housing, or any other social welfare legislation. In each case liberal scholars and analysts proposed programs, and later, usually much later, centrist politicians adopted them and put them into effect.

However, we are still far from having disposed of poverty in America. In this incredibly rich country we should not be boasting that *only* 12 percent of the population live below the poverty line. This represents 26 million people who subsist in conditions that the majority would find intolerable. But even this figure does not reveal the total number of people whose living conditions are far short of what we normally think of in America as a reasonable standard. If we raise the official 1976 poverty level by $1000 to $6500, we arrive at an income on which it is a heart-breaking task to provide decently for a family of four. And at that level we have not 26 million, but close to 40 million who might well be classified as poor.

Furthermore, say the liberals, the gains that have been made toward the reduction of poverty are precarious. Every time unemployment rises, more people fall into poverty. And, because of the preoccupation with keeping inflation down, we are tolerating higher levels of unemployment than were considered acceptable in the past. This, together with the cuts that have been made in the antipoverty programs, account for the fact that the gains of the 1960s have not continued into the 1970s. We began the decade with an official estimate of about 12 percent living in poverty, and, after some fluctuations up and down, the 12 percent figure was still there in 1976.

The liberals' proposals.   Liberals make a number of proposals for dealing with the uneven distribution of wealth in America. First, they want to continue in the general direction charted by the New Deal and expanded in the War on Poverty. They agree that many of the programs undertaken thus far have been defective in various ways, but they are not prepared to write off the programs of the thirties and the sixties as total failures. The most serious shortcoming they perceive is that too many of them have been half measures. Thus Medicare helps the elderly; but the health problems of younger people can only be attended to through a comprehensive national health program. The public housing program was too limited and too sterile, and should be expanded into a much greater involvement of the federal government in the housing field. Without this involvement we shall see a further deterioration of our stock of housing, for the cost of construction and of credit is so high that nobody can afford to buy a new home unless he is in the upper-middle-income group.

As for the Community Action Programs, the liberals do not deny they had their share of problems. Management failures, incessant squabbling, nepotism, and corruption showed up in a number of projects run by the local poverty boards. But all these are very much in evidence in other segments of American political and managerial life. Thus it was inevitable that programs which were partly controlled and run by the poor would reflect their lack of managerial and organizational experience as well as those cultural traits which had in the first place limited their chances of being successful. Wherever failures in the local poverty programs emerged, they were prominently and mercilessly publicized, and critics of the program gleefully pointed to these confirmations of what they had been contending all along. It appears that in political life we prefer to punish those who make mistakes rather than to enable them to learn from their errors. This is especially so when the poor are participants in the process.

Nonetheless, CAP should not be written off as a total failure. A number of highly effective leaders emerged from the community programs; and, in the liberals' view, intensified efforts should be made to involve the poor in the design and management of poverty programs.

Next, we need a guaranteed annual income. In a country of such abundance we should be able to provide to all of our people a minimum standard below which no one should be allowed to fall. The fact is that we already accept this in principle. But, because we are afraid to recognize it as a basic right, we surround it with bureaucratic restrictions and paperwork that is enormously expensive, infuriates and humiliates the recipients, and invites evasion and cheating. Benefits under the programs vary enormously from state to state, and they impose a burden on state and local budgets that makes the programs—and the poor—the target of widespread hostility. What is needed is a federal program that will cut through all the red tape and offer an assured subsistence level for all of those people who, for whatever reasons, are simply unable to provide adequately for themselves.

Nixon's Family Assistance Plan was intended to be a step in this direction. But he was unable to face its full implications. So concerned was Nixon with reassuring the country—and himself—that this was not really a guaranteed income, that it became increasingly unclear exactly what it was. And so insistent was he that the work ethic was not being abandoned that welfare recipients and their supporters were bound to see the program as punitive. The president insisted that people on welfare must work or accept training. But, with unemployment running at high levels, it was unclear where the jobs were to come from. "Workfare," in other words, was to be a means of forcing the recipients of the program to provide cheap, exploited labor as a means of punishing them. Carter's Program for Better Jobs and Income still put too much emphasis on the work requirement; but it did have the merit of proposing an expansion of public service jobs.

This brings us to the essence of the liberals' proposals—an expanding economy with full employment. Economic growth is necessary because it provides the resources to improve the living standards of the poor and the total environment in which they live. It also generates the abundant supply of jobs without which many people will continue to languish in poverty. And, say the liberals, most of the poor want to work, as long as the job pays them a reasonable wage. Some—the aged, the incapacitated, large families headed by the mother alone—cannot work, and they need the guaranteed income and other government assistance. Some who can work do not want to; but these constitute a small minority, not much larger proportionately than the shiftless element to be found at any economic level of the society. If there are plenty of jobs, and training programs to develop the necessary skills, there will be a strong demand for workers, just as during World War II, when there were hardly any unemployed.

But we do not have plenty of jobs. Under the Nixon and Ford policies the unemployment level reached close to 9 percent. Even when the economy picked up, the jobless rate remained at an obstinate 7 to 8 percent. This led to the rationalization that we could not get below 5 or even 6 percent unemployment, for many of the unemployed were actually only looking for part-time jobs, and to try to wipe out unemployment totally would lead to severe distortions in the economy. Liberals recognize that full employment does not mean that 100 percent of the work force should have jobs, for there will always be some people between jobs and there will be shifts in the economy that temporarily will cause some dislocation. But liberals contend that, given a vigorous economy, there need be no more than about 4 percent out of work at any given time. This means that we must pursue monetary policies that do not choke off the supply of money needed by an expanding economy; fiscal policies that provide the needed infusion of government spending whenever the economy lags; and a program of federal, state, and local government jobs that makes government the "employer of last resort" when the private sector fails to put people to work.

In all these respects the liberals complained that Jimmy Carter, though an improvement over his Republican predecessors in the presidency, was not acting boldly enough. He was too heavily committed to the war against budget deficits and against inflation.

But can we ignore the danger that, as a result of the liberals' measures, the economy could pick up too much steam and produce a new surge of inflation? Liberals have a three-pronged answer to this question. First, large-scale government spending is inflationary only if the economy is working at close to full capacity. If it is not, the infusion of government funds simply provides the stimulus to get idle resources to work. In fact, our economy usually operates well below capacity, and we lose tens of billions of dollars annually because we function so far below our potential. Second, we can live with a certain amount of inflation. Price increases of 4 to 5 percent a year are not particularly disruptive, for wages, profits, and Social Security payments usually keep abreast of them. Certainly the damage done to some groups by such increases is not as great as that caused by high rates of unemployment, which cause severe disruption in people's lives and leave them with a sense of humiliation and personal failure. If, however, inflation gets out of bounds—at a rate of, say, 8 percent or more—then something must be done. Spending on some government programs—highway or government building construction, for example—can be deferred for a while. But, most important, government must intervene to control price rises by direct action. Nixon's wage and price control efforts did not commend themselves to liberals, for they contend that the controls were biased in favor of business, and that they were imposed and removed so abruptly that they were followed by further soaring increases in prices. What we need is a firm, sustained program of government restraints on pricing directed particularly at the biggest corporations. These corporations are so dominant that they are no longer subject to competitive market forces. Thus, even when business falls off, they raise their prices. What we are faced with, then, is not a competitive price structure but "administered" prices—prices imposed upon us by administrative decision of the managers of the corporations. This, liberals argue, is a large part of the story of the double-digit inflation of 1973–74, and they insist that the fear of inflation should not be used in a manipulated effort to force the reduction of government spending and the acceptance of an increase in unemployment.

Finally, liberals look to two particular sources to help pay for the cost of programs for low-income people. The first is the defense budget, which can be cut by tens of billions of dollars. The second is the closing of the tax loopholes, which enable the rich to keep most of their money while preserving the illusion of a just and progressive tax system. As Jack Newfield and Jeff Greenfield have pointed out, "The American tax system is a fraud. It has been so manipulated by the legal and political hired guns of rich that it *reinforces*, rather than equalizes, the power of wealth in America."[8]

Wealth, and the power that goes with it, is excessively concentrated at the top, say the liberals, and poverty will not be eradicated until we bring about a degree of redistribution that has not so far been undertaken.

The Radical Left: Rule by the Rich

However critical the liberals' attack on the inadequacies of past and present antipoverty programs, they are still denounced by the left for their failure to see that no fundamental redistribution can come about within the existing framework.

Certainly some concessions have been made by the ruling group. The moderate wing of the power elite is capable of "reacting to pressure from below and granting some degree of satisfaction to the unhappy," says Domhoff. But it is always on their own terms. In fact, it is the power elite who are behind the studies by such groups as the Brookings Institution and the Committee for Economic Development which influence social legislation. And "it is the power elite who take advantage of the expertise trained at the universities they finance and direct. In short, it is the power elite that develop the plan to deal with the pressures of domestic discontent."

They do this in order to provide a safety valve for that discontent. They make concessions that provide some amelioration of the conditions of the poor. But those concessions do not challenge the privileges of the rulers or narrow the range of inequality. They maintain "the wealth distribution intact, and with it the privileges, prestige, and prerogatives of the few tenths of a percent of the population making up the American upper class."[9]

The liberals, by persisting in their fight for reform measures, prevent the people from seeing the basic realities and inequalities of the system. Gradualism does not lead us toward a just society. It moves us farther away from it. For, by moving a proportion of the population out of acute poverty into a slightly more tolerable condition, gradualist reform lessens the hostility needed to create a revolution.

Of all the antipoverty proposals considered in this chapter only one is perceived by the left as containing acceptable values. The idea in CAP that the poor must be helped to organize themselves to develop a sense of power and meaning, to free themselves from the inferiority to which they had been assigned, and to challenge existing bastions of power is very much in line with the strategies advocated by the radical left.

However, in the left's perspective CAP was doomed to failure. Beyond a point, government would not allow structures created by itself to challenge its own authority. Once the administration realized that it had unleashed forces that could be dangerously abrasive, it was inevitable that it would quickly rein in those forces.

So, at the heart of the matter, is the fact that we are controlled by a ruling class that is ready to make some concessions from time to time but never to relinquish its power or to change its cherished values. Accordingly, it cannot undertake the measures that alone can abolish poverty. As long as the acquisitive, competitive ethic, which is fostered by corporate capitalism, remains, it is inevitable that the poor will be derided and scorned by the rest of the society. Only when the corporations become servants of the community, rather than of large shareholders, will they be turned away from frivolous and even dangerous purposes toward the task of ending poverty. Only when we care less about success and ambition and more about building a community in which everyone is accorded dignity and respect can the curse of poverty be lifted. Poverty today exists not for lack of production but because of distortions in distribution. We have long had enough wealth to bring everyone up to a full sufficiency if we cared to. What is needed is more equality, rather than increased gross national product.

"In these days, when it takes a great deal of money to live, I feel damn farsighted in having a great deal of money."

Drawing by Wm. Hamilton: © 1974 The New Yorker Magazine, Inc.

The Conservatives:
Some Poverty Is Inevitable

To conservatives the persistence of inequalities of property and income is no cause for alarm. On the contrary, the opportunity to make and bequeath a great deal of money is an important conservative value. Without it they believe that an essential source of incentives for effort and creativity would be lost and society would settle down into a drab, static uniformity. Moreover, ours is not a feudal society with a small number of weathy aristocrats ruling a great poverty-stricken mass. The masses in the United States are middle-class property owners.

Admittedly we still have our poor. But their numbers are much fewer, and their plight much less serious, than the liberals and the radicals allege. Thus, if we are to take the official definition, an annual income of $5500 for a family of four would not sound like deprivation, let alone poverty, to most of the peoples of Latin America, Africa, India, and even the Soviet Union. To those who suggest that comparisons should be limited to the United States context, conservatives still insist that the official poverty line is unduly high, that a more realistic figure would be about three-quarters of the federal government's level—which would cut the number said to be living in poverty by almost a half.[10] Still, even if a true estimate is closer to 7 or 8 percent of the population than the official 12 percent, poverty is a problem that affects several million people, and the conservatives do not propose that we ignore it.

What should be done.   In a large part the conservatives' answer to what we should do about poverty is to stop doing most of what we have been doing. For one thing we should not repeat rabble-rousing programs such as the Community Action Program of the Economic Opportunity Act. Indeed, the CAP provisions of the Act offered a perfect illustration of a liberal establishment, comprised of left-wing intellectuals, university professors, foundation officials, and bureaucrats, working its will without Congress's realizing what was going on. The result of their labors was disastrous. The program was riddled with incompetence, waste, and corruption. Absurdly misguided efforts were made to secure the participation of the poor through special elections for the local poverty agency boards. The turnout among the qualified electorate (to qualify one had to declare oneself to be poor) was a tiny fraction of those eligible. Worse yet, CAP, by organizing discontent and encouraging protest and confrontation as techniques for giving the poor self-respect, was an important contributing factor in the outbreaks of rioting between 1965 and 1968 in Los Angeles, Cleveland, Newark, and Detroit—all cities that received substantial funds from the poverty program.

As for the other liberal proposals, the conservatives find them all fallacious. They do not agree that the way to economic growth is through high government spending and huge budgetary deficits. They were horrified when President Nixon declared that he was a Keynesian. They were angered, too, when, despite their proclaimed intention of reducing government spending, the Nixon and Ford administrations repeatedly incurred enormous budgetary deficits. When Nixon imposed price controls, they declared that he had lost his nerve, that if he had waited a little longer prices would have declined anyway, and that controls ultimately damage the economy.

Nor will the poor gain much from tax reform. Some of the loopholes for the rich are undesirable, but many serve a specific social purpose. Tax-free municipal bonds (which usually offer a low rate of interest) facilitate borrowing by local governments and keep their costs down. Private charity, which is better than more federal programs, is encouraged by the system of tax deductions. And so on. Moreover, it is not only the rich who benefit from tax loopholes. Lower-income people are helped by loopholes such as the deduction allowed for the homeowners' property tax. In any case, if the loopholes that are of advantage to the rich alone were closed, the revenues generated would be far less than is commonly assumed and would certainly not be sufficient to abolish poverty and reduce the taxes of middle-income people.

Conservative proposals point in a very different direction. They advocate the removal of most constraints on private enterprise. Business, left largely to pursue its own interests, will generate more and more wealth. Only a rising gross national product can provide enough for all, including the poor, and only business has the genius to accomplish this.

Consequently, government spending should be cut. The national debt should be reduced. Taxes should be slashed; confiscatory tax rates on the upper-income groups and on business corporations take away their incentive to produce more, and without that incentive everyone suffers, including the poor.

Inflation is the great threat to economic growth, stability, and justice. It unfairly penalizes people on fixed incomes, notably the elderly. It pushes up the cost of government. It unleashes an ever-upward wage–price spiral which, at some point, leads businesspeople to lose confidence in the economy's stability and cut back on inventories and new orders. This induces a recession—which involves high rates of unemployment. Thus the conservatives argue that their concern with inflation is not a heartless disregard of the suffering caused by unemployment but a necessary condition of preventing unemployment.

Their analysis does assume a somewhat higher level of unemployment than liberals are prepared to accept, for otherwise the economy would lose a necessary degree of flexibility, and inflation would be encouraged. Conservatives would deal with this in a number of ways. One would be to lower or abolish the minimum wage. By imposing an artificial minimum wage, government forces some employers of unskilled labor out of business or makes them substitute machines for people. Then, the federal government should not be quite as open-handed in providing unemployment benefits. The ease with which people can qualify for these benefits, the increase in their scale, and the extension of the period for which they are given have encouraged a considerable number of people to go on the unemployment rolls rather than look for work.

However, conservatives agree that government should provide some financial aid to people who have diligently tried to find work but have been unsuccessful. Milton Friedman is among those conservatives who have proposed that this be done by a negative income tax program. This would simply establish a minimum level of income, and it would use the Internal Revenue Service mechanism to provide anyone whose income fell below that level (even people who would not normally have to file an income tax return) the amount needed to bring them up to the prescribed minimum. Money earned above the absolute minimum would not disqualify a recipient from any benefits; it would be taxed but only at a gradually increasing rate so that the incentive to work would remain. This was an essential feature of the Friedman plan, and the incentive to work was, as we have seen, a component of the Family Assistance Plan.

However, as the details of FAP were spelled out, Friedman became doubtful that it incorporated the work incentive adequately. The supplementation of FAP by a number of other federal programs, such as food stamps, complicated the issue and, by Friedman's analysis, would result in a very high tax on any earnings above the minimum. Moreover, Friedman's proposal was intended not to supplement other forms of federal aid to the poor but to replace them. He believed that poverty was simply a lack of money. He wanted to get money into the hands of the poor and let them do what they wanted with it, exercising the free choice that was the essential virtue of the free economy. To liberals the income programs were supplements to, rather than substitutes for, other poverty programs. On this Friedman dissented vigorously.

Even in its pure form, Friedman had considerable difficulty in persuading other conservatives to support his idea. To many of them any proposal that would hand out money to the poor as a right, without conditions, was immoral. Whatever constraints were imposed on the program at the outset would soon be abandoned as the FAP beneficiaries, the bureaucracies, and the liberals brought their pressures to bear.

To those conservatives who cannot accept Friedman's unadorned negative income tax plan, the alternative is to continue to provide welfare programs of various kinds but to restore the responsibility to state and local governments. These should crack down on the abuses and widespread frauds that beset AFDC, food stamps, Medicaid, and so on and that allow some people to receive aid far greater than the income of many working people. What would remain would be a reasonable and humane response to the needs of those who are simply unable to shift for themselves. The poor will always be with us. Fortunately, in America they are far fewer than in almost any other country. We must do what is necessary for them to ensure that they do not go without the simple necessities of life.

But we should not raise the responsibility of public and private charity to the level of a right which the recipients are encouraged to assert aggressively. As for those who try to take the easy way out of poverty by engaging in criminal activity, the response should be the tightening and stricter enforcement of the laws.

The Radical Right:
Stop the Rush to Socialism

In their diagnosis of who makes the decisions on social legislation, the right comes to many of the same conclusions as the left. The Committee for Economic Development, the Brookings Institution, and the universities provide the long-range plans. These are paid for by the "insiders, such as the Rockefellers, Fords, or Kennedys."

But the intent of this conspiracy is differently perceived on the right than on the left. The right believes that the purpose is to move the country in the direction of socialism. But why should the rich want socialism? It is because "socialism is not a share-the-wealth program, but in reality a method to *consolidate* and *control* the wealth."[11] This is true in the Soviet Union, which is not an egalitarian society but a highly stratified system in which a few at the top live very well indeed. In this country, the rich design programs that hand out money to the poor at the expense not of themselves but of the great majority of the country, including businesspeople who are not part of the club of superrich insiders.

Poverty, the extent of which is vastly exaggerated by the intellectuals, the media, and the other opinion molders of the country, should be dealt with by private charity and by strictly administered state and local action. The problems of the poor should not be used as a rationale for moving the country faster and faster toward socialism. Instead, government spending should be slashed, budget deficits ended, and the income tax abolished by repeal of the Sixteenth Amendment.

The Centrists:
The Great American Middle Class

When the centrists look at the American record on the distribution of wealth, they see a remarkable success story. "Something has happened in the United States in recent years," says Ben Wattenberg, "that has never happened before anywhere: The massive majority of the population of a nation is now in the middle class."[12] Wattenberg's definition of middle class starts with families of four who have a little "discretionary" income—income that can be spent on things people want as against what they absolutely need. In 1972 the family income that produced an initial amount of discretionary money was $7000. Almost three-quarters of all American families had an income that year of over $7000. Even if we take the more ample figure of $10,000 as our defining figure for the middle class, 56 percent of American families qualified as middle class in 1972. And even allowing for inflation, the proportion in the middle class has gone up a little since 1972.

How has this excellent record been achieved? First, the economy has grown sufficiently to provide something for everybody. Business, labor, and agriculture have been the prime movers, but government has played an essential role.

Economic growth in America is a product of the partnership between the private and public sectors.

Second, we have established a reasonable degree of economic stability. Most especially we have learned to prevent any recurrence of the Great Depression, which could never happen again. We still have recessions, and unemployment is periodically higher than it should be. We must recognize that some of the increase in unemployment in recent years has resulted from long-term changes in the labor force. There has been an enormous increase in the number of women seeking full-time or part-time work. And the situation is complicated by including in the un-employed many college students and other teenagers who are looking only for part-time or temporary jobs. Thus the liberals' demand that we reduce unemploy-ment to 4 percent or less is no longer realistic. Still, by the judicious use of monetary and fiscal policy we should be able to bring unemployment down to a level of 5 or 6 percent.

We may have more difficulty in finding the tools needed to control inflation. When prices rise at the rate of 10 to 12 percent, the result is not only damage to people on fixed incomes but also a serious undermining of the people's confidence in the economic and political order. Inflation at those levels is not only unjust and inconvenient; it is also dangerous. Fortunately, there is considerable evidence that the sharp increases of 1973 and 1974 were the consequence of special circum-stances—the economic consequences of Vietnam and the doubling of oil prices. Subsequently, the rate of inflation has slowed considerably and was brought down to below 6 percent in 1976. Even at its worst, inflation in this country was less severe than in most other nations. In the year ending August 31, 1974, prices in the United States rose 11.2 percent. The average increase for all noncommunist industrial countries was 13.5 percent. In Britain the rate was 17 percent, in Italy over 20 percent. In Chile consumer prices rose 340 percent in 1975, which represented real progress over 1972, when the rate was over 1000 percent. So in-flation is a problem for us—a greater problem than we had imagined a few years ago. But our economy is too strong, and our government sufficiently sophisticated, to prevent anything like the disastrous phenomenon we have witnessed in Chile and a number of other countries at various times.

As for the poor, the liberals keep on stretching the data and adjusting their definitions to hide the essential fact: poverty in America was cut in half in the 1960s, and now afflicts no more than about 12 percent of the population. This still represents an important problem—more so than the conservatives admit. But the progress achieved is impressive, and in part it is attributable to the development of a number of government programs for the people in the lower half of the in-come scale. Not all of these programs are working well, and it is time they were subjected to a thorough reassessment and pruning. Community Action programs, for example, are too abrasive. They produce demands that cannot possibly be met, and they provoke hostile attitudes toward the poor. They have been wasteful and incompetently managed, and they have contributed little toward the reduction of poverty.

Then, too, it is time to get rid of AFDC and replace it with something more effective and humane. Although Nixon's Family Assistance Plan may not have been perfect, it is a great pity that it was rejected. This happened because it was caught in a crossfire between left and right factions committed to rigid ideologies instead of sensible problem solving; thus a program that represented a genuine breakthrough was vetoed. However, sound ideas do not die in the American system. Carter has presented his own version, and the prospect is that some kind of major welfare reform will be undertaken within the next few years.

Other changes, too, are needed in such fields as health insurance and the tax system. These questions will be hotly and extensively debated. But out of the controversy the necessary reforms will be shaped.

The middle class in America will continue to grow, and its living standards will go on rising. Gradually we shall keep on reducing the number of the poor until the only ones left in the poverty category will be those who, because of individual disabilities of body or character, would never be able to make it in any system. The only thing that can jeopardize the continuation of this steady progress is the social tension that could be generated by strident, impossible demands of liberals and the left, or the unwillingness to accept reasonable changes by conservatives and the right.

Conclusion

There is no dispute from any point on the spectrum with the fact that there has been a substantial reduction of poverty in America over the past 40 years. The centrists celebrate this reduction as a magnificent achievement. Left of center the critics complain that the extent of the decline is overstated by the official figures, that it has not gone far enough, and that our society suffers from the persistence of gross inequalities. Right of center the argument is heard that the extent of poverty is overstated by the official figures, that some inequality is inevitable and desirable, and that our economy and our free society are threatened by trying to create an artificial equality. But if there is disagreement over the scale and the consequences of the reduction of acute poverty, there is at least a significant measure of agreement that its extent has been reduced.

From here onward it is likely that substantial further declines in the proportion of people living below the poverty line will be more difficult to achieve than in the past. There are two reasons for this. First, as we get down below 12 percent of the population, we come closer to what may be an irreducible minimum, a hard core of people who simply will not be able to make their own way in the world without support from the community. Second, the recent changes in our economic circumstances make it harder to secure the majority support needed for new social welfare programs. The fear of unemployment and recession has now been matched, if not overshadowed, by the fear of inflation. This creates stronger resistance to government spending, budget deficits, and higher taxes, which are all associated in the public mind with efforts to help the poor.

A faster pace of economic growth could resolve this dilemma. But, as we shall see in our discussion of energy and the environment in Chapter 13, the abundant natural resources that have fueled our incredible growth until now cannot be taken for granted in the future. As recently as the early 1960s, commentators on American society were telling us that we had reached the end of the age of scarcity and were moving into the "postindustrial society"—a society of technologically assured abundance. Somehow that dazzling scenario has had to be postponed for at least a decade or two. Meanwhile the hard political and economic choices continue to haunt us, and they will not always be decided in favor of the poor.

Still, it is unlikely that politicians will stop proposing programs to help the poor. Whether the poor actually constitute 12 percent of the population, 20 percent, or only 8 percent, their plight will continue to be discussed in the political arena; for it represents not only a source of programs through which some politicians might make their reputation, but also a perennial cause of tension and instability in the social order. This becomes especially clear when we relate it to the subject of our next chapter—the relationship between the races in America.

Notes and References

1.   "The Richest Men in America," *Newsweek*, August 2, 1976, pp. 56–59.

2.   Oscar Lewis, *La Vida* (New York: Random House, Inc., 1966), pp. xlv–xlviii, li–lii.

3.   Leonard Goodwin, *Do the Poor Want to Work?* (Washington, D.C.: The Brookings Institution, 1973).

4.   Daniel P. Moynihan, *The Politics of a Guaranteed Income* (New York: Random House, Inc., 1973), p. 74.

5.   See John Bibby and Roger Davidson, *On Capitol Hill* (New York: Holt, Rinehart and Winston, Inc., 1967), pp. 219–38; Richard Blumenthal, "The Bureaucracy: Antipoverty and the Community Action Program," in Allan P. Sindler, *American Political Institutions and Public Policy* (Boston: Little, Brown and Company, 1969), pp. 129–79; John C. Donovan, *The Politics of Poverty* (Indianapolis, Ind.: Pegasus, 1967), pp. 27–38; Daniel Patrick Moynihan, *Maximum Feasible Misunderstanding* (New York: The Free Press, 1969).

6.   Daniel P. Moynihan, "Comments: What Is 'Community Action'?" *Public Interest*, No. 5 (Fall 1966), p. 6.

7.   Donovan, *The Politics of Poverty*, p. 42.

8.   Jack Newfield and Jeff Greenfield, *A Populist Manifesto: The Making of a New Majority* (New York: Paperback Library, 1972), pp. 96–97.

9.   G. William Domhoff, *The Higher Circles: The Governing Class in America* (New York: Random House, Inc. [Vintage Books], 1970), p. 250.

10.   See Rose D. Friedman, *Poverty: Definition and Perspective* (Washington, D.C.: American Enterprise Institute for Public Policy Research, 1965).

11.   Gary Allen, *None Dare Call It Conspiracy* (Rossmoor, Calif.: Concord Press, 1971), p. 32–33.

12.   Ben J. Wattenberg, *The Real America: A Surprising Examination of the State of the Union* (New York: G. P. Putnam's Sons, [Capricorn Books], 1976), p. 51.

Race:

The Critical Test

Of all domestic issues the relationship between the races poses the most critical test of American government and politics. For most whites it is a problem of how to deal with the claims of black people. For blacks it is what James Baldwin called "the white problem." For all of us it forces a further examination of those enduring questions about equality introduced in Chapter 1 and pursued in the context of poverty in Chapter 11.

The race problem in America has a long, unhappy history, beginning in the sixteenth century when blacks were brought here as slaves from Africa, chained and packed together in such dreadful conditions that great numbers of them died on the voyage over. Once here they were sold and bartered, and became the work force for the plantation economy of the South. There have been some recent suggestions by economic historians that the life of the slaves, though harsh, was not as bad as most accounts have suggested—better in many respects than the conditions under which many factory workers lived in the North.[1] Other historians have bitterly disputed these findings, both on methodological and factual grounds. But no one questions the central core of the problem—whatever their living conditions, black people were slaves. Apparently, the wording of the Declaration of Independence, that "All men are created equal," did not apply to blacks, for they were property rather than people under the law.

This denial of the blacks' humanity worried more and more people as the nineteenth century progressed, and a move for the abolition of slavery slowly gained ground. At the very least, the northern states, which did not allow slavery, wanted to stop the spread of the institution from the South into the newly developing regions of the West. The tension built, and was brought to fever pitch by the Supreme Court's *Dred Scott* decision in 1857, in which Chief Justice Roger

Taney, ruling on the rights of a runaway slave, declared that he had no constitutional rights since he was not a citizen under the Constitution.

The South seceded over the slavery issue. The Civil War was fought primarily over the determination of Lincoln and the North to restore the Union. But when it was over, the issue that had precipitated the war had to be dealt with. The South was for slavery, and the South lost. The Thirteenth Amendment abolished slavery in 1865; the Fourteenth Amendment in 1868 reversed the *Dred Scott* decision and made citizens of the former slaves; in 1870 the Fifteenth Amendment gave black males the right to vote (see Appendix 1).

Reconstruction and Reaction

These amendments were passed during the Reconstruction era along with the Civil Rights Act of 1875, which provided for equal public accommodations for blacks. But eight years after its passage the Supreme Court ruled the act unconstitutional. Southerners took this as the signal they had been waiting for. Reconstruction, they felt, was a vengeful effort to destroy the South's way of life. Striking back, they segregated the blacks and passed "Jim Crow" laws to make segregation and discrimination official. Blacks who challenged segregation in any way were intimidated, sometimes terrorized, sometimes even lynched. (In the 1880s and 1890s there were over 100 lynchings a year.)

Any possibility that black people might try to use the vote to advance their cause was effectively prevented despite the guarantees of the Fourteenth and Fifteenth Amendments. Blacks were kept from the polls by registration requirements, including literacy tests that were interpreted in favor of whites and against blacks; by a "poll tax" that most blacks were too poor to pay; and if all else failed, by physical threats. Then, too, the South was dominated by the Democratic party, whose political monopoly was sustained partly by tradition, partly by the fear that a genuine two-party system might lead to bidding for black people's votes by one of the parties. Thus the only real competition took place in the primaries; and the primaries were private affairs for whites only.

There was not much for blacks to do if they wanted to improve their conditions but to move from the South. Increasing numbers of them did so, hoping to make a better life in the cities of the North. Although they were not confronted there by segregation laws, most of them encountered discrimination, poverty, and living conditions sometimes more squalid than those they had left behind.

Politically weak, they found that government would do little for them. Only in the 1930s with the New Deal did they begin to share in some of the benefits that federal government programs provided. World War II brought them jobs; and the nation sought their help as fighting men—in segregated units. With the war over steps were taken to reduce discrimination in the armed forces, federal employment, and government-backed mortgages. But there was still no momentum behind the efforts to obtain equal rights for black people.

The Civil Rights Breakthrough

Gradually, however, that momentum developed, and it moved on several fronts. First there were the courts. From the late 1930s black leaders had begun to file suits in which they challenged the "separate but equal" doctrine, which had been established by the Supreme Court in *Plessy* v. *Ferguson* (1896). In 1950 the Supreme Court made two decisions[2] reducing the obstacles to blacks' getting into graduate schools. Then in 1954 came the momentous decision in *Brown* v. *Topeka Board of Education* that separation solely on grounds of race inherently denied the constitutional guarantee of equal protection of the laws. From there the Court went on in subsequent years to strike down state laws requiring segregation in public accommodations, public facilities, juries, and other fields where government action resulted in discrimination.

Concurrently with the help they were getting from the courts, black people took direct action to seek redress of their grievances. In December 1955, in Montgomery, Alabama, a black working woman, Rosa Parks, refused to follow the rule that black passengers give up their seats in the front of the bus to whites and move to the back. She was arrested and fined; but blacks conducted a year-long boycott of the Montgomery buses led by an extraordinary Baptist minister, Martin Luther King, Jr. King's home was bombed, and he went to jail. But in November 1956, a federal court injunction put an end to bus segregation in Montgomery. The issue had captured the imagination of the country, and so had Martin Luther King.

On the basis of this experience King built an organization, the Southern Christian Leadership Conference (SCLC), and developed the strategy of non-violent civil disobedience. Sit-ins and demonstrations spread throughout the South, and "freedom rides" brought white and black civil rights activists from the North. Then came the events in Birmingham, Alabama, in the spring of 1963. "Bull" Connor, the Birmingham police chief, set police dogs on a crowd of civil rights demonstrators. Television covered the event, and a shock wave swept the nation. Demonstrations and protests, in some cases riots, followed in cities throughout the country. The mood of outrage was turned to dedication by a great march on Washington, where King told more than 200,000 people of his dream of an America free from prejudice and discrimination.

The impetus was established for federal legislation. After an intensive lobbying campaign by civil rights forces, the Civil Rights Act of 1964 passed. The act expanded the federal protection of voting rights; gave the attorney general authority to bring civil suits against discrimination or segregation in public facilities and such public accommodations as restaurants, lunch counters, gas stations, theaters, stadiums, hotels, or lodging houses (except for owner-occupied units with five rooms or less); empowered the attorney general to file suit for the desegregation of public schools; authorized the U.S. Office of Education to report on desegregation progress and give technical and financial assistance, on request, to school systems embarked on desegregation; extended the life and expanded the jurisdiction of the Civil Rights Commission; created an Equal Employment Opportunities Commission charged with the task of promoting and enforcing equal job opportunities in businesses or unions with 25 or more workers; and created a Community Relations Service to work in local communities. One other significant provision was set forth in Title VI of the bill: "No person in the United States shall, on the ground of race, color, or national origin, be excluded from participation in, be denied the benefit of, or be subjected to discrimination under any program or activity receiving federal financial assistance."

Congress, spurred by demonstrations for black voting rights in Selma, Alabama, and other southern communities, followed the 1964 act with the Voting Rights Act of 1965. This banned the use of literacy or other tests to qualify voters and authorized the appointment of federal voting examiners empowered to order the registration of blacks in districts where there was an obvious pattern of discrimination. (Districts affected were those where less than 50 percent of voting-age citizens had been registered in the 1964 election, which was the case in six southern states and a few counties in other parts of the country.) The effects of the act were dramatic. By 1966, black registration in the South had increased by half a million to 2.7 million.

Thus the Civil Rights Act of 1964 had finally spelled out in specific terms the provisions of the Fourteenth Amendment of 1868. And the Fifteenth Amendment's promise of the right to vote, made in 1870, was given the full weight of governmental power by the act of 1965. It had taken almost a hundred years; but at last it seemed that the courts, the executive and legislative branches of government, and the civil rights movement had succeeded in ending the barriers against the full enjoyment of their constitutional rights by black people.

Violence in the Cities

Euphoria was not to last. The hopes of certain progress toward a fully integrated society were soon to be shattered by a series of traumatic events. In the summer of 1964, the year of the great Civil Rights Act, riots broke out in the black neighborhoods of seven cities, including New York, Chicago, and Philadelphia. In the summer of 1965, the year of Voting Rights, there was an eruption of violence in the Los Angeles black ghetto of Watts which far surpassed previous outbreaks elsewhere. It lasted six days, achieving a scale that led some commentators to use words like "revolt" or "rebellion" rather than riot. The National Guard was finally called in to restore order. The violence in Watts left 34 dead and over 1000 injured. Property damage was estimated at about $40 million, and there were almost 4000 arrests.

Up to 15 percent of the black adult population of the immediate area involved in the rioting were active at some point in the outbreak. In addition, 35 to 40 percent were "active spectators"; and "while the majority expressed disapproval of the violence and destruction, it was often coupled with an expression of empathy with those who participated or sense of pride that the Negro has brought worldwide attention to his problem."[3]

In 1966 there were outbreaks in several other cities, smaller in scale than Watts but enough to destroy the assumption of whites in the communities in which they occurred that they were free from serious racial tensions. Then came the summer of 1967—the most violent the nation had experienced since the Civil War. There were 41 serious disorders, 8 of which assumed major proportions. Eighty-three people were killed, most of them in Detroit and Newark and most of them blacks. Local police were unable to contain the major uprisings, and peace was restored only when the National Guard had taken over the affected areas.

The repeated experience of the total breakdown of order in whole sections of major cities; of murderous exchanges of gunfire; of city blocks set to the torch; of uncontrolled looting—and all of this carried live on television—led to the appointment by President Johnson of a commission under Governor Otto Kerner of Illinois to study the riots and make recommendations to prevent their recurrence. In March 1968, the National Advisory Commission on Civil Disorders submitted its report.[4] Its basic conclusion was, "Our nation is moving toward two societies, one black, one white—separate and unequal." Further, the report asserted that massive corrective measures must be undertaken to offset the "white racism" that was at the heart of the problems. Programs must be launched to improve conditions in the inner cities, and the trend toward segregation must be reversed. Otherwise, said the Commission, "Large-scale and continuing violence could result, followed by white retaliation, and ultimately, the separation of the two communities in a garrison state."

Black–White
Disparities in the 1970s

The catastrophic situation which the Kerner Commission warned against has not yet come about. There have been no further outbreaks on the scale of Watts in 1965 and Detroit in 1967. However, there have been sporadic outbreaks of violence. Tensions, resentments, and counterresentments persist.

At the root of the problem are the differences referred to in the previous chapter: differences in the quality of life between the majority of whites and the majority of blacks. In significant respects these differences have narrowed. But they have not been eliminated, and they remain as sources of discontent for the 11 percent of the population who are black. The differences and the progress made in reducing them can be seen in official Census Bureau figures on income, jobs, education, housing, and health, and also in the area of political power.

Income.   Average black family income in 1975 was about three-fifths of white family income. This was down a little from 1970, but up from 1959, when the ratio had been only a little more than a half. The proportion of blacks living in poverty (about 30 percent) is about four times the proportion of whites. Close to one black family in five receives federal Aid to Families with Dependent Children. This is closely related to the fact that about a third of black families are headed by women, a proportion which has doubled in 20 years. About 40 percent of all food stamp purchases are made by blacks.

Jobs.   The unemployment rate for blacks is almost double that of whites, and a third or more of black teenagers are unemployed.

The 1960s saw a significant upgrading in the occupations of black people, more of them moving into clerical, sales, craft, and technical jobs. But they are still much less likely than whites to hold positions in the professions and in the middle and upper ranks of managers and technicians. In an effort to correct this federal, state, and local governments established "affirmative action" programs aimed at increasing the proportions of minorities and women in government and government-aided employment. These programs require that institutions set targets for increases in the proportion of minorities and women employed at each level, and move toward these targets on an agreed-upon schedule. In addition, business and labor unions have launched programs directed toward the same ends.

Education.   The gap between blacks and whites in years of education has declined sharply over the last three decades. For blacks the figures are shown in Table 12–1.

TABLE 12–1   *Median School Years Completed,*
Age Group 25–29

Year	Blacks	All Races
1940	7.0	10.3
1950	8.6	12.1
1960	10.8	12.3
1970	12.2	12.6

SOURCE: Data from U.S. Census Bureau; cited in Ben J. Wattenberg, *The Real America* (New York: Capricorn Books, 1976), p. 133.

Since 1970 there has been a further slight gain to bring the figure within a few percentage points of the proportion for whites. The result is that the proportion of blacks finishing high school was 72 percent in 1974, up from 65 percent in 1970. Eighty-five percent of whites finished high school in 1974.

Black college enrollment has also been increasing at a rapid rate. In 1965, 10 percent of blacks aged 18 to 24 were enrolled in college as compared with 26 percent of the whites. By 1972 the white percentage was unchanged, but 18 percent of young blacks were in college, and the proportion was still rising. The gap at the graduate school level was much higher, however, and here again the affirmative action principle was applied by many colleges and universities in an effort to increase the proportions of minorities and women.

With respect to school integration, major gains have been made in the South, where less than one black child in 10 attended an all-black school by 1973. But these gains have not been matched by integration in the North and West, for, in a number of big-city school districts, blacks constitute a majority of the students and sometimes the entire student body. Thus in 1972 the percentage of black children in schools that were predominately black was approximately 95 in Newark, 93 in Chicago and St. Louis, 90 in Cleveland and Kansas City, 85 in Baltimore, and 80 in Philadelphia and Detroit. Houston, San Francisco, Los Angeles, Boston, Fort Worth, and Birmingham were other cities with a high degree of school segregation.

Under pressure from the courts a number of northern districts have been adopting a variety of devices to reduce the extent of segregation, the most controversial of these being the busing of both black and white students to schools outside their immediate neighborhoods.

Housing.   Blacks are much more likely than whites to live in substandard housing conditions. However, there has been substantial improvement in this respect. In 1960, 41 percent of housing occupied by blacks was lacking in some or all plumbing facilities. By 1970 this was down to 17 percent, as compared with 5 percent of whites. Home ownership among blacks is also on the increase, rising from about a quarter of black families owning homes in 1940, to a third in 1950, to about two-fifths by 1970. About two-thirds of whites owned their own homes in 1970.

Here again, however, the problem of segregation has persisted, despite governmental efforts to eliminate discriminatory practices in the sale and rental of housing. As blacks moved into the northern cities, whites moved out to the suburbs, and an increasing number of cities came to have black majorities. Among these were Washington, Newark, and Atlanta; and it was likely that before long Baltimore, Detroit, St. Louis, New Orleans, and Philadelphia would join the list of predominately black cities.

Health.   Black Americans tend to have more problems with their health than whites. This appears to result partly from lower incomes and poorer housing, and partly from the less than adequate quality of medical facilities and the insufficient number of health-care personnel in the black ghettos. (Blacks constitute 2 percent of the nation's doctors, 2.6 percent of the dentists, 5.7 percent of the nurses.)

On the average, blacks live six years less than whites. The life expectancy of black men is 62, of white men 68; for women the figures are 70 for blacks, 76 for whites. The black infant mortality rate—that is, the proportion dying before the age of one—has declined significantly in recent years, but is still almost twice the rate for whites, and the proportion of women who die in childbirth is much higher among blacks than among whites.

Political power.   With one senator, 16 members of the House of Representatives, one Supreme Court justice, and less than 1 percent of all the state and local elected officials in the country in 1977, it was clear that blacks were very much underrepresented in the political system. However, the number of state and local officeholders has almost tripled since 1970. They have included the mayors of Newark, Gary, Washington, Atlanta and Los Angeles; a black lieutenant governor in California; and a secretary of state in Pennsylvania. The gains have been particularly impressive in the South, where the surge of black voters enfranchised by the 1965 Voting Rights Act has brought a jump in the number of black sheriffs and other local officials, as well as members of state legislatures.

Racial Issues and the Policy-making Process

Here again we see many of the political forces we have described throughout this book coming into play in the process of shaping governmental policy on race and minorities. The elements affecting policy making that are particularly important here are the climate of public opinion, the array of interest groups, the Supreme Court, president and Congress, and the federal bureaucracy.

Public Opinion

The year 1963 was a critical one in establishing the importance of the race issue in the public mind. In March of that year a survey indicated that only 4 percent of those interviewed mentioned race as the top issue facing the country. By September, after riots in Birmingham, the assassination of black leader Medgar Evers, and Governor George Wallace's headline-catching efforts to prevent the desegregation of higher education in Alabama, 52 percent of the public put race at the top of the list of significant issues. Since then various other issues, including Vietnam, inflation, unemployment, and crime, have pushed race out of top place. But it has never receded to the position of relative unconcern that it occupied in March 1963. And not only is the race issue deeply troubling to the majority of the people; it is also divisive. Although it would be a gross oversimplification to explain racial attitudes simply in terms of black versus white views, it does appear to be the case that the majority of blacks see the reality of life in America differently than do the majority of whites.

The blacks' attitudes.   The clearest indication of a growing divergence from majority white attitudes among blacks was the emergence in the late 1960s of the concept of "black power." There have been many versions of this doctrine. In some versions it proposes that there must be a separate black state, carved out of the deep South and providing a permanent solution for a black race that must no longer seek accommodation with a hopelessly corrupt and exploitative white society. Others advocate black power as a temporary expedient to enable blacks to build a more adequate base from which to bargain for their full rights in America. But all of them begin with the notion that in white America the black man is powerless. He occupies none of the critical positions in the society—the top posts in the executive branch, big industries and banks, law firms, foundations, universities, or the media—and he cannot realistically aspire to them, since he occupies too few of the middle-level positions from which the top might eventually be reached. Worse than this, black people have been deeply imbued by white America with a sense of inadequacy, of not being qualified to exercise power. From the time of slavery, whites have systematically and calculatedly stripped black people of their cultural heritage and their identity. With no picture of themselves except that which the white has foisted upon them—that of a docile, subservient group equipped for no more than a subordinate role in society—black people have been deprived of the character traits that can bring them out of their bondage.

The time has come, say black power spokespersons, to make virtue out of necessity. White liberals pay lip service to the ideal of integration but are unable to prevent America from becoming increasingly segregated. This being so, blacks should abandon, at least temporarily, the phantom hopes of being fully integrated. Since blacks are concentrated in ghettos, three kinds of opportunities present themselves. The first is to build the ghetto into a political power base. When most members of a group live in one part of town, the task of political organization is made easier. Accordingly, segregation can help blacks to select and work for their own black candidates, rather than merely throwing support to the least objectionable of the white candidates; it can also enable them to press for community control of governmental institutions and schools in the ghettos. Second, black economic power can be developed by compelling white owners of ghetto businesses to appoint blacks as managers and by promoting black ownership of businesses. The third opportunity that segregation provides is to enable black people to rediscover their identity. Only thus will they be able to assure themselves that they are not merely tools for the white man's purposes but proud, self-motivating people who must be dealt with and bargained with on their own terms.

The idea of building pride in their racial identity has won the strong support of the great majority of blacks.[5] However, this support does not extend to black separatism. Opinion surveys show that most blacks still favor integration. By overwhelming margins black people want the schools to be integrated. Busing is not the preferred method. Although national polls tend to show that more blacks are for it than against it, the margins for busing are much smaller than the margins for school integration.

"*How come I'm colored,
you're black, and Freddy is
Akbar Ahmed?*"

Drawing by Sidney Harris

In general, the majority of black people are not pessimistic about the future. Opinion surveys indicate that they believe their conditions have improved and will continue to do so and that they have a similarly hopeful view of race relations. According to a 1970 poll, the majority of blacks felt that the most effective way of changing the system was to use the means provided by the system itself, including a variety of political techniques. And the same poll showed that 58 percent of blacks supported the view that violence was unnecessary to achieve their purposes.[6]

Yet this was only part of the story. In 1966, 21 percent of black Americans believed that "blacks will probably have to resort to violence to win rights." This proportion had risen to 31 percent by 1970. The 1970 poll revealed that 63 percent of blacks believed that "the system is rotten and has to be changed completely for blacks to be free." The intensity of feelings behind such statements was described by black psychiatrists William H. Grier and Price M. Cobbs as "black rage."[7] They spoke of black people being driven to the brink of paranoia by the need to be "ever alert to danger from their white fellow citizens." They described an educated black woman, working quietly in an integrated setting for 15 years, making an annual contribution to the NAACP; and then, during a period of racial turmoil, becoming "alarmed at waves of rage that swept over her as she talked to white people or at times even as she looked at them." They told, too, of a black professional man, always a "nice guy," who suddenly began to experience "almost uncontrollable anger" toward his white colleagues. And, if this is increasingly the case with "successful" blacks, asked Grier and Cobbs, what of the mass of black people who did not have the education to gain jobs that brought status and high pay?

In sum, the larger numbers of black people believe that their lot has improved considerably and will continue to do so, and that the civil rights cause, with its focus on integration, should still be supported. But they also want greater emphasis than in the past on ethnic pride; they are angry at what they conceive to be their continued humiliations at the hands of white people; and they contend that the full emancipation and equality of black people cannot be achieved without major changes in the present system.

The whites' attitudes.   The majority of whites continue to believe that blacks have been unfairly treated; that laws discriminating against them should be repealed; that the living conditions of black people should be substantially improved. According to surveys conducted by the University of Michigan's Institute for Social Research between 1964 and 1974, the proportion of whites favoring strict segregation has fallen from 23 percent to about 10 percent. Support among whites for equal access to public accommodations for blacks rose from 56 percent in 1964 to 75 percent in 1974, and approval of the principle that blacks should have the right to live in any neighborhood they could afford went up from 65 percent to 87 percent. The proportion of whites who perceive the civil rights movement as violent has dropped sharply since 1968. And in 1974, 58 percent of whites believed that race relations were getting better. Support for this figure can be found in the fact that, when Tom Bradley, a black man, was elected mayor of Los Angeles in 1973, only 18 percent of the city's population was black; and in the substantial increase in the number of black–white interactions in jobs, schools, and neighborhoods that have occurred over the last decade.

Nonetheless, the majority of whites have resisted any but the most gradual change. And polls indicated that attitudes hardened in the aftermath of outbreaks of violence, substantial white majorities supporting tougher treatment of black militants and more power to the police.[8] The demands for black power caused acute discomfort among whites. Although a majority of whites supported the notion of black children's being taught subjects in school that would add to their feeling of pride in being black, the sudden transformation of their perception of the black as a shambling, placid, shiftless fool to an aggressive, self-assertive, even threatening figure was profoundly disorienting to them. There was growing resentment at the increased federal spending in the inner cities, because less affluent whites felt that their own interests were being neglected in the preoccupation with the blacks.

Consistently, there has been much more support for improving the quality of education in the ghetto areas than in integration of the schools. According to the University of Michigan survey, there has been a decline in the proportion of whites favoring federal government action to produce school integration from about a half in 1964 to about a third in 1974. Busing in particular arouses overwhelming opposition among whites. In Boston in 1975 and 1976 this opposition took the form of outbreaks of violence as whites tried to prevent busloads of children from black communities being brought into the predominately Irish working-class neighborhoods of South Boston. Efforts to break down patterns of housing segregation have also provoked bitter hostility in suburban areas of the country. Thus one of the main reasons for the resistance to public housing and other housing programs for low-income people was that their administrators tried to locate the programs, which included many black people, in predominately white communities.

It is also clear that much of the white middle class's resentment at having to pay rising taxes for welfare has racial implications since a high proportion of the people on welfare are blacks. Again, as a result of federal pressures for "equal opportunity" employment and affirmative action programs, an increasing number of whites have come to perceive blacks as rivals for opportunities previously the preserve of the white man. This perception has contributed in some of the cities of the East and Midwest to a resurgence of white ethnicity. The descendants of Italian, Polish, Irish, and other European immigrants could summon from their own heritage powerful sources of community and identity. The resentments that these groups articulated were directed not only at the blacks but also at upper-income white people, who tend to be sympathetic to the claims of the blacks. It was the feeling of working, lower-middle-class people that the affluent stratum—characteristically Protestants, Jews, professionals, intellectuals, college students—was not free from prejudice, but that its prejudices were directed at lower-status whites (including the police) rather than at blacks. As one white policeman told psychologist Robert Coles:

> I wish I could take some of these student radicals and send them out with some of my men that work in the Negro sections. . . . They'd see that if you pulled the police out of the Negro sections, like the white radicals say you should—*they* don't live there!—then the ones who would suffer would be the poor, innocent, colored people. . . .
>
> It's not the average colored man who's to blame for all the trouble we're having in this country. It's a handful; well, it's more than a handful of troublemakers. There are the crazy agitators, and the college crowd, the students and the teachers, and worst of all, if you ask me, the rich people who support them all, and come into the city to march and demonstrate and wave their signs.[9]

Then, with the expansion of affirmative action programs, resentments grew even among formerly sympathetic whites, who began to express indignation at governmental and educational agencies which, they contended, were giving black people unfair advantages over whites.

Interest Groups

A considerable number of organizations speak for the interests of black people: the National Association for the Advancement of Colored People (NAACP), and the NAACP Legal Defense Fund, which is particularly active in bringing court cases to enforce integration; the National Urban League, which works in the field of jobs and other economic areas; the Congress of Racial Equality (CORE), which was active in civil rights politics in the 1960s; and the group founded by Martin Luther King, the Southern Christian Leadership Conference (SCLC). More militant groups have included the Student Non-Violent Coordinating Committee (SNCC), which in the 1960s aggressively promoted black power under the leadership of Stokely Carmichael and H. Rap Brown; and the Black Panthers, whose consciously created image of guerrilla soldiers sparked a series of armed raids by the FBI and other law enforcement agencies. Recently, the Panthers have become much less militant, turning their attention to city politics and programs to help poor children, though they still believe in fundamental social change.

The more moderate groups have participated directly in the kind of pressure-group tactics designed to produce reform measures from the federal government. Thus the NAACP has lobbied for the civil rights cause in Washington, has brought the case to the Supreme Court that resulted in *Brown* v. *Board of Education*, and has opposed antibusing forces before the courts. But these groups have not had the resources or the power to go it alone. The NAACP is the only one of them to maintain a full-time professional lobbyist in Washington. No civil rights or black community leader is regarded by decision makers in Washington as being among the most influential voices in such fields as education or housing.[10]

Coalitions and civil rights legislation.   To have an impact, then, black and civil rights interest groups have joined with other groups, such as the AFL–CIO, the Americans for Democratic Action, and leaders of civic and church social action groups. Groups of this kind came together in the Leadership Conference for Civil Rights and mounted the massive pressure operation that was instrumental in passing the 1964 Civil Rights Act. It was essentially the same combination of groups that went on the next year to lobby successfully for the Voting Rights Act of 1965, and then again for the Fair Housing Act of 1968.

Lined up against the Leadership Conference for Civil Rights was the Coordinating Committee for Fundamental American Freedoms, whose officers were right-wing conservatives and whose money came mostly from the Mississippi Sovereignty Commission, an organization created to preserve segregation. The National Association of Manufacturers and the Chamber of Commerce had reservations about some sections of the 1964 bill, but they were busy on tax and other legislation, and did little to help the southern segregationist opposition.

In later years there was very little in the way of an anticivil rights lobby. But this is not to say that the civil rights forces had the field to themselves. On the contrary, as attention in the 1970s moved away from the South and turned toward the problem of segregation in the schools of the North and West, the civil rights coalition was forced onto the defensive. Sentiment in the communities was strongly against busing, and Congress was receptive to proposals to limit the power of the Courts to mandate busing as a tool of desegregation. And whenever a bill came up against the interests of particular business groups, as in the field of housing, the civil rights coalition had to contend with the lobbying efforts of organizations like the National Association of Realtors.

The civil rights groups still had enough influence to force through a seven-year extension of the 1965 Voting Rights Act when it expired in 1975, and to expand its protection to Spanish-speaking people. The principle of the right to the vote still commands a broad national consensus. But the consensus is on the other side on such issues as busing and housing integration in the North. And, no matter how skillfully the civil rights groups apply pressure, they have been able to do no more than moderate slightly the congressional urge to heed the voice of angry grass-roots organizations in white communities.

The Courts

As we have noted, the courts have played a critical role at various stages of the struggle over civil rights. In the nineteenth century the key Supreme Court decisions went against blacks. The *Dred Scott* case came down on the side of slavery. In 1883 the Court found the Civil Rights Act of 1875 unconstitutional. And *Plessy* v. *Ferguson* in 1896 put the seal of approval on the South's "Jim Crow" laws that reversed the efforts of the Reconstruction era to force acceptance of the rights of black people on the South.

School segregation.   From the 1930s, however, Supreme Court decisions began to move in favor of black people. Then came the great breakthrough of 1954. The case that the Warren Court had to consider was brought by Oliver Brown, a black working man, of Topeka, Kansas, and the NAACP. Brown's daughter was bused some distance away to an all-black school. He wanted to get her into a school a few blocks from home. But the Topeka board of education refused to allow a black girl to enroll in an all-white school.

Chief Justice Warren spoke for a unanimous decision in the *Brown* case. "To separate [children] from others of similar age and qualifications solely because of their race," said Warren, "generates a feeling of inferiority as to their status in the community that may affect their hearts and minds in a way unlikely ever to be undone." In public education, "the doctrine of 'separate but equal' has no place. Separate educational facilities are inherently unequal," and are a denial of the Fourteenth Amendment's guarantee of the equal protection of the laws.

But it was one thing for the Supreme Court to make a constitutional finding. It was another to enforce the decision in the face of the declared intention of southern states to use massive resistance. In 1955 the Supreme Court announced a followup to the 1954 case, a second decision on *Brown* v. *Topeka Board of Education*. School districts must move toward desegregation, if not immediately, at least "with all deliberate speed." Almost everywhere in the South the school systems moved with deliberation rather than with speed.

At last in 1969, 15 years after *Brown*, the Court, now headed by Chief Justice Burger, ran out of patience. In the 11 states of the South, only 20 percent of black children attended schools that contained at least 50 percent whites. School districts, said Burger, in *Alexander* v. *Holmes County Board of Education*, must get the job done "at once," and keep it done "now and hereafter." The South complied to such an extent that within a few years only a small proportion of black children in the southern states still went to all-black schools. Efforts by some southern districts to escape the impact of the Court's decisions by providing public funds for all-white private schools were struck down by the courts; and in 1976 the Supreme Court even upheld the right of a black child to be admitted to a white private school that was not underwritten by public funds.[11]

De jure *and* de facto *school segregation.*   As the 1970s began, however, the legal issues became more complicated. The *Brown* case had dealt with *de jure* segregation—that is, situations resulting from laws deliberately calculated to require segregation. But suppose that segregation came about *de facto*—that is, from the factual reality of blacks living in one part of town and whites living in another?

In one sense, this situation might not be covered by the *Brown* principle, since it was not brought about by state or local laws or policies deliberately and openly aimed at establishing segregation. On the other hand, the result was the same—segregation of the races, and in *Brown* the Supreme Court had said that "separate educational facilities are inherently unequal." Furthermore, even if government had not passed laws or declared policies that were openly segregationist in intent, there might be other ways in which official decisions were implicated in producing segregated schools. For example, there is the way government agencies draw the boundary lines between school districts, or group neighborhoods within a district. If the lines are drawn to put adjoining black and white communities in the same area for assignment of children to the schools, integration will result. But if the lines are drawn *between* the two communities, the consequence will be segregated schools. Then, too, housing patterns are affected by zoning laws, which may be designed to keep poor blacks out of affluent white neighborhoods; or by the prejudices of realtors, who are licensed by the state; or by federal housing programs, which have sometimes reinforced segregation by providing money for white suburbs on the one hand and black ghettos on the other, thereby reinforcing segregation.

The Burger Court's response to the problem of what constitutes unconstitutional school segregation has evolved in a number of cases since 1971, and has sometimes upheld mandatory desegregation, sometimes not. The Court ruled in favor of lower court decisions requiring desegregation, even where this had required a substantial amount of busing, in Charlotte, North Carolina[12]; Pontiac, Michigan; Denver[13]; Wilmington, Delaware[14]; and Boston. In each of these cases the Court based its findings on the conclusion that *racial separation had clearly resulted from actions of governmental bodies.* Thus in the Denver case the Court declared that Chicano and black students were in segregated schools because of the way the school board had drawn boundary lines and selected school sites; and even though this affected only a few schools in the system, the Court decided that the whole district was required to participate in a desegregation plan. The Court found that similar factors had produced school segregation in Boston, and twice refused to consider appeals against a federal judge's order to integrate some of the Boston schools. And in the Wilmington case the Court ordered integration across school district lines, ruling that white schools in suburbs outside Wilmington must integrate with predominately black schools in the city, because a 1968 Delaware law required small districts to consolidate with each other yet forbade Wilmington to expand its boundaries to take in a nearby white district.

However, *where the link between governmental policy and school segregation could not be clearly established to the Court's satisfaction*, then the Court did not require desegregation. This was true of Richmond, Virginia,[15] and Detroit,[16] in both of which cases plans to integrate city and suburban schools across school district lines were rejected. What distinguished these cases from the Wilmington case in the minds of the Court was the lack of clear evidence that governmental policies rather than the basic housing patterns of the community were the principal cause of segregation. "Boundary lines may be bridged," said Chief Justice Burger in the Detroit case, "where there has been a constitutional violation calling for interdistrict relief, but the notion that school district lines may be casually ignored or created as a mere administrative convenience is contrary to the history of public education in our country." In its 1976–77 term the Supreme Court seemed to be signaling that an even more stringent criterion must be met before it would force desegregation and busing on a community. In sending back to lower federal courts two cases involving Indianapolis and Austin, Texas, which had come to it on appeal, the Supreme Court asked the lower courts to require proof of *intentional discrimination* by governmental bodies. The mere fact that segregation resulted from the actions of government might no longer be enough to prove unconstitutionality; *intent* as well as *impact* had to be demonstrated. By this test the Supreme Court also found that a lower court order requiring the busing of 18,000 of Dayton, Ohio's 42,000 pupils went much too far. In the absence of proof of intentional segregation, said Justice Rehnquist for the Court, the remedy was "entirely out of proportion" to the problem, and a less drastic plan must be devised.[17]

In reviewing the role of the courts in achieving school desegregation, we must not overlook the fact that state as well as federal courts may take action in this field. Thus civil rights organizations in California turned to the state courts to compel integration of the public schools in Los Angeles. They received a favorable ruling in the local county superior court, and when the issue came before the California Supreme Court, in 1976, that court agreed that the existing state of school segregation in Los Angeles ran counter to the *state* constitution's provision for equal protection of the laws. The state supreme court's ruling seemed to allow a wide range of possibilities in achieving integration, and did not require a precise mathematical representation of the various races in each school. But substantial steps toward desegregation were clearly indicated, and it was clear also that some busing would be necessary to accomplish this objective.

Since the decision was an interpretation of the California constitution, it was unlikely that the U.S. Supreme Court would intervene in the state court's ruling.

The Supreme Court and other civil rights decisions.   Apart from its decisions regarding the schools, the Supreme Court has been an important factor in a number of other areas affecting the rights of black people. *Brown* v. *Board of Education* was followed in the 1950s and 1960s by a number of decisions that forbade segregation of various kinds of public facilities. Citing the Thirteenth Amendment abolishing slavery and an 1866 Civil Rights Act giving blacks as well as whites the right to buy, sell, and hold property, the Court forbade discrimination in the sale of private housing.[18]

In the field of employment, the Burger Court has upheld the complaints of blacks on the issue of seniority. Blacks who had been denied jobs in the past because of their race could now be moved ahead of whites who had more seniority than they did; the blacks were not hired earlier, and thus lacked seniority, said the Court, because of clearly discriminatory hiring practices.[19]

However, under Chief Justice Burger the picture has become increasingly ambiguous in the fields of housing and education. Thus, while the Court ruled that government-subsidized housing for low-income people in the suburbs is an appropriate means of attacking housing segregation, it drew the line at forcing a predominately white suburb to change its zoning laws to permit housing for low-income minorities, for the Court was not convinced that the zoning laws had been deliberately contrived to keep blacks out.[20] In the latter case, as in its school desegregation rulings, the Court was insisting that discriminatory intent must be proved.

Then, blacks are concerned about the spate of litigation challenging federal and state programs requiring affirmative action in favor of minorities and women. The first major test of affirmative action came in 1974, when Marco DeFunis, a white honor graduate of the University of Washington, was twice turned down for admission to the university's law school though he had scored higher on the admission test than 36 minority students who had been admitted (most of whom had scored below the school's normal admissions standard). DeFunis brought the case before a state court, which ruled in his favor; but the state supreme court reversed the decision, saying that the school was within its rights in treating minority applicants separately. By the time the case reached the U.S. Supreme Court, the justices decided 5 to 4 that they would not rule on the issue because, in the years that had passed, the law school had changed its mind and admitted DeFunis, who was about to graduate. The case, therefore, was "moot," that is, it was no longer a live issue. Thus affirmative action, a matter of surpassing concern to minorities, had to await other decisions on other cases—such as the *Bakke* case, taken on appeal to the U.S. Supreme Court after the California Supreme Court had upheld the claim of a white applicant to the University of California at Davis Medical School that he had been rejected in favor of much less qualified minority students. (The special admissions program at Davis reserved 16 of 100 openings for minorities.)

The President and the Congress

It was a long time after the Reconstruction era before the elected representatives of the people in the federal government again ventured into the civil rights field. The South used its control of committee chairmanships and the filibuster to hold off any action that might be proposed in Congress. No Republican president after Lincoln had an appetite for civil rights issues, and not much more could be hoped from Democratic presidents.

At last, Franklin Roosevelt moved the black vote away from its historical allegiance to the Republican party established by Lincoln, securing it firmly for the Democratic cause. Yet Roosevelt introduced no civil rights legislation. Beyond establishing a civil rights division in the Department of Justice, his program for black people was a facet of the economic and welfare measures designed to help the poor as a class.

Harry Truman did propose civil rights legislation. He asked Congress to strengthen the federal government's civil rights enforcement powers and its machinery for studying the race issue. There was no response. Consequently, he used his executive powers to establish a Commission on Human Rights, to abolish segregation in the military, and to issue orders against discrimination in government and in federally aided housing programs. These were important advances. But the proponents of civil rights were unable to move Congress. And whatever hopes they had cherished during the Truman era vanished with the election of Dwight Eisenhower, who clearly had no desire to become entangled in the legislative politics of civil rights.

Nonetheless, Eisenhower's hand was forced by events. When a federal court ordered the integration of Central High School in Little Rock, Arkansas, in 1957, Governor Faubus refused to cooperate. Eventually, with acute reluctance, the president enforced the court's instruction by sending federal paratroops to Little Rock to restore order and see to it the school was integrated. The governor closed all the Little Rock high schools for a year; but, when they finally reopened, they were integrated.

Meantime the Congress, which was in Democratic hands, was prevailed upon to see that the problem could not be left to the courts alone. Courts move case by case, the results come slowly, and may or may not apply to the whole country. So Congress passed two civil rights bills in 1957 and 1960. However, they were weak bills, of little more than symbolic value.

With John Kennedy in the White House, although there was no civil rights legislative activity at first, he showed none of Eisenhower's reluctance to deal with southern opposition to federal court orders. Kennedy sent federal marshals and 16,000 troops to Mississippi when riots broke out after James Meredith, a black student, enrolled in the University of Mississippi at Oxford in 1962. And in 1963 Kennedy forced Governor George Wallace to back down by federalizing the Alabama National Guard after Wallace had stood in the doorway of the University of Alabama at Tuscaloosa to block the entry of two black students.

But on the legislative front Kennedy was afraid that if he tried to push hard for a civil rights bill he would jeopardize the precarious congressional support for the rest of his program. His strategy was to wait for his second term. Then, with a larger margin in Congress, he could aim for major civil rights legislation.

Once again, however, the pace of events changed a president's plans. The police dogs in Birmingham, Martin Luther King's inspired leadership, the March on Washington, all told Kennedy that he could delay no longer. In June 1963 Kennedy addressed the nation and asked for a far-reaching civil rights bill. He was killed before he could carry out his proposal, but Lyndon Johnson moved the plan ahead, and the bill that finally emerged in 1964 was even more far-reaching than the one Kennedy had proposed.

The next step was the Voting Rights Act of 1965. Johnson himself had not been personally very active in the passage of the 1964 Civil Rights Act, leaving the administration efforts mostly in the hands of the Justice Department. But the voting rights cause he took as his own. He addressed Congress himself, making an impassioned plea for action. He prevailed. Moreover, the whole thrust of Johnson's "War on Poverty" was to produce the kind of programs that would be helpful to black people.

One more piece of important civil rights legislation was to come out of Congress during the Johnson presidency. In the aftermath of the assassination of Martin Luther King in 1968, and the riots that this event provoked in some cities, Congress passed a strong "open housing" law, which prohibited discrimination in the sale and rental of housing, and which applied to about 80 percent of all the housing in the country.

But this was the end of the line for vigorous action by president and Congress to advance civil rights. After that, the message coming into Washington from constituencies in all parts of the country was: there have been enough laws and too many court decisions. In fact, the only new laws we need are those which will roll back those court decisions which force busing on communities as a tool for integration.

That message was heard loud and clear by the incoming president, Richard Nixon. His election in 1968, and his reelection in 1972, owed little to the votes of black people, who remained overwhelmingly in the Democratic column. The South, on the other hand, supported him both times. Several of the Nixon administration's policies appeared to reflect the president's debt to southern whites rather than to blacks. The administration pleaded with the Supreme Court in 1969 to allow the South more time to desegregate. Nixon tried to nominate a southerner to the Supreme Court. There was an unsuccessful attempt to dilute the impact of the 1965 Voting Rights Act when it came up for renewal. A series of raids on the Black Panthers late in 1969, though undertaken by local police forces, was defended by Attorney General John Mitchell.

Then there was the busing issue. The president made his position clear in a statement in 1970. *De jure* segregation must be ended, North and South. "The constitutional mandate will be enforced." But *de facto* segregation was another matter. It was undesirable but not necessarily illegal. Desegregation plans should be devised community by community, and drastic busing plans should not be used to break the tradition of neighborhood schools. Funds should be provided to improve the quality of education in the ghetto schools. These views were reflected in legislation proposed in 1972 to put $2.5 billion into poverty-area schools but allow only very limited busing, and then as a last resort.

In the field of housing, Nixon in 1971 indicated that, although he would enforce federal laws barring discrimination in the sale, rental, or construction of housing, he would not use federal power to compel communities to accept low-income housing.

This is not to say that the Nixon administration's policies were totally hostile to the interests of black people. The president appointed a black commissioner to the Federal Communications Commission, seven black ambassadors, a number of blacks at the sub-Cabinet level and in White House staff positions, and there was a substantial increase in the number of blacks promoted to the higher ranks of the armed services. Funds for civil rights enforcement were increased, and so were federal contributions to black colleges and small businesses. The president signed legislation authorizing the Equal Employment Opportunity Commission to bring suits in federal court to enforce federal laws against job discrimination. Efforts were made to enlarge training and job opportunities in private business, and administrative pressure was applied to encourage hiring and promoting minority people in universities and other recipients of federal funds.

The Justice Department brought several suits to enforce the fair housing legislation of 1968. And, although Nixon asked the Supreme Court to give the South more time to comply with desegregation rulings, he acted to enforce court orders once they were final. During his first term the administration filed suits to desegregate 225 school districts, as compared with 116 between 1965 and 1968 during the Johnson administration.

Nonetheless, Nixon's major pronouncements on race questions were about busing and housing integration; and the majority of blacks concluded that their concerns were not high on his list of priorities. Blacks came to similar conclusions about the Ford administration. Again the major racial controversy on which Ford took a stand was busing, and he didn't like it. He proposed legislation that would limit the amount of busing in a district to those parts of the district which had been deliberately segregated and would also set a life span of five years to a particular court-ordered busing program.

The Congresses that confronted both Nixon and Ford were, as we have seen, strongly Democratic. But on busing there was not very much difference between Republican presidents and Democratic Congresses. In 1972 Congress passed a bill, which Nixon signed, requiring the postponement of busing until all court appeals had been exhausted and limiting the use of federal funds for busing purposes. In 1975 both House and Senate included provisions in the appropriations bills for the Department of Health, Education and Welfare that would prohibit HEW from ordering the busing of children to achieve desegregation. In the same year a proposed constitutional amendment to ban busing for racial integration picked up a good deal of support in the House from Democrats from all parts of the country until the Democratic caucus voted against it and the Judiciary Committee shelved it.

Congress was not about to repeal *Brown* v. *Board of Education* or the 1964 Civil Rights Act. But as popular opposition to court-imposed busing has mounted, Congress showed itself to be very responsive to constituency feelings. The liberal Congress that resulted from the 1974 elections was ready to demonstrate its liberalism through measures that would create more jobs and thus help black people. But there was no appetite for new legislation specifically directed toward the concerns of blacks.

Would Jimmy Carter's elevation to the White House move Congress and the country toward new initiatives to help minorities? This question was raised with a mixture of doubt and hope by black leaders, for Carter's record in the race relations field was full of contradictions. He had played to the racism of many white Georgians in winning the governorship of his state; but no sooner was he elected than he called for an end to prejudice and discrimination and hung a portrait of Martin Luther King in his office. In his 1976 campaign for the presidency he made it clear that he did not like busing. However, in the end, well over 80 percent of black voters resolved their doubts in favor of Carter in the election; and without their votes in some key states, particularly in the South, Carter would have lost.

So blacks were an essential component in Carter's constituency. He pleased them by appointing two blacks to high positions in his administration, Patricia Roberts Harris as secretary of Housing and Urban Development and Andrew Young as United Nations ambassador, as well as a number of others to lesser posts. They also approved of his sending his daughter Amy to a public school in Washington whose enrollment was 60 percent black. But they looked for much more than this. They wanted action on jobs, housing, education, and other critical areas. Carter insisted that he supported their goals. He pointed to his plans for welfare reform and public service jobs, and his administration opposed moves in Congress to restrict court-ordered school busing plans. Still, by the summer of 1977 a number of black leaders were expressing dissatisfaction with the Carter administration, claiming that he was a fiscal conservative who was not moving fast enough to deal with the needs of the minorities who had put him in office.

The Bureaucracies

Federal agencies, as we noted in Chapter 8, respond to many forces—from their particular constituencies and the ideas and practices of their own staffs to the president, the Congress, and the courts. Given the turmoil that has surrounded the relationship between the races it was inevitable that the bureaucracies should find themselves caught up in fierce crosscurrents, and should be the subject of attacks from various quarters.

A large number of federal agencies are involved in the implementation of

laws and the disbursing of funds concerned with programs of particular importance to black people. Notable among these are units within the Department of
Health, Education and Welfare, the Department of Housing and Urban Development, and the Justice Department. Some of these agencies have reflected the
wishes of constituencies opposed to integration. Thus until 1947 the Federal
Housing Agency's official manual had warned federal officials not to insure
property unless it was protected from "adverse influences" such as "inharmonious
racial groups." It took a firm order from President Truman to expunge this policy
of reinforcing housing segregation in the communities.

Still, there have been other groups within the bureaucracy who saw as their
first responsibility the advancement of the cause of minorities. Clearly this has
been the mandate of the Equal Employment Opportunity Commission. And
HEW and the U.S. Office of Education have persisted in demanding that school
districts develop plans to integrate their faculties, and in compelling universities
and colleges to submit affirmative action plans a condition of receiving federal
aid. School and university officials complained and brought pressure on the
bureaucracies directly and through Congress. During the Nixon and Ford administrations there were few instances of federal funds actually being withheld
from educational institutions for lack of compliance with civil rights regulations.
However, Joseph Califano, Jimmy Carter's HEW secretary, announced early in
1977 that he would order the suspension of federal funds from any school or
school district found to be in violation of federal laws against race or sex
discrimination.

Whereas most federal agencies with responsibilities in the civil rights field
have fluctuated in their degree of enthusiasm for the integration cause, there is
one that has been consistently on the side of civil rights action and enforcement.
This is the body established during the presidency of Harry Truman, the United
States Civil Rights Commission. Through the years it has called for stronger
measures by the federal government, industry, labor, education and other groups
to step up the pace of integration. By conducting public hearings around the
country and issuing reports on civil rights progress in such fields as housing, jobs,
and education, the commission has provided a forum for voices often highly
critical of the administration.

Five Perspectives on Race

The Centrists: Not the
Millennium But Real Progress

To the centrists the race problem is still a serious social, political, and moral
dilemma for America. However, great progress has been made and will continue
to be made if we act with intelligence and restraint.

The seriousness of the problem is there in the cold, harsh statistics on income, jobs, welfare, broken families, quality of schooling, and residential and school segregation. The gap between black and white, says the centrist political analyst Ben J. Wattenberg, "is still a national disgrace."[21] The situation is bad for black children and black mothers, who are stigmatized as welfare recipients, suffer from all the ailments of poverty, and are trapped in the "deteriorating neighborhoods that are havens for addicts, criminals, drunks, prostitutes, vandals, rapists and muggers."[22] It is also bad for our politics, for it creates tensions and hostilities that make it difficult for political leaders to work out those reasonable compromises on which a democratic society depends for its progress.

But, say the centrists, we must set the present problem in perspective. The fundamental point to bear in mind is that the gap in the standard of living between blacks and whites has been narrowing. By the end of the 1960s, says Wattenberg, the majority of blacks had become "middle class," as defined by income, occupation, and education. Wattenberg contends "that the emergence of such a substantial number of blacks into the American middle class is nothing less than a revolutionary development."[23]

To make his point Wattenberg draws attention to the statistics showing the social, economic, and political progress of blacks mentioned earlier in this chapter. Further, he cites the fact that, although white family income went up by 69 percent between 1960 and 1970, black family income doubled. By the early 1970s over half of black families earned more than $7000 a year. One-third earned over $10,000 a year, as compared with only 4 percent in 1950, and 13 percent in 1960 (allowing for inflation). The income gains are most dramatic when we look at young, black, husband-and-wife families outside the South. Their median income moved up to 93 percent of the comparable white family income by 1971, as compared to 79 percent in 1959. And, if we look at families in the same age group in which both husband and wife work, we find that the white advantage had disappeared by 1970.

The census figures showing higher unemployment among blacks obscure some positive trends. Among black married men the jobless rate dropped much more steeply than for whites. The increase in blacks working in middle-class jobs—clerical, craft, and so on—from 1960 to 1970 was very much greater than among whites. The gap in number of years of schooling is now very small, and blacks today comprise about 9 percent of the college population—not much short of their 11 percent of the total population. There have also been dramatic gains in home ownership; infant mortality has declined by one-third; and the difference in average life expectancies of blacks and whites has narrowed considerably.

Even in those fields where the gap is not closing the situation is not quite as disastrous as it appears, say the centrists. Thus more blacks on welfare does not mean more black poverty. More people are on welfare because more black families are headed by women—and because welfare is easier to get than it used to be. Actually, the proportion below the poverty line has declined from 48 percent in 1959 to 28 percent in 1974. As for the black teenage unemployment figure, much of this is accounted for by young people who are going to school and are looking for *part-time* work. The numbers who are not in school, are looking for full-time jobs, and cannot find them, represent less than 7 percent of black teenagers.[24]

In sum, we have been through a period of impressive progress for black people. Their economic conditions are considerably better than they were. There is still a gap between blacks and whites, and some blacks have been left behind in the general progress of black people. But the improvement is undeniable and impressive.

Moreover, segregation and discrimination have been dramatically reduced in the South in a few short years. The extent of segregation in northern cities is deplorable; but much of it is due to the preference of blacks, like any other ethnic group, to live among people of their own background. Nor should we overlook the fact that more and more blacks are moving out of the inner cities into the suburbs. Chicago, Detroit, Milwaukee, St. Louis, Washington, D.C., Newark, and Los Angeles are all experiencing "black flight" into the suburban areas—an indication that large numbers of blacks are achieving middle-class status and, like the white middle class, want to move into better neighborhoods. As this trend continues, it will help blur the confrontation predicted by the Kerner Commission between white suburbs and black cities. And white stereotypes of blacks will continue to change as more blacks rise into the middle class, become media celebrities, and establish themselves as successful, moderate political leaders.

In politics, blacks have a long way to go to achieve full representation, but every election brings large percentage increases in the number of elected black officials. And as blacks win offices in the lower ranks of politics, they gain footholds from which they will rapidly move up the ladder.

There is every reason to believe that the progress achieved thus far can be sustained if we proceed intelligently. But full economic parity and total integration cannot be accomplished overnight. The prospect of future gains will be gravely jeopardized if we raise expectations that cannot possibly be fulfilled and if we undertake measures that arouse the antipathy of the majority of the population.

The centrists' program for racial justice.   Thus the *right* way to achieve continued economic advances is to promote the expansion of the economy and to provide government funds in reasonable amounts for carefully designed programs of job training, housing rehabilitation, welfare reform, and so on. The *wrong* way to achieve further progress is to throw vast amounts of federal funds into hastily conceived projects that do little or nothing for the larger number of poor blacks.

The *right* way to improve the education of black children is (1) to provide funding at substantial but not lavish levels for programs that improve basic learning skills; and (2) to encourage integration by voluntary busing programs, redrawing those boundary lines which were aimed at separating the races, and developing "magnet" schools—schools that are made so attractive that white parents no less than blacks want to send their children to them because of their academic superiority. The *wrong* way is large-scale mandatory busing. It is wrong for three reasons. First, it undermines the enormously popular principle of the neighborhood school. Second, busing is detested by the great majority of whites who do not want their children bused to inner-city schools where performance levels are low and violence is frequent. Although racist hostilities are undoubtedly provoked by forced busing, it is unfair to describe as racism a reluctance to have one's children bused many miles to get an inferior education and to be exposed to abuse and physical danger. In any case, many black parents, too, have no enthusiasm for having their children bused out of their communities. Third, forced busing does not work. It does not improve the quality of education for either black or white children, for time is wasted by the process of transportation, and the tensions resulting from forced integration inhibit effective learning.

Busing does not even produce integration. This is now conceded by the very same scholar, James S. Coleman of Johns Hopkins University, on whose work the proponents of busing to achieve integration had depended most heavily. In 1966 the Coleman report, based on a survey commissioned by HEW, had concluded that differences in school facilities and curricula made little difference in the quality of education.[25] The key factor was the difference in socioeconomic backgrounds; poor children, coming from "culturally deprived" homes, generally doing worse than children from more affluent families. The conclusion that many, including Professor Coleman, drew from this study was that only by mixing poor children with more affluent children could the performance of the poor be improved. Whether or not this is correct (and there is much debate about this), we cannot tell from the results of forced busing, say the centrists. For what court-imposed compulsory busing does is to provoke white parents to move away from the communities affected by busing, or put their children into private schools, thus leaving the schools under busing orders to become predominately black. When James Coleman realized that this was happening he withdrew his support of extensive busing programs in large school districts. He still believed that ultimately integration was needed to improve the education of black children. But the courts were not the way to achieve this.[26]

Finally, the *right* way to promote increases in the number of blacks on the faculties of universities and in the professions is to provide funds for special training programs that enable talented blacks to overcome the disadvantages associated with a background of poverty. The *wrong* way is to establish affirmative action programs, which are essentially programs of reverse discrimination. These programs establish quotas that promote less qualified over more qualified people, and create a sense of resentment and injustice that can only harm the relationship between the races.

Thus the centrists are pleased with the gains that have been made, particularly in the last 20 years or so; hopeful about the future; but concerned that further progress may be endangered by rigid and ill-conceived efforts to force the pace of change.

The Conservatives:
Now It's Up to the Blacks

Until the 1960s the conservative position on race in America was mostly identified with southern segregationists. This group argued for generations that blacks were inherently inferior to whites and incapable of undertaking the responsibilities that must accompany the granting of rights. In time the southern conservatives modified their position. Ultimately, blacks might be capable of full participation in the system, but they are not ready as yet. Nor are southern whites ready to accept them. The problem is not race prejudice, but a matter of cultural differences. More time should be given for both black and white communities to prepare themselves for integration.

This position is still alive in the South. Moreover, southerners seized the opportunity to drive their arguments home as northerners became not spectators but participants in the race problem. When northern school districts began to appeal court decisions to integrate their schools, gleeful offers of help poured in from the South, and full page ads were taken out by southern political leaders in northern newspapers asking the North to support the South's claims to "equal treatment." Southerners also made the point that northern liberals have always claimed to be morally superior to the South on the race issue; but this claim was exposed as hypocrisy by the willingness of the more affluent among them—including some of New York and Washington's most ardent liberals—to send their children to private schools rather than allow them to go to public schools where the majority of students are black.

Today, however, the South does not provide the most effective sources of conservative arguments on race. In large measure the South has been beaten on this issue, and the decline of George Wallace and the parallel rise of Jimmy Carter provides clear political evidence of the undermining of southern segregationist conservatism. Instead, a number of northern conservatives have been gaining more attention for their position. People such as William Buckley have never accepted a segregationist position. They argue that black people should be given every opportunity to assume their full human rights, and that the federal courts have an important role in striking down *de jure* segregation.

However, they insist that ending segregation must take time; they do not believe that *de facto* segregation calls for court interference; they are strongly opposed to mandatory busing, to affirmative action programs, and to huge injections of federal money as a means of improving the conditions of blacks. In these respects the arguments they make are similar to those presented by the centrists. There are, however, differences in tone between the conservatives and the centrists on this issue.

Centrists see busing as a foolish idea which we have been pushed into by a number of well-meaning but misguided idealists. To conservatives such as M. Stanton Evans there is more to it than that. The federal government is trying to put into effect the plan of the "social engineers"—sociologists and educationists who have determined that the root of the problem facing black people is the environment in which black children grow up. Therefore, everything possible must be done to reduce the influence of the culturally deprived home and the slum neighborhood. "The object is to break into the Negro family and culture pattern and remold black children according to guidelines preferred by middle-class (and predominately white) social planners who think they have a commission to tinker around with the psychic makeup of the human species."[27] Busing is an essential tool to achieve this, for time on the bus is time away from home and neighborhood, and it takes the black child to distant schools removed from the influence of the black parents. Affirmative action programs provide another example of manipulative social engineering, an effort to solve an alleged injustice by an even greater injustice, contrived by federal bureaucrats who work with their minority constituencies and ignore the declared wishes of the majority of the people.

Although centrists are still willing to spend a good deal of federal money on improving living and educational standards of black people, conservatives believe that this is not the answer. As we saw in Chapter 11, some conservatives favor a negative income tax as a means of providing the poor with the money for their basic needs and thus solving the welfare problem. Generally speaking, however, conservatives believe that blacks, like all other Americans, are best served by the private enterprise system. The incomes of blacks have been rising not because of the muddled efforts of the federal government, but because the economy has been expanding under the impetus of private businesses. If government will stop trying to help blacks by paternalism and social engineering, business will create plenty of opportunities for jobs and rising incomes. The rest is up to the individual. Those who want to take advantage of those opportunities will do well. Those who do not, whether they be white or black, should not expect favored treatment from the government or the society.

It is true, say the conservatives, that blacks have been discriminated against, and they still do not live as well as whites, on the whole. But the legal barriers have been removed. It is time to stop dwelling on the sins of the past. Other groups—Irish, Jews, Poles, Italians, and so on—came to this country with nothing and suffered discrimination. But in time they made it into full participation in the American system. Black people have their chance to do the same. They may need a little help; but, by and large, it is up to them now.

The Radical Right: Civil Rights and the Communist Conspiracy

A central theme—sometimes *the* central theme—in the history of radical right movements in America has been racial purity. The Ku Klux Klan from its beginnings organized fears of black demands for equality and allied this with warnings against Jews, Catholics, and everyone except fundamentalist Protestant whites.

Various ministers from the South have sounded the same notes ever since the white man's world was turned upside down during the days of Reconstruction.

Very strong antiblack attitudes are still held in America by substantial numbers of people, and not only in the South. Frequently, these attitudes are part of a syndrome that includes anti-Semitism, anti-Catholicism, and hostility to any groups that do not descend from the first waves of northern European immigrants to America. However, except for the American Nazi party, the Ku Klux Klan, and a variety of small groups that circulate angry pamphlets and mimeographed sheets, direct antiblack sentiments are rarely expressed in public by radical right groups today. At a meeting of the Christian Crusade against Communism in 1963, Major General Edwin Walker raged against "niggers, for whom the best thing, for their own good, is to be separated." An observer reported, however, that "some leaders of ultra-conservatism were obviously uncomfortable about the anti-Negro emphasis in Walker's outburst."[28]

The John Birch Society's approach is of a different nature. They bitterly oppose the civil rights movement, which has been the subject of repeated attacks in publications of the society. Yet the focus of these attacks has not been blacks but communists. The Civil Rights Act of 1964 was "part of the pattern for the Communist takeover of America. . . . the whole racial agitation was designed and is directed by the international Communist conspiracy."[29]

As Robert Welch sees it, blacks have made great gains in America.[30] They are better off in terms of their standard of living and their basic freedoms than most other people in the world. Progress will continue if we recognize that "not hatred but love is the Christian and the American way of life" and that "good will towards all men of all races is as much a part of the greatness of America as are its prosperity and its freedom." Unfortunately, Welch told the black people, "some of you are beginning to listen to rabble-rousing pro-Communist criminals who want to rise up and play a leading role in destroying this whole great American system!" Blacks should not allow themselves to be made into dupes. They have benefited enormously by their own efforts and by the opportunities provided by white America. They should not throw this all away by listening to the false promises of the communists.

Welch explains that "there are agitators now trying to stir up the white people to hate *all* Negroes because of the riots being fomented by Negro troublemakers." Years ago he had warned white friends in the South against falling for this, instead of placing the blame where it belonged, "on the shoulders of the Communists." By and large his friends had seen the truth of this warning. Now he asked blacks to see it, too.

The Liberals: Some Progress, But Not Nearly Enough

We have already looked at a number of areas in which the liberals have found events overtaking their positions and forcing them into uncomfortable dilemmas.

Nowhere is the liberals' agony more acute than on the race issue. They fought hard for civil rights, and it was their fondest desire that the legislation of 1964 and 1965 would usher in a new era of racial harmony and progress. But at the very moment of their greatest triumphs, Watts exploded in violence, its example soon to be followed in other major cities. Then came the reaction against those events—the white "backlash"—opening up smouldering resentments and prejudices and the furor over busing. Liberals were dismayed, too, by the doctrine of black power, whose spokespersons spat upon the integrationist ideal and demanded that blacks look only to blacks for leadership. Painfully, the liberals have pieced together an analysis and a strategy that tries to take account of these new circumstances.

First, they agree with the centrists that the condition of black people has improved greatly. In large measure, they argue, this is the result of the pressures from the civil rights movement in which the liberals played a principal role. However, they question whether the gains have been as great and as secure as people such as Wattenberg suggest. For one thing, the Census Bureau figures on which Wattenberg relies underestimate the number of poor blacks. In 1973 the bureau admitted that it had missed over 5 million persons in taking the 1970 Census, including almost 1.9 million blacks—7.7 percent of the black population. As the bureau explained, the undercount of blacks resulted from the fear of many of the Census takers of knocking on doors in the inner city.

Then Wattenberg puts particular emphasis on the incomes of young, black, married couples in the North and West having achieved parity with counterpart

"Yes, we feel our little old town has clearly moved forward with the times."

Drawing by Sidney Harris. Reproduced by special permission of *Playboy* Magazine; copyright © 1969 by Playboy.

white families. But in the young, black families, the wife is more likely to be working full time than in the white family. Moreover, about half of black people live in the South (with more of them moving back in a reversal of the previous trend); and very large numbers of blacks are not young or part of a stable family unit. Taking into account all blacks in all parts of the country, there is still a wide gap in incomes and in the incidence of poverty. The gap has narrowed, but with 28 percent of blacks living in poverty we have not established grounds for complacency.

The unemployment problem is also worse than the official figures indicate. The official black–white gap is serious enough, with over 14 percent joblessness among blacks in 1975 compared to about 7.6 percent for whites. But, if we take into account workers who became discouraged and dropped out of the labor market and others who held part-time jobs because they could not find full-time work, we reach a black unemployment rate of close to 26 percent.[31] As for black teenagers, the official count of unemployment is over one-third, but the unofficial count can be as high as 50 percent—even two-thirds in many of the inner city poverty areas. Some analysts are suggesting that these unemployed teenagers are coming to represent a "permanent underclass"—a group of people told by society that it has no need for them. Furthermore, the income and employment gains that the figures showed in 1970 are precarious. From 1970 to 1975 the weak state of the economy took a particularly heavy toll on black people. The closing of the black–white gap stopped, and in some respects widened a little.

With respect to schooling, blacks are catching up with whites in the number of years in the classroom, but not in the quality of education. The sharp increase in black higher-education enrollment is much more evident in the community colleges than in the major universities, and the gap at the graduate level—the real entry point to professional and managerial positions—is still very wide. In housing and health there has been improvement, but there are still large differences in the facilities available to black and white communities.

As for the political gains that blacks have been making, these are but minor inroads into the total system of power in America. The most dramatic political advances are in the cities (mostly small southern cities and a few metropolitan areas in the North). But control of cities is no longer a prime asset. Although other ethnic groups moved into the American system through city politics, the times are different now. As the black Georgian legislator, Julian Bond, has observed, "the city itself is just not a healthy animal any more. So we are taking it over at a time when no one wants it. We are seizing on a dead horse."[32]

And the very fact that blacks are gaining power in so many cities is a consequence of the most insidious aspect of the race problem today—the desertion of the cities by the whites, their occupation by the blacks, and the growing separation of the races that ensues. This is not to deny that many blacks have also been leaving the poverty ghettos. But, as they move out, few of them are allowed to settle in predominately white communities. They occupy other areas that whites leave. The ghetto remains a ghetto. It simply expands.

No doubt many black people prefer to live with other black people. But in large measure this is because they and their families must pay such a heavy psychic cost for moving into predominately white neighborhoods. Moreover, it is absurd to suggest that the prime reason for the separation of the races is that blacks want it that way. They are not free to choose. Real estate practices, zoning laws, the entire system is rigged to keep them from going wherever their incomes might take them.

The liberals' program for racial justice.   So liberals do not think that we are now well along the way to solving the race problem. Much more needs to be done. What are their proposals? They argue for a major federal government economic effort; programs to enable blacks to move up the professional and managerial ladder; a broad attack on segregation; and a renewed push in the political arena.

In the economic area, say the liberals, we need a continuing effort on a very large scale to abolish poverty and urban blight. This will be of special significance to blacks, but it should not be identified as a program to help blacks only. Thus in 1973 families of Mexican origin earned little more than two-thirds of the national median, with 23.5 percent in the poverty category, and Puerto Rican families even less, with over a third below the poverty line. These groups had also completed fewer years of education than the national median—a problem made more difficult in many cases by the fact that English is not spoken in the home. Disproportionate numbers of American Indians suffer from poverty, poor housing, inadequate education, and all the other disabilities common to racial and ethnic minorities in the United States.

It is true that government spending on programs to help blacks and other minorities may be taken by the white majority as a threat to their own rights and opportunities. But, if these programs can be presented as part of a general governmental attack on a whole range of deficiencies in our society, the danger of conflict can be greatly reduced. After all, great numbers of whites are not so securely above the poverty line that an illness, an injury, or the loss of a job could not result in economic calamity for them and their families. They need programs in the fields of health insurance, employment, job training, and so on, which are as important to the majority as to the poor.

Conflict arises out of the economics of scarcity. When there are not enough jobs to go around, when incomes are not keeping up with prices, hostilities grow as people jostle each other for the limited supplies available. In an economy of abundance, stimulated by well-conceived federal programs, there will be less reason for conflict, and people—white, black and brown—discover their shared interests rather than their differences.

As for affirmative action programs aimed at moving minorities faster into the upper ranks of industry, government, education, and the professions, liberals are, in principle, favorably disposed toward them. No doubt these programs do represent a kind of discrimination in reverse. But blacks have struggled under greater liabilities than other ethnic groups in our history. Poles, Italians, Irish, and Jews may have come to this country in poverty, but not in chains. They did not live here as slaves and suffer the legally imposed segregation, discrimination, and humiliation imposed on blacks until quite recently. So equality cannot be obtained merely by ending the discrimination. For a time it has to be reversed. Blacks must be given a chance to catch up to overcome the unfair advantage that society has given to whites over blacks throughout our history.

At the same time, liberals are made uncomfortable by the fact that, in order to put affirmative action programs into effect, statistics have to be compiled listing employees by race, and schedules have to be established for reaching agreed-upon quotas of minority employees in various ranks. After all, liberals have always argued for color-blind laws. At best, then, liberals see affirmative action programs as temporary expedients that can deal with the problem only to a small extent. The larger part of the answer is not to argue over who should get the limited number of positions, but to increase the total number of opportunities. Thus it is absurd to suggest that we have a surplus of college teachers. Federal and state governments should not be cutting funds for higher education, but expanding them so that we can have more minority faculty without cutting into the number of white faculty.

Next, liberals continue to call for rapid advances toward an integrated society. Separate cannot be equal, particularly in the field of education. Integration remains a moral imperative and is the essential condition for improving the quality of minority schools. To bring this about, busing is necessary in some cities. The extent to which it is needed is exaggerated by its opponents. As the U.S. Civil Rights Commission argued in a report in April 1970,

> substantial desegregation can be accomplished through relatively simple devices such as alteration of existing school attendance areas, school pairing, and the establishment of central schools. . . . To be sure, transportation is necessary in giant urban centers as it is in smaller cities, but here, too, it is false and defeatist to assume that the bus rides must be lengthy or that the education of our children will be disrupted.

As for the Coleman argument that busing has caused the departure of whites from the urban centers, civil rights spokespersons insist that this phenomenon has little to do with busing, and is simply part of a trend to get away from the inner cities and their problems into the suburbs. Moreover, although the examples of violent resistance to busing have captured the headlines, some major cities have been peacefully integrating their schools, using many methods including busing. This was the case in Dallas and Milwaukee, where community leaders and white and black parents worked together to create a climate of acceptance. And after bitter resistance and disruption during the first year of court-ordered busing in Louisville, integration proceeded smoothly in the second year.

In any case, say the liberals, busing and other such policies are merely partial correctives to the underlying problem—the segregation of the races by residential patterns. As long as blacks are compelled by live in separate communities, school integration can be accomplished only by artificial means. What is needed is an enormous increase in the opportunities for black people to live with whites in integrated neighborhoods. In some measure this calls for providing low-cost housing in the suburbs—small numbers of scattered units to minimize resistances and the disruption of community styles. More significantly, it simply means removing the hindrances to the growing number of black people who want to move into white suburbs and can afford to do so.

Finally, say the liberals, political strategies must be devised to accomplish these policies. We have to elect a president and Congress who will exercise the necessary moral leadership, make the right kind of Supreme Court appointments, push the bureaucracy out of its natural timidity, and approve the funding needed to get the job done.

All this will require a vast organizational job of getting out the vote, working for black candidates and for white candidates attuned to the interests of blacks, and applying group pressure to ensure that once the candidates are elected they do not backslide. This job requires that blacks enter into coalitions, for they constitute only one-ninth of the population, and the majority of them still do not have the money and education that are the keys to power in America. Their allies can be drawn from many sources, depending on the particular purpose to be served—liberal organizations, church groups, labor, and even on occasion the more enlightened wing of the business community. But, although alliances may shift from program to program, long-range policy changes favorable to black people will be possible only if broad coalitions are built of the various groups in American society dedicated to the achievement of greater equality, freedom, and power for deprived minorities.

The Radical Left: Capitalism Breeds Racism

In the eyes of the left the analyses of the other four perspectives are at worst masks the repression and at best a thin veneer to protect established privileges. The reality of repression has at last been exposed in the revelations of the way the FBI deliberately set out to harass black leaders and their organizations. There was the bugging of Martin Luther King's telephone. And a 1968 memorandum of FBI chief J. Edgar Hoover, which became public in 1975, revealed the FBI's plan to stir up the rivalry between two black groups, the Black Panther party and Ron Karenga's US party (a rivalry that finally led to the shooting of two Black Panther leaders by two US members after a meeting on the UCLA campus). This kind of provocation is a standard method of the capitalist ruling class, which keeps dissenters under control by the tactic of divide and conquer.

Defenders of the system make much of the progress toward desegregation in the South. Although the desegregation of schools and other public facilities may upset the old-line southern conservatives, it is entirely satisfactory to the southern industrial interests, whose dominance in the region is increasing, and who prefer to get away from the crudities of the past. But, like their northern counterparts, they continue to exploit their black workers even more than the whites.

As for the liberals, the inadequacies of their analysis and of their actions is revealed with particular clarity in the context of race. The Kerner Commission produced an essentially liberal manifesto. Accurately, it declared that "white racism" was largely responsible for the existence of the black ghettos and for the abominable conditions therein. But the report's recommendations—integration and more money—were the standard liberal answers, which fail to come to grips with the root causes of racism. The root problems are the division of America into profoundly unequal classes; the need of the dominant class to perpetuate an underclass that provides cheap manufacturing and domestic labor; and the deliberate playing on race prejudice to sow division among the masses. The liberal attempts to appeal to conscience and to use legislation and the courts to give the blacks their rights can produce only superficial accomplishments. Even these are incredibly slow in coming; thus, despite the apparently clear declaration of policy by the Supreme Court in 1954, whole generations of black children continued to go to segregated schools in the South before the policy was implemented. And further generations will receive segregated educations in the North. Beyond the liberals' puny achievements in this area, they are not likely to gain many more concessions. For corporate capitalism can no more agree to the abolition of racism than it can accept the end of class exploitation.

Then, too, labor, a key element in the liberal–civil rights coalition, is a prime practitioner of racism, by establishing apprenticeship programs and other barriers to entry into craft jobs that discriminate against blacks. Finally, liberals covertly resist the claims of black people through "institutional racism." Thus liberals support affirmative action programs that increase the number of minorities hired in police and fire departments and other such jobs. But in universities, where liberals hold many of the administrative and faculty jobs, their support of affirmative action is less enthusiastic. They say they are eager to see more blacks appointed, but very few black people can meet the qualifications that the institution requires. This is not discrimination, say the liberals, but a necessary protection of standards. For black people, the results are the same.

Consequently, says the left, there is no hope for black people in their traditional alliance with liberals. Instead, blacks should join with other alienated elements to force a radical reconstruction of American society.[33] These alienated groups include the poor, other profoundly disadvantaged ethnic minorities, such as Mexican Americans, Puerto Ricans, and American Indians, and the young —especially the leftist militant students. And beyond the national context one should look to the entire Third World—the world of poor people who, whether or not they are nominally independent of colonial rule, are still subject to neocolonial, imperialist oppression, including that which emanates from the United States. The Third World consists predominantly of nonwhites; and the nonwhite population of the world far outnumbers the whites. Thus, in the international perspective, American blacks are not a minority but part of a great, nonwhite, ultimately antiwhite majority. Blacks in the United States should therefore identify with people everywhere in the world who are fighting against American imperialism.

There are different views among the radical left on the tactics to use in contemporary America. Some of the more militant blacks and their white counter-parts believe in guerrilla warfare, terrorism, and ultimately revolution. The number of these on the left is on the decline, however, and most radical black leaders argue that the time is not ripe for revolutionary violence. All agree, however, that reform measures do not go to the root of the problem of racism and that sooner or later confrontation with the ruling elite is inevitable.

Conclusion

It is clear from this chapter that the nature of the race problem in America has changed dramatically in recent years. For one thing, the debate on the issue has shifted toward the right since the mid-1960s. Until then the focus was on the South, and centrists tended to ally themselves with the liberals in opposition to southern segregation. But now the problem is focused in the North and West, and busing and affirmative action have moved centrists' opinion in a more conservative direction. Thus the presentation of the conservative position in this chapter is relatively brief, since it follows the centrist perspective, which has adopted a modified conservative argument. Another indication of the shift away from the left is the tendency of black leadership to become somewhat more moderate than it was during the upheaval of the urban riots in the 1960s.

Second, race prejudice as such seems to have declined. One indication of this is that in 1977 the American Broadcasting Company presented on eight consecutive evenings a televised version of Alex Haley's extraordinary book *Roots*, Haley's imaginative recreation of his family's origins in Africa through slavery and Reconstruction in the American South—and the series was watched by the largest audience in all of television history. Such massive attention to the history of black people in America would have been inconceivable even a few years earlier.

So there has been change since 1944, when Gunnar Myrdal, a Swedish sociologist, published a major study of black people in America. He called his study *An America Dilemma*,[34] implying the conflict between the high moral principles we profess as a people and the persistence of group prejudice. Nonetheless, despite the various indications of growing maturity on the race issue, the material we have reviewed in this chapter suggests it would be rash to assume that the American dilemma has been resolved, or even that it is on its way to resolution.

Notes and References

1.   Robert William Fogel and Stanley L. Engerman, *Time on the Cross: The Economics of American Negro Slavery* (Boston: Little, Brown and Company, 1974).

2.   *Sweatt* v. *Painter*, 1950; *McLaurin* v. *Oklahoma*, 1950.

3.   Nathan E. Cohen, *Los Angeles Riot Study: Summary and Implications for Policy* (Los Angeles: Institute of Government and Public Affairs, UCLA, 1967), pp. 3–4.

4.   National Advisery Commission on Civil Disorders, *Report* (Washington, D.C.: Goverment Printing Office, March 1, 1968).

5.   See "White and Negro Attitudes toward Race-related Issues and Activities" (New York: Columbia Broadcasting System, 1968).

6.   Time–Louis Harris Poll, *Time*, April 6, 1970, pp. 28–29.

7.   William H. Grier and Price M. Cobbs, *Black Rage* (New York: Basic Books, Inc., Publishers, 1968).

8.   Gallup Poll, *Newsweek*, October 6, 1969, p. 35.

9.   "A Policeman Complains," *The New York Times Magazine*, June 13, 1971, pp. 11, 73–75, 78–80.

10.   Harold Wolman and Norman C. Thomas, "Black Interests, Black Groups, and Black Influence in the Federal Policy Process: The Cases of Housing and Education," *Journal of Politics*, November 1970.

11.   *Ruyon* v. *McCrary*, 1976.

12.   *Swann* v. *Charlotte-Mecklenburg*, 1971.

13.   *Keyes* v. *Denver School District*, 1973.

14.   *Buchanan* v. *Evans*, 1975.

15.   *Richmond* v. *State Board of Education*, 1973.

16.   *Milliken* v. *Bradley*, 1974.

17.   *Dayton* v. *Brinkman*, 1977.

18.   *Jones* v. *Mayer*, 1968.

19.   *Frank* v. *Bowman Transportation Co.*, 1976.

20.   *Arlington Heights* v. *Metropolitan Housing Corporation*, 1977.

21.   Ben J. Wattenberg, *The Real America: A Surprising Examination of the State of the Union* (New York: G. P. Putnam's Sons [Capricorn Books], 1976), p. 124.

22.   Ibid., p. 139.

23.   Ibid., p. 124.

24.   Ibid., p. 130.

25.   James S. Coleman et al., *Equality of Educational Opportunity* (Washington, D.C.: Government Printing Office, 1966).

26.   Paper presented to the American Educational Research Association in Washington, D.C., May 1975, reporting on a study by James S. Coleman, Sara Kelly, and John Moore. See also "Integration Yes; Busing No," interview with James S. Coleman, *The New York Times Magazine*, August 24, 1975, pp. 10–11+.

27.   M. Stanton Evans, *Clear and Present Dangers: A Conservative View of America's Government* (New York: Harcourt Brace Jovanovich, 1975), p. 184.

28.   Stan Twardy, "Carnival of Hate," *The Progressive*, October 1963, pp. 24–26.

29.   Quoted by William F. Buckley, "The John Birch Society," *The National Review*, October 19, 1965, pp. 916–18.

30.   Robert Welch, "To the Negroes of America," reprinted in Gilbert Abcarian, *American Political Radicalism* (Waltham, Mass.: Xerox College Publishing, 1971), pp. 94–100. See also Robert Welch, *The New Americanism, and Other Speeches and Essays* (Boston and Los Angeles: Western Islands Publishers, 1966).

31.   Vernon E. Jordan, "The State of Black America," National Urban League, January 1976, p. 5.

32.   Julian Bond, *Time*, April 6, 1970, p. 24.

33.   See, for example, Carl Wittman and Thomas Hayden, "An Interracial Movement of the Poor," in *The New Student Left*, Mitchell Cohen and Dennis Hale, eds. (Boston: Beacon Press, 1967), pp. 182–211.

34.   Gunnar Myrdal, *An American Dilemma: The Negro Problem and Modern Democracy*, Twentieth Anniversary ed. (New York: Harper & Row, Publishers, 1962).

Energy

and the Environment

The issues we examined in Chapters 11 and 12—the distribution of wealth and the relations between the races—have been prime sources of contention throughout our history. But the problems considered in this chapter—the deterioration of our natural environment and the dwindling of our sources of energy—did not become central concerns of most politicians until very recently. Actually, the problems had been there all along, but we had not done very much about them. Then a few dramatic events suddenly projected them into our national consciousness as full-blown crises. After a brief period in which everyone feared that each of these crises would overwhelm us, the panic receded and the crises were renamed "problems." Nonetheless, these two interwoven issues, the protection of the environment and the quest for energy sources, continue to be recognized as important matters demanding attention from the American political system. Their political salience—the extent to which they must be taken seriously by politicians—rises and falls as circumstances change. But they will never again be relegated to the status of questions of minor importance, of interest only to a few groups and a few regions.

The Environment:
A Brief History of the Issue

There are two main strands to the environmental issue. The first is *conservation*—the need to protect natural resources of land, minerals, fossil fuels, timber, water, and so on whose supply (at least in easily accessible form) is limited and will eventually run out. The second strand is *pollution*—the damage inflicted on the environment by human effluents, or waste products. At first, little attention was paid to either of these problems. Although writers have cried out against the "rape of the earth" since the beginnings of industrialization, their voices were not heeded in America during the long period in which the land was seen as a great cornucopia, its riches available to anyone who wanted to seize them. Government, far from providing checks against private exploitation, sold off or even gave away the public domain to encourage the settlement of the land.

Then, in the latter part of the nineteenth century, as the era of the expanding frontier ended, attitudes on the use of natural resources began to change. Pressure for conservation built as whole forests disappeared; more people wanted to enjoy outdoor recreation and scenic beauty; industry needed assurance of a long-term supply of natural resources; and new scientific knowledge was gained of how to replenish the forests and husband other resources. The federal government began to enter the picture, especially from Theodore Roosevelt's time, by establishing national parks and national forests, reclaiming arid lands through irrigation projects, constructing dams, preserving wildlife, and regulating the production of oil and other mineral resources. Then Franklin Roosevelt's New Deal, bringing a spate of government regulation and seeking ways of putting people to work, undertook a huge expansion of programs in all of these fields. Still, as America became increasingly urbanized, only a minority of the population were directly interested in the conservation issue—farmers, mining, logging, and oil companies, and campers, mountain climbers, and others with a special love of open spaces and wildlife.

Gradually the concern of few groups widened into a general concern not only about conservation but also about pollution, and at the end of the 1960s the two strands merged into the issue of the environment. A number of writers, organizations, and political leaders helped bring this about, as we shall see a bit later in the chapter. But the context in which they worked was shaped by two primary factors: population and technology.

At the time of the American Revolution the population of the American colonies numbered about 3 million. By 1976 it had passed 215 million. So, although the land area of the United States has increased in the last 200 years, its resources today have to sustain far more people per acre. This in itself is not the problem. The land could easily sustain the needs of 215 million people—living in the style of the eighteenth century. But we are now a technological society. Technology, while bringing immense increases in the gross national product, also requires enormous inputs of energy and resources and spews forth millions upon millions of tons of waste. Both its voracious appetite and its massive wastes impose intense pressures on the environment.

The Damage Becomes Clear

By the 1960s the damage was painfully apparent. The air, the inland waters, and the oceans were being polluted. The danger to health from the smog in Los

Angeles was notorious; but it affected many other cities, including communities throughout the western states, that had long boasted about the purity of their air. Noise pollution, always a problem in an industrialized society, achieved ruinous proportions in neighborhoods bordering on jet airports. Effluents from industry and homes poured into the rivers and the lakes. Lake Erie came close to death, acids from nearby factories killing everything in the water except sludge worms and a mutant of the carp. In the summer of 1969 the Cuyahoga River in Cleveland, laden with city wastes, burst into flames. The disposal of solid wastes became an ever more complicated problem for municipalities as garbage sites were filled and as industry and consumers made increasing use of plastics and other nonbiodegradable materials—those which are not broken down through natural biological processes.

Not only was man polluting his environment. He was also engaged in a relentless exploitation of its resources—some of them irreplaceable. Forests were cut down faster than they were replanted, and minerals were stripped from the soil. The supply of dependable fresh water in the United States is estimated at about 650 billion gallons a day (BGD). By 1970, cities, industry, and agriculture consumed about 350 BGD. By 1980 consumption may well reach 600 BGD, and by the year 2000, 1000 BGD. Accessible open space diminished as land developers and industry pushed the urban sprawl interminably outward to suburbs and suburbs of suburbs and debased the natural splendors of coastal areas.

Eventually, human efforts to combat those features of the environment that threatened our health or convenience brought forth some unpleasant surprises. The most obvious example was the use of pesticides, especially DDT, which wiped out mosquitoes and protected crops from blight but which also killed fish, birds, and beneficial insects—and had harmful effects on humans, who store up pesticide residues in their body tissues. The unlooked-for damage wrought by pesticides, in fact, focused attention on the fundamental issue of our relationship to nature. Would we seek ways of living harmoniously with our natural environment, or must we seek to subdue it? If the latter, we might be made to suffer grievously for our arrogance. This was the central teaching of the ecologists, those who studied "ecosystems"—the natural patterns of interrelationships between animals (including humans) and plants, and between them and their environment.

Nor was the consequence of these problems limited to the United States. For one thing, the United States, with less than 6 percent of the world's population, used more than 40 percent of the world's scarce or nonreplaceable resources. Then population growth was a worldwide problem—much worse in fact in many other countries than here. By the mid-1970s world population reached 4 billion. Some estimates suggested that it might double by the end of the century, and most of the increase would occur in the poorest nations. Moreover, technology proceeded apace in many parts of the globe. The pressures of people and technology on the environment played havoc universally. Pollution in the Volga River and the Caspian Sea threatened to wipe out the sturgeon, the source of caviar. The Aswan Dam replaced periodic flooding with controlled irrigation. It also cut down the natural fertilization of the soil of the Nile Valley; increased the salinization of the soil; reduced the sardine catch in the eastern Mediterranean; multiplied the incidence among Egyptians of schistosomiasis, a debilitating disease carried by snails; and led to an increase in the population.

According to some ecologists these localized problems were merely precursors of greater disasters to come. Famine, they said, would strike down vast populations. In the eighteenth century the British economist Thomas Malthus argued that periodic plagues and famines were nature's way of reacting when population growth outstripped the available food supply; the Malthusian nightmare, said the ecologists, would become a terrible reality in the latter part of the twentieth century. This view was supported by a 1972 analysis called the "Club of Rome" study. Conducted by a team of MIT scientists and engineers using a computer, the study predicted that, unless economic growth was halted soon, the world economy faced collapse within 70 years, bringing pestilence and starvation.[1] Nor was this the gloomiest of the forecasts being made. Some scientists suggested that the man-made increase in carbon dioxide in the atmosphere could eventually destroy the human race.

By the late 1960s these dire warnings by scientists were made available to the general public in an outpouring of books and articles. Then came two developments, one in 1969, the other in 1973, which dramatically brought home the dangers that faced us from the damage to the environment on the one hand and the depletion of resources on the other.

The Santa Barbara oil spill.   On January 28, 1969, the pollution problem was brought into focus by an incident off the coast of Santa Barbara in California. A leak developed in an offshore well of the Union Oil Company, and hundreds of thousands of gallons of oil spilled into the ocean, spreading a slick extending over hundreds of square miles and fouling beaches and harbors. The president of Union Oil insisted that, unfortunate though the accident was, it should not be referred to as a disaster. After all, no one had been killed. "I am always tremendously impressed at the publicity that [the] death of birds receives versus the loss of people in our country in this day and age."[2] Nonetheless, the accounts of beaches saturated with oil, of dead and dying birds, of the inability of a great corporation, armed with its array of technologies, to stop the leak quickly or to prevent the spread of the slick, catalyzed in the public imagination all the growing unease about the despoiling of the environment. A fundamental question was raised. Passing over the obvious question of why the regulations governing offshore oil drilling were so ineffectual, people began to wonder why oil derricks, *however safe*, should be allowed to mar the beauty of the coastline. Aesthetic values, in other words, had become a matter of prime public concern and were not to be automatically subordinated to financial advantage.

For some time in America there had been a groping toward a shift of emphasis from the quantitative accumulation of wealth to the quality of life. The Santa Barbara oil slick seemed to symbolize the threats to the quality of life resulting from the pursuit of economic gain; and Union Oil, despite its vast payrolls and contributions to economic growth, found itself fighting desperately to counter its new public image as a careless and destructive predator.

At last the issue had been projected into the forefront of the public consciousness. Politicians at all levels, local, state, and federal, were galvanized into action. At the apex of the system, President Nixon in his 1970 State of the Union address declared that, next to world peace, the major concern of the next decade might well be the quality of the environment: "The real question of the seventies is, shall we surrender to our surroundings, or shall we make our peace with nature and begin to make reparations for the damage we have done to our air, to our land, and to our water?"

Thus the pollution side of the environmental problem became a top political priority and brought about some basic changes in public policy. Controls were imposed on industrialists and land developers. State and local government agencies were brought under regulations that required them to seek approval of an Environmental Impact Assessment Report as a condition of receiving federal funds for new construction or purchase of existing buildings.

And the environmental issue was a major factor in the banning of the construction of the Supersonic Transport (the SST) in 1971. Intense pressures from Boeing and other corporations, labor, the House leadership, members of Congress from the areas where the plane would be built, and the White House failed to overcome the environmentalist arguments about sonic boom, intolerable levels of noise around airports, extremely high fuel consumption, and a possible increase in skin cancers caused by the depletion by the plane's exhaust of the ozone barrier protecting the earth from the sun's rays.

The 1973 oil embargo—and its consequences.   The other element of the environment problem, the dwindling of natural resources, leaped into the headlines in 1973. Abundant, cheap energy had always been taken for granted by the American people with only occasional warnings of the possibility of breakdowns, as in power shortages in New York and a few other cities. But now there were warnings that this could happen all over the country, for the construction of new electric power plants had not kept up with the accelerating demand resulting from economic growth and rising standards of living, and the accompanying demand for air conditioners and sophisticated appliances of all kinds in homes and offices.

By 1973, gasoline shortages began to appear. Prices rose. Some gas stations went out of business for lack of supplies. Others closed early or limited the number of gallons per customer. Cities and counties that had previously chosen among several competing bids for their gasoline needs suddenly found only one oil company bidding for their business at much higher prices. And sometimes there were no bids at all. This situation would not improve, said the oil companies. Demand was outstripping supply.

Then the supply shrank further. In October 1973, the Middle East erupted in war. The United States helped replace the severe losses in weapons that the

Israelis sustained. Saudi Arabia and other Arab states retaliated by cutting off all oil supplies to the United States. Although the United States was less dependent than Japan or several Western European countries on Arab oil, the embargo intensified alarmingly an already serious, long-term problem. According to government and industry sources, we were running out of domestic supplies of oil and natural gas.

Something had to be done, and a number of measures were put into effect immediately. Cutbacks were imposed on home heating oil and airplane fuel. Speed limits on the highways were reduced nationally to 55 mph. The price of gas and heating oil went up sharply. Limited allocations of gasoline were made for each region of the country. In many areas, long lines formed at the gas pumps, and motorists were permitted to buy gas only every other day. Nothing could have shocked the American people into an awareness of the resource problem more than being forced to wait in line for gasoline. The automobile has become a projection of our personality; and to be denied easy, instantaneous access to gas was a profoundly disorienting experience.

Moreover, the media were full of grim news about the rising cost of oil imports. In 1970 our oil imports cost us less than $3 billion a year. By 1973 the figure was up to about $8 billion and by 1975, to $24 billion. The figure had reached more than $35 billion by 1976, and was still rising sharply. These increases reflected two developments: the steep price rises imposed by the oil-producing nations and the United States' growing reliance on oil imports as domestic production fell. Thus by the end of 1976 we were importing over 40 percent of our oil, and the proportion could reach 50 percent before long.

Now the search began in earnest for alternative sources of power—coal, oil shale, nuclear, synthetic fuels, hydroelectric, solar, and geothermal (steam generated by the earth's internal heat). But here, too, costs were high. We have plenty of coal, but converting it to gas is expensive. Nuclear energy costs are rising at an alarming rate. Solar energy can make a significant contribution to our total energy needs only after very large developmental costs. Altogether research and capital outlays needed for these alternative sources will cost at least $100 billion over the next decade. Still, the oil embargo generated a national determination to launch a frontal attack on the energy problem. This, by all accounts, was the newest top national priority.

A respite—and then the natural gas crisis.   As happens with so many crises, as soon as the immediate urgency passes, the media, the public, and the politicians find it difficult to sustain their commitment to the problem. Soon after the embargo ended, gasoline became abundantly available again. Its price had gone up steeply and continued to creep upward, but this did not break the dependence of most people on the automobile, and long summer vacations at the wheel of a car became commonplace again.

However, another sharp blow at complacency was struck early in 1977, this time not by foreign countries but by nature. An especially harsh winter froze the

Midwest, the East, and much of the South. The supply of natural gas, the clean, efficient fuel used by much of industry and a high proportion of homes, ran short as production declined (Figure 13-1). More than a million workers were laid off as industrial plants and many other kinds of businesses ground to a halt for lack of fuel. Emergency measures were undertaken to divert gas supplies from the West; and, as the worst of the cold subsided, business gradually resumed, and workers were able to get back to their jobs. Still, the crisis had effectively riveted the public's attention on the fact that the energy problem was not limited to oil alone but was a pervasive threat affecting another of the fuels on which industry and the economy had so long depended.

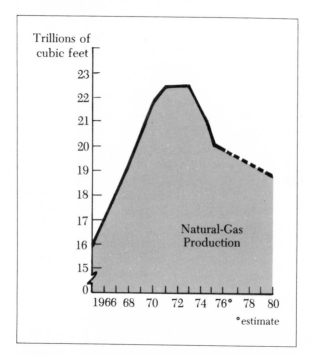

FIGURE 13–1   Domestic Natural Gas
Production   (Data from U.S. Bureau of Mines.)

Obviously, then, we must change our patterns of energy consumption and reduce the extent of our reliance on oil and natural gas. This can be accomplished in two ways. The first is conservation; significant reductions in energy use can be made by the avoidance of waste through the insulation of homes and the more efficient use of energy by industry, to cite just two examples. The second method is to shift to other sources of energy. According to government estimates, by 1985 there will, in fact, be a relative decline in the use of oil and natural gas and an increase in the use of coal and nuclear power (Figure 13-2).

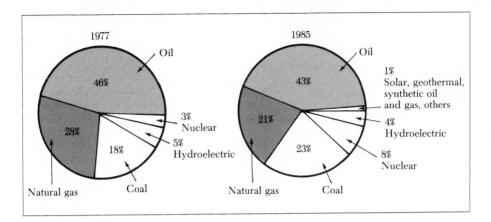

FIGURE 13–2   How the Energy Pie Is Cut — Present and Future   (Data from the Federal Energy Administration.)

The Clash of Issues: Environmentalism versus Energy

At last the American people and their leaders are forced to confront the energy problem as a matter demanding unrelenting and expensive attention. But what does this mean for environmentalism? In one sense the two problems are compatible. Environmentalists worry about pollution on the one hand and the depletion of natural resources on the other. As long as the energy problem is dealt with by conservation programs, the environmentalists can only applaud. Conserving energy by reducing the amount of gasoline required by an automobile lessens the smog-producing emissions and other harmful pollutants thrust into the atmosphere. And recycling waste products conserves energy, since methane gas from garbage dumps can be used as a fuel.

However, there are other respects in which the goals of protecting the environment and dealing with the energy shortage can come into sharp conflict with each other. Antipollution devices on automobiles may cut gasoline mileage. Of the alternatives to oil and natural gas imports, only solar and geothermal energy are nonpolluting. Offshore drilling to exploit our own coastal oil reserves runs the risk of producing more oil spills. Building a pipeline from major new oil fields in Alaska endangered the delicate ecological balance of the tundra. Coal strip mining from coal beds close to the surface could lay waste vast areas of the land. Nuclear power plants produce large quantities of radioactive waste materials. They could endanger many lives in the event of an accidental explosion. And they raise the temperature of streams and rivers they use for cooling, thus upsetting freshwater ecocycles. Coal and oil with a high sulphur content are cheaper and more abundant than the low-sulphur supplies, but they cause more air pollution.

Moreover, antipollution and energy programs came into conflict in another way. They compete for funds. The President's Council on Environmental Quality estimated in 1973 that it would cost industry and government more than $275 billion over 10 years to reverse the deterioration of the environment. This would have to be paid for from higher prices and taxes—the same sources paying for energy outlays that, according to the federal administration, could amount to a trillion dollars between 1975 and 1985.

Is There Really an Ecological Crisis?

There is no difficulty in establishing the case for outlays at these or higher levels if we are to be guided by the warnings, which we described earlier, of the grave environmental threats to the survival of man. However, the experts who uttered these warnings have been challenged by other experts. Some of them have thrown cold water on the predictions that the earth's population will soon exceed its available resources. Population growth in the United States and some other industrial countries has slowed dramatically, and there are signs of significant reductions in the growth rates in several of the poorer nations, too. Consequently, earlier estimates that world population would hit 6.3 billion or more by the year 2000 and would continue to rise have now been revised downward to a projection of 5.4 billion by 2000 and not much growth after that (Figure 13-3).

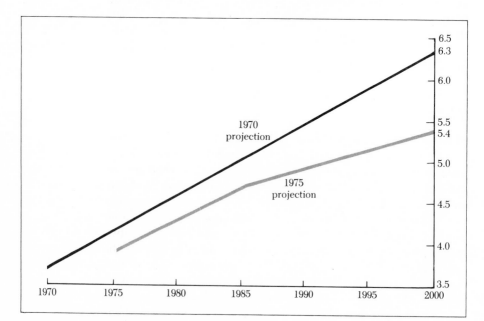

FIGURE 13-3   World Population: Estimated
Increase by the Year 2000, in billions   (Data from
Lester R. Brown, Worldwatch Institute.)

Futurologist Herman Kahn insists that there will be ample resources to take care of any projected increase in world population.[3] And in 1975 the Club of Rome sponsored a new report based on further study, which modified their apocalyptic view of three years before, and suggested that with careful, selective growth we need not outstrip the earth's resources or make our environment uninhabitable.

Yet the problems are not over. Although there are large differences of interpretation, no careful student of these questions suggests that we need not worry about pollution or world food supplies. As for the United States' energy needs, complacency hardly seems justified as long as oil imports increase each year, and there is an international cartel with a considerable degree of control over world prices. Consequently, political decision makers continue to spend a good deal of their time trying to cope with these issues, and protagonists at the various points on our spectrum continue to debate them vigorously.

Energy and the Environment: The Policy-making Process

The major political forces that shape governmental policy on the issues of energy and the environment are the interactions of the president and Congress; bureaucracies; state and local government (for much of the action took place at the local level); the climate of public opinion, particularly the role played by scientists and the media and by students on college campuses; and the lineup of interest groups on each side of the issue.

The President and the Congress

The traditional rivalry between the president and Congress, which we described at some length in Chapters 6 and 7, will be particularly visible as we discuss policy making in energy and the environment—especially when one institution is in the hands of the Republicans and the other in the hands of the Democrats. We shall see further the inability of Congress to provide decisive leadership.

As long as the issues were in the exploratory stages, these problems were not acute. During the 1960s, despite jurisdictional conflicts between several congressional committees, valuable work was done in preparing the ground for antipollution legislation, and Congress and the White House worked together in passing a number of statutes related to controlling air and water pollution as well as commissioning research and development on solid-waste disposal.

Sharp differences emerged, however, after the Santa Barbara oil spill in 1969, when the quality of the environment suddenly became a highly charged political issue. Congressional leaders demanded strong action, and at first President Nixon held back. Then, the issue intensified, and in February 1970 Nixon presented a

37-point program aimed at purifying rivers and lakes, cleaning up the landscape and the air, and enlarging the amount of land available for recreation, all this to be accomplished by harnessing the efforts of government and industry.

The Democratic Congress was not to be outdone. It passed the Clean Air Act of 1970, which required that most new automobiles be made 90 percent free of polluting emissions by 1975. Then, in legislation passed in 1972, Congress called for the expenditure of almost $25 billion to clean up the nation's waters by 1985, starting with $5 billion in 1973 and $6 billion in 1974. This was too much for Nixon, who vetoed the measure as inflationary. Congress overrode his veto, but the president impounded some of the funds. Subsequently, as we saw in Chapter 6, Congress won this battle, for the courts declared impounding unconstitutional, and the funds were released.

Although the main source of conflict in the antipollution field was money, more fundamental differences of principle emerged over the energy problem following the 1973 oil embargo. The response, first of Nixon, then of Ford, was to cut our reliance on oil imports by three kinds of measures. First, energy must be conserved by consumers, by the production of cars with better gasoline mileage, and by increases in fuel prices. The price of gasoline and fuel oil had been controlled since 1971; and for many years the price of natural gas, other than that distributed within the state in which it was produced, had been regulated. These controls, said the administration, should be phased out, and prices allowed to rise to levels established by the free market.

Second, alternative sources to the imports—Alaskan and offshore oil, coal, oil shale, nuclear, geothermal, and solar energy—must be developed. And, third, antipollution programs must be modified wherever these impede energy conservation and the development of alternative sources. Thus, to help Detroit achieve better mileage, there should be a five-year delay in the schedule for 90 percent pollution-free engines; more high-sulphur coal should be allowed; and restraints on the production of offshore oil should be removed.

Bitter opposition to the White House proposals arose from the Democrats in Congress, who particularly disliked the idea of using sharp price increases to choke off demand, for they believed the result would be both rising prices and increased unemployment when the country was already mired in "stagflation." The immediate aim should be moderate cuts in imports, and the cuts could grow deeper as the economy picked up. But how was this to be achieved? Here Congress showed itself to be well equipped to criticize, poorly organized to propose solutions.

The complexity of the committee structure of both houses of Congress showed up very clearly in the context of energy policy. The administration's energy recommendations had to be referred to four committees in the House—Commerce, Armed Services, Ways and Means, and Banking—and nine in the Senate—Commerce, Armed Services, Interior, Public Works, Government Operations, Finance, Banking, Labor, and Judiciary. As a result, in the first two months of 1974, federal energy officials had to testify at 35 committee or subcommittee hearings. Each committee produced its own recommendations, some dovetailing with others, some competing.

When at last each chamber hammered out an agreed program, Senate and House saw matters differently. The debates dragged on and on. Eventually, all the factions got together. A bill was passed that would hold oil prices down at first, then allow them to rise gradually until 1979, when controls would be lifted—if Congress allowed them to be; the auto industry was to be ordered to produce only cars averaging 27.5 miles to the gallon by 1985. President Ford was unhappy with the bill, but, reluctantly, he signed it.

The president and Congress did manage to produce some other agreements in the field of energy production. There was the pipeline to transport oil from new fields in Alaska, which Congress finally approved after a long period of hesitation; further delays were forced by court suits initiated by environmentalist groups, but at last the courts gave their approval, and construction proceeded. Then, too, Congress forced on a reluctant White House in 1975 the repeal of the "oil depletion allowance," a special tax break for the oil industry dating from 1926. In 1969 the depletion allowance had been reduced from 27.5 percent to 22 percent; and in 1975 the enormous oil company profits resulting from the sudden jump in prices led to the virtual elimination of the allowance.

Moreover, the president and Congress worked together in 1976 to provide substantial research and development appropriations for energy sources, the emphasis being heavily in the nuclear energy area. But taken all together these various measures fell far short of a comprehensive energy program.

Thus it was left to the Carter administration to devise and implement an energy policy commensurate with the nation's needs. In April 1977, Carter presented a comprehensive set of energy programs.

The energy problem facing the American people, said Carter, must be treated as "the moral equivalent of war." So we must take strong measures to reduce the annual energy growth by over 2 percent; to cut gasoline consumption by 10 percent and imports of foreign oil to less than 6 million barrels a day (from almost 9 million barrels in 1977); to establish a strategic petroleum reserve sufficient to last about 10 months; to increase coal production by more than two-thirds; to insulate most American homes and all new buildings; and to step up the use of solar energy in homes.

Among the devices proposed to achieve these goals were:

Removing price controls on gasoline and boosting federal taxes if use exceeded the government's targets.

Penalizing gas-guzzling cars with surcharges, and providing rebates for cars with good mileage.

Allowing the price of domestic oil to rise to the world price by 1980, with rebates to the public to prevent damage to the economy.

Controlling natural gas prices, but allowing the prices to rise.

Imposing taxes to encourage industry to switch from natural gas to coal, and expanding research and development in nonpolluting uses for coal.

Stepping up the output of nuclear energy under strict safeguards, but ending support for the "fast breeder" reactor that produces its own raw material by generating plutonium.

Providing tax credits to homeowners to encourage more insulation and the installation of solar-heating equipment.

All this was to be accomplished, said Carter, without allowing energy companies to make unreasonable profits. Nor must we abandon our commitment to protecting the environment, he insisted, and he called for vigorous action on air and water pollution, solid-waste disposal, and the preservation of wilderness areas.

Congress was now of the same party as the president; the Senate in 1977 established a Committee on Energy and Natural Resources; the House set up an Ad Hoc Select Committee on Energy. But still the struggle for energy legislation was bitter and prolonged. The House approved most of Carter's program; but the Senate, following the lead of Russell Long and his Finance Committee, balked at the key tax proposals in the program. Long argued that Carter's approach was punitive, and should be replaced by measures to stimulate energy production by giving tax incentives to industry and by ending price controls on natural gas as well as oil. A compromise program had to emerge at last from extended bargaining between House and Senate in conference committee. But the process provided the President with one more sharp reminder that in the post-Vietnam, post-Watergate era Congress was not about to rubber-stamp proposals from the White House, but was insisting on reasserting its authority.

The Federal Bureaucracies

The development of antipollution and energy policies by the federal administration has been bedeviled by cross-purposes and infighting among the agencies. Thus the Soil Conservation Service has battled against developmental proposals of the Agricultural Extension Service and the Tennessee Valley Authority. The Army Corps of Engineers has pursued flood control projects in face of efforts by other agencies to advance more broadly conceived projects; and Congress has taken such a proprietary interest in the Army Corps of Engineers, whose projects benefit their local constituencies, that the Engineers have been able to defy not only other federal agencies but sometimes even the president himself.

Other conflicts arose between the agencies responsible for producing energy and those concerned with protecting the environment. In the field of nuclear energy the conflict was concentrated within a single agency, the Atomic Energy Commission (AEC), which was responsible for development and production and, at the same time, safety and pollution control.

In the case of the Santa Barbara oil spill in 1969, the antipollution forces had to contend not only with the country's need for energy but also with the federal government's budgetary pressures. Secretary of the Interior Stewart Udall had approved the oil leases to private industry in 1968, though for years he had been in the forefront of the fight for the conservation of natural resources. Later Udall described that decision as "a sort of conservation Bay of Pigs."[4] Udall had agonized for some time before he accepted the proposal, for he was worried about the risks of leakage in an area prone to earthquakes. But he had been subjected to two kinds of pressure. First, the experts in his own department were insisting that, without the offshore oil, the West Coast would face shortages. (This was before the Alaskan pipeline changed the picture.) Second, the Bureau of the Budget was demanding more revenues to help pay for the Vietnam war. The federal government's leases to Union Oil raised $602 million.

A further problem facing the federal agencies in the energy and environmental fields is that they have lacked the resources needed to obtain information and have had to rely heavily on industry sources. In the Santa Barbara case the Interior Department's Geological Survey did not have the funds to do its own test drillings and used the reassuring reports presented by the oil companies. The head of the Geological Survey accepted the companies' conclusions and assured Udall that the risk was minimal.

As pollution problems and energy shortages reached crisis proportions and thus became political issues, governmental efforts began to address these problems. In 1970, President Nixon established the Environmental Protection Agency, which brought together antipollution enforcement authority previously distributed among a number of federal agencies, and he further set up a Council on Environmental Quality in the Executive Office of the President. Similarly, a Federal Energy Administration was established when the energy crisis hit the country, and the functions of the Atomic Energy Commission were absorbed into a new Energy Research and Development Administration. A Nuclear Regulatory Commission was established to solve the problem that had existed under the AEC—the neglect of nuclear safety considerations because these were subordinated to the nuclear development mission of the AEC. Then, to direct his administration's energy program, Jimmy Carter created a Cabinet Department of Energy under James Schlesinger, a former defense secretary and AEC head. The new department took over the functions of the Federal Energy Administration, the Energy Research and Development Administration, and the Federal Power Commission as well as the energy-related activities of a number of other federal departments and regulatory agencies. The Nuclear Regulatory Commission remained as an independent agency. So did the Environmental Protection Agency, whose staff was expanded; the Council on Environmental Quality remained in the Executive Office of the President; and the Interior Department was given expanded responsibilities in the environmental field, responsibilities that were vigorously exercised by Carter's interior secretary, Cecil Andrus.

State and Local Government

The issues considered in this chapter highlight both the strengths and the weaknesses of the federal system. On the positive side, several of the states assumed strong leadership in the fight against pollution. For example, the state of California and the county of Los Angeles took strong regulatory action to ban the burning of trash in backyard incinerators, control industrial effluents, and force the car manufacturers to move toward the reduction of harmful auto emissions. And Oregon banned the use of "no-return" bottles for soft drinks and other non-biodegradable containers.

Still, the fact remained that many of our forests, mountains, and rivers are not conveniently contained within state boundaries. And the profusion of sub-federal government agencies, "each jealously guarding its prerogatives and each diligently ignoring and working at cross-purposes with its neighboring governments," was a serious barrier to antipollution programs.[5] Though there were a number of interstate compact agencies concerned with such problems as the control of wastes discharged into rivers crossing several states, their effectiveness was limited.

The energy crisis intensified the problems of intergovernmental relations. State interests clashed with federal interests. States that produced oil and natural gas resented federal price controls. Coastal states fought the federal government over who controlled offshore oil and gas beds.

There was also conflict among states. Oil- and gas-producing states acted to protect their supplies from the demands of consuming states. Texas banned shipments of natural gas out of state if these were needed at home. New Mexico put a tax on any electricity generated within the state that was sold outside the state. States in the West, Southwest, and Northeast formed separate energy groups to look after their regional interests. Western states such as Montana, Colorado, New Mexico, and Wyoming, which contained great quantities of coal, feared that wide-scale strip mining would destroy the scenic beauty of their land. And almost everyone preferred to have nuclear power plants in adjoining states rather than their own.

Public Opinion

Of the various factors influencing public opinion on environmental and energy questions, scientists, the media, and students were of particular importance.

Scientists.   A few books and articles by scientists in various fields first alerted segments of the public to the environmental issue. In 1962 marine biologist Rachel Carson uttered an urgent warning against the indiscriminate use of pesticides in her book *Silent Spring*. Other experts and officials complained that her argument was grossly overstated. But the book was a best seller and was serialized in the influential *New Yorker* magazine. Its theme was taken up by more and more writers and public figures, and its general findings were endorsed in 1965 by a presidential advisory panel. Other scientists wrote widely read books on the environment and resources—Barry Commoner warning of the threat to human survival represented by the havoc inflicted on the environment by man, Paul Ehrlich making dire predictions that the earth's resources could not sustain the expansion of population. And the Ford and Rockefeller foundations funded scientific studies on energy and the environment.

The media.   With the Santa Barbara oil spill, the audience for discussions of the environment was enormously expanded. The Santa Barbara incident provided dramatic television material. There was color coverage of magnificent beaches soiled by filthy oil; frantic efforts to save the lives of birds unable to fly because their wings were soaked with oil; a few solitary individuals in rowboats hampering the efforts of a great corporation to install a new oil rig; the same rig accidentally capsizing; and angry citizens organized into GOO (Get Oil Out), articulating the frustrations of people all around the country whose environment, in one way or another, was being spoiled by the ravages of technology. Nor did the networks drop the issue after the Santa Barbara leak was plugged and the damage finally repaired.

The printed media were no less involved. Newspaper stories on environmental problems increased exponentially. Magazines, which had been carrying more and more articles on pollution even before Santa Barbara, now gave the issue sustained attention. This meant that the media were running the risk of offending some of their biggest advertisers, particularly the oil and automobile companies. Nonetheless, the coverage was persistent and often scathing. Although the media are interested in profits, their business is news; and ecology, they discovered, was eminently newsworthy.

Students.   Of all segments of the public none responded with greater enthusiasm to the utterances of scientists and journalists than college students. April 22, 1970, was proclaimed "Earth Day," and in colleges and universities all over the country teach-ins and demonstrations were held, gas masks worn, auto engines buried, mounds of garbage strewn and then meticulously collected. Ecology provided the student movement with a focus of activity for organized student expression. The topic brought together under one rubric several of the sources of dissatisfaction that troubled students and had moved them toward the left. Many of them were intensely critical of the great corporations, both because they were big and because they were capitalistic; of technology, perceived as the enemy of human values; of Western civilization itself, which had set itself up so arrogantly as superior to other cultures and even to nature.

Like the earlier objects of student attention—the civil rights movement and the Vietnam war—the environmental issue lost some of its appeal in time, and there was no revival of enthusiasm when the energy crisis struck. However, if the crowds attending courses in ecology on college campuses have thinned, concern about the quality of the environment still persists in the student culture, reflected in the interest in organically grown foods and ecological studies.

The general public.   Although the public at large did not respond as dramatically as did students and the media, surveys showed significant increases in public concern about pollution from the mid-1960s. By 1970, when a Gallup poll asked people to name the three topics they thought should receive the most governmental attention, air and water pollution were mentioned by 53 percent, second only to crime. Another Gallup survey in 1972 showed that about half of all automobile owners were willing to pay $50 or more out of their own pockets to reduce the pollution caused by their cars.

However, there was a limit to the support the majority were to give to measures to attack these problems. The 1972 Gallup survey showed also that only 3 in 10 were willing to pay $50 or more to purify the waters. Moreover, the acid test came in a question in another survey: "If you had to choose, would you favor or oppose the U.S. deliberately limiting economic and technical growth in this country?" Twenty-seven percent were for limiting growth. Sixty percent were opposed.[6]

When the energy shortage struck, this problem confronted the people in immediate form. The majority did not believe that a choice had to be made. A 1975 Harris survey found that 65 percent felt that solutions to the energy crisis could be found without interrupting antipollution efforts. This might not always be true, however, as became clear in 1976 when proposals were placed on the ballot in a number of states to halt the construction of nuclear power plants pending the elimination of hazards. The proposals were all defeated.

In sum, the public grew confused about what to do about the energy problem and how to relate it to the pollution issue. In the immediate aftermath of the Arab oil embargo, a climate existed that might have made it possible to enact strong new programs of conservation and resource development. But when the immediate shortage disappeared, and gas was available in abundance, though at higher prices, the backing for drastic measures dwindled. Indeed, as rumors spread of oil tankers anchoring outside ports because the storage facilities were already overloaded (reports later denied by administration officials), skepticism became widespread that the oil crisis had ever existed. So the gathering consensus on the need for decisive action seemed to be breaking up; and it fell to Jimmy Carter to reactivate the public concern over energy. For a time, at least, he had some success. Polls taken just before he presented his energy program in April 1977 indicated that about half the people did not believe that the energy situation was really serious; but, following Carter's presentation, the proportion accepting that the problem was critical increased significantly.

Interest Groups

The importance of the environmental and energy issues is attested to by the intense pressures applied by a broad range of interest groups—business (especially the energy producers and the automobile manufacturers), environmental organizations, labor, and civil rights groups.

Business.   A *Fortune* magazine survey published in early 1970 revealed that 57 percent of the nation's top industrial executives supported an increase in government regulation to combat pollution.[7] Yet there were limits to industry's enthusiasm for the fight against pollution. Oil companies with an investment of over $400 million in the Alaskan pipeline could hardly be expected to applaud the delays that environmentalists forced upon them before approval for the construction was finally given. Automobile manufacturers fought hard for postponement of the deadlines for pollution-free emissions set by antismog laws, and managed to secure a series of extensions of time. Throughout industry, concern spread about the burden of cost increases imposed by the installation of environmental-protection devices and about the projects delayed or abandoned because elaborate studies would have to be undertaken and reviewed by governmental agencies to prove that the projects did not have an adverse effect on the environment.

Pressures by business groups did not reach their peak, however, until the struggle over energy legislation after the 1973 oil crisis. The oil industry is the most influential of the business groups in the energy field for a number of reasons. Seven of the major oil companies are listed among the 20 biggest business corporations in America. These major oil companies have engaged in "vertical integration"—that is, controlling the oil industry all the way down the line from the initial exploration and production, through refining, and then selling their products. Some have also invested profits in what is known as "horizontal integration"—reaching out to acquire holdings in coal and other energy fields. And some oil companies have become conglomerates, venturing into fields totally unrelated to energy.

The oil companies spend a great deal of time and energy promoting their legislative interests. They are represented in Washington by the American

"We create it, we clean it up —business couldn't be better."

Drawing by Sidney Harris. Reproduced by special permission of *Playboy* Magazine; © 1971 by Playboy.

Petroleum Institute, headed by lobbyist Frank Ikard (who previously served for seven years on the tax-writing Ways and Means Committee of the House). As we have mentioned before, business—and especially the oil industry—is among the major sources of money for political campaigns. And some of the oil industry's contributions have been illegally drawn from corporate funds, as was the case with Phillips Petroleum, which admitted in 1974 to having contributed $685,000 to political campaigns over a 10-year period from corporate coffers, including $100,000 in 1972 to the Committee to Reelect the President.

The oil industry is well represented in Congress through the congressmen from oil-producing states. As we have seen, Russell Long of Louisiana is chairperson of the Finance Committee in the Senate.

Apart from lobbying and campaign contributions, the oil industry has spent heavily in getting its case before the public through taking full-page ads in newspapers and magazines.

The industry has not agreed unanimously on all energy issues. The smaller, independent companies, represented by the Independent Petroleum Association of America, have fought against legislation that they felt was designed to help the major companies put them out of business. Among the majors there have been differences over a number of issues, including the desirability of conservation rather than stepped-up production. However, the industry has been generally united in fighting off moves in Congress which, they contend, would reduce their profits and thus their ability to develop new sources of supply.

Other energy industries—coal, nuclear, natural gas, electric utilities and so on—sometimes compete with oil; but they usually join forces when the issue is energy versus the environment. For example, an effort to pass legislation in 1975 to set severe limits to strip mining was defeated by a joint effort by the coal industry and electricity utilities, who wanted the low-sulphur coal produced by strip mining.

Another major business interest, the automobile industry, took no pleasure from the high profits that came to the oil industry in the wake of the embargo. On the contrary, the sales of new automobiles were hard hit by rising gas prices. But the conservation of oil and the protection of the environment could not be high priorities for the automobile manufacturers, and they lobbied heavily to protect their interests, sending Henry Ford and other corporation presidents on visits to Capitol Hill, to the top levels of federal executive departments, and even to the White House.

The environmental lobbies.   Several organizations have engaged in the fight against pollution and increasingly against business. Traditionally, this effort was in the hands of such associations as the Sierra Club, the Friends of the Earth, and the National Audubon Society, whose members have a deep commitment to the preservation of the land, waters, and wildlife of America. Then, when the environmental issue came to the fore in the early 1970s, new conservationist groups proliferated. The Environmental Defense Fund, a coalition of scientists and lawyers, brought cases before the courts and government agencies. Environmental

Action, Inc., published lists of members of Congress it considered hostile to the environmental cause and worked for their defeat. Effective reinforcement for these specifically environmental groups came from the other public interest organizations, Common Cause and the Ralph Nader groups. Thus the defeat of the supersonic transport in 1971 was at least partly attributable to the pressure applied by Common Cause, working with the Friends of the Earth and the tiny but influential Citizens League against the Sonic Boom.

According to the oil companies' chief lobbyist, Frank Ikard, these groups have been extremely effective in their opposition to the oil companies. "Common Cause and Nader," he said, "are the two most powerful groups in the United States. They generate a kind of fear technique that no business groups can use. If you don't follow their lead, they publicize the fact that you're listening to the wrong voices. Their public relations arm is very substantial."[8] The repeal of the oil depletion allowance and other antiindustry energy legislation of 1975 were evidence of the enhanced power of the public interest groups. On the other hand, the oil industry was successful in fighting off several of the proposals that they regarded as most damaging to their interests.

Labor.   The effectiveness of the antibusiness forces might have been considerably greater had it not been for the fact that labor, usually a potent element on the liberal side of domestic issues, was ambivalent on environmental and energy questions. On the one hand, labor was active in some aspects of the environmental cause. The AFL–CIO and the United Auto Workers joined a number of other groups to form the Citizens Crusade for Clean Water, which led Congress in 1969 to vote considerably more funds to fight water pollution than President Nixon had asked for. The AFL–CIO came out in favor of strip mining controls. And in 1975 the AFL–CIO called for antitrust legislation to force the major oil companies to divest themselves of their marketing operations and their holdings in coal, natural gas, and uranium, as well as to treat them as public utilities subject to strict federal regulation.

However, labor organizations could not ignore the possible threat to jobs represented by antipollution and energy conservation laws. Some companies, unable or unwilling to pay for the installation of required antipollution equipment, closed their doors and threw their employees out of work. In 1969, when a proposal was presented in the House to force the automobile industry to bring exhaust emissions under control on pain of abolition of the internal combustion engine, a cry of anguish went up from one of the congressmen from Michigan:

> There are more than 25,000 workers in one city alone in my district who work directly for one company in the auto industry. I would point out to the members that in this nation of ours one out of every seven workers' jobs is traceable to the auto industry in some way or another. . . . This industry means an awful lot to an awful lot of people in America, and I would consider that very carefully before we tamper with writing standards that would affect it on the floor of this House.[9]

The Environmental Protection Agency declared in 1975 that the problem of lost jobs was grossly exaggerated; that in five years of antipollution laws only 75 plants had closed with a loss of 15,710 jobs (mostly in the fields of iron and steel, paper, and chemicals); that, in fact, the antipollution industry that these laws had brought into existence already employed 1.1 million workers. Still, these figures did not take account of the new jobs that would have been created by construction and other projects that had to be abandoned or were never started because the new laws would have made them too costly. And the AFL–CIO's president, George Meany, lobbied energetically on behalf of the supersonic transport because it would provide a considerable number of jobs in the economically depressed Seattle area, and in various other locations.

The United Auto Workers (UAW) were particularly embarrassed by the pollution and energy threats represented by their product. The UAW is among the more liberal unions, frequently criticizing George Meany for being insufficiently concerned with the broad public interest. UAW president Leonard Woodcock spoke in the established tradition of his union when, in 1975, he attacked the major corporations for using "environmental blackmail" to avoid the application of antipollution regulations, and holding "workers or at least their jobs in hostage" by playing on fears of lost employment if laws protecting the environment are passed. Still, he pleaded with environmentalists not to ignore the threat to jobs they represented, and he asked for compensation for workers displaced by antipollution rules. The UAW also resisted policies aimed at reducing the public's dependence on the automobile. Instead, Woodcock and his union favored requiring the companies to build nonpolluting automobiles with economical fuel consumption.

Civil rights organizations.   Another of the traditional components in the liberal coalition could not be counted on when it came to environmental protection. Low-income blacks living in squalid tenements are not likely to be especially horrified by an oil slick off Santa Barbara. They are more inclined to be interested in the extermination of rats and roaches in urban slum areas than in the survival of salmon and sea gulls. To most blacks, in fact, the environmental issue is a diversion from efforts to deal with the urban crisis rather than an opportunity to build a broad coalition that could work to solve the urban crisis as part of the general environmental crisis. As Clarence Mitchell, the NAACP's Washington lobbyist, put it, spending on pollution should come "after we take care of the problems of low income, poor housing, and inadequate medical care. Once we get these accomplished, then we can go into the fringe areas such as cleaning up rivers and air." [10]

Five Perspectives on
Energy and the Environment

The Liberals:
Don't Leave It to Business

Environmentalism has a natural attraction for liberals. It captures the essence of some of their central values, especially the belief that we should move beyond our preoccupation with quantitative, material advancement to a concern with the quality of life.

However, the liberals have some difficulty with the ecologists' advocacy of a slower rate of economic growth as a means of lessening the strain on the environment and conserving the earth's natural resources. With less economic growth the liberals know that it becomes more difficult to fund social welfare programs. Although they favor redistribution of income as a means of abolishing poverty, they see the political resistances as too great to allow the job to be done by redistribution alone. Thus we also have to push for increases in the GNP. Liberals try to resolve this dilemma by proposing that, instead of the reckless, uncontrolled growth of the past, we should plan for careful, controlled growth; and they want to see the larger part of this come *not* in the production of material goods that create pollution and squander resources but rather in the form of educational, cultural, recreational, health, and other services that contribute to the well-being of the community and do little damage to the environment.

As the liberals see it, the chief culprits in the deterioration of the environment are business corporations. The greed of industrial enterprises for profit, no matter what the cost to the public interest, is incompatible with the effort to sustain a reasonable relationship with the natural environment. It is the same with the energy problem. The massive lobbying efforts of the oil cartels, natural gas, nuclear and coal industries, together with the automobile companies, have corrupted the political system with their money, and made it difficult to adopt a rational, environmentally sound approach to the energy problem.

So deep is the liberals' distrust of big business that, when the energy crisis was proclaimed in 1973, some of them doubted its existence. They noted that the administration was heavily dependent on industry for its information on oil production and reserves. Ralph Nader told a congressional committee in January 1974 that reserve figures quoted by government represented only about 10 percent of proven reserves and that the world was "drowning in oil." Similar suspicions were voiced during the natural gas crisis in the winter of 1977. The gas producers, said the liberals, were deliberately holding back supplies and refusing to explore new sources in order to force the removal of price controls.

Just the same, the liberals, although skeptical about the immediate oil and gas crises, welcome the public's awakening to the long-range energy problem. They do not see how we can go on heedlessly despoiling the earth of its limited supply of fossil fuels and other natural resources. They believe that we must move as quickly as possible to a lower resource-consuming economy. And we must take the leadership to encourage nations around the world to move in the same direction. Although liberals welcome the indications of the decline in population growth, they still do not see any prospect of holding the increase below a billion people by the end of the century—and they wonder how we shall find the food and fuel for another billion people.

The principal culprit in creating the energy crisis, say the liberals, is business. Long before the oil embargo the corporations were engaged in practices that were bound to produce a shortage eventually. For decades business aggressively pushed the sale of energy. The consumer has been bombarded with messages from electricity companies identifying "the good life" with electric gadgets. The automobile and oil lobbies have combined to make the private automobile the principal means of transportation, with the result that public transportation, which is far more economical in its use of energy, has suffered gross neglect.

Then, too, the oil industry has been concerned more with keeping prices up than with increasing the supply. So it persuaded Congress and the administration to shelter it behind import quotas that limited the use of foreign crude oil while draining domestic reserves. American companies, aided by favorable tax laws that they helped write, invested heavily in Middle Eastern oil production and refining, owned much of the oil until the Arab countries confiscated it or brought them out —even then continued to work closely with the Arabs in providing technical assistance and equipment. And these measures were undertaken by a small number of huge corporations whose relationships, said the liberals, were characterized not by competition but by collusion.

This argument received strong support in July 1973, when a Federal Trade Commission staff report charged that anticompetitive practices by the biggest oil companies were a major contributor to the shortage. Subsequently, the FTC filed a complaint alleging that the eight largest oil companies—Exxon, Arco, Texaco, Gulf, Mobil, California Standard, Indiana Standard, and Shell—had engaged in monopolistic practices that forced prices up. In February 1976 Gulf Oil pleaded guilty to four counts of deliberately violating government oil-price regulations, and was fined $20,000. And even among the lesser oil companies who claimed to be the principal source of price competition in the field, there was price fixing, for in 1975 Phillips Petroleum Company and Douglas Oil Company of California entered "no contest" pleas to charges that, with four other oil companies, they had conspired in 1970 and 1971 to fix the wholesale price on hundreds of millions of gallons of gasoline sold by independent stations.

What should we do about the energy problem? First, we should reject the type of proposals that came out of the Nixon and Ford administrations to use sharp increases in prices as a means of cutting demand, and to pull back from our commitment to the war against pollution. In fact, gasoline consumption has continued to grow despite the large increases in prices. Higher energy prices do little, it seems, except punish the poor. They give the producing companies enormous profits which they do not necessarily invest in developing more sources of energy.

Nor can we afford to reduce our concern with pollution. Tearing apart vast areas of magnificent terrain in the West through strip mining or oil shale development is too high a price to placate our insatiable demand for energy. The multiplication of nuclear power plants sharply increases the prospect that someday, somewhere, a disastrous accident will occur, killing hundreds of thousands of people. It also greatly aggravates the problem of disposing of nuclear wastes, a problem for which we still have nothing but temporary solutions. And there is the additional question of security. A study by the General Accounting Office published in July 1976 reported that: ". . . Serious deficiencies in both the material accountability and the physical security systems were found. . . . The evidence raises serious questions as to the ability of [the Energy Research and Development Administration's] facilities to detect and prevent a theft of bomb quantities of special nuclear materials."

Liberals further deplore the fact that already the pace of offshore oil drilling is being stepped up, and new leases have been granted off the coast of southern California. Although more stringent safeguards have been adopted since the Santa Barbara spill in 1969, the growing number of offshore oil wells means that sooner or later more accidents will happen. In other respects, too, the great environmental advances of the beginning of the decade are being undermined in the name of the energy shortage. So liberals reject the idea of relying on business to solve the energy problem and of backing away from the commitment to save the environment. Instead, they recommend a series of measures that involve the federal government very heavily in the production and distribution of energy. This is in accordance with their belief (as explained in Chapter 1) that, although liberty is a core value, it does not extend to the right of huge corporations to manage the economy in their own interests. Accordingly, the liberals offer both short-run and long-run proposals that set severe limits to the freedom of major corporations.

The liberals' proposals: short-run measures.   Liberals argue that we should maintain price controls. Under controls prices might be allowed to rise in order to encourage conservation; but the increases should be moderate and they should come in the form of higher taxes on fuels rather than simply higher prices charged by business to add to their already inflated profits.

If local shortages of particular fuels should occur, we should handle them through government planning and the allocation of supplies between the various regions of the country. If another oil embargo is imposed, we should resort to rationing, thereby ensuring everyone a fair share of the limited supplies. Rationing worked well enough in World War II, and it can work in another emergency.

Long-run measures.   Over the long haul liberals begin with conservation. Conserving resources is ecologically sound and economically the best way of reducing the problem to manageable proportions. Next we should explore and develop oil and gas reserves in the lands and offshore waters owned by the federal government. This would provide a yardstick by which to measure costs and prices in private companies, and would reduce the government's dependence on the corporations for energy data.

Then we must develop alternative, pollution-free energy sources. Ultimately, the nuclear fusion process, harnessing the power now available only in thermonuclear weapons, would be the complete solution. But this is still some way off. In the meantime we should undertake the massive development of solar energy, devoting to this and other nonpolluting energy sources the same kinds of national commitment used to produce the A-bomb in World War II and to put men on the moon by 1969.

Liberals also propose splitting up the giant oil corporations, denying them the ability to corner the market by producing, refining, and selling their products, stopping them from buying up solar energy companies to hold down solar development as a means of keeping up oil prices, and preventing them from putting their profits into fields unrelated to energy. They should be treated like public utilities, subjected to close government regulation of production and pricing. If, despite these steps, they persist in evading regulation and rigging the market, they should be nationalized.

Only through strong measures of this kind, say the liberals, will it be possible to stop the energy corporations from thwarting the public interest. Of course, their power is great and will be very difficult to break. Still, liberals view the defeat of the SST and the repeal of the oil depletion allowance as encouraging indications of what can be accomplished by determined effort. So, the liberals contend, we must step up these efforts by electing people to public office who care about the environment; by effective grass-roots lobbying campaigns; and by the kind of lawsuits that force such delays on business that it became uneconomic to proceed with environmentally harmful projects.

The Radical Left:
The Corporate Rape of the Earth

Some of the themes of the ecology movement strike responsive chords on the far left. They approve of the accusations heaped upon the business corporations for their alleged disregard of the environment in their drive for profits. And the new left counterculturists approve of the rejection of the single-minded pursuit of uncontrolled technological progress.

But the new left go much further than the liberal environmentalists. They seek a return to simpler social forms and a unity between man and nature. Theodore Roszak, the leading spokesperson for this position, argues that ecology is important not just because the human species is in danger of extinction, but because nature, like humankind, is sacred.[11]

The liberals' attack on the corporation is stated in harsher terms by the radical left. It is not enough, says one writer of the left, to blame the oil companies, destructive though their policies have been. We must look at the entire system, which reflects their purposes. The governments of the United States and other Western powers backed the companies "not merely, as is often alleged, because of political pressure from the 'oil lobby,' but, more fundamentally, because the prosperity and even the working of the economic system were geared to the flow of cheap oil." It was cheap because the producing companies were exploited by the Western countries—treated as colonies whose sole purpose was to provide the advanced countries with the energy they needed. Those days are gone. There will be no more cheap energy, food, or raw materials of any kind. So it is true that we face an energy crisis. But it cuts much deeper than the oil embargo. And this crisis "can only be solved by a radical change in the whole existing economic system."[12]

Thus the tactics of the liberal environmentalists designed to produce stronger laws and enforcement powers are largely beside the point. The environment cannot be saved from the ravages of the corporations, and a rational energy problem cannot be shaped by the actions of our legislatures or executive agencies or courts or pressure groups. Nothing but the transformation of the system can accomplish that: "We must . . . junk the business system and its way of life, and create revolutionary new institutions to embody new goals—human and environmental."[13]

The Conservatives:
Leave It to Business

Among the members of conservationist groups are people of strong conservative leanings. Senator Barry Goldwater, for example, is a long-standing member of the Sierra Club. To be conservative, after all, is to support the preservation of the inheritance from the past, including the heritage bequeathed to us by nature. Conservatives also tend to be skeptical about claims that all change, including technological change, means progress. Yet conservatives disagree with the analysis of liberals and the left of the pollution and energy problems on three grounds: First, it exaggerates the gravity of the problems; second, it is wrong about their causes; and third, its proposed solutions are fallacious and destructive of our liberties.

Undoubtedly, the problems exist. There is pollution, and the 1973 oil embargo did show us to be dangerously dependent on imported oil. But neither of these problems is as potentially disastrous as the left-of-center critics suggest. It is absurd to argue that pollution threatens to bring the human race to an end. We may well face more impurities in the air and water, and this is undesirable. But industrialization has always brought impurities with it, and in some respects our environment is purer than it was in earlier periods of history. Certainly we should not be complacent, and we must do all we can to preserve the natural beauties of our environment. But the Santa Barbara oil spill did not portend the end of the world.

Then there is the great population scare. M. Stanton Evans observes: "It is significant, indeed, that so much of the uproar about population comes from government, media, and academic types who live in Washington, New York, and other areas around the nation's seaboards. These places are congested, of course —in considerable measure by the people who complain about their congested status."[14] In fact, the United States as a whole is among the least densely populated countries in the world; and its birthrate has already fallen to the levels advocated by the zealots of Zero Population Growth—with the result that we are heading for an aging population that will lack the dynamism provided by a more youthful society. As for the world at large, it can sustain a population far beyond the present projections—and these projections may well be scaled down as the birthrate begins to fall in the poorer countries. What will make it fall—what always makes the birthrate fall—is a rising standard of living. It is within the capacity of the poorer nations to accomplish this, if they display the energy and the will to do so. All that is necessary to defy the predictions of Malthus (and somehow the imminent doom forecast by Malthus is always being postponed) is to make effective use of the tools of technology, which were lacking when Malthus wrote in 1798.

Nor is there any reason why we should run out of energy. Eventually the supply of fossil fuels will be used up. But that is far off in the future. Our still considerable quantities of oil and natural gas are backed up with enough coal to last from 300 to 900 years. And we are still in the early stages of the uses of nuclear power.[15]

Still, in the short term we do have problems. The reasons for this are not at all what the liberals and the left suggest. They put almost all the blame for pollution and the energy shortage on private business. But business is not the only culprit. With respect to pollution there is no single scapegoat. All of us pollute. Industry manufactures cars and produces oil, but we drive cars—two or more to a family—and we burn the gasoline. Industry produces cans and bottles, but we produce the litter.

In the energy field, government is the principal source of scarcity. Government price controls on oil and natural gas have kept prices down artificially. This provided energy at rates so cheap that it was squandered. If prices had been allowed to find their natural level, we would have conserved energy more carefully. Moreover, with higher prices, business would have made bigger profits and thus would have had more money to invest in exploration and production of the needed additional resources.

Clearly, then, the solutions to our problems lie in the opposite direction to the liberals' panacea. First, energy must be given a higher priority for the time being than the attack on pollution. This is not to say that we should ignore the pollution problem. Government has a role to play in setting standards for the quality of air and water which everyone may be required to respect. But these standards should not be impossibly high. We cannot have a 100 percent pollution-free environment. As long as man exists on the earth, some damage will be inflicted on the environment. In fact, many of the hazards that we blame on man are also found in the state of nature. Recent research shows that carcinogens (cancer-

Drawing by Conrad; © 1977. Reprinted with permission,
The Los Angeles Times.

causing agents) exist, at least in small quantities, in a number of plants in their
pure organic state.

So we must stop suggesting that even the slightest impurity in our surroundings is intolerable. We must not allow ourselves to be frightened out of the
use of beneficial technological discoveries because of exaggerated allegations
about harmful side effects. For example, the insecticide DDT has been sharply
curtailed in the United States because of claims that it retards the reproduction of
fish, makes birds' eggs thin, and builds up harmful residues in animals and in
humans. Yet an exhaustive official hearing on the subject concluded that "DDT is
not a safety hazard to man when used as directed," and, if properly used, it need
not do much damage to wildlife; the limited harm caused "is not unreasonable on
balance with its benefits." [16]

Not content with denying DDT to many farmers in the United States, the environmentalists have carried their crusade to the United Nations, trying to secure
a worldwide ban. But the World Health Organization and the Food and
Agriculture Organization pointed out that without DDT about half of the poor nations' cotton production would be destroyed; India's plans for increased
agricultural output could never be realized; and tens, perhaps hundreds, of thousands of people would die of malaria. Although the World Health Organization
was testing alternative pesticides, none had appeared that was effective enough
and cheap enough to replace DDT. Yet the liberals, the great champions of the
poor, were fighting to inflict this terrible damage on the poor countries.

The environmentalists were also asking the United Nations to organize an international crusade against pollution in order to head off the threat to the environ-

ment caused by the industrialization of the newly developing countries. But antipollution equipment is expensive. Suppose, said the representatives of the poorer nations, the advanced industrial countries had been forced to accept severe pollution controls during their earlier industrial history. How far advanced would they be today? And why should the poor nations deny themselves an opportunity to pull themselves out of their poverty?

The liberals' obsession with the environment is also making it impossible for us to solve our energy problem. The delays they forced in the construction of the Alaskan pipeline forced up our oil import bill by $2 billion a year; and, if they had had their way, we should never have gotten any oil from Alaska. More billions of dollars in imports resulted from the closing down of the Santa Barbara oil fields and from the cost of removing lead from gasoline and other forms of emissions controls. No matter what proposals are made, the liberals find them unacceptable. The development of vast reserves off the coasts will, they say, cause oil spills and ruin the coastline. Coal, strip mining, oil shale, nuclear energy, all are unacceptable to them.

They see our salvation in solar energy, though this cannot handle more than a small fraction of our needs for decades to come. Even hydroelectric development is hindered by the absurdities of liberal-sponsored environmental legislation. In 1976, a $600 million hydroelectric project in New England was held up because botanists found some specimens of the furbish lousewort in a remote area of northern Maine. Nobody claims that the furbish lousewort, a fernlike wild snapdragon, is beautiful or even pretty, and it has no commercial value. But it is rare; in fact, it had been assumed to be extinct before its discovery in Maine. And the Endangered Species Act bars federal projects from destroying rare and endangered species of plants and animals. So the project could not proceed until the lousewort was discovered in another area. The consequence of this kind of nonsense, say the conservatives, together with the general obstructionism of the environmental extremists, can only be either to place us completely at the mercy of the Middle East oil countries or to bring all economic growth to a halt.

Since most of the liberals are not prepared to accept the consequences of their proposals, they seek a way out of their dilemma through massive intervention in the energy problem by the federal government. This is undesirable in two respects, say the conservatives. First, it will be a major step toward the end of our freedoms and the complete takeover of the economy by government. Second, it will not work. Government does not know how to produce and market efficiently. And, when government tries to interfere in the free market, it makes a mess of the situation. Planning and controls create rigidities and delays in the system. Rationing (which is the real preference of some of the liberals) produces an immense bureaucracy and immediately establishes a black market in which gasoline coupons are sold illegally to those who can afford them. (So much for the argument that rationing is the only equitable solution!)

The answer is to get rid of government price controls. Prices will rise. Demand will fall as the higher cost cuts down frivolous uses of energy. Higher profits will give the energy companies the funds they need to explore for more oil and natural gas, discover more effective ways of transforming coal into gas and oil, and even bring down the price of solar energy. It is true that in the past some of the oil companies' profits have been diverted into unrelated fields of investment. But this is because government price controls and harassment by the environmentalists have made the future of their industry so uncertain. Once they are given a more hospitable environment, they will find ways of tapping our vast energy resources, just as they did in the past.

So private business must be given its head, unhampered by bureaucratic restrictions and regulations—and unsupported by government. "Time and again," says Milton Friedman, "I have castigated the oil companies for their hypocrisy, for loudly proclaiming their allegiance to free enterprise yet simultaneously undermining free enterprise by seeking and getting special governmental privilege." [17] Thus the end of the oil depletion allowance is to be welcomed, and there should be an end to import quotas and sheltering behind tariffs. Free enterprise can solve our energy shortages, so long as it is truly free and fully competitive.

The Radical Right: Environmentalism Equals Revolution

In their campaigns against fluoridation of water some elements of the radical right have sounded themes that contain an interesting similarity to environmentalist arguments: man and his science should not tamper with nature by adding dangerous chemicals. This similarity, however, has not led the radical right to find common cause with the ecologists. On the contrary, they are bound to be hostile to a movement that has drawn its sustenance from all the institutions and organizations the right detests: the Rockefeller and other foundations; the federal government; the media; intellectuals; liberal and left-wing students.

Thus in 1970 the Daughters of the American Revolution found the purposes of Earth Day "distorted and exaggerated," if not subversive. Voices were raised on the far right suggesting that April 22 had been deliberately selected for Earth Day because it was Lenin's birthday.

Environmentalism, to the radical right, has been adopted by the radical left as a means of destroying faith in the American system and replacing it with state socialism, otherwise known as communism. As one writer for the John Birch Society put it:

> Give me a breath of dirty air! I would prefer it, I really would—at least if laundering the air means that the ecology charlatans are going to hustle us into dictatorship. Which is exactly what it means. At the moment, they want to bury the private automobile in exchange for air as fresh as was ever drawn by the god on Olympus. And, if they bring it off, these con artists of a past that never was (and a future that never can be) will in the process destroy the nation's economy and cut our liberties to the bone. [18]

The Centrists:
A Time for Trade-offs

On environmental and energy issues, centrists hold to their preference for a middle ground between the analyses offered from both sides of the spectrum. Thus on the environment centrists believe that pollution represents a serious problem—more serious than conservatives usually admit—but that the warnings of the imminent collapse of our civilization, or even the end of the human race, are exaggerated.

In looking at the causes of pollution centrists do not find business blameless. They believe that businesspeople have been insufficiently concerned with the public interest and must bear a major part of the responsibility for the damage that has been inflicted on our environment. But then, so must everyone else. As Max Ways put it in *Fortune* magazine, ". . . all men are polluters—and all living Americans are big polluters. . . . At the root of our environmental troubles we will not find a cause as simple as the greed of a few men. The wastes that besmirch our land are produced in the course of fulfilling widespread human wants that are in the main reasonable and defensible." Capitalism is not the root of the trouble, for the Soviet Union, "organized around central planning, has constructed some of the most terrifyingly hideous cityscapes on earth, while raping the countryside with strip mines, industrial pollutants, and all the other atrocities that in the U.S. are ascribed to selfish proprietary interests." And the Japanese, "though their basic culture lays great stress on harmony between man and nature," are not doing much better than the Russians or Americans.[19] So it is unprofitable to look for scapegoats. Instead, we should concentrate on the quest for solutions.

A variety of solutions are available, and we need not adopt remedies that are worse than the disease. We are, in fact, already embarked on the needed courses of action through the dramatic increase in federal laws, enforcement of the laws, and federal spending since the late 1960s. The federal example is being duplicated by states and cities all around the country, and in a variety of ballot measures voters have displayed a new attitude toward the environment and a readiness to accept the slowing of growth by such means as halting construction along coastlines. In fact, the pendulum may have swung too far in the direction of government controls. Early in 1977 the Dow Chemical Company, after spending $6 million to buy a site in northern California and $4 million more on environmental studies, decided not to proceed with the construction of a $500 million petrochemical complex that would have employed 1000 workers. The reasons they gave were that since they had first applied for approval in 1975, they had been required to obtain 65 separate permits, including several related to the environment, from 12 local, regional, state, and federal agencies; and, furthermore, they were now so enmeshed in lawsuits brought by environmentalists and confused and contradictory signals from the various governmental agencies involved that they had no assurance they would ever be able to proceed with construction.

So, whereas some controls are desirable, we must avoid the danger of halting growth by bureaucratic red tape and inertia. We need economic flexibility no less than environmental protection; and this suggests that we should look for other ways of achieving our purposes than relying solely on controls and enforcement. Rewards provide an alternative to punishments, and subsidization of antipollution measures and of antipollution industries offers one possibility. Taxation should be utilized, too, both to discourage activities that increase pollution and, in the form of tax relief, to reward those who protect the environment.

Of course, there is still resistance. And the energy shortage has complicated the problem immeasurably. For centrists it means that more compromises will have to be accepted by the environmentalists than earlier seemed necessary or desirable. Still, the centrists insist that we can adjust to the energy shortage; that serious dislocations should occur only in the short run, and can be handled by a combination of conservation and somewhat higher prices; and that over a period of 10 to 15 years the further development of existing resources combined with technological breakthroughs will give us sufficient energy to meet all reasonable needs.

What the energy crisis has done, as these centrists see it, is to force us to face up to hard choices realistically. Even before the energy problem was upon us we could not give the ecologists everything they were demanding. Already we were coming to grips with tough issues, and the course of events seemed to be following the sequence suggested in a congressional committee report.[20] After some preliminary stages, the report suggests, environmental quality issues typically reach the point of a public cry for action. This leads to the setting of stringent targets for the reduction of pollution. But these are crudely established on the basis of insufficient knowledge, and the polluters—local governments and individuals, as well as industry—are able to show that the controls are harsh, inefficient, and exorbitantly costly. Next, compromises begin to emerge; the polluters find new ways of reducing the harm they inflict on the environment, much of the cost is passed on to the consumers, and restrictions are made more flexible and sophisticated as government gains experience in operating them. Finally, "as the climate for discussion becomes less emotional, less polarized, and based on greater knowledge, society begins to accept common-sense tradeoffs."

We have now arrived at the point at which concern for the environment is a weighty factor in the consideration of trade-offs, whereas a few years ago there was very little to trade off. But it does not embody all the values that will concern American society in the future, and it cannot therefore escape the process of bargaining.

In the centrists' view, the American political system is extremely well adapted to precisely that process of bargaining and arranging trade-offs between conflicting interests and values. They concede that the outcome is not always perfect, and that it sometimes takes longer than it should. Fortunately, the terrible urgency of 1973 has passed. We still have some time, and Congress and the president have been shaping a program that will make us much less vulnerable to any future crises.

Conclusion

The problems related to environmental protection and energy production make heavy demands on our decision-making processes and institutions. The respective roles of business corporations and government, the liberties of the individual versus the needs of the total community, the demands of the present weighed against the claims of the future, all these perennial controversies enter into the politician's efforts to grapple with environmental and energy problems.

But even if there were no such value conflicts and everyone were agreed on what should be done, it is by no means certain that we would be able to achieve our objectives. These are extraordinarily balky problems. No matter how successful our conservation measures, energy use will increase in the United States, and we shall not be able to achieve both our environmental and energy goals to the full, since the one will consistently interfere with the other.

Then there is the difficulty of getting at the facts. Experts with impeccable credentials are found on either side of every question discussed in this chapter. Thus we do not know whether pollution confronts us with serious threats to the survival of the race. Are we to be swayed by the first Club of Rome report, or the second? Is economist Robert Heilbroner right when he tells us that we cannot avoid great disasters from "large-scale fatal urban temperature inversions, massive crop failures, resource shortages," and that these will lead eventually to the end of democratic freedoms, since only authoritarian regimes can act decisively enough to prevent total extinction?[21] Or shall we be guided by the cheerful scenarios of Herman Kahn, who tells us we are heading toward a future of abundance? What world population shall we plan for when expert predictions for the end of the century differ by a billion or more? What do we do about specific pollutants when a leading environmental scientist, René Dubos, warns us that "even if we had limitless resources we could not formulate really effective control programs because we know so little about the origin, nature, and effects of most air pollutants," and even less about chemical pollutants in water supplies?[22]

Experts also disagree bitterly on the extent of the danger of a nuclear explosion, some suggesting that if we keep on building new plants a disaster is inevitable sooner or later, others insisting that the risk is miniscule.

In the energy field we do not know with any precision the extent of world reserves of fossil fuels. A CIA study quoted by President Carter to support his energy conservation proposals predicted world production of oil falling seriously behind demand by 1985, with severe shortages and soaring prices resulting; and an international study team, the Workshop on Alternative Energy Strategies, reiterated the warning of a coming crisis. On the other hand, a United Nations conference study in 1976 predicted that the world had enough oil and gas for another 100 years; and a 1977 Stanford Research Institute analysis insisted that the worldwide trend was toward a slowing in the rate of energy increase.

As for U.S. reserves the U.S. Department of the Interior has estimated that we have between 40 and 60 years before we run out of oil and natural gas.

However, a study by a group of National Research Council scientists concluded that we will run out in less than 25 years. Then again, such estimates of possible reserves have been wrong in the past; the U.S. Geological Survey predicted during World War I that we would run out of oil in 10 years.

Confronted by such uncertainties, the ordinary citizen may well be inclined to feel bewildered and turn away from the subject in despair. However, out of the welter of conflicting facts and opinions it is possible to suggest the following conclusion: It would be folly to ignore the warnings that the future is full of dangers from the pollution of the environment and the depletion of resources. We are not compelled to accept the most gloomy of the predictions; in fact, they are being treated with skepticism by a growing body of expert opinion. But the pessimists include a large number of scientists and other specialists of considerable reputation. The stakes are so high, the consequences if they are even partially correct are so serious, that a prudent society will assume that a finite risk exists, and that it should take out insurance against that risk. This means that we dare not go back to the lack of concern about pollution and energy that existed before the 1970s. It also means that we would be well advised to commit much greater resources to trying to get more authoritative data than we have today so that we can propose solutions to our problems with more assurance.

Notes and References

1.   Dennis L. Meadows et al., *The Limits of Growth* (New York: Universe Books, 1972). The study was commissioned by the Club of Rome, a worldwide group of scientists, economists, and industrialists, as well as the Smithsonian Institution, Potomac Associates of Washington, and the Woodrow Wilson International Center for Scholars.

2.   Statement of Fred Hartley, Hearings before the Subcommittee on Air and Water Pollution of the Committee on Public Works, U.S. Senate, 91st Congress, 1st Session, on S7 and S544, February 5 and 6, 1969, *Water Pollution—1969, Part 2* (Washington, D.C.: Government Printing Office, 1969), pp. 342–43.

3.   See Herman Kahn, William Brown, and Leon Martel, *The Next 200 Years: A Scenario for America and the World* (New York: Morrow Books, 1976).

4.   Hearings, *Water Pollution—1969, Part 4*, p. 1280.

5.   J. Clarence Davies III, *The Politics of Pollution* (Indianapolis, Ind.: Pegasus, 1970), p. 130.

6.   William Watts and Lloyd A. Free, eds., *State of the Nation* (New York: Universe Books, 1973), pp. 150–53.

7.   See Robert S. Diamond, "What Business Thinks," *Fortune*, February 1970, pp. 118–19, 171–72.

8.   Congressional Quarterly, *Guide to Current American Government*, Fall 1975, p. 67.

9.   James Harvey, *Congressional Record*, September 4, 1969, 91st Congress, 1st Session, p. 7518.

10. Quoted in Douglas Ross and Harold Wolman, "Congress and Pollution: The Gentleman's Agreement," *The Washington Monthly*, Vol. 2, No. 7 (September 1970), p. 17.

11. Theodore Roszak, *Where the Wasteland Ends* (Garden City, N.Y.: Doubleday & Company, Inc. [Anchor Books], 1973), pp. 367–71.

12. Geoffrey Barraclough, "The End of An Era," *The New York Review of Books*, January 23, 1975, pp. 23–24.

13. Editorial, *Ramparts*, May 1970, p. 4.

14. M. Stanton Evans, *Clear and Present Dangers: A Conservative View of America's Government* (New York: Harcourt Brace Jovanovich, Inc., 1975), p. 222.

15. Ibid., p. 249.

16. Environmental Protection Agency, *Hearing Examiner's Recommended Findings, Conclusions and Orders*, 40 CFR 164.32, April 25, 1972, cited in Evans, *Clear and Present Dangers*, p. 242.

17. *Newsweek*, November 19, 1973, p. 130.

18. Richard E. Band, "Ecomaniacs: Your Car Is Driving Them Crazy," *American Opinion*, October 1973, p. 27.

19. "How to Think about the Environment," *Fortune*, February 1970, pp. 100 ff.

20. Managing the Environment, Report of the Subcommittee on Science, Research, and Development to the Committee on Science and Astronautics, U.S. House of Representatives (Washington, D.C.: Government Printing Office, 1968), pp. 9–12.

21. Robert Heilbroner, *An Inquiry into the Human Prospect* (New York: W. W. Norton & Company, Inc., 1974), pp. 132–33, 136.

22. René Dubos, "We Can't Buy Our Way Out," *Psychology Today*, March 1970, p. 20.

14 Foreign Policy:

A New Era?

As we turn our attention to foreign policy, we find ourselves in a very different setting than prevails in domestic politics. At home regular procedures have been devised for creating domestic policy and for dealing with conflicts over that policy. These procedures include a system of courts and a machinery of law enforcement to carry out the decisions of the courts.

International politics is much more fluid. The participants are nations, or nation-states; each of them is sovereign, in the sense that each nation controls its own affairs through its recognized government; and each pursues its foreign policy, or its relations with other nation-states, largely on the basis of what it determines to be its own national interest. A body of international law has grown up out of a combination of custom and treaties among these nation-states.

In addition, the United Nations (created at the close of World War II) and the International Court of Justice, or World Court, were both established with the objective of encouraging cooperation among the nations. There are also alliances into which groups of nations form themselves from time to time—to ensure mutual economic or military cooperation. And in the midst of all this there is a constant process of bargaining and compromise among nations, which constitutes the greater part of international, as it does of domestic, politics.

Yet when negotiations break down, nations tend to assert their separate and sovereign interests, even if this means defying international law. The United Nations can try to bring them to account; but it may not be able to do so unless the major powers agree to take concerted action. The International Court can intervene only where its jurisdiction has been accepted by all the parties concerned. Given the weakness of these constraints on the actions of individual nations, conflicts sometimes lead to confrontations and—periodically—to war.

In this chapter we shall examine the foreign policy that the United States has evolved to find its way through the semianarchy of world politics. We shall devote the larger part of our discussion to American policy—mostly an adversary policy—in relation to the Soviet Union and other communist nations since the end of World War II, paying particular attention to the nuclear arms race and to the lessons of the Vietnam war. After looking at the precepts of American foreign policy we shall discuss the policy makers. Although the preeminent role of the president in making foreign policy will quickly become apparent, we shall also consider the roles of Congress, the foreign policy and military bureaucracies, interest groups, and public opinion. Then we shall turn to our five perspectives for contrasting views of the merits and the flaws of American foreign policy.

Fundamentals
of U.S. Foreign Policy

A generally *isolationist* mood prevailed at the beginning of our history as a nation, a mood that was captured in George Washington's warning against involvement in any "permanent alliance." The Monroe Doctrine in 1823 told the European powers to stay out of our territory—the Western Hemisphere—and promised that we would not meddle in European affairs. Of course, we could not do entirely without a foreign policy, since we were embroiled in wars with Britain (in 1812); with Mexico (in 1846), which led to our annexation of Texas; and with Spain (in 1898), which led to our acquisition of the Philippines, Puerto Rico, and Guam. Moreover, our trade and overseas investments led us into various kinds of international economic involvements.

Still, with so much land to settle in our early days, we did not need to follow the European example of building empires at great distances from our shores, and the prevailing attitudes remained introverted. When at last we did intervene on a massive scale in European affairs by entering World War I in 1917–18, the aftermath was a powerful desire to untangle ourselves from the Old World and its troubles. Thus Woodrow Wilson's desperate attempt to persuade the country to join the fledgling League of Nations, which its supporters hoped would put an end to war for all time, was rejected by the Senate, and the United States stayed out of the League, drawing back into its former state of isolationism.

We continued to stay out of the turmoil that engulfed Europe in the 1930s. We watched while Spain fought a civil war that resulted in the establishment of an extreme right-wing, Fascist, dictatorship. We did nothing while Fascist Italy attacked an African state, Abyssinia. We did not become involved when Germany, under Hitler's Nazi party, took over Austria, then part of Czechoslovakia. Britain and France, too, wanted to stay out of it, and at Munich in 1938 they signed an agreement with Hitler that accepted his conquests in return for a promise of no further expansion. The result was to be "peace in our time." The next year Hitler marched eastward again, overrunning Poland. Britain and France declared war on

Germany, and World War II had begun. France, Belgium, Holland, Denmark and Norway were occupied by Germany, Britain stood in grave danger, and the Germans invaded the Soviet Union. Still, the dominant sentiment in this country favored sending supplies to the British but not to get into the war. At last the Japanese attack on Pearl Harbor in 1941 led to our declaring war on Japan, Germany's declaring war on the United States, with the consequent alliance of the United States, Britain, the Soviet Union, and the nations overrun by Germany, against Japan, Germany, and Mussolini's Italy.

The war in Europe ended with Germany's capitulation in April 1945. In August the Japanese surrendered after the first two nuclear bombs ever to be used in war destroyed Hiroshima and Nagasaki. The U.S. role in the war—especially the production of vast quantities of weapons and the possession and deployment of nuclear weapons—established this country as a military power of unparalleled might.

From this time onward isolationism was to give way to *internationalism*. The selection of New York as the headquarters for the United Nations symbolized the leading part that the United States would henceforth play in world politics. A great many elements have gone into shaping the foreign policy that grew out of this leadership role. Paramount among them has been the concern over the rival power represented by communist countries, especially the Soviet Union.

When World War II ended, communist governments backed by great numbers of Russian troops were in control of most of Eastern Europe, including East Germany and East Berlin. Only Czechoslovakia retained a degree of independence, and this was swallowed up in a communist coup in 1948. To our top policy makers the extension of Soviet power represented a direct military threat to our Western European allies and thus to our national security. Because communism is a system that abolishes the private ownership of the means of production and distribution and that takes the form of a one-party dictatorship, it has no use for capitalist democracy. And the diagnosis of communist intentions by the U.S. government was that the Russians and their allies planned to spread their ideology and power throughout the world.

Containment

The problem of resisting the expansion of communist influence had to be approached carefully. Soviet troops could not be dislodged from Eastern Europe without an all-out war; but after the end of World War II most American troops were quickly withdrawn from Europe. So the doctrine of *containment* was adopted. If communism could not be rolled back, at least it could be prevented from spreading. Greece received American military help to forestall a communist takeover, and military aid was granted Turkey to discourage any Soviet ambitions there. Berlin became a crisis point. It was a partitioned city: the eastern part was Soviet territory, and the western part of the city, though surrounded by East German territory, was incorporated into West Germany and thus independent of communist rule. The Soviets tried to break the connection between West Berlin and West Germany in 1948 by imposing a blockade, cutting off all land routes from West Germany to Berlin. The United States airlifted food and supplies into the western part of the city and eventually broke the blockade.

These actions were the forerunners of a long-term strategy to contain communism, a strategy that incorporated five main components: (1) creating a series of alliances; (2) giving economic and military aid to foreign countries; (3) carrying on clandestine activities, notably by the Central Intelligence Agency; (4) building stockpiles of nuclear weapons, known as "mutual deterrence"; and (5) engaging in "conventional," or nonnuclear, wars.

Alliances

Since the end of World War II, the United States has taken the initiative in setting up a network of alliances with other countries who share our determination to resist the expansion of communism. These alliances are based on collective security treaties, formal agreements that bind each of the member nations to come to the aid of any ally attacked by a communist power.

The most important of these alliances is the North Atlantic Treaty Organization (NATO), founded in 1949. Initially, NATO consisted of the United States, Canada, the United Kingdom, France, Italy, Luxembourg, the Netherlands, Belgium, Denmark, Norway, Iceland, and Portugal, which were later joined by West Germany, Greece, and Turkey. Other treaty alliances of the United States include the Southeast Asia Treaty Organization (SEATO), set up in 1954 and comprising Thailand, the Philippines, Pakistan, Australia, New Zealand, France, and Britain; and the Organization of American States (OAS), formed in 1948 and encompassing 20 Latin American countries along with the United States. (Cuba was suspended from the OAS in 1962 because of allegations of Castro's aggressive intentions against some of the organization's members.) Through these various alliances U.S. troops, numbering over half a million in 1975, have been stationed at bases around the world for the purpose of preventing communist expansion (Figure 14-1).

Foreign Aid

Another primary instrument aimed at holding back the advance of communism has been foreign aid. This has taken two forms. First there is economic aid in the form of grants, loans, and technical assistance to help build other countries' economies in the belief that this will prevent their turning to the Soviets for help, and that building their prosperity will do away with the social and political tensions on which communism thrives. This belief was the driving force behind the Marshall Plan, proposed by Truman's secretary of state George Marshall, which brought billions of dollars to the European economies that had been ravaged by

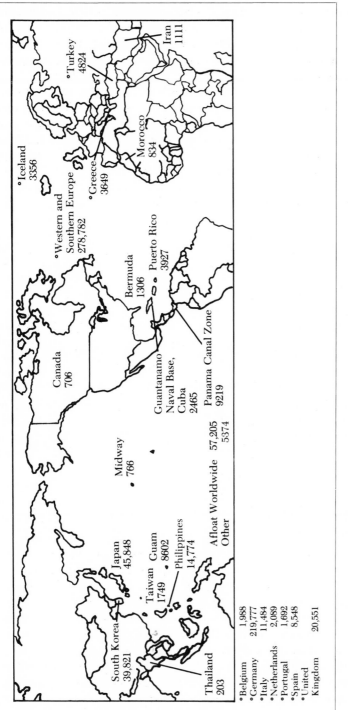

FIGURE 14–1   U.S. Military Personnel Stationed Abroad (Total: 471,868)   (Data from Congressional Quarterly, Guide to Current American Government, Fall 1975, p. 19, and U.S. Department of Defense, Directorate for Management Information Operations and Control, Selected Manpower Statistics [May 1977], pp. 36–38.)

World War II. Subsequently, large amounts of economic aid were made available to many of the poor, or "developing," nations of the world. The other kind of foreign aid is direct military assistance—supplying arms and training military forces, again with the objective of enhancing the ability to resist communism.

From the end of World War II through 1976, the United States contributed a total of about $220 billion in economic and military aid, according to the Agency for International Development. About two-thirds of this was for economic aid, one-third for military assistance (though the dividing line between these two categories is often hazy). Regionally, the largest amounts went to the Far East ($67 billion) and Europe ($58 billion), followed by the Middle East and South Asia ($42 billion), and Latin America and Africa (each with over $20 billion). By individual country, South Vietnam received easily the largest amount of U.S. aid ($23 billion), followed by South Korea ($13 billion). Britain, France, and India each received around $10 billion, and others who have been given between $5 billion and $10 billion each are Israel, Turkey, Taiwan, Japan, Italy, West Germany, Greece, Pakistan, and Brazil.

Clandestine Activities

Through its various intelligence agencies, the United States has sought to find out the strength of the Soviet's military forces and its strategic and political plans. In addition, we have undertaken "covert" operations through the use of secret agents and the provision of money and arms to foreign groups in an effort to undermine or overthrow governments we believed sympathetic to communism. In at least a few cases, U.S. agencies also prepared plans to assassinate foreign leaders who were either communists, or, in our view, friendly to the communists.

Mutual Deterrence:
The Balance of Terror

Far transcending in importance any other method of containing communism has been our building a huge armory of atom and hydrogen bombs and missiles. The Soviet Union has also engaged in a similar buildup of nuclear and thermonuclear weapons. (*Nuclear* refers to the atom bomb; *thermonuclear*, to the hydrogen bomb.) The existence of these awesome stockpiles has changed the nature of world politics. The scale of destructive capacity they represent is of a different order than anything that came before. The atom bomb that was dropped on Hiroshima exploded with the force of about 20 *kilotons*—the equivalent of 20,000 tons of TNT—and gave off deadly radiation as well as a huge fireball. The official number of civilian casualties was 306,000, including 78,000 killed. Only three buildings were left standing in the city.

The hydrogen bomb multiplied even this destructive force by a factor of a thousand, for now the calculations were in *megatons*. Nikita Khrushchev, Stalin's successor, once told the Supreme Soviet a joke about these magnitudes. Soviet scientists, he said, had made an error in a hydrogen bomb test. They had intended to set off a 50-megaton explosion. Instead, the blast had amounted to 58 megatons. However, he explained gleefully, the scientists would not be punished for their little mistake. The 8-megaton error Khrushchev boasted about represented far more explosive force than had been detonated in all the wars in human history to that time.

Brooding over foreign policy since the early 1950s has been the dread of an ultimate, thermonuclear holocaust. And the possession of these weapons has acted as a restraining factor, for each side has known that the other possessed these fearsome weapons and was able to deliver them to the other's territory. Each has also known that it *could not by unleashing a surprise attack wipe out the other side's ability to hit back.*

In the case of the United States, the ability to retaliate if the Soviets struck first depended on the dispersion of bombers on bases in several parts of the globe. Then we moved into the age of missiles. These included intercontinental ballistic missiles (ICBMs), maintained on our own territory, kept underground in silos "hardened" by deep layers of concrete, and vulnerable only to an almost direct thermonuclear hit. There were also intermediate-range ballistic missiles (IRBMs) at European bases, and thermonuclear weapons on Polaris missiles carried by nuclear submarines moving around the depths of the ocean on random courses and capable of firing their weapons without having to surface.

"*The Russians are gaining! The Russians are gaining!*

"*The Americans are gaining! The Americans are gaining!*

Drawing by Conrad; © 1977. Reprinted with permission, *The Los Angeles Times.*

The Russians, too, had bombers, hardened ICBMs, and missile-carrying nuclear submarines. The number of warheads available to them was considerably less than the number in the American armory. Still, it was more than could possibly be knocked out by us; and, even if they hit only a few of our cities, the consequences would be catastrophic, for many of their warheads had bigger megatonnage than ours.

Consequently, both sides could suffer a "first strike" by the other and still retain an "assured destruction capability" sufficient to inflict "unacceptable damage" on the other side. Opinions might vary as to what was "unacceptable." But by the late 1960s Defense Department estimates of the havoc that a U.S. retaliatory strike would wreak on the Soviet Union ranged from a minimum of 37 million killed and 59 percent of industrial capacity destroyed up to almost 120 million deaths and 77 percent of industry wiped out. Calculations of potential damage to the even more urbanized and industrialized United States were of a similar order. Some experts insisted that, however terrible the idea of thermonuclear war, a clear possibility remained that, if such a war occurred, either or both protagonists could survive and even recover.[1] But in the minds of most political leaders the death of a minimum of 37 million of their own people could not be considered an "acceptable" hazard.

Thus emerged the state of "mutual deterrence," both sides being deterred from attacking the other because of the inevitability of a shattering counterattack. In Winston Churchill's graphic phrase, there existed a "balance of terror . . . in which by a process of sublime irony, survival is the twin brother of destruction." Peace was preserved through fear. It was an abominable condition—but at least the peace was preserved. Moreover, one of the tenets of communist ideology had been changed. Stalin had proclaimed that, as long as there was large-scale capitalism, there would be large-scale war, and that in the long run capitalism would destroy itself or be destroyed by war, leaving communism to take over as the final stage of social evolution. But by the early 1960s the thermonuclear stockpiles drove Khrushchev to the conclusion that total war was too dangerous for communism as well as for capitalism. Wars between great powers were no longer inevitable or tolerable, he said, so that even the Soviet Union and the United States must seek the paths to "peaceful coexistence."

A precarious balance.   This balance of terror between the United States and the Soviet Union avoided direct confrontation of the two countries. Yet these nations did not enjoy genuine security. As long as the stockpiles existed, the possibility of holocaust could not be overlooked. One side might misread the other's intentions, pushing hard in the belief that the opponent would back down, then discovering it was mistaken at the point at which both sides were committed too deeply to withdraw. Or each side might back a different country in a local war; then find themselves getting more deeply embroiled; then become direct protagonists. If this were so, and if one party appeared to face defeat, the temptation might increase to move on from "conventional" to nuclear weapons. These need not be H-bombs, nor even devices on the Hiroshima scale. "Tactical" nuclear weapons that could be used by infantry against battlefield targets were available to provide a new range of military options. But, if the introduction of such weapons turned the tide of battle, the pressure would be great for the losing side to introduce similar devices. The steps from there to an all-out thermonuclear exchange, if not inevitable, would be very easy to imagine.

Then, too, with so much explosive potential around, the possibility of a war breaking out through an electronic malfunction or human error could not be completely ruled out. Although the most elaborate "fail-safe" precautions were taken by the United States against this danger, no humanly devised system can be infallible. Nor could we be sure that the safety requirements of other countries with hydrogen bombs were as rigorous as our own. Although the precautions might be adequate in normal periods, the danger of accidents increased in times of crisis.

The dreadful danger implicit in the balance of terror was vividly revealed in the Cuban missile crisis in 1962. Photographs taken by U.S. reconnaissance planes revealed that the Soviet Union was constructing missile bases in Cuba, capable of delivering an initial salvo of 40 thermonuclear warheads on U.S. targets and killing up to 80 million Americans.

It was a calculated attempt to change the balance of power, for at the time the United States had a clear advantage in the number of thermonuclear missiles that could reach the other's territory. Prior to Cuba the Soviets had no bases from which they could launch IRBMs to match those we maintained in Europe. Apparently, Khrushchev assumed that President Kennedy would not risk a thermonuclear confrontation over the matter. It was a miscalculation. He presented Khrushchev with an ultimatum to stop shipping missiles and to withdraw those already in Cuba. At the same time he let Khrushchev know that, if the missiles were withdrawn, there would be no American attempt to oust Castro. This gave Khrushchev a chance to save face, for he had installed the missiles after Castro had appealed to the Soviet Union for protection against the United States. Kennedy's assurance he would leave Castro alone would allow Khrushchev to say he had achieved his purpose and could therefore withdraw the missiles. However, by this stage of the confrontation Soviet credibility and prestige were deeply involved, and for several tense days it was not clear whether or not Kennedy had calculated correctly. Finally, Khrushchev withdrew his missiles. But for a time the leaders on both sides had looked into the abyss.

After the Cuban missile crisis, the two powers began to take tentative steps away from the brink. Kennedy spoke of the need to "reexamine our attitude toward the cold war." A treaty was signed between the two, forbidding further testing of nuclear weapons in the atmosphere. Other treaties were entered into later, banning the use of nuclear weapons in outer space and discouraging nuclear proliferation to other countries.

These agreements did not prevent the continuation of the arms race. The two nations continued to build more weapons and work on new systems, such as the antiballistic missile (ABM), designed to shoot down attacking missiles before they hit their targets. This competition raised fears on both sides that the other was forging ahead in the arms race and might even achieve a breakthrough that would put the opponent at its mercy. Thus the situation was acutely unstable, and the prospects of war by miscalculation or accident remained high. It was also enormously expensive, placing severe burdens on the two economies.

At last, negotiations were begun in an effort to slow down the arms race and eventually reduce the stockpiles. The end of the first stage of the Strategic Arms Limitations Talks (SALT) came in May 1972, when President Nixon and the Soviet Union's leader Leonid Brezhnev signed agreements that stabilized the levels of strategic offensive missiles for five years at about 2400 for each side and limited ABM systems to two sites for each country—one for the purpose of defending a major city and the other to defend an offensive-missile base.

Still the arms race went on. The Russians had been engaged in an intense effort to catch up with the Americans, for at the time of the Cuban missile crisis we had far more nuclear power than the Soviets. By the early 1970s the Soviets had succeeded in narrowing the gap sharply, and had almost as many ICBMs and SLBMs (submarine-launched ballistic missiles) as the United States had. By 1977 the Soviets had actually forged ahead in the number of strategic missiles—about 2370 to our 1710. Moreover, they now had more *megatonnage* in their arsenal than we had, for their biggest missiles carried much larger warheads than our ICBMs. And the Soviet Union was spending even more on armaments than was the United States.

But this does not mean that the United States was falling hopelessly behind in the arms race. In the mid-70s we still had about 400 long-range, strategic bombers, over three times the Soviet force. And although we had done very little to build our strategic missile strength toward the allowable SALT limit of 2400, we had not been idle. Rather than increase the number of *missiles*, we had been increasing the number of *warheads*. This we were accomplishing by transforming some of the missiles into MIRVs—multiple, individually targeted reentry vehicles. The MIRV is a kind of space bus carrying several warheads which it can direct to a number of separate targets either individually or in clusters. Through "MIRVing," despite our having fewer strategic missiles than the Soviets, we had far more deliverable warheads by 1976—between 7500 and 8500 to about 2500 to 3000 for the Soviets.

Now, the Soviets set their sights on overcoming this disadvantage and began to gear up for MIRVing, too. Thus it was obvious that the 1972 limits established by SALT could be rendered meaningless unless a new agreement were arrived at. In 1974 the two sides reached an agreement in principle to set a new limit. Each side was allowed 2400 strategic carriers, 1320 of which could be MIRVed.

As the two sides negotiated to pin down this tentative agreement, new sources of contention developed. The Russians had a medium-range bomber, the *Backfire*, which they wanted to exclude from the 2400 SALT limit because it did not have intercontinental range. We rejected their proposal because the bomber could be refueled in the air. On the U.S. side we wanted to leave out of the 2400 SALT limit the cruise missile, a slow, low-flying robot aircraft which can be carried by a bomber or a submarine and guided to its target by its carrier, and which can fly below radar. It is also much less expensive than other nuclear weapon systems. The Soviets objected to this, though they, too, had a similar system under development. Both sides proceeded with refinements of their present systems. The Russians developed new versions of their ICBMs; they built their submarine fleet rapidly, and successfully tested an SLBM with a range of 6000 miles. The U.S. administration proposed a new generation of bombers (the B-1 to replace the B-52) and nuclear submarines (the longer-range Trident to replace the Poseidon, which had already updated the Polaris). Also under consideration by the United States was development of a much bigger and more accurate missile (the MX); and a tactical nuclear weapon, the neutron bomb, designed to kill people primarily through short-lived radiation, and thus not doing much damage to buildings and the terrain.

So the arms control discussions proceeded, with periodic agreements quickly followed by new sources of dissension. And the inherent instability of this situation was compounded by the fact that the United States and the Soviet Union were not the only members of the nuclear club. By the mid-1970s Britain, France, China, and India had nuclear weapons; Israel could make them any time if it had not already; and, though there was an international treaty to discourage the spread of the weapons, the urge to possess them could prove irresistible to several more nations.

"*Conventional*" War: Korea and Vietnam

A peace preserved by a nuclear balance of terror is far from being a condition of tranquility. It still assumes hostile attitudes between the superpowers. The prevailing situation of restrained belligerency came to be known as a "cold war"—a state of belligerency in which the conflicting parties refrained from attacking each other's territory.

However, the nuclear standoff did not cover all eventualities. For one thing, there could be many localized situations in which the use of atomic bombs would be totally out of proportion to the scale of the problem. In fact, nobody would believe that we would wipe out a country over some minor dispute—especially since that might invite massive retaliation upon us by the Soviet Union. And even at major confrontation points, like Berlin and West Germany, our leaders felt that we should be able to mount the kind of "conventional," or nonnuclear, military force that would discourage a Soviet invasion and thus provide at least a temporary alternative to nuclear war.

As part of our NATO agreements of 1949 we have maintained over 250,000 troops in Western Europe. Although we have not had to use these troops in battle, we have used military force elsewhere—for example, in Lebanon in 1958 and the Dominican Republic in 1965. And, faced with the takeover of China by communists in 1949, the United States extended the containment principle from Europe to Asia and engaged our troops in two wars—Korea and Vietnam.

The Korean war began in June 1950, when the post-World War II division of Korea into two nations was challenged by an invasion of South Korea from the communist North. The United Nations Security Council (in the absence of the Soviet Union, which was boycotting the council) declared North Korea an aggressor, and the United States sent troops to lead the United Nations forces to repel the invasion. The tide of battle swung back and forth, first driving the North Koreans almost to the Chinese border, then driving the U.N. forces deep into South Korean territory as Chinese troops entered the war, then moving up again as the U.N. army counterattacked. After prolonged truce talks during which the fighting went on, the war came to an end in July 1953, with an agreement to divide Korea again along the 38th parallel.

A still larger and more devastating war was to come in Vietnam. France had been the colonial ruler of Indochina, but its defeat at Dien Bien Phu at the hands of communist forces in 1954 ended French power in Vietnam. Here again there was a partition into the communist North and the noncommunist South. The government of South Vietnam was threatened by armed insurrection which, said the South Vietnamese, was controlled by the communist North. Under Eisenhower (who had refused to help the French at Dien Bien Phu), a limited amount of economic and military aid was sent to the South Vietnamese government. President Kennedy expanded this aid considerably, dispatching 16,000 "advisors" to train the South Vietnamese army and back them up militarily. This was not sufficient to halt the communist forces, and in 1965 Lyndon Johnson decided that South Vietnam must not be allowed to fall. So Johnson launched a full-scale war against the National Liberation Front, or Viet Cong, and their supporters in North Vietnam. More men and more bombings were called for by the generals and military advisors. Escalation followed escalation; but as more U.S. troops were sent and more bombs dropped, the other side also stepped up its efforts. At last, in March 1968, Johnson rejected another request from the Joint Chiefs of Staff for more troops, and began the process of scaling down our involvement in the war.

As president, Richard Nixon continued that process, pursuing a policy of "Vietnamization" of the war—turning it over to the South Vietnamese, while still giving them strong backing with bombers, supplies, and a diminishing number of American troops. However, the process lasted through Nixon's entire first term; and along the way U.S. forces invaded neighboring Cambodia and Laos (which provided sources of refuge for communist troops), intensified their bombing attacks, which came to include the North Vietnamese capital, Hanoi, and mined Haiphong harbor. At last an agreement was reached early in 1973 that resulted in the withdrawal of all U.S. troops from Vietnam. However, the hope that this agreement would lead to the survival of a noncommunist government in Saigon was soon to be dashed. Fighting resumed among the Vietnamese, resulting in the total collapse of the regime we had been supporting and the takeover of South Vietnam by the National Liberation Front in April of 1975.

Détente

Armed confrontation with communist powers had had mixed results, at best. But, even while the Vietnam war raged, other approaches to dealing with communism were being developed. The United States was coming to the conclusion that it was no longer dealing with an implacably hostile, completely united communist bloc headquartered in Moscow. Now the communist world was becoming *polycentric*—split into several centers of power. The most significant feature of polycentrism was the growing rivalry between the Soviet Union and the People's Republic of China, which had rejected Moscow's leadership, and proposed its own version of communism, "Maoism" (named after Chinese Communist party chairman Mao Tse-tung). Consequently, the Chinese decided to unsettle the Russians by making an overture to communist China's great enemy, the United States. The Chinese let it be known that they would welcome a visit from President Nixon; and in 1972 Nixon met the Chinese leaders in Peking, from where he went on to Moscow to consult with Brezhnev and the other Soviet leaders.

The era of *détente*—of defusing the tensions and seeking areas of agreement—had begun, and was pursued in a series of informal discussions with communist leaders conducted by Henry Kissinger. Among the products of détente was an increase in trade, including a massive sale of U.S. grain to the Soviet Union. Another outcome was a conference on Europe in Helsinki in 1975 at which the West gave up its opposition to Soviet dominance in Eastern Europe in exchange for Soviet promises to ease its restrictions on foreign journalists and visitors, encourage more cultural exchanges, and loosen its restraints on emigration from the Soviet Union.

It must be emphasized, however, that détente has not meant the end of conflict between the superpowers. The Soviet Union still insists that communism must eventually supersede capitalism. And the United States remains committed to the containment of communism. Thus, when there were threatening sounds from North Korea in 1975, the United States reemphasized its commitment to South Korea, not even excluding the possible use of nuclear weapons. When the Cambodian regime seized an American merchant ship, the *Mayaguez*, in 1975 (they said the ship was in their territorial waters; we claimed it was in international waters), President Ford ordered a gunboat into Cambodia, and the crew was rescued after an exchange of gunfire. And in the Middle East, when the Soviet Union took the side of the Arab states in the 1973 Arab–Israeli war, the United States warned the Soviets to stay out, alerted U.S. forces around the world, and replaced the weapons the Israelis had lost in the war.

So détente means not the end of tensions between the United States and the communist nations nor even the abandonment of military confrontations, but rather an effort to reduce the tensions and confrontations and prevent their leading to large-scale war—most especially thermonuclear war.

Other Dimensions
of U.S. Foreign Policy

The containment of communism, we have seen, has been the most important element in U.S. foreign policy since World War II. But we must not conclude from this fact that nothing else has mattered to us. If communism had never appeared in the world, we would still have a foreign policy; and, even though the anticommunist theme seems to have touched almost every aspect of our international behavior, it is possible to discern some other motives of considerable importance.

Thus our relationships with affluent, industrialized countries such as Britain, Germany, France, Japan, and Canada have not been shaped exclusively by our mutual interest in restraining communism. We are heavily involved in trade with these countries, and many of the major U.S. corporations are multinationals, with large holdings in industrialized nations abroad. These economic ties create common interests that our foreign policy has protected and advanced. Then the developing nations of Latin America, Asia, and Africa, sometimes called the Third World, are of interest to us for more reasons than their potential for being taken over by communism. The poverty of many of these countries, bringing with it the danger of periodic famines and pestilence, is a source of international instability. And, although most of these areas are now freed from the colonial status that was common before World War II, they still complain that the rich countries are exploiting them and buying their raw materials too cheaply. Their resentment must be a source of concern to us, for their raw materials are important to our economy, and some of our multinational corporations have large investments in developing nations, particularly in Latin America.

Next there are the newly rich, nonindustrialized countries, whose affluence results from their ownership of large supplies of a scarce resource. The obvious examples here are the Arab oil nations. Although the United States is concerned about Soviet infiltration in the Middle East, a more important concern for our economy, and thus for foreign policy, is to ensure the continued flow of critically important fuel.

Finally, we are beset by the difficulties of trying to solve world political, economic, energy, and environmental problems in a context of separate, competing nation-states. The United States, having turned away from isolationism to internationalism, has been seeking ways of replacing international conflict with cooperation. To this end we helped found the United Nations in 1945, and the United States is one of the five permanent members of the Security Council, the executive committee of the United Nations. (The other permanent members of the Security Council are the USSR, the People's Republic of China, Britain, and France, and there are 19 others chosen for two-year terms.)

However, the United States has been disappointed in its hopes that a spirit of amity and mutual cooperation would prevail in the United Nations. Conflicts have repeatedly broken out in the world organization, and both the United States and the Soviet Union have resorted to the use of the veto (to which permanent members of the Security Council are entitled) over U.N. decisions. In the General Assembly of the United Nations, no country has such veto power; and since every nation, however large or small, has one vote in the assembly, the United States and the affluent nations are often outvoted by Third World countries. Similarly, in some of the specialized agencies and councils that deal with economic, social, and cultural matters, positions are sometimes adopted that the United States strongly opposes. American opposition has been particularly strong with respect to actions taken by a combination of Third World, Arab, and communist nations against Israel, a close ally of the United States. Even so, the United States continues to declare that support for the United Nations is a cardinal element in its foreign policy, since the world body provides a vital forum for discussion and negotiation.

To sum up, U.S. foreign policy consists of many networks of relationships. Of all the themes that sustain these networks the containment of communism has been the most significant and the most persistent since the Second World War. But we cannot fully understand American foreign policy without taking into account some of the other elements mentioned here.

Who Makes Foreign Policy?

The Presidency

As we saw in Chapter 6, as chief diplomat and commander in chief of the armed forces, the president has the prime responsibility for making and carrying out foreign policy. Only Congress has the constitutional authority to declare war. Yet, without clear authority from Congress, Truman intervened in Korea in 1950 and stationed seven U.S. divisions in Germany in 1951; Eisenhower sent troops to Lebanon; Kennedy approved the Bay of Pigs invasion; Johnson took military action in the Dominican Republic and Vietnam; Nixon attacked Cambodia and Laos. Each executive could point to many precedents.

Jefferson, who is often quoted by senators who want to limit the president's power, made the Louisiana Purchase and told the Senate about it later. Polk got into a war with Mexico in 1846, then secured Congress's declaration of war. Wilson sent troops to Siberia to fight the Bolsheviks in 1918, though the United States was not at war with Russia. Roosevelt provided protection for British convoys in 1940–41 and sent them some old U.S. destroyers before we entered World War II and before getting Congress's sanction. Not one of these actions was challenged by the Supreme Court.

The Senate, says the Constitution, must review all treaties and may nullify them. But presidents, using the power they say is implied in the constitutional roles of principal foreign policy spokesperson, commander in chief, and chief executive, have made "executive agreements" with foreign countries that do not require the approval of the Senate. Every year there are far more executive agreements made than treaties. Most of them are on routine technical matters. (Eisenhower's secretary of state, John Foster Dulles, once said that "every time we open a new privy, we have to have an executive agreement.") But some agreements, to establish military bases abroad, for example, can have great importance and consequences.

In exercising their great authority in foreign affairs presidents have been guided by two main principles since the end of World War II. The first, as we have seen, was to demonstrate enough military strength to contain communism. This inspired Kennedy's refusal to accept the emplacement of missiles in Cuba in 1962 and to refuse to agree immediately to a Soviet demand to pull U.S. bases out of Turkey in exchange for the withdrawal of missiles from Cuba. Kennedy had actually given the order for dismantling the Turkish bases some time before and was appalled to discover that his instructions had not yet been carried out. But he felt that to accept the demand now, under pressure, while the world watched would be taken as an indication of weakness and would compromise the credibility of America's position everywhere. The same insistence on avoiding the appearance of weakness was seen when Nixon, explaining his decision to invade Cambodia in 1971, declared that the United States must not act "like a pitiful helpless giant."

The second principle guiding presidential foreign policy was the avoidance of thermonuclear war. This led to our doing nothing when Soviet troops marched into Hungary in a brutal suppression of an uprising in 1956; and to Kennedy's allowing Khrushchev to save face as he withdrew the Cuban missiles by giving him a guarantee that Castro would remain (and that the Turkish bases would be dismantled after a suitable period of time had elapsed). It set limits to how far we were prepared to go in escalating Vietnam; it led to the SALT agreements; and it was an important factor in the steps toward détente with the communist powers in the early 1970s.

Political considerations have been a factor in these decisions, of course. Presidents are interested in improving their own prospects for reelection or for their parties' electoral fortunes. But presidents have also had their eye on the judgment of history. To ensure that judgment will be favorable, they have not wanted to be the first American president in history to lose a war. On the other hand, if recklessness or misjudgment should plunge the world into a thermonuclear war, there might not be anybody in the future to award them their place in history.

These conflicting considerations weighed heavily on Jimmy Carter as he took over the presidency. He called his visit to the "flying command post" from which he might some day have to direct a nuclear war a "very sobering experience." Among his stated objectives was a desire to hold down military spending. Next, he called on the Russians to agree with the United States to halt all nuclear testing as part of a broader program to curb the spread of nuclear weapons and eventually ban them from the earth. Then he expressed his eagerness to pin down the SALT II agreement, indicated his willingness to make concessions, and appointed Paul Warnke, a dove from the Vietnam war and a critic of proposals for major increases in nuclear armaments, as director of the Arms Control and Disarmament Agency.

Carter also decided to cancel the development of the B-1 bomber (the proposed successor to the B-52); to reduce foreign arms sales; and to undertake a phased withdrawal of troops from South Korea. And he negotiated an agreement with Panama that would lead to the end of U.S. sovereignty over the Panama Canal by the end of the century.

On the other hand, Carter explained that U.S. arms control concessions must be matched by Soviet concessions; although he tried to prune the military budget, it continued to rise; and his national security adviser, Zbigniew Brzezinski, had been a hawkish member of the Johnson administration at least until the later stages of the Vietnam war, and had warned on many occasions of the need to maintain our military strength in the contest with the Soviet Union. Moreover, in an unprecedented move, Carter wrote a personal letter in February 1977 to Soviet scientist Andrei Sakharov, who was infuriating the Kremlin by his public criticisms of their suppression of dissidents. Carter's letter promised to "continue our firm commitment to promote respect for human rights." The Soviet leaders warned that Carter was interfering in their domestic affairs and that this could jeopardize détente and the SALT discussions. But Carter insisted that he must, as president, express his nation's concern for individual liberties and press the Soviet Union to fulfill the commitments that it had solemnly made in the Helsinki agreements. Thus Carter was indicating that his fervent desire to continue and broaden détente was contingent on a fuller recognition by the Soviet Union of the interests and values of the United States.

Congress

Between the end of World War II and the late 1960s Congress rarely challenged the dominance of the executive branch in foreign policy. When the president called for the support of Congress, he usually obtained it. Only in the field of economic aid were the administration foreign policy budgetary proposals regularly cut by Congress.

With Vietnam, however, the Senate Foreign Relations Committee began to exercise its constitutional authority. In June 1969, the Senate approved the National Commitments Resolution, which declared that "a national commitment by the United States results only from affirmative action taken by the executive and legislative branches of the United States Government by means of a treaty, statute, or concurrent resolution of both Houses of Congress specifically providing for such commitment."[2] The Senate was thus putting presidents on notice that they must make no more military commitments abroad without involving Congress. Subsequently, Congress repealed the Tonkin Gulf resolution, which had given Lyndon Johnson a free hand in Indochina.

The challenge to administration policies became even stronger over Nixon's continued involvement in Cambodia after the withdrawal from Vietnam. Both houses of Congress threatened to deny approval of any federal monies unless the bombing of Cambodia was stopped, and the president eventually capitulated.

Later that year Congress pressed its advantage home. The War Powers Act of 1973 set a limit of 90 days to the President's authority to send U.S. troops into a combat area without specific congressional approval; failing that approval the troops must be withdrawn. The War Powers Act was vetoed by President Nixon, but both houses of Congress overruled the veto. There were to be no more Vietnams, Congress was saying, without the full involvement of Congress required by the Constitution.

Subsequently, Congress infuriated President Ford and Secretary of State Kissinger by cutting off military aid to Turkey while Kissinger was trying to settle a conflict between Turkey and Greece over Cyprus. The administration was angered again in 1976 when Congress insisted that the United States stop intervening in a civil war in the African state of Angola against a faction backed by troops from Castro's Cuba. Then, too, investigating committees of the Senate and House played a major role in publicizing and cutting back the CIA's covert activities abroad.

The president still retains a great deal of autonomy, however, in his conduct of foreign affairs. Where the safety of American troops is threatened, the president can claim that he will be derelict in his responsibilities as commander in chief if he does not do everything in his power to protect them. If the troops have all been withdrawn, he can still argue that he must do everything necessary to protect an ally or preserve the integrity of a treaty or an executive agreement in accordance with his constitutional responsibility to maintain peace and the national security. And giving the president authority to commit troops to combat for 90 days may leave Congress with little opportunity to cancel the commitment once it is made.

Still, it now appears that a persistently assertive Congress can set much sharper limits to a president's freedom of action in foreign affairs than has typically been the case since the end of World War II.

The Federal Bureaucracies

We noted in earlier chapters that, in making their decisions, presidents have not relied only on the traditional structures of government. They have built their own staffs in the Executive Office and turned to people they trusted for advice wherever they were located. This has been especially the case in foreign policy, where the need for speed and confidentiality in the decision-making process leads presidents to seek as much flexibility and informality as possible. This has resulted in the increased authority of the assistant to the president for national security affairs.

Still, foreign policy cannot be formed or carried out by a few people operating in a free-wheeling, impromptu fashion. There have to be elaborate sources of information and analysis, and large numbers of people to carry out the myriad details of policy. In other words, there have to be institutions.

The National Security Council.   The National Security Council (NSC), located in the Executive Office and directed by the president's adviser for national security, is the principal instrument for pulling together all the various sources of advice and information a president needs to integrate "domestic, foreign, and military policies relating to the national security." The president chairs the NSC, and its members include the vice-president and the secretaries of state and defense. The chairperson of the Joint Chiefs of Staff and the director of the CIA are advisers to the council, and other officials, such as the secretary of the treasury and the director of the U.S. Information Agency, attend at the president's invitation. The NSC was a small agency when it was established under the 1947 National Security Act; but in time it behaved in typical bureaucratic fashion, spawning committees and subcommittees in all directions, and issuing mountains of paper. Kennedy downplayed the NSC, but it was revived during the Nixon era, especially when it was headed by Henry Kissinger before he was named secretary of state in 1973.

The State Department.   The impatience of some presidents with the NSC has been far exceeded by their frustration with the State Department. In some cases this has resulted from dissatisfaction with the performance of the State Department's head, the secretary of state. As the State Department sees it, "the Secretary of State is the President's principal advisor in the formulation of foreign policy and the conduct of foreign relations."[3] This was true enough of Eisenhower's secretary of state, John Foster Dulles, and, of course, of Henry Kissinger. But, as we have seen, it was far from true of Dean Rusk under Kennedy, or William Rogers under Nixon, both of whom had less influence than the White House national security assistant.

However, even the more powerful secretaries of state have rarely been able to provide the kind of speedy response, initiative, and coherent planning that presidents sorely need. The problem is that the State Department is a sprawling, poorly coordinated agency. As Figure 8–1 (page 274) indicated, the State Department encompasses an enormous range of agencies and activities, including a policy planning staff; five geographical bureaus headed by assistant secretaries; a variety of bureaus concerned with specific functional areas, such as international organizations, congressional relations, economic and business affairs, and protocol; the group of professional diplomats who constitute the U.S. Foreign Service; and about 275 overseas consulates and embassies.

Other foreign affairs units.   The Agency for International Development (AID) operates as a semiautonomous arm of the State Department. Its job is to administer programs of financial and technical assistance to developing nations.

The Peace Corps, created by President Kennedy in 1961, sends Americans (mostly, though not exclusively, young) to provide various kinds of organizational and technical help to poorer nations. Under President Nixon the Peace Corps became part of ACTION, which administers a variety of domestic and overseas volunteer programs.

The United States Information Agency (USIA) is the overseas information and propaganda arm of the U.S. government. It operates libraries and information centers abroad and produces and distributes films and magazines. The USIA also operates the Voice of America, a worldwide shortwave radio network broadcasting in 35 languages.

The Department of Defense.   With responsibility for spending over $100 billion a year, the Department of Defense (DOD) is clearly a force to be reckoned with in the field of foreign policy.

Although DOD is concerned with building military strength, the American political tradition requires that the military be subject to civilian control. Thus the president is commander in chief of the armed services. Heading the Department of Defense is the secretary of defense, to whom report the deputy secretary; several assistant secretaries; and the secretaries of the Army, Navy, and Air Force (who head up the three armed forces departments). Working for DOD, in the Pentagon in Washington and in other U.S. and foreign locations, are over a million civilian employees.

Despite the ultimate civilian control of the DOD, the military has a major voice in shaping foreign and national security policy. The armed services include close to 2 million members. They are led by the chiefs of the Army and the Air Force, the chief of naval operations, and the commandant of the Marine Corps. Each reports to the secretary for the Army, Navy, or Air Force. But each is also a member of the Joint Chiefs of Staff (JCS), who, through their chairperson, report directly to the secretary of defense.

Some 400 officers, selected from the different branches of the armed services, constitute the Joint Staff of the Joint Chiefs. And there are large numbers of military officers working in the many departments, agencies, and bureaus of DOD, responsible for areas such as communications, intelligence, mapping, supplies; for the Strategic Air Command and the Continental Air Defense command; and for the European, Pacific, Atlantic, and other geographic commands.

Periodically, there have been sharp conflicts between civilian and military leaders in the shaping of defense policies. The military's role was particularly threatened when the thermonuclear era arrived; for military officers were trained for battles between armies, navies, and air forces, not for planning the mutual annihilation of whole countries with a few missiles. Consequently, in the early 1960s President Kennedy's secretary of defense, Robert McNamara, brought into the Pentagon a group of brilliant young civilian systems analysts—"whiz kids" they called them—who seized the initiative from the resentful generals in designing and coordinating new military strategies. Civilians continue to be involved at the upper levels of Pentagon strategic planning; but today there is a new breed of military officers, trained in the latest tools of strategic analysis and exposed in a 10-month program at the National War College to a sophisticated curriculum that explores the social, economic, political, and even ethical context of military policy.

The Arms Control and Disarmament Agency.   An independent agency established by Congress at the request of President Kennedy in 1961, the Arms Control and Disarmament Agency (ACDA) advises the president and the State Department on disarmament and arms control questions, manages the conduct of negotiations in those fields, and carries out programs of long-range research. It has played a major role in the various treaties, including the 1963 nuclear test ban, the Nuclear Nonproliferation Treaty, and the SALT talks.

The intelligence agencies.   Conducting foreign policy in a world of separate, sometimes mutually hostile, nation-states involves a constant effort to discover the extent of the strength, resources, and intentions of other nations. Some of the data are openly available, but some are not. The United States maintains a number of agencies that spend billions of dollars a year gathering and analyzing information from abroad. The principal ones are the Central Intelligence Agency (CIA); the Pentagon's Defense Intelligence Agency (DIA) and its National Security Agency (which makes and breaks codes); and the State Department's Bureau of Intelligence and Research.

The CIA has been assigned the key leadership role among these agencies, for the director of the CIA also has broad responsibility for all foreign intelligence activities. The CIA has two main divisions. One gathers and interprets data from published material and from such other sources as photographs taken by orbiting satellites and high-flying U-2 planes. The other engages in overseas operations.

It is these overseas activities that have involved the CIA in intense controversy. On the one hand, the agency undertakes espionage, the secret collection of intelligence, and this sometimes involves methods that break the laws of other countries and arouse criticism at home. Much more contentious, however, are the CIA's clandestine or covert activities, which entail active intervention in the politics of other nations. Thus in Iran in 1953 and in Guatemala in 1954 the CIA was directly involved in overthrowing governments. The Bay of Pigs in 1961 was an abortive CIA-directed plan to bring about the end of the Castro regime in Cuba.

Between 1963 and 1973 the CIA spent over $13 million in subsidizing political parties and newspapers in Chile, first to prevent the election of Salvador Allende and then to contribute to his overthrow. The CIA participated in efforts to overthrow the regimes of Rafael Trujillo in the Dominican Republic and Ngo Dinh Diem in South Vietnam in the early 1960s. There was a plot to assassinate Congolese leader Patrice Lumumba in 1960 and several schemes to kill Cuban president Fidel Castro. Special toxins were prepared for Lumumba to be injected on "anything he could get to his mouth, whether it was food or a toothbrush." The plans for Castro included exploding seashells, poisoned cigars, and a poisoned diving suit, and CIA operatives talked with U.S. organized crime figures about doing the job. CIA money was spent to underwrite the political activities of anticommunist party leaders in Italy; to support the regime of King Hussein of Jordan for 20 years; to provide payoffs to government leaders in several other countries; and to subsidize organizations and publications by anticommunist intellectuals in Western Europe.

A further dimension of the controversy that has enmeshed the CIA is its activity within the United States. Despite the fact that the legislation establishing the CIA limited its role to foreign affairs, the agency interpreted this broadly, and it worked secretly with domestic American organizations that might be able to contribute to the fight against communism abroad. Thus from 1952 to 1967 the CIA provided funds to the National Student Association to help American students compete with the Soviet Union in the world student movement. Activities by individual students were also supported by the CIA; over 250 U.S. students were sponsored by the CIA to attend youth festivals in Moscow, Vienna, and Helsinki, and were asked to observe Soviet security practices and report on Soviet and Third World personalities.

Then, too, the CIA has funded the research of many college and university professors. According to a 1976 report of Senator Frank Church's Select Committee on Intelligence Activities, thousands of academics at hundreds of U.S. academic institutions were then in contact with the CIA. Most of those contacts were limited to asking professors about their travels abroad or consulting them on subjects on which they were recognized experts. But large numbers of research grants have been provided by the CIA; and, although some of these merely funded work that the professors wanted to do anyway and involved no editorial interference by the CIA, there have been a number of instances in which academics wrote books or other materials for use as overseas propaganda.

Between 1953 and 1964 the CIA also undertook close to 150 secret experiments with drugs and the control of human behavior in efforts to determine how to protect U.S. agents from interrogation techniques.

As these various revelations came to light, a public outcry led to changes in the top leadership of the CIA and the structure of the intelligence services, and first President Ford and then President Carter undertook reforms of the CIA aimed at preventing any further abuses and reducing covert activities.

We should not conclude that the CIA has been consistently on the side supported by the military and conservative groups. During Vietnam the CIA was more critical of the wisdom of escalation and much less inclined than the Pentagon to underestimate the strength and the will of the Vietcong and the North Vietnamese. And the CIA has also been less prone than the military to argue that the Soviets are forging ahead in the nuclear arms race. In fact, in 1976 Secretary of Defense Donald Rumsfeld and other members of the Ford administration felt that the CIA was not taking a serious enough view of Soviet military advances, and for the first time the administration appointed a group of seven outside experts, headed by Harvard professor Richard Pipes, to join with the CIA in preparing the annual national intelligence estimate of Soviet strategic strength and intentions. The result was that the CIA draft of the intelligence report was changed considerably to show greater concern with the Soviet buildup.

Interest Groups

The many facets of foreign policy attract intense pressures from a large and varied array of interest groups. In the area of foreign trade, for example, industries engaged in exporting and importing usually favor free trade, and business study groups such as the Committee for Economic Development advocate a policy of removing all artificial barriers to the flow of commerce between nations. On the other side, business and farm groups, sometimes backed by labor, who feel threatened by foreign competition press for Congress and the administration to impose tariffs or quotas on imports.

On defense issues, industries that manufacture weapons lobby long and hard for federal contracts. Close to $40 billion is spent on weapons and equipment by the armed services each year. About two-thirds of the contracts for major weapons systems go to about 15 major corporations, such as Lockheed, General Dynamics, and Boeing. These companies work closely with the Department of Defense and with the senators and congressmen whose constituencies stand to benefit from the contracts for weapons production, as well as from military installations. Thus the California, Texas, and New York delegations engage in bitter battles to keep contracts in their states or attract them away from the others. The committees of Congress concerned with the military, the Armed Services and Appropriations committees, have generally been highly receptive to the views of the military, their chairpersons especially so. Mendel Rivers of the House Armed Services Committee used the campaign slogan, "Rivers Delivers," and he was instrumental in delivering to Charleston, South Carolina, a military payroll of $200 million a year from a variety of installations, including two Polaris missile facilities, a shipyard, and Army, Navy, and Marine centers.

Moreover, the defense contractors support the efforts of the Pentagon to use arms sales as a means of tying other countries to U.S. policies. In 1976 over $8 billion worth of American arms was sold abroad. More than half this total went to Arab countries (especially Saudi Arabia and Iran), over $900 million worth to Israel, and about $625 million worth to South Korea. The 10 leading defense contractors engaged in foreign arms sales for 1975 were McDonnell Douglas, Grumman, Northrup, Textron, General Electric, United Technologies, Raytheon, Lockheed, Hughes Aircraft, and Boeing. All had annual arms sales of over $100 million, and McDonnell Douglas's sales were over $400 million. Some of their multimillion-dollar sales, notably those of Lockheed in Japan and Northrup in Saudi Arabia, were helped along by large payoffs to officials of the foreign governments by the contractors involved.

Against this formidable array of industrial power supporting high levels of defense spending we find no specific economic interest groups. Nonetheless, substantial campaigns of opposition are mounted by a variety of liberal and antiwar groups to the defense budget in general and to particular weapons programs.

The battle over the antiballistic missile (ABM) in 1969 brought out a typical lineup of groups on both sides. In favor of the program were the Nixon administration; the major companies that would participate in ABM production—Western Electric (a subsidiary of AT&T), Raytheon, McDonnell Douglas, Martin-Marietta, General Electric, Texas Instruments, Sperry-Rand, RCA, Motorola, Hercules, IBM, and Thiokol; several members of Congress from the 16 states in which these corporations were located; the Committee to Maintain a Prudent Defense Policy, formed by Truman's secretary of state, Dean Acheson, Johnson's deputy secretary of defense, Paul Nitze, and Dr. Albert Wohlstetter (a nuclear war strategist from the University of Chicago); and the American Security Council, a conservative group financed by private corporations including some of the leading defense contractors, which had been advocating the ABM since 1967 through mailings and radio broadcasts.

Against the ABM were the National Committee for a Sane Nuclear Policy (SANE); the Coalition for National Priorities, a loose alliance of more than 20 liberal and religious groups; the Council for a Liveable World, which organized seminars on disarmament for senators and raised campaign funds for some of them; the National Citizens Committee Concerned about Deployment of the ABM, headed by former Supreme Court Justice Arthur Goldberg and former Deputy Secretary of Defense Roswell Gilpatrick. Though some labor unions favored the ABM, for it would provide jobs for their members, the United Mine Workers, the United Auto Workers, and the Teamsters joined the anti-ABM lobby. The battle was close-fought. The administration prevailed, but the division on two key votes in the Senate was 51 to 50 and 51 to 49.

Then in late 1976, amid growing warnings by the military of Soviet gains in the nuclear arms race, another group, the Committee on the Present Danger, was formed to persuade the incoming Carter administration to take a strong stand against the Russians. Leaders of this organization included three top members of the Johnson administration and the AFL–CIO secretary-treasurer. Paul Nitze, who acted as an adviser to Jimmy Carter during his election campaign, and Albert Wohlstetter were moving forces behind this committee as they had been in the fight for the ABM. The group undertook a nationwide campaign with a budget of about $250,000 a year to alert public opinion to the seriousness of the Soviet danger. A contrasting interpretation came from the Center for Defense Information, headed by a retired rear admiral, Gene LaRocque, who insisted that the United States was not falling behind the Soviet Union in the arms race, and, further, that the United States could reduce its defense spending to $85 billion a year without any damage to our national security.

Another kind of interest group is heard from as we consider American policy toward countries or regions. Ethnic groups, immigrants or the descendants of immigrants, voice their concerns over the fate of the country from which they or their forebears came. Pressure from Greek Americans was at least partly responsible for Congress's cutting off arms aid to Turkey in the Turkish–Greek conflict over Cyprus. Black leaders push for action against white-supremacist South Africa and Rhodesia. Refugees from Castro's Cuba resist proposals for détente with Castro.

In the case of the Middle East the cause of Israel has been effectively argued by such organizations as the American Israel Public Affairs Committee, the Anti-Defamation League of B'nai B'rith and the American Jewish Committee. These organizations have constituencies of considerable political effectiveness, for Jews tend to be politically active; they are well represented among journalists, academics, and lawyers, and their votes are concentrated in northern and western states such as New York and California, which are particularly important in presidential election strategies. In 1977 there were five Jewish senators and 18 Jewish members of the House.

Historically, the Arab side has been not nearly so well represented in American politics as the Israeli cause, for there are only 1.5 million Americans of Arab heritage as against 5.7 million Jewish Americans. Still, the National Association of Arab Americans has a Washington staff, and five American cities have Arab Information Centers financed by the League of Arab states. Moreover, the oil money of the Arab states is becoming a factor to be reckoned with domestically. A good deal of that money is being invested in American bonds and businesses, and several former Cabinet officers, including Clark Clifford, Richard Kleindienst, William Rogers, and John Connally have done legal and financial work for Arab countries. Moreover, those major oil corporations which have heavy investments in the Middle East have generally offered advice in Washington favorable to the Arab side.

We saw another example in our discussion of Congress in Chapter 7 of the lobbying by a foreign government to secure its position in the United States. Money, gifts, and entertainment were lavished on some members of Congress by South Koreans in a crass effort to influence the level of U.S. military and economic aid to South Korea.

Public Opinion

The policy leadership of the executive branches of government and of interest groups always has to be set within a context of mass public opinion. Thus the effectiveness of the pro-Israel lobby results more from the persistent support of Israel revealed by opinion polls than from the budget of the American Israel Public Affairs Committee. Even the Arab oil boycott did not shake pro-Israel sentiment in the country. A Louis Harris poll in January 1975 showed that, when asked if the United States should stop military aid to Israel if this proved necessary to get Arab oil, 64 percent of the public said no. Without this kind of attitude, the less than 3 percent of the population who are Jewish could hardly force a pro-Israeli policy on the United States.

But what factors shape public opinion on foreign policy? To a considerable extent it is the leadership exercised by the president. Until recently almost every major presidential initiative since World War II, whether toward war or peace, has been followed by a surge of public support. This was true of both the Marshall Plan to rebuild Europe's war-shattered economy during the Truman administration and the Bay of Pigs invasion approved by President Kennedy. It was true of all of Johnson's escalations during the Vietnam war, including the mining of North Vietnam's harbors, and of Nixon's visit to Peking.

However, there are limits to how far the majority will follow the president. Before the end of the Korean war there was little support left among the electorate for continuing our involvement. In Vietnam there was more and more sentiment for getting out as time went on. Students and other antiwar activists launched furious demonstrations; and, although a majority of the public were critical of the demonstrators and their tactics, the air of tension and passionate protest that was generated created a pervasive sense that the war was controversial and politically unpalatable. This attitude was intensified as the media, particularly television newscasters and commentators, turned away from their earlier neutrality or support for the war and became openly critical. Johnson's standing in the opinion polls plummeted.

Under Nixon the polls showed disapproval of our invasion of Laos; the Nixon administration might have tried to hold on longer in Southeast Asia but for the tide of hostile opinion in the country; and the Ford administration was similarly unable to find any support for its apparent desire to help the South Vietnamese government in the final stages of its collapse in 1975.

After Vietnam a trend set in toward reducing our overseas involvements. According to studies by William Watts and Lloyd Free,[4] there was a marked shift away from internationalism and toward isolationism between 1964 and 1974. In 1964, 65 percent of the electorate leaned toward the internationalist position and only 8 percent toward isolationism. By 1974 the more-or-less internationalists were down to 41 percent, and the more-or-less isolationists had risen to 28 percent of the voters. A 1975 Harris poll indicated that Americans were simply not prepared to get into any more wars if it could possibly be helped. Only 39 percent favored use of the American military if Western Europe was invaded; 34 percent if the Russians took over West Berlin; 32 percent if Castro's Cuba invaded the Dominican Republic; 16 percent if communist China invaded India or Taiwan; 14 percent if North Korea invaded South Korea. Despite the strong sympathy for the Israeli cause in the United States, only 27 percent favored going to Israel's aid militarily if Israel were losing in a war with the Arabs. The only country that a majority of Americans would want to protect with our troops in the event of an invasion was Canada. In other words, in every one of the areas in which America has, at one time or another since World War II, been prepared to go to war there was no longer public support in 1975 for doing anything of the kind. Moreover, in 1976 more people in America thought that too much was being spent on defense (36 percent) than thought too little was being spent (22 percent).

However, there were also limits to the extent of noninvolvement that Americans were calling for. The majority, according to the 1975 Harris survey, strongly favor international cooperation in such fields as food, energy, and economic problems. The proportion feeling that we are spending too much on defense fell by about 10 percentage points between 1974 and 1976. And there remains widespread suspicion of international communism and a reluctance to give ground to it.

Five Perspectives
on Foreign Policy

The Liberals:
Too Much Nationalism,
Too Much Anticommunism

To the liberals there have been two great flaws in American foreign policy since World War II—an obsession with the danger of international communism and a persistent attachment to an outmoded nationalism. With respect to communism, liberals have been among its harshest critics. They were bitterly opposed to many of the policies of the Soviet Union during the Stalin era. They are deeply critical of the continued persecution of Russian writers, scientists, and other intellectuals in the 1970s. They do not believe that all the troubles of the world have been caused by the United States; nor that in an age of nuclear weapons, when the Soviets have vast stockpiles, we can unilaterally dispense with our entire nuclear armory.

What they do believe is that the cold war is the result of actions, some planned, some blundered into, by both sides and that we and the Russians must both bear some of the blame. Our part of the blame lies in our having adopted a rigidly ideological hostility to the Soviet Union; in refusing to see until many years had passed that Moscow was losing its control over communist parties in other parts of the world; and in pursuing a policy dedicated primarily to the preservation of the privileges of the "have" nations of the world against the "have-nots" and of corrupt dictators against the aspirations of the masses of the people.

The second defect in our policy, as the liberals see it, is the obstinate reluctance to depart in any significant degree from the belief that the solutions to world problems can be found through the pursuit of our separate national interest rather than focusing on the needs that all people have in common. The world may not be ready, liberals recognize, to abandon the nation-state. But our problems now are global, and the greatest nation in the world should be helping all the others to see that simply national solutions are irrelevant and obsolete. Instead, our foreign policy has clung fearfully to the symbols of nationalism and super-patriotism.

There have been three damaging consequences of this combination of anticommunism and nationalism. First, we have engaged in a buildup of nuclear and thermonuclear weapons far exceeding the needs of our national security. Second, we have allowed ourselves to take on a series of military involvements, some on a very large scale. Third, we have interfered in other countries' politics through particularly vicious and degrading secret activities.

The arms race.   We have been spending ruinous amounts of money on our stockpiles of thermonuclear weapons. All we require is "minimum deterrence"—the very least amount needed to guarantee that the Soviets would not unleash an attack upon us because to do so would mean their destruction as well as ours. Instead, we have gone on and on to build "overkill"—the capacity to destroy any potential enemy's population several times over.

Thus we now have over 25,000 nuclear and thermonuclear warheads, far more than the Russians. 7500 to 8500 of these are big, "strategic" weapons that could destroy whole cities and missile sites. The rest are "tactical" weapons, many of them in Western Europe, others in Asia, for use in battlefield engagements. Our nuclear-powered submarines alone contain far more destructive power than can be needed in any conceivable circumstances. We are MIRVing (placing multiple warheads in each missile) 31 of our 41 submarines. Each of these 31 Poseidons carries 16 ballistic missiles, each of which is being equipped with 10 to 14 warheads by the MIRVing process. Thus our submarines will be able to fire between 5000 and 7000 warheads, each containing an explosive power of at least three times the TNT equivalent dropped in that first bomb on Hiroshima. Each of them, in other words, can destroy any country on earth from a range of about 2800 miles.

But this, it seems, is not enough. We have plans for a new generation of nuclear-powered submarines, the Tridents. These could fire from a greater range than the Poseidons, about 4000 miles. They would carry not 16 but 24 missiles, each with perhaps 17 warheads, thus almost doubling the number of warheads carried by the Poseidon. Each Trident could deliver well over 1000 times the destructive force unleashed on Hiroshima.

And this is by no means the full extent of the plans being prepared by our policy makers. Our security, it is said, cannot be guaranteed without the cruise missile in addition to everything else. Then there is concern that our land-based ICBMs might be wiped out in a sudden attack. So proposals are put forward to make the missiles mobile, moving them around in long trenches so that the Soviets could never be sure where they are. And we must have, say the military, smaller bombs as well as big ones, for our tactical nuclear weapons may be a little too big for the safety of our own troops if used in a battlefield encounter; so we develop the neutron bomb with its terrible capacity for killing people and sparing property.

This pressure for more and more weapons comes in the first place from our leaders' ideological and nationalistic obsessions, which were brutally expressed by the late Senator Richard Russell, chairperson of the Armed Services Committee, in an exchange with Senator Joseph Clark during a closed-door debate over the ABM in October 1968:

Senator Clark: There comes a time when the tens of millions of casualties are so enormous that civilization is destroyed, and if there are a few people living in caves after that, it does not make much difference.

Senator Russell: If we have to start over again with another Adam and Eve, then I want them to be Americans, and I want them in this continent and not in Europe.[5]

But, in addition to the anticommunist, nationalistic ideology, there are the internal political pressures from what President Eisenhower in his farewell address called "the military–industrial complex." This includes the various branches of the military themselves, each presenting its own shopping list every year to protect its own position not only from the Soviets but also from each other. The Air Force wants more MIRVing, new bombers, fighters, helicopters, and radar systems. The Navy insists on more and better nuclear submarines and nuclear-powered aircraft carriers. The Army asks for more and smaller tactical nuclear weapons, tanks, guns, troops, and a great deal of almost everything else usable in war.

Working hand in hand with the military are the defense industries that profit from the production of these weapons systems. They hire retired senior military officers to present the case for *their* company to the Pentagon. They take out lavish advertisements in magazines (charged to the taxpayer as a business expense) making the case for a new missile or plane. They work on Congress both indirectly, through the Pentagon, and in direct discussions with the legislators from the districts in which their plants are located. Thus Congress, too, becomes part of the military–industrial complex.

And most presidents have been part of the complex. Thus under Kennedy a vast increase in nuclear weapons took place until Secretary of Defense McNamara decided we had enough by 1967–68. Under Nixon we moved ahead with MIRVing. His administration also mounted a tremendous pressure campaign on behalf of the ABM. To the liberals this was an immensely dangerous idea, for, if it worked (which they thought very unlikely), it would unleash another round in the arms race, since the other side would work on new devices that could outwit the ABM; then we would have to have a new ABM to beat the new missile; and so on, and so on. Yet this foolish, immensely expensive idea was put forward by the administration, and all the power of the presidency was joined with the military-industrial complex to force the ABM through the Senate by a narrow margin.

As it turned out, nothing much came of the great ABM furor. As part of the first SALT agreement each side accepted a limitation of one ABM system to protect its capital city and one to guard a single strategic missile base. In the event, Congress never appropriated the money for an ABM around Washington. (It would not look good in the country to provide protection only for the government.)

After Vietnam, resistance to the demands of the military grew. Even conservatives complained about waste in military programs, and about the repeated cost overruns that resulted in the country's having to spend double or even triple the amounts originally budgeted for a weapon. The result was that, for the first time since the end of World War II, Congress imposed some significant cuts in the military budget. However, by 1975 pressures for increased outlays were again becoming intense, and the defense budget started shooting up again to a projected figure of $120 billion for 1978.

So the arms race went on. And, as the United States and the USSR built up their stockpiles, they threw away their ability to persuade other countries not to join the nuclear club. And each time another nation got The Bomb, the grim prospect that a nuclear war would break out some time in the next decade or two grew significantly greater. Perhaps possession of the weapons would have the same sobering effect on the smaller countries that it had on the United States and the Soviet Union. But for all of them there was the danger pointed to by the British historian A. J. P. Taylor:

> If weapons exist they will one day be used. The deterrent will work ninety-nine times out of a hundred. At the hundredth time it will not. One side will judge that it can win or, even worse, that without immediate action it will lose. Such is the lesson of history, and I see no reason to suppose that the present situation is fundamentally different from past ones.[6]

Vietnam and the arrogance of power.   At least, say the liberals, we have not, since World War II, used any of the nuclear weapons on which we have been spending so much of our substance. But we have used conventional weapons, and in the two cases of Korea and Vietnam on a very large and bloody scale. In the case of Korea there was at least the rationale that an army had launched an invasion across an established frontier, and the United Nations joined in the condemnation of the attack and in the efforts to stop it militarily. This was not so in Vietnam.

We got into and expanded the war in Vietnam primarily because of our fervent anticommunism and our nationalistic arrogance. The fear of communism was the point of departure. Any other regime, no matter how reactionary or corrupt, was to be preferred to communism. Our leaders had given some grudging recognition to the fact that communism was not now an international monolith, and they had agreed to a limited increase of contacts and trade with some Eastern European countries. Nonetheless, we were faced with the fact that communists had taken over in China, North Korea, and Cuba. It was now an obsession with our leaders that communism must not be allowed to advance further. In Asia, Vietnam was the vital test, the domino that must not fall, a battleground in the contest between the "free world" and the world of communism.

This was the outlook of almost all of President Johnson's advisers. Dean Rusk, who had gained his foreign policy experience during the Stalinist era, allowed his concern about Russia to be overshadowed only by his alarm over China. McGeorge Bundy was a vigorous exponent of the 1965 escalation. In 1966, however, he left the White House to head up the Ford Foundation and later began to harbor doubts about the policy, doubts that grew steadily. W. W. Rostow took over his job, and Rostow had no doubt that Vietnam was part of the global communist effort to take over through wars of national liberation. Johnson also consulted regularly with the Joint Chiefs of Staff, who pressed constantly for more and more troops and wider and wider bombing, and with the director of the CIA. Outside his official circle the president sought advice from a group of men who had held high public office as Cabinet members, diplomats, and military leaders.

Constituted as the "Senior Advisory Group on Vietnam," it was not surprising that the advice they offered favored the escalation in Vietnam.

The second reason given by the liberals for our escalation in Vietnam was nationalistic pride. It seemed inconceivable to the men who made American policy that the enormous might of America would not be able to overwhelm an enemy drawn from an essentially agrarian country or that any opponent would be willing to absorb enormous losses year after year without backing down. Robert McNamara was one of those most guilty of this miscalculation. He had qualms at several points along the way, until at last they reached the point at which the president preferred to have him out of the way and arranged for him to move to the World Bank. Nonetheless, Vietnam was very much a product of McNamara's belief that any problem must respond to the new technologies and modes of analysis that he and his aides had brought with them into the Pentagon and which the United States was supremely well equipped to apply once outmoded strategic doctrines had been swept aside.

Clearly the men who were involved in the key Vietnam decisions were not uneducated or inexperienced. McGeorge Bundy was a Harvard dean. W. W. Rostow was a professor at MIT. Rusk was a college teacher and foundation president. McNamara had been an enormously successful industrial executive and possessed a remarkable mind. And all were committed, they believed, to rationality, not to ideology.

Yet they did have an ideology that warped their judgment. It prevented their seeing the obvious absurdity of the involvement in the first place. It led them to screen out any information that failed to fit their preconceptions.

Reinforcing these factors was the character of Lyndon Johnson himself. The situation fitted his personality all too well. He was not a man to be easily thwarted. At first, he had been unenthusiastic about large-scale intervention, undertaking it only because almost all his close advisers recommended it. But once he had committed himself to the idea, it was his characteristic behavior to carry it through at whatever cost. His vast ego would not allow him to admit failure.

At last, the Johnson administration had to call a halt to escalation. The military asked for 206,000 more troops. Secretary of Defense Clark Clifford undertook a study of the demand. He came to the conclusion that more effort on our side would be canceled out by still more commitments from North Vietnam. He was impressed by intensifying opposition in the Senate and by a disenchanted public watching the horror on television every night—influenced further by editorial judgments against the war by Walter Cronkite of CBS and Frank McGee of NBC. He worried about the anger of young people at home: "I was more conscious each day of domestic unrest in our country. Draft card burnings, marches in our streets, problems on school campuses, bitterness and divisiveness were rampant."[7]

The president was furious at first with Clifford's defection. But other elder statesmen, including Dean Acheson, supported Clifford's recommendation not to go along with the generals. With Eugene McCarthy's taking 42 percent of the vote in a primary race against Johnson in New Hampshire, and bleak prospects ahead in other primaries, the president at last decided that he could no longer stand out against all the forces in the system that would not tolerate our getting further into the quagmire, and he started the process of scaling down the war.

But then there was Richard Nixon. He continued the process of winding down the war, but, for the liberals, the pace was agonizingly slow. Gradually, he and Kissinger played out the game of Vietnamization, launching savage strikes each time it became obvious that the Saigon forces could not pick up the slack left by our troop reductions, and spreading the carnage to Cambodia and Laos.

Our *credibility* was at stake, said Nixon. We had made commitments as a nation. No one would believe our word in the future if we defected on our commitments to stand by South Vietnam. The fact that the commitments should never have been made in the first place and were impossible to fulfill made no impression on Nixon. A further factor was Nixon's own political advantage. Since Vietnam had destroyed Johnson's prospects of reelection, Nixon knew he had to be close to the end in Vietnam by the fall of 1972 if he wanted to be reelected. Yet, if our getting out quickly led to the installation of a communist government in Saigon before that time, he would be subjected to bitter attacks from conservatives, and might not even get his party's nomination. So gradual withdrawal, getting us out not too early, not too late, was the right strategy for a man as dominated by political calculation as Richard Nixon.

The cease-fire, when at last it came, was hailed as a masterpiece of patient negotiation and as the achievement of "peace with honor." But there was no honor, the liberals charged, in the use of our overwhelming military might to inflict devastation on a tiny, mostly agrarian country; in the defoliation of its forests; in the use of napalm against women and children; in brutal massacres of civilians like those at My Lai.

Moreover, Vietnam had inflicted devastation on our own political system. The misuse of presidential power was demonstrated in its most arrogant form. Instead of open government we had insulated, secret decision making. The president brazenly lied to Congress and the people about the prolonged bombing of Cambodia. And the passion for secrecy, the obsession with security that the Vietnam war spawned, led to the insidious growth of a grave threat to democratic institutions. When Daniel Ellsberg released a copy of the Pentagon Papers, and when antiwar activists engaged in acts of civil disobedience, the Nixon administration showed its contempt for democracy and even for "law and order" by forming a group charged with domestic spying and the undertaking of flagrantly illegal projects.

The final irony was that it was all for nought. The Vietnam cease-fire held up only briefly. The army we had supported for so long was forced into a disastrous retreat and collapse. Saigon was overrun and became Ho Chi Minh City. Our commitments had not prevailed. Yet the dire warnings of the consequences have not proved correct, for the dominoes have not fallen. The world goes on, and much of it is still noncommunist.

Looking back on it all, some of our policy makers admitted that they had blundered. Cyrus Vance, who had been Lyndon Johnson's secretary of the Army and deputy secretary of defense, told the Senate Foreign Relations Committee during his 1977 confirmation hearings as Carter's secretary of state, "In the light of hindsight I believe it was a mistake to have intervened in Vietnam. I made a number of mistakes but I hope we have learned from our mistakes." And Henry Kissinger said in 1975, "We probably made a mistake in Vietnam in turning Vietnam into a test case for our policy. . . . We should have seen the Vietnam problem in Vietnamese terms," he conceded, "rather than as the outward thrust of a global conspiracy."[8] We and the Vietnamese, said the liberals, had paid a terrible price so our leaders could learn such a transparently obvious lesson.

The CIA.   Nothing could illustrate better the abandonment of all moral standards and the contemptuous disregard for the American public than the clandestine operations of the CIA. Liberals do not deny that in a world of nation-states it is necessary for each nation to get the best information it can on the plans of other countries. But they cannot stomach the way the CIA has overthrown foreign governments by plotting and arming coups; debased other country's systems by putting politicians on their payroll; planned (however unsuccessfully) the assassination of foreign leaders; and raised, paid, and led small armies—all in the name of preserving democracy from totalitarianism. And of course they find intolerable the CIA's meddling in our domestic political affairs.

Liberals are pleased that Congress has at last investigated the CIA and wants to do something to bring its activities under control. But they charge that leaders of Congress either knew what was going on and did nothing about it, or preferred not to know what was happening. In either case, Congress is culpable, along with a whole succession of presidents who have allowed the CIA to grow into a monstrous undertaking, an "invisible government" in its own right.[9]

What should be done.   The liberal criticisms of the arms race, Vietnam, and the CIA led them for a time to a straightforward, fairly uncomplicated set of proposals for a new foreign policy. First, we must cut the nuclear arms budget. By some calculations we could reduce it by a third or even a half and still provide the minimum deterrence needed to prevent the Soviet Union from launching a strike against us. This would set a much-needed example for other nations and start the process of reducing world outlays on armaments, which had reached about $350 billion a year by 1977. Second, we should sharply reduce the number of American troops abroad. We do not need over a quarter of a million men in Western Europe, for the notion that the Russians will send an invading army across any of the borders of our allies is pure fantasy. Third, we must stop the indiscriminate sale of American armaments. We should not be the munitions maker to the world. Fourth, we should work toward a reduction of the gross inequalities that separate the rich from the poor nations. This means supporting the aspirations of the developing countries without demanding anticommunist allegiance in return, and siding with black people against white supremacists in Rhodesia and South Africa. It also means providing more economic and humanitarian aid, but less military aid to right-wing dictators. Fifth, we should channel more of our diplomacy and economic aid through the United Nations, and work toward international cooperation instead of national conflict.

By the mid-1970s, however, this basic liberal prescription had been complicated by events. First, increasing accounts of Soviet repression of intellectuals, artists, and scientists brought an indignant reaction from liberals, whose belief in civil liberties was offended by this evidence that, though Stalin was long departed, the intolerance of dissident ideas lived on. Some of the liberals' enthusiasm for détente has therefore been blunted. Second, in 1973 Egypt attacked Israel in the "Yom Kippur" war; and although the Israelis were on the offensive when the war stopped, they had suffered severe losses and some sobering setbacks. This was very disturbing to liberals. A considerable proportion of liberal intellectuals are Jewish. Moreover, Israel is the kind of democracy very much admired by liberals. Consequently, some liberals have argued that it is important not to draw the wrong conclusions from Vietnam. That war has told us that we should not become involved on behalf of a country that does not have the will and capacity to fight for itself, and in which the government does not represent the will of the people. But Israel, with its traumatic memory of Hitler's deliberate extermination of 6 million Jews, has left no possible doubt of its will to fight for its survival. And its freely elected government has had the full support of its people in the wars that have been forced upon it. Moreover, the repeated condemnation of Israel by the Third World majority in the United Nations has brought great distress to liberals, and shaken their faith in the desirability of working through the United Nations.

So, although the liberals' critique of American foreign policy remains essentially unchanged, some aspects of its proposals for the future have been modified. If its general principles remain, more allowance is now being made for exceptions.

The Radical Left: Imperialist America

The left agrees with much of the liberals' critique of American foreign policy, but they go further. They also refuse to absolve the liberals from some share of the blame for what has gone wrong.

Radical left critics declare that the cold war is largely the creation of the United States. With the end of World War II we proceeded to encircle the Soviet Union with military bases. In answer to this encirclement and to our possession of the new weapons of terror, the Soviet Union constructed its own nuclear weapons; and again following us, developed the hydrogen bomb. It was natural then that the People's Republic of China, faced with our active enmity, should create its own weaponry.

What is the driving force of American foreign policy? Some on the left interpret it as a straightforward expression of private business interests. At home, military spending is the essential underpinning of the economy, the principal device for preventing another Great Depression. Abroad, our foreign policy is a simple form of economic imperialism, protecting the overseas investments of American corporations, especially the multinationals. One example of this occurred in 1970, when ITT twice approached agencies of the U.S. government, including the CIA, with an offer of $1 million to be used in Chile to prevent the election of a man of the moderate left, Salvador Allende, as president; for, under Allende, ITT's large holdings in Chile's telephone system were likely to be taken over by the Chilean government with very little compensation to the corporation.

However, there is another, more complex analytic view of American foreign policy on the part of the radical left. Although this view allows an important place for direct financial exploitation, it sees as the primary motivating force the ideology of corporate capitalism. At the heart of this ideology is the fear of revolution, particularly communist revolution. This fear has permeated American domestic as well as foreign policy and has poisoned our political atmosphere, leading to McCarthyism, Watergate, and all the other manifestations of repression of dissent. And the liberals, who now criticize our foreign policy makers for being obsessed with anticommunism, were themselves among the prime contributors to the obsession in the early years of the cold war; for, fearful that they might be accused of being soft on communism, liberal organizations such as the Americans for Democratic Action stridently attacked the Soviet Union as the principal source of world tensions.

What these liberals failed to recognize was that, in subscribing to the ideology of anticommunism, they were supporting a doctrine that would not only undermine their policies at home but also create a profound threat to world peace. This threat, in fact, was much more pervasive than that represented by the mere advancement of American financial interests abroad. For example, we would not have plunged into Vietnam merely to support the rather limited investments of U.S. companies in Indochina. It was the more general fear of communist gains that pulled our leaders further and further into that shameful war.[10]

The danger inherent in the anticommunist paranoia reached its most acute form at the time of the Cuban missile confrontation. In that crisis, Kennedy was prepared to unleash thermonuclear annihilation to compel the Soviet Union to withdraw some missiles which even Robert McNamara declared did not really threaten our security. "A missile is a missile," said McNamara, and whether it was based on Cuba or the Soviet Union made little difference to the balance of terror. A willingness to bargain away the Turkish bases, already declared obsolete, could have resolved the crisis quickly. But this would have damaged our prestige and was therefore unacceptable.

Kennedy, no doubt, did not want war. But as a last resort he was ready to order it with the consequent annihilation of vast populations. Nothing—certainly not mere prestige—could justify such a decision. Although the new left today does not admire the Soviet Union, it does not believe that life under communism (whose undesirable features would be no more difficult to change than are those of corporate capitalism) would be worse than the horrors of all-out thermonuclear war.

As the left sees it, anticommunism is absurd as the basis of foreign policy. Although some variants of communism, including that of the Soviet Union, have themselves become repressive, communist powers have generally favored the aspirations for social justice and a decent standard of living of the dispossessed peoples of the world and have supported the revolutions that are the indispensable condition for achieving those aspirations. Our foreign policy should adopt at least benevolent neutrality toward those revolutions, and preferably should actively support them.

The policies we have followed worldwide are the natural product of the power elite that rules this country. At every one of the major decision points, the men the president called on for advice shared power-elite values; and the elder statesmen of the power elite—John McCloy, Clark Clifford, Dean Acheson—were called in at times of crisis. Usually the decisions on which these men were consulted involved imperialist aggressions, and most of the time they were on the belligerent side of the issues. It is true that, on Vietnam, Acheson and Clifford, who had favored the earlier escalations, told Johnson in 1968 to reverse the process. This was not because they had suddenly become peace lovers. It was simply because they realized that their policy had failed. It was affecting the balance of payments and the dollar was threatened. Economics had become more important than ideology, as it ultimately must for the power elite when the two come into conflict.

Economics was also an important component in the decision to seek a lowering of tensions with the People's Republic of China. Anticommunism is not abandoned. Even as Nixon visited Peking, the Vietnam war continued; and, as he prepared to go on to Moscow, Haiphong Harbor was mined. Moreover, the buildup of MIRVs has continued unabated. But there are now two new compelling factors. First, China and the Soviet Union represent enormous markets; and capitalism, Lenin showed, must eventually collapse unless there are foreign markets to exploit. The second factor is strategic: policy can be directed toward making mischief between China and Russia, thereby widening the differences between them.

Détente might tend, for a time at least, to lessen the intensity of the ideological opposition between the great powers. But it does nothing to advance the cause of the Third World. On the contrary, these countries might find that the Soviet Union and the Chinese People's Republic can no longer be relied on to protect them against the encroachments of American imperialism.

The election of Jimmy Carter did nothing to change the left's gloomy assessments of the prospects for international peace and justice. Carter talked about the need to stop the arms race; but even his election promise to cut defense spending by a mere 5 to 7 billion dollars was adjusted by his administration to mean a reduction in the growth that would have occurred had Ford won. Carter also hurt the prospects for arms agreements by his pious protestations on behalf of Sakharov and other Soviet dissenters. Although the new left has been critical of Soviet repression of its scientists and writers, they see Carter as being disqualified from making such protests, since he presides over a system that is itself basically intolerant of radical dissent.

Then, too, Carter's top appointments showed that nothing had changed. Secretary of State Vance and National Security Adviser Brzezinski had served in the Johnson administration during the worst of the Vietnam war. So had Secretary of Defense Harold Brown, who had presided over much of the savage bombing of Vietnam as Air Force secretary. All of them had now recanted, saying that Vietnam had been a terrible "mistake." But how much hope is to be found in a system that takes the men who have been responsible for an unmitigated, brutal disaster and, after giving them other prestigious jobs for a while (Vance in corporate law, Brown as president of the California Institute of Technology), brings them back to the top policy-making arena in even higher positions than before?

Moreover, their period out of government had not taken them far from those circles in which foreign policy attitudes are shaped in America. Not only was Brzezinski a director of the Council on Foreign Relations and Columbia University professor, he was also the director of the Trilateral Commission. The commission was founded by David Rockefeller in 1972 to bring together representatives of the United States, Western Europe, and Japan to develop a common posture in their dealings with the rest of the world. In part this was an effort to replace disunity among these nations with cooperation in face of the pressure on oil prices imposed by OPEC, the major oil-exporting nations. But, as the left saw it, the Trilateral Commission also sought to preserve the advantages of the rich nations over the Third World of poor nations.

Among Brzezinski's associates on the commission were several other men who were to become members of the Carter administration, including Cyrus Vance, Harold Brown, Treasury Secretary Michael Blumenthal (formerly president of Bendix Corporation), Vice-President Walter Mondale—and Jimmy Carter himself. Indeed, Carter got to know these people through the Trilateral Commission; and the fact that the key members of the Carter administration came from an elite group whose purposes were to protect the privileges of the established, rich powers, asserted beyond doubt in the minds of the left that the Carter administration would, with only minor variations, perpetuate the old, discredited foreign policy of the United States.

The Conservatives: Nationalism and Anticommunism

Two principal strands of thought go into the conservatives' approach to foreign policy. The first is nationalism. Whereas liberals see nationalism as an outmoded, increasingly dangerous concept, conservatives cherish it as a means of maintaining diversity in the world and as an expression of pride in our own system and its accomplishments. Thus conservatives are hostile to any proposal that might undermine our national sovereignty, our right to run our own affairs without interference from abroad.

The second element in conservative foreign policy is a passionate anticommunism. To the conservatives the arguments of the left that the United States started the cold war and of the liberals that both sides started it are arrant nonsense. It was started by the Soviet Union. It has been sustained by the Soviet Union and aggravated by Red China and other communist countries. The communists have acted this way because, as Barry Goldwater put it in 1960, "the Communists' aim is to conquer the world."[11]

Since the 1960s our leaders have been increasingly impressed by two arguments put forward by the liberals. The first is that communism has changed since Stalin passed from the scene and now seeks genuine accommodations with the West. The second is that there is no longer a single communist bloc and that the divisions among the communist powers are more significant than their common ground. Both these assumptions are false.

It is true that, from time to time, communist tactics change. But Lenin, the master communist theoretician of this century, laid down the principle that a communist country might, whenever the circumstances were unfavorable, pull back from direct confrontations with capitalist powers. But the strategy must remain the same. Capitalism must be overthrown. Time is on the side of communism. Patience is necessary sometimes, and major concessions might have to be made, but the long-range purposes must remain implacable. This, in fact, has been the case. Faced with massive thermonuclear power, a change in tactics was decided upon. But Stalin's successors have not changed their central intent, which is world domination.

As for disunity among the communist countries, they have developed differences which, over the short run, may be significant. China and Russia do disagree and have been hurling abuse at each other. But this is essentially a family quarrel. They are both communist powers. Maoism is only a further refinement of Leninism. Both the major communist countries stood against us in Vietnam. In every area where the vital interests of this country are challenged, they adopt the same posture against us and depict us as the representatives of aggressive imperialism against the masses of the people.

Confronting this combination of power—the greatest threat to American interests and survival we have ever encountered—we have shown weakness and vacillation. We have hoped for the best. We have put faith in the word of communist leaders when their practice and their Marxist–Leninist theory have presented us with undeniable evidence that their word is not to be trusted, that truth or lies are equally available as weapons to achieve their purposes. Our central preoccupation has been peace. Certainly we all want it. But we have not understood that the communists' prime objective has not been peace but victory. Unfortunately, "our leaders have not made *victory* the goal of American policy. And the reason that they have not done so . . . is that they have never believed deeply that the Communists are in earnest."[12] The consequences of this attitude have been demonstrated in every major area of foreign policy.

The arms race.   Consider, in the first place, the relative nuclear strength of the two sides. For a time we were the only nuclear power. Then, as we entered the thermonuclear age, we possessed an overwhelming lead. Now that lead is gone and the Soviet Union is forging ahead. In 1967 we were warned by an association of military and scientific experts known as the American Security Council that by 1971 "a massive megatonnage gap will have developed" in favor of the Soviet Union.[13] That prophecy proved to be correct. Much is made by our leaders of our having more warheads through the process of MIRVing. But they say little about the advantages possessed by the Soviet Union.

To begin with they have more strategic weapons than we do. They, too, have started the MIRVing process. They have much bigger warheads than we do—nothing in our armory comes close to matching the destructive power of their SS-9 thermonuclear missile so the total amount of megatonnage on their side is much greater than ours. Then, they are building submarines much faster than we are, and they can already fire their SLBMs 6000 miles. They have an ABM system around Moscow, whereas we have none around Washington. And, finally, they have very likely been cheating on the SALT agreement, so the official figures underestimate their true strength.

In face of these obvious indications that the Russians are ahead of us, and gaining a wider margin all the time, the liberals continue to lobby against our trying to catch up and tell us that we cannot afford to protect our vital interests. Yet for some years our defense budget hardly increased at all. This meant that *as a proportion of our gross national product* military spending was actually declining. And the recent modest increases in defense outlays have done little more than keep abreast of inflation and provide for raises in military salaries and pensions rather than more weapons. So much, then, for the vaunted power of the military–industrial complex.

But, the liberals say, what difference does it make if the Soviets pull ahead of us, so long as our own force is sufficient to keep them intimidated? Conservatives are not persuaded that the Russians are going to be intimidated much longer. It is possible, in fact, that they could actually be building toward a "first-strike" capacity—the ability to launch a surprise attack that destroys the other side before it can hit back. It is conceivable that at some point the Russians may decide that their huge weapons could wipe out most of our retaliatory power, which has not been tested under operational conditions and might be subject to widespread malfunctions caused by radioactivity unleashed by the atmospheric explosion of a large number of thermonuclear missiles. Of course, we would still have our nuclear-powered and nuclear-armed submarines. But the Soviets are engaged in the development of tracking systems that could make our submarines vulnerable to a concerted sudden attack. The Soviets may even be developing high-energy particle beams capable of neutralizing U.S. missiles. And, even if the Russians assume that we would be able to hit back with some of our missiles, we must remember that communism is a fanatical doctrine. Individual human life is less important than the ultimate triumph of communism. The leaders of this doctrine—if not today's leaders then tomorrow's—might well decide that a few cities, a few million people, are a necessary sacrifice to ensure the victory of communism throughout the world.

If a Soviet first-strike remains a possibility rather than a probability for the near future, another danger in the Soviet megatonnage lead cannot be denied. This is the threat of "nuclear blackmail." Given the advantage we have allowed them to accumulate, they can now press us hard in any area of the world and know that our resistance will be shadowed by fear that we will provoke them into a nuclear attack. The fact that the Soviets withdrew their missiles from Cuba in 1962 was the result of the lead that we possessed at that time in nuclear armament. That lead is gone. Thus if anything like the Cuban missile crisis were to occur today, it is extremely unlikely that the Soviets would back down.

Even in 1962, conservatives point out, we did not press our advantage home. We could have seized the opportunity to get rid of Castro and make amends for our pathetic showing at the Bay of Pigs. But we were afraid of running the small risk involved. Today, given the Soviet buildup, the risk would be much greater, and we would lack the will to prevent the Soviets from having their way.

It is not the conservatives' contention that we should provoke a thermonuclear war. But they argue against a policy of peace at any price. Peace is not the only value. Freedom, the avoidance of the slavery that is communism, must not be jettisoned out of fear. In any case, the best way to preserve the peace is to counter communist power with even greater power. The only language they understand is strength; to allow ourselves to become weak is the surest path to war.

The decline of the West.   Finally, the communists have left a vital escape clause in their doctrine of "peaceful coexistence." They would prefer for the time being not to have a direct thermonuclear confrontation with the free world. But they have left themselves free to support "wars of liberation"—especially guerrilla wars conducted against "colonialist" powers. This kind of war is almost risk-free for the Soviet Union and communist China. They need not commit their own troops but merely send military and technical assistance. They can compel us to commit our forces all over the world on terrain unsuited to conventional military tactics. They can harass and embarrass us, knowing that we will not commit nuclear weapons to small-scale hostilities. The objective will be to take over one small area at a time by the use of what has been called "salami tactics"—taking one thin slice, then another, then another, until the whole salami is gone.

Vietnam was the case in point, the critical test of our will to stand against the doctrine of wars of liberation. We made one of our half-decisions. We decided that something had to be done, but we lacked the will to do enough. At the Bay of Pigs we had supported an invasion by Cubans but withheld the air power that was an indispensable component of the original plan. Again in 1962 during the Cuban missile crisis we compromised. Now in Vietnam we sent in great numbers of troops but constrained them within a "no-win" policy. Over and over again military leaders told us what we had to do to win, including such steps as closing the port of Haiphong, destruction of railroads and the irrigation system, and cutting off the supply trails through Laos and Cambodia. Ironically, some of these measures were finally adopted but at a stage of the war when our purpose was merely to cover our withdrawal and force the enemy to negotiate the terms of our withdrawal.

The outcome of our weakness has been a grave deterioration in our international position. At the end of World War II we were easily the world's dominant power. But we did not use our strength to protect our interests. At the Yalta Conference between Roosevelt, Churchill, and Stalin in 1945, Roosevelt gave away Eastern Europe to the communists. Then we evolved the doctrine of containment, which resulted in our standing by helplessly while the Russians took over Czechoslovakia, built the monstrous Berlin wall, then brutally suppressed the efforts of the people of Hungary to loosen their subjection to Soviet imperialism. Subsequently, the Soviet Union and its East European allies (the members of the Warsaw Pact) have built up much greater military strength than the NATO allies.

We can see from Table 14-1, the conservatives insist, that only in the number of tactical nuclear weapons is the West ahead—and there is grave doubt that these devices would be used for fear of setting off a total thermonuclear war. The communists have more troops (and could mobilize their forces much more quickly than the West), more aircraft, and far more tanks than the West. This offers a very strong temptation to the Soviet Union to press home their military advantage. At the very least, it increases the Soviets' ability to encourage internal communist takeovers in Western European countries such as Italy. So even in Europe, where the doctrine of containment began, its maintenance is increasingly in jeopardy.

As for other regions of the world, containment has failed dismally. Almost a quarter of the entire population of the earth fell under communism in China. North Korea, North Vietnam, and finally South Vietnam went communist. Close to our own shores we allowed Cuba to become a communist country, a Soviet protectorate, and a base for subversion in Latin America and Africa; and now we are bargaining away our long-established rights to the Panama Canal. Elsewhere we condoned, even encouraged, neutralist doctrines that leaned toward communism and lavished foreign aid on unstable regimes that repaid us by abusing us and voting against us in the United Nations. We have treated shabbily any nation

TABLE 14-1   *Comparative Military Forces in Europe, 1976*

Defensive System	NATO Nations	Warsaw Pact Nations
Troops	792,000	899,000
Tanks	6,755	15,700
Tactical aircraft	1,700	3,000
Tactical nuclear warheads	7,000	3,000

SOURCE: Newsweek, February 7, 1977, p. 37.

accused of colonialism or racism, though these countries have been bulwarks against communism. We have meekly accepted charges of immorality and brutality in Vietnam despite the massive corruption and brutality that characterizes the regimes of many Third World countries.

We have pinned too many hopes on a United Nations that is heavily influenced by the communist countries and that represents a threat to our sovereignty as a nation. And for the political advantage of presidents and the doubtful gains from some trade deals, we have negotiated with the Russians and the communist Chinese, in the foolish belief that the communists will stick to their agreements and that being nice to them can lessen their dedication to destroying us.

These are the fruits, say the conservatives, of our being ruled by the liberal establishment. Democratic and Republican regimes have succeeded each other. But essentially the same men, all members of the Council of Foreign Relations, all favored by Wall Street and eastern industrialists and bankers, have set the basic policies in foreign affairs. They have pushed aside the counsel of those few in high places who have warned against the Soviet menace. The liberals and their supporters in government have also subordinated the military leaders, the professionals whose job it is to study the intentions of their counterparts abroad, and have replaced their advice with a reading of communist intentions that persistently puts them in the most favorable light possible.

As for the CIA, conservatives have criticized some of its blunders and excesses and incursions into domestic affairs, and they believe that the CIA should be brought under more effective control by the president. But the Russians have their secret police (the KGB), their spies, and their clandestine activities agencies. The British and the French and every other major country (as well as many minor ones) have organizations that conduct espionage and undertake "dirty tricks" abroad. Ours is the only country in history that has exposed the workings of its foreign intelligence agency to day-after-day screaming headlines. This has caused great damage to our national security, and has led directly to the deaths of at least several of our CIA operatives.

To sum up, our problem is not that we are run by a military-industrial–espionage complex. Foreign policy is in the hands of the liberal establishment. In the mid-1970s that establishment was shaken by the passionate pleas of exiled Russian intellectual leaders such as Aleksandr Solzhenitsyn that we not listen to the siren song of détente. In *The Gulag Archipelago*[14] and other works, Solzhenitsyn documented from his own experience the horrors of Stalin's concentration camps about which liberals had for so long been mute; and he argued that, if repression in the Soviet Union was no longer as murderous as it had been, that country was still the sworn enemy of freedom. But if the liberals were made uncomfortable by the repression of dissenters in the Soviet Union, they were also still intent on dealing with the totalitarians in Moscow and Peking. And so great was the liberals' influence even on Republican administrations that President Ford, at the urging of Kissinger, refused to invite Solzhenitsyn to the White House.

So it is time, say the conservatives, to put people into office who understand what communism is all about, who will stand firm for American interests in the world, and seek alliances with those countries who share our interests. These would include Canada, most of Western Europe (unless Italy and France take communists into their governments), Japan, South Korea, the Philippines, Taiwan, Rhodesia, South Africa, anticommunist nations in Latin America, some of the nonradical Arab countries, and Israel.

Working with such allies, and making clear to the communist powers that the security of our allies is part of our own security, it will be possible to reverse the policy of political expediency and conciliation of our enemies which has been the hallmark of our leaders, Republicans and Democrats alike, for so many years.

The Radical Right: The Betrayal of America

As we have noted, the radical right sees international communism as the prime source of the world's problems. As one spokesman for the right puts it, "We have been temporizing with the Communist menace instead of 'coming to grips' with it as the first order of our moral and political duty. An elementary perception of the true nature of Communism clinches the conviction that we cannot coexist with cholera, namely, that it is virulent, contagious and deadly."[15] Communism is predatory, amoral, criminal, and atheistic. Clearly, then, it would be immoral to bargain with this inherently evil force.

In this respect, the radical right analysis is a somewhat more extreme version of the conservatives' analysis of communism and of the defects of American foreign policy. The radical right, however, goes much further than the conservatives in their assessment of how far communism has already succeeded in accomplishing its purposes. To the far right, communists have already taken over a large part of the world; the U.N. is totally a communist agency; and, since our own country is being rapidly infiltrated by communists and their sympathizers, they are on the verge of taking us over, too.

This has come about because our leaders have either been blind to the realities of communism or they have actively connived in advancing the communist cause. Vietnam was a perfect illustration of this. "Does anyone doubt," asked Robert Welch in August 1965, "that we could have wiped the North Vietnamese Communists out of South Vietnam within three months, at any time during the past several years, and made them glad to stay out, if we had really wanted to do so?"[16] But we had not wanted to do so because the war served our leaders' purposes by enabling "the Communists in government, in the press, in the pulpit, and in every other division of our national life, to label all criticism of their captive Administration as treasonous." Thus they were setting up a phony anticommunist war that they had no intention of winning in order to establish controls over the lives of the people, which would culminate in the establishment of a police state. If this were not so, a war against communism in Vietnam would be highly desirable, and we should be seeking and obtaining a rapid victory. In the absence of a will to win, however, we should never have gotten into such a war.

Why is it that our leaders, the Rockefellers and the rest of the eastern internationalist bankers and industrialists, are so ready to play the communists' game? It is because they have been working out deals with the communists to carve up world markets between them. Now, they are getting together to exploit each other's markets, and the distinction between Soviet communism and American welfare-state socialism becomes ever murkier.

The Council on Foreign Relations is the most important American institution for producing these policies. Another is the United World Federalists, "whose membership is heavily interlocked with that of the Council on Foreign Relations. The UWF advocate turning the U.N. into a full-fledged world government which would include the Communist nations."[17] Richard Nixon was working in precisely this direction. He was "far too clever to actually join the UWF, but he has supported their legislative program since his early days in Congress."[18]

More recently we have the Trilateral Commission, through which David Rockefeller is advancing the interests of his family and the Chase Manhattan Bank and has the entire Carter administration at his service. Henry Kissinger, Nelson Rockefeller's agent, has left the White House and the State Department; but Zbigniew Brzezinski, David Rockefeller's man, has taken over at the president's elbow. The "insiders" have changed chairs for a while.

It is almost, but not quite, too late to stop the complete takeover of America by communism. We must get out of the United Nations—and get the United Nations out of this country. We must fight against the deals with communist China, which are the culmination of the initial betrayal of China to communism by our leaders. We must stop trading and negotiating with the Soviet Union. We must prevent the surrender of our vital interests in the Panama Canal. We must end the give-away programs to the alleged neutralists, who hardly bother to conceal their affection for communism. Our foreign policy must be based on friendship only for those nations—and there are very few left in the world—who are dedicated to holding out against a world communist government. To do these things, we must break the power of the Council on Foreign Relations. We must also try to elect candidates who understand the nature of the communist conspiracy and work to bring its power to an end.

The Centrists:
Strength and Restraint

Given the broad range of ideas that the centrist band of opinion encompasses, it is obvious that there would be sharp disagreements among centrists over a field as important and as multifaceted as foreign policy. However, American foreign policy, as we defined it at the beginning of this chapter, is essentially the work of centrists, most of whom persist in defending the general lines they have taken against the attacks of the critics from both sides.

Thus they have argued that we have followed a prudent middle course between strength and restraint. On the whole the conservatives' diagnosis of Soviet intentions was regarded by centrists as more accurate than the liberals' perception. On the other hand, the liberals' warnings that military power must be held in check and that military leaders must not be given all they ask for have been heeded. Evidence of this balance is found in a number of areas.

The arms race.   In the arms race, for example, we had no alternative but to build our strength as long as the Soviets were increasing theirs. Only by increasing our might, in fact, was it possible to compel the Russians to bargain seriously.

In the final analysis, the balance of terror has worked. Despite the ideological and strategic differences between the communist countries and the West and despite the recurrence of confrontations, any one of which would have led to war in the past, there has not been a major military clash between the major powers.

Then our posture in crisis after crisis shows that, although we would not allow the Soviets and the Chinese communists to take over the world, neither would we plunge into thermonuclear war. A war would probably have started if we had tried to knock down the Berlin wall. But when the Russians tried to cut off supplies to the people of West Berlin, we took the reasonable risk of supplying them through an airlift. Our handling of the Cuban missile crisis was a masterpiece of firm but restrained decision making. We forced the Russians to pull their missiles out; yet we avoided war by refraining from pushing Khrushchev beyond the point at which he would have no alternative but to fight.

The Vietnam war.   What about Vietnam? Centrists supported the war at least through 1966. With the wisdom of hindsight they are now prepared to admit, with Kissinger, that it was a mistake to throw ourselves into a war that the local population was not prepared to fight. But hindsight vision is always remarkably clear. Projecting ourselves back into the context of the time we can explain the Vietnam war as an understandable error of reasonable men doing their best to cope with an extraordinarily difficult situation.

Communist forces in South Vietnam were gaining ground. If they took power without any U.S. opposition, it would encourage communists in the rest of Indochina—indeed, throughout the world—to believe that they could act with impunity. So Eisenhower pledged some support to the anticommunist forces, and Kennedy provided military supplies and "advisers." Once this was done—and in the light of the time it seemed an eminently sensible course of action—we had made a commitment. If we did not follow through on that commitment, our word would no longer be believed, and communists everywhere would be reinforced in the conviction that they were "the wave of the future."

In the circumstances of the time it seemed entirely reasonable that substantial intervention by U.S. military forces would be enough to turn the tide of battle. It was not assumed that this would take very long to achieve; we did not intend to go on increasing our commitment; we sought only to force the communists to come to the peace table. The problem was that the North Vietnamese refused to do this and continued to send more troops. As we became more heavily committed, we found it harder to retrace our steps; for a great power cannot easily withdraw from such a situation without doing grave damage to the credibility of its foreign policy.

Moreover, the critics' charge that our Vietnam policy was one of unrestrained militarism was untrue. The Joint Chiefs of Staff were always given less than they asked for. Vietnam, indeed, was a strategy carefully balanced between the application of strength and the avoidance of direct confrontations with the Soviet Union and with China. We did not accept the demands of the right wing in America to invade North Vietnam.

The Nixon administration did take much longer to withdraw from Vietnam than many centrists thought necessary, and there was much criticism of the Cambodian and Laotian incursions. In the end, the fall of Saigon made a mockery of the hopes for a stable peace that had been raised by the cease-fire negotiated by Kissinger. But here again, we had made a goodwill effort. It was unsuccessful because the communists broke the agreement, and because the Saigon government, despite all our help, collapsed with a suddenness and completeness that surprised even the communists.

Some impressive successes for foreign policy.   But it would not be fair to take Vietnam as the typical example of the way we conduct our foreign policy. In the Middle East crisis in the fall of 1973 our diplomatic performance was brilliant. Conservatives had warned that, having lost the nuclear superiority we possessed earlier, we would no longer dare confront Soviet power in a tense situation. Yet when the Arabs attacked Israel with arms supplied by the Soviet Union, we resupplied Israel. And when the Russians sent a belligerent note to Nixon threatening to send Russian troops to prevent Israel from destroying the Egyptian army, the president refused to be intimidated, put American forces on alert—and the Russians backed down.

Similarly, the liberals were nonplussed by Nixon's visit to Peking. He was stealing their thunder. Yet it was easier for a relatively conservative president to take this initiative than it would have been for a more liberal man. This is one of the special attributes of the American political system—that it enables conservative men to do liberal things, and liberal men to do conservative things.

Nor is there much substance in the complaints from liberals, conservatives, radical left, and radical right that foreign policy is made by the few without reference to the wishes of the majority. Given the multiplicity of decisions that must be made, the speed that is frequently required, and the secrecy without which neither military action nor negotiation can be successful, it is inevitable that the mass of the people cannot be included at all stages of foreign policy making and that a great deal of latitude will be given the executive branch. There are dangers implicit in this, and sometimes wider consultation and less secrecy would be healthy. However, the majority's views on the broad direction of policy are heard by the policy makers, and in general the policies have paralleled those views quite closely. On those occasions when a wide gap between policy and opinion in the country appears, the mechanisms exist to bring the former back into line with the latter. This was clearly the case on March 31, 1968, when Johnson announced his decision not to send any more troops to Vietnam and to try to bring Hanoi to the peace table. In large measure, this was the accomplishment of men derided by the left as members of a warmongering power elite—Clark Clifford especially—who had compelled the president to face reality.

What we must do now is to continue to maintain the balance between conflicting forces in the world. We must undertake a further modest buildup of our armed strength yet keep the way open for mutually agreed upon reductions of nuclear forces. We must continue to seek to relax tensions with the Soviet Union and the People's Republic of China, but not lose sight of their hostility to capitalism or their oppression of basic freedoms. We must work for closer cooperation with the noncommunist advanced industrialized countries while not ignoring the needs of the poverty-stricken nations of the world. And we must support the United Nations as an international forum and symbol of world order, while protecting our own national interest and the interests of our friends in the world.

Conclusion

By the mid-1970s it appeared that the American people had grown weary of trying to straighten out the affairs of other countries. The opinion polls that testified to this seemed to confirm the suggestion of some scholars that there is a cycle of involvement followed by withdrawal in our relation to the world, and that we are now in a withdrawal phase. Thus one scholar writing in 1952 found that since 1776 there had been four "extroverted" or outward-looking periods in our attitude toward foreign affairs and three intervening periods of introversion. He speculated that some time in the 1960s America would swing back from the extroverted period which began in 1940 and look inward again.[19] The prevailing attitudes we have described since Vietnam seem to bear out this prediction.

Still, it will not be as easy to withdraw from the world as it was in early periods of introversion. We are one of the two leading military powers in the world. If our power is challenged directly in some part of the world, it is by no means certain that the president, reading polls on the people's reluctance to get involved militarily, will do nothing. Those polls deal with vague, hypothetical possibilities. An actual crisis, and bold presidential action to meet it, could once again induce the people to rally behind the president in support of our national interest and prestige.

Then, too, we have far more wealth and resources than any other country. Fluctuations in our economy have repercussions on the economies of many other countries. Our grain production keeps vast numbers of people from starving. At the same time we need resources from other countries. Robert W. Tucker suggested in 1972 that we are not really dependent on anybody else's raw materials, and for this and other reasons we should consider a modified version of isolationism.[20] But, when the Arab oil boycott struck, he changed his mind and called upon us to give serious consideration to the use of armed force to ensure our supplies of oil.[21]

Moreover, ideological hostilities, though reduced, are still very much alive. And they are complicated by national rivalries. Ethnocentricity—the attachment to one's own ethnic group—may well be a more fundamental source of international conflict than ideology. Ethnocentricity has been the key to the struggles, for example, between India and Pakistan, and between Israel and the Arab countries—both of which have been caught up in the vortex of great power rivalries. And a parallel source of conflict between nations is race. The tension between black and white in southern Africa had reached crisis proportions in Rhodesia by the mid-1970s, and the Union of South Africa might not be far behind as a focus of international conflict. The Soviet Union, the People's Republic of China, and Cuba made it clear that they stood for the end of white rule. The United States, declaring its sympathy with black aspirations, but concerned about maintaining stability (and about substantial U.S. investments in South Africa), pursued a mediator's role. But if war came to southern Africa, could we remain completely uninvolved? And if we became involved in a small way (perhaps with a limited number of advisers), could we be drawn in deeper and deeper? And on whose side?

Beyond even these sources of instability lie further international dangers that can hardly be ignored by the United States. There is the widening gap between the rich and the poor nations of the world. We have provided several billion dollars in economic aid. But today the proportion of our national income devoted to foreign economic assistance has fallen below that of several smaller and less affluent nations. It is true that our foreign aid program has suffered from a confusion of purposes—some military, some political, some humanitarian[22]—and a great deal of the money has been wasted. Yet, given the grinding poverty endured by a high proportion of the world's population, to cut back our foreign aid program even further will not free us of the moral and political dilemmas involved in the world income gap.

Finally, we must take into account the issues of energy and the environment, which we raised in Chapter 13. If the ecologists are even partly right, we face a crisis that is international in scope and entails an imminent confrontation between technology and the global environment. On a worldwide scale it is difficult to see how the population increase is to be brought under control or how the intention of the poor nations to improve their lot through industrialization can do anything but intensify the environmental problem immeasurably. If this be so, Americans will not be able to insulate themselves from the increasing tensions resulting from a struggle for dwindling natural resources nor from the threat of nature's retaliation against the intolerable pressures placed upon her by human beings. To counter this danger, the United States would have to allocate a large part of its energies to an intensive global effort. This would require a new kind of national commitment transcending anything in our history.

Thus in the post-Vietnam era of international politics the United States cannot avoid intervening in the affairs of the world. The question is only what forms the intervention will take and whether it can be based on different premises than those which emerged from the experience of the fifties and sixties.

Notes and References

1.   See, for example, Herman Kahn, *On Thermo-Nuclear War* (Princeton, N.J.: Princeton University Press, 1960).

2.   U.S. Congress, Senate Resolution 85, 91st Congress, 1st Session, June 25, 1969.

3.   U.S. Department of State, "Foreign Policy and the Department of State," Publication 8869 (Washington, D.C.: Government Printing Office, September 1976).

4.   William Watts and Lloyd Free, eds., *State of the Nation* (New York: Universe Books, [Potomac Associates Book], 1974), pp. 200ff.

5.   Quoted in Seymour M. Hersh, "The Military Committees," *The Washington Monthly*, Vol. 1, No. 3 (April 1969), p. 87.

6.   A. J. P. Taylor, "Rational Wars?" *The New York Review of Books*, November 4, 1971, p. 37.

7.   Clark M. Clifford, "A Vietnam Reappraisal," *Foreign Affairs*, July 1969, p. 612.

8.   Henry Kissinger with Barbara Walters on NBC's Today program, May 6, 1975.

9.   See David Wise and Thomas B. Ross, *The Invisible Government* (New York: Random House, Inc., 1964).

10.   See Gar Alperovitz, *Cold War Essays* (Garden City, N.Y: Doubleday & Company, Inc. [Anchor Books], 1970); Gabriel Kolko, *The Roots of American Foreign Policy* (Boston: Beacon Press, 1969); Carl Oglesby and Richard Shaull, *Containment and Change* (New York: Macmillan Publishing Co., Inc., 1969); and William Appleman Williams, *The Tragedy of American Diplomacy*, rev. ed. (New York: Dell Publishing Co., Inc. [Delta Books], 1962).

11.   Barry Goldwater, *The Conscience of a Conservative* (New York: Macfadden Books, 1960), p. 91.

12.   Ibid., pp. 91–92.

13.   "The Change in Strategic Military Balance: U.S.A. vs. U.S.S.R.," prepared at the request of the Committee on Armed Services, U.S. House of Representatives, 90th Congress, 1st Session, July 1967. The Council included retired generals Bernard Shriever, Curtis LeMay, Thomas Power, and Albert Wedemeyer, and professors Edward Teller and Stefan Possony.

14.   Aleksandr Solzhenitsyn, *The Gulag Archipelago* (New York: Harper & Row, Publishers, 1973).

15.   Clarence Mannion, *The Conservative American* (Shepardsville, Ky.: Victor Publishing Co., 1966), p. 190.

16.   Robert Welsh, *Bulletin of the John Birch Society*, August 1965.

17.   Gary Allen, *None Dare Call It Conspiracy* (Rossmoor, Calif.: Concord Press, 1971), p. 122.

18.   Ibid., p. 122.

19.   Frank L. Klingberg, "The Historical Alternations of Moods in American Foreign Policy," *World Politics,* January 1952, pp. 239–73.

20.   Robert W. Tucker, *A New Isolationism: Threat or Promise?* (New York: Universe Books [Potomac Associates Book], 1972), pp. 32, 46–47.

21.   Robert W. Tucker, "Oil: The Issue of American Intervention," *Commentary,* January 1975, pp. 21–31.

22.   See Hans J. Morgenthau, *A New Foreign Policy for the United States* (New York: Praeger Publishers, Inc., 1969), pp. 88–106.

Power and Politics:

A Review of the Five Perspectives

We have now spent 14 chapters examining the electoral and political processes, the institutions, and the policies of the American system of government and politics. We have considered masses of data on each of the topics into which our subject has been divided. But we have done much more than present a compilation of facts. We have been dealing with highly charged information that lends itself to widely divergent and passionately argued interpretations. From the almost limitless number of possible analyses, we have selected five ideological groupings, or perspectives, and each of these has been represented in relation to every subject we have discussed (though for reasons given in Chapter 1, some of the perspectives have been given more attention than others).

Now the time has come to sum up. Let us begin by reviewing the attitudes and postures of each perspective, using the framework of the political spectrum that we established in Chapter 1. We open our discussion of each perspective by reminding ourselves of its basic values or ideals. Then we ask how each ideological grouping sees the reality of power in America today. Next we examine how much change is required to bring the reality close to the ideal. And finally we shall assess the prospects for achieving those changes.

The Liberals

The America that liberals would like to see is a country in which there are no enormous disparities of income, wealth, power, and status; in which government expresses the needs of the many, not just the few; and in which individual expression and personal freedom flourish. The liberals' ideal America would also act as a beacon to the world, seeking to replace competing nationalisms with a cooperative effort to bring social justice and individual liberty to people everywhere.

The America that liberals see is quite different from this ideal. They see some people enjoying vast amounts of money and possessions while millions are condemned to abysmal poverty. They believe that the wealthy maintain their privileges by the disproportionate influence they exert on government. Business and monied interests are excessively represented in elections as a result of their campaign contributions and in the decision-making process as a result of their lobbying.

Liberals also believe that government has all too often ridden roughshod over the rights of individuals. The fragility of our First Amendment freedoms was vividly demonstrated by the Nixon administration's abuses of power, which might not have been curbed but for a series of lucky accidents. These domestic shortcomings have all been reflected in American foreign policy, which has repeatedly put us on the side of corrupt dictators and privileged classes, and squandered resources on the military in an absurd and recklessly dangerous effort to assert our superiority over the exaggerated power of communism.

To change all this is a difficult task in view of the obstacles imposed by the nature of our governmental and political system. This system provides abundant opportunities for vested interests to resist reforms. The constitutional separation of powers fragments decision making so that stalemate and inertia take the place of action. Genuine alternatives to the existing policies are rarely offered because political parties and elections confuse the issues rather than clarify them. It is no wonder that trust in government and voting turnouts have fallen to shamefully low levels. And, as long as people are alienated from politics, they do not create the pressure of opinion needed to force government to act decisively. Consequently, generations must pass before we are able to put through even modest improvements like Medicare, federal aid to education, and tax reform.

Yet if the liberals' reading of the situation is predominately negative, it is not one of unrelieved gloom. They believe that it is still possible to accomplish change within the system, and they point to many of the reforms that we have discussed in this book. The programs of the New Deal in the 1930s and the Great Society in the 1960s have helped reduce poverty in America. Laws and court decisions have addressed the claims of black people. Serious attention has at last been given to the needs of the consumer and to the protection of the environment—both attributable in large measure to the efforts of public interest groups such as Common Cause and the Nader organizations.

The politicians most detested by liberals—Richard Nixon and his associates—fell from power and in many cases went to jail. And in the aftermath of Watergate a series of reforms was pushed through which had previously seemed unattainable—public financing of presidential campaigns and other limits on campaign abuses; a new ethics code in Congress; cutting back the power of congressional committee chairpersons; and setting limits to the seniority rule and the filibuster. Also in the aftermath of Watergate huge Democratic majorities were elected to Congress.

Although Jimmy Carter was certainly not the liberals' first choice for president, and they had strong reservations about many of his policies, they could hope that a Democratic president and Congress would produce at least some reforms of the welfare and tax systems. As for foreign policy, liberals welcome the lessening of the anticommunist obsession of the cold war years; they hope that the experience of Vietnam has prevented any more Vietnams for at least a generation; and they believe it possible that the arms race will at last be slowed down and eventually brought under control.

These improvements do not cause liberals to believe that everything is going their way. On the contrary, they fear that the changes, though important, are not nearly far-reaching enough to give any assurance that democratic self-government can survive in the face of all the dangers we have talked about in this book—economic fluctuations, racial tensions, ecological deterioration, the dwindling of natural resources, nationalist hostilities, and thermonuclear confrontations. The liberals' attitude, then, is far from optimistic. But they stop short of despair. And they make the point that, to achieve their purposes, they do not have to wait for a vast increase in the number of people who participate in politics. Active minorities make the difference in American politics. If the size of the minority actively working for liberal causes can be increased even by a few hundred thousand, the potential for change might be far-reaching.

Liberals hope that this increase in political participation is attainable from among the people who gained their first political experience in the civil rights movement and the antiwar protests of the 1960s; from the black, Chicano, and other racial and ethnic minorities; from the movement for women's rights; and from professional people in their thirties and forties who, tired of the mediocrity and corruption of the old politics, are ready for a new politics of integrity that deals effectively with the great issues facing us. With a coalition of this kind, liberals believe that America would have at least a reasonable chance of coping with the problems that confront her and the rest of the world.

The Radical Left

The goal of the left is to establish a socialist society. Such a society is based on the principle of equality. It is a society in which distinctions based on income, class, and race have disappeared. Property, except for a few personal possessions, is communally owned. Cooperation is the principle mode of human relations; and everyone participates in the decision-making process. To make this possible institutions are decentralized and reduced to human scale.

Nor is this ideal limited to the United States. The radical left envisions a world made up of socialist communities, so the objective of our foreign policy should be to support those forces in other countries which are pressing for socialism.

As the members of the radical left look at the United States, they see a system totally antithetical to their ideal. From their perspective, America is a living symbol of corporate capitalism. The dominant values of corporate capitalism are gross inequality, class discrimination, racism, exploitation of workers, ruthless competition, and obsession with material accumulation. These values are maintained by a small ruling elite. The masses of the people, while given the illusion of participation by the sham of elections and the empty game of party politics, are shut out of all the important decisions.

While the power elite works through the enormously overgrown institutions of the presidency and the federal bureaucracies, the ultimate power centers are the corporate boardrooms. The intimate relationships between economic and political power are well illustrated throughout this book: ITT's successful effort to hold on to Hartford Insurance; the great oil companies' dominance over energy policy; the huge corporations' contributions to Nixon's reelection campaign; and on and on.

Abroad, U.S. foreign policy serves the interests of American capitalism in general and the multinational corporations in particular. It is a policy of imperialism, driven by a near-paranoic hostility toward communist countries and bent on subjugating the economies of poor nations to our own. Thus foreign policy has led to brutally immoral wars, such as Korea and Vietnam; has taken us to the brink of thermonuclear annihilation, particularly during the Cuban missile crisis; and, through the vehicle of the CIA, has encouraged methods that reveal the complete moral bankruptcy of the American political system.

In challenging the ruling elite's power, the liberals' method of reform *within the system* is pathetically inadequate. Even where it achieves minor improvements in the conditions of the people (and these typically take decades to bring about), reformism does nothing to alter the fundamental injustice of the system. In fact, by throwing a sop to the masses, these improvements lower the prospect of fundamental change, for they reduce the level of dissatisfaction just enough to impede the potential for radical or revolutionary change.

The activists of the left are fully aware of the obstacles to radical change. The ruling elite controls the military and the police. Through the rulers' power over the media and the educational system, the people are manipulated into believing that they are free. With the end of the Vietnam war, there seem to be no sharp issues to galvanize students and other potential sympathizers into action against the system. So the number who have developed a revolutionary consciousness is small.

Just the same, the radicals of the left are convinced that the obstacles are not insurmountable. They point to the evidence of declining trust in institutions—not just governmental institutions but business, too—and the polarization of opinion among the electorate. The traditional forms of politics, they argue, are worn out, discredited. Corporate capitalism is less and less able to cope with the problems of unemployment, inflation, declining energy and other resources. Once the people, especially the disenchanted young, are shown that real alternatives exist, they will turn to them.

What methods are needed to provide these alternatives? Militant confrontations are one tactic. Violence is not as attractive to most radicals as it was in the sixties, for the force available to the ruling class is overwhelming, and the masses are alienated and antagonized when innocent bystanders are hurt. But demonstrations, marches, occupations of buildings, picketing, and other shows of strength and forms of civil disobedience are useful means of attracting the media's attention. In fact, very few important changes have ever come about in America without the use of abrasive and disruptive tactics.[1]

Then radical groups have created new grass-roots institutions to involve people in the effort to change conditions in their communities. We saw in our discussion of state and local politics that the radical left has sometimes engaged in electoral politics; but in most cases this involvement has been outside the existing two-party structure and designed to show people that political action does not have to be undertaken under the meaningless labels of Democrat and Republican.

Finally, the establishment of small communities, either in rural areas or in urban neighborhoods, gives the left the opportunity to demonstrate the possibilities of cooperation rather than competition, common ownership rather than private property, and a sufficiency for all rather than riches for some and poverty for others.

Through these methods, the left radicals believe that—slowly at first and then with gathering momentum—a revolution of power and styles of living will overtake America. And in many other countries where corporate capitalism is less powerfully entrenched, the revolution may proceed faster. The old communist left still looks to the Soviet Union to act as the vanguard for the worldwide socialist revolution. The new left regards the Soviet Union as too heavily bureaucratic and centralized to serve as a proper model for socialism. But all factions on the left share the belief that the days of the capitalist systems everywhere are numbered, and that they will give way to a different and superior form of social organization.

The Conservatives

The conservative vision of America is of a land in which individuals are encouraged to improve themselves by hard work, initiative, and imagination; and, if they do so, they are rewarded by the right to acquire property, use it with a minimum of interference, and pass it along to their children. The conservatives' ideal America is a country where power is exercised primarily at the state and local levels. It is also a society that prizes traditional beliefs and customs, a culture firmly rooted in family, religion, and neighborhood. Finally, America, to conservatives, should be a leader among nations, proud of its own history and traditions, respecting the integrity of other nations and ready to take a firm stand against those who, like the communist countries, threaten the rights of others to live in freedom.

America was once like this, the conservatives believe; but that America has been corrupted beyond recognition. At first gradually, and then with breakneck speed from the 1930s, America has become a welfare state. Everyone is being leveled to a condition of drab uniformity. Incentives to advance oneself are destroyed. The rights of property owners and businesspeople are impinged upon by punitive rules and regulations and confiscatory tax rates. Rewards are provided not for enterprise and effort but for laziness and incompetence. There is a general debasement of moral standards. All other sources of authority—family, church, state, and community—are undermined by the power of the central government, which standardizes and regiments our lives. Patriotism, too, is a declining force. As we lose respect for ourselves and our traditions, the world loses respect for us, and our international position deteriorates in inverse proportion to the surging power of communism.

This debasement of our freedoms at home and our strength abroad is the direct consequence of the power that has been assumed in America by an elite of intellectuals, the liberal establishment. These people have no respect for the values and moral standards on which the greatness of this country was founded. Through the New Deal, the Great Society, and now through the programs of the Carter administration, they have built so much power into the presidency and the federal bureaucracy (aided and abetted by the Supreme Court, particularly during the Warren era) that the separation of powers and the federal division of powers have become almost meaningless.

The liberal establishment has proceeded almost unchecked in its "social engineering," its experiments in centralized, national planning, producing bureaucratic monstrosities like the War on Poverty, school busing, affirmative action, and so on, all of which serve only to create antagonisms between classes and races. Problems such as the energy shortage are in large part created by governmental bungling. And the obvious solutions, so readily available through the free-market system and the efforts of private business, are ignored in favor of the cumbersome administrative schemes of the planners.

This same liberal establishment has persistently refused to face the true meaning of communist aggression, responding only when the danger becomes particularly menacing and then—as in Korea, the Cuban missile crisis, and Vietnam—with pallid half-measures instead of the decisive actions needed for victory. Now we are in a situation in which even these half-measures must fail, for they were based on our superiority in nuclear weaponry. But this no longer exists because of our leaders' refusal to provide the military with the resources it needs.

To change these policies and restore America to its former virtues and greatness is a difficult task, say the conservatives, for three primary reasons. First, the federal government now subsidizes, underwrites, and protects so many interests—including, unfortunately, a large segment of the business community—that a habit of dependency has been established. Second, through its control of the media, the universities, and the philanthropic foundations, the liberal establishment biases the climate of opinion in the country in favor of its own plans. Third, Watergate struck a savage blow to the conservative cause, even though true conservatives had nothing to do with it.

Just the same, conservatives have not given up. In fact, they believe that their prospects over the long haul are excellent. The very fact that the liberal establishment has been in control for so long has given the people an opportunity to see the full consequences of its policies. And there is increasing evidence that, despite the steady process of brainwashing by the liberal opinion molders, the people at large are growing dissatisfied. The tax burdens of the welfare state are becoming oppressive not only to the wealthy but also the the vast middle class. Busing and affirmative action are deeply unpopular. The attacks on traditional values and the spread of the most vicious types of pornography are arousing intense resentment. The insidious increase in violent crimes is producing a demand for stronger measures to protect the community rather than the criminal; and there is widespread approval for the decisions of the Burger Court which have strengthened law enforcement.

There is a reaction, too, against the loss of jobs and the energy shortages inflicted by the environmental extremists. And the repudiation of foreign involvements that followed Vietnam should not be read as a willingness to allow communism to take over the world. Rather, the people have quite rightly refused to be drawn into any more foreign confrontations unless we are willing to build our strength to the point at which we can force the communists to give up their aggressive plans. Thus the mood of the electorate is increasingly conservative, and the polls give clear evidence that opinion in the country has moved away from the middle of the road toward the right of the political spectrum.

The time is ripe, then, for the conservatives to rid themselves of their feelings of inferiority, assert themselves more effectively, and develop the organizational strength needed to win political power. They are now applying themselves vigorously to this task with the establishment of new conservative groups. Whether through a realigned and revitalized Republican party, building on the conservative party platform of 1976, or through a new party untrammeled by the present electoral weakness of the Republicans, the conservatives believe that the time is not far distant when they can launch a successful bid to replace the policies of the liberal establishment with their own.

The Radical Right

We noted in our opening chapter that it is difficult to distill a single set of values out of the two differing strands of thought on the radical right. On the one hand, there is the more elitist position, typified by the John Birch Society, which believes in an America of competitive individualism and unrestricted business enterprise. Government in their ideal society would be delegated to those best qualified to rule by their ability and their economic success. As these rightists see it, the Founding Fathers established the perfect model to achieve this. But on the other hand, the populist rightists seek a much broader base for their ideal system, in which large numbers participate in shaping policy.

Nonetheless, there are certain values to which both of these strands of thought subscribe. These are values already suggested in our statement of the conservative perspective, but expressed in more extreme form. Thus all groups on the radical right work toward an America in which the people are devoutly religious and attached to family life. And all take a fervent pride in their country; patriotism, or Americanism, is the most intense and frequently articulated of their values.

This is the key to their international as well as their domestic aspirations. All on the radical right call for a foreign policy that asserts the strength and prestige of America, looks for allies only among those countries that support similar ideals to our own, and displays undying hostility to atheistic, imperialistic communism.

There is little disagreement among the various factions on the radical right about their perceptions of the reality of America today. All insist that we are heading pell-mell for socialism–communism. They believe that through civil rights and antipoverty legislation we have created a new privileged class, in which the poor, blacks, and other minorities are rewarded for sloth, irresponsibility, and hostile behavior. They see the total degradation of traditional values and institutions, and warn that, just as the Roman Empire wallowed in corruption and debauchery before it fell, so our intellectuals and our counterculturists are pushing America toward its decline by attacking the Bible, the family, and traditional male–female roles, and by urging permissiveness toward drugs, pornography, sexual licentiousness, crime, civil disruptions, and treason.

Power, say the radicals of the right, is almost completely in the hands of a small, affluent elite who are either communists or "insiders" working hand in hand with the communists. They work their will through the White House, the bureaucracies, the Supreme Court, the Congress, the media, the intellectuals, organized labor, and other special-interest groups. The left-wing elites manipulate public opinion by stirring up exaggerated fears of damage to the environment and the depletion of energy and other natural resources, all the while insisting that the problems can be resolved only by placing even more power in their hands.

Nor is the present situation the result, as the conservatives seem to suggest, of the efforts of misguided though probably well-meaning people. It is all part of a malign plan, a conspiracy of power by the Rockefellers and their fellow insiders. And the conspiracy is worldwide. Insiders in the United States are working with their counterparts in the Soviet Union, China, and the other communist powers to divide the world up into mutually profitable spheres of control.

Somehow the mass of the people must be roused out of their apathy to take a stand against the totalitarians who rule them. Perhaps it is already too late. The damage done to the cause of Americanism by the communists and their allies may be irreversible. But the growing distrust of governmental institutions is a signal that at last the people are tiring of the corruption and moral delinquency of our rulers and their policies of favoring the poor against the middle class, blacks against whites, patriots against draft dodgers, communist and Third World nations against our few friends abroad.

The leadership needed to capture these resentments cannot be found in the ranks of the conservatives. Despite their attacks on the establishment, most conservatives are too busy playing the old political games to be trustworthy. For the

"Go ahead, put *your faith in the American people. Let's just see where* that *gets us."*
Drawing by Weber; © 1976 The New Yorker Magazine, Inc.

moment, the radicals of the right cannot point to a standard-bearer of the caliber needed to help America recapture her former glory. But they note that George Wallace was building nationwide support until he was cut down by a bullet. And they have no doubt that, when the opportunity arrives, the leaders will be there. In the meantime there is work to be done educating the people through speeches and publications, entering the electoral arena wherever the right candidates and issues present themselves, and enlisting in organizations all those who understand the extent of the present danger.

The Centrists

Centrists aspire to a land of moderation and reasonableness. They want a country of diversity and multiple interests. Conflict, therefore, is inevitable. But conflict should be handled by negotiation and resolved by compromise. Thus the centrists' values fall between the opposing ideals to their left and right. They believe in equality of opportunity but allow substantial variations in income and property. They respect property rights but would subject them to social controls. They support freedom of expression but not moral anarchy or the disruption of law. This careful balancing of values they apply to the international scene, too, arguing that foreign policy should be a judicious mixture of firmness and restraint. And the governmental system through which these values are put into effect should be pluralistic, with power checked and restrained, and diffused among many centers.

Centrists do not claim that we have attained this ideal condition in America today. They recognize that, especially since the early 1960s, we have suffered some significant failures both at home and abroad. They concede that for a time the system became unbalanced, and too much power gravitated toward the presidency. And they are somewhat concerned about the decline of trust in government.

But centrists do not agree with the sweeping criticisms of the system by liberals and conservatives, let alone the total condemnation by the radicals of left and right. If the system has not performed perfectly, this does not startle the centrists; the world to them is an imperfect place and the ideal is never fully realizable. Nor are the failures nearly as serious as the critics contend. The American system, after all, has produced unequaled benefits for large numbers of people, including a high standard of living, abundant opportunities for higher education, and an expanding array of public services. And progress continues to be made, for in the last 20 years poverty has declined, the middle class has expanded, the condition of black people and other minorities has improved in every respect.

Clearly, then, the shrill warnings heard from left and right have been proved wrong. We have not been turned into a garrison state by racial war, as the liberals predicted, nor brought to the edge of collapse by leftist terrorism, as the conservatives seemed to suggest. Although we face serious problems in the fields of energy and inflation, our difficulties in these areas are less acute than those of many other industrialized countries.

Similarly, in foreign policy, events have not borne out the dire prophecies of the critics. Liberals and the radical left repeatedly charged that the world was about to blow up because of the arms race, the pressure of the military–industrial complex, and so on. Yet World War III has not broken out; the danger of thermonuclear confrontations seems to have receded; and we will not have any more Vietnams. At the same time we still possess enormous military power, despite the charges from conservatives and the radical right that we have allowed our strength to decline disastrously.

As for our governmental institutions, they have survived all the challenges of recent years. The perpetrators of Watergate were brought down because of the checks and balances of the system. While these checks and balances can be thrown out of kilter temporarily, eventually they reassert themselves. And in the aftermath of Watergate the necessary corrective measures have been taken.

America is still a country firmly committed to self-government, to free elections, to providing people with moderate choices of leaders and policies. In a word, the system works.

This does not rule out the need for change. Moderate, step-by-step change is an integral part of the system. And gradualist change is exactly what the people want. Despite the suggestions of polarizing ideologies in some studies, when the time comes to choose candidates for high office, the majority persistently favor the proponents of moderate change. Psychologically, we resist more radical advances, for we can absorb only a given amount of change without becoming disoriented and subject to acute anxiety. And, politically, our institutions would break down if they had to deal with too many changes too fast. In fact, the time may well have arrived for us to reduce the demands we have been placing on our psyches and our institutions. Through executive action, new laws, and court decisions we have been flooding the system with new burdens. Although we may need to move forward carefully in some areas, such as welfare reform and health insurance, we would do well to pull back from our efforts to force the pace of change in such fields as school integration, affirmative action, and election finances.

For, if it is necessary for government to respond to the legitimate claims of important segments of the population, it is no less vital that government abandon the tendency of recent years to raise expectations and promise the unattainable. If we are to restore faith in government, we cannot have many more broken promises. What we need above all else is a period of solid, constructive government performance. So we should establish reasonable expectations by which to judge the record of government. And if our leaders can avoid setting overly ambitious goals at home and abroad there is no reason why they should not be able to satisfy the people's expectations and thus restore confidence in the institutions of our political system.

Why Bother with Politics?

However wide the differences between our five perspectives, they all agree on one point: the importance of political activity. This message is not universally understood. Some people say: "I don't care much about politics, so I guess that makes me a centrist." But this is a misreading of centrist views. Although centrists see less need for the expansion of political participation than, say the liberals, they are devout believers in the practice of politics. Others may present a pseudoradical rationale for not being involved: "The whole system is run by a small clique; there is nothing we can do; so why try?" But radicals of both left and right are attacking politics *as it is now practiced*, and plead with people to become deeply committed to *their* kinds of politics.

Still, it is unquestionably clear that a considerable, and perhaps increasing, number of people have turned away from politics. This fact comes as no surprise in the light of the material we have reviewed in this book. We have seen examples of tawdry and venal behavior, of betrayals of the public trust, of gross abuse of power. We have examined vast institutions that seem to have become too big and cumbersome to serve individual human purposes. We have talked about policy issues of bewildering complexity, in which the search for solutions is made even more difficult by the inadequacy of the methods available to analyze the problem and the simple inability to determine the basic facts. Finally, we have demonstrated that every topic, every issue, is the subject of bitter disagreement, with ideological squabbling pushing aside the possibility of effective problem solving.

But if these arguments against politics seem compelling, we must still ask: What is the alternative to politics? Shall we turn policy making over to a small group of wise, dispassionate people who will make the decisions for us? But even if this were desirable, who are these people? Do any of us know even one person of such exalted qualities? Should we, then, try to eliminate the element of human self-interest entirely by developing the ultimate computer, programmed to solve all our problems? But we know that no technological device can make decisions for human beings on what kind of world they want to live in or how they should choose among alternative ways of reaching their goals. There are always choices to be made; and we cannot escape the responsibility for choice.

And that, in the last analysis, is what politics is about—the making of choices among competing purposes and values. We have set forth in this book five alternative sets of purposes. They do not exhaust the list of possibilities. You may prefer some variation or combination of them, or even an entirely different solution to the problem. But for anyone who cares in the least about the survival of the human race and about the need to prevent the degradation and debasement of life, some kind of commitment—fraught though it may be with the perils of corruption, inconsistency, and frustration—is indispensable.

Notes and References

1.   See Jerome Skolnick, *The Politics of Protest* (New York: Ballantine Books, Inc., 1969); and William A. Gamson, "Violence and Political Power," *Psychology Today*, July 1974, pp. 35–41.

The Constitution of
the United States of America

We the People of the United States, in Order to form a more perfect Union, establish Justice, insure domestic Tranquility, provide for the common defence, promote the general Welfare, and secure the Blessings of Liberty to ourselves and our Posterity, do ordain and establish this Constitution for the United States of America.

Article I

Section 1   All legislative Powers herein granted shall be vested in a Congress of the United States, which shall consist of a Senate and House of Representatives.

Section 2   The House of Representatives shall be composed of Members chosen every second Year by the People of the several States, and the Electors in each State shall have the Qualifications requisite for Electors of the most numerous Branch of the State Legislature.

No Person shall be a Representative who shall not have attained to the age of twenty five Years, and been seven Years a Citizen of the United States, and who shall not, when elected, be an Inhabitant of that State in which he shall be chosen.

Representatives and direct Taxes shall be apportioned among the several States which may be included within this Union, according to their respective Numbers, which shall be determined by adding to the whole Number of free Persons, including those bound to Service for a Term of Years, and excluding Indians not taxed, three fifths of all other persons. The actual Enumeration shall be made within three Years after the first Meeting of the Congress of the United States, and within every subsequent Term of ten Years, in such Manner as they shall by Law direct. The Number of Representatives shall not exceed one for every thirty Thousand, but each State shall have at Least one Representative; and until such enumeration shall be made, the State of New Hampshire shall be entitled to chuse three, Massachusetts eight, Rhode-Island and Providence Plantations one, Connecticut five, New-York six, New Jersey four, Pennsylvania eight, Delaware one, Maryland six, Virginia ten, North Carolina five, South Carolina five, and Georgia three.

When vacancies happen in the Representation from any State, the Executive Authority thereof shall issue Writs of Election to fill such Vacancies.

The House of Representatives shall chuse their Speaker and other Officers; and shall have the sole Power of Impeachment.

Section 3   The Senate of the United States shall be composed of two Senators from each State, chosen by the Legislature thereof, for six Years; and each Senator shall have one Vote.

Immediately after they shall be assembled in Consequence of the first Election, they shall be divided as equally as may be into three Classes. The Seats of the Senators of the first Class shall be vacated at the Expiration of the second Year, of the second Class at the Expiration of the fourth Year, and of the third Class at the Expiration of the sixth Year, so that one third may be chosen every second Year; and if Vacancies happen by Resignation, or otherwise! during the Recess of the Legislature of any State, the Executive thereof may make temporary Appointments until the next Meeting of the Legislature, which shall then fill such Vacancies.

No Person shall be a Senator who shall not have attained to the Age of thirty Years, and been nine Years a Citizen of the United States, and who shall not, when elected, be an Inhabitant of the State for which he shall be chosen.

The Vice President of the United States shall be President of the Senate, but shall have no Vote, unless they be equally divided.

The Senate shall chuse their other Officers, and also a President pro tempore, in the Absence of the Vice President, or when he shall exercise the Office of President of the United States.

The Senate shall have the sole Power to try all Impeachments. When sitting for that Purpose, they shall be on Oath or Affirmation. When the President of the United States is tried, the Chief Justice shall preside: And no Person shall be convicted without the Concurrence of two thirds of the Members present.

Judgment in Cases of Impeachment shall not extend further than to removal from Office, and disqualification to hold and enjoy any Office of honor, Trust or Profit under the United States: but the Party convicted shall nevertheless be liable and subject to Indictment, Trial, Judgment and Punishment, according to Law.

Section 4   The Times, Places and Manner of holding Elections for Senators and Representatives, shall be prescribed in each State by the Legislature thereof; but the Congress may at any time by Law make or alter such Regulations, except as to the Places of chusing Senators.

The Congress shall assemble at least once in every Year, and such Meeting shall be on the first Monday in December, unless they shall by Law appoint a different Day.

Section 5   Each House shall be the Judge of the Elections, Returns and Qualifications of its own Members, and a Majority of each shall constitute a Quorum to do Business: but a smaller Number may adjourn from day to day, and may be authorized to compel the Attendance of absent Members, in such Manner, and under such Penalties as each House may provide.

Each House may determine the Rules of its Proceedings, punish its Members for disorderly Behaviour, and, with the Concurrence of two thirds, expel a Member.

Each House shall keep a Journal of its Proceedings, and from time to time publish the same, excepting such Parts as may in their Judgment require Secrecy; and the Yeas and Nays of the Members of either House on any question shall, at the Desire of one fifth of those Present, be entered on the Journal.

Neither House, during the Session of Congress, shall, without the Consent of the other, adjourn for more than three days, nor to any other Place than that in which the two Houses shall be sitting.

Section 6   The Senators and Representatives shall receive a Compensation for their Services, to be ascertained by Law, and paid out of the Treasury of the United States. They shall be in all Cases, except Treason, Felony and Breach of the Peace, be privileged from Arrest during their Attendance at the Session of their respective Houses, and in going to and returning from the same; and for any Speech or Debate in either House, they shall not be questioned in any other Place.

No Senator or Representative shall, during the Time for which he was elected, be appointed to any civil Office under the Authority of the United States, which shall have been created, or the Emoluments whereof shall have been encreased during such time; and no Person holding any Office under the United States, shall be a Member of either House during his Continuance in Office.

Section 7   All Bills for raising Revenue shall originate in the House of Representatives; but the Senate may propose or concur with Amendments as on other Bills.

Every Bill which shall have passed the House of Representatives and the Senate, shall, before it become a Law, be presented to the President of the United States; if he approve he shall sign it, but if not he shall return it, with his Objections to that House in which it shall have originated, who shall enter the Objections at large on their Journal, and proceed to reconsider it. If after such Reconsideration two thirds of that House shall agree to pass the Bill, it shall be sent, together with the Objections, to the other House, by which it shall likewise be reconsidered, and if approved by two thirds of that House, it shall become a Law. But in all such Cases the Votes of both Houses shall be determined by Yeas and Nays, and the Names of the Persons voting for and against the Bill shall be entered on the Journal of each House respectively. If any Bill shall not be returned by the President within ten Days (Sundays excepted) after it shall have been presented to him, the Same shall be a Law, in like Manner as if he had signed it, unless the Congress by their Adjournment prevent its Return, in which Case it shall not be a Law.

Every Order, Resolution, or Vote to which the Concurrence of the Senate and House of Representatives may be necessary (except on a question of Adjournment) shall be presented to the President of the United States; and before the Same shall take Effect, shall be approved by him, or being disapproved by him, shall be repassed by two thirds of the Senate and House of Representatives, according to the Rules and Limitations prescribed in the Case of a Bill.

Section 8   The Congress shall have Power to lay and collect Taxes, Duties, Imposts and Excises, to pay the Debts and provide for the common Defence and general Welfare of the United States; but all Duties, Imposts and Excises shall be uniform throughout the United States;

To borrow Money on the credit of the United States;

To regulate Commerce with foreign Nations, and among the several States, and with the Indian Tribes;

To establish a uniform Rule of Naturalization, and uniform Laws on the subject of Bankruptcies, throughout the United States;

To coin Money, regulate the Value thereof, and of foreign Coin, and fix the Standard of Weights and Measures;

To provide for the Punishment of counterfeiting the Securities and current Coin of the United States;

To establish Post Offices and post Roads;

To promote the Progress of Science and useful Arts, by securing for limited Times to Authors and Inventors the exclusive Right to their respective Writings and Discoveries;

To constitute Tribunals inferior to the Supreme Court;

To define and punish Piracies and Felonies committed on the high Seas, and Offences against the Law of Nations;

To declare War, grant Letters of Marque and Reprisal, and make Rules concerning Captures on Land and Water;

To raise and support Armies, but no Appropriation of Money to that Use shall be for a longer Term than two Years;

To provide and maintain a Navy;

To make Rules for the Government and Regulation of the land and naval Forces;

To provide for calling forth the Militia to execute the Laws of the Union, suppress Insurrections and repel Invasions;

To provide for organizing, arming, and disciplining the Militia, and for governing such Part of them as may be employed in the Service of the United States, reserving to the states respectively, the Appointment of the Officers, and the Authority of training the Militia according to the discipline prescribed by Congress;

To exercise exclusive Legislation in all Cases whatsoever, over such District (not exceeding ten miles square) as may, by Cession of particular States, and the Acceptance of Congress, become the Seat of the Government of the United States, and to exercise like Authority over all Places purchased by the Consent of the Legislature of the State in which the Same shall be, for the Erection of Forts, Magazines, Arsenals, dock-Yards, and other needful Buildings;—And

To make all Laws which shall be necessary and proper for carrying into Execution the foregoing Powers, and all other Powers vested by this Constitution in the Government of the United States, or in any Department or Office thereof.

Section 9   The Migration or Importation of such Persons as any of the States now existing shall think proper to admit, shall not be prohibited by the Congress prior to the Year one thousand eight hundred and eight, but a Tax or duty may be imposed on such Importation, not exceeding ten dollars for each Person.

The Privilege of the Writ of Habeas Corpus shall not be suspended, unless when in Cases of Rebellion or Invasion the public Safety may require it.

No Bill of Attainder or ex post facto Law shall be passed.

No Capitation, or other direct, Tax shall be laid, unless in Proportion to the Census or Enumeration herein before directed to be taken.

No Tax or Duty shall be laid on Articles exported from any State.

No Preference shall be given by any Regulation of Commerce or Revenue to the Ports of one State over those of another: nor shall Vessels bound to, or from, one State, be obliged to enter, clear, or pay Duties in another.

No Money shall be drawn from the Treasury, but in Consequence of Appropriations made by Law; and a regular Statement and Account of the Receipts and Expenditures of all public Money shall be published from time to time.

No title of Nobility shall be granted by the United States: And no Person holding any Office of Profit or Trust under them, shall, without the Consent of the Congress, accept of any present, Emolument, Office, or Title, of any kind whatever, from any King, Prince, or foreign State.

Section 10   No State shall enter into any Treaty, Alliance, or Confederation; grant Letters of Marque and Reprisal; coin Money; emit Bills of Credit; make any Thing but gold and silver Coin a Tender in Payment of Debts; pass any Bill of Attainder, ex post facto Law, or Law impairing the Obligation of Contracts, or Grant any Title of Nobility.

No State shall, without the Consent of the Congress, lay any Imposts or Duties on Imports or Exports, except what may be absolutely necessary for executing its inspection Laws: and the net Produce of all Duties and Imposts, laid by any State on Imports or Exports, shall be for the Use of the Treasury of the United States; and all such Laws shall be subject to the Revision and Control of the Congress.

No State shall, without the Consent of Congress, lay any Duty of Tonnage, keep Troops, or Ships of War in time of Peace, enter into any Agreement or Compact with another State, or with a foreign Power, or engage in War, unless actually invaded, or in such imminent Danger as will not admit of delay.

Article II

Section I   The executive Power shall be vested in a President of the United States of America. He shall hold his Office during the Term of four Years, and, together with the Vice President, chosen for the same Term be elected as follows:

Each State shall appoint, in such Manner as the Legislature thereof may direct, a Number of Electors, equal to the whole Number of Senators and Representatives to which the State may be entitled in the Congress but no Senator or Representative, or Person holding an Office of Trust or Profit under the United States, shall be appointed an Elector.

The Electors shall meet in their respective States, and vote by Ballot for two Persons, of whom one at least shall not be an Inhabitant of the same State with themselves. And they shall make a List of all the Persons voted for, and of the Number of Votes, for each; which List they shall sign and certify, and transmit sealed to the Seat of the Government of the United States, directed to the President of the Senate. The President of the Senate shall, in the Presence of the Senate and House of Representatives, open all the Certificates, and the Votes shall then be counted. The Person having the greatest Number of Votes shall be the President, if such Number be a Majority of the whole Number of Electors appointed; and if there be more than one who have such Majority, and have an equal Number of Votes, then the House of Representatives shall immediately chuse by Ballot one of them for President; and if no Person have a Majority, then from the five highest on the List the said House shall in like Manner chuse the President. But in chusing the President, the Votes shall be taken by States, the Representation from each State having one Vote; A quorum for this purpose shall consist of a Member or Members from two thirds of the States, and a Majority of all the States shall be necessary to a Choice. In every Case, after the Choice of the President, the Person having the greatest Number of Votes of the Electors shall be the Vice President. But if there should remain two or more who have equal Votes, the Senate shall chuse from them by Ballot the Vice President.

The Congress may determine the Time of chusing the Electors, and the Day on which they shall give their Votes; which Day shall be the same throughout the United States.

No Person except a natural born Citizen, or a Citizen of the United States, at the time of the Adoption of this Constitution, shall be eligible to the Office of President; neither shall any Person be eligible to that Office who shall not have attained to the Age of thirty five Years, and been fourteen Years a Resident within the United States.

In Case of the Removal of the President from Office, or of his Death, Resignation, or Inability to discharge the Powers and duties of the said Office, the Same shall devolve on the Vice President, and the Congress may by Law provide for the Case of Removal, Death, Resignation or Inability, both of the President and Vice President, declaring what Officer shall then act as President, and such Officer shall act accordingly, until the Disability be removed, or a President shall be elected.

The President shall, at stated Times, receive for his Services, a Compensation which shall neither be encreased nor diminished during the Period for which he shall have been elected, and he shall not receive within that Period any other Emolument from the United States, or any of them.

Before he enter on the Execution of his Office, he shall take the following Oath or Affirmation:—"I do solemnly swear (or affirm) that I will faithfully execute the Office of President of the United States, and will to the best of my Ability, preserve, protect and defend the Constitution of the United States."

Section 2   The President shall be Commander in Chief of the Army and Navy of the United States, and of the Militia of the several States, when called into the actual service of the United States; he may require the Opinion, in writing, of the principal Officer in each of the executive Departments, upon any Subject relating to the Duties of their respective Offices, and he shall have Power to grant Reprieves and Pardons for Offences against the United States, except in Cases of Impeachment.

He shall have Power, by and with the Advice and Consent of the Senate, to make Treaties, provided two thirds of the Senators present concur; and he shall nominate, and by and with the Advice and Consent of the Senate, shall appoint Ambassadors, and other public Ministers and Consuls, Judges of the Supreme Court, and all other Officers of the United States, whose Appointments are not herein otherwise provided for, and which shall be established by Law: but the Congress may by Law vest the Appointment of such inferior Officers, as they think proper, in the President alone, in the Courts of Law, or in the heads of Departments.

The President shall have Power to fill up all Vacancies that may happen during the Recess of the Senate, by granting Commissions which shall expire at the End of their next Session.

Section 3   He shall from time to time give to the Congress Information of the State of the Union, and recommend to their Consideration such Measures as he shall judge necessary and expedient; he may, on extraordinary Occasions, convene both Houses, or either of them, and in Case of Disagreement between them, with Respect to the Time of Adjournment, he may adjourn them to such time as he shall think proper; he shall receive Ambassadors and other public Ministers, he shall take Care that the Laws be faithfully executed, and shall Commission all the Officers of the United States.

Section 4   The President, Vice President, and all civil Officers of the United States, shall be removed from Office on Impeachment for; and Conviction of Treason, Bribery, or other high Crimes and Misdemeanors.

Article III

Section 1   The judicial Power of the United States, shall be vested in one supreme Court and in such inferior Courts as the Congress may from time to time ordain and establish. The Judges, both of the supreme and inferior Courts, shall hold their Offices during good Behavior, and shall, at stated Times, receive for their Services, a Compensation, which shall not be diminished during their Continuance in Office.

Section 2   The judicial Power shall extend to all Cases, in Law and Equity, arising under this Constitution, the Laws of the United States, and Treaties made, or which shall be made, under their Authority;—to all Cases affecting Ambassadors, other public Ministers and Consuls;—to all Cases of admiralty and maritime Jurisdiction;—to Controversies to which the United States shall be a Party—to Controversies between two or more States;—between a State and Citizens of another State;—between Citizens of different States;—between Citizens of the same State claiming Lands under Grants of different States, and between a State or the Citizens thereof, and foreign States, Citizens, or Subjects.

In all cases affecting Ambassadors, other public Ministers and Consuls, and those in which a State shall be Party, the supreme Court shall have original Jurisdiction. In all the other Cases before mentioned, the supreme Court shall have appellate Jurisdiction, both as to Law and Fact, with such Exceptions, and under such Regulations as the Congress shall make.

The Trial of all Crimes, except in Cases of Impeachment, shall be by Jury; and such Trial shall be held in the State where the said Crimes shall have been committed; but when not committed within any State, the Trial shall be at such Place or Places as the Congress may by Law have directed.

Section 3   Treason against the United States, shall consist only in levying War against them, or in adhering to their Enemies, giving them Aid and Comfort. No Person shall be convicted of Treason unless on the Testimony of two Witnesses to the same overt Act, or on Confession in open Court.

The Congress shall have Power to declare the Punishment of Treason, but no Attainder of Treason shall work Corruption of Blood, or Forfeiture except during the Life of the Person attained.

Article IV

Section 1   Full Faith and Credit shall be given in each State to the public Acts, Records, and judicial Proceedings of every other State. And the Congress may by general Laws prescribe the Manner in which such Acts, Records, and Proceedings shall be proved, and the Effect thereof.

Section 2   The Citizens of each State shall be entitled to all Privileges and immunities of Citizens in the several States.

A Person charged in any State with Treason, Felony, or other Crime, who shall flee from Justice, and be found in another State, shall on Demand of the executive Authority of the State from which he fled, be delivered up, to be removed to the State having Jurisdiction of the Crime.

No person held to Service or Labour in one State, under the Laws thereof, escaping into another, shall in Consequence of any Law or Regulation therein be discharged from such Service or Labour but shall be delivered upon claim of the Party to whom such Service or Labour may be due.

Section 3   New States may be admitted by the Congress into this Union; but no new State shall be formed or erected within the Jurisdiction of any other State; nor any State be formed by the Junction of two or more States, or Parts of States, without the Consent of the Legislatures of the States concerned as well as of the Congress.

The Congress shall have Power to dispose of and make all needful Rules and Regulations respecting the Territory or other Property belonging to the United States; and nothing in this Constitution shall be so construed as to Prejudice any claims of the United States, or of any particular State.

Section 4   The United States shall guarantee to every State in this Union a Republican Form of Government, and shall protect each of them against Invasion; and on Application of the Legislature, or of the Executive (when the Legislature cannot be convened) against domestic Violence.

Article V

The Congress, whenever two thirds of both Houses shall deem it necessary, shall propose Amendments to this Constitution, or, on the Application of the Legislatures of two thirds of the several States, shall call a Convention for proposing Amendments, which, in either Case, shall be valid to all Intents and Purposes, as Part of this Constitution, when ratified by the Legislatures of three fourths of the several States, or by Conventions in three fourths thereof, as the one or the other Mode of Ratification may be proposed by the Congress; Provided that no Amendment which may be made prior to the Year One thousand eight hundred and eight shall in any Manner affect the first and fourth Clauses in the Ninth Section of the first Article; and that no State, without its Consent, shall be deprived of its equal Suffrage in the Senate.

Article VI

All Debts contracted and Engagements entered into, before the Adoption of this Constitution, shall be as valid against the United States under this Constitution, as under the Confederation.

This Constitution, and the Laws of the United States which shall be made in Pursuance thereof; and all Treaties made, or which shall be made, under the Authority of the United States, shall be the supreme Law of the Land; and the Judges in every State shall be bound thereby, any Thing in the Constitution of Laws of any State to the Contrary notwithstanding.

The Senators and Representatives before mentioned, and the Members of the several

State Legislatures, and all executive and judicial Officers, both of the United States and of the several States, shall be bound by Oath or Affirmation to support this Constitution; but no religious Test shall ever be required as a Qualification to any Office or public Trust under the United States.

Article VII

The Ratification of the Conventions of nine States, shall be sufficient for the Establishment of this Constitution between the States so ratifying the Same.

Done in Convention by the Unanimous Consent of the States present the Seventeenth Day of September in the Year of our Lord one thousand seven hundred and eighty seven and of the Independence of the United States of America the twelfth. In witness whereof We have hereunto subscribed our Names.

Articles in addition to, and amendment of, the Constitution of the United States of America, proposed by Congress, and ratified by the several states, pursuant to the Fifth Article of the Original Constitution:

Amendment I

Congress shall make no law respecting an establishment of religion, or prohibiting the free exercise thereof; or abridging the freedom of speech, or of the press; or the right of the people peaceably to assemble, and to petition the Government for a redress of grievances.

Amendment II

A well regulated Militia, being necessary to the security of a free State, the right of the people to keep and bear Arms, shall not be infringed.

Amendment III

No Soldier shall, in time of peace be quartered in any house, without the consent of the Owner, nor in time of war, but in a manner to be prescribed by law.

Amendment IV

The right of the people to be secure in their persons, houses, papers, and effects, against unreasonable searches and seizures, shall not be violated, and no Warrants shall issue, but upon probable cause, supported by Oath or affirmation, and particularly describing the place to be searched, and the persons or things to be seized.

Amendment V

No person shall be held to answer for a capital, or other infamous crime, unless on a presentment or indictment of a Grand Jury, except in cases arising in the land or naval forces, or in the Militia, when in actual service in time of War or public danger; nor shall any person be subject for the same offence to be twice put in jeopardy of life or limb; nor shall be compelled in any criminal case to be a witness against himself, nor be deprived of life, liberty, or property without due process of law; nor shall private property be taken for public use, without just compensation.

Amendment VI

In all criminal prosecutions, the accused shall enjoy the right to a speedy and public trial, by an impartial jury of the State and district wherein the crime shall have been committed, which district shall have been previously ascertained in law, and to be informed of the nature and cause of the accusation; to be confronted with the witness against him; to have compulsory process of obtaining witness in his favor, and to have the Assistance of Counsel for his defense.

Amendment VII

In Suits at common law, where the value in controversy shall exceed twenty dollars, the right of trial by jury shall be preserved, and no fact tried by a jury, shall be otherwise reexamined in any Court of the United States, than according to the rules of the common law.

Amendment VIII

Excessive bail shall not be required, nor excessive fines imposed, nor cruel and unusual punishments inflicted.

Amendment IX

The enumeration in the Constitution, of certain rights, shall not be construed to deny or disparage others retained by the people.

Amendment X

The powers not delegated to the United States by the Constitution, nor prohibited by it to the States, are reserved to the States respectively, or to the people.

Amendment XI [January 8, 1798]

The Judicial power of the United States shall not be construed to extend to any suit in law or equity, commenced or prosecuted against one of the United States by Citizens of another State, or by Citizens or Subjects of any Foreign State.

Amendment XII [September 25, 1804]

The Electors shall meet in their respective states and vote by ballot for President and Vice President, one of whom, at least, shall not be an inhabitant of the same state with themselves; they shall name in their ballots the person voted for as President, and in distinct ballots the person voted for as Vice President, and they shall make distinct lists of all persons voted for as President and of all persons voted for as Vice President, and of the number of votes for each, which lists they shall sign and certify, and transmit sealed to the seat of the government of the United States, directed to the President of the Senate;—The President of the Senate shall, in the presence of Senate and House of Representatives, open all the certificates and the votes shall then be counted;—The person having the greatest number of votes for President, shall be the President, if such number be a majority of the whole number of Electors appointed; and if no person have such majority, then from the persons having the highest numbers not exceeding three on the list of those voted for as President, the House of Representatives shall choose immediately, by ballot, the President. But in choosing the President, the votes shall be taken by states, the representation from each state having one vote; a quorum for this purpose shall consist of a member or members from two-thirds of the states, and a majority of all the states shall be necessary to a choice. And if the House of Representatives shall not choose a President whenever the right of choice shall devolve upon them, before the fourth day of March next following, then the Vice President shall act as President, as in the case of the death or other constitutional disability of the President.—The person having the greatest number of votes as Vice President shall be the Vice President, if such number be a majority of the whole number of Electors appointed, and if no person have a majority, then from the two highest numbers on the list, the Senate shall choose the Vice President; a quorum for the purpose shall consist of two-thirds of the whole number of Senators, and a majority of the whole number shall be necessary to a choice, but no person constitutionally ineligible to the office of President shall be eligible to that of Vice President of the United States.

Amendment XIII [December 18, 1865]

Section 1   Neither slavery nor involuntary servitude, except as a punishment for crime whereof the party shall have been duly convicted, shall exist within the United States, or any place subject to their jurisdiction.

Section 2   Congress shall have power to enforce this article by appropriate legislation.

Amendment XIV [July 28, 1869]

Section 1   All persons born or naturalized in the United States, and subject to the jurisdiction thereof, are citizens of the United States and of the State wherein they reside.

No State shall make or enforce any law which shall abridge the privileges or immunities of citizens of the United States; nor shall any State deprive any person of life, liberty, or property, without due process of law; nor deny to any person within its jurisdiction the equal protection of the laws.

Section 2   Representatives shall be apportioned among the several States according to their respective numbers, counting the whole number of persons in each State, excluding Indians not taxed. But when the right to vote at any election for the choice of electors for President and Vice President of the United States, Representatives in Congress, the Executive and Judicial officers of a State, or the members of the Legislature thereof, is denied to any of the male inhabitants of such State, being twenty-one years of age, and citizens of the United States, or in any way abridged, except for participation in rebellion, or other crime, the basis of representation therein shall be reduced in the proportion which the number of such male citizens shall bear to the whole number of male citizens twenty-one years of age in such State.

Section 3   No person shall be a Senator or Representative in Congress, or elector of President and Vice President, or hold any office, civil or military, under the United States, or under any State, who, having previously taken an oath, as a member of Congress, or as an officer of the United States, or as a member of any State legislature, or as an executive or judicial officer of any State, to support the Constitution of the United States, shall have engaged in insurrection or rebellion against the same, or given aid or comfort to the enemies thereof. But Congress may by a vote of two thirds of each House, remove such disability.

Section 4   The validity of the public debt of the United States, authorized by law, including debts incurred for payment of pensions and bounties for services in suppressing insurrection or rebellion, shall not be questioned. But neither the United States nor any State shall assume or pay any debt or obligation incurred in aid of insurrection or rebellion against the United States, or any claim for the loss or emancipation of any slave; but all such debts, obligations, and claims shall be held illegal and void.

Section 5   The Congress shall have power to enforce, by appropriate legislation, the provisions of this article.

Amendment XV [March 30, 1870]

Section 1   The right of citizens of the United States to vote shall not be denied or abridged by the United States or by any State on account of race, color, or previous condition of servitude.

Section 2   The Congress shall have power to enforce this article by appropriate legislation.

Amendment XVI [February 25, 1913]

The Congress shall have power to lay and collect taxes on incomes, from whatever source derived, without apportionment among the several States, and without regard to any census or enumeration.

Amendment XVII [May 31, 1913]

The Senate of the United States shall be composed of two Senators from each State, elected by the people thereof, for six years; and each Senator shall have one vote. The electors in each State shall have the qualifications requisite for electors of the most numerous branch of the State legislature.

When vacancies happen in the representation of any State in the Senate, the executive authority of such State shall issue writs of election to fill such vacancies: Provided, That the legislature of any State may empower the executive thereof to make temporary appointments until the people fill the vacancies by election as the legislature may direct.

This amendment shall not be so construed as to affect the election or term of any Senator chosen before it becomes valid as part of the Constitution.

Amendment XVIII [January 29, 1919]

Section 1   After one year from the ratification of this article the manufacture, sale, or transportation of intoxicating liquors within, the importation thereof into, or the exportation thereof from the United States and all territory subject to the jurisdiction thereof for beverage purposes is hereby prohibited.

Section 2   The Congress and the several States shall have concurrent power to enforce this article by appropriate legislation.

Section 3   This article shall be inoperative unless it shall have been ratified as an amendment to the Constitution by the legislatures of the several States, as provided in the Constitution, within seven years from the date of the submission hereof to the States by the Congress.

Amendment XIX [August 26, 1920]

The right of citizens of the United States to vote shall not be denied or abridged by the United States or by any State on account of sex.

Congress shall have power to enforce this article by appropriate legislation.

Amendment XX [February 6, 1933]

Section 1   The terms of the President and Vice President shall end at noon on the 20th day of January, and the terms of Senators and Representatives at noon on the 3rd day of January, of the years in which such terms would have ended if this article had not been ratified; and the terms of their successors shall then begin.

Section 2   The Congress shall assemble at least once in every year, and such meeting shall begin at noon on the 3rd day of January, unless they shall by law appoint a different day.

Section 3   If, at the time fixed for the beginning of the term of the President, the President elect shall have died, the Vice President elect shall become President. If a President shall not have been chosen before the time fixed for the beginning of his term, or if the President elect shall have failed to qualify, then the Vice President elect shall act as President until a President shall have qualified; and the Congress may by law provide for the case wherein neither a President elect nor a Vice President elect shall have qualified, declaring who shall then act as President, or the manner in which one who is to act shall be selected, and such person shall act accordingly until a President or Vice President shall have qualified.

Section 4   The Congress may by law provide for the case of the death of any of the persons from whom the House of Representatives may choose a President whenever the right of choice shall have devolved upon them, and for the case of the death of any of the persons from whom the Senate may choose a Vice President whenever the right of choice shall have devolved upon them.

Section 5   Sections 1 and 2 shall take effect on the 15th day of October following the ratification of this article.

Section 6   This article shall be inoperative unless it shall have been ratified as an amendment to the Constitution by the legislatures of three-fourths of the several States within seven years from the date of its submission.

Amendment XXI [December 5, 1933]

Section 1   The eighteenth article of amendment to the Constitution of the United States is hereby repealed.

Section 2   The transportation or importation into any State, Territory, or possession of the United States for delivery or use therein of intoxicating liquors, in violation of the laws thereof, is hereby prohibited.

Section 3   This article shall be inoperative unless it shall have been ratified as an amendment to the Constitution by conventions in the several States, as provided in the Constitution, within seven years from the date of the submission hereof to the States by the Congress.

Amendment XXII [February 26, 1951]

Section 1   No person shall be elected to the office of the President more than twice, and no person who has held the office of President, or acted as President, for more than two years of a term to which some other person was elected President shall be elected to the office of President more than once. But this Article shall not apply to any person holding the office of President when this Article was proposed by the Congress, and shall not prevent any person who may be holding the office of President, or acting as President, during the term within which this Article becomes operative from holding the office of President or acting as President during the remainder of such term.

Section 2   This article shall be inoperative unless it shall have been ratified as an amendment to the Constitution by the legislatures of three-fourths of the several States within seven years from the date of its submission to the States by the Congress.

Amendment XXIII [March 29, 1961]

Section 1   The District constituting the seat of Government of the United States shall appoint in such manner as the Congress may direct:

A number of electors of President and Vice President equal to the whole number of Senators and Representatives in Congress to which the District would be entitled if it were a State, but in no event more than the least populous State; they shall be in addition to those appointed by the States, but they shall be considered, for the purposes of the election of President and Vice President, to be electors appointed by a State; and they shall meet in the District and perform such duties as provided by the twelfth article of amendment.

Section 2   The Congress shall have power to enforce this article by appropriate legislation.

Amendment XXIV [January 23, 1964]

Section 1   The right of citizens of the United States to vote in any primary or other election for President or Vice President, for electors for President or Vice President, or for Senator or Representative in Congress, shall not be denied or abridged by the United States or any state by reason of failure to pay any tax.

Section 2   The Congress shall have the power to enforce this article by appropriate legislation.

Amendment XXV [February 10, 1967]

Section 1   In case of the removal of the President from office or of his death or resignation, the Vice President shall become President.

Section 2   Whenever there is a vacancy in the office of the Vice President, the President shall nominate a Vice President who shall take office upon confirmation by a majority vote of both Houses of Congress.

Section 3   Whenever the President transmits to the President pro tempore of the Senate and the Speaker of the House of Representatives his written declaration that he is unable to discharge the powers and duties of his office, and until he transmits to them a written declaration to the contrary, such powers and duties shall be discharged by the Vice President as Acting President.

Section 4   Whenever the Vice President and a majority of either the principal officers of the executive departments or of such other body as Congress may by law provide, transmit to the President pro tempore of the Senate and the Speaker of the House of Representatives their written declaration that the President is unable to discharge the powers and duties of his office, the Vice President shall immediately assume the powers and duties of the office as Acting President.

Thereafter, when the President transmits to the President pro tempore of the Senate and the Speaker of the House of Representatives his written declaration that no inability exists, he shall resume the powers and duties of his office unless the Vice President and a majority of either the principal officers of the executive departments or of such other body as Congress may by law provide, transmit within four days to the President pro tempore of the Senate and the Speaker of the House of Representatives their written declaration that the President is unable to discharge the powers and duties of his office. Thereupon Congress shall decide the issue, assembling within forty-eight hours for that purpose if not in session. If the Congress, within twenty-one days after receipt of the latter written declaration, or, if Congress is not in session, within twenty-one days after Congress is required to assemble, determines by two-thirds vote of both Houses that the President is unable to discharge the powers and duties of his office, the Vice President shall continue to discharge the same as Acting President; otherwise, the President shall resume the powers and duties of his office.

Amendment XXVI [July 5, 1971]

Section 1   The right of citizens of the United States, who are eighteen years of age or older, to vote shall not be denied or abridged by the United States or by any State on account of age.

Section 2   The Congress shall have power to enforce this article by appropriate legislation.

Presidents of

the United States

Year	President	Party
1789	George Washington	
1792	George Washington	
1796	John Adams	Federalist
1800	Thomas Jefferson	Democratic-Republican
1804	Thomas Jefferson	Democratic-Republican
1808	James Madison	Democratic-Republican
1812	James Madison	Democratic-Republican
1816	James Monroe	Democratic-Republican
1820	James Monroe	Democratic-Republican
1824	John Quincy Adams	Democratic-Republican
1828	Andrew Jackson	Democratic
1832	Andrew Jackson	Democratic
1836	Martin Van Buren	Democratic
1840	William H. Harrison	Whig
°1841	John Tyler	Whig
1844	James K. Polk	Democratic
1848	Zachary Taylor	Whig
°1850	Millard Fillmore	Whig
1852	Franklin Pierce	Democratic
1856	James Buchanan	Democratic
1860	Abraham Lincoln	Republican
1864	Abraham Lincoln	Republican
°1865	Andrew Johnson	Democratic
1868	Ulysses S. Grant	Republican
1872	Ulysses S. Grant	Republican
1876	Rutherford B. Hayes	Republican

Year	President	Party
1880	James A. Garfield	Republican
°1881	Chester A. Arthur	Republican
1884	Grover Cleveland	Democratic
1888	Benjamin Harrison	Republican
1892	Grover Cleveland	Democratic
1896	William McKinley	Republican
1900	William McKinley	Republican
°1901	Theodore Roosevelt	Republican
1904	Theodore Roosevelt	Republican
1908	William H. Taft	Republican
1912	Woodrow Wilson	Democratic
1916	Woodrow Wilson	Democratic
1920	Warren G. Harding	Republican
°1923	Calvin Coolidge	Republican
1924	Calvin Coolidge	Republican
1928	Herbert C. Hoover	Republican
1932	Franklin D. Roosevelt	Democratic
1936	Franklin D. Roosevelt	Democratic
1940	Franklin D. Roosevelt	Democratic
1944	Franklin D. Roosevelt	Democratic
°1945	Harry S. Truman	Democratic
1948	Harry S. Truman	Democratic
1952	Dwight D. Eisenhower	Republican
1956	Dwight D. Eisenhower	Republican
1960	John F. Kennedy	Democratic
°1963	Lyndon B. Johnson	Democratic
1964	Lyndon B. Johnson	Democratic
1968	Richard M. Nixon	Republican
1972	Richard M. Nixon	Republican
°°1974	Gerald R. Ford	Republican
1976	Jimmy Carter	Democratic

°Completed term upon death of the incumbent.
°°Completed term upon resignation of the incumbent.

Selected
Bibliography

Chapter 1 (Five Perspectives on the American Political System)

°Gary Allen, *None Dare Call It Conspiracy* (Rossmoor, Calif.: Concord Press, 1971). A radical right statement by a freelance journalist arguing that a wealthy elite in America is in collusion with the Soviet Union to control domestic and world decisions.

Carl L. Becker, *The Declaration of Independence* (New York: Alfred A. Knopf, Inc., 1942). An examination of the Declaration and its historical context.

°Daniel Bell, ed., *The Radical Right* (Garden City, N.Y.: Doubleday & Company, Inc., 1963). Critical commentaries on the radical right by centrist, liberal, and conservative scholars, including Daniel Bell, Richard Hofstadter, David Riesman, Nathan Glazer, Peter Viereck, Talcott Parsons, and Alan F. Westin.

°James MacGregor Burns, *The Deadlock of Democracy*, 2nd ed. (Englewood Cliffs, N.J.: Prentice-Hall, Inc., 1966); °*Uncommon Sense* (New York: Harper & Row, Publishers, 1972).

°Edward S. Corwin et al., eds., *The Constitution of the United States* (Washington, D.C.: Government Printing Office, 1964). A line-by-line analysis of the Constitution.

°Ralph de Toledano and Karl Hess, eds., *The Conservative Papers* (Garden City, N.Y.: Anchor Books, Doubleday & Company, Inc., 1964).

°Kenneth M. Dolbeare and Patricia Dolbeare, *American Ideologies: The Competing Political Beliefs of the 1970s*, 3rd ed. (Chicago: Rand McNally & Company, 1976). An examination of the role of various contemporary ideologies in America, with categories that are slightly different from these in *Power and Politics in America*.

°G. William Domhoff, *Who Rules America?* (Englewood Cliffs, N.J.: Prentice-Hall, Inc., 1967); °*The Higher Circles* (New York: Random House, Inc., 1970).

°Available in paperback.

°Thomas Dye and L. Harmon Zeigler, *The Irony of Democracy*, 3rd ed. (North Scituate, Mass.: Duxbury Press, 1975). An analysis of the American system by two political scientists, one of the left, the other conservative, based on the proposition that "Elites, not masses, govern America."

°Henry Etzkowitz and Peter Schwab, eds., *Is America Necessary?* (St. Paul, Minn.: West Publishing Co., 1976). A reader presenting conservative, liberal, and socialist perspectives on American political institutions.

°M. Stanton Evans, *Clear and Present Dangers: A Conservative View of America's Government* (New York: Harcourt Brace Jovanovich, Inc., 1975).

°Milton Friedman, *Capitalism and Freedom* (Chicago: University of Chicago Press, 1962). An economist's argument that capitalism is an indispensable condition for the free society.

°Barry Goldwater, *Conscience of a Conservative* (New York: Macfadden-Bartell, 1960, 1964).

°Robert A. Goldwin, ed., *Left, Right and Center* (Chicago: Rand McNally & Company, 1965). Essays on liberalism and conservatism in the United States by such proponents as Frank S. Meyer, Stephen C. Shadegg, David Spitz, Martin Diamond, and Samuel H. Beer.

°Arthur N. Holcombe, *The Constitutional System* (Glenview, Ill.: Scott, Foresman and Company, 1964). A centrist scholar's explanation of the principles embodied in the Constitution.

Matthew Holden, Jr., ed., *Varieties of Political Conservatism* (Beverly Hills, Calif.: Sage Publications, 1974).

Willmoore Kendall, *The Conservative Affirmation* (Chicago: Henry Regnery Company, 1963). A critique of liberal ideology from the perspective of a conservative political scientist.

James Madison, Alexander Hamilton, and John Jay, *The Federalist* (available in various editions). The basic exposition of the principles embodied in the U.S. Constitution by some of the men who shaped it.

°C. Wright Mills, *The Power Elite* (New York: Oxford University Press, Inc., 1956).

°Carl Oglesby, ed., *The New Left Reader* (New York: Grove Press, Inc., 1969). Selections from some of the central figures of the new left, including C. Wright Mills, Herbert Marcuse, Mark Rudd, Frantz Fanon, Huey Newton, Rudi Dutschke, and Daniel Cohn-Bendit.

°Marcus Raskin, *Notes on the Old System: To Transform American Politics* (New York: David McKay Company, Inc., 1974).

°Arnold M. Rose, *The Power Structure* (New York: Oxford University Press, Inc., 1967). A sociologist's analysis of American politics as a pluralist system. Rejects Mills's power-elite analysis as "a caricature of American society."

°Robert A. Rosenstone, ed., *Protest from the Right* (Encino, Calif.: Glencoe Press, 1968). Articles by and about the extreme right.

°Lyman T. Sargent, *New Left Thought: An Introduction* (Homewood, Ill.: The Dorsey Press, 1972). A sympathetic analysis of new left ideas.

Robert A. Schoenberger, ed., *The American Right Wing: Readings in Political Behavior* (New York: Holt, Rinehart and Winston, Inc., 1969).

Chapter 2 (Public Opinion: Who Cares about Politics?)

°Gabriel A. Almond and Sidney Verba, *The Civic Culture* (Princeton, N.J.: Princeton University Press, 1963). Comparative study of political attitudes in the United States, Mexico, Great Britain, Germany, and Italy.

Patrick Buchanan, *The New Majority* (Philadelphia: Girard Bank, 1973).

°Angus Campbell, Philip E. Converse, Warren E. Miller, and Donald E. Stokes, *The American Voter* (New York: John Wiley & Sons, Inc., 1960 [abridgement, 1964]; Chicago: University of Chicago Press, 1976).

°Albert H. Cantril and Charles W. Roll, Jr., *Hopes and Fears of the American People* (New York: Universe Books, 1971).

Fred I. Greenstein, *Children and Politics*, rev. ed. (New Haven, Conn.: Yale University Press, 1970). The formation of political attitudes in young children.

°Bernard C. Hennessy, *Public Opinion*, 2nd ed. (Belmont, Calif.: Wadsworth Publishing Co., 1970).

V. O. Key, Jr., *Public Opinion and American Democracy* (New York: Alfred A. Knopf, Inc. 1961). Standard work in this field. °*The Responsible Electorate* (Cambridge, Mass.: Belknap Press of Harvard University Press, 1966).

°Robert E. Lane and David O. Sears, *Public Opinion* (Englewood Cliffs, N.J.: Prentice-Hall, Inc., 1964). Impact on political opinions of family, groups, and other societal influences.

°Paul Lazarsfeld, Bernard Berelson, and Hazel Gaudet, *The People's Choice: How the Voter Makes Up His Mind in a Presidential Campaign*, 3rd ed. (New York: Columbia University Press, 1968).

Warren E. Miller and Teresa E. Levitin, *Leadership and Change: The New Politics and the American Electorate* (Cambridge, Mass.: Winthrop Publishers, Inc., 1976). Voting behavior and attitudes from 1948 to 1974.

°Norman H. Nie, Sidney Verba, and John R. Petrocik, *The Changing American Voter* (Cambridge, Mass.: Harvard University Press, 1976).

Elmer Eric Schattschneider, *The Semisovereign People: A Realist's View of Democracy in America* (Hinsdale, Ill.: The Dryden Press, 1975). An analysis of the role of the people at large in contemporary democracy.

°William Watts and Lloyd A. Free, eds., *State of the Nation* (New York: Universe Books, 1973). An account of public opinion on various topics in Gallup polls, together with a summary of the background events.

Chapter 3 (Political Parties: Do We Need Them?)

°David S. Broder, *The Party's Over: The Failure of Politics in America* (New York: Harper & Row Publishers, 1972).

°Fred I. Greenstein, *The American Party System and the American People*, 2nd ed.

(Englewood Cliffs, N.J.: Prentice-Hall, Inc., 1970). Synthesis of research on parties "in terms of their contribution to democracy, stability, and 'effective policy-making.'"

°(Edward) Pendleton Herring, *The Politics of Democracy* (New York: W. W. Norton & Company, Inc., 1965).

V. O. Key, *Politics, Parties and Pressure Groups,* 5th ed. (New York: Thomas Y. Crowell Company, Inc., 1964); °*Southern Politics in State and Nation* (New York: Alfred A. Knopf, Inc. 1949).

Daniel A. Mazmanian, *Third Parties in Presidential Elections* (Washington, D.C.: The Brookings Institution, 1974).

Austin Ranney, *Curing the Mischiefs of Faction: Party Reform in America* (Berkeley, Calif.: University of California Press, 1975). Study of three periods of major reforms in the party system.

°William A. Rusher, *The Making of the New Majority Party* (New York: Sheed and Ward, 1975).

°Richard M. Scammon and Ben J. Wattenberg, *The Real Majority* (New York: Coward McCann & Geoghegan, 1970).

Elmer Eric Schattschneider, *Party Government* (New York: Farrar and Rinehart, Inc., 1942).

Frank J. Sorauf, *Party Politics in America,* 3rd ed. (Boston: Little, Brown and Company, 1976).

°James L. Sundquist, *Dynamics of the Party System: Alignment and Realignment of Political Parties in the United States* (Washington, D.C.: The Brookings Institution, 1973). Historical survey of the relative strength of political parties.

Chapter 4 (Elections: Majorities, Media, and Money)

Herbert E. Alexander, *Political Financing* (Minneapolis, Minn.: Burgess Publishing Co., 1973).

Herbert E. Alexander et al., *Financing the 1972 Election* (Lexington, Mass.: Lexington Books, 1976).

°Walter DeVries and V. Lance Tarrance, *The Ticket-Splitter: A New Force in American Politics* (Grand Rapids, Mich.: William B. Eerdmans Publishing Co., 1971). Analysis of the increase in ticket-splitting as party ties weaken.

Alexander Heard, *The Costs of Democracy* (Chapel Hill, N.C.: University of North Carolina Press, 1960). Study of money in campaigns.

William R. Keech and Donald R. Matthews, *The Party's Choice* (Washington, D.C.: The Brookings Institution, 1976). How presidential candidates were nominated from 1936 to 1972.

°Stanley Kelley, Jr., *Professional Public Relations and Political Power* (Baltimore, Md.: Johns Hopkins Press, 1966). The role of public relations firms in elections.

°Norman Mailer, *Miami and the Siege of Chicago* (New York: World Publishing Co., 1968); °*St. George and the Godfather* (New York: The New American Library, Inc., 1972). Brilliantly written studies of the 1968 and 1972 Republican and Democratic conventions.

Ernest R. May and Janet Fraser, eds., *Campaign '72: The Managers Speak* (Cambridge, Mass.: Harvard University Press, 1973). A colloquium by the people who managed the campaigns of various candidates in 1972.

°Joe McGinniss, *The Selling of the President 1968* (New York: Trident Press, 1969).

°Dan Nimmo, *The Political Persuaders* (Englewood Cliffs, N.J.: Prentice-Hall, Inc., 1970). Techniques of modern election campaigns. Includes discussion of television, the role of campaign consultants, and the implications of the new communications technologies for democratic politics.

°Dan Nimmo and Robert L. Savage, *Candidates and Their Images: Concepts, Methods, and Findings* (Pacific Palisades, Calif.: Goodyear Publishing Co., Inc., 1976). Suggests that campaigns and campaign techniques are of growing importance in influencing voters.

°Nelson W. Polsby and Aaron B. Wildavsky, *Presidential Elections*, 4th ed. (New York: Charles Scribner's Sons, 1976). Analysis of alternative strategies for winning nomination and election. Includes a case study of the 1964 election and consideration of reform proposals.

°Gerald M. Pomper, *Elections in America* (New York: Dodd, Mead & Company, 1968). Study of our electoral processes both at federal and state levels from a generally favorable perspective.

°Gerald M. Pomper et al., *The Election of 1976: Reports and Interpretations* (New York: David McKay Company, Inc., 1977).

°Theodore H. White, *The Making of the President, 1960* (New York: Atheneum Publishers, 1961); *The Making of the President, 1964* (New York: Atheneum Publishers, 1965); *The Making of the President, 1968* (New York: Atheneum Publishers, 1969); *The Making of the President, 1972* (New York: Atheneum Publishers, 1973). The 1960 study is the best of the four, but all are interesting, blow-by-blow accounts of the elections and their context of political and social forces.

Jules Witcover, *Marathon: the Pursuit of the Presidency: 1972–1976.* (New York: The Viking Press, 1977). A newspaper reporter's story of the 1976 campaign.

Chapter 5 (Interest Groups and the Public Interest)

°Congressional Quarterly, *The Washington Lobby*, 2nd ed. (Washington, D.C.: Congressional Quarterly, Inc., 1974).

Robert Engler, *The Brotherhood of Oil* (Chicago: University of Chicago Press, 1977). Study of the impact of the oil industry on the legislative and political process.

°Jo Freeman, *The Politics of Women's Liberation* (New York: David McKay Company, Inc., 1975). Analysis of the women's liberation movement and the various groups participating in it.

°John Kenneth Galbraith, *The New Industrial State*, 2nd rev. ed. (Boston: Houghton Mifflin Company, 1971).

°Carol S. Greenwald, *Group Power* (New York: Praeger Publishers, Inc., 1977). Analysis of interest groups which argues that they are an important and legitimate part of the making of public policy.

Abraham Holtzman, *Interest Groups and Lobbying* (New York: Macmillan Publishing Co., Inc., 1966).

°Gabriel Kolko, *Wealth and Power in America* (New York: Praeger Publishers, Inc., 1962).

°Sanford A. Lakoff and Daniel Rich, eds., *Private Government* (Glenview, Ill.: Scott Foresman and Company, 1973). Readings on the internal government and political attributes of business, labor, professional associations, and universities.

°Theodore J. Lowi, *The End of Liberalism: Ideology, Policy, and the Crisis of Public Authority* (New York: W. W. Norton & Company, Inc., 1969). Critical analysis of the interest group process and its consequences for the making of public policy.

°H. R. Mahood, *Pressure Groups in American Politics* (New York: Charles Scribner's Sons, 1967). Reader offering a variety of perspectives and some case studies.

Lester W. Milbrath, *The Washington Lobbyists* (Chicago: Rand McNally, Inc., 1963).

Ralph Nader, Mark Green and Joel Seligman, *Taming the Giant Corporation* (New York: W. W. Norton & Company, Inc., 1976).

David B. Truman, *The Governmental Process*, 2nd ed. (New York: Alfred A. Knopf, Inc., 1971). Government and politics in America as an expression of the group process.

Chapter 6 (The Presidency: A New Despotism?)

°James David Barber, *The Presidential Character: Predicting Performance in the White House* 2nd ed. (Englewood Cliffs, N.J.: Prentice-Hall, Inc., 1977).

Edward S. Corwin, *The President: Office and Powers*, 4th rev. ed. (New York: New York University Press, 1957).

°Thomas E. Cronin, *The State of the Presidency* (Boston: Little, Brown and Company, 1975). The modern presidency, with particular reference to the personality cult that surrounds the chief executive.

°John Dean, *Blind Ambition* (New York: Simon and Schuster, 1976). An indictment of the Nixon White House by one of its occupants.

°Erwin C. Hargrove, *The Power of the Modern Presidency*, (Philadelphia: Temple University Press, 1974).

Stephen Hess, *Organizing the Presidency* ((Washington, D.C.: The Brookings Institution, 1976). Proposals for reorganizing the president's office.

°Doris Kearns, *Lyndon Johnson and the American Dream* (New York: Harper & Row, Publishers, 1976). The story of Johnson's life and presidency as seen by a former White House intern.

°Louis W. Koenig, *The Chief Executive*, 3rd ed. (New York: Harcourt Brace Jovanovich, Inc., 1975).

°Richard Neustadt, *Presidential Power* (New York: John Wiley & Sons, Inc., 1976).

°Dan Rather and Gary Paul Gates, *The Palace Guard* (New York: Harper & Row Publishers, 1974). The Nixon White House as seen by media correspondents.

George E. Reedy, *The Twilight of the Presidency* (New York: World Publishing Co., 1970).

°Clinton Rossiter, *The American Presidency* (New York: Harcourt, Brace & World, 1960). The historical development of the several roles of the president.

William Safire, *Before the Fall: An Inside View of the Pre-Watergate White House* (Garden City, N.Y.: Doubleday & Company, Inc., 1975).

°Arthur M. Schlesinger, Jr., *A Thousand Days* (Boston: Houghton Mifflin Company, 1965). The Kennedy presidency described by a liberal historian who worked in the White House during the Kennedy era. *The Imperial Presidency* (Boston: Houghton Mifflin Company, 1973). A reassessment of the presidency, in which Schlesinger expresses his concerns about the trend toward a monarchical presidency.

°Garry Wills, *Nixon Agonistes: The Crisis of the Self-Made Man* (Boston: Houghton Mifflin Company, 1970). A caustic review of the career of Richard Nixon.

Chapter 7 (*The Congress: How Much Has It Changed?*)

°Stephen K. Bailey, *Congress in the Seventies*, 2nd ed. (New York: St. Martin's Press, Inc., 1970). Updated version of *The New Congress*.

°Richard Bolling, *House Out of Order* (New York: E. P. Dutton & Company, 1965). A liberal congressman's diagnosis of what is wrong with the House of Representatives and what should be done about it.

°Lawrence C. Dodd and Bruce I. Oppenheimer, eds., *Congress Reconsidered* (New York: Praeger Publishers, 1977). Readings on Congress in change.

°Richard F. Fenno, Jr., *Congressmen in Committees* (Boston: Little, Brown and Company, 1973). Study of decision making in committees.

°Lewis A. Froman, Jr., *Congressmen and Their Constituencies* (Chicago: Rand McNally & Company, 1963). Congressional elections and the impact of the constituency on the congressman's actions.

°Mark J. Green, James M. Fallows, and David R. Zwick, *Who Runs Congress?* (New York: Bantam Books, Inc., 1972).

°John F. Manley, *The Politics of Finance: The House Committee on Ways and Means* (Boston: Little, Brown and Company, 1970).

Donald R. Matthews and James A. Stimson, *Yeas and Nays: Normal Decision-Making in the U.S. House of Representatives* (New York: John Wiley & Sons, Inc., 1975). Study based on voting patterns and interviews with members of Congress.

°Gary Orfield, *Congressional Power: Congress and Social Change* (New York: Harcourt Brace Jovanovich, Inc., 1975). Study of Congress in the making of policy. Argues that Congress is more important and less conservative than is generally believed.

°Nelson W. Polsby, *Congress and the Presidency*, 3rd ed. (Englewood Cliffs, N.J.: Prentice-Hall, Inc., 1976).

°David B. Truman, ed., *The Congress and America's Future*, 2nd ed. (Englewood Cliffs, N.J.: Prentice-Hall, Inc., 1973). Essays by Truman, Samuel P. Huntington, Richard F. Fenno, Ralph K. Huitt, Richard E. Neustadt, and prospective roles of the Congress.

Chapter 8 (The Federal Bureaucracy: A Fourth Branch)

°Anthony Downs, *Inside Bureaucracy* (Boston: Little, Brown and Company, 1967). An attempt to build a theory of bureaucratic decision making, starting from the premise that "bureaucratic officials, like all other agents in society, are significantly—though not solely—motivated by their own self-interests."

Peter F. Drucker, *The Age of Discontinuity* (New York: Harper & Row, Publishers, 1969).

°Robert Fellmeth, *The Interstate Commerce Commission* (New York: Grossman Publishers, 1970); °James S. Turner, *The Chemical Feast* (New York: Grossman Publishers, 1970). Two of the Ralph Nader study group reports on the ICC and the Food and Drug Administration.

°A. Lee Fritschler, *Smoking and Politics: Policy-Making and the Federal Bureaucracy* (New York: Appleton-Century-Crofts, 1969).

John Kenneth Galbraith, *Economics and the Public Purpose* (Boston: Houghton Mifflin Company, 1973). Galbraith pulls together and revises many of the ideas he expressed earlier in *The Affluent Society* and *The New Industrial State*, and makes some proposals for a limited kind of socialism.

°Herbert Kaufman, *Are Government Organizations Immortal?* (Washington, D.C.: The Brookings Institution, 1976). Examines the self-perpetuating tendencies of federal agencies.

°Grant McConnell, *Private Power and American Democracy* (New York: Alfred A. Knopf, Inc., 1966).

°Francis E. Rourke, *Bureaucracy, Politics and Public Policy*, 2nd ed. (Boston: Little, Brown and Company, 1976).

°E. F. Schumacher, *Small Is Beautiful: Economics As If People Mattered* (New York: Harper & Row Publishers, 1973). A British economist's argument for smallness of scale in human organization.

°Herbert A. Simon, *Administrative Behavior: A Study of Decision-Making Processes in Administrative Organizations*, 2nd ed. (New York: The Free Press, 1957).

Dwight Waldo, *The Administrative State: A Study of the Political Theory of American Public Administration* (New York: The Ronald Press Company, 1948).

°Aaron Wildavsky, *The Politics of the Budgetary Process*, 2nd ed. (Boston: Little, Brown and Company, 1974). The shaping of the federal budget viewed as a prime function of the bureaucracy and a key to the political process.

°Peter Woll, *American Bureaucracy* (New York: W. W. Norton & Company, Inc., 1963).

Chapter 9 (The Supreme Court and Constitutional Rights)

°Henry J. Abraham, *Freedom and the Court: Civil Rights and Liberties in the United States*, 3rd ed. (New York: Oxford University Press, Inc., 1977).

°Gordon E. Baker, *The Reapportionment Revolution: Representation, Political Power and the Supreme Court* (New York: Random House, Inc., 1966).

°Daniel S. Berman, *It Is So Ordered* (New York: W. W. Norton & Company, Inc., 1966). An introduction to the judicial process by an examination of the steps leading to *Brown* v. *Board of Education.*

Alexander M. Bickel, *The Supreme Court and the Idea of Progress* (New York: Harper & Row, Inc., 1970). A centrist scholar's view which suggests some reservations about the activism of the Warren Court.

°Archibald Cox, *The Role of the Supreme Court in American Government* (New York: Oxford University Press, Inc., 1976). Lectures on the Supreme Court by the law professor who, as Watergate special prosecutor, was fired in the "Saturday night massacre."

°Robert F. Cushman, *Leading Constitutional Decisions*, 15th ed. (Englewood Cliffs, N.J.: Prentice-Hall, Inc., 1976). Excerpts from key decisions of the Supreme Court.

°Anthony Lewis, *Gideon's Trumpet* (New York: Random House, Inc., 1964).

°Alpheus Thomas Mason, *The Supreme Court from Taft to Warren*, rev. ed. (Baton Rouge, La.: Louisiana State University Press, 1958). An examination of four decades of the Court which attacks "the fiction that judges operate in a nonpolitical vacuum, above any personal considerations, and beyond political influences."

°Robert G. McCloskey, *The Modern Supreme Court* (Cambridge, Mass.: Harvard University Press, 1972).

John R. Schmidhauser, *The Supreme Court* (New York: Holt, Rinehart and Winston, Inc., 1960).

Chapter 10 (Federalism: States and Cities)

Martin Anderson, *The Federal Bulldozer: A Critical Analysis of Urban Renewal* (Cambridge, Mass.: The MIT Press, 1964).

°Edward C. Banfield, *The Unheavenly City* (Boston: Little, Brown and Company, 1970); *The Unheavenly City Revisited* (Boston: Little, Brown and Company, 1974).

°Edward C. Banfield and James Q. Wilson, *City Politics* (Cambridge, Mass.: Harvard University Press, 1963). Systematic exposition of the nature of city politics, its structures and styles, and the political roles of various groups and classes. Posits a shift from the "immigrant ethos" to the "middle-class ideal."

°Alan K. Campbell, ed. *The States and the Urban Crisis* (Englewood Cliffs, N.J.: Prentice-Hall, Inc., 1970).

°Robert A. Dahl, *Who Governs?* (New Haven, Conn.: Yale University Press, 1961). Study of New Haven leading to pluralist conclusions.

°Daniel J. Elazar, *American Federalism: A View from the States*, 2nd ed. (New York: Thomas Y. Crowell Company, Inc., 1972).

°Robert A. Goldwin, ed., *A Nation of States* (Chicago: Rand McNally & Company, 1963). Contrasting perspectives on federalism in America by Morton Grodzins, Martin Diamond, Russell Kirk, Herbert J. Storing, James J. Kilpatrick, Harry V. Jaffa, and Walter Berns.

Morton Grodzins, *The American System* (Chicago: Rand McNally & Company, 1966).

Floyd Hunter, *Community Power Structure* (Chapel Hill, N.C.: University of North Carolina Press, 1953). Study of the concentrated power structure of Atlanta.

Duane Lockard, *The Politics of State and Local Government*, 2nd ed. (New York: Macmillan Publishing Co., Inc., 1969).

Carol Estes Thometz, *The Decision-Makers: The Power Structure of Dallas* (Dallas, Tex.: Southern Methodist University Press, 1963).

Chapter 11 (Economic Policy: Sharing the Wealth)

°The Brookings Institution, *Setting National Priorities: The 1978 Budget* (Washington, D.C.: The Brookings Institution, 1977).

Richard A. Cloward and Frances Fox Piven, *The Politics of Turmoil: Essays on Poverty, Race, and the Urban Crisis* (New York: Pantheon Books, Inc., 1974).

John C. Donovan, *The Politics of Poverty* (New York: Pegasus, 1967).

°Leonard Freedman, *Public Housing: The Politics of Poverty* (New York: Holt, Rinehart and Winston, Inc., 1969). The trials of the public housing program from 1949 and why it fared so badly.

Rose D. Friedman, *Poverty: Definition and Perspective* (Washington, D.C.: American Enterprise Institute for Public Policy Research, 1965).

°John Kenneth Galbraith, *The Affluent Society*, 3rd rev. ed. (Boston: Houghton Mifflin Company, 1976).

°Michael Harrington, *The Other America*, rev. ed. (New York: Macmillan Publishing Co., Inc., 1969).

Oscar Lewis, *La Vida* (New York: Random House, Inc., 1966).

Daniel P. Moynihan, *Maximum Feasible Misunderstanding* (New York: The Free Press, 1969); *The Politics of a Guaranteed Income* (New York: Random House, Inc., 1973).

Gilbert Y. Steiner, *The State of Welfare* (Washington, D.C.: The Brookings Institution, 1971). Review of governmental welfare programs and prospects for reform.

Ben J. Wattenberg, *The Real America: A Surprising Examination of the State of the Union* (New York: G. P. Putnam's Sons, 1976).

Chapter 12 (Race: The Critical Test)

°Dee Brown, *Bury My Heart at Wounded Knee* (New York: Holt, Rinehart and Winston, Inc., 1970).

°Stokely Carmichael and Charles V. Hamilton, *Black Power* (New York: Random House, Inc., 1967).

James S. Coleman et al., *Equality of Educational Opportunity* (Washington, D.C.: Government Printing Office, 1966).

°John Hope Franklin, *From Slavery to Freedom*, 4th ed. (New York: Alfred A. Knopf, Inc., 1974). History of blacks in America.

°William H. Grier and Price M. Cobbs, *Black Rage* (New York: Basic Books, 1968).

°Martin Luther King, Jr., *Why We Can't Wait* (New York: Harper & Row, Publishers. 1964). A compilation of essays, including the "Letter from a Birmingham Jail."

°Malcolm Little, *The Autobiography of Malcolm X* (New York: Grove Press, Inc., 1965).

°Gunnar Myrdal, *An American Dilemma: The Negro Problem and Modern Democracy*, 20th ed. (New York: Harper & Brothers, 1944, 1962).

°Michael Novak, *The Rise of the Unmeltable Ethnics* (New York: Macmillan Publishing Co., Inc., 1972). A plea for recognition of the aspirations of ethnic white groups—Poles, Italians, Greeks, and Slavs.

Armando Rendon, *Chicano Manifesto* (New York: Collier Books, Macmillan Publishing Co., Inc., 1972).

°*Report of the National Advisory Commission on Civil Disorders* (Washington, D.C.: Government Printing Office, 1968).

John S. Shockley, *Chicano Revolt in a Texas Town* (Notre Dame, Ind.: University of Notre Dame Press, 1974).

°C. Vann Woodward, *The Strange Career of Jim Crow*, 3rd rev. ed. (New York: Oxford University Press, Inc., 1974). Post-Civil War segregation in the South.

Chapter 13 (Energy and the Environment)

°Walt Anderson, ed., *Politics and Environment*, 2nd ed. (Pacific Palisades, Calif.: Goodyear Publishing Company, Inc., 1976). Reader on various aspects of the ecological crisis. Includes a number of case studies.

Rachel Carson, *Silent Spring* (Boston: Houghton Mifflin Company, 1962).

°J. H. Dales, *Pollution, Property, and Prices* (Toronto: University of Toronto Press, 1968).

°J. Clarence Davies, III, *The Politics of Pollution* (New York: Pegasus, 1970). Survey of the problem, the governmental machinery that is supposed to deal with it, and alternative policies for the future.

°David Howard Davis, *Energy Politics* (New York: St. Martin's Press, 1974).

Paul R. Ehrlich and Anne H. Ehrlich, *Population, Resources, Environment: Issues in Human Ecology*, 2nd ed. (San Francisco: W. H. Freeman and Company, Publishers, 1972).

°John C. Esposito, *Vanishing Air* (New York: Grossman Publishers, 1970). The report of the Nader study group on air pollution.

°Roy L. Meek and John A. Straayer, *The Politics of Neglect, The Environmental Crisis* (Boston: Houghton Mifflin Company, 1971). A reader on various aspects of the ecological crisis.

°David F. Paulsen and Robert B. Denhardt, eds., *Pollution and Public Policy* (New

York: Dodd, Mead & Company, 1973). A reader on the environmental policy-making process, with particular reference to air and water pollution.

°Walter A. Rosenbaum, *The Politics of Environmental Concern* (New York: Praeger Publishers, 1973). Study of the forces arrayed against each other on environmental issues; the role of various governmental agencies; and an assessment of future prospects.

°Carol E. Steinhart and John S. Steinhart, *Blowout! A Case Study of the Santa Barbara Oil Spill* (North Scituate, Mass.: Duxbury Press, 1972).

Chapter 14 (Foreign Policy: A New Era?)

Philip Agee, *Inside the Company: CIA Diary* (New York: Stonehill Publishing Company, 1975).

°Graham Allison, *Essence of Decision: Explaining the Cuban Missile Crisis* (Boston: Little, Brown and Company, 1971).

°Gar Alperovitz, ed., *Cold War Essays* (Cambridge, Mass.: Schenkman Publishing Co., 1970).

°Richard J. Barnet and Ronald E. Müller, *Global Reach: The Power of the Multinational Corporations* (New York: Simon and Schuster, 1974).

°James Clotfelter, *The Military in American Politics* (New York: Harper & Row, Publishers, 1973).

°David Halberstam, *The Best and the Brightest* (New York: Random House, Inc., 1972).

Roger Hilsman, *To Move a Nation* (Garden City, N.Y.: Doubleday & Company, Inc., 1967). The politics of foreign policy during the Kennedy administration.

°Townsend Hoopes, *The Limits of Intervention* (New York: David McKay Company, Inc., 1969).

°Samuel P. Huntington, *The Soldier and the State: The Theory and Politics of Civil–Military Relations* (Cambridge, Mass.: Harvard University Press, 1959, 1957).

Herman Kahn, *On Thermonuclear War* (Princeton, N.J.: Princeton University Press, 1961).

George Kennan, *The Cloud of Danger* (Boston: Atlantic–Little, Brown and Company, 1977).

°Robert F. Kennedy, *Thirteen Days* (New York: W. W. Norton & Company, Inc., 1969). Memoir of the Cuban missile crisis.

°Henry A. Kissinger, *Nuclear Weapons and Foreign Policy* (New York: Harper for the Council on Foreign Relations, 1957). An influential analysis of the consequences of nuclear weaponry for foreign policy.

Seymour Melman, *Pentagon Capitalism* (New York: McGraw-Hill Book Company, 1970).

Hans J. Morgenthau, *A New Foreign Policy for the United States* (New York: F. A. Praeger for the Council on Foreign Relations, 1969).

°New York Times, *The Pentagon Papers* (New York: Bantam Books, 1971).

Eugene V. Rostow, *Peace in the Balance* (New York: Simon and Schuster, 1972). Defense of U.S. foreign policy, including the Vietnam war.

Robert Strausz-Hupé et al., *Protracted Conflict* (New York: Harper, 1959). A call by conservative scholars for a stronger stance against international communism.

°Robert W. Tucker, *A New Isolationism: Threat or Primise?* (New York: Universe Books, 1972).

°William Appleman Williams, *The Tragedy of American Diplomacy*, 2nd ed., rev. ed. (New York: Dell Publishing Company, 1972).

°David Wise, *The Invisible Government* (New York: Random House, Inc., 1964).

Daniel Yergin, *Shattered Peace: The Origins of the Cold War and the National Security State* (Boston: Houghton Mifflin Company, 1977).

Chapter 15 (Power and Politics: A Review of the Five Perspectives)

°Robert Dahl, *After the Revolution?* (New Haven, Conn.: Yale University Press, 1970).

°Hugh Davis Graham and Ted Robert Gurr, *Violence in America: Historical and Comparative Perspectives* (Washington, D.C.: Government Printing Office, 1969, and Bantam Books, 1970).

°Charles Reich, *The Greening of America* (New York: Random House, Inc., 1970).

°Theodore Roszak, *The Making of a Counter Culture* (Garden City, N.Y.: Doubleday & Company, Inc., 1969); *Where the Wasteland Ends* (Garden City, N.Y.: Doubleday & Company, Inc., 1972).

Jerome H. Skolnick, *The Politics of Protest* (Washington, D.C.: Government Printing Office, 1969).

Index